NAM

THE VIETNAM EXPERIENCE
1965-75

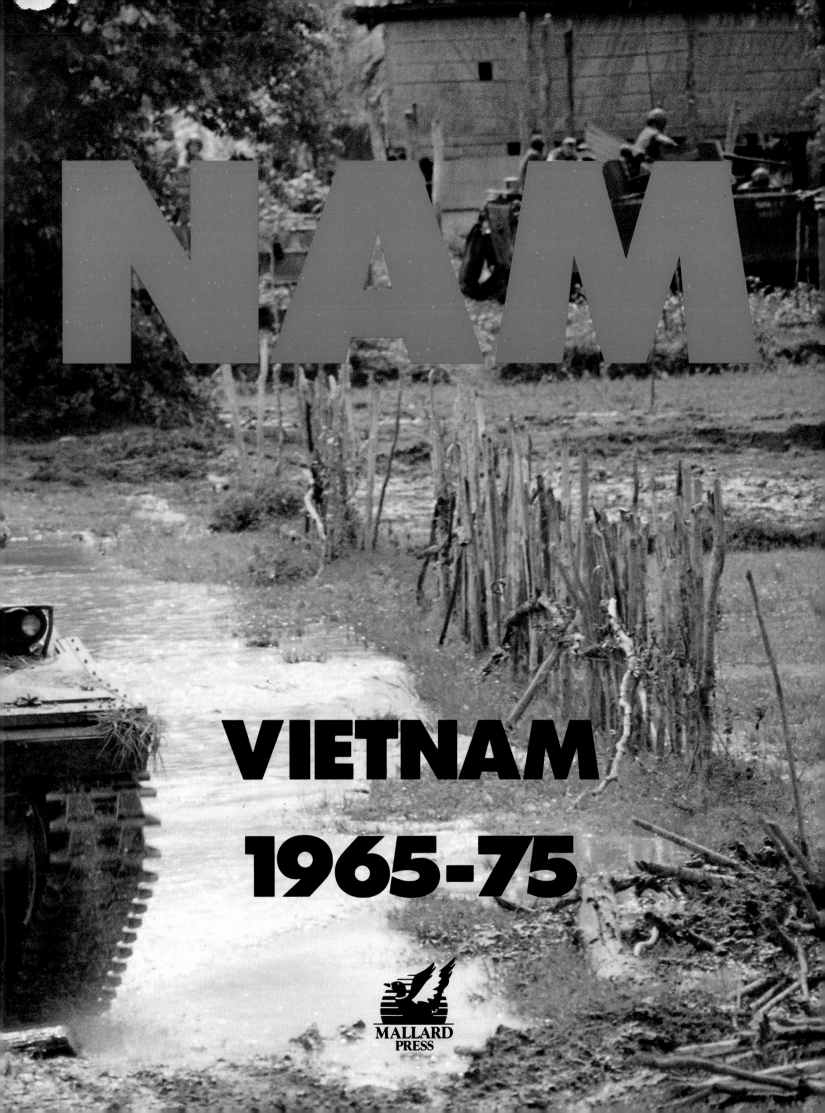

NAAM

VIETNAM 1965-75

MALLARD PRESS

MALLARD PRESS
An Imprint of BDD Promotional Book Company, Inc.
666 Fifth Avenue
New York, NY 10103

Mallard Press and its accompanying design and logo are
trademarks of BDD Promotional Book Company Inc.

Copyright © 1988 Orbis Publishing

First published in the United States of America
in 1989 by The Mallard Press

ISBN 0-792-45003-5

Printed in Hong Kong

Acknowledgments

Photographs were supplied by:
Aviation Photographers International, T Arbuckle, Barr G. Ashcraft, Associated Press, AWM, D Berretty/Rapho, Camera Press, Philip Chinnery, Philip Chinnery/ M Fanning, Bruce Cole, M Connolly, DoD, Robert F. Dorr, T. Fincher, John Frost, Helen Gibson, John Hillelson Agency/Don McCullin, Robert Hunt Library, George McKay, Magnum, Tom Mangold and John Penycate, NHPA, Tim Page, Rod Paschall, Photographers International, Photo Int, Photosource, Photri, James Pickerell, Popperfoto, The Research House, Sgt. Pete Rejo, Rex Features, Robert Hunt Library, Frank Spooner Pictures, Frank Spooner/Gamma, Leroy Thompson, Topham, TRH Pictures, TRH Pictures/US Army, US Air Force, US Army, US Marine Corps, US Navy, *Veteran* magazine.

Artwork by:
Russell Barnet, Beckett/Nolan, Graham Bingham, Tony Randall.

Photographic retouching: Roy Flooks.

All cartoons and photographs from *Grunt Free Press* are by courtesy of Ken Sams.

The Publishers would like to thank the following for kind permission to reproduce extracts from their respective books and articles:

Collins for extracts from the book *In The Presence Of Mine Enemies*, by Howard Rutledge.

The Embassy of the People's Republic of Vietnam for their kind permission to reproduce extracts from *The Ho Chi Minh Trail*, published by the Red River Press.

Roslyn Targ Literary Agency, McFarland & Co and Sphere Books for permission to reproduce extracts from Wallace Terry's *Bloods*, W D Ehrharts's *Vietnam Perkasie* and Mark Baker's *NAM*.

Associated Press for permission to reproduce Peter Arnett's report on Hill 875 and extracts from Neal Ulevich's account of Operation Frequent Wind.

Monthly Review Press for permission to reproduce extracts from *Our Great Spring Victory*.

CONTENTS

ONE MAN'S VIEW

Twenty years have elapsed since I was drafted into the US Army and found myself undergoing the ultimate male rite of passage: being thrust out of a comfortable life at home and into a war zone. What I did in Vietnam was so unlike anything that happened to me before or since that the events are etched indelibly in my consciousness. It's difficult to believe that two decades have passed. The memories are as sharp as if my year in Vietnam occurred – well, not yesterday, but perhaps a year or two ago.

Historians call it the 'Second Indochina War', the first being the 1945-54 conflict in which the communists fought against their French colonial rulers. The Second Indochina War is commonly known in the United States as the Vietnam war. The fact that 'war' is not written with a capital 'w' is a reminder that we never officially declared war.

Officially declared or not, the Vietnam war was the longest and most controversial conflict in US history. As was the case with millions of other young American men, the war in Vietnam became the pivotal point of my life. I was 22 years old when I was drafted on 11 July 1967, a recent college graduate about to face life in the real world. But the world I found myself in turned out to be light years away from the nine-to-five environment I'd envisioned for myself. Instead of entering the workforce, I turned into a shaved-head draftee who barely made it through the physical and emotional torture of basic training. Six months after I was drafted I found myself in a leased commercial jetliner with 250 other green recruits flying over the Pacific Ocean to a place I could barely find on a map. Being 22, I was a bit older than most of the others. I'd been exempt from the draft during my four years of college. But thousands of men who either could not, or did not want to attend college were drafted or signed up voluntarily soon after they were eligible at age 18. I was older than most,

but not wiser. I knew next to nothing about Vietnam.

That was mainly due to the fact that the nation was not exactly on a total war footing. In fact, things at home went on pretty much as usual. Millions of men were exempt from serving for one reason or another. Those guys took jobs, went to law school, married and had kids and otherwise started normal adult lives. Only in those families with a relative in Vietnam was daily life affected by that far-off war in that far-off country.

My ignorance about what was happening in Vietnam hadn't stopped me from supporting the war. I figured that if my country was involved the cause must be just. I soon learned otherwise. My feeling that I was serving my country in a good cause vanished within six weeks after I landed in Vietnam on 13 December 1967.

I was lucky. I took my chances with the draft and the Army made me a clerk. I got a good assignment in Vietnam, too. Some clerks wound up in infantry units, doing paperwork and carrying rifles as well. I was assigned to a personnel company near the city of Qui Nhon. The area, once a hotbed of communist guerrilla activity, was very quiet during my year there. We had to pull guard duty every third night or so, but otherwise life for the clerks in our company consisted mainly of doing long hours of boring paperwork.

Our camp was attacked only once, by sappers during the Tet holiday on 30 January 1968. It was part of the infamous Tet Offensive, when the Viet Cong guerrillas and the North Vietnamese Army attacked every major city, town and military base in South Vietnam. The Tet Offensive was a shattering military defeat for the communists, but they won an important psychological victory. Up until Tet, American officials had been confidently predicting that the war was being won. But Tet caused American public opinion to turn against the war for the first time. Two months later President Lyndon

Qui Nhon, S Vietnam
March 1968
The bunker I lived
in for 7 days on
the mountain

Johnson announced he would seek peace talks with the communists.

The Tet Offensive affected me similarly. In my first six weeks in Vietnam I'd seen firsthand and learned from others that the massive American troop commitment (more than 500,000 men at the time) seemed to be the only thing keeping the communists from taking over South Vietnam. I remember very clearly agreeing with my buddies that had the Americans somehow disappeared, the communists would take over in a matter of hours – days at most. The South Vietnamese Army seemed to be riddled with corruption and incompetence, as was the South Vietnamese government.

I didn't know any GIs in Vietnam who were zealous anti-communists. Most of us just wanted to put in our time and get home alive. Each guy had a year's commitment, and believe me, every one of us was aware every day of that year of how many days he had to go in Nam. We lived for the day when we would get back to what we called 'the World'.

The day I left Vietnam was the happiest day of my life. But soon after I returned home the happiness changed. I wasn't jeered at and called a baby killer as others were. But I soon got the message from friends, family and strangers that Vietnam was a taboo subject. It was an embarrassment. I – being someone who took part in the war – was an embarrassment. Like most vets, I simply shut up about the war and went about my business. If people didn't want to hear about it, that was fine with me.

Twenty years later Vietnam vets are no longer embarrassments. Beginning in the early 1980s the American public changed its mind about the men who took part in that dirty little war. Even most former anti-war activists stopped blaming the warrior for the war. A memorial to all Vietnam veterans was erected in Washington, DC, in 1982. Dozens of others have been built across the country.

At my wife's 20-year high school reunion two years ago, Vietnam vets were asked to stand. We were given an ovation.

To me, the new praise seems shallow. No, Vietnam vets never were the villains we were once made out to be. But we're not the superheroes some want us to be today. We deserve recognition – so does anyone who serves his or her country in whatever capacity. Vietnam was a big part of our lives, but only a part. We should not shrink from talking about it. But we should also get on with our lives and not dwell too much on the past.

While I distrust the recent shower of praise for Vietnam vets, I heartily welcome the wealth of written material that has been published on the war and its veterans in recent years. In many ways that war is not over. Most of the big questions – Was it in the US national interest to get involved? Why did we fight a self-imposed limited war? Was it possible to defeat the communists, given their tenacious commitment? Did 58,000 Americans die in vain? – have yet to be answered. The more the was is discussed, the closer we will come to answering some of those important questions.

Over the coming weeks *NAM* will look in detail at every aspect of the Vietnam war. It will look at it from the viewpoint of those who were involved in it directly and will shed new light on an experience that touched an entire generation of Americans and continues to have an influence today.

Marc Leepson

MARC LEEPSON is typical of the hundreds of thousands of young Americans who served in Vietnam. Some would agree with him, some would not. We hope we can reflect their views.

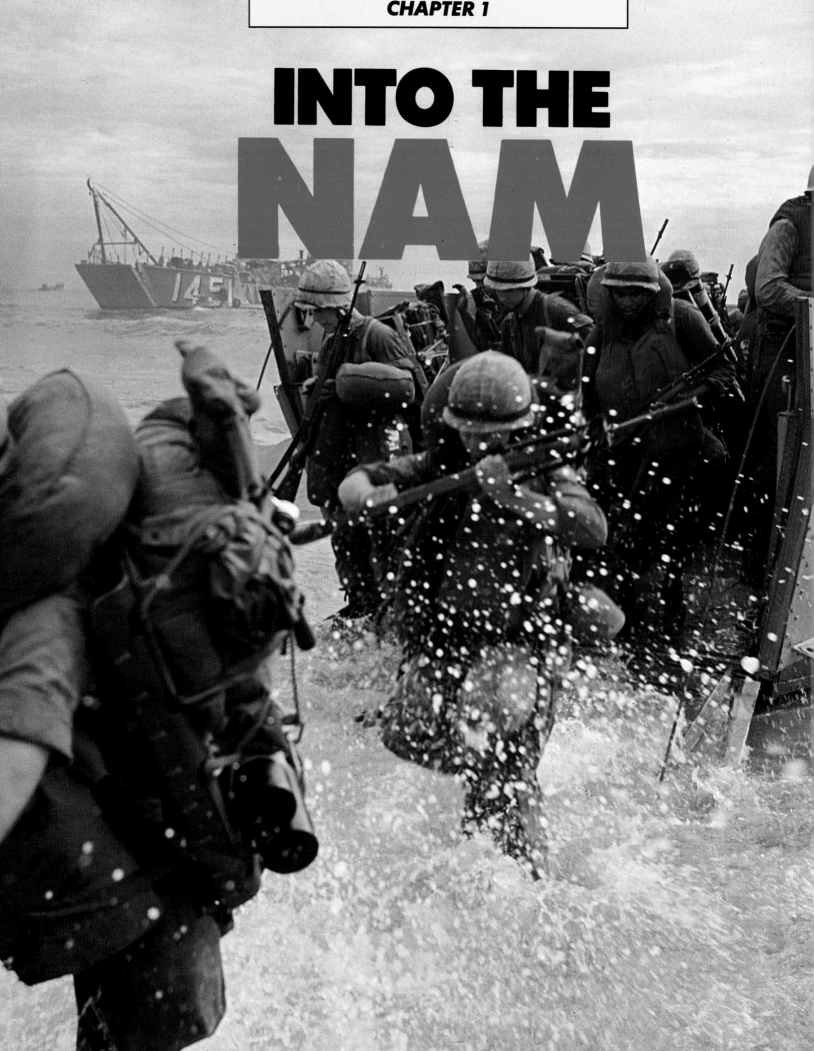

INTO THE NAM

8 March 1965: Marines storm ashore at Da Nang, first US combat troops to be committed. They've come to defend democracy – but they're in a war like nothing they've ever experienced

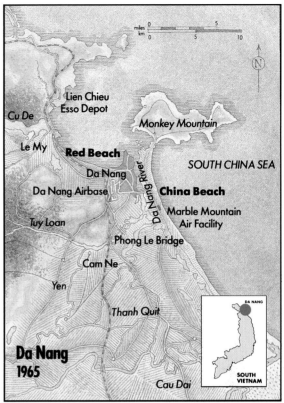

Da Nang 1965

On the morning of 8 March 1965, the American airbase at Da Nang did not look much like a place destined to become one of the three busiest airports in the world. There were the bunkers left by the Japanese in 1945. There were the blockhouses left by the French. And there was the single 3000yd runway aiming out towards the golden beaches of the South China Sea.

Out to sea were 3500 US Marines, ready to take the undefended beach of a friendly nation in a full frontal assault. This bizarre event was the farcical curtain-raiser to the greatest tragedy in American history. Until then Vietnam had been the sleepy setting for a Graham Greene novel. Soon it would become a name that no-one would ever forget. For the first time, US combat troops were going there with permission to shoot back if fired on. Half a world away, in the White House, that decision had taken President Johnson weeks of agonizing thought.

March sees the tail end of the monsoon in Vietnam and the weather gets feverish. The four ships of Amphibious Task Force 76, after six weeks en route from Japan, had spent the last day pitching up and down in vile seas – 'the worst weather we had encountered in the South China Sea ever' was the verdict of the commanding general, Frederick J. Karch, veteran of the battles against the Japanese for Saipan, Tinian and Iwo Jima. Now the Marines on board USS *Mount McKinley*, *Henrico*, *Union* and *Vancouver* stared ashore with tense anticipation. The news was that Viet Cong were everywhere in Da Nang: that attack could come from any quarter. Thinking ahead to the coming assault on the beach, many young Marines recalled World War II movies.

In Da Nang, the town the French called Tourane when this was a colonial provincial capital, a steady drizzle fell. In the cool of the morning you could even imagine the French café awnings and stucco buildings of Vietnam's second largest town were somewhere along the Mediterranean coast. The town was teeming – refugees from the war had poured in from the countryside to double its population to 200,000.

Below: General Frederick J. Karch fails to see the humour when, having committed 3500 Marines in an assault, he is greeted with a garland of dahlias.

Left: US Marines charge through the rolling surf on the beach at Da Nang, M14s at the ready. Right: To their great surprise, they are met, not by armed resistance, but by pretty Vietnamese school girls who festoon them with flowers. They were soon to learn that this was to be no ordinary war.

The truth was, Da Nang was one of the few safe places in the border regions these days. Out in the countryside, in the 10,000 square miles that made up what the military called I Corps Tactical Zone, the land belonged to the Viet Cong: Charlie, the gooks, the VC – the enemy. Out there, the South Vietnamese Army, the ARVN, clung to safety in a few outpost garrisons. Mostly, they didn't venture far beyond the defended perimeter of bamboo stakes and mud walls.

And even in Da Nang, safety was only relative. The Viet Cong were extremely elusive, and trying

1965

THE REASON WHY

Were 2.7 million young Americans tricked into fighting in Nam?

The USA slipped gradually into the Vietnam war, like a man sliding into quicksand. For a generation of Americans, the finger of guilt pointed at Lyndon Baines Johnson. But was he responsible?

US interest in Vietnam was straightforward – successive presidents believed that there was a world-wide communist threat and it was their job to resist it. This threat had a particular Asian dimension: China had gone communist in 1949; the North Koreans had invaded the non-communist South in 1950; during the 1940s and 1950s there were communist revolts in the Philippines and Malaya, and in 1954, the communist-dominated Viet Minh had defeated the French colonial forces in Vietnam.

In 1960, President John F. Kennedy saw Southeast Asia as under imminent threat, and increased aid to South Vietnam. It was this commitment that Lyndon Johnson inherited in November 1963. He declared that he would not let South Vietnam go the way of China.

But giving more and more aid to the corrupt regime of President Ngo Dinh Diem in South Vietnam merely resulted in more corruption – not military success. So the US became intimately involved in the internal politics of the South – a murky, secretive business. US Special Forces in the Central Highlands found they were fighting the government in order to protect their Montagnard forces. On 2 November 1963 a group of ARVN officers overthrew and then murdered President Diem with the permission of the US Ambassador.

Plans drawn up in January 1964 for covert operations against North Vietnam included sabotage and spying within the North, secret bombing raids in Laos and naval missions off the North Vietnamese coast.

During 1964, because much of what the US was involved in would not bear open scrutiny, Johnson assumed blanket powers that enabled him to act as he pleased in this dirty little war. Already, advisors were being used more or less as combat troops.

On 6 August 1964, Johnson and his advisors got the powers they needed when the US Congress passed what became known as the Gulf of Tonkin Resolution which gave Johnson the right to take 'all necessary measures' to repel attacks against US forces. Johnson himself described the resolution as 'Like Grandma's nightshirt – it covered everything.'

The background to the resolution was attacks on US naval vessels by the North Vietnamese. Shortly after 1500 hours on 2 August 1964, the destroyer USS *Maddox*, steaming 10 miles off the coast of North Vietnam in the Gulf of Tonkin, was attacked by three communist patrol boats. Two patrol boats launched torpedoes (which missed) while the third approached even closer before being blown out of the water. No American casualties had been suffered.

Johnson authorized the carrier USS *Constellation* to join *Ticonderoga* in the South China Sea and agreed that the *Maddox*, with another destroyer, the USS *C. Turner Joy*, should return to the Gulf of Tonkin. As the two destroyers approached the coast late on 3 August, a violent thunderstorm broke out, causing their sonars to act erratically. Captain John J. Herrick of the *Maddox*, convinced that an attack was imminent, requested air cover and, once again, Crusaders from the *Ticonderoga* complied. As they flew over at about 2100 hours, the two warships suddenly began to zig-zag wildly and to open fire in all directions, reporting that they were under attack from a fleet of enemy patrol boats. Sonar operators warned of 22 incoming torpedoes and gun-crews claimed to have hit three enemy craft.

As soon as reports of this second incident were received, Johnson decided to act. He ordered retaliatory airstrikes against coastal targets in the North and appeared on nationwide television to inform the people of his 'positive reply' to North Vietnamese aggression. But was Johnson's action a justifiable response to aggression or merely a cynical ploy in election year? No authorities believe there is any clear evidence of a second attack – Johnson himself said, 'Hell, those dumb stupid sailors were just shooting at flying fish' – but he obviously saw a way of manipulating opinion to suit himself and escape from any possible accusations of being soft on communist aggression in the coming presidential election. His right-wing opponent, Senator Barry Goldwater, was forced to agree that he approved of Johnson's actions.

But however worthwhile Johnson's motives, the fact remains that the US had taken a decisive step down a dangerous road. In the words of the cliche, truth had become the first casualty.

to track them down, as the American advisors already in Vietnam knew, was like looking for tears in a bucket of water.

There were 23,000 US soldiers in Vietnam already this morning: advisors, Special Forces, Air Force personnel. For them, firefights with the enemy were forbidden – at least, that's what the rule book said. The best they could do was put backbone into South Vietnam's own troops. Otherwise, you could easily end up fighting the Vietnamese war *for* them.

A new pattern of war

Until recently, as wars go, this had not been a bad one. Certainly, in Saigon, you could have an action packed day and be back on base by five o'clock for cocktails. Until last month, when they'd been ordered home, you could have your family along. But the reason General Karch was about to become the 14th US general in Vietnam this morning was because the advisors were not succeeding in their mission. The idea had been to train Vietnam's own forces to deal with the Viet Cong back north.

Just one battle that week showed why this was proving so difficult. At an isolated government forces camp near Binh Dinh, the Viet Cong had hurled themselves at the perimeter for six hours. An estimated 500 had died. Certainly the defenders had picked 100 corpses off the wire when the assault force withdraw.

Such pitched battles were becoming more common. But the small men in black pyjamas knew how to strike silently too. On 31 October 1964, they had floated on sampans past the US airbase at Bien Hoa, disguised as farmers. The mortar attack they suddenly let loose killed four Americans, destroyed five bombers and damaged eight more. And on Christmas Eve 1964, a driver parked an explosive-crammed truck by the Brink Hotel in Saigon, where US soldiers were crowded, waiting for Bob Hope to entertain them. The explosion tore through the building, killing two Americans and wounding more than 70 others.

But the event that, above all else, had brought the Marines to Da Nang had shattered the night of 7 February 1965. At Camp Holloway, near a provincial capital called Pleiku, some 400 Americans of the 52d Combat Aviation Battalion were asleep when 300 Viet Cong guerrillas crept up on them. The VC had spent the last week's official ceasefire for a religious festival stockpiling captured US mortars and ammunition. At 0200 hours they let loose a bombardment that turned the base into a conflagration of exploding ammunition and burning aircraft and left seven Americans dead and 100 wounded. 'They are killing our men while they sleep in the night,' President Johnson raged. 'I can't ask our American soldiers to continue to fight with one hand behind their back.'

The Marines who stormed the beach at 0903 on 8 March were supposed to have both hands unleashed. 'We've been ready to do this job for some time,' said General Karch. 'There's a sense of

relief at the prospect of getting some action.'

The frogmen were the first to reach the land, pulling themselves out of the surf, aiming up the beach to the line of palm trees and firs. Hard behind them, 11 Marine amphibious tractors (LVTPs) thrust their 45-ton steel hulks through the white foam. This was a 'high surf' landing – utilizing the heaviest landing craft to cope with the ten-foot swell out in the transport area. There were 34 men packed into each LVTP; 200 into each of the bigger, 61-ton LCM-8s. As they hit the beach, they opened their steel jaws. It took just 15 minutes to disgorge the four waves of the assault force onto the sands, fully armed, mean and ready for action. In 65 minutes, 1400 combat soldiers – carrying rifles, machine guns, and rocket and grenade launchers – were on dry land.

Marines are indoctrinated at boot camp that there is no such thing as a friendly beach. And as they hit Red Beach Two, the Leathernecks were ready for anything – except for what actually happened.

The mayor of Da Nang, with his Polaroid camera, was there to welcome them. So were the television

Above: Christmas Eve in Saigon sees a fresh wave of bomb attacks.

cameras and a gaggle of news-hungry pressmen, eager for quotes from the Marines who went scuttling for cover.

Warriors welcomed with flowers

Banners proclaimed: 'Vietnam welcomes the US Marines Corps' and 'Happy to welcome the Marines in defense of this free world outpost.' And then there was the winsome welcoming committee of pretty, smiling Vietnamese school girls who shyly hung garlands of dahlias and gladioli around the thick necks of the towering Marines. Even straight-backed Annapolis-trained General Karch was hard put to maintain his composure while being festooned with posies. A picture survives of General Karch, flower bedecked and unsmiling. 'That picture has been the source of a lot of trouble for me,' Karch later said. 'People say, 'Why couldn't you have been smiling?' But you know, if I had to do it over, that picture would be

Top: The Leathernecks brought to Da Nang the new Ontos anti-tank weapon. Mounting six recoilless rifles and one 50-calibre machine gun, it gave added punch to the Marine forces. Above: Marines begin patrols in the area around Da Nang as part of their 'security' mission.

the same. When you have a son in Vietnam and he gets killed, you don't want a smiling general with flowers around his neck as the leader at that point.'

The landing did not go entirely unopposed though. A Viet Cong sniper managed to put a bullet through the wing of a C-130 Hercules transport as it made its approach to Da Nang with more Marines from camps on Okinawa. But no real damage was done.

Fighting an unseen enemy

But why had the Marines stormed this tranquil beach in such a comic-book fashion when Da Nang had a perfectly good airstrip and a deep-water harbour? It was partly because the Marines were trained and ready to operate that way. A beach landing got the maximum amount of men and machines deployed in the shortest amount of time. Nam O Beach in the Bay of Da Nang – now renamed Red Beach Two – had been an amphibious-assault training beach before World War II. The port was not equipped with even the simplest facilities and the airstrip, at that time, would not have been able to handle the landing of such a large body of men – let alone 105mm howitzers, M-48 medium tanks and Ontos fighting vehicles. But the real reason for the high-profile amphibious assault was to send a very public message to the North Vietnamese – and their Russian and Chinese allies – that the US was not prepared to stand by and watch South Vietnam fall to the communists.

For a few days, no-one got killed. When the ARVN government forces had a firefight not two miles from the airbase perimeter on the first night, they did not ask the Marines to assist. Penned up in the eight square miles of the airbase, it was easy to wonder why you were here. Especially when rounds of fire from the training ranges of the nearby ARVN base whistled dangerously overhead. Or when the ARVN patrol you had been sent to relieve either refused to budge or ran away on your approach.

Some of the South Vietnamese troops did impress though, up to a point. 'The Vietnamese seemed to know their business all right,' said Lieutenant Donald H. Hering, 'but we were a little shook up when they started lighting cigarettes and listening to jazz on their transistors while we were patrolling.'

You could wonder, too, as you collapsed with heat exhaustion hauling equipment ashore, why the Japanese or the French or the Vietnamese had never bothered to provide a port of 100,000 people with simple facilities – like a single crane. And when the Marine pilots began to get to work they didn't expect, back at camp, that they would be flying helicopters full of live chickens and cows up-country. But that's what the remote outposts of the hard-pressed Vietnamese troops needed.

If the war was happening, it was not – so it seemed – around Da Nang. The Marines began to venture abroad. They ran patrols in the hills to the west. It was easy, in the mysterious tropical night, to imagine strange shapes, to hear strange noises. The first Marines to die did so on just such a patrol. Two of them, in a three-man patrol, ventured out, lost their way and came up behind their companion in the dark. He turned, fired, and wounded both of them mortally. The killing fields of Vietnam had begun to claim their victims.

FIRST BLOOD TO THE MARINES

When the Marines were finally let off the leash in Operation Starlite, they scored an early victory – but did the Viet Cong learn the most valuable lessons?

Time passed slowly for the Marines at Da Nang. They filled sandbags to make bunkers and they patrolled the airbase perimeter. The heat was thick and oppressive and the men on guard duty were plagued by mosquitoes, but the worst of it was that nothing was happening. Every now and then a monkey would set off a trip flare, or rattle the line of rock-filled beer cans the Marines had strung out to warn them of any Viet Cong creeping up on the base . . . another false alarm. It was boring and very frustrating.

Below: A Marine gunner cuts loose with an M60 machine gun. After months of boredom the Marines were eager to get into action and take on the VC face to face.

Their thoughts turned back 20 years, to the legendary Marine assaults on the beaches of Tarawa and Iwo Jima. Marines, or 'Leathernecks' as they called themselves, were fighting men, not babysitters. They'd been sent to Nam to fight a war, but what kind of war was this when there was no-one to fight? The Marines at Da Nang grumbled a lot.

Patrolling in the hills west of the base, looking for Viet Cong guerrillas, was equally tedious and very hard work. Heavily loaded with weapons and equipment, men dropped like flies from heat exhaustion. Occasionally, they would make a chance contact with the Viet Cong – a brief exchange of shots, perhaps a fleeting glimpse of a black-clad figure disappearing into the trees, and then nothing. The Viet Cong were masters at vanishing into thin air. To everyone concerned, from the lowliest Marine to the commandant of the US Marine Corps himself, General Wallace M. Greene, it was quite obvious that the limited defensive role they had been assigned was proving to be worse than useless. 'The Marine mission is to kill Viet Cong,' complained Greene on his return

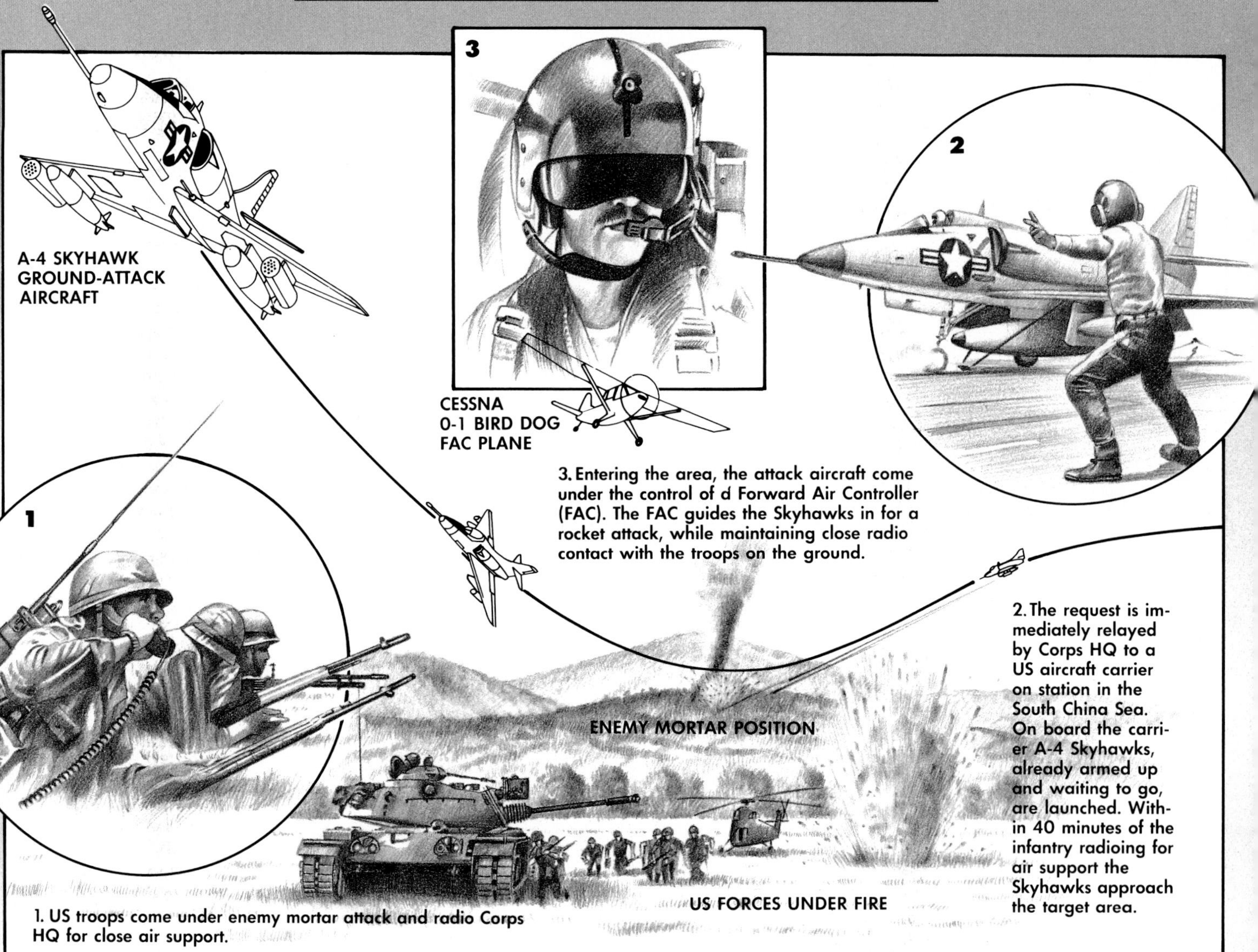

1965

A-4 SKYHAWK
GROUND-ATTACK
AIRCRAFT

3

CESSNA
0-1 BIRD DOG
FAC PLANE

3. Entering the area, the attack aircraft come under the control of d Forward Air Controller (FAC). The FAC guides the Skyhawks in for a rocket attack, while maintaining close radio contact with the troops on the ground.

2

1

ENEMY MORTAR POSITION

2. The request is immediately relayed by Corps HQ to a US aircraft carrier on station in the South China Sea. On board the carrier A-4 Skyhawks, already armed up and waiting to go, are launched. Within 40 minutes of the infantry radioing for air support the Skyhawks approach the target area.

US FORCES UNDER FIRE

1. US troops come under enemy mortar attack and radio Corps HQ for close air support.

CLOSE AIR SUPPORT

from an inspection tour of the Da Nang base. 'They can't do it by sitting on their ditty boxes.'

For a full five months after the Marines swept ashore at Da Nang the Viet Cong carefully avoided a full-scale confrontation with their new enemy. They watched as more and more Marines arrived on the coast to set up further enclaves at Chu Lai and Phu Bai, and they watched them build a new airstrip at Chu Lai. In the very early hours of the morning on 1 July they decided to shake the Marines up a little.

At about 0130 hours a Marine sentry heard a suspicious noise out on the perimeter wire of the Da Nang base. He tossed an illumination grenade in the direction of the sound and as it exploded, so did half the airbase. A furious VC mortar barrage swept across the field as a team of Viet Cong sappers charged through a hole they had clipped

Below: Into action. Marines are lifted into LZ White. Starlite gave the Marines their first opportunity to exploit their superior mobility and firepower to full effect. Right: A wounded Marine receives treatment on the battlefield.

in the fence and lobbed explosive charges onto some of the parked aircraft. As quickly as they had come, they were gone again. The damage caused was not particularly extensive, and only one American was killed in the attack, but because it was so spectacular, it received world-wide publicity. It also hardened the resolve of the Marines at Da Nang to hunt out and destroy the enemy before he could do it again.

They did not have to wait long. Through July and early August countless intelligence reports had been reaching the office of General William Westmoreland, overall commander of the American Army in Vietnam, of a build-up of VC troops close to the Marine enclaves. But locally gathered intelligence had to be treated with a large pinch of salt. Most of it was low-level stuff, passed on to the Americans by South Vietnamese informers

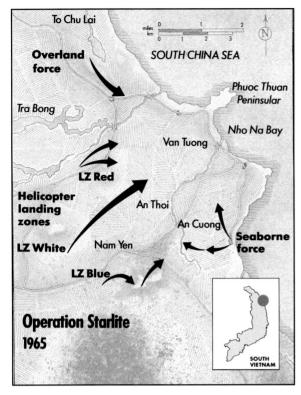

Overland force

SOUTH CHINA SEA

To Chu Lai

Tra Bong

Phuoc Thuan Peninsular

Van Tuong

Nho Na Bay

LZ Red

Helicopter landing zones

An Thoi

An Cuong

LZ White

Nam Yen

Seaborne force

LZ Blue

Operation Starlite 1965

SOUTH VIETNAM

whose word was notoriously dubious. But, as the scraps of incoming information were painstakingly collated, a definite picture of a VC build-up in the area around Chu Lai, 60 or so miles south of Da Nang, began to emerge. It was finally clinched by the arrival out of the blue of a Viet Cong deserter on 15 August.

During his interrogation, the VC defector revealed that the 1st Viet Cong Regiment – a force numbering some 1500 men – had set up base in the hamlets around Van Tuong, only 12 miles south of the Marines at Chu Lai. And, that they were preparing for a full-scale attack on the American enclave. For the virtually unblooded Marines, this was too good an opportunity to pass up.

Up until now, the Marines had been unable to bring the full power of their military machine into gear. A Marine battalion was organised to be highly self-sufficient – it could move at great speed, packed into the bellies of HH-34 helicopters, and could call up heavy artillery and close air support if it ran into a large enemy force or found itself pinned down. This was how the Marines were trained to fight, and it was how they decided to take on the VC on the Van Tuong peninsula.

They walked into a wall of fire

For the operation to succeed they would have to move quickly. Staff officers assembled and an overall plan for the action was drawn up. It was essential for the Marines to surround the enemy regiment before the elusive Viet Cong soldiers could make a getaway. So they decided to launch the attack from three separate directions. One Marine company would move overland and dig in along the Tra Bong river to block any VC attempts to break out to the north, while a whole

battalion of men would be put ashore on the southern side of the peninsula at An Cuong. The final axis of the attack would be lifted in by helicopter to landing zones to the west. With their backs to the sea, the VC would be trapped. Operation Starlite, as it was codenamed, was set to go on 18 August.

On the morning of the 18th the giant 40-ton amtrac landing vehicles of the 3d Battalion, 3d Marines, rose up out of the surf and clawed their way up the soft sands of the beach at An Cuong. Pouring from their holds, the Marines advanced towards the thatched huts of the nearby hamlet. Suddenly, the Marines up front walked into a wall of Viet Cong machine-gun fire and exploding mortar shells, and all attempts to continue the advance up the coastline were brought to a standstill. Out at sea, the light cruiser USS *Galveston* moved into action. Her six-inch guns were brought to bear on the slopes of the hill where the VC were entrenched and a merciless barrage of shells rained down on the Viet Cong positions. Through the smoking debris of shattered trees came the Marines, only to be greeted by another volley of VC fire. A pitched battle developed as the Marines surged forward into the VC trenches and bunkers and took on the enemy hand-to-hand. After several hours of savage fighting, the hillside was secured.

Out at the helicopter landing zones on the western side of the operational area, the fighting was equally tough. At LZ Blue, Company H of the 4th Marines landed almost on top of the 60th Viet Cong Battalion, dug in on a low hill. The VC held their fire as the first choppers touched down and then opened up with everything they had. Rocket-propelled grenades and machine-gun rounds poured into the LZ as the incoming Marines fought desperately to secure the area. Three

FROM DEFENSIVE TO OFFENSIVE

When the decision was taken in February 1965 to commit 'main force' US units to Vietnam, their task was seen as a purely limited one – to create 'enclaves' of American military presence on the coast, partly to protect existing airbases, but also to ensure that pockets of organised force would remain if the Army of the Republic of Vietnam (ARVN) collapsed. Thus, when the 9th Marine Expeditionary Brigade (9MEB) arrived at Da Nang in early March, the Marines merely threw a cordon around the airfield and dug in, occupying no more than eight square miles of South Vietnamese territory.

This was unlikely to last. The Marines, trained for more offensive operations, found the task irksome and, as reports of communist infiltration increased, they gradually expanded their 'tactical areas of responsibility' (TAORs) to ensure defence in depth. General Westmoreland was also keen on his troops undertaking more aggressive action. He was already developing the concept of 'search and destroy' that was to have such an effect on the conduct of US operations.

By mid-April Westmoreland was able to announce a less rigid 'concept of operations' which permitted aggressive patrolling – something which led to the first clashes between Marines and Viet Cong (VC) guerrillas. As VC attacks on the enclaves at Da Nang, Phu Bai and Chu Lai became a threat, Westmoreland was granted permission, on 26 June, to use his forces as he saw fit and, with TAORs now covering 600 square miles, the move towards aggressive action, designed to seek out North Vietnamese as well as VC formations, became inevitable. The communist forces stepped up their action; early in July, the actual airbase at Da Nang was attacked by a demolition squad. By August, the Americans in their turn were ready to strike. The first of the major 'search and destroy' operations (Starlite) was being prepared.

THE WRONG STRATEGY?

Operation Starlite may have been Westmoreland's first step down the road to defeat

The shift from a strategy of defending enclaves to one of 'search and destroy' wedded the American forces to a conventionally fought war in Vietnam. General William Westmoreland wished to use the American forces, with their weight of firepower, to take on large communist concentrations, while the ARVN contained the guerrillas.

Many members of the US defence establishment had different ideas. They believed in the concept of Counter Insurgency (COIN), as an answer to guerrilla warfare. COIN involved a close co-ordination of political, military and social policies, in order to isolate the guerrilla from the general population. When the allegiance of the population was won, then the guerrillas could be defeated.

The US Marines, moreover, had their own theory, known as the Combined Action Program (CAP). It involved, for example, a specially trained Marine squad protecting a village, while civic and medical aid was provided.

Westmoreland rejected this type of strategy partly because one such policy - the 'Strategic Hamlet' programme - was proving unworkable in Vietnam, and also because he believed that his combat troops were needed to meet an immediate threat of large concentrations of the enemy breaking through.

Influential voices opposed Westmoreland, but he got his way, and Starlite was the result. Whether it was the right result is another question entirely.

UH-1B helicopter gunships did what they could to suppress the VC fire and a Marine platoon was sent up the hill to root out the enemy. The first attack was beaten back but, reinforced and with the support of massive airstrikes and tanks, the infantry finally succeeded in taking the hill.

Further north at LZ White, Company E ran into similar trouble. The LZ was long and flat, overlooked by a ridge to the east on which the VC had set up firing positions. Coming in, the HH-34s were hit by a barrage of rifle and machine-gun fire. The Marines made for the slope and began a steady push upwards in the face of intense resistance. Again, Navy firepower was brought down on the VC, but not before they had managed to inflict considerable casualties on the Americans clawing their way up through the scrub on the slope. The battlefield was littered with dead and wounded as the Marines finally took the crest.

For the rest of the day, in brain-boiling heat, the Marine companies advanced steadily, closing the vice on the VC regiment. Fighting was heavy, especially in the area around the hamlets of Nam Yen (3) and An Cuong (2). An amtrac force with

Below: A medic claws his way up the slope from LZ White to aid a wounded soldier. But the man was already dead, and the medic himself was hit moments after this picture was taken.

three tanks, on its way to re-supply the men of Company I, 3d Battalion, 3d Marines, became lost in a maze of trails and stumbled into a devastating VC ambush. A hastily dispatched force from Company I was also hit as it tried to relieve the pressure on the knocked-out column and a savage battle ensued. Staying close to their vehicles, the Marines fought tooth and nail to avoid being overrun by the Viet Cong soldiers coming at them from the treelines and hidden fortifications around the settlements. Both sides suffered many casualties but the Marines managed to hold out.

Digging out the stragglers

The next day, the last pockets of VC resistance were finally wiped out. The mopping up that followed was particularly unpleasant. Any VC who had not managed to slip through the Marine cordon were holed up in a mass of hidden bunkers, caves and tunnels scattered throughout the area. As the Marines swept through, trying to winkle out the stragglers, they would often be hit by sniper fire coming from the rear. Sometimes, they literally had to dig them out. But by nightfall on

Above: Pouring with sweat in the intense heat, a Marine trudges uphill as the vice closes on the VC.

the 19th the Viet Cong were beaten.

Operation Starlite, the first major US engagement of the war, had been a great success. It had claimed the lives of 614 VC soldiers for the loss of 45 Americans dead. The key to the Marines' victory was undoubtedly the weight of firepower they were able to call up – artillery, heavy mortars, naval gunfire and ground-attack aircraft – a way of fighting that would win the Americans many a pitched battle in the years to come. But while the Americans celebrated their first real victory, what of the defeated Viet Cong? They had been cornered, this time, forced to stand up and fight a face-to-face battle on ground of their enemy's choosing. Trapped on the Van Tuong peninsula their cunning and expertise in the ways of guerrilla warfare could not hope to match the sheer destructive power of American military technology. But in the villages and the paddy fields, or deep in the forests of the Central Highlands – places where the VC could move undetected and at will, spring ambushes, lay booby traps – would the Americans be able to cope with *their* special brand of warfare?

1965

DELTA DAWN

As the US and ARVN troops moved from their defensive enclaves, seeking out the enemy in search and destroy operations, it should be remembered that the destroyers were far from invulnerable. Photojournalist Tim Page captured the reality of an ARVN mission as they step into enemy territory. That first leap into the unknown could be met by anything from a punji stake to an onslaught of automatic fire.

EYE-WITNESS

One of the war's premier photographers, Tim Page was in Vietnam from 1965-69, and was wounded four times.

Above, left to right: After de-assing from the choppers, the LZ is secured and the objectives checked, before heading out. Right: the sweep bears bitter fruit: dead and wounded. The hat of a fallen comrade lies ignored.

A MEAN PLACE TO FIGHT

In the Vietnamese jungle, you could die in 30 minutes from a snake bite. Veteran Leroy Thompson describes the horrors of fighting among leeches, ants and cobras

EYE-WITNESS

The author Leroy Thompson is no ordinary Vietnam Vet. During the war, he served as an officer with a Ranger-trained special-mission unit that operated extensively in the jungles of Southeast Asia.

The Southeast Asian jungle had many smells, most bad. As I pressed my nose into the fetid undergrowth skirting the emergency extraction zone, I couldn't help wondering if it was the last thing I'd ever smell. The perspiration coursed down my face and arms, making the grip of the silenced High Standard pistol I clutched slimy and slick, while the festering insect bites which covered my body had begun to itch in unison.

The other members of my reconnaissance team formed a perimeter around me facing outward to provide 360 degree security as we waited for the Huey 'slick' extraction helicopter to pull us out. As the slick came gliding over the jungle canopy towards our LZ, I re-holstered my pistol and picked up my CAR-15 carbine. The time for silent killing was past. Our radio crackled as the chopper pilot's voice boomed, 'Tiger Leader. Mark your Lima now with smoke. Over.' Then, after the M18 smoke grenade spewing violet smoke was tossed into the clearing, 'I have violet. Tiger confirm'.

Damn right, I confirmed, as the slick roller-coastered in to hover just above the LZ. Quickly, we pulled in the perimeter, me as the team leader the last one aboard. As the slick began to rise, the door gunner grabbed my harness to pull me

aboard the swaying helicopter.

Jinking right and left to avoid possible ground fire, the chopper pilot poured on the power. As I lay on the floor I could smell the combination of hot oil, grease, gasoline, sweat, mildew, hot brass, and stale cigarette smoke that was the essence of the chopper. Even the closely packed, unwashed bodies of my team could not cover that beautiful smell, nor the lovely 'whump, whump' of the chopper blades as we left the jungle behind. 'Bye, bye, Laos,' I thought as my eyes took in the slick's door gunner manning his M60 machine gun, its cartridge belt snaking out over a can of peaches to keep it from jamming. His 'chickenplate' armour and scarred helmet made him seem a somewhat seedy knight, and the legend painted on his helmet like a coat of arms – 'If I die here, bury me face down so Vietnam can kiss my ass' – seemed to summarize the war perfectly for me right then. I thought he was beautiful, and so was that ugly green Huey chopper that was pulling us out of the jungle.

For the American soldier fighting in Southeast Asia perhaps the hardest lesson to learn was that summarized by Chapman in the title of his classic work on jungle warfare – *The Jungle is Neutral* – which, indeed, it is. Even those trained as I was in special operations and jungle warfare found it difficult to adjust to the realities of the hell of fighting in the jungle; for conscript infantrymen it was even worse. Coming from an industrialized society, it was hard to accept that in the jungle

1965

Left: Tired and exhausted, a Marine shows the strain of fighting in a hostile jungle – the fear of ambush, the discomfort of rotting uniforms and the daily threat to health. Right: Widespread in the thick jungles of Vietnam, the Krait could prove deadly if stepped on - suddenly flipping its head to one side for a single, lethal bite.

SNAKE BITE

There are 133 species of snake in the jungles of Vietnam. Of these, 131 are poisonous. And the most poisonous - kraits, cobras and bamboo vipers - are among the most common. Everyone knows how to avoid antagonising a snake: keep calm, move slowly, the snake is more frightened than you are … Good advice, but not too helpful if you're walking point on patrol, tense and wary, ready to wheel round swiftly at the slightest sound. That swift wheel around is when the krait gets you.

A bite from a small, black and yellow coloured krait, a bright-green bamboo viper or a 5ft-long cobra could kill within hours, and so the first move was always to make an 'H'-shaped cut in the wound, to suck out as much poison as possible. Then, a tourniquet could be applied using a belt or gunsling, tied tight enough to make the victim's veins stand out. And during this process the patient had to be kept as calm as possible - panic would increase his heartbeat and make the venom circulate all the faster.

Where possible, a medevac helicopter would be called in. In order to help the doctors assess the right treatment, the snake itself had to be caught and sent back with the wounded soldier. Grunts didn't carry special containers for snakes, and a dead snake moving around on the floor of a pitching helicopter could look remarkably lifelike.

All in all, snakebite was bad news for all concerned.

American technology was no longer king. You could die in minutes if a snake like a krait bit you. When you walked around at night, a branch might pull the pin on one of your grenades.

Training, and the fact that we operated in small groups was our way of keeping the jungle neutral. Our job was to convince the enemy that the jungle was ready to bring death at any moment by setting ambushes. Our 'Hunter-Killer' teams of six men set ambushes using Claymore anti-personnel mines, detonator cord and automatic weapons. Our fields of fire were set to sweep a trail, with Claymores primed to pulverize anyone in our killing zone. Our job was to inflict messy enemy casualties and then blend back into the jungle. But whether we were the hunters or the hunted was often hard to determine; frequently we were both. For the VC also wanted the jungle to be on their side.

The burden of fear

We moved through the jungle in single file – 'ranger file' – to minimize the chances of hitting a booby trap. We avoided trails for the same reason, though it made movement far more difficult. Our pointman frequently carried a shotgun so that he could sweep the area in front of him should he walk into an enemy patrol or ambush. In some cases, we had sawn-off M79 grenade launchers clipped to our harness and loaded with cannister rounds. Fear and discomfort were our constant companions in the jungle. But we had one advantage over the enemy. We knew that for us the key was to survive for those few minutes until the firepower available to back us up could be brought into action. That's why we burdened ourselves with extra ammo, even though humping it in the jungle was agony.

Eventually, humping anything in the jungle became agony. The standard-issue clothing became filthy and stiff, and during the monsoon it went sodden and chafed against the skin. On recon missions we never even took our boots off, or removed our rucksacks for days at a time. During the monsoon my fingers would become white and wrinkled until they looked like some of the slimy crawling things which called the jungle home. Cleanliness was important but impossible to maintain. As a result, minor problems became major ones. Jungle sores, small cuts, and insect bites would not heal and at times, as we saw the rot crawling up our thighs, we worried that our testicles would fall off.

The ants were constant, always there, always crawling, and always biting. But we would have gladly taken the ants over the leeches. Leeches were everywhere in the jungle and especially all over our bodies. Frequently, cigarettes couldn't be lighted to burn them off so the only recourse was to drench them in 'bug juice' and wait for them to fall off. At any given time I hated leeches more than the VC or NVA, but I kept reminding myself, 'the jungle is neutral; the VC have leeches, too, but without the benefit of American bug juice'.

Above: For soldiers wading through the streams and rivers of Vietnam, the leech (inset) was often an unwelcome and painful travelling companion.

Because of the constant filth, spots and boils also became a problem, and you could tell short-timers – men about to leave the Nam – by the peroxide baths they began to give their faces in an attempt to clear them up before returning to the outside world.

Wandering in a dead land

The scientists or Pentagon planners, no doubt, thought defoliation was a great idea as they sat in their air-conditioned offices – but it wasn't. Even forgetting the problems with Agent Orange, which none of us knew about then, we hated moving through defoliated areas. We had no cover and were easy prey for an ambush. Worse still, the dead leaves crumbled into a powder which got into our clothes and chafed our skin intolerably. The dried creepers in defoliated areas also seemed to reach out to trip us. The skin between my fingers and toes, cracked and bleeding anyway, would become especially sensitive to the corrosive powder from the dead vegetation of the defoliated areas.

In the jungle the smell of death soon became mixed with the smell of stagnant pools, rotting vegetation, and our unwashed bodies. Normally, even before we left on a recon mission, we avoided washing with soap for a couple of days since the VC had a finely developed sense of smell for US

Below: The eerie wasteland of a defoliated forest freed US soldiers from a surprise attack, but exposed them to untold risks.

18

soap. Lack of cleanliness affected health and comfort in the jungle but there was, in reality, little comfort, just survival.

Eating was mostly a chore, at best a chance for a slight rest. C-rations were often known as 'Charlie'-rats, a pun on the radio code for 'C' and the implication that C-rats must have been wished upon us by the enemy. Only someone who's tried to eat a cold can of 'beef slices with potatoes and gravy' as the monsoon rain pours into the can mixing water with grease can appreciate a meal in the jungle. Of course, the rain did drown some of the insects which had crawled into the can. The monsoon rains had other, far worse, side effects, however. They chilled us after our bodies had grown used to the tropical heat. During the monsoon, slopes became mudslides which were impossible to climb, and before noon the jungle was often shrouded in fog.

A walking nightmare

Sleep in the jungle was, at best, tortured and intermittent except when you virtually collapsed from exhaustion. But that was dangerous, too, since you might have to come awake instantly and start E & Eing (escaping and evading). While I slept, one hand was usually on the detonator for the Claymore mines surrounding our sleeping position, the other hand on my weapon. It may be a flaw in my character, but I never dreamt the guilty dreams they portray in the movies about killing the enemy. My bad dream was about trying to kill the enemy and not being able to, my rifle jamming or refusing to go off. No doubt Freudian psychologists would have seen this related to fears of impotency; big deal, let them try deep penetration missions in the jungle, then they can judge my dreams!

Our weapons, of course, were very important to us in the jungle. In the early days the high-residue powder and lack of proper lubricants caused a lot of problems with the M16. Our version of the M16, the Colt Commando CAR-15, held up well: I

Above: His face contorted in pain, a soldier suffers from a mass of Hornet stings - a potentially fatal injury. Below right: a Marine nurses his feet, plagued by the constant wetness which causes 'trench foot' - a common menace in Vietnam.

required my teams to maintain them carefully and to tape them to avoid metallic sounds. We would only load 18 rounds in 20-round magazines or 27 rounds in 30-round magazines. Every fifth round was a tracer. In addition, I carried a Browning 9mm pistol, a Smith and Wesson stainless steel 0.38 revolver, a High Standard 0.22 silenced pistol, a Randall knife, and assorted M26 and 'Willie Pete' (white phosphorus) grenades. Paranoid? Over-insured? On the contrary, I wished I could have carried more.

The Southeast Asia jungle was indeed a mean place to fight, but when I think back now almost 20 years later I'm proud of the fact that we learned to survive there and made it an even meaner place for the VC.

CHAPTER 4

1965

In the mountainous border country of Vietnam, Green Berets fought an undercover war, lying in wait on the Ho Chi Minh Trail that kept the Viet Cong supplied

When the Marines landed at Da Nang in 1965, they were far from the first of our troops to set foot in Vietnam. The Green Berets had been there since 1957. As the US Special Forces, they had been sent as military advisors to train and assist the South Vietnamese Army – the ARVN. We also began to equip and train the primitive Montagnard tribesmen who lived along the border with Laos and Cambodia.

The infamous Ho Chi Minh Trail ran from North Vietnam down through the mountains of Laos and eastern Cambodia. It was the Viet Cong's supply route and the strategic key to the war. Along it trudged North Vietnamese Army

CUTTING THE

EYE-WITNESS

The author Colonel Rod Paschall served with the Green Berets and the 25th Infantry Division in Laos, Vietnam and Cambodia during the war in Southeast Asia.

Rod Paschall leads a patrol of Montagnard tribesmen who have been armed and trained by the Green Berets. Their aim, in the border regions, was to cut the VC's supply lines and intercept troops coming in from Cambodia and Laos.

officers, South Vietnamese communists returning home, and simple bearers who carried what they were told to carry. These infiltration parties usually numbered between 10 and 15 people. Armed with Russian AK-47s, Chinese copies of Soviet weapons or captured French kit, they humped medical supplies, radios and ammunition on their backs. The Ho Chi Minh Trail was no six-lane highway. It was a tortuous path of high mountain passes, rivers to be forded and narrow tracks through dense jungle.

For the fledgling ARVN to stand a chance against the battle-hardened Viet Cong, it was vital that this supply route was cut. In 1963, my Special Forces detachment, along with four others, had armed and trained 200 Montagnard

Most of Paschall's Mnong company was moved up to Ban Don by truck. The equipment was airlifted by H-21 helicopter, then off-loaded with the help of several elephants and their keepers from a nearby village.

VC LIFELINE

1965

Colonel Rod Paschall was with a Special Forces detachment in South Vietnam in 1962. His job was to arm and train the primitive mountain – or Montagnard – tribesmen on the Darlac plateau. The VC were already operating in this area. Four-man agitation and propaganda teams were levying rice taxes and 'conscripting' recruits. Reprisals were taken against villages that resisted.

To the Saigon government the loyalty of these tribesmen in the border areas was vital. But arming them was a risky business. Had they gone over to the VC, the arms would have fallen straight into enemy hands. However, the Montagnards hated the Vietnamese – communist and non-communist – who had always treated them as inferiors. But they were prepared to be loyal to Americans who gave them weapons.

Rod Paschall headed a 12-man team in Darlac. But these 'A' teams were not organised as a fighting force. They comprised two officers and ten sergeants, specialists in communications, weapons, demolition, intelligence and medicine. The idea was to operate with the tribesmen, training them and assisting them in action.

The problem was that regional VC companies of between 80 and 100 men, armed with AK-47s, World War II submachine-guns and mortars, were also at work in the area. This meant that the Americans had to work fast to mould the tribesmen into an efficient fighting force.

At Lac Thien, the first village Paschall and his team visited, 10 local Mnong tribesmen had already been armed. They wore loin clothes but they carried US carbines and a few grenades. The village itself was defended by a couple of strands of barbed wire and a few

THEY TOLD ME: 'LEAVE OR DIE'

When calling in an airstrike at night the Green Berets lit cans of petrol, arranged in the form of an arrow, to direct the incoming aircraft.

punji sticks. And it was badly sited under a hill.

Within an hour of being in Lac Thien, Paschall received a note from the local VC telling him to leave – or die. With four Rhade tribesmen who had been seconded to the team, Paschall laid an ambush. Three of the agitprop team – who had sent the note – were killed and the leader captured. Under interrogation he revealed that the VC regional company intended to attack.

By the time they did, three weeks later, Paschall's team had armed 25 more villagers, set up an outpost on the nearby hill top, trained and equipped two other villages, set up a simple radio net and organized a strike force of 75 Mnong tribesmen. Normally, two or three Americans accompanied the patrols and always at least a platoon of the company were outside the base camp.

The attack came at night. It began with a barrage of mortar rounds. Within minutes, village defences were fully manned and guard positions re-inforced. The perimeter was breached but the VC were repulsed by an airstrike, directed by a fire arrow. One tribesman was killed and several wounded. The VC left three dead. Marks indicated others had been dragged away. Bullet holes in village huts indicated that the VC were not very proficient and had not set up a base of fire to support their advancing troops.

Within a year, Paschall's team had equipped 20 more villages and the local VC company had dwindled away through desertion. When Paschall and his team left Vietnam in 1963, they thought the war was over. In fact, it had only just begun. The Politburo in Hanoi realised that the VC were losing the war in the hills and in December 1963 they began sending regular NVA forces south.

villages in the Darlac border province and we moved a company of about 80 armed tribesmen up to the old French fort at Ban Don. Our assignment was to patrol some 50 miles of the Cambodian border.

The terrain was a pleasant surprise. The foliage was relatively sparse, the ground generally flat and there were a few clear streams. Ban Don itself was sited on a fairly substantial river. We crossed the river in sampans under the cover of a machine gun position on the fort and set off for the Cambodian border.

I had taken with me one other American, my medical sergeant, and 10 Rhade tribesmen, thinking they would know the area. They did not. They had only been on patrols of three or four miles. We planned to cover 25 in two days and one night.

There were plenty of trails through the bush and they looked well used. We travelled quickly, mostly at a dog trot, off-setting the trails by 20 to 50yds. Two men travelled about 20yds in front as point and one man was kept about 10yds to the flank, between us and the trail. We would stop every hour or so and move down to the trail, looking for footprints or other signs of use. The idea was to get a feel for the ground, avoid contact and study the trail network in this sector.

The Saigon government had had no military presence in this area for three or four years, so the North Vietnamese and the Viet Cong were taking few precautions. The trails avoided dense terrain and there were no booby traps or punji pits full of sharpened bamboo sticks. Camp sites and rest areas were at trail intersections, near streams. We were plainly in the enemy's back yard.

An enemy base area

As it grew dark, we moved away from the trail. Finding a slight rise in the ground, we set up a 50 per cent alert for the night. The Rhade squad leader was nervous. My medic, Sergeant Young, joked with him to calm his fears.

We were on the move again before day-break and we had only gone about half a mile when I came on one man from the point. He had his finger pressed to his lips. They had found an enemy base area and the other point man had sent him back to warn us. Five minutes later the other point returned, reporting in a whisper that there were several huts ahead. He could see no-one, but he could smell smoke.

Sergeant Young and I decided to take a look. We found six or seven bamboo huts with thatched roofs. There was no-one in sight but the smell of the smoke sent a shiver down my spine. It came from doused cooking fires. The coals were still warm. The enemy had not been gone long and they

Paschall's squad leaders (top) and their men (centre) wait in the dry creek bed 200yds from the VC way station. Left: Taken completely by surprise, only one VC survived the attack.

could be watching us.

Moving back into the brush, I began to feel more confident. If the enemy had known we were there, he would have hit us already. There was every indication that they had used the trails. We had not, so it was unlikely that they would come across signs of our presence later. What we had stumbled across was most probably a way station for Viet Cong and North Vietnamese infiltration parties. One had spent the night there, leaving – probably – about the same time we had left our overnight position. It was at the junction of the trails for Ban Don and Ban Me Thuot, on a small stream about five miles from the border – one day's march from Ban Don, maybe two days with a heavily laden carrying party.

We found fresh tracks

Sergeant Young and I used brush to cover our tracks. With the rest of the patrol we headed due south through the jungle to hit the trail leading from the way station towards Ban Me Thuot There we found what we expected – fresh tracks. I reckoned there were about 12 of them. It was hard to tell, it had not rained in some time. A Montagnard pressed his foot into the earth next to one of the tracks. It made no more of a mark which meant they were travelling light.

The tracks also indicated that they were walking. At a dog trot we would intercept their

rear in the late afternoon. But we would have to use the trail and there would be no time to cover our tracks. I had a better idea.

We brushed away all traces of our presence and backed into the jungle. Then we followed a direct compass bearing back to the fort. Next day we sent out the regular close-in security patrols in full view of the villagers. But there would be other patrols. These would go out after midnight, carrying ammunition and rations for four days. They would go out every 72 hours, returning under cover of the night.

At 0100 hours that night I took 26 men – both Rhade and Mnong – back across the river. Every other man carried an entrenching tool. But there was no radio. It would have been useless at the range we intended to travel. We moved a couple of miles into the brush and waited till daylight. Then we moved off towards the way station, avoiding the trails.

We placed the way station under surveillance while the patrol holed up in a dry creek bed nearby. Mid-afternoon the second day, the observation post watching the way station came back to the creek out of breath. Ten enemy soldiers were making camp for the night in the huts.

I called the Americans together and we moved the patrol up to the way station, travelling in single file. Twenty five yards short of the position we deployed the Montagnards in a simple assault line, facing the enemy. The plan was to inch forward as far as possible, firing only on discovery. It was vital that every enemy soldier was killed or captured. If one darted off, he must be hunted down immediately.

They disappeared without trace

The enemy were taken completely unaware. They had put out no security and saw us only when we were less than 10yds from them. We could have taken them all prisoner, but one reached for his AK-47. The Montagnards pulled the triggers on their sub-machine guns. As soon as firing started I was yelling 'cease fire!' Nine enemy were killed. The sole survivor was taken prisoner. There were no friendly casualties.

We bound the prisoner, stripped the dead of their weapons, documents and anything else which could be of use. Half the Montagnards were detailed to carry the bodies away. They were buried in a heavily wooded area at some distance. The other half of the patrol were detailed to do a clean sweep of the way station. Every sign of our presence was to be taken away. Each of the brass casings from expended bullets was carefully found and collected. Our tracks were brushed over. Then we backed away into the jungle, leaving the enemy way station apparently undisturbed.

During the next few months, this action at the way station was repeated several times. The infiltration groups making their way across the border had no way of communicating while they were on the move. They simply disappeared without a trace.

THE GREEN BERETS

The US Special Forces were formed in 1952, and in 1953 the 77th Special Forces Group (Airborne) became the nucleus of the Special Warfare Center in Germany. But most US commanders would gladly have traded these 'Sneaky Petes' for a few more tanks, and manpower in Europe dwindled. The very idea of elite units and special forces of any kind was completely alien to the organization of the US armed forces. However, in June 1957 the 1st SFG began to train the South Vietnamese army – the ARVN – in Okinawa and teams from 7th SFG made six-month tours in Vietnam from May 1960.

In October 1964, the Green Berets 5th SFG took over Special Forces operations. Some 951 strong on arrival in Nam, their strength grew to 1828 by October 1965.

The most important of their missions was to organize Civilian Irregular Defense Groups (CIDG) among the Montagnard tribesmen. This began with a pilot project at Buon Enao in December 1961, and by October 1965 there were 30,400 'cidgees'. A more aggressive role began with the Border Surveillance (BS) Program in October 1963.

But the Green Berets were expected to use more than their combat skills. As part of a programme to win the 'hearts and minds' of the villagers, they were on hand to provide medical care (above) for the people.

Special Forces deployment 1965

By 1965, the US Special Forces were well established in South Vietnam with a large number of camps

The Buon Enao area

- Buon Ho
- Buon Tah
- Ban Me Thuot
- Buon Enao
- Lac Giao
- Lac Thien

located in border areas such as the Buon Enao district. Their role was to train local tribesmen and prevent infiltration.

- Hue
- Da Nang
- Kontum
- Pleiku
- Ban Me Thuot
- Nha Trang
- SOUTH VIETNAM
- Saigon
- SOUTH CHINA SEA

Key

★ Special Forces headquarters
● Special Forces detachments

Viet Cong assassination and government water torture: South Vietnam was being torn apart by a vicious guerrilla war long before the US Army appeared on the scene

It's a blisteringly hot afternoon in a small Mekong Delta village. There's no-one in sight – every human being is in the shade of the simple, straw-thatched huts. Suddenly there are shouts. Running into the village come a group of South Vietnamese government soldiers, wearing American style uniforms that are slightly too large for them. They're dragging along a painfully thin teenager, who looks younger than his 18 years and wears the loose black cotton pyjamas of the ordinary peasant. He's already been bloodied up – they found him hiding in a drainage ditch, and suspect him of being a VC guerrilla.

DIRTY WAR

In the struggle for South Vietnam, both the VC (left) and the South Vietnamese Army (below) used brutal methods to get what they wanted. Below right: Two victims of VC terror, killed in 1960. Right: A ritual Buddhist suicide.

An officer strolls out of one of the huts, and the villagers – thin and black-clad like the prisoner himself – gather round as the fingers of the youth are wired to a field telephone. While the officer interrogates him, the phone is cranked – causing excruciating pain. His body stiffens and dances with the current, and he finally blurts out answers. The villagers watch impassively as he is led away – perhaps to be shot, perhaps to be tortured again later.

At about the same time in a northern province, near the former imperial capital of Hue, a Catholic school teacher, active in anti-colonial politics during the early 1950s but strongly anti-communist, is giving instruction on Vietnamese

history to a class of children. The door opens, and four men with guns walk in. They explain that they are here because of false propaganda being disseminated by the puppet regime in Saigon. One of the gunmen shoots the teacher in cold blood – but there follows an even more shocking atrocity. As a warning to others who might be willing to accept instruction from pro-government teachers, the assassination squad hammer pencils into the ears of some of the children.

These incidents were not unusual; they were only too typical of the war being fought in Vietnam before the American ground troops arrived. Ever since the nationalist/communist Viet Minh had begun their war against the French rulers of their country in the 1940s, an underground struggle of a peculiarly vicious kind had been part of the everyday life of the Vietnamese peasantry. When the French were finally defeated in 1954, Vietnam was divided along the 17th Parallel. The North was taken over by a nationalist/communist regime headed by Ho Chi Minh. The South was placed under the control of Ngo Dinh Diem, a fiercely anti-French nationalist. He was a tough and shrewd politician, and within a year had fought off several attempts to unseat him. Diem's main victory, however, was in persuading the Americans to back him – the first head of the US Military Mission in Saigon had recommended that US aid be stopped, but Diem's ruthless manoeuvring soon gave him sufficient credibility to justify a continued flow of funds. By the end of the 1950s South Vietnam was receiving more US aid per capita than any country in Asia, and a US Military Assistance Advisory Group was training and equipping Diem's army – the ARVN (Army of the Republic of Vietnam).

A savage regime

The partition of Vietnam had been, in theory, only temporary. It had been originally intended to hold elections that would reunite the country; but Diem cancelled those in the South. To strengthen his position, Diem issued a series of severe laws and decrees, ostensibly directed against communist agents, and put in motion a campaign to root out the remaining members of the Viet Minh. Most notorious among these edicts was 'Law 10-59', which permitted roving military tribunals to try suspects and carry out summary executions. Initially, this ruthless policy was successful in some areas – particularly in the Mekong Delta – but it would soon backfire.

Communist cells kept their activities on a small scale during the late 1950s, and did not risk large-scale encounters with ARVN troops. But in effect, Diem's measures allowed his officials to launch a reign of terror against former Viet Minh members, and to suppress any form of opposition to his regime. Thousands of innocent villagers were beaten and tortured, or held in prison camps in the most terrible of conditions. The result was, inevitably, resentment and hatred – something the communists could readily capitalise on.

THE VIET CONG

The Viet Cong was the common name for the armed forces of the National Liberation Front (NLF). Founded on 20 December 1960, the NLF was ostensibly a broad coalition. Its President, Nguyen Huo Tho, was a non-communist and members of religious sects as well as national minorities (such as the hill tribesmen) were represented.

In fact, as the communist rulers of Vietnam have since admitted, the NLF was in effect a communist front, run by the members of the politburo in Hanoi, and its armed forces were directed by experienced guerrilla commanders like Vo Nguyen Giap, who had directed the defeat of the French at Dien Bien Phu in 1954.

The core of the Viet Cong was the 10,000 or so former members of the Viet Minh who had remained in the South after the partition of the country in 1954. The North formed two transport commands in 1959, and these had infiltrated at least 28,000 trained personnel into the South by the end of 1964. Together with local recruitment, this process resulted in a guerrilla army of some 300,000 men under orders.

The Viet Cong were divided into two main sections. First of all, the paramilitary units were villagers who might undertake sabotage by night, act as intelligence gatherers or porters or, in the case of the young, become members of assassination or suicide squads. Secondly, there were full military units: the regional forces, which provided back up, and the main force. By 1965 this was some 50,000-80,000 men strong, able to act in large, self-contained formations.

A vexed question, and one that assumed enormous propaganda importance, was the role of the North Vietnamese Army (NVA). By March 1965, it is now accepted that three complete NVA regiments (some 5800 men) were operating with the Viet Cong, in addition to support units and political cadres. At the time, this was a statistic that could not be verified, and both sides made claims that bore little relation to the truth, purely to justify their actions.

In 1960, the communists formally established a National Liberation Front to fight the government. This rapidly started to extend its influence in the countryside, and experienced fighters moved down from the North to form tough cadres in the South. The Viet Cong, as the new communist military organisation was known, was selective in its terror, and efficient in its propaganda.

Terror tactics

NLF cadres or VC agitprop teams would visit a village at dusk. They would discuss, argue, and explain how Diem was a puppet of the imperialist forces that had been driven out of the North. Hidden within the agitprop teams' velvet gloves, however, were steel talons. Government officials were quietly disposed of, and the next day their heads might be found left on stakes to greet government troops entering the village. Special 'Security Squads' were used for larger-scale terror if selective moves failed to work.

One eyewitness in Long Kanh Province, just northeast of Saigon, recalled a classic incident. He was travelling on a bus along a quiet road when it was suddenly halted. Six members of the Viet Cong walked through the bus, collecting the government-issue identity cards. Two men were then taken off the bus – they were plain-clothes policemen. The leader of the VC cadre said to them: 'We've been waiting for you. We've warned you many times to leave your jobs, but you have not obeyed. So now we must carry out sentence.'

The two men were then forced to kneel by the roadside and were decapitated with machetes.

Right: Beating and torture were expected as routine if taken prisoner in Vietnam. Disregard for the rules laid down by the Geneva Convention for the conduct of war were the norm, for both the VC and the ARVN. This worried prisoner seems only too aware of this fact.

1965

MURKY WATERS

South Vietnamese politics was nasty and corrupt. Why did the Americans choose to support such questionable allies?

On 15 July 1965, the Prime Minister of South Vietnam, Air Vice-Marshal Nguyen Cao Ky (seen below in typical pose), caused something of a stir when he announced that Adolf Hitler was one of his heroes. On the eve of mounting their first major combat action against the communists, the Americans had once again been severely embarrassed by the men they were supposed to be helping.

The rulers of South Vietnam were a varied group of politicians. Some may have started out with high ideals, but they were operating within a corrupt society, and they all wanted to insure against defeat.

The keynote for South Vietnam's leaders had been set by the Diem clan. President Ngo Dinh Diem, who had come to power in 1955, was himself a tremendously hard worker, but he gradually lost touch with reality, partly by trying to do everything himself. He became a compulsive talker: one US reporter spent over six hours as the victim of one particularly lengthy monologue.

But if Diem himself talked, his brothers acted with great decision - in their own interests. His eldest brother, Ngo Dinh Thuc, was Catholic Archbishop of Hue. He dealt very successfully in real estate. ARVN soldiers in the area around Hue were employed cutting wood for him rather than fighting the Viet Cong. Another brother, Ngo Dinh Can, ran a smuggling operation.

Most notorious, however, were Ngo Dinh Nhu and his wife 'Madame Nhu'. Nhu ran areas of central South Vietnam like a warlord, meting out his own punishments and rewards. He and his wife took out full-page newspaper advertisements denying they were involved in illegal activities - a forlorn hope. Known as the Dragon Lady, or Queen of Saigon, Madame Nhu was renowned for her tight dresses and showy jewels. She also tried to impose her view of personal morality on the Vietnamese, including the banning of playing cards; people were arrested for wearing 'cowboy clothing'.

Diem was assassinated in 1963 and a series of short-lived military governments succeeded each other over the following two years as political instability reigned. Meanwhile, US aid poured into the country, creating an imbalanced economy in which the small urban middle class could do extremely well out of the purchase of consumer goods. Much-needed agricultural reform took second place to buying expensive status symbols.

The US government still dabbled in internal Vietnamese politics: General Duong Van Minh (nicknamed 'Big Minh') who was one of the dominant military figures, and was prepared to try to come to a settlement with the Viet Cong, was labelled 'drifting and indecisive' and shuffled from the centre of the political stage. In 1965, the Americans did manage to find a political leader they could trust, in Nguyen Van Thieu. He ruled initially in tandem with Air Vice-Marshal Ky, and remained in power until 1975.

Thieu may have provided some stability, but he did little to stop the corruption that had spread throughout the ruling classes. At the Cirque Sportif, the club patronised by leading lights in Saigon society, the poolside would be adorned daily by the exquisitely dressed wives of generals and politicians. They would show off their latest purchases - diamonds or gold jewellery - as their husbands discussed how their businesses (maybe in prostitution, or perhaps in bogus antiques) were going.

Meanwhile, in Hanoi, ruthless, simply clad men were planning their next move in the long war to create a united, communist Vietnam. They had been fighting since 1945; they were prepared to fight into the 21st century to achieve their goal. There is no doubt which set of men was the more likely to win.

FIELD OF COMBAT

South Vietnam, covering an area of some 66,200 square miles and with a population of some 16 million in 1965, presented a wide variety of terrain and climatic conditions. Stretched like a bow from the Demilitarized Zone (DMZ) on the 17th Parallel in the north to the low-lying Mekong Delta in the south, the country was hot and humid, with average daily temperatures of 27C and a heavy annual rainfall, produced by monsoons which came from the south in the summer and the north in the winter.

In the south was the Mekong Delta, interlaced with a myriad of unmapped waterways. The ricebowl of the country and heavily populated, it had always been a hotbed of communist activity. No central government forces had ever been able to assert themselves fully in the region, although President Diem had done his best to root out those members of the Viet Minh who had remained there after the partition of Vietnam in 1954.

Further north, lay the capital, Saigon, with about 1.5 million inhabitants. Past Saigon going north was an area of 'piedmont' – forested, sparsely populated rising ground, the beginning of the Châine Annamitique mountains that spread like a backbone virtually the full length of the country (750 miles). Steep-sided mountains up to 8000ft in height created the Central Highlands, where jungle-covered valleys ran down to the coast. In the Highlands, the population consisted of scattered nomadic tribesmen – the 'Montagnards'. The Viet Cong made strenuous attempts to woo the Montagnards; the South Vietnamese government tended to treat them with contempt.

Along the coast, from the DMZ in the north to the southern coast, heavy, but unpredictable rainfall again led to concentrations of population in lush agricultural land. The major cities in this area were the former Imperial capital Hue (with over 100,000 inhabitants) and Da Nang, with about 200,000 inhabitants. The great US bases – Da Nang itself and Cam Ranh – were situated on the coast.

Previously printed 'verdicts' were pinned to each of the dead men. The VC reboarded the bus, and returned the identity cards to each passenger, explaining, 'You'll get into trouble with the authorities without these, and we don't want that to happen.'

Cold and vengeful – but efficient – in the early 1960s the VC were conducting a campaign of terror that the government seemed incapable of countering. Diem, once an energetic nationalist, was increasingly isolated from real events, and the efficiency of his regime began to plummet. He preferred to rule through members of his family, the government became corrupt and, critically, he and his entourage were Catholics.

Ritual suicide of the Buddhists

The majority of the Vietnamese people were Buddhist – the organisation of families and villages was based on Confucian lines, with obedience to elders an important characteristic. But there was an important Catholic minority in Vietnam, many of whom had reached high administrative rank under the previous French rulers. Some 900,000 Catholics had also fled south to escape almost certain communist persecution in the North when the country was partitioned. A clandestine organisation, known as the Can Lao, soon blossomed. Comprising members of Diem's family, high government officials and senior Catholic churchmen, the Can Lao had members in all government agencies. Its members levied an unofficial tax on many aspects of Vietnamese life. Land reform was blocked, but large areas of land were granted to Catholic refugees – especially in the Central Highlands, which enraged the Montagnards, the hill people who lived in this region.

The first that many in the West knew of Vietnam was when this religious conflict between Buddhist and Catholic came to a head. In a symbolic gesture that was captured by the world's press, the elderly Buddhist monk, Thich Quang Duc, calmly squatted down by a road junction in Saigon, poured petrol over his robes and then set light to himself.

The immediate result of the Buddhist protests was the fall of Diem himself – his failure to cope with the situation led to his assassination by army officers. These same officers then took over the reins of power. But the confused, violent whirl of events had gone too far to be turned around.

By 1965, Vietnamese villagers had a long experience of violence – they expected the worst, and it was often meted out to them. Any individual – women and children included – were potential weapons in this struggle.

How could farm boys from New Mexico, taking the caps off their mosquito-repelling aerosols and unwrapping their compo rations from San Francisco, be expected to understand the meaning of clan structure within a Vietnamese village? Or the symbolic meaning of children having pencils hammered into their ears? Or the fact that pacifist monks could sit immobile while they roasted to death in public to make a political point? The Vietnam War was to be a real clash of cultures – and it was already very dirty before the Americans even got involved.

Embarking on his extraordinary career as a combat photographer at the age of 18, the author, Tim Page, captured on film some of the most dramatic and haunting images of the entire Vietnam war.

AMBUSH!

On patrol in a Viet Cong stronghold riddled with mines, booby traps and tunnel systems: in August 1965, as the fighting moved south towards Saigon, US troops began operating in the notorious communist sanctuary known as the 'Iron Triangle'

At the end of summer '65, the Allied Command in Vietnam decided to throw a massive search and destroy operation into the Viet Cong's major sanctuary near to Saigon – the 'Iron Triangle'. Two battalions of the 173d Airborne Brigade, reinforced by a battalion of the 1st Royal Australian Regiment, would launch an assault and block operation near Ben Cat, the district capital. Tactical air support, helicopters and artillery were on constant standby.

What had attracted *LIFE* to assign me to the story was that, in an effort to push Charlie out of the known labyrinth of tunnels in the area, the airborne was to deploy a new weapon that would unleash a mixture of CS gas and smoke into the tunnel entrances. It promised to be a colourful assignment.

We kicked off late one Friday morning in the

monsoon season – the weather was a sod. The 173d's battalions required 110 lift ships since the old B-model Hueys could only carry eight fully laden troopers. The LZs were hot, but light incoming fire was soon suppressed by a combination of artillery based at Ben Cat and Bien Hoa, and the heavy firepower of B-model gunships and rocket-firing 'hogs'. Four miles west of Ben Cat, Charlie Company – to whom I had been assigned – formed the extreme left flank of the Tactical Area of Responsibility (TAOR). The area to be searched was 40 square miles of scrub land and old rubber plantations.

The choppers did not sit down to let us off – we jumped from a few feet up as the door gunners pumped rounds into the surrounding tree-lines. The LZ was rapidly secured. As the sun set over Cambodia, we got a re-supply of C-rations and water. Navy and Air Force planes then put on a display of tactical support a few hundred yards from our perimeter. Throughout the night, artillery banged away on harassment and interdiction

comfortable way to spend a spooky night when the teeming rain turned the poncho hammocks into hip baths and deadened the giveaway noises of the hostile bush.

It was a grimy, damp and bedraggled company that greeted the dawn. The odd radio was tuned to Armed Forces Radio Vietnam – AFRVN was beaming the World Series baseball finals live to our boys in green. The Los Angeles Dodgers had the Minnesota Twins on the rack.

'All Americans read this die'

When a lookout spotted shapes flitting along the opposite tree-line, fire was brought down and the enemy disappeared into the undergrowth without trace. We moved out under the cover of a creeping barrage, a lot of which was woefully short. Chunks of jagged hot shrapnel landed among us and curses abounded.

Our point man was soon turning up old bunkers and fighting holes, and the next clearing was found to be heavily studded with anti-helicopter

A WIDENING WAR

Operations by the 173d Airborne around Saigon were being conducted as part of the US attempt to stem the effects of the Viet Cong early summer offensive. The communists aimed to push through the Central Highlands to cut South Vietnam in two, and to threaten Saigon.

Already, on 11 May, the provincial capital Song Be, some 80 miles north of Saigon, was occupied by Viet Cong forces for a short time. As the summer monsoon began to build up, the Viet Cong readied themselves for major assaults.

On 29 May, there was a series of attacks in the Central Highlands. The ARVN forces did not acquit themselves well: only US air power had saved the whole of Quang Ngai province from being overrun. In the middle of June, two Viet Cong regiments occupied a Special Forces camp at Dong Xoai, only 70 miles from Saigon, and cut to pieces the ARVN relief forces.

General Westmoreland (above) felt he had no alternative but to use US troops to plug the gap. A battalion of the 173d Airborne, holding a defensive enclave at Bien Hoa airbase near Saigon, moved out to retake Dong Xoai. The ARVN had performed poorly, to say the least, during June; casualties had been heavy, with many units unable to return to action after suffering severe losses, and the inept leadership that many senior officers had displayed had only been equalled by the lack of enthusiasm of the troops – desertion rates increased.

For the rest of the summer and into the autumn, the Americans of the 173d would be in action in earnest against the communist strongholds near Saigon.

Left: Into the 'Iron Triangle'. Crouching low and peering into the thick scrub that lies ahead, a trooper of the 2d Battalion helps to secure the perimeter of the LZ while choppers land and take off in a storm of dust and smoke. Right: One day into the operation, and still no sign of the VC.

missions. Although it was reassuring to know that Charlie was being softened up, the noise was particularly disruptive to any sleep pattern – especially in a mosquito-infested, Viet Cong-contested piece of scrub in the Iron Triangle.

After cold 'C-rats' that served as an impromptu breakfast, we moved out shortly before dawn. The going was dense brush, and the man on point had to hack through the thorns and creepers with a machete. He was 'spelled' every 10 minutes or so, with another man coming forward to take his place.

The day's objective, a large 300yd meadow-like area, was reached at 0100 hours. We were re-supplied by some quirk at G4 stores with a ship load of ice blocks, 20 cases of chocolate milk and the same of grape juice. Enough for a battalion, much less a company of 130 men. The guys could not believe their luck and scoffed the lot. We all fell victim to a serious case of the trots – not the most

stakes. We moved cautiously on towards the next objective – a disused rubber plantation road just north of the Saigon River. We were to wait for a leaflet drop before moving through the inhabited zone between road and river. These leaflets would advise all civilians to be ready to move out for screening at Ben Cat. There were also 'chieu hoi' leaflets, offering Viet Cong guerrillas the opportunity to surrender in any one of five languages. Charlie used them for toilet paper.

We made it to the road by 1300 and waited for Company B on our right to come on line. We flopped into the shade, loosening rucksacks and gear. The leaflet drop was scheduled for 1430. At three o' clock, as we moved up, there was an enormous explosion at the front of the column and the screech of smallarms echoed down the track. I found out later that the lead elements of Company B had stopped to read a sign by the side of the road. It was written in Vietnamese and, as the troopers

Left: Brown foliage at the head of the trail raises the suspicions of two troopers, but neither man realises that the trap is about to close. Moments after Page took this picture, the VC opened up on the lead elements of Company B from the cover of their camouflaged ambush position. Below left: In the aftermath of battle, medics work feverishly to prepare the wounded for medevacing out of the combat zone (far right). Guided down by a red smoke flare, these 'dust-off' choppers meant the difference between a hospital bed and a body bag for many of the battalion's wounded.

clustered around their interpreter, the message – 'All Americans read this die' – exploded with devastating results.

Simultaneously, the VC ambush opened up from camouflaged trenches and bunkers. For the guys on the road, there was no place to go. Using remote control, the VC had detonated a Claymore-type mine based on one of our dud 105mm shells. Their machine gun began spewing bullets at the same instant. The lead platoon was decimated.

We moved into the fire zone to retrieve the wounded and dying. I sprinted forward. On one side of the road, an NCO, his own leg shattered, was shielding a badly wounded and shocked man with his own body. A trooper, his face half shot away and his arm and leg at an ungainly angle, screamed and spat blood in his death throes while his buddies held him down. People were claiming they had shot gooks before being hit themselves, but it was difficult to get an accurate picture of what was going on. Victor had done his homework and executed the perfect ambush.

It was intense and insane

For more than 200yds, the road was a scene of terrifying carnage; we had taken six dead and 19 wounded right there, and it looked as though it could be more. Chunks of body writhing, shredded guys just laying back, limbs at strange bloody angles, white jagged bone protruding. It was intense and insane. By this point, the M16s were blasting back a constant stream of the high velocity chatter, accompanied by the rattle of M60 machine guns and the thump of M79 grenade launchers. There was not enough time to help, to shoot frames, to survive, to think – I just went over to rock 'n' roll, picking off frames, stumbling back with a leg in one hand, a Nikon in the other. Bent double, then going forward again, ducking, falling, shooting feet and bodies from the horizontal –

THE IRON TRIANGLE

A 'dagger' pointing at Saigon, which was only 35 miles to the southeast, the 'Iron Triangle' had earned its name and reputation long before US forces arrived in Vietnam. An area of 60 square miles, it was defined by the Saigon river to the southwest, the Thi Tinh river to the east and the Than Dien forestry reserve to the north. Its corners were anchored on the villages of Ben Cat, Phu Hoa Dong and Ben Suc. Most of the 6000 inhabitants lived in Ben Suc; they were later resettled by US forces being regarded as VC sympathisers. US intelligence reckoned that Ben Suc provided the VC with four rear-service transport companies.

Although generally elevated about 40m above water level, the Iron Triangle was cut by marshes, swamps and open rice paddies, and there was also densely packed secondary forest, barely penetrated by a few ox-cart roads and foot trails. Ever since World War II it had been a refuge for anti-government forces, and by 1965 the area was the HQ of the VC Military Region IV, a staging post for assaults on Saigon.

The Iron Triangle was literally a 'human anthill' riddled with tunnel and bunker complexes, concealed storage rooms and mined and booby-trapped trails. In 1967, during Operation Cedar Falls, over 1100 bunkers and 525 tunnels were located and destroyed while the supplies captured included 3700 tons of rice, 800,000 phials of penicillin, 7500 uniforms, 60,000 rounds of ammunition, and hundreds of military documents.

South Vietnam
Main operations, 1965

On 8 March 1965, the first US combat troops were deployed in South Vietnam. During April and May, as US forces established enclaves in the Da Nang, Quang Ngai, Qui Nhon and Saigon areas, the ARVN launched a major offensive against the Viet Cong in the south. Beginning on 29 May, the Viet Cong struck back, mounting an offensive in the Central Highlands and in the area north of Saigon.

Phu Bai
Da Nang
Chu Lai
Quang Ngai
Kontum
Qui Nhon
Pleiku
Central Highlands
Nha Trang
Song Be
Dong Xoai
SOUTH VIETNAM
Bien Hoa
Iron Triangle
Saigon
Vung Tau
SOUTH CHINA SEA

Key
→ Ho Chi Minh Trail
■ US enclaves
✸ ARVN offensive, April-May
✸ VC Spring offensive, May-June

a lot of dud pix.

The VC backed off quickly. They were hip to the fact that there would be an incoming inferno very soon. The first artillery rounds sailed over two minutes later, creeping forward to chase Mr Charles. When the 'arty' lifted, Air Force F-100 Super Sabres screamed overhead and pitched in a load of napalm canisters. All incoming stopped and, out on the flanks, only the odd sniper round and burst of US fire could be heard.

There was a stunned interlude before the first 'dust-offs' started to flutter in, their landing positions on the road marked by swirling red smoke grenades. The dead and wounded were piled in and the birds lifted off for the medical station at Bien Hoa, 10 minutes' flying time away.

I had my story. Re-supply choppers started to arrive as the lead elements pushed on, chasing the victors. I hopped an empty Huey back to Bien Hoa and stumbled into the *LIFE* office an hour later, covered in gore and dirt and suffering from shock.

The story poured out over three stiff cognacs with beer chasers. The following week it ran to four pages. On the cover of that issue was news of the musical *Hello Dolly*, which had opened at Nha Trang air force base at precisely the same moment that Company B, 2d Battalion, 503d, had walked into Dante's inferno. After that the unit kind of adopted me. I went out on a dozen more ops with them, always hitting contact. More war stories.

RPD LIGHT MACHINE GUN

Calibre: 7.62mm
Weight: 7.1kg (unloaded)
Length: 1036mm (overall); 521mm (barrel)
Feed: 100-round belt
Maximum rate of fire: Cyclic, 700 rounds per minute
Muzzle velocity: 700 metres per second
Sights: 1000m
Maximum effective range: 800m

HARDWARE OF THE VC AMBUSH

The early Viet Cong used a combination of Chincom weapons and deadly improvisation to lay ambushes for US ground forces

Drawing on experience gained during World War II, Soviet weapon designers developed the M43 7.62 x 39mm intermediate cartridge for use in a new breed of gun – the assault rifle. The first adopted weapon to fire this new cartridge was the SKS self-loading Simonov, a gas-operated, 10-shot carbine that resembled a conventional bolt-action rifle in its outward appearance.

Equipped with a hinged folding bayonet under the muzzle, the SKS was certainly built to last. Laminated beech woodwork and heavy steel enabled the carbine to stand up to rough treatment on the battlefield, and the new cartridge offered powerful and accurate firepower to a range of 450m – ideal during an ambush.

The Viet Cong made extensive use of an SKS copy during the early years of the Vietnam war, receiving their supplies of the Chincom Type 56 carbine from communist China. Simple to operate and maintain, the robust Simonov semi-automatic was eventually superseded by the ubiquitous and more compact Kalashnikov AK-47 assault rifle.

Another Soviet-designed weapon that found its way into the hands of Viet Cong main force units was the RPD fully automatic light machine gun, introduced into Warsaw Pact service during the 1950s as a squad support weapon. The Chincom Type 56 and 56-1 copy of the RPD won great favour with both the Viet Cong and NVA; light, uncomplicated but capable of sustained heavy fire, the RPD light machine gun was ideally suited to a conflict where stealth, cunning and shock action were seen as essential.

The problem of ammunition belts picking up dirt or snagging on nearby obstacles was overcome by equipping the RPD with a 100-round drum into which the belt could be coiled when the gun needed to be employed in a mobile role. The RPD could therefore be operated by one man, compared with the two-man crew of the American M60 machine gun. The only real drawback of this design is that the gas-operated mechanism required to lift and feed a fully-loaded belt into the chamber is liable to malfunction if the belt is even slightly damaged.

Another potential problem with the RPD is the danger of the barrel overheating and jamming the weapon. Since the barrel cannot be removed for changing when hot, Viet Cong gunners had to be trained to fire only in short bursts, never exceeding 100 rounds per minute during an ambush or firefight. To achieve the accuracy desired on the battlefield or for an ambush, the gunners also had to make allowances for the vibration caused by the recoil of the lightweight RPD.

One of the more macabre group of weapons employed by the Viet Cong was that of booby traps. Unexploded bombs from US artillery and aircraft provided the VC with a staggering 800 tons of explosives each month from which they were able to fashion a plethora of remote-controlled death traps. Used as much for their psychological impact on US troops as the physical damage they inflicted, these homemade bombs were usually placed along roads where American patrols and convoys passed regularly.

Above: VC extract the explosive filling from a US shell.

SKS SIMONOV CARBINE

Calibre: 7.62mm
Length: 1020mm
Weight: 3.86kg
Operation: Gas
Feed: 10-round box
Sights: 1000m
Maximum effective range: 450m
Muzzle velocity: 735 metres per second

LANDING ZONE UNDER FIRE!

Helicopters and gunships spearheaded victory in the battles of November 1965 – but riding a Huey into a hot LZ was always a terrifying experience

1965

A rifle company of the 1st Cavalry Division (Airmobile) have spent a long hot morning slogging through second-growth jungle. After five days in the field they are heading back to base camp for a day's rest. They aim to reach the pick-up zone – the PZ – by noon. They dream of mail from home, a cold – OK warm – beer, a tepid shower. But that's for later. Right now, the platoon leader is up front with the point man checking the PZ. Everything is quiet.

The silence is broken by a crackle on the radio. The radio operator hands the headset over to the platoon leader. The company commander wants to talk. It's bad news. The entire outfit has been alerted for a quick-reaction 'eagle flight'. The platoon is to secure the PZ.

Ten minutes later the company commander and three other platoons come stomping through the jungle. Sweat is pouring from their faces. The men are formed into five- or six-man groups ready to load up on a slick. Leaders check weapons, ammunition, water, while the platoon commanders are briefed. The Air Cavalry have located a VC force near a village. They don't know how big the enemy unit is but the VC fired on the scout helicopter. Gunships are raking the enemy. The Cav's infantry platoon has been committed, but the enemy is pouring heavy fire on them. The company is designated to make a combat assault on the battle zone. The company commander will take charge of the battle, develop it and secure a landing zone for a larger force if necessary. A battalion commander is already over the scene.

Previous page: A door gunner lays down suppressive fire from his M60 as the grunts run into trouble in a hot LZ.

BIRD DOWN

John B Morgan III was a chopper jock in Vietnam. He was shot down. He survived his 12-month tour and he went back for more – flying Cobras. But that's another story.

I was shot down on 15 February 1967. My unit had been in-country about 40 days and operational for only about two weeks. I was a WO-1, a Warrant Officer, flying as co-pilot for Major Charles A Neal, 1st Platoon Leader. Our mission that day was to re-inforce a battalion of US infantry who were surrounded and under heavy fire by the NVA. Ours was the second attempt that day.

We were flying 15 UH-1D slicks, organized in five Vs of three in trail formation. The LZ was only large enough to accommodate three aircraft so we only had a 30-second interval drops. We had picked up units of the 1st Battalion, 12th Infantry, 10 miles south of the LZ. Major Neal and I were flying the lead ship and had five Pathfinders aboard who would co-ordinate communications on insertion.

The LZ was about 75yds in diameter, surrounded by trees and heavy brush. The American unit was dug in around the perimeter, leaving the centre clear for birds. As we approached from west to east the artillery prep was shut off and the last round marked by smoke.

At that time our two pairs of UH-1C helicopter gunship escorts started their racetrack firing loop and our door gunners were told to open fire. The gunships were firing 2.75in diameter folding fin air-to-ground rockets with nine-pound high explosive warheads and quad flexible M60s into the area surrounding the LZ.

I was 22 years old, in the lead ship on my first hot combat assault – but I was not the only one with sweaty palms and eyes as big as horse turds. As we started our deceleration and approach the noise was impressive. We could hear the machine guns and rockets launching second hand through our headsets as the gunship drivers chattered

over the air-to-air VHF. Impacting rockets and our own door guns added to the roar of battle.

All this did not seem to impress the NVA though. They were dug in and merely fired straight up as we passed overhead, adding another new sound to the din – the sound of bullets passing through aluminium aircraft skin. One round came through the chin bubble an inch forward of my left foot. It passed through the radio console and Major Neal's right calf, and ricocheted off his control stick. The force of the bullet knocked his right foot off the right tail rotor pedal. His other foot slid the left rotor pedal forward to the mechanical stop. At this point, I was just along for the ride.

The aircraft yawed hard left and hit the ground near the middle of the LZ at around 15 knots. The toe of the right skid hit first. The aircraft rolled 360 degrees to the right. As the main rotor blades hit the ground the transmission and attached parts departed – luckily to the rear and not through the cockpit as they would have done if the bird had rolled to the left. I remember watching the LZ and the tree line do a beautiful slow roll to the sound of crumpling metal, and I remember wishing that this would come to an end.

What was left of our slick – Old 888 – came to a rest sitting upright in a cloud of red dust. This sight was enough to convince whoever was in charge to call time out and the remainder of the ships aborted.

Our passengers were deposited on the ground as the aircraft rolled away from them. Some had injuries. But the door gunner on the right-hand side was not so lucky. He had been crushed and died of internal injuries without regaining consciousness.

When the ship stopped moving I hauled ass outta there like my tail was on fire. Before I remember I was in a good-sized foxhole about 20yds away. Then I remembered my buddies and slunk back to help free them from the wreckage. Major Neal was still strapped in his armoured seat, struggling to get free and obviously in a lot of pain. I unbuckled his seat belt and dragged him back to the foxhole. Adrenalin was shooting out my ears. There, his leg was attended by a medic who did what he could for the door gunner.

As the noise of the other helicopters faded, we settled down in the crowded foxhole to wait. We heard M16s, returning the fire of Russian-made AK-47s.

On the other side of the LZ, the engine of an H-23 wrecked earlier that morning churned on. What was left of its rotor blades thrashed what remained of the fuselage and bubble.

An air force forward air controller appeared overhead in an O-1 Bird Dog. He co-ordinated with a pair of F-100 Super Sabres who did a mighty fine job of bringing napalm as close to the perimeter as I cared to have it. We could feel the heat on our faces.

Within three hours the first 'Dust-Off' medevac Hueys arrived. Major Neal was one of the first to go out – he had gotten his ticket all the way to the USA. I was flying again the next day.

Above: John B. Morgan and hootchgirl.

The landing zone – the LZ – is big enough for 10 slicks. The company will go in in two lifts, with two minutes between. The first lift is in five minutes. On landing, three platoons will fan out from the LZ. Company headquarters and the fourth platoon will remain in the centre, then move towards the heaviest fighting. 'Brief your men,' barks the company commander, 'and let's get going.'

All men aboard

This may seem like a shaky way to mount an airmobile assault, but it works. The riflemen and the helicopter crews have worked together before, countless times. They trust each other. The men are well trained and know what to do. They smoke a quick cigarette then, in the distance, comes the 'wop-wop-wop' of the approaching helicopters. They look like a swarm of dragonflies.

through the engine.

The troops clamber aboard and sit on the diamond-patterned aluminium floor. Some units sit on their steel helmets to protect their butts from ground fire. Most are ordered not to. The pilots have their .45 holsters slung between their legs. Many are 19-year-old volunteers who joined the army because they wanted to fly. It's a dangerous job. By the end of the war, 926 pilots and 2005 aircrew are dead.

Often the grunts recognize the door gunners and chopper pilots from other eagle flights. The door gunners pat their M60 machine guns reassuringly and yell greetings. Like the pilots, they often wear chickenplates – or chest armour. If there are any spare, they lay them in the vulnerable plexiglass chin bubbles under the Huey's nose or the gunners sit on them. The army

The company commander pops a green smoke grenade to mark the touchdown point of the lead helicopter. The beat of the rotor blades rises in pitch as the slicks fly in. On their flanks are helicopter gunships, darting and swooping to protect the pick-up. The slicks raise their noses as they 'flare' to slow their forward motion. Then they hover and drop on their skids. The engines idle but the rotors keep turning. Everyone is vulnerable now. The downdraft riffles the thick grass and the stench of kerosene wafts across the PZ. The whine of the engines is deafening, but there is no need for orders now. The grunts are on their feet, hunchbacked under the weight of their rucksack, weapons and ammunition. Leaders hold tight to their maps in the swirl. Weapons are on safety so some dumb jerk doesn't put a round

Top: Warrant Officer Skipper of the 361st Aviation Company was one of the many chopper jocks to risk his life in one of the most hazardous jobs in Vietnam. Above: A Huey slick dips its nose to pick up airspeed on its way out.

aviator in charge of the first lift checks with his flight leaders on his command radio net. They report all men aboard. He orders the pilots to power up. They rotate the throttles and watch the gauges.

Drop the nose and go

The leader orders lift-off and the pilots lift their birds into a low hover about three feet off the ground. Over the radio comes the order to go. In unison the pilots lower the choppers' noses and pick up airspeed.

The column remains low until they reach 60 knots to minimize the risk of ground fire. Then the pilots press back on the control stick and climb to 1200ft. This cruising altitude is high enough to be out of effective rifle range but low enough for quick

descent to the landing zone.

A minute later 10 more Hueys flare into the PZ. The platoon leader pulls in security and the men clamber aboard. Then the second lift follows the first.

There are no doors on the slicks. The wind whips through the open troop compartment. It feels good after the oppressive heat of the jungle at noon. Some men dangle their feet over the edge, like kids cooling their toes in a stream. Others crane over their buddies' shoulders for a peek at the scenery. Some watch the door gunners – or sit quietly, wondering what awaits them at the LZ.

On order, the door gunners test fire their M60s. The chatter of the guns sounds good. It makes everyone feel better. The smell of cordite is lost quickly in the 100 knot wind.

Nearer the landing zone, the men perk up and get ready. The artillery are already 'prepping' the LZ with 105mm shells. On its flanks, the battalion's forward air controller is bringing in the airstrikes. Gunships are pounding the VC with rockets and machine guns.

'First lift is in the LZ,' squawks the intercom. The company commander's radio operator calls. He and the old man are running off the LZ. His voice is breathless. In the background there's the noise of the first-lift slicks taking off.

It's a hot LZ

Now the grunts can see the LZ. There's coloured smoke in the centre and black and grey smoke from artillery and bombs around the perimeter. The pilot wires the door gunner on the intercom: 'It's a hot LZ.' Someone mouths: 'Oh shit, not another one.' Why couldn't it be a cold LZ, a nice helicopter ride and a walk in the sun? The grunts check their weapons, take a swig of water, steel

Above left: An eagle flight gives the grunts a cool break from the oppressive heat of the jungle. Above: Helicopter gunships and artillery prep the LZ. Main picture: The slicks go in.

themselves for the assault.

One of the first lessons learnt by a rookie chopper jock is that landing under enemy fire is a no-no. But sometimes it is unavoidable. Even a cold LZ can turn hot in seconds. The working assumption is that all LZs are hot and as many slicks as the LZ can accommodate are landed at one time. This deploys the maximum number of troops in the fastest possible time. All the ships will then take off together to prevent the enemy from concentrating on one target.

As added insurance, gunships would prep the LZ. If there is return fire, they will fly a racetrack loop over the LZ with one gunship coming on station as the first breaks away. This gives continuous fire on the target as the slicks come in to land.

But despite these precautions, a hot LZ is a terrifying place, with bullets smashing through the airframe, plexiglass chin bubbles bursting and instrument panels erupting in smoke and sparks. Both pilots must keep their hands on the control stick in case one is hit.

Open up with the door guns

The pilots' worst nightmare is the 50-cal machine gun. It spews bullets half-an-inch in diameter and an inch long at 2700ft per second. One or two hits from this weapon could spoil your whole day.

The column of choppers loses altitude rapidly as it approaches the LZ. The rotor pitch changes and the noise deepens as the slick loses airspeed. The engine whine hurts inside your head. The flight

fragile rotor blades beating over head. An F-4 Phantom, screaming up after dumping its bomb load, flashes by. The grunts try and visualize the combat scenario. They still can't see anything yet.

The door gunners begin blazing: They are aiming aft and the grunts cannot see what they are firing at. It could just be suppressive fire to make any enemy keep his head down. No, wait. The grunts spot the muzzle flash. It's the twinkling strobe of an AK-47 automatic – not the single flash of a local VC's rifle. And it's in the 4- to 8-o'clock sector that the third platoon have been assigned.

Everybody out

The column of helicopters flare in unison as they reach a low hover about three feet off the ground. The pilots settle the birds vertically, carefully feeling for the turf. But the grunts don't wait for the skids to touch. Before the platoon leader can yell they are un-assing from both sides.

By the time the platoon leader and radio operator have un-assed, the helicopters are already lifting to get the hell out of there. They barely reach a hover, dip their noses and haul ass. As the rotor noise fades, the grunts catch the sound of a firefight in progress.

The platoon leader turns to the 6-o'clock direction and herds his men back in the direction the helicopters came in. The platoon sergeant and squad leaders fan the men out into combat formation. The platoon leader reports to the company commander by radio, then he spots enemy muzzle flashes. He directs fire against

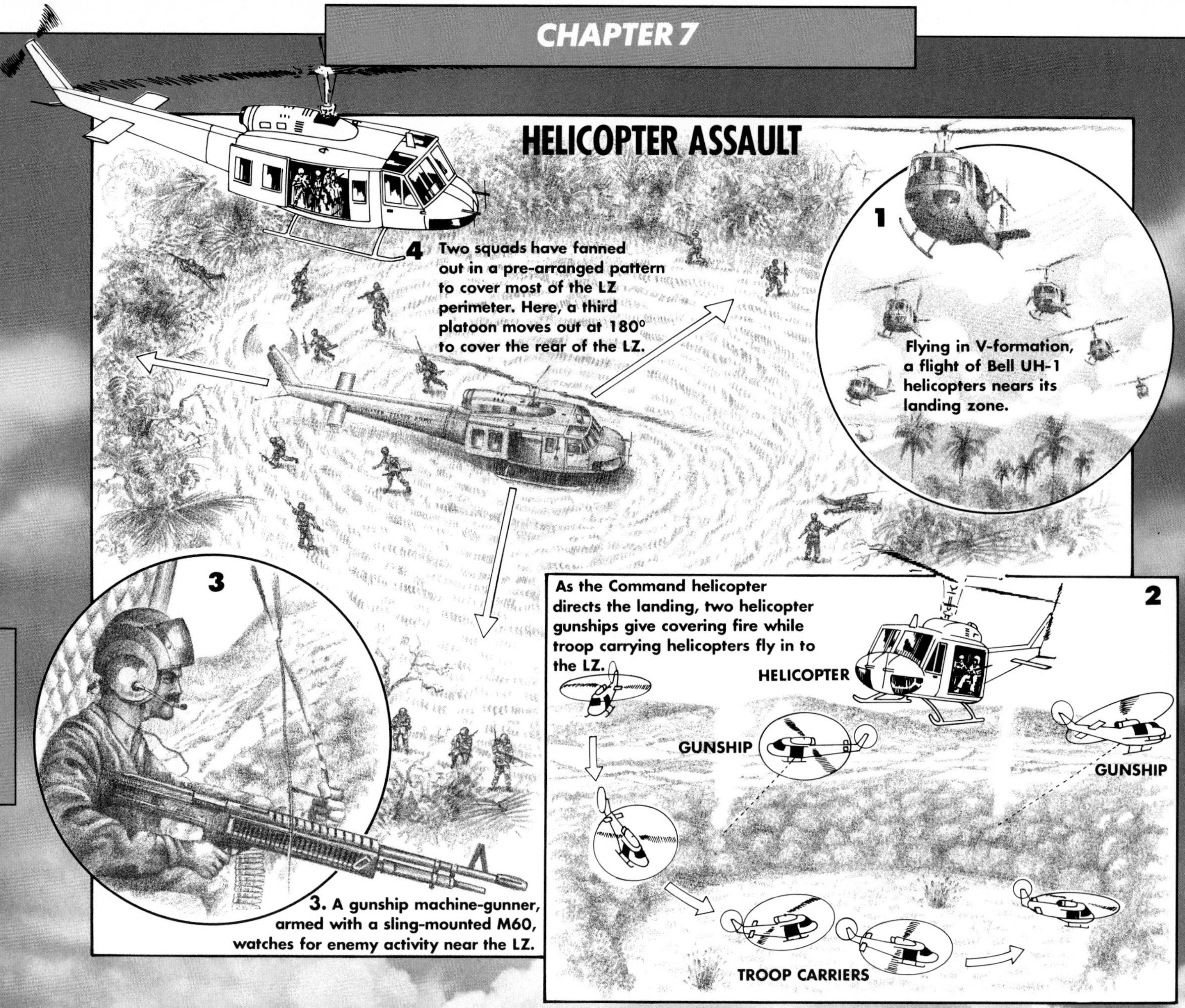

HELICOPTER ASSAULT

1965

1 Flying in V-formation, a flight of Bell UH-1 helicopters nears its landing zone.

2 As the Command helicopter directs the landing, two helicopter gunships give covering fire while troop carrying helicopters fly in to the LZ.

HELICOPTER

GUNSHIP

GUNSHIP

TROOP CARRIERS

3. A gunship machine-gunner, armed with a sling-mounted M60, watches for enemy activity near the LZ.

4 Two squads have fanned out in a pre-arranged pattern to cover most of the LZ perimeter. Here, a third platoon moves out at 180° to cover the rear of the LZ.

TACTICAL PROBLEMS

The helicopter provided the Americans with what they called 'airmobility' - speed, freedom of movement and firepower on the battlefield. But was airmobility all it was cracked up to be?

Vietnam was the first helicopter war. At the height of the conflict the Americans fielded some 5000 machines, able to transport whole battalions of infantry into a combat zone at a moment's notice. For the infantry commander, the helicopter seemed an answer to all his prayers. He could move his men from one crisis point to another over any terrain, bring in ammunition in an emergency, ship out his wounded, and provide fire support for his embattled troops on the ground by calling up gunships.

Another advantage of the helicopter was that the enemy were totally unfamiliar with this type of weapon and the tactics that went with it. The North Vietnamese Army and the Viet Cong preferred to fight a war with no recognisable front lines, launching all-out attacks and then melting away when the going got tough. The helicopter, however, was a threat to this way of fighting.

The first real test of the airmobility idea came during the Ia Drang Valley campaign in October and November 1965. There, helicopters were an invaluable asset, lifting in over 5000 tons of cargo to the troops in the field and moving whole battalions of men and artillery batteries during the course of the battle. In all this flying only four choppers were shot down, proving to many sceptics that the helicopter was not as vulnerable as they had first thought.

On paper, the airmobility idea looked great. But there were several very real and practical problems with making it work. For all their versatility, helicopters always had to land somewhere, and the troops on board had to fight on the ground. Suitable landing zones were not all that easy to find and incoming shells from US artillery, intended to soften up a landing zone, did not make the approach any less hazardous for the choppers and those on board.

There were also problems with the men. Once they had been lifted in, troops were often reluctant to move away from the landing zone where they knew that they could be resupplied, or evacuated if they got wounded. In short, mobility in the air often proved a poor substitute for mobility and firepower on the ground.

Left: Troopers form a tight defensive perimeter after a Huey has touched down on the LZ. Above right: Some of the grunts don't even wait for the skids to touch mother earth. Before the platoon leader can yell an order, they are 'un-assing' from their Huey on both sides.

Overhead helicopter gunships swoop along the flank. The platoon leader pops a coloured smoke grenade to mark his position. One of the squad leaders shoots a white phosphorous rifle grenade at the enemy. The gunships spot the bright white Willie Pete and take up the attack. They pour firepower onto the enemy. It is important to seize the combat advantage quickly. A hot LZ can turn into a mess in a hurry if a helicopter is downed.

Men are hit

As the platoon moves off the LZ, the grunts watch, smell and listen for the enemy. They listen for the swish of incoming mortar rounds and the crack of rifle fire. Their stomachs tighten. Sweat rolls down their faces in the close heat, soaking into the olive drab towels around their necks.

So far there have been no enemy mortars, but there's plenty of small arms and automatic fire. Men are hit. Medics rush from trooper to trooper, slapping on field dressings, fighting to stop the bleeding. Other men yell and chant as they lean into the firefight.

The gunships are low on fuel and the enemy is still firing. The platoon leader orientates his map with the terrain and calls for artillery support. Trust between infantrymen and the artillery is all important. If the gunners 'drop one short' and put a shell smack in the middle of the platoon, a lot of guys are going to get killed. The artillery forward observers recognize the radio operator's voice. He knows them too. They pass the fire request to the 105mm batteries that have already been pounding the LZ. The guns shift aim. Soon friendly shells swish comfortably overhead. Then there is the heavy crump as 105s pound into the enemy's position.

The grunts are hot, thirsty, tired and scared. But there is still work to do. They grab another swig of water from their canteens and press forward. On the big status board in the Pentagon, this is just another combat assault. But it is life and death to the men on the ground – on both sides – in this little piece of Vietnamese real estate. Airmobility exists to bring combat power to bear on the enemy. But for the grunt, the helicopter ride is just a pleasant interlude, a pre-amble to the dirty, deadly business of infantry combat.

A battalion from the 28th Infantry, under Lieutenant-Colonel Robert Haldane, were advancing through the rubber trees around their landing zone. Suddenly, bursts of sniper fire spattered out from within the jungle. Haldane's men began taking casualties, but the battalion swept on, determined to silence the guerrilla attack. It turned into an impossible task. Each time the enemy were surrounded they would somehow evaporate into the dense jungle air, leaving Haldane taunted and confused. He pressed on, but once again his unseen tormentors vanished.

Haldane's experience during Operation Crimp in January 1966 – the first big search-and-destroy sweep into the Viet Cong sanctuaries northwest of Saigon – was to become all too familiar to ground commanders in Vietnam. It was not until several days into the operation that Sergeant Stewart Green accidentally sat on what he thought was a scorpion but turned out to be a nail, and part of a

EYE-WITNESS

John Penycate (left) and Tom Mangold were the first BBC journalists to enter Vietnam after the war and make contact with VC commanders. Travelling the world to talk to survivors from both sides, their research revealed for the first time the full and shocking drama of the tunnel warfare waged beneath the jungles of Vietnam. The complete story is recorded in their best-selling book, The tunnels of CuChi.

WAR IN THE

VC guerrillas lived for years underground in amazing underground complexes, and US tunnel rats had to go in and fight it out with flashlight and pistol

wooden trapdoor. Beneath it was a narrow shaft that led to a tunnel. Green explored a small part of the tunnel, but darkness and claustrophobia soon drove him out. When coloured smoke was blown into the tunnel entrance, it reappeared unexpectedly from openings all over the surrounding countryside. The GIs had discovered the secret of the Viet Cong's ability to fight with the hidden menace of ghosts – a vast and labyrinthine tunnel complex deep below the jungles of South Vietnam.

At the height of the Vietnam war, the tunnel network stretched for hundreds of miles, linking whole districts and provinces from the Cambodian border to the gates of Saigon itself. 'No-one has ever demonstrated more ability to hide his installations than the Viet Cong,' wrote General

William Westmoreland. 'They were human moles.' The tunnel system housed an army at war and contained everything they needed to take on the most powerful military nation in the world – workshops and depots to hide arms and supplies, headquarters to plan their battle strategies, hospitals to care for the wounded, as well as kitchens, conference rooms and dormitories. For the poorly-armed guerrillas to sustain a war against enemies winged into battle by helicopter, they had no choice but to burrow underground. Hidden by day, the Viet Cong emerged at night as a shadow government.

In the tunnels, major operations like the Tet Offensive of 1968 were planned and prepared in complete secrecy; large units moved around undetected. The Viet Cong's local guerrillas had a special attachment to their ancestral soil, and their subterranean strongholds were an essential symbol of their resistance to those they saw as invaders.

Building a world beneath the jungle

The tunnel system was started during the anti-colonial war against the French (1945-54), but expanded fast when the Americans arrived. It was carved with hoes and baskets by 'volunteer' village labour out of the laterite clay which, when dry, set as hard as concrete. Where the water table permitted, there were several levels, each separated by watertight trapdoors which sealed the rest of the system against gas or explosives – as did the water trap, a water filled U-bend in the tunnel floor. Upward or downward trapdoors were often undetectable, leading explorers to believe that a tunnel was short when in fact it gave access to a huge system. There were false tunnels and apparent dead ends. The passages were a few feet in diameter, allowing only the lithest of men to wriggle forward, and zigzagged to deny a line of

was almost unimaginably harsh. The air was bad, and food – which was always scarce – rotted quickly. Spiders, ants and mosquitoes proliferated, and a parasite called the chigger burrowed under the skin to cause intense irritation. Many guerrillas suffered malaria or vitamin deficiency. In spite of that, a whole underground lifestyle developed. There were weddings, and babies were born. There were entertainments and morale-

boosting lectures. A huge cottage industry grew up making mines out of unexploded American bombs and other odds and ends of war. The Viet Cong's hospitals had to be close to the fighting. There were both forward aid stations and larger hospitals complete with operating theatres; parachute nylon covered the walls, offering a makeshift protection to the wounded and dying as the surgeons worked by candlelight. A constant shortage of medical supplies meant that anaesthetics were rare and operations often turned into agonizing ordeals. Wounded guerrillas in the underground wards would plead to see the daylight again, their muffled cries shrouded under the thick banks of clay.

One of the US Army's biggest bases in South

Left: Tense and alert, a tunnel rat stares cautiously above him as he emerges safely into the daylight.

1965

TUNNELS

fire. The tunnels were sown with booby-traps, from grenades and sharpened punji stakes to tethered poisonous snakes.

Tunnel entrances were skilfully concealed. Access even to a major headquarters complex such as that at Phu My Hung was through a one-foot-six trapdoor aperture. The Viet Cong normally placed mines near their important tunnels – an American unit that suffered deaths or injuries from mines was less likely to linger in the area. Indeed, there is ample evidence that the American high command never fully appreciated the size of the tunnel system, though it acknowledged the Viet Cong's endurance and tenacity in maintaining the war.

For the Viet Cong guerrillas, life in the tunnels

Above: Stripped to the waist, and armed only with a flashlight and a pistol, a tunnel rat prepares for another deadly incursion into the Viet Cong's underground world. Booby traps, bullets and punji stakes will threaten his every move.

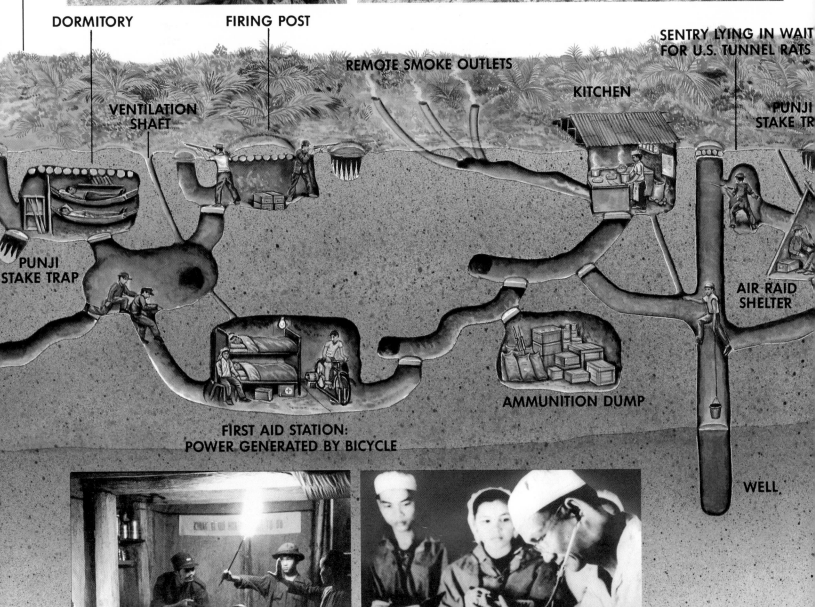

CHAPTER 8

DORMITORY

FIRING POST

SENTRY LYING IN WAIT
FOR U.S. TUNNEL RATS

REMOTE SMOKE OUTLETS

KITCHEN

VENTILATION
SHAFT

PUNJI
STAKE TR

PUNJI
STAKE TRAP

AIR RAID
SHELTER

AMMUNITION DUMP

FIRST AID STATION:
POWER GENERATED BY BICYCLE

WELL

VC TUNNEL COMPLEX

During the Vietnam war, the Viet Cong built up highly complex tunnel systems over large parts of South Vietnam. Whole companies of Viet Cong were able to survive and fight for long periods of time within these systems.

NVA OFFICERS DISCUSS TACTICS

SUBMERGED ENTRANCE

WATER TABLE

Far left: A 'cultural troupe' gives a performance. Throughout the 1960s, uplifting entertainments were presented in the tunnels. Left: A medical team at work. First-aid stations were often powered by a bicycle-driven generator.

Top far left: A sniffer dog discovers a hidden tunnel entrance, and the tunnel rats are once again faced with the problem of going into the lair of the enemy. Top left: A dead VC, one of the few bodies found. The skill of the Viet Cong in the tunnels was legendary.

Vietnam, Cu Chi, was built right on top of a Viet Cong tunnel system. The altitude and relative dryness of the land, which made it suitable for vehicles, also made it ideal tunnelling terrain. When the American 25th Infantry Division first arrived in 1966, an enterprising Viet Cong called Huynh Van Co hid with two comrades underneath the camp for a week, emerging at night to wreak havoc and steal food. The newly arrived 25th were baffled by the attacks, assuming that mortar fire was coming from outside their perimeter. But (in the words of one general) they had bivouac'd on a volcano. After causing psychological damage out of all proportion to its military importance, Huynh Van Co and the others withdrew to the 'belt' of tunnels surrounding the base. Neither they nor their tunnel were ever detected.

Enter the tunnel rats

After Operation Crimp, the extent and importance of the tunnel system dawned slowly on the American commanders. As more tunnel entrances were found, attempts were made to destroy the tunnels with explosives or by burning acetylene gas. These had limited success owing to the hardness of the earth and the VC's capacity for making instant repairs overnight. Dogs were sent down to find the Viet Cong, but were killed or maimed by booby traps. Soldiers ordered down tunnels tended to come up rapidly, reporting that the tunnel went nowhere. It became clear that the army would have to develop specialist volunteers for this unique problem. The result was the birth of the infantrymen who rejoiced in the undignified but menacing title of 'tunnel rat'.

The father of the tunnel rats was Captain Herbert Thornton, a bald and round-faced man from the Deep South. He was the Chemical Officer of the 1st Infantry Division at Di An, responsible for contaminating tunnels with CS gas. He's lucky to be alive. He was once crawling in a tunnel behind a rookie tunnel rat who set off a booby trap mine. Thornton was blown out of the tunnel and into the open air above, uninjured but deafened in one ear. His companion was never found.

'It took a special kind of being'

Thornton's superiors soon realised that tunnel destruction was a short-sighted policy when they learnt that this underground network could contain the key to the Viet Cong's battle plans – a treasure trove of documents and plans hidden deep below the jungle floor. Thornton was detailed to set up a tunnel team. Not only would special skills be needed, but an unusual type of temperament and courage. 'It took a special kind of being,' said Thornton. 'He had to have an inquisitive mind, a lot of guts, and a lot of real moxie into knowing what to touch and what not to touch to

1965

US troops tried everything to flush the VC out of their complex tunnel network. **Top** : Rifles cocked and at the ready, two Marines take no chances as they approach a tunnel entrance. **Above:** Smoke and CS gas usually failed to penetrate the inner recesses of the tunnels. **Above Right:** Marines join arms to heave a buddy out of the ground.

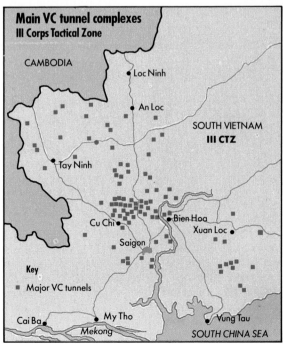

Main VC tunnel complexes
III Corps Tactical Zone

CAMBODIA

Loc Ninh

An Loc

SOUTH VIETNAM
III CTZ

Tay Ninh

Cu Chi • Bien Hoa
Xuan Loc
Saigon

Key
■ Major VC tunnels

Cai Ba • My Tho
Mekong
Vung Tau
SOUTH CHINA SEA

stay alive – because you could blow yourself out of there in a heartbeat. At first we tried having tunnel teams all over the Division, but we had people getting zapped because they didn't have enough knowledge to go into a tunnel right.' There were 'non-combat' deaths. Men suffocated when the oxygen underground had been burned away with explosives.

Flushing out the VC

It was the most unnatural and stressful mission: crawling for hours through pitch dark earthen tunnels facing sudden death at any moment. A wire or root could trigger a grenade, or release a viper. Viet Cong guerrillas would lie in wait silently to garrotte a tunnel rat as he peered through a trapdoor, or impale him with bamboo spears as he descended a shaft. The tunnel rats needed iron nerves and heightened senses. Men sometimes broke down underground. They were dragged to the surface crying and screaming, to be absolved of tunnel duties from then on.

Former tunnel rat Harold Roper recalled: 'I felt

information to the surface by telephone wire though many dispensed with all communication, preferring to keep their ears attuned for the slightest sound below ground that might herald danger. 'Kit Carson scouts', or former Viet Cong who had defected, accompanied the rats to talk out cornered VC. The rats adopted their own codes and procedures: you never fired more than three shots underground without rearming, as the enemy would know you were out of ammunition. When emerging from a tunnel you would whistle 'Dixie' – a muddy figure from the earth could easily be taken for a VC by your own side.

Underground heroes

What sort of man volunteered for this hazardous duty? Obviously, smaller men were at an advantage, and many were Hispanic or Mexican. All were oddball heroes who knew they would advance in their comrades' esteem for undertaking such a harrowing mission. Theirs was the ultimate confrontation with the enemy, face to face, one on one. For the rat the light at the end of the tunnel was usually a Viet Cong with a candle.

Staff Sergeant Pete Rejo was a tall wiry Cuban who volunteered to serve two extra tours of duty with the tunnel rat squad of the 1st Infantry Division. For him, tunnel warfare became an obsession. 'I loved it. The enemy hit us, then they went down the holes. I knew we were going to get them down there. Where else were they going – deeper? When they told me they had a VC down there, I came unglued.' Rejo would pursue the Viet Cong or North Vietnamese into the recesses of the system until he cornered them. His favoured weapons were the knife or the bayonet. Rejo took no prisoners in the tunnels.

No rat was ever left in a tunnel dead. A wounded rat was both an obstacle to his comrades and gave the VC a chance to escape. Such was the cameraderie of the rats that men would break the rules and go back alone to finish off a VC who had shot a comrade. Sergeant Pete Rejo not only defied the orders of his squad commander, Lieutenant Randy Ellis, but wilfully kept him in ignorance of an enemy's continued presence in a tunnel in the Iron Triangle when another rat had suffered grievous wounds underground. On the pretext of going down to destroy the tunnel with an explosive charge, Rejo descended alone to finish off the North Vietnamese soldier he knew was cornered. Rejo also knew that the communist soldier would be sitting with his AK-47 cocked, ready to turn subterranean night into day with the blast of his automatic weapon in the confined space. As Rejo drew near, he chose caution; he set his charge at the entrance of the tunnel where he knew the enemy was lurking. When it exploded, the tunnel collapsed. Rejo could say nothing to Ellis, and will never know if his enemy had been entombed as he intended, or – which is just as probable – had scurried off down some secret passageway, crawling to freedom through the dank soil of South Vietnam.

Above: Sergeant Pete Rejo in action. One of the most fearless and determined of the tunnel rats, Rejo became a self-styled expert in tunnel warfare.

more fear than I've ever come close to before or since. The Viet Cong would take their dead down the tunnels after a battle because they knew we were big on body count. Finding them wasn't pleasant. It was worse if they'd been there for a week – it stank! Everything rotted quickly because of the humidity. I came across rotting bodies several times. It didn't revolt me. I was just an animal – human beings don't do the things we did. I was trained to kill and be killed. Looking back, it's unreal. I wouldn't even think of doing anything close to that again.' The tunnel rats became an elite in Vietnam, with their own ad hoc badge and other privileges. Their nonsense Latin motto meant 'not worth a rat's arse'.

With flashlight, handgun and knife

When the infantry came across a tunnel, the rats were helicoptered in to explore it and flush out the VC. Despite belonging to the world's best equipped army, their techniques were simple. All they carried was a flashlight, a handgun and a knife. They operated in small teams, relaying

CHAPTER 9

1965

FIRE FROM THE SKY

Sleeping out under the wings of their planes, always ready for action, the Phantom pilots sent to Vietnam in summer 1965 had to go in low, down where it hurt, to give the grunts close support

EYE-WITNESS

Flying with the callsign 'L'il John', the author, Warrant Officer John D. Cummings, became one of the Marine Corp's most experienced Radar Intercept Officers. He returned to Vietnam in 1972 for a second tour of duty.

We were the first fliers in-country, Marine fighter jocks with the 'Gray Ghosts' of VMFA-531. We arrived at Da Nang in April 1965 at the start of the big build-up, long before the easy-living Air Force guys got their Phantoms to Nam.

Our F-4B Phantoms were new but everything else in-country was primitive. When we arrived, Da Nang was a backwater. I remember choking clouds of dust everywhere. The only other fliers at Da Nang were the Marine UH-34 helicopter guys who'd flown in the Shu Fly operation supporting the ARVN in the Mekong Delta since 1963. They lorded it over us, living well in cool colonial buildings while we slept in tents or on the flightline, under the wings of our Phantoms. And we'd arrived with only what we could carry in our fighters – our toilet bags, our flight gear and maybe a spare pair of socks.

The fiction was that the Marines landed in Da Nang to protect the airfield. The fact was that we were girding for our first encounters with the veteran Viet Cong forces in the area – the first test between our grunts and Charlie's best.

At first though, we just flew around making a lot of black smoke. The Phantom was famous for its long plume of cruddy exhaust, which was handy for VC gunners. They could zero-in from a mile away.

But it was on the ground that we were suffering the real hardship. We built a 16-holer 'public comfort station' near the tents. Right, you had to crap outdoors with everyone looking at you. Public it was, comfortable it was not. And the Goddamn dust got everywhere. To eat and wash up, we had to take a 30-minute ride on a six-by-six truck to the other side of the field.

We flew all sorts of missions but our main job was to help the grunts on the ground with close-air support. We did this for the ARVN, but in May and June we switched support to our own boys. We were all Marines – riflemen, first and foremost – so when they were involved in a fight we could not just sit on our bayonets and watch. The weather was abominable. But we gave the grunts close air support all over the country, whatever the conditions.

Fighting in the dark

We had the new low-drag bombs rather than the box-finned World War II stuff the Marine units Stateside used. But we never had enough. Secretary of Defense Robert McNamara called it the 'non-bomb shortage'. Believe me, it was real. Our guys would go out with a six-bomb multiple ejector rack with only three bombs in it. We were so desperate we actually snitched ordnance from Navy carrier planes diverted to Da Nang with battle damage. Some of it we didn't even know how to use, like Snakeye fin-retarded bombs. The rules were very strict. We were not allowed to drop a

Left: Napalm strikes home. A Phantom ground-attack mission (right) could last up to four hours. But on one occasion, when Da Nang came under mortar attack, an F-4 pilot logged the shortest mission on record. He launched, flew the pattern, dropped his bombs and landed – all within 17 minutes.

VMFA-531

First flown on 27 May 1958, the McDonnell Douglas F-4 Phantom was designed as a carrier-borne, long-range high-altitude interceptor for use by the US Navy and Marine Corps. In a complete break from tradition, it was armed with air-to-air missiles (AAMs) instead of cannon, and was equipped with powerful radars that necessitated the addition of a second crew member – the Radar Intercept Officer (RIO).

With a top speed of 1485mph provided by two General Electric J79-8B afterburning turbo jets, the production F-4B had been fully adapted to carrier operations by the beginning of US involvement in Vietnam, seeing action for the first time in August 1964 as part of the retaliatory strikes in the aftermath of the Gulf of Tonkin incident.

Normally, the F-4 was used to provide top cover for strike aircraft, seeking out and engaging North Vietnamese MiGs in traditional aerial dogfights. Equipped with four AIM-7 Sparrow and two AIM-9 Sidewinder AAMs, the F-4 was an extremely effective interceptor – 'locking on' to the enemy before he was even aware of American presence.

But the F-4 could also be adapted to other roles, most notably that of ground attack. Marine Corps and Air Force squadrons, stationed at airbases in South Vietnam, often flew support missions for US and ARVN ground forces, being called into action by Forward Air Controllers (FACs). Each F-4 could carry up to 16,000lb of rockets and bombs beneath its fuselage or on underwing points.

the shadows. Both Air Force guys radioed that their bombs had hung – a statistical impossibility – and that they were leaving us to do the job.

My pilot took us in and I got a good sighting on a column of men moving along a creek bed. We released. One of our bombs did hang, but I was told later that the others scored good hits. I couldn't see a thing at the time – we were climbing in a high-G turn to get away from the ridgelines.

Rob Hanke and his Radar Intercept Officer (RIO), Fred Schwartz, went in behind me and what they did was phenomenal. We banked out of the turn in time to see their bombs walk straight along the rows of men who'd only just begun to scatter. Rob was officially credited with the highest kill rate of the war up till then, an estimated 250 in a single bomb run. Most were VC but, sadly, some were South Vietnamese prisoners. Our intelligence guys said the VC planned to kill them anyway.

We had a problem with G forces when the Phantoms were manoeuvring rapidly. One time Rob Hanke went in really low – so low that back at Da Nang they found a piece of tree embedded in his air intake – and the enemy started shooting 12.7mm stuff at him. He pulled up so abruptly that Ed Janz in the back seat lost consciousness for a few moments. Later we learned that the back seat of a Phantom gets more Gs than the front in a pull-up, and we adjusted our flying to take this into account.

Above: While groundcrew conduct a pre-flight check, the pilot and RIO run through the details of their mission before climbing aboard the Phantom and heading into action (right). The effect of an F-4 low-level strike could be devastating, with air-to-ground rockets and bombs delivered with pinpoint accuracy.

bomb unless we had a confirmed hot target.

In the early days, no-one knew much about night work. Charlie ruled the night. He had complete freedom to run patrols, set up ambushes and reposition his units. But we flew the occasional night mission, called a Blue Blazer.

Rob Hanke and I were wakened up sleeping in the heat under our planes one night. We were sent down south of Da Nang. There were two Air Force F-100 Super Sabres ahead of us in the darkness. Charlie had taken some South Vietnamese prisoners, and an old C-123 supply plane was dropping million-candlepower flares around them that nearly burnt our eyes out.

We'd had no briefing. We'd never flown with flares. We didn't even know the level of the ground and had an excellent chance of colliding with it – if we didn't fly into an Air Force 'weenie' in an F-100 first. The F-100s dropped down into the mountain pass where Charlie was herding the prisoners, then decided that they did not like it down there in

By June, it was in the air. The United States Marines, not tested on the battlefield since Korea, were going to be up against Charlie in a major, set-piece battle. We wanted to be up there above our grunts. But our squadron had been out in Westpac – the Western Pacific – for nearly two years and we were crestfallen by the news that 531 might be recalled before the first major land battle.

Meanwhile we choked on dust in Da Nang and cursed our abominable living conditions. I had discovered a genuine flush toilet on the far side of the field but was kind of quiet about it. While I crapped in comfort the rest of the guys continued squatting over the 16-holer.

The supply ship eventually arrived and we moved into 12-man expeditionary tents, but we still slept under the planes because it was cooler. The showers were set up but they never worked well, so we stayed dirty.

Rob Hanke had a 32in waist, but after two months in a single set of underwear he 'requisitioned' a pair of 44in skivvies from the Shu Fly guys. He spent the rest of his tour walking round hitching his underpants up. I only had two sets of underwear.

'Ho Chi Minh ain't gonna win'

As Marines, we were hardened to these conditions. Sure, we were fighter jocks, but we did not expect our circumstances to be any better than the grunts on the ground. The flightline was overcrowded with ordnance guys painting 'Ho Chi Minh ain't gonna win' on the bombs, guys satisfying nature in the 16-holer surrounded by mosquitoes and blue flies, and everyone was trying to get me to reveal the whereabouts of the coveted flush crapper. We had a club – a wooden shack with the sign 'No coats, ties or Navy wives allowed' on it, brought in from our peacetime garrison in Japan. There was a running argument whether it was the Navy or the Air Force who had least in common with us Marines, but in Da Nang any women, even a Navy wife, would have been welcome. The one time the enlisted guys had been allowed downtown, one of them was sold a booby-trapped cigarette lighter that blew his head off. After that the town – and the girls – were off limits.

Missions would begin with a pre-dawn wake-up – the time might vary but we always called it 'zero dark thirty'. Weather and intelligence briefings were limited. Mostly we'd launch without being told what the target was until we were in the air. The Forward Air Controllers who spotted targets for us were Marine aviators like us, only they were on the ground with radios. Coming in low and close, we'd often hit Charlie when he was within easy range of the ARVN or our own Marines.

Early July we were relieved by another Marine squadron – the 'Flying Nightmares' of VMFA-513. Marine Phantoms stayed in Southeast Asia until the 531st departed Nam Phong, Thailand, in July 1973. But though some of us felt bad about missing the main event and most returned for another combat tour, the Gray Ghosts of 531 were the first in and nobody else can claim that.

WAR IN THE AIR

In 1954, on the eve of the French defeat in Indochina, there were several hundred US Air Force personnel stationed in Vietnam, whose job it was to help maintain a fleet of C-47 transport aircraft for the French forces. When Vietnam was divided into North and South, American advisors, mechanics and training personnel remained in the South to work with the South Vietnamese Air Force.

By 1961 the advisory role had been extended and a special US training squadron, known as Farm Gate, was instructing South Vietnamese pilots in combat flying skills. A year later, American pilots themselves were getting involved in the war, flying experimental defoliation missions, and it was not long before reports were coming in that American pilots were flying actual combat missions when the Vietnamese pilots proved unable to cope.

In the aftermath of the Gulf of Tonkin incident in August 1964, the full force of American airpower was unleashed as carrier-based aircraft of the US Seventh Fleet launched retaliatory air strikes against North Vietnamese coastal targets. These raids were followed by the deployment of US fighters and bombers to bases in Thailand and South Vietnam.

The steady escalation of American involvement in the air war reached a new peak in February 1965 when a series of air raids, codenamed Flaming Dart, were mounted against targets in North Vietnam in reply to the Viet Cong attacks on US personnel at a base near Pleiku and in Saigon.

In March American air activity increased even further as US warplanes began a sustained bombing campaign against the North – Operation Rolling Thunder.

As the bombing campaign in the North continued, US aircraft also began flying close air support missions for troops engaged on the battlefields of the South, and attacked the convoys of enemy troops and supplies coming down the Ho Chi Minh Trail. The sledgehammer of US air power was in full swing.

49

WOUNDED IN ACTION

1965

For America, the human cost of war reached new proportions in 1965. 5300 US troops were wounded and 1350 killed. But behind the statistics, each casualty had his own gruelling tale to tell

Right: Hit in the foot, a soldier receives emergency first aid while the rest of his patrol try to work out where the enemy are.

Right: When time was tight, pole stretchers were difficult to use in the dense vegetation of Vietnam. Here four soldiers carry an unconscious buddy to an LZ by the seams of his clothes.

Left: Bringing the wounded back into the Landing Zone so they can be heli-lifted back to base.

Right: In the aftermath of battle, a Marine pauses to offer an injured buddy a drag on his cigarette before the medevacs arrive.

CHAPTER 10

STOP THE WAR

Was it right for the US to get involved in Vietnam? Already in 1965, millions of Americans believed it was wrong, and started a wave of public protest that spread throughout the nation

Opposite: John Seltz, 25, makes a one-man stand in front of a troop train at Berkeley, California, 24 August 1965. Right: Soon draft card burning became the most visible symbol of protest against the war.

In mid-October 1965 David Millar, a 22-year-old Jesuit charity worker in a Bowery soup-kitchen, held up his draft card at a Manhattan anti-Vietnam rally. 'I believe the napalming of villages is an immoral act,' he said, holding a match to the corner of the card. 'I hope this will be a significant act – so here goes.' And he lit it. At the end of October, Millar became the first American to be arraigned under a new law that made draft-card burning a Federal offence with a maximum penalty of five years in prison and a $10,000 fine.

Vietnam was the world's first television war. Night after night, as American families sat down to their evening meals, they were confronted with the horrors of modern warfare on the 6 o'clock news. In sophisticated cocktail lounges and low-life bars alike, the war was the deadly backdrop to a pre-prandial highball or an early evening beer. Even in the streets, TV showrooms played out scenes of mesmerizing violence for any passing bum.

In 1965, 93 per cent of American homes had TV. Colour sets had started making an impact on the mass market the year before. Soon everyone in the country would be all too familiar with the flaming orange of napalm, the vivid greens of Asian jungle, the dull yellow of monsoon mud and the deathly black of burnt skin.

It was compulsive viewing. It ran nightly like a macabre soap opera. And the action was more thrilling than anything Hollywood could produce. This was real. Many people had friends in the cast. And without John Wayne on the screen, the average American could not be 100 per cent sure that the good guys would win out.

But it was not just images of the war that burnt their way into the national consciousness. The peace protests soon began to become nightly news too. When America had gone to war in March 1965, the response on the home front had been immediate. In Washington, DC, 25,000 anti-war demonstrators took to the streets. Many of them had been protesting against America's role in Vietnam for some years, but their opposition had been confined to faculty rooms of colleges, Quaker meeting houses and the letters columns of small-circulation pacifist magazines.

Some of the protesters were old-fashioned pacifists, often with a religious background. Others were college instructors and students already involved in other forms of political protest in academic institutions. And there were radical writers and middle-of-the-road liberals who were against the war, but also opposed violent protest.

David Dellinger, the pacifist leader who became the first American to visit wartime Hanoi, recalls '...the heady sense, after the lonely vigils, that the country was beginning to wake up to what was happening'.

Stopped in their tracks

At the end of June, when the men of the 173d Airborne Brigade began search-and-destroy operations in War Zone D northeast of Saigon, they had already seen action – against protesters. Anti-war activists had delayed their troop trains by blocking the line. Later that summer, the Vietnam Day Committee, formed on the campus of the University of California at Berkeley in the spring, organized further attempts to stop troop trains, but these were unsuccessful. Only a handful of hard-core radicals were in favour of physical confrontation. Most protesters were only prepared to picket local induction centres and march in demonstrations.

But with Joe Six-Pack the war was never more popular. In January 1965, a Harris poll showed that 59 per cent of Americans were cool on the Administration's commitment in Vietnam. By summer, a solid two-thirds majority of Americans supported the war. 'There's too much involved for us to back out now,' said a 29-year-old labourer from Greensboro, Indiana. 'We have to finish the job.'

However, there was a moral battle going on in America that was being fought and won by committed pacifists. Since the early 1960s, non-violent civil rights marchers – both black and

1965

Above: Anti-war protest was widespread and worldwide. This scathing graffiti appeared in the US officers club in Hanau, West Germany.

they could win through whatever the Administration ranged against them. And when the civil rights leader and pacifist Dr Martin Luther King spoke out against the war, he brought with him not just overwhelming moral authority but also the power of his commanding, charismatic – and very televisable – oratory.

Though the civil rights movement had done much for the constitutional position of the rural southern black, those crammed in the seething slums of the northern and western cities didn't want dreams, they wanted jobs. In August 1965, the ghetto of Watts, in Los Angeles, exploded into violence. The cry went up to 'Burn, baby, burn' and 'Get Whitey'.

Fighting for Whitey

In post-Watts meetings, black groups dropped Martin Luther King's tactics of non-violence while voting to oppose the war. Already many had noted the disproportionately high number of blacks in the front line. While 8 per cent of US military personnel were black, in 1965 blacks made up some 23 per cent of the enlisted soldiers killed in action.

Meanwhile, in affluent white suburbs, the sons of the well-off could easily get a deferment by staying on at college, getting married, feigning homosexuality or faking medical conditions. Some took drugs to raise their blood pressure. Others punctured their arms to simulate needle tracks. Doctors were often sympathetic. 'I save lives by keeping people out of the army,' said one. With their sons safely at home, some white middle-class Americans saw the war as a convenient way to clear ill-educated and uppity blacks out of the ghettos.

Some kids, desperate not to be drafted, took the most drastic step of all and went into exile – mainly in Canada, Mexico and Sweden. In the

white – had been beaten, abused and even killed protesting against segregated schools, housing, transportation and the unfair literacy and civics tests that barred many southern blacks from voting. But despite the murderous assaults of policemen like Alabama's Bull Connors, who set dogs on protesters, baton-wielding state troopers, Ku Klux Klan snipers and rock-throwing racists, by August 1965, with the passing of the Voting Rights Act, the non-violent civil-rights protesters had won. This left radical activists with a wealth of organizational experience and the feeling that

LBJ was widely identified as a warmonger, blamed for the Vietnam debacle.

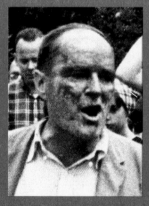

Dr Benjamin Spock, the child-care expert, voiced the concern of middle America.

Dave Dellinger, editor of *Liberation*, smeared with paint thrown by young fascists.

Norman Morrison, 31, father of three, burned himself to death in front of his baby daughter.

Martin Luther King, the voice of black protest, brought moral authority to the anti-war cause.

course of the war Canadian immigration authorities registered some 30,000 draft evaders but, according to one exile organization, another 50,000 settled there illegally.

But draft-card burning was the favourite method of dramatizing resistance to the war. It became a regular feature of anti-war demos and the nightly news. It often infuriated hostile onlookers who frequently physically attacked the protesters or doused the flames with water or fire extinguishers. The leading ranks of the New York march were drenched in red paint. In Chicago and Oakland demonstrators were pelted with eggs. In Detroit marchers' chants of 'Hey, hey, LBJ! How many kids did you kill today?' were drowned by counter-protesters singing *The Star-Spangled Banner*. And in Berkeley 12,000 marchers on their way to the Oakland Army Terminal were turned back by police and tear gas.

In October in Britain, police removed demonstrators who blocked the road outside the US Embassy in Grosvenor Square – 78 were arrested. And in Sydney, Australia 50 demonstrators were arrested, just days after Australia had increased its contingent in Vietnam to 1300.

A burning issue

On 2 November, Norman Morrison, a Quaker, burned himself to death outside the Pentagon. Already several Buddhist monks and a young girl had burned themselves to death on the streets of Saigon. Now this potent – and unanswerable – gesture brought the horror of the war to American soil. A week later, on 9 November, Roger Allen LaPorte burned himself to death outside the United Nations building in New York.

On 19 November, total US fatalities of 1000 in Vietnam were published. There were no figures for the Vietnamese dead.

The year's protest culminated on 27 November with a demonstration of 30,000 older, quieter protesters in Washington, DC. It was organized by SANE, the Committee for a Sane Nuclear Policy, whose most famous member was Dr Benjamin Spock. He was the author of *Baby and Child Care*, the bible for parents of the post-World War II baby boom. His presence was a major boost to the movement's respectability in the public's eyes and attracted many older moderates.

More exuberant left-wing participants with banners calling for immediate surrender and withdrawal were persuaded to keep a low profile. Demonstration leaders made speeches condemning both sides for not making any serious attempts to find a peaceful settlement. They called for an immediate end to the US build-up – now approaching 200,000 men – and an end to the bombing. As they marched around the White House, their moderate banners called for a 'Supervised cease-fire' and claimed that 'War erodes the Great Society'.

'Dissent,' said LBJ in a statement issued next day, 'is a sign of political vigor.'

Instead, it was tearing the country apart.

Right: Urged on by a patriotic press, counter demonstrations escalated. In October, a 10,000-strong anti-war parade in New York was attacked by 'hard-hats' - tough construction workers whose beer-swilling macho image became a symbol for popular patriotism compared with the effete, pot-smoking beatnik image of Anti-war protesters.

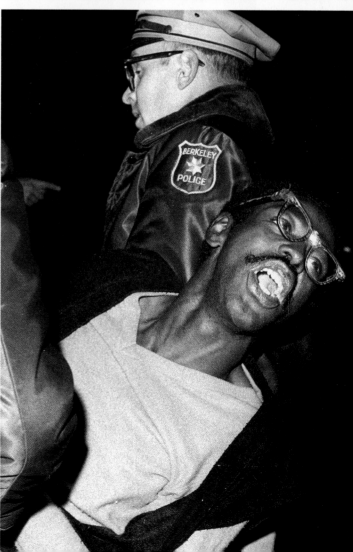

Right: August 1965, Watts. The cry went up 'Burn, baby, burn' and 'Get Whitey'. Riots left 35 dead, 900 injured and $46m worth of damage. In October, Al Harrison, black organizer at Detroit's Wayne University, proclaimed: 'We got no business fighting a yellow man's war to save the white man.' And later: 'If there was no Vietnam, the American Government would have to invent one.' Both sentiments were to be expressed over and over during the next few years.

Ambushes were something of an obsession for American infantrymen in Vietnam. After any contact with enemy forces, a soldier was liable to report 'We were ambushed', even if his unit had been sent to the location on hard intelligence that the enemy was there. If you asked him whether his squad or platoon was in single file, he would say 'Naw...we don't do that'. If you asked where the fire came from, as likely as not he would tell you that the fire was delivered from the front. Yet he would still insist on calling the action an ambush.

The reason for this insistence was that we always had ambush on our minds. It was a favourite technique of the Viet Cong (VC), though less so for the North Vietnamese Army (NVA). Naturally, we always guarded against it. We would invariably keep men out wide as flank security and rarely used a narrow column in 'indian territory'. But it was usually the enemy who initiated contact, even though we were the ones looking for a fight.

As a matter of fact, even if the enemy pulled off a real ambush, he was not likely to live through it, because most of his ambushes were on the roads against our vehicle convoys. Since we used a lot of

THE ART OF AMBUSH

A Claymore anti-personnel mine can shoot out 700 ball bearings at waist height, shattering bone and tearing soft flesh. In the dense jungles of Vietnam, both sides lay in wait with booby traps primed for action - but just who was hunting who?

armour with our convoys in VC or NVA territory, the enemy often bit off more than he could chew. I knew a number of armoured cavalry and tank commanders who just loved to run the roads looking for an ambush. They would immediately counter-attack the enemy ambush force, call in artillery, and know that helicopter-borne infantry would be on the way.

The truth is that we ambushed our enemy about as many times as he ambushed us. The best ambush outfit I ever fought beside was an American mechanized infantry battalion, the 1st Battalion of the 5th Infantry Regiment. They usually worked the Iron Triangle, War Zone C and War Zone D – areas north of Saigon crawling with Viet Cong. My outfit, B Company, 2d Battalion, 27th Infantry, would often be attached to one of

Top: A US special advisor goes up river to lay an ambush. Opposite: A Green Beret lies in wait with an M16, spare clips and grenades.

1965

SPECIAL FORCES AMBUSH

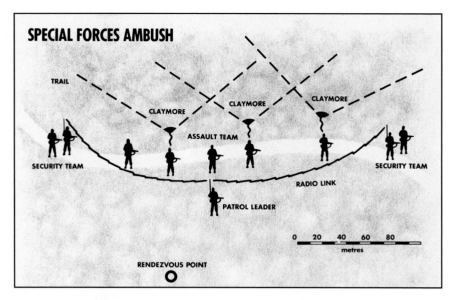

TRAIL

CLAYMORE CLAYMORE CLAYMORE

ASSAULT TEAM

SECURITY TEAM SECURITY TEAM

RADIO LINK

PATROL LEADER

0 20 40 60 80
metres

RENDEZVOUS POINT

Above: This diagram illustrates the various elements involved in a Special Forces ambush.

their M113 armoured personnel carrier units. Their trick was to beat the bush all day in search of enemy contact and then ring up the vehicles for the night in a defensive perimeter. At dusk, one platoon of five M113s would go roaring off in the twilight. When they hit the right spot, one of the vehicles would drop the rear exit door and an infantry squad would roll out into the gathering darkness. The M113s would then speed back to the

perimeter. An ambush party had just been dropped off and the enemy did not have the vaguest idea where it was. Tactics like these made the 5th 'Mech' the star of the 25th Division in successful ambushes for a long time.

As Special Forces, we carried out a lot of ambushes, simply because we were normally out in regions of the country that our enemy claimed as much as we did. He would feel confident in those areas and would do dumb things like using trails and travelling in single file without flank security.

An enemy speciality

We divided ambushes into two categories, hasty and deliberate. The hasty ambush was when you suddenly became aware of the presence of the enemy and grabbed the chance to bushwack him. You just got everybody into some sort of firing line, trying to keep as quiet as possible. That was all there was to it, really. In fact, the hasty ambush was perhaps more of an enemy speciality.

The Special Forces, on the other hand, usually ran the deliberate ambush. Let's say you had a 10-man patrol. First you selected a location for your ambush and planned exactly what you were going to do. On the way to the ambush site, you designated a series of rally points – if anything went wrong, everyone would make it back to those points any way they could. After you passed the

THE CLAYMORE MINE

last rally point, you put the site of the ambush under surveillance for 20 to 30 minutes, and if it was all clear you then moved your people to their positions. Two pairs of soldiers, designated as the security element, would go in first. One pair would be up the trail, 50yds more or less from the ambush site depending on the terrain. The other pair would be down the trail from the site about the same distance. The main job of the security element was to tell you when the enemy was coming, how many there were in the enemy force, and the length of the column. It also had the mission of picking off any enemy soldier who was so far in advance of the column that he would otherwise slip through the killing zone before the trap was sprung. But knowing the length of the column and the number of enemy troops was the most important thing. If the 320th NVA Division was trotting down the trail, you just might want to declare a moratorium on violence for the day.

After the security element, the assault element would take up their positions—five men in the case of our 10-man patrol. The remaining man would be the patrol leader, free of any duties except command. He would place every man and would determine if and when you were going to spring the ambush. Once everyone was in position, you waited and waited , sometimes for 24 to 48 hours. Another rule of the ambush was patience. But the most important was KISS – Keep It Simple, Stupid.

When the enemy did at last arrive, the prime weapon the assault element used to destroy him was not the M16 rifle, it was the 2.5lb Claymore anti-personnel mine. The Claymore did the killing. The spread on that weapon was about 60 degrees and the optimum effective range was 50yds, although in close terrain with trees and other obstacles it would be less, and you would need more mines to do the job. Let's say you needed three Claymores for a 20- to 30-man enemy infiltration unit coming down the trail. The assault team would then consist of three Claymore firers who would kick off the mines on signal from the patrol leader, then pick up their M16s fast in case anyone was still fighting in the killing zone. The other two members of the assault element on the flanks of the Claymore firers would start blasting away with their M16s as soon as they got the signal. Few survived an ambush.

Hunter could become hunted

Once the action was over, the patrol leader would supervise the search of the bodies and then direct the withdrawal. The last part was vital. If you were operating in enemy territory, you could easily become the hunted instead of the hunter. The rule was to put as much distance as possible between you and the scene of the action as quickly as possible—covering your tracks as you went. The security element would be the last to pull out, remaining to discourage enemy pursuit.

That was how we conducted ambushes in Special Forces. But then, everyone carried out ambushes in Vietnam. I remember a notable one. I was in 27th Infantry attached once again to the 5th Mech. The M113s were about 6 miles from us and we had slipped into Bo Loi Woods, apparently unnoticed amid all of the noise and dust of the mechanized vehicles. The plan was just to wait until the afternoon when the vehicles would suddenly turn on the flank and push towards us, hopefully with some enemy in between.

I had my company in the jungle in a wide perimeter that straddled a trail. We were just keeping quiet and waiting. All of a sudden, here comes a VC on a bicycle down the trail with an AK-47 slung over his back. This guy was actually singing. Obviously he hadn't seen us – we were fairly well camouflaged. He peddled right through my forward element and then he stopped singing and stopped peddling. He just coasted with this dumb look on his face. He knew he was right in the middle of a company of the 'Wolfhounds'. We were dumbstruck. Everyone just had their mouths open, eyes transfixed on this fellow. I finally blurted out 'catch that son-of-a-bitch' and my radio operator leaped on the back of the VC with a flying tackle. When the dust cleared, people regained their senses and the whole company started laughing. The dazed VC looked around at us and couldn't control a sheepish grin... That is what I would call a hasty ambush.

STRUGGLE FOR THE HIGHLANDS

The Central Highlands, an area of rugged mountains and heavily forested valleys running down the 'spine' of South Vietnam, was an extremely vulnerable region. Communist attacks from southern Laos or eastern Cambodia towards the coast threatened to cut South Vietnam in two.

US Special Forces had been operating in the Highlands (above) since 1961, training and leading Montagnard tribesmen and establishing fortified camps astride likely enemy infiltration routes. In 1965 these camps came under sustained attack by both the Viet Cong and the North Vietnamese Army. The bitter, fighting that developed during these encounters made it obvious that more direct military action was essential.

In August and September 1965 the 173d Airborne Brigade conducted operations in the area. The 1st Brigade of the 101st Airborne Division was also in action here during August, sweeping along Highway 19 from Qui Nhon to An Khe during Operation Highland and along the Song Con river valley to the north of the An Khe Pass a month later during Operation Gibraltar. Gibraltar involved fighting against NVA main-force units. In October and November the fighting in the Highlands reached a new peak as the 1st Cavalry Division (Airmobile) launched Operation Silver Bayonet, culminating in the fierce battle for the Ia Drang Valley in November. In 1965 the Americans won the first round in the struggle for the Highlands, but it was only the beginning of a long campaign for control of this vital area.

The M18A1 Antipersonnel (Claymore) Mine (below) was one of the most lethal pieces of military hardware used during the Vietnam war. Particularly effective as a means of executing an ambush along jungle tracks used by the Viet Cong and NVA, the Claymore mine comprised a rectangular cast-iron box, with spikes fitted to the base for stability. An ominous instruction - 'FRONT TOWARDS ENEMY' - was embossed on the outside.

It contained 700 steel balls set in an explosive bed and was detonated by remote control - hidden in the undergrowth, some distance away from the lethal zone, a trooper (left) would complete a simple electrical circuit to set off the mine. Alternatively, the M18A1 could be set off by a tripwire hidden along the track. Once detonated, the Claymore sprayed its contents in a 60 degree fan-shaped pattern that was lethal to a range of 50yds.

CHAPTER 12

FIGHTING WITH THE PIG

1965

A platoon is moving through thick vegetation. Suddenly, shots ring out – they're under attack. In this situation, all US troops depended upon the M60 machine gun for protection and covering fire. And the M60 gunners bore a heavy responsibility for their buddies' lives

In a close-range firefight in the jungle, a veteran grunt, a man who had paid some dues in the Nam, could identify a particular weapon in action by its own distinctive sound signature. Through the chaos of battle, the thump of grenades and mortar bombs exploding, he could distinguish the high-pitched rattle of his buddies' M16s from the coarser, staccato ripping noise of enemy AK-47s. But when the M60 gunners cut loose with their weapon, everyone – even the new guys – knew about it.

The M60, commonly known as 'the pig', was the main American general purpose machine gun of the Vietnam war. In bursts of six or seven rounds, the M60 poured out 7.62mm slugs at a devastating rate, chewing up the dirt, splintering trees and shredding flesh. Superior to anything the enemy could field in the machine-gun department, M60 firepower often gave infantry platoons the edge they needed in a dire situation. A reliable machine gun is a great confidence builder, and the M60 was very, very reliable.

For many troops in the Nam, the M60 was a

relatively new piece of kit. It was brought into service in 1961 to replace the old warhorses of World War II and Korea – the Browning M1919A6 and A4 machine guns, and the Browning Automatic Rifle. In their own way, these older weapons were OK. Tried and tested on the battlefields of World War II and Korea, they provided a respectable rate of fire but lacked some of the more 'user friendly' features that made the M60 so popular with the gunners in the Nam. Both the A6 and A4 weighed more than 30lb apiece, a

Below: An M60 gunner unleashes a stream of automatic fire, relying on the assistant gunner beside him to ensure an uninterrupted flow of ammunition into the chamber. Great care is needed when firing from this position - the recoil from an M60 is powerful enough to dislocate a man's shoulder.

lot of weight to hump around in the jungle, and that was without ammunition. The M60, weighing in at 23.75lb, was less of a drag to carry and could be fired from the hip, provided that the company commander picked big, strong men for the job.

Don't lose that glove!

It was gas operated and had a fixed headspace, which meant that gunners did not have to waste a lot of time stripping the weapon down and adjusting the space between the face of the bolt and the face of the firing chamber. The result of these improved features was that the M60 suffered fewer stoppages and malfunctions than its predecessors.

But the M60's main selling point was its quick-change barrel. When an automatic weapon is fired continuously in heavy combat, the barrel heats up very quickly, causing expansion of the metal which can lead to malfunctions and stoppages at critical moments. The way to beat the problem

and keep firing is to pack a spare barrel. On the M60, a hot barrel can be changed for a cool one in seconds: flip up the lock-lever at the front end of the receiver, and pull out the barrel. Every M60 gunner and assistant gunner carried spare barrels, and an asbestos glove to protect their hands when making the change. (Don't lose that glove!)

The 42-man rifle platoons were authorized two, two-man M60 crews. In the attack they provided a base of fire while the rifle squads manoeuvred, or they walked right along with the riflemen and grenadiers. Moving through open country, platoon leaders deployed their men in open formation, with the machine gunners alternately moving ahead to lead each flank so that one team was always ready to shoot from a stable position. In action, the M60 could be fired from a tripod mount for long-range, accurate defensive fires, but out on patrol, the gunner stabilised with the folding bipod legs fitted at the muzzle. These could be propped up on anything that came to hand – a fallen tree, a wall or an earth bank – and allowed

Above: Swathed in ammunition and standing upright to improve his cone of fire, an M60 gunner lays down suppressive fire before his platoon can advance. At a range of 100yds the M60 was one of the most potent weapons available to US ground troops in Vietnam - in a firefight, or tough night defence, everyone wanted plenty of ammo for the M60.

Above: A Huey gunner sights his pintle-mounted M60D. An improvised addition to the ammunition feed prevents twisted belts from jamming. Right: On board an APC, a trooper uses grease to service his M60. Below: Letting loose.

the M60 team to manoeuvre quickly in a firefight and get the weapon into action on cue.

A well-sited machine gun in the hands of a good gunner can cut an infantry attack to ribbons, and the M60 crews were always a primary target during an enemy assault. Their ability to move quickly from firing position to firing position, shooting from the hip, greatly improved their chances of survival. Some gunners even fired in three-round bursts so that the sound signature of their weapon was closer to that of the M16 and would not give away their position.

In the assault, the machine gun could move right along with the rifle squads. When a platoon went in, with troops on line blazing away with everything they had, the M60 gunners and their assistants were the main thrust of the attack. The gunners rigged nylon webbing straps across their shoulders to take the weight of the weapon and leaned into the attack as if they were struggling against the full force of a gale. When a gunner squeezed the trigger of his M60 with his right index finger, he leaned forward even further and held the muzzle down with his left hand and forearm. With the barrel protruding almost four feet in front of him, he could adjust his fire very precisely by keeping an eye on where his bursts hit the enemy or kicked up the dirt. The assistant gunner paced alongside him, feeding the belt of shiny 7.62mm cartridges into the receiver group. Platoon leaders usually directed the fire of the M60, but when firing for effect the gunner himself spotted enemy positions and poured successive 'bursts of six' into them.

Packing a mean punch

Being a gunner was hard work. Apart from the machine gun itself, a great deal of ammunition had to be carried on operations and a typical gunner's load could weigh as much as 80lb. Before going out on a combat operation, the gunner festooned himself with 200 or so rounds of 7.62mm in a linked belt. The assistant gunner was also swathed with belts, loaded up with 400 rounds, and on top of this he carried a can of linked ammunition. Further supplies were hauled by other men in the platoon, along with their rifles, grenades, Claymore anti-personnel mines and water canteens.

At night, the M60 moved over to its defensive role. Well before nightfall, after a hard day of sweating it out in the jungle, the platoon set about constructing its night defensive perimeter. Claymores were laid, trip flares set and foxholes dug. If the men were in for a night action, the M60s would play a crucial role in knocking down the waves of enemy infantry as they tried to overrun the position. Before siting the machine guns, the platoon leader and gunners analyzed the surrounding terrain and selected spots that would cover the most likely avenues of enemy advance. The gunner and his assistant would then dig the firing position and block the M60 into a firm stance, ready for trouble.

Versatility, like reliability, was another hall-mark of the M60 – a number of variants on the basic weapon were produced to cater for the offensive and defensive needs of helicopters, jeeps, trucks and armoured personnel carriers. Even the M60A3 main battle tank packed an M60E2 machine gun, mounted to fire along the same line as the main armament.

On transport helicopters going into a threatened LZ, the door gunners on both sides of the chopper listened on the intercom for the command to open up with suppressive fire. When it came, they fired their M60s into actual or suspected enemy positions as the helicopter pilots steered their machines through the final hair-raising 200ft of the descent. The gunners mixed tracer with the armour-piercing rounds in the belt – usually one tracer every five rounds – and the blazing streak behind the tracer helped them adjust their fire as the helicopter pitched and yawed into the LZ.

In a firefight, the M60 was always in the thick of the action – a prime target for the enemy, a major source of firepower for the embattled platoon. It is not surprising, therefore, that an extraordinary number of machine gunners fighting in the Nam earned Medals of Honor. PFC Carlos J. Lozada was one of them.

Last stand at Dak To

On 20 November 1967, on a hill near Dak To in the Central Highlands, Lozada added a heroic chapter to the combat history of the 173d Airborne. An M60 gunner with Company A, 2d Battalion, 503d Infantry, he and three other grunts were staked out 360yds from the company perimeter, an outpost to warn of enemy approach. The rest of the 2d Battalion were starting up Hill 875 when they ran into a bunch of entrenched NVA regulars who poured out a stream of fire from well-concealed fighting positions. Company A, near the base of the hill, became exposed. As an NVA company moved along a trail towards Lozada's outpost, he sounded the alarm, and then opened fire with his M60. Twenty North Vietnamese were mowed down and the attack was broken up.

But the battle was far from over. Other NVA units were enveloping the company and Lozada's outpost was ordered to move back into the perimeter. By now, it was too late, as the NVA pressed another assault against the beleaguered men. Lozada broke up the attack on one side of the trail and then leapt across it with his M60 to take on another group of NVA soldiers. His wounded comrades were being pulled back inside the company perimeter, which was now threatened with imminent destruction.

Lozada must have realized that if he withdrew from his position, the way would be open for the enemy to overwhelm his company. Urging his wounded comrades to work their way back to safety, he held off the NVA on three sides, cutting down waves of enemy troops as they charged to within yards of his position.

Above: Weighed down with both belted and boxed ammunition, an assistant gunner with the 173d Airborne prepares to move out on patrol.

Company A was badly mauled that day, but its survivors were able to make their way into the beleaguered battalion perimeter, thanks to Lozada's courage and skill with the M60. On the next day, a relief force from the 4th Battalion, 503d Infantry, found scores of NVA bodies littering the trail where Lozada had made his stand. Carlos Lozada's body lay face up, his hands crossed on his chest, M60 at his side.

COMBAT ORGANIZATION

The basic fighting unit of the US Army in Vietnam was the rifle platoon. At full strength a platoon fielded 41 men and one officer, divided into three rifle squads (10 men each), a weapons squad (9 men) and the platoon HQ (the officer and 2 men). Platoons were normally commanded by a lieutenant, with squads led by second lieutenants or senior NCOs.

These rifle platoons were organised into companies, commanded by captains. Each company would normally have three rifle platoons, a mortar platoon, and a rifle HQ consisting of two officers and 10 men.

The next step up the organizational structure was the battalion. This unit was commanded by a lieutenant-colonel and consisted of an HQ and an HQ company, and four front-line fighting companies. In 1965, battalions also had a combat support company, responsible for heavy weapons such as 4.2in mortars and flamethrowers. Once in Vietnam, however, it was found that such weapons were a liability rather than an asset, particularly in close jungle terrain, and the men were re-assigned to form a fifth rifle company.

Battalions were grouped in threes to form brigades, commanded by full colonels.

The main tactical formation was the division, commanded by a major-general, comprising three brigades as well as artillery and other support elements.

By December 1965, five US Army formations - the 173d Airborne Brigade, the 1st Brigade of the 101st Airborne Division, the 1st Infantry Division, the 1st Cavalry Division (Airmobile) and the 3d Brigade of the 25th Infantry Division - had been deployed to Vietnam. They were responsible for the security of existing bases and lines of communication, and for taking the war to the enemy in the war zones north of Saigon and in the Central Highlands.

M60 GENERAL PURPOSE MACHINE GUN

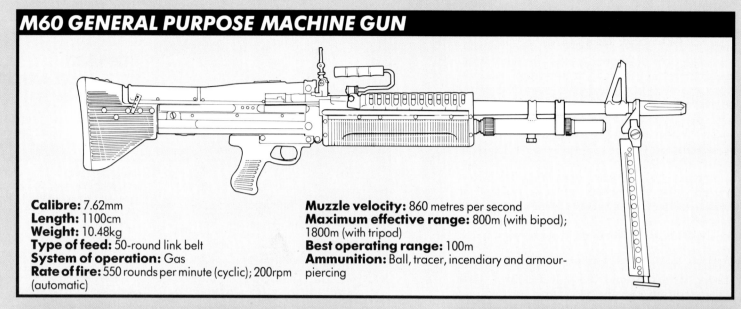

Calibre: 7.62mm
Length: 1100cm
Weight: 10.48kg
Type of feed: 50-round link belt
System of operation: Gas
Rate of fire: 550 rounds per minute (cyclic); 200rpm (automatic)

Muzzle velocity: 860 metres per second
Maximum effective range: 800m (with bipod); 1800m (with tripod)
Best operating range: 100m
Ammunition: Ball, tracer, incendiary and armour-piercing

M60 AUTOMATIC FIREPOWER

During countless patrols and firefights, the ubiquitous M60 became the symbol of US presence in South Vietnam

The M60 General Purpose machine gun (GPMG) evolved as a result of designs started at the end of World War II, and replaced the Browning light and heavy machine guns in the US armoury. The Allies had been impressed with the flexibility provided by the German GPMGs, and the American M60 thus incorporated a modified feed mechanism based on that of the German MG42, with the operating mechanism of the FG42 assault rifle.

The first prototype was the T44. When this proved disappointing, however, the feed mechanism was improved on a further two variants before the T161 emerged and was pronounced ready to enter service as the M60 GPMG.

Moving away from the recoil mechanism of the Browning machine guns, the M60 was designed as a gas-operated weapon. As the first round travels down the barrel, it pushes gas into the gas cylinder through a hole in the bore. The pressure generated in the cylinder then forces a piston down the chamber, moving the bolt back and bringing the next round into place. Once the firing pin hits the bullet and sends it speeding out of the barrel, the cycle is repeated for as long as the trigger is depressed.

With no gas regulator on the gun, however, there were drawbacks to this mechanism. Accumulated dirt or dust would slow the piston down and result in the M60 either jamming or 'running away'. The latter term refers to the weapon continuing to fire even when the finger is removed from the trigger. An extremely unnerving problem to deal with during the heat of battle, the assistant M60 gunner would have to hold on to the ammunition belt in order to stop it feeding.

Besides the advantage of a quick-change barrel, one of the best features of the M60 was that the chromium-plated barrel itself had stellite liners for the first six inches along the muzzle from the chamber. This non-ferrous lining, combined with precision engineering, considerably increased the life-span of each barrel.

As a result of the practical experience gained during the Vietnam war, a modified version of the basic M60 was introduced into service. Issued as the M60E1, this improved weapon remains the standard GPMG in the US Army.

The M60E1 differs from the original M60 in a number of respects, including the attachment of the bipod to the rear of the gas cylinder, a modified rear sight, the addition of a die-cast feed cover and a new feed tray. A further improvement has been the addition of a hanger assembly that can be used in conjunction with a 100-round ammunition box. Known as a 'bandolier', this enables the M60 gunner to lay down fire while on the move.

Above: Field-stripping the M60. Below left: The M122 tripod.

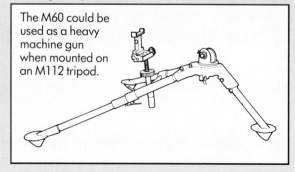

The M60 could be used as a heavy machine gun when mounted on an M112 tripod.

SEARCH AND DESTROY

Out in the sun, used as live bait for VC ambushes – grunts had a hard time on the endless sweeps through rice fields and jungle

Previous page: A Vietnamese village goes up in flames as American forces search for caches of Viet Cong weapons and supplies. Above: A soldier of the 1st Infantry Division prods a log pile with a length of bamboo. Searching villages was an extremely dangerous business. A perfectly innocent-looking stack of wood could hide anything – an explosive booby trap or a Viet Cong guerrilla with a sub-machine gun. Left: Humping the boonies. Search and destroy missions in tough terrain were hard on the men, and nine times out of ten achieved nothing.

The men of Charlie Company awoke to a dreary, wet morning. It had been raining heavily for hours and they were soaked to the skin after a miserable night spent on a marshy patch of ground in a valley, just north of Dak To in the Central Highlands. As the troopers mooched around, getting themselves together for the coming day's operations, their company commander called together his platoon leaders to put them in the picture. During the night, the men in their sister unit - Alpha Company - had taken a heavy pounding from the NVA, and one of their gun positions had been overrun during a massed attack. Today, Charlie Company would move out and work their way up the flank of the valley in search of the enemy.

The date was 6 June 1966. The men of Charlie Company were part of a large 'search and destroy' operation, codenamed Hawthorne, being conducted by the 1st Brigade of the 101st Airborne Division. It was a day in the Nam they would not forget.

As soon as they moved out, the point man up ahead began to hear sounds of the enemy. Captain William Carpenter, the company CO, immediately organized his three platoons in a chequerboard pattern, hoping for a contact. Every now and then they spotted a khaki-clad soldier and pumped off a few rounds in his direction, but no firefight developed.

Fire in the bamboo

By mid-afternoon the company was pushing hard through dense bamboo as it continued in its search. A few men had fallen back, exhausted by the hard work in the boiling heat. Suddenly, a North Vietnamese soldier was spotted heading for a creek below with a roll of toilet paper in his hand. More Vietnamese came into view, washing out clothes and bathing in the creek. Charlie Company opened fire.

The NVA took some time to realise what was happening but were soon scrambling for their weapons. Minutes later, Charlie Company began to take a lot of incoming as the the whole hillside erupted in a mass of fire. NVA heavy machine guns cut through the wall of bamboo like a scythe and Carpenter's men were pinned down, unable to move an inch. First Sergeant Walter Sabalauski described the situation:

'The terrain, with all that bamboo, was so thick you couldn't get out of the line of fire. To pull back – suicide. You can't pull back and shoot too. You can't be ducking and throwing your roundhouse at the same time. Then they started lobbing grenades – and when you start lobbing grenades, you're pretty damn close.'

It was then that Carpenter decided to call in a napalm strike: 'Lay it right on top of us,' he radioed, 'We might as well take some of them with us.'

The scream of low-flying fighter bombers reverberated through the valley as the hillside dissolved into a fiery sea of napalm. Men leapt to their feet, their clothing ablaze, howling and running like madmen – but the strike gave them the breathing space they needed to regroup and set up some sort of defensive perimeter while the NVA licked their wounds.

Throughout the night, the NVA plastered the battered remnants of Charlie Company with mortar fire, but were held at bay by US 'Puff the Magic Dragon' gunships and the fire from several batteries of heavy artillery that we located well to the rear.

For three days the men remained where they were, unable to get out, while driving rain turned the shell-blasted ground into a mud-bath. In these appalling conditions the wounded were made as comfortable as possible. Finally, the troopers managed to slip away to be evacuated by helicopter. The following day, American B-52 bombers

and was a considerable success. The men of the 1st Cavalry Division, veterans of the Ia Drang campaign of the previous November, succeeded in locating and destroying more than 2000 enemy soldiers for the loss of only 228 Americans. On paper, the figures looked good, but there was a major problem that the US high command had not taken into account.

Trouble with the ARVN

Westmoreland's search and destroy concept was part of a larger, long-term strategy for bringing South Vietnam back under government control. Once the American forces with their helicopters and massive firepower had routed an enemy unit, the South Vietnamese Army was supposed to take over and clear the area of any survivors of the search and destroy operation. They were then to secure the area against any further infiltration

Often, a firefight would break out without warning. Below: Troopers of the 1st Cav return fire on an enemy bunker during Operation Masher. Below left: Troops provide fire support with M79 grenade launchers during a contact.

flattened the whole area.

Operation Hawthorne was an example of a strategy for fighting the war the Americans called 'search and destroy'. General Westmoreland believed that if the enemy would not come out and fight, then you had to get out there and make him fight. This meant large units going into the field to 'find, fix in place, fight and destroy' enemy forces and their base areas. It was a strong, aggressive approach, but would it get the results Westmoreland was looking for?

Into the An Lao Valley

In the early months of 1966 search and destroy went into top gear with the launch of Operation Masher in the An Lao Valley on the coastal edge of the Central Highlands. The operation, later renamed 'White Wing' after President Johnson complained that the codename 'Masher' was a trifle tactless, stretched over a period of 41 days

THE BODY COUNT

Did American units deliberately exaggerate the number of enemy soldiers they claimed to have killed to enhance their reputation?

It is usual during wartime for military commanders to try to calculate the exact level of success they have achieved on the battlefield. In Vietnam, they chose to measure their success with a method known as the 'body count'.

At first, only confirmed NVA or Viet Cong dead were to be included; possible or probable kills did not count. But how could you count the number of dead enemy soldiers when there was a battle raging?

The American high command issued guidelines to offset these problems. It was assumed that for every 100 dead counted there would be at least 30 enemy disabled or dying of wounds. Units were very keen to exaggerate their statistics.

During the war some notorious cases came to light. Major-General Julian J. Ewell, commander of the 9th infantry Division between 1968 and 1969, was obsessed with the count. He even set his subordinates quotas and graded their effectiveness accordingly. The division had an unsurpassed record of enemy casualties – but a very low ratio of weapons captured to enemy dead.

1966

and build up of enemy forces so that civilian programmes to improve the lives of the South Vietnamese in the villages could get under way without interference from the enemy. The reason for this division of responsibility was that Westmoreland just did not have the manpower on the ground to hold on to areas once they had been cleared – the troops were always needed elsewhere. On the whole, the Americans performed well in battle; the problem was the South Vietnamese Army – the ARVN.

Within a week of the completion of Operation Masher/White Wing, intelligence sources reported that enemy units were already moving back into the An Lao Valley. The South Vietnamese forces had been unable to follow through after the initial Air Cav operation. This failure to exploit a military advantage was to plague military commanders in Vietnam throughout the coming years of the war.

For the grunts on the ground, search and destroy meant a lot of hard work, and a lot of boredom. They soon christened these operations 'a walk in the sun' since on most days nothing happened. They went out into the boonies carrying a mountain of kit, they got tired, their feet hurt and they achieved nothing. But while they were bored, they were also afraid.

With every step they could be killed. Crude, but highly effective, Viet Cong booby traps lay in wait for them on jungle trails, in streams, in the

BROTHERS IN ARMS

If the Americans came to fight this war with and for the South Vietnamese, it wasn't long before they looked as if they were fighting it for themselves. Instead of willing the South Vietnamese Army (ARVN) to defend themselves, the massive increases in US troop presence gave them the impression that Uncle Sam would do the job for them. During the first nine months of 1966, only 46 per cent of the ARVN's large-scale operations resulted in contact with the enemy, against the 90 per cent achieved by US forces. Over the same period, ARVN desertions were running at an annual rate of 130,000 – a massive 21 per cent of the total.

Poor leadership and a shortage of equipment have been cited as reasons for the ARVN's

growing distaste for combat. Equally important was the suspicion amongst US commanders that communist infiltration of the AVRN would compromise any jointly planned operations. The result was that although the four US field force commands exactly matched the ARVN's four Corps Tactical Zones (CTZs), the two sides fought separate wars. By December 1965, Westmoreland's search and destroy strategy assigned the ARVN a merely secondary role. While US forces were given the task of finding and engaging the enemy, it was the ARVN's job to conduct 'clearing operations' – looking for guerrillas who remained after the major operations had ended. It was an assignment commonly nicknamed 'search-and-avoid'.

Above: Heavy fire support was an important part of search and destroy. The infantry patrols out in the field would run into a contact and immediately call in artillery fire from batteries of 105mm guns (above). Right: Troops of the 1st Infantry Division tear open sacks of rice found during a search and destroy operation. The destruction of enemy base areas, including food supplies, was part of the mission and during large operations units uncovered massive caches of food, weapons and equipment. Far right: Two troopers of the 1st Cav drag a half-dead VC from a bunker during Operation Masher.

villages, everywhere. One wrong foot, and a squad could be blown away by the explosion of a well-hidden land mine.

Good officers kept their men alert and stuck to the rules. To walk down the middle of a trail invited disaster – ambush or land mine – so the grunts struggled through the brush on either side of the route. It was a hard slog, but it saved lives. Around 4 o'clock in the afternoon was generally reckoned to be the worst time for mines and booby traps. As evening drew in on a hard day, a patrol's defences would be down and the men would become careless.

Going into villages could be extremely danger-

1966 was destined to be a year of bloody fighting in the highlands area between Chu Lai and Ban Me Thuot. As the strategy of 'area warfare' developed, General Westmoreland wanted to seize the offensive by taking on the enemy's main forces at his base camps and sanctuaries. Harbouring major enemy units, the 20,000 square-mile region was a prime target for the biggest assaults of the war so far.

Operation Masher/White Wing was mounted to attack enemy strongholds in the Binh Dinh province. Joining up with Marines from I Corps, already engaged in Operation Double Eagle in the Quang Ngai province, the 1st Cavalry Division, along with ARVN and Korean forces, swept through Binh Dinh in six weeks of almost continuous fighting. By 6 March, a massive 2389 enemy casualties were reported.

But although the operation was a success, the VC were quick to re-establish control. The 1st Air Cav was destined to return to the area several times throughout the year in Operations Davy Crockett, Crazy Horse, Irving and Thayer, as the struggle for Binh Dinh continued.

Further south, the 3d Brigade of the 25th Infantry Division struck out near the Cambodian border, first in Operation Garfield in March, and later, in an effort to protect the Special Forces border camps at Duc Co and Plei Me, in Operation Paul Revere — the first time US forces had entered the Chu Pong-Ia Drang area since the campaign of 1965.

In the northern part of the region, the 1st Brigade of the 101st Airborne mounted Operation Garfield near Dak To on 2 June. Finding themselves completely surrounded by the 24th NVA Regiment, it took two weeks of almost constant air bombardment, including 36 B-52 bombing sorties, to crumble the NVA resistance. But as with other operations in this front, it was difficult to convert a successful battle into a permanent, strategic gain.

ous. No-one could be trusted. A peaceful, rural scene with peasant farmers going about their business could suddenly be shattered by a hail of fire from a VC ambush position, or a small child might rush playfully in among the soldiers – but with two live hand grenades.

Human bait for the VC

Out in the field, at the sharp end of search and destroy, the grunts were in effect human bait for the VC. As they made their way through paddy fields, villages or jungles they would suddenly run into a contact. A few men might go down in the opening burst of enemy fire, and then the unit would call in artillery or close air support to pulverise their attackers. From their commander's point of view, if the men ran into trouble they had succeeded in their mission. But the men didn't always see it that way.

The strategy of search and destroy was the basic method by which the US Army engaged the enemy on the ground in Vietnam. By 1968, however, like Operation Masher, its name was dropped when it became associated with aimless searches in the jungle and the destruction of property. From then on, operations were described in basic military terms – reconnaissance in force, helicopter assault – but the men still had the same job to do.

1966

In Vietnam, nowhere was safe. Even fairly short grass could hide lethal booby traps like the simple cartridge trap shown above. A round in a bamboo sleeve was buried in the ground, with its tip just protruding and its primer resting on a nail or firing pin.

If you stepped on a toe-popper, a bullet would blow your foot off; if you stood on a punji trap you'd get a spike through your boot. Every inch of ground in Vietnam could kill or maim

Vietnam was a very nasty war and booby traps were one of its nastier aspects. They scared the hell out of me. The thought of my leg being punctured by a fæces-smeared spike and turning gangrenous frequently crept into my mind as I moved through the boonies. I was extremely cautious and paid attention to every booby-trap update that came down the turnpike. I was also very vindictive and placed as many booby traps for the Viet Cong as I could.

The booby trap was certainly not an innovation of the Vietnam war. In fact, the most feared of booby traps, like punji stakes, had been used in World War II against the Japanese. It is naive to assume that the VC were not playing fair by using booby traps. Guerrilla warfare doesn't play by the rules – except those laid down by Chairman Mao in *On Protracted War* – that's why it is so effective. We just had to learn caution. After all, war is a dangerous business.

Fear is the primary result of a booby-trap

EYE-WITNESS

Leroy Thompson served in a Ranger-trained special unit, and spent long periods on deep-penetration patrols.

VIET CONG BOOBY TRAPS

Below: The sharp end of a Viet Cong punji stake trap. Although punji stakes were not very effective as killing devices, they had a terrible psychological effect on the American troops. Even if a soldier never ran into one, the very thought that there might be punji pits around would make him hesitate over every step.

campaign. Seeing a bloody stump where a buddy's foot had been blown off, or his torso punctured by the spikes of a bamboo whip, sapped the morale of the US troops. But it also created another bonus for the VC. It increased the likelihood of US troops committing atrocities. An 18-year-old grunt who's seen his buddy's leg blown off is far more likely to waste a peasant who failed to point out the booby traps to his patrol. And any US atrocity rallied more peasants to the VC's side and won a political and a propaganda victory.

Personally, I admit to using villagers I believed to be VC sympathizers as human booby-trap detectors. I felt no compunction about it then and I don't feel any now. To me, my men were more valuable than those villagers who, whether they were VC or not, knew where the booby traps were.

The simplest VC booby traps were often the most effective. They made widespread use of booby traps consisting simply of a grenade and trip wire. Usually, these were stretched across the trail. To counter them we avoided the trails and walked very deliberately. At the slightest pull on our foot or leg, we froze. But it was the unreliability of VC grenades that saved many Americans. Many are walking around today who tripped the wire to a dud grenade.

Grenades were also used to booby trap gates.

The grenade would be buried shallowly and a short trip wire attached to the bottom of the gate. Even the slightest movement of the gate would detonate the grenade under the victim's feet.

Grenades attached to bamboo arches over trails, with trip wires fixed to the ground, were especially feared. Their shower of fragments caused messy face and head wounds. Fortunately, this type of booby trap was fairly easy to spot – during the day. But at night they were deadly. Frequently the VC would detach the trip wire during the day so that they and the local peasants could move freely up and down the trail. At night, they would come back and re-set them.

Trip wires criss-crossing the LZ

Armoured cavalrymen were so afraid of mines they covered the bottoms of their armoured personnel carriers with sand bags and rode on top. The VC got wise to this and would sling a string of grenades between two poles across the road.

As the war progressed, the VC and the NVA became surprisingly adept at picking likely helicopter landing zones and booby trapping or pre-zeroing mortars on them. Large stakes carrying grenades were driven in around the perimeter of a possible LZ. Trip wires criss-crossed the clearing. Since the pilots would be unlikely

1966

1966

Below: A Viet Cong 'armaments factory' in Quang Ngai province. Baskets are loaded with fearsome metal spikes, mounted on wooden boards, ready to be distributed along the jungle trails around the village. The spikes were often coated with poison or smeared with human excrement to increase the likelihood of their victim developing blood poisoning. This picture was released at the time of the war through Chinese communist sources.

Left: These grunts do not look one bit happy as they follow a narrow trail through the jungle, where a simple grenade and trip-wire device (below) could take out a man at any moment. For this trap, the VC would push a grenade (with the pin pulled but the safety handle still in place) into a can. The can was then fixed to a tree, with a wire tied to the grenade stretched across a trail.

to see the trip wires, these could be very effective. The VC and NVA troops would receive a huge bonus for destroying a helicopter so it was well worth their while booby-trapping potential LZs.

Command detonated grenades, daisy-chained along a trail and set off by a hidden VC, were also used to good effect against US troops, especially if the patrol was bunched up. But being Ranger-trained special ops troops, my men would not make this mistake. Instead they encouraged me to wear my rank insignia. The VC would usually go for an officer or radioman with their command detonation mines. Such was the gallows humour of the Nam.

The VC improvised traps too. Punji stakes inflicted gruesome wounds. Made of sharpened

At the Mines, Booby Traps and Tunnel Training Centre in Vietnam, the soldiers were introduced to a whole range of deadly devices: the sideways closing trap (left); a detonator for mines (below); a punji trap (below, far left); and the terrible swinging man trap (below left).

THE ESCALATING ROLE OF THE NVA

Not only were the Americans fighting an unseen enemy in Vietnam, they were also fighting an unknown quantity. No-one could ever accurately estimate the number of North Vietnamese combat forces who were assisting the Viet Cong in their struggle, nor how many more were being prepared for future action. A lack of detailed knowledge meant that, whatever the success of individual operations, it was often hard to tell who was actually winning this war. Confusion was not only the lot of the soldiers in the firing line.

Closer estimates are now available. North Vietnamese infiltration into the South began as far back as 1959, and by 1964 28,000 military personnel had begun to reinforce the Viet Cong as a fighting force. In the latter months of 1964, the build up of North Vietnamese Army (NVA) troops intensified as three further NVA regiments moved south.

Although NVA forces accounted for only a proportion of communist troops (79,900 out of a total of some 300,000 in the winter of 1967, for example) all operations were masterminded by the brilliant Hanoi General, Vo Nguyen Giap. It was Giap who had organised the expansion of the NVA to 15 divisions plus regimental units, and the massive channel of arms and supplies that flooded down Ho Chi Minh trail. As the war developed Giap devised two distinct kinds of tactics – small scale guerrilla attacks which were designed to have a cumulative effect and large assaults on vulnerable regions which would limit the manoeuvrability of enemy reinforcements.

Giap's strategy depended upon a close interplay of NVA and Viet Cong units, with the VC leading the guerrilla warfare and their northern allies mounting most of the main-force assaults. In spite of the massive build-up of US forces, Giap's astute manoeuvres maintained the initiative.

bamboo sticks, barbed wood or metal spikes, these were designed to inflict puncture wounds which would become infected – because the spikes were smeared with human excrement.

Spikes through the leg

Though the steel inserts in my jungle boots were a great comfort – I did not fancy a poisoned spike through my foot – there was little American technology could do to counter such booby traps. Also a punji beartrap got round the problem of our inserts. It consisted of two boards or steel plates with spikes driven through them. They were designed to pivot when stepped on and drive their spikes through the leg.

Spikes were also placed in pits which were concealed under a mat with a covering of dirt and vegetation. And they were placed in the grass on the banks of gullies or streams so that someone jumping from one bank to the other would impale themselves.

Bridges over streams or rice paddies might be sawn through the middle and the cut covered with mud. Underneath, just where the troops would tumble into the water, there would be punji stakes. Giant punji stakes would also be used to booby trap LZs.

The VC would often booby trap their tunnel complexes to maim or kill American tunnel rats. They would place spikes or stakes at the point where a tunnel rat would enter from above. Entrances might also be mined with command-

1966

The thousands of streams and waterways running through the jungles of Vietnam were ideal places for the Viet Cong to set their traps. In the muddy water, troops crossing (left) had great difficulty in spotting trip wires attached to grenades under the surface (below). Once tripped, the pressure wave from the exploding grenade would cause grievous internal damage to anyone in the water. But if their suspicions were aroused, American and South Vietnamese troops sometimes used human mine detectors— suspected or captured VC— to test the water (below left).

detonated grenades. But the most diabolical booby trap of all was at an entrance where the tunnel rat would have to hang by his hands from the edge before dropping into the tunnel. There would be a slit at eye level. Through it, a spear would be driven into the face of the victim by a waiting VC or a trip wire arrangement.

Bamboo whip booby traps used a piece of bamboo bent taut and wedged in place. It would have spikes embedded in it. When a trip wire released the wedges, the whip would sweep across the trail impaling anyone in its path.

The mace was a variation on the whip. A spiked rock on a camouflaged rope would be held overhead. It would be released by a trip wire and swing down the trail with devastating effect.

Other field expedient booby traps used by the VC included a mine made from a coconut shell filled with gunpowder, and a trap, created by burying a cartridge with its primer against a nail and only the top of the bullet protruding. A heavy footstep would set it off, firing the bullet through the victim's foot.

Though the VC were perhaps not as creative as the Germans or Japanese in booby trapping 'souvenirs', great care had to be taken when picking up enemy equipment. Of course, we too made great use of the fact that the VC loved to scrounge US supplies, often leaving C-rations rigged to a claymore when we vacated a campsite.

Better to injure than to kill

When we found VC or NVA supply dumps we would salt them with doctored rifle ammo and mortar rounds which would blow up in the weapon. Not only did this cause casualties, but it eroded the enemy's confidence in his weapons.

My favourite use of a grenade was to pull the firing pin and wedge it in a tin with the safety handle depressed. I'd wedge the can between rocks or in the fork of a tree and fix a trip wire to jerk the grenade from the can. Since VC medical facilities were primitive, we actually preferred a seriously injured VC to a dead one, as it put more of a strain on their limited resources.

In most cases, VC booby traps were extremely cost effective. For a few grenades or some hastily fabricated spikes, the VC could cause debilitating injuries to American troops but, more importantly, they eroded the American will to fight. And the caution which this fear caused slowed operations and prevented US troops responding quickly.

On the positive side, the fear of booby trapping often forced US troops to move more carefully and avoid trails, making them more effective in the jungle. But it must be said that the outrage over booby trapping probably caused US troops to commit a certain number of atrocities. The fear of booby traps permeated the minds of some troops so much that rumours of Saigon hookers who had even booby trapped their sexual parts with broken glass were rife. On the political level, Vietnam may have been limited war. But for those fighting it, it was total war, on both sides.

GETTING OUT THE WOUNDED

Being a medevac pilot was a dangerous job – but rescuing the wounded was crucial to morale

Warrant Officer Phil Marshall was dozing on his bunk in the alert hooch as the call for 'DUST-OFF!' – the nickname for a medical rescue mission – came from the radio shack next door. Instantly awake, he leapt up and ran to the radio room to get the mission sheet as the co-pilot, crew chief and medic ran to the Huey nearby. With the details of the location and radio frequency of the unit requesting dust-off in his hand, he emerged from the shack at a dead run.

Night scrambles were less traumatic than daytime missions, when the aircraft commander would often run from the mess tent, shovelling

Above: As rotor blades cut through the humid air south of Da Nang, a dust-off pilot waits for his human cargo, a young Marine maimed by a Viet Cong booby trap, to be carried aboard.

food into his mouth, followed invariably by such examples of combat pilot humour as, 'If you don't make it back, can I have your fan?'

The co-pilot's shout of 'Clear!' and the slowly increasing whine of the helicopter turbine greeted Marshall as he jumped into the darkened left seat. Repositioning his .38 revolver in its waist holster between his legs, for extra protection of the vital areas, he crammed the mission sheet into his shirt pocket. It joined the letter from his girlfriend he had received that evening, but had only been able to read three or four times.

He fastened his seat belt and shoulder harness

Dust-off missions came in many shapes and sizes, but most followed the same pattern. Stage One: After making a priority-one call for a medevac chopper, troopers rush a casualty from the fire zone (left). Stage Two: Having administered basic first aid to the wounded man, medics brace themselves against the dust-off's 'prop-blast' and wait for the skids to touch down (below). Stage Three: The casualty is taken on board (right).

and slid his armoured chickenplate under the shoulder straps. He pulled on his helmet and continued the engine run-up to 6600rpm while Don Study, the co-pilot, buckled up and reached down to the side for his helmet. Marshall continues the story:

'Immediately upon reaching proper rotor speed, my intercom call of "Coming Up" was instantly answered by a "Clear Left" from the crew chief, Specialist Fourth Class Zeb Dulin behind me, and a "Clear Right" from the medic, Spec 4 Randy Love on the opposite side. The crew always sat on armoured pads on the floor, with their backs to our armoured seats for maximum protection. Their rear facing positions gave us 360 degrees of eyesight in any situation.

'Time was running out'

'As we got light on the landing skids and lost contact with the ground, Don informed Quang Tri tower of our departure and direction. A dust-off aircraft on an urgent medical evacuation mission – or medevac – was rarely questioned or asked to wait. A low-level departure generally gave us a chance to scan the area and stay under the traffic pattern until we were well away from the city.

'While departing, the co-pilot normally made a call to the artillery command centre for clearance, or at least a report of where arty was firing from and where it was impacting, so that we could avoid or fly under the rounds. An artillery shell through the cabin could spoil your whole day.

'As Don made the call, I noticed the dim glow of flares on the northwest horizon. I didn't even have to look at my map under the red lights – I knew where we were going.

'The 101st Airborne was making a night combat assault out near the northern firebases along the DMZ (Demilitarized Zone). The arty info was coming in over the radio, but it didn't register...my mind was about 40 klicks away.

'The crew was quiet. We knew what we had to

do. Here we were – a very green 21-year-old aircraft commander, a 22-year-old co-pilot, in-country for less than two months, a new crew chief all of 20-years-old on his first trip to the field and a 19-year-old medic who had a nice safe job back in some hospital in Da Nang, but was bored and wanted to fly. Young as we were, we had already flown together two days without a hitch and it felt like we had known each other for years. We were professionals and we had a job to do.

'I'm hit and going down'

'When we arrived over the area we realised that things were kind of bad. The assault was still going on and gunships were trying to suppress the ground fire. The ground commander, 'Click 66', informed us that he had three wounded that he wanted evacuated; one had a sucking chest wound – the next worst thing to being dead – and time was running out.

'We had trouble locating the correct LZ. There were flares going off and three or four strobe marking lights flashing at the same time. One of the gunships said he would fly over the LZ and switch his position lights on as he overflew it. This he did, but, as we flared over the LZ, I looked out of my left window and saw a slick making an approach at the same time. He was 50ft away and coming straight in, so I pulled pitch and got out of there as fast as I could.

'I asked Click 66 to turn his strobe light on and

WOUNDED

Between 1961 and 1973, a total of 47,244 US servicemen were killed and 303,704 wounded by direct enemy action in Vietnam. If only a small proportion of Americans fought against large enemy units, no less than 56 per cent witnessed their comrades being killed or wounded. For those on patrol or on search and destroy missions, death would often come unawares.

Because of the enemy's use of booby traps, mines and ambushes, 10,000 US servicemen lost at least one limb – more than all those in World War II and Korea put together. While 11 per cent of deaths and 15 per cent of injuries came from this source, the percentage was often much higher in periods of low combat intensity.

In a firefight with the VC or NVA, an American soldier was most likely to be killed by smallarms fire: according to the statistics, 51 per cent of combat deaths and 16 per cent of wounds came from such a source. Nearly as dangerous were the effects of exploding shrapnel fragments which caused 36 per cent of deaths and 65 per cent of injuries. Direct hits would completely dismember the victim, but soldiers in the arc of shrapnel could, and often did, survive. Death was most commonly caused by head wounds, although advanced medical facilities meant that 82 per cent of Americans seriously wounded were saved.

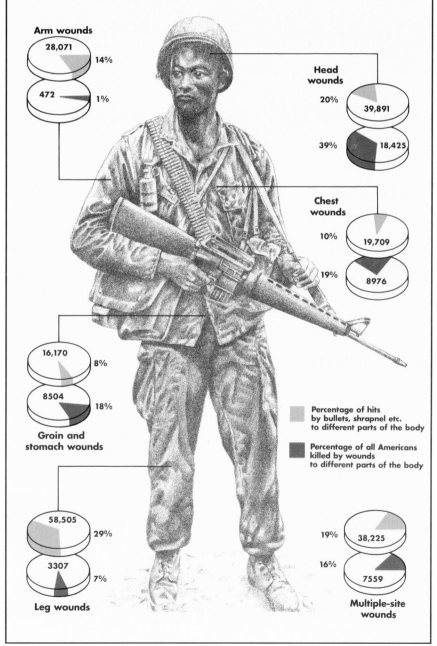

Arm wounds
28,071   14%
472   1%

Head wounds
20%   39,891
39%   18,425

Chest wounds
10%   19,709
19%   8976

16,170   8%
8504   18%
Groin and stomach wounds

58,505   29%
3307   7%
Leg wounds

19%   38,225
16%   7559
Multiple-site wounds

Percentage of hits by bullets, shrapnel etc. to different parts of the body

Percentage of all Americans killed by wounds to different parts of the body

1966

1966

In densely forested areas, where insufficient time prohibited the clearing of a landing zone, the men on the ground had to improvise to get their wounded out quickly. Above: The casualty's stretcher would be fastened to the 'skyhook' of a helicopter hovering above the tree-line, in this case an HH-43 Huskie (top). Seconds later, the dust-off would be en route to the nearest field hospital.

off and eventually we found the correct LZ among some defoliated trees in a bomb crater on the side of a hill. I could not land and had to hover about six feet above the ground, with the rotor blades turning within a foot of the trees. We got the wounded on board and departed from the LZ to the south.'

As Marshall cleared the LZ, one of the Viet Cong aimed his AK-47 assault rifle in the direction of the tell-tale 'wop-wop-wop' of the Huey rotor blades and fired off his whole clip. One of the rounds came through the left door, struck the armoured seat and shattered, sending shrapnel and jagged pieces of metal from the seat into Marshall's left arm, severing the nerves.

'My left arm went completely numb from the elbow down and my arm jerked upwards. The engine began to die as I rolled off the throttle and the low-rev audio warning began to sound. It felt like I had the whole of my left hand blown off and the explosion was so great that I thought we had been hit by a rocket-propelled grenade. I looked across at Don Study and shouted, "I'm hit, I'm hit." He grabbed hold of the controls as the aircraft began to fall like a stone. Although my life did not begin to flash before my eyes, I remember thinking "This is it Phil", and wondered how the folks back home were going to take it.

'Don bottomed the pitch and rolled the revs back on as I turned the radios from the ground to the gunship frequency. I called "Dust-Off 711. I'm hit and going down." We continued to descend and were heading for the ridgeline, although by now the power was beginning to return. We hit one tree going over the ridgeline and severely damaged both rotor blades, but thankfully they stayed together and we headed for the hospital ship *Repose*, followed by one of the "Batman" gunships.'

Ideal prey for the VC

Don Study made a very good approach to the helicopter pad on the ship, and the Navy medics rushed to take the wounded off. A doctor looked at Phil Marshall's arm and told him that he would be home for Christmas. The paratrooper with the sucking chest wound died on the way in.

This had been a typical dust-off mission. Phil Marshall and his crew went in on their own at night, without gunship cover. They brought out the wounded, despite an unsecured LZ and at great personal risk to themselves.

The dust-off helicopters were ideal prey for the Viet Cong, who knew for sure that they would come in after a firefight, or even during one. The Red Cross emblems on the Hueys made ideal aiming points for the enemy gunners and, being usually unarmed, they made tempting targets. The 'Eagle' dust-offs of the 101st Airborne and those of the 1st Air Cav took exception to this lack of respect for the Geneva Conventions and mounted door guns on their aircraft.

The first five medevac UH-IAs arrived in Vietnam in April 1962 with the 57th Medical Detachment (Helicopter Ambulance). They were

Stage Four: Once on board the dust-off, the casualty is hooked up to an intravenous drip while the extent of his injury is assessed by one of the qualified medics (right, above). The medic would relay this information to the pilot, who would then set course for the facility best equipped to deal with the wounded man's injury.

Stage Five: Once the chopper has touched down at one of the field hospitals stretcher-bearers rush towards the helicopter pad (right centre).

Stage Six: A team of surgeons provide the last link in an unbroken sequence of events that usually began with a priority-one call for a dust-off. The average elapsed time between an injury and surgery during the Vietnam war was little more than 100 minutes. Of the wounded who reached medical facilities alive, nearly 98 per cent survived. Much of the credit for this must go to the rapid response of the dust-off crews.

later given the name 'dust-off', after the call-sign of Major Charles Kelly, a famous pilot killed in action in 1964. The name stuck for the rest of the war. But in those early days before the arrival of American combat troops, the South Vietnamese were the dust-off's main customers. They were not easy to work with: ARVN units often insisted that the dust-offs took out the dead before the wounded, because the soldiers believed that the soul lingers between this world and the next if not properly buried. In later years, dust-offs would be mobbed by ARVN troops trying to escape combat, regardless of the wounded requiring evacuation. During Operation Lam Son 719, the Laos incursion of 1971, the problem was so great that dust-off crews had to grease their landing skids to prevent would-be deserters from hitching a ride out of the battlefield.

The evacuation of the wounded was supposed to be carried out according to the seriousness of their wounds. They were classified as either routine, priority or urgent. Urgent patients were those in imminent danger of loss of life or limb; they required an immediate response from any available air ambulance. Priority patients were those with serious but not critical wounds or illnesses; they could expect up to a four-hour wait.

Anytime, anyplace, anywhere

Many dust-off crews worked according to their own categories of urgent or non-urgent. If it was urgent, they went in – anytime, anyplace, anywhere. Many a bullet-ridden Huey arrived at an aid station, full of wounded and with the medic and crew chief exhausted, but still working to their own priorities of 'Stop the bleeding and keep 'em breathing.' It was a decided boost to troop morale to know that they could be evacuated from a firefight and in an army hospital quicker than someone involved in an automobile accident on a highway back in the States.

The busiest year for the air ambulances was 1969, when 140 dust-offs were stationed around the country. Fifteen per cent belonged to the 101st Airborne and the 1st Air Cav, the rest to various medical detachments. Each aircraft was flying four missions per day and, for such service, someone had to pay the price. The tab was usually picked up by the dust-off crews. By the end of the war, 88 pilots had been killed and around 380 wounded, with their crew chiefs and medics suffering a similarly high casualty rate.

By 1969 two dust-off pilots had won the Medal of Honor, Major Patrick H. Brady in 1968 and Michael J. Novosel in 1969. Statistics showed that dust-off aircraft suffered triple the losses to hostile fire than all other types of helicopter mission. Air ambulance work was a good way to get killed. But it was also very rewarding work. By the end of the war, some 390,000 Allied and South Vietnamese wounded had been evacuated by helicopter to a medical facility. Without the skill, devotion and bravery of the dust-off crews, the final number of American dead would have been much higher.

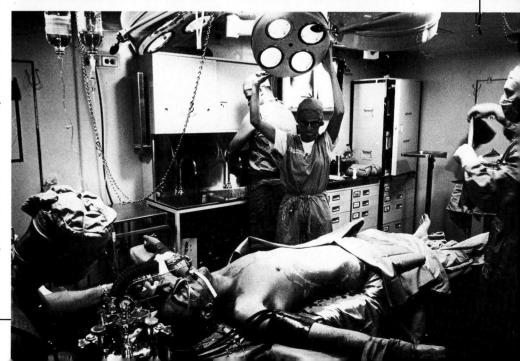

ROLLING THUNDER

One of the costliest bombing campaigns in history, Operation Rolling Thunder raged for three shell-shocked years. In more than 300,000 sorties over North Vietnam, the Americans dropped 860,000 tons of bombs, killed 52,000 civilians and lost 922 of their own planes

A B-52 and its bomb load. These iron-clad death loads were dreaded by the North Vietnamese 2: Snakeye 500lb bombs are prepared for loading. On average, the equivalent of one 500lb bomb was dropped every 30 seconds during the three-year operation. 3: F-105D Thunderchiefs drop six 750lb bombs each during a Rolling Thunder mission. 4: An F-4 Phantom prepares for

2

3

take-off from *USS Midway*.
5: The hospital at Thai Binh, near Hanoi, was bombed three times by the Americans. In 1967, it was estimated that 80 per cent of the North Vietnamese casualties were civilian.

4

5

1966

EYE-WITNESS

Marc Leepson (above) was a 22-year-old college graduate when he was drafted to serve in Vietnam. He did his tour with the 527th Personnel Service Company at Camp Granite. He is now books editor and columnist for *Veteran* magazine.

HANGING OUT

Above: For troops stuck in camp pop music was a nostalgic reminder of the world they had left behind. Here the 'Oklahoma Kid' picks out a tune on a guitar.

Right: Soldiers line up for a plate of Army food during the construction of a base area. Food was never good back at camp – but it was a damn sight better than the rations men carried on combat missions.

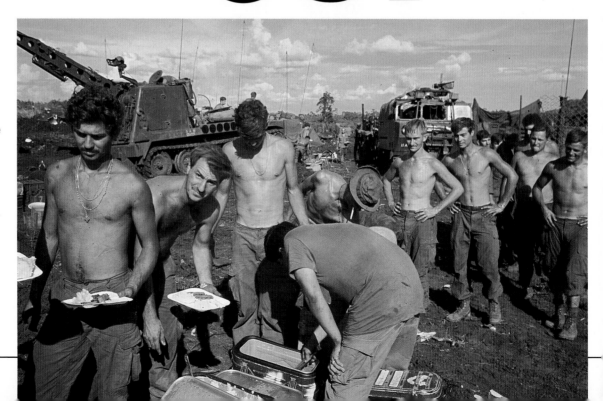

Life at a base camp in Nam – junk food, beer and ice-cream from the PX, games of basketball, parties with drugs and porno movies, listening to Jimi Hendrix, the Beatles and the Rolling Stones, and fights every Saturday night...

Watching the movies about the Vietnam war you'd think that just about every GI put in a solid year's worth of jungle fighting – but most of those who served in Vietnam never saw combat. No official figures of the so-called 'tooth-to-tail' ratio exist, and the number of support and combat personnel tended to vary during the years of the American involvement. But it is reckoned that for every combat trooper there were around five or six remfs – rear echelon motherfuckers – like me.

Most American soldiers worked in rear areas as truck drivers, engineers, telephone operators, stevedores, warehousemen, mechanics, payroll clerks, computer operators, chaplain's assistants and various other non-combat jobs. I knew one guy whose job consisted of tending a golf course. The largest single major command group in Vietnam during the height of the war was not the 1st Infantry Division or the 3rd Marines, but the 1st Logistical Command, aka the 1st Log, which had 55,000 men – mostly clerks, cooks and truck drivers and other support personnel.

Even the infantry troops didn't spend all their time humping the boonies. Some had weeks at a time of rear-echelon duty, others only days. It depended on where you served and when you were there. But no matter what your job, life in the rear had its attractions.

Rear-area base camps varied greatly in size and amenities. Some consisted of little more than a few tents surrounded by rutted, unpaved roads.

Others, such as the mammoth Long Binh Post near Saigon, had modern, air-conditioned office buildings and movie theatres. But every rear area, no matter how rudimentary, stood as an oasis from the fighting. Base camps were the targets for sappers and snipers, but most were well fortified and GIs felt safe inside the camps' barbed wire fences.

Most camps had showers – sometimes only with cold water, but after all this was a war zone. There were toilets too, some of which even had running water. There were PXs not unlike the all-purpose stores on military bases back home. A few bases even had swimming pools. A couple of the bigger

Above: Author Marc Leepson poses outside Camp Granite.

coastal facilities, including the giant base at Cam Ranh Bay, had beaches complete with life-guards and snack bars. In our compound – Camp Granite, the home of the 527th Personnel Service Company, about a mile outside the coastal city of Qui Nhon – we had a makeshift basketball court at the side of the supply sergeant's building, a softball field tucked in beside a Buddhist cemetery and several volleyball pits in sandy areas between the barracks.

Then there were the clubs – segregated by rank, of course. As you might expect, the officers' clubs tended to be air-conditioned and have cute little Vietnamese waitresses and upholstered bar stools. The enlisted men's clubs typically were on the dingy side with dirt floors, ceiling fans and 'ornery corporals acting as bartenders. At both

THE US BUILD-UP IN 1966

1966 was the year of the 'big build-up' of US forces in Vietnam. On 31 December 1965, there were 184,300 US servicemen in-country; 12 months later, that figure had risen to 385,300, with little sign of a reduction in the flow. As new units arrived, they were sent to areas throughout South Vietnam, proving that America was now fighting to win.

Vietnam had been blocked off into four military areas with the Marines given responsibility for the north, the army handling the central regions and the ARVN operating in the far south. In the northern province of I Corps Tactical Zone (ICTZ), the 1st Marine Division ('The Old Breed') was fully deployed by April 1966, joining the 3rd Marine Division as part of the III Marine Amphibious Force. Comprising the 1st, 5th and 7th Marine Regiments, the 1st Division was based at Chu Lai, with responsibilities for the provinces of Quang Tin and Quang Ngai.

Further south, in the Central Highlands (IICTZ), existing US Army units were reinforced steadily as the year progressed. First to arrive was the 25th Infantry Division in April, tasked with the defense of Pleiku; by then, the region had come under command of I Field Force Vietnam, a corps-level headquarters based at Nha Trang. In October the 4th Infantry Division ('The Ivy Division') also moved to Pleiku.

II Field Force Vietnam, set up at Long Binh in March 1966, was responsible for US units in IIICTZ (Saigon) and IVCTZ (Mekong Delta). In August, it was reinforced by the 196th Infantry Brigade (Light), sent to Tay Ninh City to the northwest of Saigon: a month later the 11th Armored Cavalry Regiment ('The Blackhorse Regiment'), equipped with M48 tanks and M113 APCs, arrived at Long Binh. The latter base received the 199th Infantry Brigade (Light) ('The Redcatchers') in December, in which month the 9th Infantry Division ('The Old Reliables') also arrived, trained for operations in the Mekong Delta. All four CTZs now contained main-force units.

More often than not the beer blast would end in the traditional fight. One time, during a beer and steak party, a close friend of mine, Specialist Fifth Class Crandell, had one – probably ten – too many and decided to chase down the beer with a few hits of marijuana. After a toke or two, Crandell started to lose control. He began shouting and running around our company area. Finally he pulled to a wobbly stop near the barbecuing steaks in the middle of the compound surrounded by our entire 200-man unit.

Fighting a drunken battle

'I am the grrr-eatest,' Crandell screeched, pretending to be Muhammad Ali. He then flung his arms out like he'd just won the heavyweight championship and collapsed on his back on the ground. The company gathered around. 'Get up, Crandell,' bawled Sergeant Grover, who'd also been drinking beer steadily for hours. 'That's an order.' Crandell shut his eyes and challenged Grover to a fistfight – never mind the fact he couldn't even stand up, much less throw a punch.

Somehow the word had gotten around that Crandell had fallen from the top of the barracks steps and someone called an ambulance. Within minutes, a World War II-vintage ambulance, complete with flopping leather top with a mouldy red cross painted on a dirty white background, came rattling into the compound and two medics whisked Crandell off to the field hospital in Qui Nhon. When I visited him next day with two buddies, he was ashen faced. Despite extensive tests, doctors found nothing wrong with him except for an excess of alcohol in his system.

It's no secret that drugs were abundant and easily available in Vietnam. When I was there, the main drug of choice was marijuana. Barbiturates were sold openly at Vietnamese drug stores in town, but only one or two guys I knew used downers regularly. Opium also was available, either in liquid form in little jars to paint on marijuana joints or in more solid form to smoke in pipes in the opium dens of Qui Nhon. Only a few of our guys smoked opium, though. It was so powerful that you risked being zonked out for a day or two if you did too much of it. In the latter stages of the war, heroin was commonplace.

Where I was, most of the recreational drug users smoked marijuana. You could buy it either loose by the jarful, rolled in joints the size of your index finger for a dollar a piece or rolled with white cigarette paper and filters and sealed in packs and cartons that looked exactly like Marlboros.

About 20 per cent of the enlisted men in our outfit smoked regularly. Probably another 20 per cent were occasional smokers. The rest either drank beer or totally abstained from intoxicants. The sergeants left the dopers alone, for the most part. There would be unannounced shake-downs every few months, when the NCOs and officers would search our lockers for dope and other bad things, like illegal weapons. But a friendly sergeant would tip off the troops in advance.

Above: Taking it easy – GIs take time out during a construction project. For soldiers spared the strain of fighting in the jungle, life in Vietnam could often be unbearably slow.

clubs the beer and liquor was very inexpensive as was the food which, in the EM clubs, consisted mainly of burgers and fries.

On occasion the beer was free. About once every six weeks our scheming staff sergeants would make some kind of deal with other wheeler-dealers and all of a sudden several big cases of steaks and a jeep-load of beer would appear in the middle of our company area. In the early evening the mess sergeants would set up big barbecue pits using discarded 50-gallon drums and begin broiling big rubbery steaks. They'd ice down the beer and we'd all chow down and try to drink as much beer as we could hold. Usually it was a brew from the Philippines called San Miguel.

A few guys fired up their first joints in the dark on the way to the mess hall for breakfast and stayed stoned all day. But most guys saved their pot smoking for the evenings, after work. They'd meet in makeshift rooms in the barracks and get high and listen to music. In the rear it was easy to get your hands on top-quality Japanese stereo equipment. Record players, tuners, amps and reel-to-reel tape decks were sold at deep discount in the in-country PXs or picked up by guys who went to Hong Kong or Tokyo for R&R. The records and tapes you could buy downtown. There were even places in town that would tape records of your choice onto reels for a ridiculously low price.

The Army ran its own radio station, Armed Forces Vietnam, but we rarely listened to the timid military disk jockeys and their six-month-old pop tunes. We were hard rock and rollers in the 527th. Our number one favourite was Jimi Hendrix. And our favourite Hendrix tune was *Purple Haze*, which somehow captured the drugged up, halfway-around-the-world, what-am-I-doing-here life we were living. Besides, word had it that Hendrix had been one of us, a trooper in the pre-Nam days with the 101st Airborne. We played a lot of Doors, too, as well as the Beatles' drug-infected *Sergeant Pepper* album and the Rolling Stones' psychedelic album of the era, *Their Satanic Majesty's Request*. When we felt like dancing we flipped on some soul music – usually the Temptations or Smokey Robinson.

Entertaining the troops

Inevitably, the pot smokers would get hungry and thirsty and GI entrepreneurs who bought small refrigerators at the PX would stock them with cold sodas and sell the chilled beverages at inflated prices to throat-parched pot heads. Other entrepreneurs borrowed the company's film projector and ran porno movies in the barracks, charging each horny viewer an admittance fee.

On special occasions we'd get shows from outside at our camp. They were nothing like the Bob Hope spectaculars with leggy starlets and Las Vegas crooners playing to tens of thousands at giant air bases. Our shows were more pedestrian. A creaky Special Forces portable stage was tugged into our company area by truck. A Filipino rock band would play fairly good cover versions of current hits. Each band had a couple of female go-go dancers. On the nights of the shows the dopers got loaded, the boozers got smashed. All of us would sit and listen to the music and watch the girls dance. Then the truck would pull out and we'd head slowly back to our barracks.

In our free time, we talked about what soldiers everywhere talked about: what we would do once we got home. Looking from Vietnam, the United States seemed like a gigantic store stuffed with good things to eat. Everything was there for the taking. All we had to do was survive a year in the deprived black-and-white nowhere of the Nam and our reward would be a return trip to the Technicolor USA – the place we called The World.

Left: Few moments at camp could compare with the arrival of a letter from home. Here, mail is handed out to members of the 5th Cav. Below: Marc Leepson (fourth from left) joins in a game of basketball.

TAIL AND TEETH

Why was the ratio of US soldiers confined to base camps to those engaged on combat service so wildly out of proportion?

All armed forces consist of frontline ('teeth') units which do the actual fighting and rear-area ('tail') units responsible for their support. It is an accepted characteristic of modern war that the more sophisticated the frontline force, the more elaborate the logistical back-up. But in Vietnam the balance got out of hand. It has been estimated, for example, that in mid-1968 only 14 per cent of US and allied ground forces were available for offensive operations, all the rest being tied down in the construction, maintenance, administration or protection of base facilities.

Such a ratio of 6 to 1 in favour of the tail was clearly unsatisfactory, but it is not difficult to see why it occurred. US armed forces in Vietnam not only used up massive amounts of ammunition and associated supplies, but demanded the 'luxuries' of food, drink and transportation, which served merely to increase the strain. By 1968, three dairies and 40 ice cream plants were dispersed around Vietnam, while over 760,000 tons of supplies were being delivered each month.

To cope with the ever-expanding supply line, the US spent $2.6 billion between 1965 and 1968 alone on new construction projects, which were carried out by 57 construction battalions and squadrons and no less than 51,000 civilians. Whatever the imbalance of teeth and tail, the logistical effort of maintaining these base facilities – where soldiers could buy everything from TV sets to Napoleon brandy – was, as Westmoreland once remarked, 'one of the more remarkable accomplishments of American troops in Vietnam.'

1966

1966

EYE-WITNESS

This article is based on the memoirs of Captain Howard Rutledge. In November 1965 Rutledge was the Executive Officer of Fighter Squadron 191, based on the aircraft carrier *Bon Homme Richard* in the Gulf of Tonkin.

Welcome to North Vietnam and the 'Hanoi Hilton' – the prison where the beds were made of concrete and the spiders were as big as a man's fist

Flying over North Vietnam in his F-8 Crusader jet fighter, Captain Howard Rutledge banked right and began his attack run on a strategic bridge north-west of Thanh Hoa. With 200 missions over Korea and North and South Vietnam under his belt, Rutledge never even contemplated the possibility of being hit. But seconds later, after a succession of anti-aircraft shells tore through the fuselage of the F-8 and sent it into an uncontrollable spin, Rutledge jerked at the ejection curtain. The parachute carried him gently towards the earth as the fighter exploded in a ball of flame. It was 28 November 1965, and the beginning of a seven-year nightmare for Howard Rutledge.

Landing safely close to a North Vietnamese village, Rutledge made a vain attempt to flee from a large crowd that had spotted his descent and was

PRISONERS OF WAR

now bearing down on him. As he saw the ring of knives, machetes and sticks closing in, Rutledge was convinced that death would not be long in coming. However, he was saved by the village commissar from summary execution at the hands of the local militia. Bound and gagged, he was manhandled into the back of a truck and driven to Hanoi, where he was to endure seven years of captivity. Howard Rutledge recounts his first three years as a prisoner of war:

'This was Heartbreak Hotel. It was one of many cell blocks of the huge Hoa Lo prison complex. Built by the French early in the century, American aircrews housed there had nicknamed the prison the "Hanoi Hilton". Needless to say, this was no hotel....

I was covered with filth and blood

'The retaining room I found myself in had knobby plaster walls that gave the place a cave-like appearance.... It was small and the filthiest place I had seen to date. It was like the worst of slums in miniature. I sat down on a pile of debris in the centre of this mess and took stock of my condition. I had no clothes. I was freezing cold. I had eaten nothing for 24 exhausting hours. My body ached. My leg and wrist were sprained and swelling badly. I was covered with filth and blood.'
When North Vietnamese interrogators demanded to know Rutledge's unit, he responded by citing the American Code of Conduct. Not content with his name, rank and serial number, the interrogators

POW CAMPS

American airmen captured by the North Vietnamese usually ended up at the old French colonial prison of Hoa Lo in the centre of Hanoi. Dubbed the 'Hanoi Hilton' by its inmates, it was made up of a series of compounds, all of which were given appropriate nicknames. 'New Guy Village' was where the prisoners were first received, 'Heartbreak Hotel' and 'Las Vegas' were the places where torture sessions were regularly held, and 'Camp Unity' was where, after December 1970, the prisoners were first allowed to meet each other in the prison compound.

But Hoa Lo was only the centre of the web. Between 1965 and 1967, some POWs lived in a compound 35 miles to the northwest of Hanoi,

known as the 'Briar-patch', and were then moved on to the 'Zoo' at Cu Loc. As the POW population increased, similar compounds appeared, graced with nothing more than American nicknames such as 'Skid Row' and 'Camp Faith'. The Son Tay camp is particularly famous for the daring American rescue mission launched in November 1970, when the raiding force found the camp empty.

In Hanoi itself, smaller compounds also existed. In 1967, POWs who had caused maximum trouble to their captors were concentrated in a building known as 'Alcatraz', while a 'model' prison, created for inspection by outside visitors, was built in the grounds of a house formerly belonging to the mayor of Hanoi.

were determined to break him.

'They forced my legs into spur-like shackles and used a pipe and strong rope to lock both ankles firmly into place. Next they forced my arms into a long-sleeved shirt and began to tie them behind me from above my elbows to my wrists. One guard put his foot on my back, forcing the laces tight enough to cut off all circulation and pulling my shoulder blades almost apart. I could see the rope cut through my wrists all the way to the bone but they did not bleed, because the bindings acted like a tourniquet, cutting off circulation entirely to my legs and arms.... The smell of human excrement burned my nostrils. A rat, large as a small cat, scampered across the slab beside me.'
Later, alone in his cramped cell, Rutledge reflected on the life of a prisoner in solitary confinement:

'Nobody can teach you to survive the brutality

Above: North Vietnamese militiawoman captures a US 'air pirate'. By the end of 1966, Hanoi was claiming that it had brought down more than 1600 US aircraft over North Vietnam and that 'hundreds of air pirates paid for their crimes'. Far left: The 'Hanoi Hilton'.

Lieutenant Robert Peel, shot down in an F105 over Than Hoa, 31 May 1965.

Major Lawrence Guarino, shot down in an F105 over Moc Chau, 14 June 1965.

Captain Murphy Neal Jones, shot down after bombing raid on Haiphong, 29 June 1966.

Major James H Kasler, shot down over Hanoi, 29 June 1966.

Lt Commander Richard Allen Stratton, shot down in an A4.E, 5 January 1967.

1966

Below: A captured B-52 pilot, downed after bombing raids on Hanoi and Haiphong, is presented to the world's press — a humiliating break from the horrors of the Hanoi Hilton.

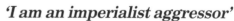

of being alone. At first you panic. You want to cry out. You fight back waves of fear. You want to die, to confess, to do anything to get out of that ever-shrinking world. Then, gradually a plan takes shape. Being alone is another kind of war, but slowly I learned that it, too, can be won.'

As the months passed, the jailers, or turnkeys as they were known, became adamant that Captain Rutledge should sign a written 'confession' that Hanoi could then use for the purpose of anti-American propaganda. He was dragged to another cell.

'As my eyes became accustomed to the dimness, I could see spiders as big as my fist hanging all around me. They may have been friendly spiders,

but they created quite a terrifying effect in the semi-darkness. Ants crawled all over me, and nine million mosquitoes were trapped inside. Gecko lizards scurried through the filth, and large rats looked me over hungrily. It is a helpless sensation to be shackled, hands and feet, in such a place. I had no way to kill the mosquitoes or frighten off the rats. I just sat and watched and trembled.'

Refusing to succumb to the indignities that were heaped upon him, Rutledge taunted his captors by declaring he would rather die than collaborate.

'As I sat there in a pile of human excrement crawling with countless moving things, I thought back upon my "bravery". It was not bravery to ask for death when the enemy needed us alive, but I knew the cost I would pay for my resistance. Again it took all the courage I could muster. Now I sat staring into the darkness, gagging on my odour, my skin crawling with pests that bit and pinched in the dark. My courage waned. Maybe they wouldn't kill me. Maybe they would just abuse me until I died.'

On 31 August 1966, after 28 days of continual torture, Howard Rutledge finally broke.

'I am an imperialist aggressor'

'When the morning dawned through the crack in the bottom of the solid prison door, I thanked God for his mercy and called the guard...."I am a Yankee imperialist aggressor," I wrote, parroting their text, knowing how little those words sounded like anything an American would write. I knew that they had not released my name yet after nine months, and that confession could be used against me to humiliate me in the camp and as propaganda around the world. I hoped my friends and family would understand.'

In May 1967, Rutledge was put back into solitary.

'He [*the guard*] shackled me to my slab in rear cuffs and irons. For five days I couldn't move. It was summer and very hot. The humidity must have been in the 90s, the temperature in the 100s. I developed one of those severe heat rashes where the red welts turn to blisters and ultimately to boils. At first I wasn't too concerned about the boils. But they wouldn't come to a head, so I had to pick them to stop the swelling. I didn't know that the pus was contagious or that the bug inside the poison caused the boils to spread. In a few days I counted at least sixty boils about one inch in diameter over my entire body – under my arms, in my nose, in my hair, on my ears, legs, arms, hands and fingers.'

In his mouth...a six inch worm

In October 1967 Howard Rutledge was transferred to a high security prison known as 'Alcatraz'. The torture and abuse continued, with the American airmen confined to tiny cells that had no windows. Fifteen hours of each day were spent in leg irons attached to the cement sleeping slabs. Rutledge describes the ordeal.

'We received almost no medicine during our entire prison terms and, because our two daily meals consisted primarily of pumpkin or cabbage soup with a few pieces of pig fat floating on the greasy surface, our protein intake was down. Therefore, our resistance to disease and infection was down. We had to be extremely careful. If we stubbed a toe, we knew we would lose a toenail....

'Our intestines were crawling with worms that would work their way through our system in surprising ways. One night Harry [*another American POW*] woke up with what he thought was a piece of string in his mouth. He pulled out a six-inch worm....We soon discovered that pepper cleaned them out....When no peppers were available, we tried to steal a drink of kerosene from a lantern. That quick snort of stolen kerosene fixed

the worms and almost fixed the thief.'
Although Howard Rutledge had no option but to adapt to the horrors of his life as a prisoner of war, it was no easy task.

'The worst part of being a prisoner is the helplessness to reach out and lift up another man in need....War is like that for both sides. I'm sure the enemy had families who bled and died. I'm sure the enemy cried when loved ones went away and did not return. I'm sure the enemy, too, were tempted to give way to anger and hatred. But revenge is God's business. When it's over, we must try to forget and forgive.'
Howard Rutledge was released on 31 January 1973, after the seven longest years of his life.

Captured American airmen were often paraded through the streets of Hanoi, where they suffered the jeers and insults of the angry local populace who — maybe only hours before — had endured US bombing.

THE GENEVA CONVENTIONS

Why were captured US pilots never given their proper rights under the Geneva Convention?

For a war that was never declared and fought without recognizable frontiers, it was perhaps inevitable that the rules of war in Vietnam were never too closely applied. Prisoners on both sides were often tortured, abused or murdered in spite of the fact that the third of the Geneva Conventions (GC3) should have protected all soldiers captured by the enemy. In a guerrilla conflict, justice stands too close to revenge.

The Democratic Republic of Vietnam had ratified the 1949 Geneva Conventions in 1957, but with the reservation that 'prisoners of war, prosecuted and convicted for war crimes against humanity...shall not benefit from the present Convention'. During the bombing of the North, the Vietnamese took the attitude that US pilots involved in bombing civilian areas were war criminals – and treated them as such.

The most important part of GC3 was Article 13, which stated that 'Prisoners of war must at all times be humanely treated'. The so-called 'Detaining Power' was not consciously to mistreat its captives, nor subject them to 'physical mutilation...medical or

scientific experiments'. It was also to protect the prisoners against 'acts of violence or intimidation and against insults and public curiosity'. Few US POWs found that these rights applied to them: most airmen captured in the North after 1965 were paraded through the streets and abused by an irate populace.

Of equal importance was Article 17, which stated that no prisoner, when questioned was required to give more than his 'surname, first names and rank, date of birth, and army, regimental, personal or serial number'. But as one survivor wrote, those who refused to give anything more did not come home. Article 17 of the conventions, which went on to state that 'no physical or mental torture, nor any other form of coercion, may be inflicted on prisoners of war to secure from them information of any kind whatsoever', was treated as an irrelevance. According to one source, about 80 per cent of US POWs were finally broken and made some form of statement for the enemy.

Other articles were similarly ignored. Most US prisoners had their clothing and possessions removed (in breach of Article 18), many of them were kept in the combat zone, particularly if they had been captured by the VC in the South (Article 19), medical and spiritual needs were not satisfied (Article 33) and threats of 'war crime trials' were regularly made, at least to captured airmen (Article 84). The rules just did not apply.

CHAPTER 18

NAMSPEAK

1966

Namspeak nam'spk, n. (neolog.) The colourful vernacular of the Vietnam war

The war developed a language of its own. It was a mixture of military terminology, GI slang from World War II and Korea, the laconic drawl of rednecks and the black mother tongue of Harlem. Forged in nape and nowhere, matured in monsoon mud, honed in hootches under hash, gruntspeak jinked through English syntax like a Thud taking incoming. But with firebases, FNGs and fraggings, bloods, birds and body bags, doughnut dollies, dopers and double veterans, it spoke eloquently of the war whose most poignant contribution was a new word for death. In the Nam to kill, be killed or just to destroy a little bitta zoo was simply – a waste.

Acid LSD, hallucinogenic drug.
Agent Orange A chemical defoliant.
Air Cav Air cavalry, helicopter-borne infantry assault teams.
Angel A helicopter that hovers near a carrier to pick up pilots who crash.
Arc-Lite Code name for B-52 bombing missions along the Cambodian border.
Arty Artillery.
Bad Good.
Beaten zone Where most bullets will hit when a machine gun is fired into bush.
The Bell Telephone Hour The 'interrogation' or torture of VC suspects using electric shocks generated by a field telephone.
Bends and motherfuckers Squat thrusts.

Big Boys Artillery.
Bird Any aircraft.
Blood A black, from blood brother.
Blooper An M79 grenade launcher, also known as a thumper.
Bode A Cambodian.
Bogart To hang onto a joint too long.
Bolter A plane that misses the arrest wire when landing on an aircraft carrier.
Boonies The boondocks, a remote rural region.
Boot A raw soldier - that is, one straight from boot camp.
Bouncing Betty A trip-wire mine, designed to explode at groin height.
Brown-Water Navy US Navy units operating in the muddy water of the Mekong Delta.
Bush Anywhere out of base where contact might be made with the enemy.

Bloods.

Busting caps Firing a weapon.
Cambodian red Local marijuana.
Cammies Camouflage fatigues.
Capping Shooting.
Charlie The Viet Cong, from military voice designation for VC.
Cherry A virgin; someone young and inexperienced.
Chinook A large transport helicopter.
Chu hoi Vietnamese for 'I surrender'.
Chopper Helicopter.
Cobra The AH-1G helicopter gunship.

Doughnut Dollies.

Concertina A tangle of barbed wire.
Condolence award Compensation paid to the family of a dead ARVN trooper.
Contact Firing on or being fired on by the enemy.
Country team US embassy personnel.
Corpsman Medic.
C-ration, C-rat Canned food carried on operations.
Dawk Neither a hawk nor a dove; someone who disapproved of the war but would not demonstrate against it.
Delta-Delta DD, doughnut dollies or nurses.
Deuce-and-a-half 2+-ton truck, also a 6x6.
Deros Date eligible for return from overseas.

Diddy bopping Walking carelessly.
Dink Derogatory term for Vietnamese.
District Mobile Company The basic VC fighting unit.
Doc Marine nickname for corpsman.
Doughnut Dollies Nurses.
Doo-mommie Anglicizaton of Vietnamese 'Duma' meaning 'Fuck your mother'.
Doper A pot smoker.
Double veteran Someone who had sex with a woman then killed her.

Dove Someone who was against the war.
Downers Depressant drugs, especially barbiturates, taken for pleasure.
Driver An aircraft pilot.
Dust-off Medical evacuation by helicopter.
Em Vietnamese for brother or friend.
Fatigues Green combat uniform.
Finger charge A booby-trapping device, named for it's size.
Firebase A temporary artillery base to support ground operations.
Fire brigade An extremely mobile unit rushed to the scene of an enemy attack.
Firefight An exchange of

smallarms fire.

FNG Fucking new guy.

Fragging The murder of an incompetent officer with a fragmentation grenade.

Free fire zone An area supposedly cleared of civilians where artillery could fire without prior clearance.

Fugazi Mad, screwed up.

Get some Kill the enemy.

Gook Derogatory term for Vietnamese.

Greased Killed.

Greenbacking Employing mercenaries.

Ground pounder A desk jockey, administrator.

Grunt Infantryman; also to shit.

Gunny Marine gunnery sergeant.

Gung-ho Uncritically patriotic, zealous, devoted or belligerent, from the Chinese 'ken ho' meaning awe-inspiring or literally 'more fiery'.

Gunship A combat helicopter armed with various weapons.

Ham and motherfuckers C-ration delicacy of ham and lima beans.

Hard hat A full-time VC soldier as apposed to a reservist or guerrilla; Stateside – a construction worker.

Hash Hashish.

Haul ass To leave quickly.

Hawk Someone who supported the war.

Head Heavily into something, e.g. pothead.

Hit A puff on a marijuana cigarette.

Hog A model B Huey with 48 2.75in rockets and four M60s.

Home Plate The airfield or carrier where an aircraft is based.

Honcho The boss.

Hootch Military accommodation or peasant shack or hut.

Hootchgirl A young Vietnamese maid.

Hot An area under fire.

Huey The UH-1 helicopter.

Hump To carry pack, equipment, armaments etc.

Incoming Incoming fire.

In-country To be in Vietnam.

I&I Intercourse and Intoxication, whimsical transliteration for R&R.

Jack/jank/jink To make evasive manoeuvres in an aircraft.

Jesus nut The mythical nut that holds the rotors onto a helicopter.

Jock, jockey A man, as in desk jock, chopper jock.

Joint A marijuana cigarette.

Jolly green giant A USAF rescue helicopter.

K-Bar Military combat knife.

Kill-zone Area around an explosive device in which 95 per cent fatalities are predicted.

Kit Carson Scout A VC

Fugazi.

defector working for the Allies.

Khmer Rouge Cambodian communists.

Klick Kilometre.

Lao green Local marijuana.

Leatherneck A Marine.

Loach A light observation and reconnaissance chopper.

Lurps Members of long-range reconnaissance patrols.

Lifer A career soldier.

Mamma-san An older Vietnamese woman.

Mike-mike A millimetre.

Mike Forces Montagnards trained by US Special Forces.

Montagnards Hill people.

Mother, motherfucker General purpose expletive.

Mustang An officer who has come up through the ranks.

Nam Vietnam.

Nape Napalm.

Nordo Someone with poor communication skills.

Number One The best.

Number Ten The worst.

Nung A mercenary, usually Chinese anti-communist or paroled prisoner working for a Mike force.

Oil spot A pacified area.

One thou, one thousand Even worse than number ten.

Payback Revenge.

Peacenik An anti-war demonstrator.

Pig The M60 machine gun.

Papa-san An older Vietnamese man.

Pathet Lao Laotian communists.

Pogue Derogatory term for those in rear echelon support.

Popular Forces Local militia forces organized within the village.

Pot Marijuana or hashish.

Puff the Magic Dragon An AC-47 gunship - a spooky.

Purple Haze A type of LSD celebrated in Jimi Hendrix's song of that name.

Rallier A VC defector who has rallied or returned to the flag of the South Vietnamese government.

Rack Bed.

Ranch Hands The special air force unit that flew defoliation missions.

R&R Rest and recreation.

Re-up Re-enlist.

Re-education camps Political prisons.

Regional forces Semiprofessional local troops.

Remf Rear echelon motherfucker, non-combat troops dealing with supply and administration.

Rock and roll Automatic fire.

Saddle Final air attack position.

Sao A repulsive, disreputable, dishonest or stupid person.

Sapper A VC soldier who infiltrated a camp for sabotage.

Short-timer's stick A notch stick a grunt would use to count down his last few days in Nam.

Shotgunning Blowing marijuana smoke down a gun barrel to enhance the effect.

Six-by A large flat-bed or dropside truck, from its wheel layout.

Short Running out of time, not long in the army.

Lifer.

Short-timer Someone with less than 30 days left in Vietnam.

Slick A troop-carrying Huey.

SNAFU Situation normal (all fucked up).

Spad An A-1 Skyraider.

Spider trap A VC foxhole.

Spooky An AC-47 gunship.

Stack trooper An exemplary soldier.

Strac Strictly adhere to regulations.

Stand downs A line unit's return to base for a short rest period.

Stash One's supply of drugs.

Steel pot Helmet.

Tanglefoot Single-strand barbed wire strung at ankle height.

Tango-boat US landing boat modified for use in the Mekong Delta.

Tet Vietnamese new year.

Thud A plane crash, especially being shot down; an F-105 Thunderchief fighter, so called because of their appalling record of losses.

Tiger suit Camouflage fatigues.

The Triangle The Iron Triangle, a VC stronghold near Saigon.

Toke A puff on a joint.

Tunnel rats US troops who flushed the Viet Cong out of their underground hideouts.

Two shop Intelligence section.

Uncle Ho Ho Chi Minh.

VC Viet Cong; by analogy, anything stupid, inept or irresponsible.

Vet A former member of the armed forces.

Victor Charlie Military designation for VC; the Viet Cong.

Viet Minh A resistance movement formed by Ho Chi Minh to fight the French, forerunners of the Viet Cong.

Vietnik A Peace protester.

Waste To Kill.

Wax To beat up, injure severly, kill or beat decisively in a sport contest.

The White Lie Ward The Da Nang hospital ward for hopeless cases.

White Mice South Vietnamese police, for their white helmets and gloves.

Willie Fudd WF-2 flying radar centre.

Willie Pete White Phosphorus or grenades.

Winchester Radio communication meaning 'I am out of ammunition'.

The World Anywhere but Vietnam.

Yard Montagnard.

Zapped Killed.

Zoo The jungle.

Zonked Drugged up.

1966

ARMOUR INTO ACTION

Sandbags on the floor of the M113 protected troopers against landmines, but a direct hit from an RPG rocket was bad news

1966

I n the early 1960s, 'wise men' on the US Army staff at the Pentagon held the view that Vietnam, just like Korea 10 years before, was no place for armoured forces. Half the country was mountainous, they argued; what was not mountain was jungle. It was soaked with monsoons for six months of every year, and rice paddies abounded. The enemy were illiterate field hands in black pyjamas. Besides, look what happened to the French a few years earlier: their armour was roadbound. As is so often the case with large assemblies of 'wise men', the Pentagon was proved wrong.

Below: Grunts pour from within the protective belly of an M113 troop carrier.

For the US and Allied forces in South Vietnam, the ubiquitous M113 armoured personnel carrier (APC) was a friend indeed. Not only was it a mobile arsenal of colossal firepower, its armour could mean the difference between life and death during a close-range firefight. Originally intended as no more than a 'battlefield taxi', responsible for ferrying troops into combat, it was issued to South Vietnamese armoured units in April 1963. The M113 was quick off the mark, and the unmistakable clatter of armoured patrols was soon heard echoing through the Mekong Delta and the Plain of Reeds.

Belching smoke, spitting venom

The secret of the M113's success lay in its simple design – a rectangular box of lightweight, welded aluminium armour set on a tracked suspension system and capable of speeds of more than 40mph. At a modest ten-and-a-half tons, compared with the 47 tons of an M48 Patton main battle tank, the M113 was a lightweight fighting machine that packed a powerful punch.

Belching smoke from its diesel engine, and spitting venom from the 0.5in and 0.3in machine guns mounted on top and to the side, the M113 was dubbed the 'Green Dragon' by its enemies. With all guns blazing, and tracks churning up the earth in its wake, most VC would flee rather than attempt to engage the Green Dragon as it raced over waterlogged paddy fields or scrub. Some stayed to fight, however, and this revealed a flaw in the M113 that had to be remedied quickly. Although the VC were often overwhelmed by the speed and firepower of the carriers, the US and ARVN troops were unnerved by the vulnerability of the machine gunners: exposed from the waist up, they were liable to be raked by enemy fire.

Salvaging for survival

After the loss of 14 gunners at the battle of Ap Bac in January 1963, the crews foraged around for a means of greater protection. At first, gunshields were improvised from the hull of a sunken ship. One crew even used the bumper of a worn out fork-lift truck.

By early 1965, the M113A1 became the standard production model and it accompanied US ground troops to South Vietnam in March. The 'wise men' at the Pentagon had been forced to

1966

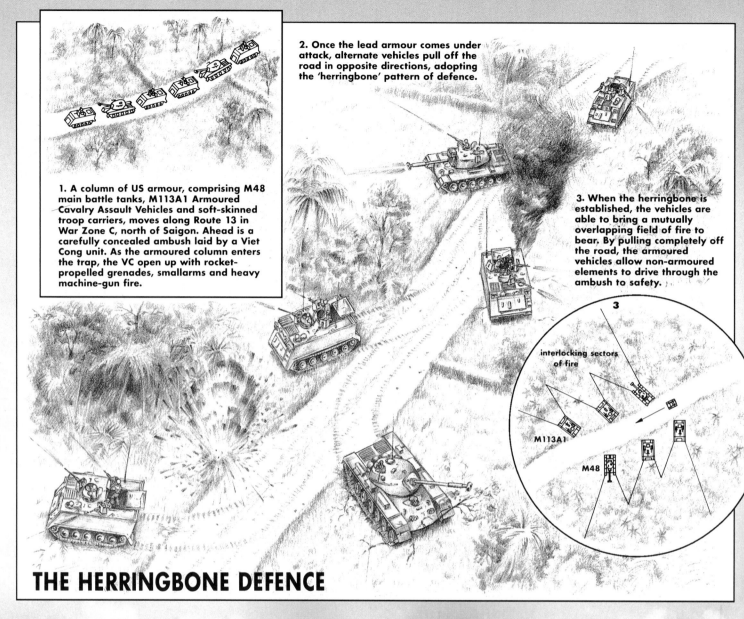

2. Once the lead armour comes under attack, alternate vehicles pull off the road in opposite directions, adopting the 'herringbone' pattern of defence.

1. A column of US armour, comprising M48 main battle tanks, M113A1 Armoured Cavalry Assault Vehicles and soft-skinned troop carriers, moves along Route 13 in War Zone C, north of Saigon. Ahead is a carefully concealed ambush laid by a Viet Cong unit. As the armoured column enters the trap, the VC open up with rocket-propelled grenades, smallarms and heavy machine-gun fire.

3. When the herringbone is established, the vehicles are able to bring a mutually overlapping field of fire to bear. By pulling completely off the road, the armoured vehicles allow non-armoured elements to drive through the ambush to safety.

interlocking sectors of fire

M113A1

M48

THE HERRINGBONE DEFENCE

recognize the potential of the basic M113 'aluminium box' as a potent weapon.

By 1965, however, the VC and NVA were armed with weapons to counter the M113 – a wealth of 57mm and 75mm recoilless rifles, together with RPG-2 rocket-propelled grenades and anti-tank mines, combined to make the M113s much more vulnerable in an ambush than they had been in the early days.

American units such as the 11th Armored Cavalry Regiment were forced to improvise tactics, based on the experience of the ARVN, to beat an enemy now armed with deadly anti-tank weapons. The crews of the 'Blackhorse' regiment

cannibalised redundant armoured vehicles to provide shields for the 0.5in machine gun, and pedestals and shields for the two side-mounted M60s. The vehicle that emerged from these modifications was known as the ACAV, the Armored Cavalry Assault Vehicle.

The series of battles along the Minh Thanh road, in June and July 1966, proved conclusively that armoured cavalry with air and artillery support could hold its own against a numerically larger force. Fought by troops of the 1st Infantry Division – the 'Big Red One' – the engagements opened Route 13 between Loc Ninh and Saigon, and successfully blocked VC attempts to withdraw their forces back into Cambodia. On 9 July, in a battle that raged from midday to sunset, the ACAVs pierced the enemy flanks and decimated elements of the 9th Viet Cong Division in a manoeuvre known as 'clover-leafing'. Over 240 VC were killed.

Every man's worst nightmare

The battles on the Minh Thanh road were not without cost, however. Anti-tank mines with charges of up to 200lb blew some of the lightweight M113s sky high, and recoilless rifle and RPG shaped charges penetrated the thin aluminium armour to create a fragment-filled hell-hole inside the carrier. One in seven direct hits punctured the carrier's skin, causing horrendous casualties to the men inside. Being trapped inside an M113 when an RPG or mine exploded was every man's worst nightmare.

To shield themselves against the ever-present threat of exploding landmines, men packed the floor of their M113A1s with anything that came to hand. Sandbags, unusable flak jackets, and ammunition boxes or C-ration tins filled with mud or sand were requisitioned by each crew to pack the floor of their vehicle. An odd assortment, perhaps, but it was a useful insurance policy against the unexpected.

Flak jackets and steel helmets were worn by all but the foolish, and the troopers usually chose to ride on top of the vehicles rather than inside. Better to be blown off the ACAV than incinerated inside it. You might fly through the air and land with a sickening thump on the ground, but the men saw this as a welcome alternative to being fried by flames or seeing their flesh shredded by steel shards.

Inside, deafened by the noise, sweltering from the heat, and constantly being jolted as the carrier threaded its way across the rough terrain, it was a different story. You had to scramble out of the rear door – often with bullets tearing through the air around you.

But whatever the risks, the fighting spirit of the troops was always reinforced by the intimidating presence of the 'Green Dragons'. Several Medals of Honor, the highest US award for gallantry, were earned by men fighting aboard ACAVs. One of these men was Lieutenant James A. Taylor.

In November 1967, Lieutenant Taylor's Troop

B, 1st Squadron of the 1st Cavalry Regiment, was sweeping through the Que Son Valley west of Sam Ky. The unit was blasting a fortified position when the enemy let loose with a stream of recoilless rifle, machine-gun and mortar fire. One of the ACAVs brewed up within seconds, erupting into a sea of flame. Without hesitating Taylor leapt off his carrier and rushed to the vehicle through an inferno of enemy fire. He pulled out five wounded men from the stricken carrier as more recoilless rifle rounds ploughed into his formation. Chaos reigned supreme.

Leading the 'Dragon' to victory

A second ACAV brewed up. Taylor dashed to the blazing vehicle and once more pulled out the wounded before the fires could cremate them. Taylor was wounded by a mortar round as he returned to his own ACAV, but he continued to direct the fight. After going on the radio net and calling for medevac choppers for the wounded, he began moving his vehicle towards the pickup zone. An enemy machine gun less than 50yds away began spattering Taylor's ACAV.

Bullets ricocheted off the protective shield as Taylor swung his 0.5in gun around and poured fire into the VC position – killing the three-man crew. When yet another ACAV was hit, he again rushed forward and pulled the men from the burning wreckage. Inspired by Taylor's bravery and determination, Troop B continued its assault and overran the enemy position. Only then did Lieutenant Taylor rest.

Once again, the ACAV had proved itself to be a valuable fighting platform from which US troops could take on the VC.

RIDING HIGH ON THE M113 ACAV

Although vulnerable to heavy weapons, the M113 provided US troops with a superb mobile fighting platform.

Today, 27 years after it was introduced into US Army service, the M113 continues to serve worldwide. Over 37,000 M113s have been produced for the US Army alone, with a further 35,000 sold to armed forces across the globe. One of the most widely deployed armoured vehicles ever built, the M113 is certain to remain in service well into the 21st century.

Initial design work on the M113 began in 1956, in response to the US Army's request for an armoured personnel carrier that was air-transportable, cheap to produce, reliable and possessing a basic design that offered full scope for specialised tasks. After rejecting five prototypes of steel construction, the army settled on the M113 and series production began in 1960. Development work continued, however, and the diesel-powered M113A1 came off the production line in 1964.

The M113 can carry 11 men in addition to the driver, who is seated on the front left-hand side of the vehicle. The commander, situated in the centre of the carrier, has a rotating cupola and is seated between two rows of five infantrymen. There is a hydraulically-operated ramp to the rear of the M113, in addition to several emergency hatches in the upper part of the hull.

The M113 hull construction and exit points are completely watertight, enabling the carrier to conduct amphibious operations without the need for any external alterations. In Vietnam, this proved a major asset during search and destroy missions in the rice paddies of the Mekong Delta.

The M113 armoured personnel carrier did have several flaws as a combat vehicle, however. Chief among these was its inability to protect troops from landmines and weapons with a greater calibre than 0.5in. A further drawback was the absence of a ventilation system in the troop compartment, making the interior of the vehicle uncomfortably hot in warm, humid weather.

The modification of the basic M113 into an Armoured Cavalry Assault Vehicle (ACAV) was an attempt to improve the firepower and protection of the vehicle in the absence of conventional turrets. All-round protection was provided for the 0.5in machine gun, and two 7.62mm machine guns and shields were mounted on the troop compartment roof.

Over 150 variants of the M113 have been produced, including mortar and TOW anti-tank guided-weapons carriers, recovery and bridgelaying vehicles, and unarmoured transport vehicles.

Above: An ACAV driver uses an improvised steering mechanism as a precaution against the threat of exploding landmines.

M113A1 ACAV

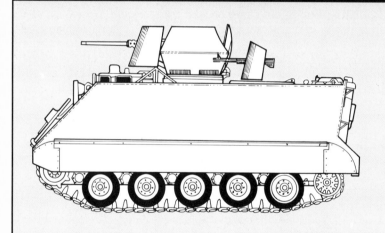

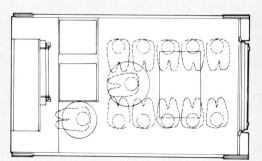

Weight: 1134kg (combat loaded)
Crew: One (driver)
Troops: 11 (including commander)
Powerplant: Six-cylinder water-cooled diesel engine
Range: 483 kilometres
Speed: 67 kilometres per hour (road); 3.6 kilometres per hour (water)
Protection: 26mm aluminium armour
Armament: One 0.5in and two 7.62mm machine guns

SOLDIERS OF THE SOUTH

Trained and armed by the US, the men of the Army of South Vietnam faced a crisis when they took on the Viet Cong

Dressed in cut-down US uniforms, boots or sandals made from rubber tyres and American steel-pots that were too big, they toted US weapons, rode in US choppers and M113s. But to many American servicemen, the ARVN looked little different to any other slope or LLDB – Lousy Little Dink Bastard. Still, in 1966, they were out in the paddy fields together.

The Americans resented the ARVN. If they had been doing their job right, the Americans thought, there would have been no need to call in Uncle Sam.

Back in January '63, an entire ARVN division – some 10,000 men – had been creamed by just three VC companies – around 350 Cong – at Ap Bac, less than 65 klicks from Saigon. The politicians said the ARVN were winning the war, but the US advisors knew different. Despite all the American kit and the air support, the ARVN couldn't read a battle any more than most of them could read a book. Their intelligence reckoned there was only one company of VC at Ap Bac – hardly a match for a full division. The ARVN plan was to land a regiment by chopper to the north, with two regional battalions foot-slogging from the south and an armoured force of M113 coming in from the west. The open farmland to the east was left clear as an artillery killing zone once the VC pulled back.

But things went wrong from the start. As the choppers came in, the VC waited, then let the fourth wave have it. Two choppers went down. Another three tried to rescue the stranded crews. They went down too. This catastrophe caused

1966

Previous page: The ARVN were not well disciplined in interrogation, or anything else. This villager has been caught with a cache of arms. But rather than being questioned in private, by the officer, he is subjected to the menacing presence of the entire platoon. Below: The ARVN soldiers' small stature caused untold problems when handling equipment designed for beefy GIs.

panic on the ground which spread quickly to other units, especially the armoured boys, churning through the paddies in their APCs. Their machine gunners, standing exposed through the top hatches, were massacred by VC fire. And, as their CO froze, the action degenerated into a slogging match. The ARVN commander decided to debus his men. This was a mistake. As they jumped down into waist-deep mud, they were cut down in droves. The ARVN officers quarrelled openly about what to do next, leaving Charlie to melt away, less three bodies. The ARVN lost 61 dead and 100 wounded. US advisor Lieutenant-Colonel John Paul Vann summed it up – 'a miserable fucking performance, just like it always is' – but his report was suppressed in the interests of allied co-operation. Officially, Ap Bac was termed an ARVN victory – after all, the VC had abandoned their position.

The landing force was pinned down

When the US ground troops arrived, the situation did not improve. At Dong Xoai in June '65, the VC attacked a base manned by Montagnard and US forces. The Montagnards fought well. They pulled back to a small HQ compound outside of town and called in support. But when the ARVN arrived by chopper, it was like a re-run of Ap Bac. The landing force was pinned down and it was not until another 40 choppers had been brought in, landing ARVN Rangers in the HQ compound, that the VC

pulled back. Even then, the ARVN failed to pursue the Cong properly, walking straight into an ambush that led to panic and the loss of Dong Xoai all over again. Three US advisors with the Rangers were left standing alone in front of the main VC attack wave. They only got out by the skin of their teeth and the skill of a chopper rescue crew.

Until the Americans began fighting the guerrillas, it was hard for them to see how the ARVN got into such a mess. They always outnumbered the enemy, even on the highest estimates of VC and NVA strength put out by the intelligence guys. In 1965, the South's armed forces – ARVN, Marines, Air Force, Navy, Regional and Provincial Forces, Police and Civilian Irregular Defense Groups – totalled the best part of three-quarters of a million men, over 30 per cent of the male population between 16 and 45. These were ranged against about 258,000 VC and NVA. In addition, for every ARVN killed, Saigon claimed four of the enemy were going down. By any normal military equation, the communists should have been losing and losing hard.

But for 20 years they'd been at war. They'd fought the French. They'd fought the Japanese. They'd fought the Viet Cong. And now they were fighting the NVA, the hard-core troops infiltrated from the North. Though they were drafted for a three-year hitch, they were essentially in for the duration with 60 or 90 days at a stretch in the field.

For Joe ARVN there was no overseas to return home to. He'd be fighting long after his American counterpart had gone home. There were no furloughs for him, no R&R in Bangkok.

By and large, the men in the ARVN were peasant farmers and may even have had a brother in the VC or even the NVA. Some may have been anti-communists, but even they probably weren't pro-government, which they saw using the ARVN simply as a political pawn. And they were disillusioned. 'I have to ask my men to go out and die,' one ARVN officer said. 'What am I supposed to ask them to die for?'

There was certainly enough to get discouraged about. Conditions of service were poor. Their diet consisted of rice, dried fish and vegetable soup. For amusement, there was once in a while some rice brandy, playing the lottery, the occasional movie and, before the Americans came, sometimes a girl. An ARVN trooper was lucky to clear 1600 piasters – about £8 – a month, more if he was married. That was little enough at the best of times, but when the Americans and their greenbacks arrived, prices soared. Soon his wife would be a hootchgirl, his sister a bar-girl, his children beggars and they'd all be dismissed as gooks – the name the Americans also gave their common enemy.

Squatting in the mud

If he was married, his family had to follow him round from base to base, squatting in the mud or living in makeshift huts constructed of discarded

Below: The ARVN did have their successes. But even though the enemy prisoners they took could have been their own brothers, this did not guarantee their good treatment.

Left: Combat was made even more difficult for ARVN troopers, like this Ranger, as their families followed them from camp to camp and even into the combat zone.

Left: This ARVN soldier is carrying an American-made Springfield M1 carbine of WWII vintage. Opposite: Joe ARVN would often spent 60 to 90 days in the field at a stretch.

Left: The ARVN drag a frightened man from his hiding place. He could be an ordinary civilian – or he could be Viet Cong. There is no way of telling at this stage.

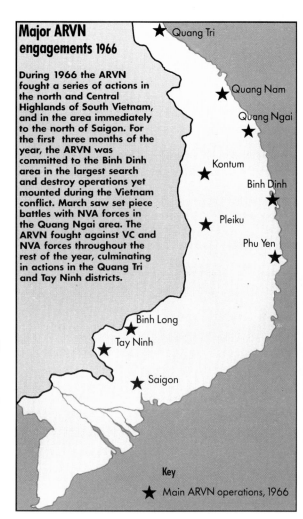

Major ARVN engagements 1966

During 1966 the ARVN fought a series of actions in the north and Central Highlands of South Vietnam, and in the area immediately to the north of Saigon. For the first three months of the year, the ARVN was committed to the Binh Dinh area in the largest search and destroy operations yet mounted during the Vietnam conflict. March saw set piece battles with NVA forces in the Quang Ngai area. The ARVN fought against VC and NVA forces throughout the rest of the year, culminating in actions in the Quang Tri and Tay Ninh districts.

★ Quang Tri
★ Quang Nam
★ Quang Ngai
★ Kontum
★ Binh Dinh
★ Pleiku
★ Phu Yen
★ Binh Long
★ Tay Ninh
★ Saigon

Key

★ Main ARVN operations, 1966

C-ration crates. Desertion rates were appallingly high – during 1966 over 115,000 ARVN deserted – more than one in five.

Some elite units, like the Airborne and Rangers, were different. They were better paid, better housed and had more of a macho mentality. They decorated their uniforms with flashy bandannas and crossed bandoliers. Some were criminals who had volunteered rather than go to jail, so at least they had a strong personal reason for fighting. But as these elite corps only made up about 5 per cent of the total strength of the South's forces, this was not a great deal of use.

Officers sold drugs and prostitutes

But the real problems went much deeper. As many US advisors pointed out, what was missing was strong leadership at every level. In some outfits, like the Airborne, Rangers and the 1st ARVN Infantry Division, US training and constant combat gradually forged a strong officer and NCO cadre, but elsewhere the situation was very different. Corruption was rife and promotions didn't depend on performance in battle, only on who you knew and who you could bribe. Mid-ranking officers sold drugs and prostitutes to the GIs and ripped off the US over lucrative construction contracts.

At combat level, local warlords sold the rice that

ARVN OPERATIONS, 1965-66

In 1966, the ARVN was out on patrol with the Americans again. Only the year before it had been close to collapse. Lacking a coherent strategy and weakened by corruption, poor leadership and desertion, it had suffered defeat after defeat, typified by the disaster at Binh Gia near Saigon in January, when the 33d Rangers and 4th Marines were virtually destroyed in a VC ambush.

US main-force units were committed to Vietnam to relieve the pressure on the ARVN, allowing it to recover its strength behind a 'shield' of friendly forces. Unfortunately, this did not work. Although some of the elite ARVN units – the Airborne, Rangers and Marines – did recover quickly, participating in search and destroy operations such as Gibraltar (near An Ninh) in September, and Harvest Moon (near Tam Ky) in November 1965, the bulk of the army merely resumed static duties throughout the country. They were supposed to be carrying out a campaign of 'pacification', persuading the people that the Saigon government was worth supporting. But their continued weakness in the face of enemy pressure often had the opposite effect.

But the Americans needed the ARVN to resume a more active role. In 1966, the policy of combined operations was extended to include less specialized ARVN units which, it was hoped, would gain experience and expertise under close US supervision. The process began in June, when the 5th ARVN and 1st US Infantry Divisions combined in Operation Lam Son II. Five months later, the 5th ARVN Ranger Group joined the 199th US Infantry Brigade in Operation Fairfax, a campaign of village clearance around Saigon which was to last until the end of 1967. In neither case was the ARVN contribution decisive. The South Vietnamese still had a long way to go before they could take on the enemy on their own.

should have gone to frontline soldiers, and the politically appointed commanders were afraid of losing too many local men in action. Often, they'd send in the Rangers – men press-ganged off city streets – to take the losses, and then steal the glory afterwards.

But this was nothing compared to the level of corruption at the top, where appointments and promotions were bought and sold, often through the wives and mistresses of top-ranking ARVN commanders. The generals were political appointees who would pay the occasional lightning visit to their men, but generally stayed as far away from the fighting as possible.

'Most of the generals had packed their bags and sent their families away and are ready to leave themselves at any time,' lamented one draftee. As a result, morale was terrible.

The soldiers knew if they were killed, their families would not get a pension and their kids would go hungry. So the troops would not risk their lives. If the communists attacked, they'd have to fight. But they didn't go chasing them into the bush. Few ARVN units would move at night for fear of ambush. They would often recess at weekends while officers whipped off to Saigon to visit their families or make a round of the bar-hostesses. Patrols sometimes played transistor radios on search and destroy missions to warn the enemy away. Sometimes they wouldn't even go to the help of other units under fire. In May 1966, a lone squad of VC, a dozen men, attacked the headquarters of the 25th division – dubbed even by General Vien as 'the worst division in the army – and perhaps in any army'. They killed 31 ARVN soldiers and three US advisors. The battalion's

three rifle companies were dug in a mere 300yds away – and stayed there listening to the shooting while their comrades died.

The defeatist mentality had been made worse when the US main-force units arrived, full of gung-ho grunts who reckoned they could zap the Cong in a month. The ARVN were shifted to 'pacification' in the villages.

The people hated them

'Soldiers stole property and grabbed women,' says one lieutenant. 'They horrified the people, who hated them.' And being tied down in static jobs that did nothing to boost morale, leaving them next to useless when, in 1966, they were sent out into the boonies with US units. There, they made contact with the enemy half as often as their US counterparts. Their claimed kill rate was pathetic by comparison and their losses per battalion less than a third.

The relationship between the American troops and the ARVN was ambivalent. Though some Americans admired the ARVN troops for their individual courage and their ability to hump heavy equipment designed for much larger men over long distances in difficult terrain, most referred to them with racist contempt – they were inscrutable, slanty-eye gooks, almost indistinguishable from the enemy. And while the ARVN were grateful to the Americans for doing the fighting for them and for their seemingly endless supplies of cigarettes, they envied their equipment and their affluence. They hated the effect they were having on their country and, after all, in the eyes of the Vietnamese they were just another bunch of foreigner invaders.

CHAPTER 21

1966

With their gatling guns firing at an incredible rate of 6000 rounds per minute, it was no wonder that fixed-wing gunships terrified the enemy

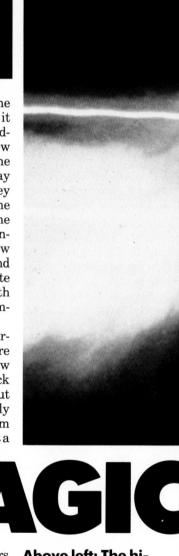

All was quiet at the Special Forces camp at Duc Lap as the duty advisors made their rounds of the camp defences. In their perimeter bunkers, the tribesmen of the Civilian Irregular Defense Group, struggling to keep awake, rubbed their eyes and stared again into the darkness. Were some of the shadows outside the compound moving?

At 1.05 am, the first mortar rounds exploded in the camp as yelling North Vietnamese sappers ran towards key positions. The whoosh of rockets reached the ears of the Green Berets as they tumbled out of their beds, grabbed their weapons and dashed outside. As the crack 95C NVA Regiment launched its first ground assault, the radio operator put out a frantic call for immediate assistance.

The II Corps Direct Air Support Centre passed the request to the AC-47 gunship on airborne alert. Within seconds, Major Daniel J. Rehm, a pilot of 'Spooky', the 4th Air Commando Squadron, pushed the throttle to the firewall as the navigator scanned his maps.

The kicker jerked the lanyard as he tossed the flare out of the open doorway and watched as it swung under its parachute, casting 200,000-candlepower illumination over the countryside below and giving a clear picture of enemy positions. The attackers looked up as the night was turned to day and began to search frantically for cover: they knew what was coming. The pilot rolled the aircraft into a left bank, squinted through the gunsight, and pressed the firing button. The interior of the rear cabin lit up with an orange glow as two of the three miniguns belched out flame and smoke. With each gun spitting out bullets at a rate of up to 6000 rounds per minute and every fourth round a tracer, the sight and sound was impressive.

The pilot of Spooky 41 recalls: 'When we arrived, the buildings in the compound were all afire and the men were grouped in a blockhouse below the burning operations centre. I set up a quick orbit of the area and began firing on targets about 200 to 300m from the camp. Almost immediately we began receiving intense anti-aircraft fire from four different points. I began with a long burst at a

PUFF THE MAGIC

Forty-five minutes after the attack began, Rehm checked in with the compound radio operator: 'Spooky 41 overhead with flares and miniguns.' They were just in time – the enemy had breached the wire and several firefights had broken out within the compound.

Three thousand feet above the defenders the pilot settled his left shoulder into the Mark 20 Mod 4 gunsight, flipped the safety off the firing button on his control column and directed the navigator to pass the order to the back of the plane, 'Flare away'.

target from my miniguns, but when the tracers started to fly close to us, I moved to another altitude and began to "peck" with short bursts at the enemy locations.'

As Major Rehms continued his attack, the crew in the back clamped their ear protectors firmly to their heads and attended to their duties; the navigator relayed orders from the pilot, the loadmaster stood by the doorway with another flare and the two gunners prepared to reload the two guns when the unused third gun took over.

Although the timely appearance of Spooky

Above left: The hi-tech interior of the AC-130 Spectre gunship, equipped with a formidable weaponry and a variety of electronic sensors.

DRAGON

Above: Angling its port wing towards the ground, an AC-47 encircles enemy targets with its miniguns in dramatic action. Right: The port side of the AC-47 reveals its three gatling-style miniguns.

prevented the camp from being overrun, it took several days of attacks by gunships, tactical fighters, B-52s and armed helicopters, before the 4000-strong enemy force broke off and withdrew. At times, up to four AC-47s were on station and in 228 flying hours they expended 761,044 rounds. As the men at Duc Lap put it, Spooky truly became their Guardian Angel.

This was a typical mission for one of the most deadly – and improbable – weapons to be used in the Vietnam war. A reconditioned Air Force cargo plane, the AC-47 had been around for 20 years

1966

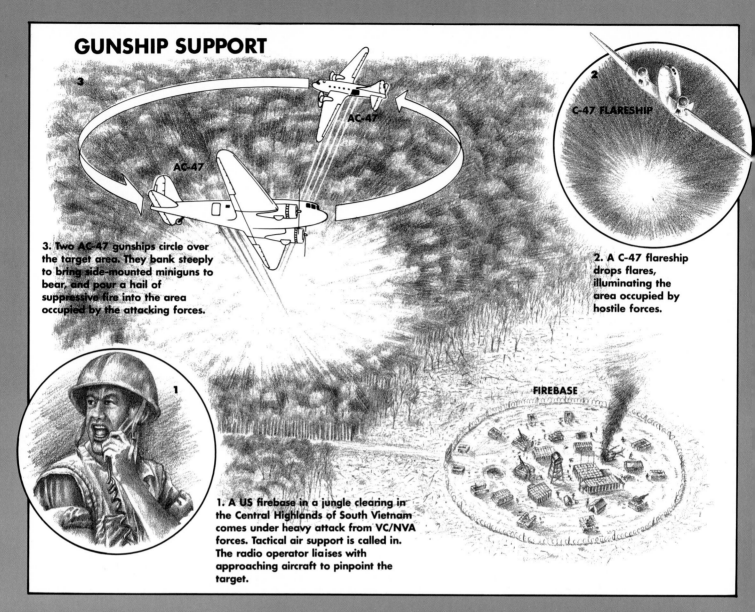

GUNSHIP SUPPORT

AC-47

AC-47

3. Two AC-47 gunships circle over the target area. They bank steeply to bring side-mounted miniguns to bear, and pour a hail of suppressive fire into the area occupied by the attacking forces.

C-47 FLARESHIP

2. A C-47 flareship drops flares, illuminating the area occupied by hostile forces.

FIREBASE

1. A US firebase in a jungle clearing in the Central Highlands of South Vietnam comes under heavy attack from VC/NVA forces. Tactical air support is called in. The radio operator liaises with approaching aircraft to pinpoint the target.

before it was decided to mount gatling-style machine guns down one side, allowing the aircraft to spit bullets into the night sky at an incredible rate. They were used largely in support of Special Forces camps – and to devastating effect. In the first year of their operation, AC-47s were reportedly responsible for the deaths of over 6500 enemy soldiers.

It had been known that an aircraft flying in a

Below: An AC-47 is loaded up on the airstrip to carry 24,000 rounds of ammunition and 45 200,000-candlepower flares.

circle around a fixed point in the ground could keep it in sight all the time. However, it took until 1964 before anyone proved that a bird with side-firing guns could continuously blast a target on the ground and keep it under fire as it circled the target in a left bank.

Testing with the new 1500-round 7.62mm General Electric SUU-11A/A minigun pod, fitted to a C-131 aircraft, produced a score of 25 hits on a

10ft rubber raft with just a one-second burst. Later tests showed that a burst could cover an area the size of a football pitch and put a round in every square foot in just three seconds. Such a weapon was to prove a life-saver to the defenders of hamlets and outposts in the countryside of Vietnam.

Originally designated FC-47 (Fighter Cargo), but changed to AC-47 (Attack Cargo) after an outcry of protest by fighter jocks, a C-47 from the 1st Air Commando Squadron was modified to carry three of the six-barreled minigun pods on the port side, 24,000 rounds of ammunition and 45 parachute flares with a burning time of three minutes each. The crew consisted of a pilot/aircraft commander, co-pilot, navigator, three gunners to maintain the guns and drop the flares and a Vietnamese observer, responsible for communications with ARVN troops.

The first AC-47 squadron, the 4th Air Commando Squadron, was given the name 'Puff the Magic Dragon', after the song by the folk trio Peter, Paul and Mary (to the singers' great annoyance), by those who had witnessed its nocturnal display of firepower. The roar of the guns and the lightning shower of tracer bullets reaching out towards the ground struck fear into the Viet Cong. Being a superstitious people, the Vietnamese took the nickname literally. Captured VC documents later told of orders not to attack the Dragon, as weapons were useless and it would only infuriate the monster.

Controlling the Dragon
The first year was a period of learning for the Spooky crews. They discovered that short bursts of three seconds were best. Very short bursts seemed to cause the guns to jam, while long bursts emptied the 1500-round magazines too fast and burned out the barrels. With practice, the pilot who aimed the guns could compensate for the many variables that went under the name of Kentucky Windage. These included the Slant Range – the distance between the gun muzzle and target, and the Airspeed – how each knot of wind would displace the bullets' muzzle velocity of 853 metres per second.

Above: With each gunship firing over 450 tracer bullets a second, a full 'Puff the Magic Dragon' assault was a stunning sight. Although the minigun firepower made the AC-47 a devastating weapon for night interdiction, a new proposal called 'Surprise Package' was introduced later in the war to improve the gunship's ability to devastate enemy troop concentrations and supply lines. This involved replacing the standard armament with two M61 cannon and two 40mm Bofors anti-aircraft guns, both incorporating improved infra-red ranging equipment.

After a disastrous attempt to employ Spooky over the Ho Chi Minh Trail in Laos, which resulted in three AC-47s being wasted, the decision was made to confine the gunship to outpost and troops-in-contact support inside Vietnam. They were out of their depth over the heavily defended trail, where the ground was thick with 37 and 57mm anti-aircraft weapons and radar-guided surface-to-air missiles. The experiment did prove, however, that 7.62mm bullets were no good for blowing out trucks, despite the effect they may have on the driver. Indeed the terrifying sight of tracers raining from the heavens did little more than freak out the VC on the ground. When fired from above 2500 ft, the tracers burnt out before reaching the ground. Aside from identifying the requirement for heavier weapons, there was also a need to equip the gunships with night-observation devices. Plans were thus made for more powerful gunships in the shape of the AC-119 Shadow and Stinger, and the AC-130 Spectre. A second AC-47 squadron arrived in 1967 and eventually all areas of South Vietnam were covered by Spooky detachments.

The Bullshit Bombers
Spooky often also worked with the PSYWAR C-47s of the 5th Air Commando Squadron. The psychological warfare aircraft flew under the call sign Gabby, although grunts called them the Bullshit Bombers. These birds flew at an orbit of around 3500 feet, and mounted a giant speaker through which an ARVN official tried to persuade the VC to come over to the side of the government. At the same time, Gabby would warn the VC not to fire at the speaker aircraft – or else. Unknown to Charlie, a Spooky gunship would be orbiting below and behind Gabby and when the enemy began to fire, the roar of the Spooky miniguns would answer them. As silence descended again, Gabby would retort 'See, I told you so!'

By the time of their replacement by the new generation of gunships in 1969, AC-47s had successfully defended over 6,000 hamlets and outposts. If they had not been able to win this war on their own, they had proved themselves the best buddy a GI facing a VC attack could ever have.

THE MINIGUN POD INSTALLATION

Used in tandem with a minigun pod, the six barrels of a GAU-2A had a combined firepower of 100 rounds per second.

In 1949, the General Electric company produced a prototype 15.24mm calibre six-barrelled gun based on an idea developed by Richard Gatling, the originator of the famous Gatling gun. This extraordinary new weapon possessed a maximum rate of fire of 6000 rounds per minute. The calibre was increased to accommodate high-explosive shells, and the M61 Vulcan 20mm cannon entered service on F-104 Starfighter aircraft in 1965.

The rotary gatling-gun principle was also extended further down the calibre scale, resulting in the M134 7.62mm minigun. In tandem with the M61 cannon, the minigun was mounted on a variety of gunships during the Vietnam war, including the AC-47 'Puff the Magic Dragon' or 'Spooky', the AC-130 'Spectre' and the AC-119 'Shadow'.

In addition to its use as a fixed, externally-powered weapon on the gunships, a self-powered variant of the M134 minigun – designated the GAU-2A – was used as the basis for the SUU-11BA pod installation. Housed inside this pod, the GAU-2 was an extremely versatile weapon system compatible for use on a variety of mountings, ranging from helicopter turrets to fixed-wing gunships.

When connected to the pilot's sighting and delivery systems (comprising target-acquisition, night-observation, infra-red and computer equipment), the concentrated firepower of the side-mounted GAU-2s was devastating. During a sweep over suspected enemy territory or a supply convoy, a battery of minigun pod installations was capable of putting one round into every square foot of an area the size of a football pitch. Fifteen seconds of sustained firepower at the high firing rate of 6000 rounds per minute was enough to ensure that nothing was left standing in the target area.

The gun pod itself utilised a MAU-57 linkless ammunition feed system, with an average stoppage rate of once every 35,000 rounds fired. A battery of three SUU-11BA pod installations would be mounted on the port side of each gunship, with a total ammunition capacity of 4500 rounds – both tracer and ball.

Extra ammunition for the minigun pod installations was stored in the forward cargo hold of the gunship, and the pod could be reloaded without the need for special ground-support equipment. Belted in standard M13 links, the rounds were loaded into the pod with the aid of an MAU-69 delinker, the latter being stowed within the pod structure itself.

The minigun's six barrels were driven by an electric motor. This derived its power from a small battery located within the pod, and required only a small charge from the aircraft. During the later stages of the war, the GAU-2 was converted for use with the new MXU-470 minigun module.

Above: Loading ammunition into an M134 minigun. Below: A battery of SUU-11BA pod installations.

GAU-2A MINIGUN

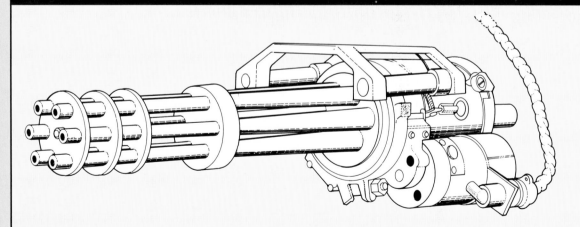

Weight: 20.64kg (minigun); 147kg (minigun and pod)
Length: 2.13 metres
Operation: Electric
Calibre: 7.62mm

Rate of fire: 6000 rounds per minute (high) 2000 rpm (low)
Muzzle velocity: 853 metres per second
Ammunition storage: 1500 rounds

越南必胜！美国必败！

Above: This propaganda poster reads: 'Better death than slavery.' Many VC got their wish. Though the style of the poster is socialist realism, the lectures at political meetings were not. As few recruits were communist, Marxism was played down and Vietnam's historic struggles against foreigners were stressed.

Although they faced certain death if wounded or captured by the enemy, the Viet Cong went into battle ready to die

WHO ARE THE VIET CONG?

What astounded the Americans most about their Viet Cong enemy was his simple endurance how could he absorb such punishment and undergo such hardship without cracking? For the individual Viet Cong guerrilla was the rock on which the American enterprise in Vietnam foundered.

He was usually a field hand. There were city dwellers in the Viet Cong, but they were only a small minority. The main force units, the true guerrilla army, were overwhelmingly recruited in the villages, from men in their teens. The villagers were almost instinctively hostile to the government of landlords, policemen and tax-gatherers, and to their American backers, who they regarded as foreign invaders. Many had personal grievances – a friend arrested by the police or their crops destroyed by defoliants. Others remembered the war against the French and saw this present round of struggle as a continuation of that conflict. In villages totally supportive of the Viet Cong, it was seen as the young men's duty to volunteer when the recruiters came around, and they were given a rousing ceremonial send-off as they marched away. Elsewhere, only the more adventurous volunteered and many were conscripted by visiting Viet Cong units, virtually at gunpoint. Yet, as with conscripts in other armies, they did not necessarily fight any the worse. The separation from home, family and friends was never easy, even for the volunteer, but he soon found a substitute for home in the bond with his comrades-in-arms. Every new recruit joined a three-man cell which included at least one veteran. These three would be close comrades for as long as they survived, sticking together through thick and thin and forming the strongest of ties. In its turn, the three-man cell was attached to a three-cell squad, and three

Above: Recruited in their teens, most Viet Cong would not get home to see their families on their occasional leaves as the war progressed and the journey home became more dangerous. Above left: VC hero Nguyen Van Danh lost the fingers of his right hand in action. He fought from the Loc Giang Village in Duc Hoa. Here, he is laying a mine.

squads formed a platoon. Within this tight-knit group a recruit was unlikely to go off the rails. The organization bred self-discipline and mutual support, a defence against demoralization and homesickness.

Robert McNamara once described the Vietnamese peasant farmer as 'no stranger to deprivation and death'. Life had always been hard for him, and frugal habits were essential for survival. He brought to the war no great hope of comfort and ease, but a tradition of day-long back-breaking work on a handful of rice and few pleasures. An acceptance of possible death was as much a part of his equipment as his rifle or helmet. But there was also a peasant resourcefulness that was put to good use in everything from building home-made weapons to foraging for food.

All the men were short by Western standards – around 5ft 3in – and most weighed about nine stone. Uniforms were the famous black pyjamas and most men carried a spare pair in their rucksacks. On his feet they wore 'Ho Chi Minh' sandals, made out of old tyres.

Like life at home

Apart from these basics, all a guerrilla owned would be a few pairs of socks and underpants, some light nylon for use as a tent or raincoat, a hammock, a mosquito net, an improvised oil lamp, a water flask, a digging tool, and a long canvas tube for carrying rice – known as an 'elephant's intestine'. With weaponry and ammunition, this was quite enough to carry, especially as the only vehicles available were bicycles. Later in the war,

some of the Honda motor bikes that were flooding South Vietnam's cities found their way out into the jungle. The VC fighter was paid about 60 piasters a month (about $2), enough to make the odd purchase of cigarettes, soap or a toothbrush through the unit's supply officer who visited Cambodian market towns about once a month.

Few were communists

Like soldiers everywhere, the Viet Cong did their best to turn a base camp into some version of life at home. Just as the American soldier watched TV and drank iced beer, given half a chance his Vietnamese enemy would plant vegetables, keep a few pigs or chickens and play volleyball or table tennis in any time left over from the endless training and preparation for combat. As well as learning practical combat skills and tactics, he spent a lot of time attending lectures by the unit's political officer. Very few of the Viet Cong peasant recruits were communists or had any knowledge of Marxism. No attempt was made to remedy this. Lectures centred on the history of Vietnam's popular struggles against foreign invaders. It was a simple approach that struck the right chord with the men. The political officer also organized public sessions of criticism and self-criticism when flagging morale or poor military performance seemed to require it. These sessions generally provided a successful and humane way of pulling the unit together by public shaming, rather than the harsh physical punishment practised by many armies.

The periods when the VC lived normally at base were brief and rare once the Americans entered

Right: Medical care was primitive. Of all the horrors of the war, what the Viet Cong dreaded most of all was a serious wound. That promised only a long, lingering, painful death.

VC AND NVA OPERATIONS IN 1966

It was in 1966 that US forces began consciously to search out the VC and NVA. Operations such as El Paso II in June and Attleboro in September were meant to carry the war into the communist forces' stronghold – War Zone C. But US post-operational reports reveal that no less than 88 per cent of all actual contacts that year were initiated by the communist forces and not by the Americans, 46 per cent of contacts beginning with the Americans being attacked. Operation Double Eagle, for example, failed to locate any NVA or VC main force units in Binh Dinh province in January. By contrast, Company C of 2d Battalion, 16th Infantry, was decimated by an unexpected ambush by the VC D8000 Battalion on 11 April during Operation Abilene. The 1st Air Cavalry's LZ Bird was only saved from being overrun by the NVA 22d Regiment during the Thayer series of operations in December by discharging two Beehive rounds – each of 8500 steel flechettes – at point-blank range into the massed NVA ranks.

While much of this activity represented reaction to US moves, NVA and VC pressure was maintained at a high level by repetitive surges in certain areas. Special Forces camps on the frontiers came under sustained attack, and the NVA overran the A Shau valley in March. The NVA was also building up its strength in the northern provinces, the arrival of the 324B Division in Quang Tri province in July heralding the beginning of direct infiltration across the DMZ as well as from Laos and Cambodia. While establishing bases from which to attack the populated areas, this also served to draw the Marines out of such areas and to frustrate any American concentration upon pacification there.

Even though US operations against them were being stepped up, the Viet Cong still held the initiative and were fighting the war on their own terms.

the war in force. Then the guerrillas were mostly either out on operations, or hiding 'like hunted animals', as one Viet Cong put it. At best they were operating among a friendly population, aided by local part-time guerrillas, fed, guided everywhere, given good intelligence and the morale boost of evident popular support in the villages. But as the war hotted up, more and more of the villages were deserted or unfriendly because of fear of reprisals, forcing the Viet Cong to spend increasing amounts of time in the remote jungles and swamps.

Snakes, mosquitoes and malaria

The jungle was as strange and threatening to the average Vietnamese as it was to the grunt from Chicago. Peasants don't live in jungles. Poisonous snakes took a dreadful toll of the sandal-shod guerrillas. Solid army boots would have saved many of them. If he was lucky, a guerrilla would have two anti-venom tablets on him when he was bitten, one to swallow, the other to chew up and plaster over the punctured skin. This was reckoned to cope with even the most venomous reptiles. But against the mosquitoes, the guerrillas had no defence. Weakened by the harsh conditions of their lives and short of medicines, they were hopelessly vulnerable to malaria. More VC died of the disease than of any other single cause, and those who survived were permanently weakened. Few escaped totally unscathed.

Nobody escaped the scourge of malnutrition. Every day, if possible, at nine in the morning and at four in the afternoon, a soldier ate a ball of cold, glutinous rice spiced up with a few small chilli peppers. For the rest he might have a little dried fish or meat and perhaps some salt. It was never enough. There were meals when a single chicken was divided up amongst 30 men. Food was an obsession that never let up. When it was possible they farmed. B-52 bomb craters, filled by the rains, became duck ponds and fish farms, and hunting brought the exotic additions of elephant – which was tough and tasteless, dog, monkey, rat and even tiger to the diet. Some ate moths, attracted by the flame of a lamp. As usual, the Americans helped out, carelessly abandoning half-eaten rations to be discovered by the scavenging guerrillas. But these were sometimes booby-trapped and usually the men went hungry.

B-52s – terror from the skies

Another ever-present companion was fear. An American air strike could come at any moment of the day, unannounced and with ferocious violence. If a unit on the move stopped for as much as half a day, the men dug trenches. In the main base areas, bunkers expanded into the famous tunnel systems that extended underground for miles. When things got really bad, aerial and artillery bombardment came in every day for weeks. Nothing could ever cure a man of the abject terror this inspired. During B-52 strikes even some of the most battle-hardened veterans lost control of their natural functions and emerged afterwards with soiled trousers, trembling uncontrollably. So many awful deaths lay in wait: to be blown apart into an unidentifiable piece of meat, buried alive

HO CHI MINH

as an explosion flattened a bunker, or gassed like vermin in a discovered tunnel. But the worst was the fear of a serious wound. These were almost always untreatable with the poor medical facilities available to the guerrillas and promised only a long and lingering death. The Vietnamese also feared lack of a proper burial, which was of the highest importance to the ancestor-worshipping villagers. Some wore a leather wristband so that, if they were killed in action, a hook could be inserted under the band by a comrade to drag their body away from the scene.

Homesick, frightened, hungry

The price of survival was constant vigilance. Where a fire was lit, elaborate horizontal chimneys carried the smoke away into the earth. Always, the guerrillas had to be ready to move out at a moment's notice, if necessary eating on the march and snatching brief spells of sleep in their hammocks slung on the branches of a tree in the forest. This constant state of readiness and need for concealment led to continual stress, and only a withdrawal to the safe side of the Cambodian border offered temporary relief. Occasional leave to visit family and loved ones was granted, but it became increasingly dangerous, and eventually impossible to carry out the journeys involved.

Yet homesick, frightened and hungry, the Viet Cong guerrilla fought on. There were desertions, of course, especially of the more unwilling conscripts, and of men whose comrades had been killed. But the vast majority were willing to fight to the death. Well led by committed officers, the Viet Cong did what peasants and infantrymen have always done best: they endured.

Above: When the Viet Cong ran short of male recruits, they enlisted women. Here a small group are taught how to fire a rifle in a quiet clearing in the jungle of South Vietnam. The rifle is American. Opposite: Not all the VC were peasant farmers who tilled the land by day and went out with a rifle at night. Here a well equipped main-force unit pose in triumph on the belly of an upturned American APC.

Standing up in the Versailles Peace Conference of 1919, a frail-looking 29-year-old Vietnamese read out a fiery petition for his country's independence from French colonial rule. It was a wildly audacious move that caused the French some embarrassment and the petition was quickly dismissed. But for the petitioner, Nguyen Ai Quoc, it was only the beginning of a long struggle. Later he was to be known to the rest of the world as Ho Chi Minh ('He Who Enlightens').

Ho had come to Europe in 1917 as a ship's cook. Like many would-be nationalist leaders from colonial nations, he was desperate for an education he could never get at home. He became a staunch communist, seeing in Marxism a philosophy that offered hope against colonialism. He joined the French Communist Party.

In the 1920s and 1930s Ho travelled and studied. He visited New York and London, but spent most of his time in the Soviet Union. He lived the life of any political exile – meetings, endless debates, grandiose plans, fear of double agents. Still in exile, he founded the Indochinese Communist Party in 1930.

He returned to Vietnam in 1941, but then fled to southern China when the Japanese invaded. It was at this time that he adopted the name which he made famous. He led guerrillas against the Japanese and occupied Hanoi when they surrendered in 1945, fought a guerrilla war against the French until he defeated them in 1954, directed a new guerrilla war in the South from 1959 and finally took on the US military machine.

Ho was single-minded and ruthless. He negiotated with both the French and the Americans while fighting them, and was prepared to sacrifice thousands of lives and endure personal hardship to achieve a united, communist Vietnam. He died in 1969, but in 1975, the victory was his. When communist tanks rolled into Saigon, it was renamed Ho Chi Minh City.

Ho was not a conventional military leader – he left details on strategy to others, such as Vo Nguyen Giap. Nor was he an autocratic dictator: he was just one of a number of individuals who made up the politburo that ran North Vietnam's affairs. But he was a dominating figure, for he embodied a fierce nationalism that struck a chord in the heart of most Vietnamese.

FIGHTING FOR

THE DMZ

Pinned down in foxholes that turned into pits of mud, the Marines braved point-blank machine-gun fire at Mutter's Ridge – during one of the fiercest firefights of the war

1966

Mountains like Korea, jungles like Guadalcanal,' grumbled one veteran. 'Only thing missing is snow.' September '66, and the men of the 3d Battalion, 4th Marine Regiment, peered out from Hill 363, across the dense jungle canopy of the Cam Lo river valley, towards their next objective. Eight hundred yards away stood the imposing granite peak known as Hill 400. Ten days out from Dong Ha, two full days without re-supply, the Marines had been scouring the Nui Cay Tre ridgeline for elements of the NVA's 324B Division for the past week. This was tough country, and each man had left base carrying only his own weapon, two canteens of water, a poncho and two socks stuffed with rations. Already the men had seen evidence of NVA presence. Ravaged bunkers, discarded ammunition and hastily dug graves – the aftermath of massive US bombardment – were sure signs that the sporadic firefights of the last 48 hours were about to hot up.

The battalion had been sent out on a search and destroy mission after photo-reconnaissance had reported NVA columns filtering through the De-militarized Zone into Quang Tri Province. The main arteries of the enemy supply line were concentrated in this valley, and Hill 400 had to be secured if the US firebase known as the 'Rockpile' was to be protected against NVA attack. In concert with a task force of three other Marine battalions, the Marines of Lieutenant-Colonel William Masterpool's 3d Battalion were about to take on the NVA in their own backyard.

After wolfing down C-rations before the mosquitoes could get at them, the two lead companies moved out at 0930 hours on the 27th and began threading their way along the ridgeline towards Hill 400. Kilo Company formed the vanguard,

113

1966

THE ROCKPILE

From the moment that the Marines landed at Da Nang in March 1965, they kept a watchful eye on the strip of land south of the Demilitarized Zone. Using infra-red cameras, reconnaissance planes flew over the area each night, returning to Dong Ha airbase to have the film developed. Each night the film was a solid sheet of black – the jungle was empty.

In May 1966, Intelligence officers noticed a handful of small white specks on the developed photographs. Each dot was formed by the heat radiating from a camp fire. During the next few days, recon planes brought back photographs that were littered with these dots – the jungles below the DMZ were swarming with North

Vietnamese troops.

The B-52 bombing operations over the Ho Chi Minh Trail had obviously forced the NVA to modify their infiltration routes into South Vietnam, and the communist troops were now crossing the DMZ en route to the populous coastal plain of Quang Tri Province. After ARVN troops captured a high-ranking NVA officer in late May, Marine Intelligence officers discovered details of Hanoi's plan to take over Quang Tri.

During the course of two major US military operations – Hastings and Prairie – one geographical feature became crucial to control of the battlefield. Known as the 'Rockpile', this 750ft jagged fang of granite lay at the intersection of three

river valleys and two enemy trails.

During Operation Hastings, the Marines established a reconnaissance post on the peak of the Rockpile. A single sniper, sustained by air drops of C-rations and water, controlled the area. By the time Operation Prairie was initiated in early August, however, Marine presence atop the Rockpile had been expanded into a firebase.

Two miles south of the Rockpile stood Hills 400 and 484, granite outcrops that were infested with NVA bunkers and mortar positions. If the strategic importance of the Rockpile within the surrounding terrain was to be safeguarded, the control of both these hills had to be wrested from the communist troops.

with the men on point using their machetes to slash a path through the six-foot layer of brush. Abrasions and insect bites can turn septic within a matter of hours in this unforgiving environment, but it was the only way the company could move forward. The canopy was so thick that scarcely any light penetrated the jungle below.

After half an hour, one of the Marines stumbled upon a human skull that had been placed at the side of the trail. Below it was a note that read: 'We come back kill Marines.' The English was flawed but the message was crystal clear. At 1000, as Captain James 'Jay Jay' Carroll led Kilo Company towards the crest of Hill 400, the point man of the lead platoon stumbled over a bamboo pole that triggered a booby-trapped Claymore mine and several hand grenades. An enemy machine gun opened up and all hell broke loose. A fusillade of bullets ripped through the air, and the sickening crump of exploding mortars drowned out the sound of M14s as the Marines returned fire to the front and flanks. Men shouted frantically for more ammo, others screamed for the medics.

A whirlwind of flying shrapnel

The Marines dived for cover in artillery craters, not sure which direction the fire was coming from. Their advance had been text-book perfect, but the NVA were not playing by text-book rules. The plan had been to probe forward and then retract

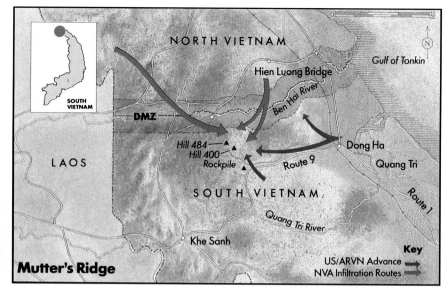

Mutter's Ridge

Key
US/ARVN Advance →
NVA Infiltration Routes →

Page 113: Badly wounded and shell-shocked by the brutal fighting for Hill 484, a mud-spattered Marine stares impassively at a buddy who reaches out to help him. Only a few days earlier, Marines of the 3d Battalion had descended into the mists surrounding the Rockpile and embarked on their search and destroy operation (above left). Carrying M14s and general purpose machine guns, the grunts were walking right into the NVA's backyard. Above: Northwest of the Rockpile, Mutter's Ridge extended from Hill 400 to Hill 484. Right: Sergeant Lee F. Jankes lays down heavy fire in an effort to prise the NVA from their network of bunkers on Mutter's Ridge.

the lead elements into an 'artillery sleeve' as soon as contact was made. Artillery and napalm would then be directed onto enemy positions. But the wily NVA had caught on to this tactic. During the last two days, the North Vietnamese troops had followed the Marines into the safety zone as soon as the shelling started. Once the explosions had ceased and the sounds of the jungle had returned to normal, the NVA would wait for the Marines to resume their advance and then start shooting again.

Plastered by mortar fire, and unable to pinpoint the location of enemy machine-gun nests, the Marines kept low and thanked God for their flak jackets and helmets as red-hot shrapnel whistled all around them. A brief respite from the shelling gave Carroll the chance to make a quick roll call – casualties were slowly filtering back to a rough

perimeter on both sides of the trail.

The perimeter slowly took shape as the incoming became more intense. Kilo Company found itself totally surrounded. 'I got a feeling they don't like us,' one Marine shouted to his buddy. 'Personality conflict,' came the laconic reply. At 1043, responding to Carroll's request for air support, two Phantoms roared over the battlefield at treetop level, dropping napalm and 500lb bombs only 200yds away from the Marines' positions. The next strike came in at 90yds and the whole area erupted into a whirlwind of flying shrapnel and foliage.

Once again, Carroll tried to lead his men forward in a desperate attempt to gain ground. NVA machine gunners unleashed a torrent of fire from close in – the nearer they were to the Marines, the safer the NVA were from the fury of Phantom air strikes that had been pounding in for the last 30 minutes. Every time the Marines moved out of their perimeter, men were cut down by a vicious cross-fire from automatic weapons.

The snipers stayed behind

After two hours the NVA broke contact, leaving only a handful of snipers behind to remind the Marines that they were still watching them. As the dust and smoke of battle cleared, the sun burst through. Carroll counted the cost: seven dead, 25 wounded.

The thin air at high altitude prevented the medevac choppers from hovering in to pick up the wounded, so Kilo Company moved back down the trail towards Lieutenant-Colonel Masterpool's headquarters, where engineers were carving out an LZ with high explosives. Hidden from sight, the NVA picked this moment to resume their ground fire with fresh intensity. It seemed that the hill was infested with a mass of 'spider holes',

1966

painstakingly dug into the hillsides over the last few weeks, from which enemy troops could lob mortars and mount ambushes almost at will. Carroll and his men took cover. Now they were pinned down 400yds away from headquarters. Many of them had been without food and water for 24 hours.

The sharp crack of sniper fire mingled with the rhythmic chatter of M60s as a blood-red sun sank over the horizon. After recovering their dead and wounded the Marines dug in for the night.

One hill down, one to go

Beginning in the early hours of 28 September, the NVA renewed their mortar attacks from the relative safety of their heavily fortified bunkers. Daylight saw no respite for the Marines, even though friendly artillery fire and air strikes were reported to be pulverising the enemy positions.

A frontal assault by Kilo Company on the NVA bunkers faltered in the face of bruising fire but, reinforced by Companies I and M from the rear, Carroll's men pushed on. Picking off NVA snipers and spotters from the trees as they advanced, the Marines used high-explosive satchel charges to prise the communists from their bunkers. Extra ammunition had to be manhandled up from headquarters to sustain the firefight, especially when the NVA infiltrated back into the area and launched a savage counter-attack. Several shrapnel casualties could be seen tearing off their WIA (wounded in action) tags and humping ammo

Below: Back at Lieutenant-Colonel Masterpool's command post, a Leatherneck mortar team cover their ears as another 81mm round is projected onto the heights of Hill 484.
Right: Marines run to the aid of a pair of radio operators hit by hostile sniper fire. Below, far right: Alone with his thoughts in the aftermath of combat, a Marine awaits evacuation from Mutter's Ridge.

grenade in their direction. There was just no way up the steep, waterlogged slope, and Company M pulled back. Air strikes and artillery continued to thunder in throughout the night.

At 1000 on the 5th, Handrahan again pushed his men forward. Advancing yard by yard through trees and scrub that had been levelled by tons of explosives and napalm, the M60 gunners laid down suppressive fire while the lead platoons threaded their way through the nightmarish terrain. The crest was reached at 1200, but still the NVA refused to retreat. To the rear, Captain Carroll was killed when a salvo of Marine tank shells strayed off-target and smashed into Hill 400. 'Jay Jay' Carroll had been in the Nam less than a month, and the artillery plateau was later renamed Camp Carroll in his honour.

Finally, at 1330, the NVA broke contact and fled into the jungle. They left behind only 10 bodies, but a series of blood-splattered trails leading off the ridge and back into the DMZ bore witness to the heavy losses they must have suffered. Yet one nagging thought stayed with the Marines: despite huge US firepower, the NVA had made good their escape. The hills had been taken, but once again true victory had proved elusive.

'Mutter's Ridge' they called it, after the radio call-sign of the 3d Battalion and in honour of the 20 Marines that were killed in action. Vietnam may have been a 'war of no fronts', but by looking at the American nicknames on any military map, you could tell where US troops fought and died.

boxes to the embattled Marines of Kilo Company.

By 1445 the battle had reached a frenzied pitch, with incoming air strikes sending tremors through the ground every 30 seconds. In swept the Huey gunships, spraying a sea of bullets into NVA positions and silencing the mortars with rocket salvoes. Hill 400 was in the hands of the 3d Battalion. A body count amounted to 50 enemy dead, for the loss of six Marines killed and nine wounded. Time for the medevacs to hover in, unloading ammunition and water and taking off with their cargo of wounded and body bags. As the Marines huddled in small groups chewing the fat in the aftermath of battle, Lieutenant-Colonel Masterpool began planning the assault on his final objective – Hill 484, 1000yds to the west. Then came the rains, turning the hillsides into a sea of mud and soaking the Marines to the skin.

They called it 'Mutter's Ridge'

Captain Robert Handrahan's Company M, alternating with the battalion's other companies as the lead unit, was the first to reach the jumping-off point – an unmarked hill 500yds north of Hill 400. At 0930 on 4 October, the final offensive to wrest control of the ridge from the NVA began.

From the cover of well-concealed stone and timber bunkers, enemy guns spewed fire at the two lead platoons as they began their tortuous advance. Occasionally the Marines would catch sight of an NVA soldier as he stood up to lob a

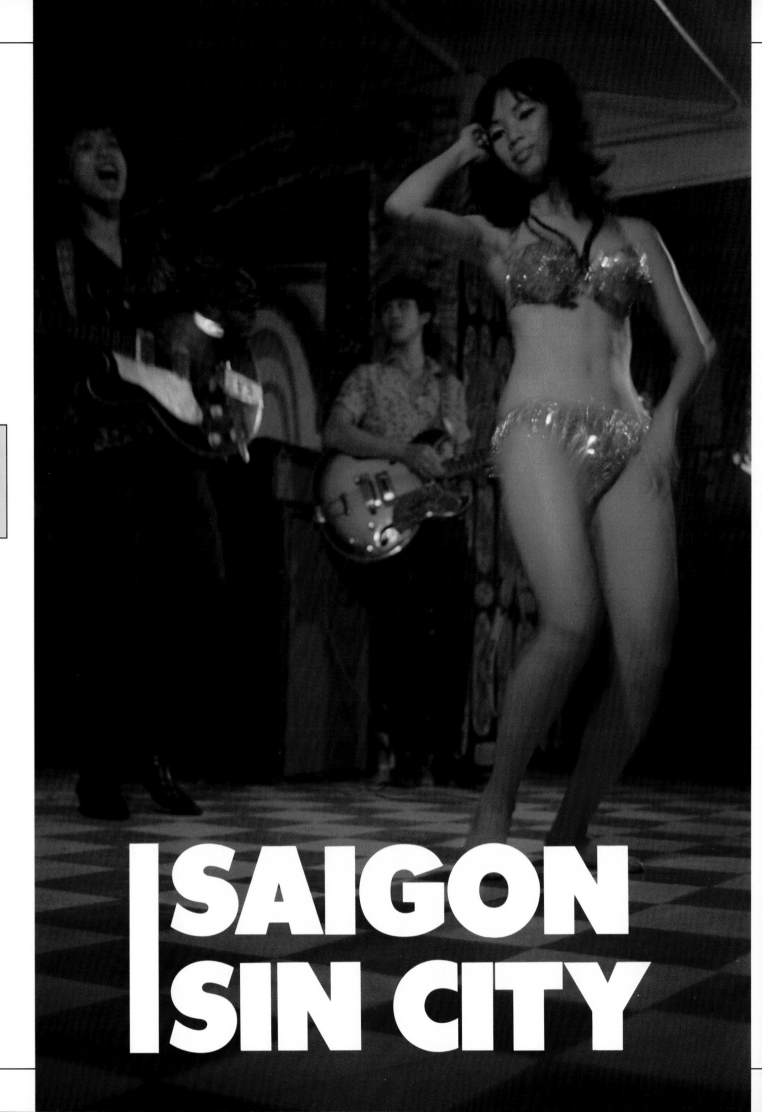

1966

**SAIGON
SIN CITY**

CHAPTER 24

Where could you get a massage and buy dope on the streets? In downtown Saigon, that's where

EYE-WITNESS

The author, Tim Page, operated out of Saigon while covering the war as a photo-journalist for *LIFE* magazine. Here he recounts his early impressions of a once sleepy colonial city.

By the end of 1966, Saigon had become as worn-out and corrupt as a blowsy old hooker, dolled up in new chrome and plastic. Back in 1965, it had the freshness of a southern French town, with stuccoed buildings in pastel shades of buff and cream, tiled roofs and gaily painted shuttered windows. The city was then still recovering from the post-Diem period when Diem's sister-in-law, Madame Nhu, had banned all forms of licentiousness, including The Twist. A spate of guerrilla bombings, like that on the floating My Cahn restaurant, meant that a night curfew had been enforced upon the US military and Vietnamese civilians. Night-life flourished, but compared to its later flowerings it was still a limited affair.

The bars opened soon after the siesta hour and

Known by the French as the 'Paris of the Orient', Saigon began to drown in a sea of vice and poverty once the Americans came to town. With dance joints (opposite) and black market profiteers (right) competing for US greenbacks, the once tranquil city changed beyond all recognition.

did their business until 11 o'clock. Then it was Cinderella time, with the Saigon Cowboys (the pimps) collecting their painted charges on souped-up scooters and Honda 50s. There remained two sophisticated night clubs with floor shows, music and dancing – the Arc en Ciel, and Maximos. Diners had a choice of over a dozen restaurants, ranging from cheap Vietnamese cafes to three-star Michelins. Much of the night-life was controlled by the Union Corse (French Mafia) and Chinese Tongs (secret societies) who in turn were obliged to pay tribute to the Vietnamese masters of the moment. The black market flourished. You could buy anything or (virtually) anybody.

The few thousand American advisors and helicopter crewmen were easily absorbed into the city, many only getting short furloughs to town from the boonies. The bars tended to cater separately to one group of military, and as the volume of men swelled, they followed their predecessors to the watering holes. The Sporting Bar on Tu Do, the main high street, was initially a Green Beret haunt, possibly one of the raunchiest. Later on it became a Lurp and hard-core bar.

In theory at least, it was forbidden to enter Saigon in jungle gear or 'camis' – camouflage fatigues. It was also against the regulations to pack a weapon unless you were an officer there on duty and could carry a sidearm. The Special Forces and country team guys blatantly disobeyed the rule, plainly uncomfortable without their pet UZIs, CARs, Swedish Ks, M16s, sawn-off thumpers or whatever. The Saigon-based Military Police, whose forlorn task it was to enforce in-town regulations on the bars, would come into

SAIGON

The chequered history of Saigon could never have prepared it for the dramatic changes of the post-war period. Originally a small fishing village, it was captured in 1859 by the French, who spent nearly 70 years developing it into a major trade centre, complete with elegant ministerial quarters, an opera house, and the stuccoed elegance of a city in the south of France. The guns of the Japanese controlled the city during World War II, but it was in 1946, when British forces, including the Gurkhas, allowed the French to take over the fighting against the Viet Minh, that the sad future of Saigon was ushered in. For 30 years, this was to be a city torn apart by war.

Always a vital strategic capital, Saigon was the nucleus of America's involvement in Vietnam and the resting ground of soldiers recovering from operations. Those who arrived in 1965 found what was already a city of extremes. Straight, tree-lined boulevards leading into spacious parks reminded them of the former style of this 'Paris of the Orient', while the makeshift dwellings of homeless refugees revealed a stinking, overcrowded urban jungle. By the time the trickle of US servicemen turned into a flood, the influx of American dollars created a booming economy for some, a paradox of poverty for others. A prostitute could earn more than a Vietnamese

major or cabinet minister; those profiting from the black market fattened as traditional Vietnamese culture gave way to a tawdry materialism.

These contrasts could be seen in a journey down Tu Do, the main high street. At the top end, near the Cathedral, stood the grand residential and ministerial buildings. Further down, the street faded into shops, cafes, hotels and restaurants and at the lower half, down to the river from the main square, it grew increasingly seedy. Tailors, curio shops and Saigon's only department store fought for space amongst the myriad of bars and brothels offering a brief respite from combat for GIs on a three-day rest and recreation leave.

What the Americans in Saigon wanted, they got, plus a little more — an army of street-walkers saw to that. Most of the black market goods were genuine, although the traders did have a habit of diluting whisky with rice wine. And, there were always the opium dens and drug parlours (below) to satisfy the dopers.

the dark, long rooms and accost boonie-rats in camis, their weapons on the bar, topless hookers draped across their knees. But if they tried to confiscate the weapons and arrest the guys for not being in A1 service dress, they got a levelled weapon, safety off, and a cheerful 'Fuck Off' in return. A regular stand off à la OK Corrall. The MPs usually backed off.

I sat once, drinking with fellow photographer Sean Flynn and members of the Cai Cai A Team, up from the Delta, when in walked the MPs. They accosted the weapons sergeant, Marachek, who was smoking an opium-painted joint, rapping to us, and fondling a young thing. Our beers were on the bar and we were perched on the vinyl-topped stools. The MP tapped Marachek on the shoulder and mumbled about weapons and camis. Marachek eased himself up to his massive six foot two, turned around, unzipped his tiger suit pants, withdrew his cock and proceeded to stir his Ba me Ba (33) beer with it. The mamasan and girls burst into shrieks of appreciative laughter and the MPs made an embarrassed exit. The other team members had only casually stirred from their booths, their ladies' heads bobbing in their laps, to show their support for their main man.

The bars that catered to the hip GIs ran a service of ready-rolled joints, or cigarettes painted discretely with opium and kept in a jar under the counter. You could find a couple in the vicinity of any BEQ (Bachelor Enlisted Quarters). Out near Tan Son Nhut airbase, there was a whole sub-strip of massage parlours, truck washes fronting 'steam and cream' joints and acid-age bars, replete with day-glo posters, ultra-violet lights and pulsating rock music.

Prostitution was no new thing in Saigon. The French had both legalised and profited from it, monopolizing a civilized system of military brothels. The Vietnamese Army continued the habit, often allowing women to travel with the

Above: On leave from combat, four servicemen take a stroll through downtown Saigon. With a myriad of whore houses, clip-joints, street-pedlars and restaurants to choose from, American money flowed like water. But, as the US presence grew, so did the frequency of Viet Cong attacks. Below: The bloody aftermath of the My Cahn bombing, in which 100 people were killed.

troops when not occupying the post barracks and frontier forts. At Dien Bien Phu in 1954, North African and Vietnamese hookers had become nurses and frontline fighters as the Viet Minh encircled and then destroyed the base.

In downtown Saigon only money mattered and the prices soon went up for a massage and a quickie, the clientele being naive out-of-towners or officers. The works could set a man back $10 green, or 15 in MSC (Military Script Currency), and to lure a bar girl out of her den for a liaison you had to buy her out. That is, you had to buy the estimated amount of Saigon teas she would have consumed in her absence. You always paid the mamasan, and whatever the girl wanted was up to you to negotiate on top of the number of 'teas' she had knocked back. She got a cut of these takings and occasionally you would meet one that actually had liquor in her glass, not coke or tea. There were always the hard core who turned on to dope too. The Bluebird, below our apartment on Tu Do, had an infamous reputation and the passage beside it harboured dirty-picture sellers as well as junk touts.

Top left: As he flicked through the service newspapers, massage parlour advertisements such as this would leave little to the grunt's imagination. Alternatively, for the more reserved, there was a wide range of cuisine available (left). Although Saigon was becoming dependent on the influx of American money, however, a climate of economic extremes was emerging. Decked out in the clothes of Western youth culture, prostitutes and bar girls (above) could pull in up to 850 dollars a month. In stark contrast, a Vietnamese policeman had to live on a mere 25 dollars. Right: US Military Police patrol the streets.

running up mufti safari suits, while curio stores knocked out desk name-plates, mounted unit insignias and endless nick-nack souvenirs. The black market blossomed, supplying the nouveau riche of the city, hairspray being a number one item, straight from the commissary shelves. You could order a fridge, a jeep or a case of panty-hose by mail order before it even entered the docks.

Neon lights and hard cash

Neon lights went up, announcing the coming of the West, and bouffant girls in miniskirts tottered self-consciously amongst the graceful Saigon women. The ranks of the working ladies were swelled by the flood of refugees from the embattled countryside. Deserters and dodgers went underground, flourishing on the black tide of goods. The traffic was overloaded by thousands of 50cc Suzukis, Bridgestones, Yamahas and Hondas. Trucks fought the diminutive four-door Renault 4 cabs for road space. Jeeps blasted through the lot, ploughing room for official Ford sedans.

In early 1965, strolling in Saigon had been like walking in Avignon. But there were only 17,000 Americans in-country at that time. By 1967 there were almost half a million, 50,000 who called Saigon home. They came replete with TV and radio stations, wallets full of hard cash, insatiable libidos and one of the worst forms of clap known to mankind – the Heinz 57 variety, for which there was no known cure, just an endless drip. And with the rapid passing of their youth, the old Saigon faded behind a ferro-concrete-clad smile and endless concertinas of barbed wire.

1966

The black guys tended to segregate themselves with their music and had established a separate quarter behind the docks in Canh Hoi. Generally it was not cool, as a white, to go over there. Those who did, found a soul sin city, the air thick with primo Cambodian Red marijuana and the rooms reverberating to the beat of James Brown, Wilson Pickett and The Temptations. The bar girls there could really move, and there was a predominance of darker Khmer ladies in the dank back rooms. It was easy to score the illicit in Canh Hoi, although most of the sidewalk cigarette sellers would carry ready-rolled joints alongside regular US and Viet brands. You could buy a carton of your favourite brand where all the cigarettes had been carefully emptied and reloaded with herb, a pinch of tobacco artfully placed next to the filter and at the tip. Perfect party camouflage at a buck a pack, tax seal intact.

The corruption of Saigon was completed by the building of multi-story military quarters, requiring endless service industries. The traditional cafes swung to providing burgers, fries and milkshakes. Tailor shops sprung up on every block,

1966

When a company of South Vietnamese troops enters a small village and discovers only two male adults, the commander makes a simple but terrifying deduction. Either they are VC, or they have information that may be of use. Far left: A vicious blow to the head brings one of the suspects to his knees. He is then dragged through the mud towards a water urn, where soldiers deliver a few well-placed kicks to the body (left).

INQUISITION

EYE-WITNESS

James Pickerell (above) spent three years covering the Vietnam war as a freelance photographer. His work has appeared in a number of publications, including *LIFE* and *Paris Match*.

The South Vietnamese Army steals, rapes, and generally treats the population in a very callous fashion...' Damning words, coming from an official US report on the climate of fear and intimidation fostered by ARVN officers. The arbitrary looting of hamlets and widespread persecution of VC suspects were often common pastimes for men who had little regard for humane codes of conduct. In a war where the enemy walked freely among villagers, this brutal sense of superiority could turn routine interrogation into a sadistic nightmare for anyone that got in their way. Photographer James Pickerell, on patrol with an ARVN unit in the Mekong Delta, recorded one such incident. The suspect survived, but only just...

Above right: Unable to resist, the 'suspect' waits for his tormentors to begin their brutal interrogation in earnest. Right: The second suspect watches as the ARVN begin their crude water torture. Far right: With a callous smirk, one of the soldiers walks away from the scene, just as the second suspect is kicked to the ground.

AGENT ORANGE

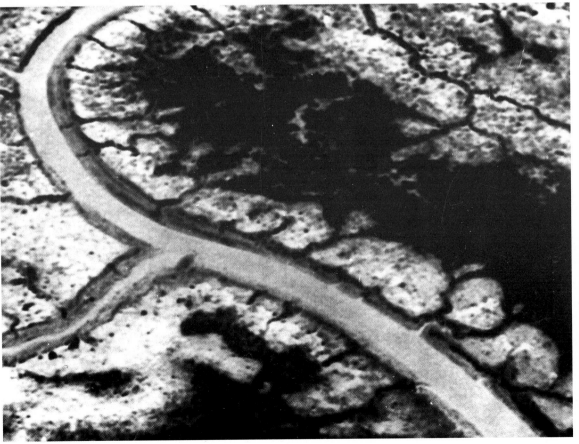

Above: 'Only you can prevent forest.' That was the motto of the Ranch Hands who flew defoliation missions over South Vietnam and the Ho Chi Minh Trail. Left: And prevent them they did. This is the result of the aerial spraying on the coastal mangrove forests.

US aircraft defoliated vast swathes of South Vietnam, trying to open up VC sanctuaries. But was this policy morally justifiable, even in wartime, and will it have disastrous longterm consequences?

The two Pratt & Whitney Double Wasp engines roar as the heavily laden converted C-123 transport lumbers down the air strip at Tan Son Nhut. It is carrying over 1000 gallons of the defoliant Agent Orange. Slowly, the screaming propellers claw their way into the hot thin air. Within minutes another plane follows. It is 1966 and the 'Ranch Hands' are out on another mission.

They arrived in Vietnam back in 1962 to help the South Vietnamese strip the forest cover from outlying VC strongholds. With no leaves on the trees, the Viet Cong would have nowhere to hide. The men on board are all unmarried and have given undertakings that they will, if necessary, fly in civilian clothing and they accept that if they are captured the US government may disclaim all knowledge of them. The first team of Ranch Hands to be sent to Vietnam were not even told where they were going.

Early flights had South Vietnamese Air Force officers on board and the Ranch Hands were simply advisors under the Farm Gate training program. But the Vietnamese officers were in command in name only.

The pilots are protected with aluminium alloy armour-plating under the cockpit, and an open-topped box, three-feet square and made of two half-inch sheets of Doron armour has been installed at the spray operator's position to give some protection from ground fire. The planes are often fired upon and sometimes brought down. On hot missions the Ranch Hands are sometimes accompanied by F-4 Phantoms, whose job it is to rocket and strafe the target area before the C-123s go in.

Spray booms are fitted under the wings and tail, and a 1000-gallon MC-1 Hourglass spray tank and pump system is fitted in the cargo hold. There is a man in back to handle the pump, but the spray operation is controlled by the flight engineer from his spray console.

Several methods of forest clearance have already been tried. Napalm has been dropped to set the jungle on fire, but the canisters have either fallen through the canopy and been smothered in the damp undergrowth, or they've caught in the upper branches and burnt just one tree. No self-sustaining fire has been created.

Bombing and bulldozing flat vast tracts of forest with giant Rome Plows has also been tried. But that approach is expensive and time consuming. It does not work well in mountainous areas and it effectively fertilizes the soil in the monsoon conditions of Vietnam, and a dense undergrowth will quickly grow back.

Agent White and Agent Purple – so called because of the colouring of the cans they come in – have also been used. But neither is as effective as Agent Orange. Orange contains a growth hormone that makes trees drop their leaves prematurely.

The use of these herbicides is not new. The year before the Ranch Hands first went in-country, more than 40 million acres of agricultural land, plus hundreds of thousands of miles of roadsides, railways and other rights of way in the United States were treated with the same herbicides. More than 10 million acres in the USA – that's around a quarter of the area of South Vietnam – were sprayed with herbicides from the air.

The Ranch Hands' C-123s turn towards Laos.

Below: On the ground, as well as from the air, defoliation left the Viet Cong and NVA nowhere to hide. Although this tactic worked in the short term, in the monsoon conditions of South Vietnam, thick undergrowth soon grew back, giving the Viet Cong even better cover. The US thought with their superior technology they could change anything. The VC worked with things as they were. The Ranch Hands went on spraying anyway. Their motto 'Only you can prevent forests' mimicks the sign seen in US national parks: 'Only you can prevent forest fires.'

1966

1966

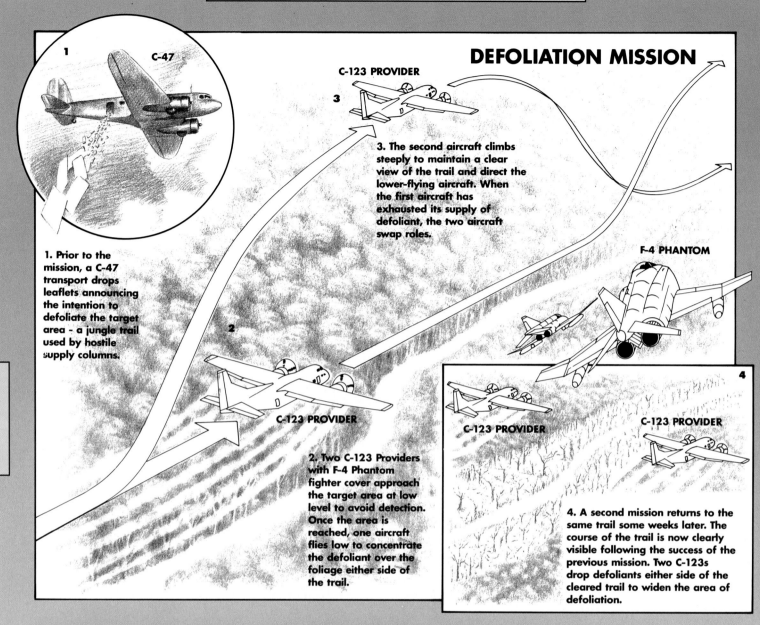

DEFOLIATION MISSION

1 C-47

C-123 PROVIDER

3

3. The second aircraft climbs steeply to maintain a clear view of the trail and direct the lower-flying aircraft. When the first aircraft has exhausted its supply of defoliant, the two aircraft swap roles.

1. Prior to the mission, a C-47 transport drops leaflets announcing the intention to defoliate the target area - a jungle trail used by hostile supply columns.

F-4 PHANTOM

2

C-123 PROVIDER

2. Two C-123 Providers with F-4 Phantom fighter cover approach the target area at low level to avoid detection. Once the area is reached, one aircraft flies low to concentrate the defoliant over the foliage either side of the trail.

4

C-123 PROVIDER   **C-123 PROVIDER**

4. A second mission returns to the same trail some weeks later. The course of the trail is now clearly visible following the success of the previous mission. Two C-123s drop defoliants either side of the cleared trail to widen the area of defoliation.

Their mission this time is to spray a section of the Ho Chi Minh Trail. It is the second mission over the same 20-mile length of road. A week ago two planes flew this way, but it had been difficult to see the road through the thick jungle canopy from the spraying altitude of 150ft.

There's no point in navigating from landmarks as the roads are very often not where they are shown on maps. Sometimes, when the jungle is particularly dense, the planes go in low, locate the road and drop smoke canisters. With the jungle canopy in some places reaching 200ft above

Below: Side by side, two C-123 Providers make a second spray run down a section of the Ho Chi Minh Trail.

ground level, the smoke takes about a minute to rise to visible height. Then the planes can turn and spray, connecting two columns of smoke with a strip of herbicide.

Normally though, on a two-plane mission, the lead plane flies high, at around 1000ft. From that height, the trail or road is usually clearly visible. The other plane follows lower, spraying. And at the end of run, the planes swap positions.

But today there are no such problems. After a week, the discolouration of the forest, caused by the first spraying, is easily visible from the air.

The two C-123 Providers can spray at the same time, following the discoloured strip and widening the defoliated area to the required 250yds on each side of the road.

Before the mission, C-47 aircraft dropped leaflets, explaining that spraying is in progress, and loudspeaker announcements were made from low-flying planes. But these did not help calm the peasants' fears. Evil-smelling purple fluid falling from the skies does not seem natural to them, whatever the government says. The VC also issue helpful little pamphlets, explaining how to avoid the bad effects of spraying. Food and other produce can be protected by burying it in holes at least six-feet deep, they say, otherwise anyone – especially nursing mothers and children – going near contaminated vegetables may suffer horrible diseases and death. But leaflet drops and loudspeakers also alert the VC. It gives them time to prepare a reception committee for the spray planes.

A crushing blow to village morale

To counteract the VC propaganda, government psychological-warfare teams roam the countryside, eating bread soaked in defoliant spray and washing their faces in it. The peasants see this merely as trickery. Rumours of the American use of chemical poisons grow. One old woman even believed her basket of vegetables was ruined when an American advisor touched it with a 'poison' stick. And two former prisoners of the VC say their captors complained more about herbicides than any weapon used against them.

Though the Ranch Hands' motto is 'Only you can prevent forests', they do not confine their activities to defoliating the jungle. Since 1962, they have also been destroying crops with Agent Blue – to prevent them falling into VC hands.

But it is not just the VC's crops that get sprayed, and if the VC are short of food they simply up the rice tax on the surrounding villages. In fact, for the VC, crop spraying is another propaganda victory.

'Almost none of the people understand the purpose of the crop destruction by the Vietnamese government,' said one of the VC. 'They can only see that their crops are destroyed. Added to that we pour propaganda into their ears. Therefore, a number of people joined us because they'd suffered from damage.'

'The farmers love their land and the things they grow,' said another. 'All their lives, they did not own anything better than their own little plot of land and a few trees. The spraying in one day killed the trees they planted 15 or 20 years before. You see how this affects their feelings and morale.'

However, crop destruction probably does persuade wavering peasants to move out of Viet Cong-dominated areas into those controlled by the South Vietnamese government.

'The truth is, if these people moved to government-controlled areas, it was not only because their crops had been sprayed with chemicals,' said a former resident of a VC-controlled area. 'Since their areas had been hit by bombs and mortars, they had already had the intention to leave and they would probably have done so had it not been for the fact that they could not decide to part with their crops. Now that their crops were destroyed by chemicals, they no longer had any reason to be undecided.'

Soon the destruction of crops became a tool for moving the peasants off the land into the cities and refugee camps, where an eye could be kept on them. Captured Viet Cong documents revealed that the VC were concerned over the number of farmers forced to move to government-controlled

Below: Flying low and straight was dangerous. The Ranch Hands often took a fighter along for protection.

OPERATION RANCH HAND

In 1966, the use of defoliants in Vietnam was reaching its height. But the use of herbicides in war started in the early 1950s, when the British used them on a limited basis to destroy the crops of communist insurgents in Malaya.

In 1961, President Diem of South Vietnam asked the United States to conduct aerial herbicide spraying in his country. In August, the South Vietnamese Air Force initiated herbicide operations with American help (above). But Diem's request launched a policy debate in the US administration. Some viewed herbicides as an efficient means of depriving the Viet Cong of jungle cover and food. Others doubted its effectiveness and were worried that it would expose the US to charges of using chemical warfare.

In November 1961, President Kennedy approved the use of herbicides, but only as a limited experiment requiring Vietnamese participation and the mission-by-mission approval of the US Embassy, the Military Assistance Command Vietnam and South Vietnam's government.

Operation Ranch Hand began in January 1962. Gradually limitations were relaxed and the spraying became more frequent and covered larger areas. In November 1962, the crop destruction programme began in earnest. By the time Operation Ranch Hand ended nine years later, some 18 million gallons of chemicals – mainly Agents Orange, Blue and White – had been sprayed on 20 per cent of South Vietnam's jungles, including 36 per cent of its mangrove forests, covering six million acres in all.

areas because of crop destruction. VC troops were generally ordered to fire on spray planes, even when firing might expose their position.

But during this particular mission, the Ranch Hands aren't concerned with crop spraying. The C-123 is carrying 1000 gallons of Agent Orange and this is a defoliation mission over the Ho Chi Minh Trail. The spray zone is now in sight. The planes go in low to avoid ground fire and pop up to 150ft above the canopy at the spray-on point. The flight engineer flicks a switch on his console. The pump operator activates the 28-horsepower pump whose 60lb per square inch pressure sprays 280 gallons of herbicide every minute onto the jungle below. In less than three-and-a-half minutes, another 350 acres of jungle will be completely destroyed.

It will not be until 1969 that a study by the National Cancer Institute reveals that dioxin, an impurity created in the manufacture of Agent Orange, causes cancer and birth defects in laboratory animals.

AGENT ORANGE – WAS IT LEGAL?

In 1966, Agent Orange was raining from the skies. There was no reason to think it was harmful, but some people in US administration opposed it. They thought it left America open to the charge of using chemical warfare.

The use of herbicides to defoliate trees seems innocent enough in the annals of war atrocities. But was it illegal? The Hague Convention of 1907 prohibited the use of 'poison and poisoned weapons' and the 1925 Geneva Protocol outlawed poisonous gases 'and all analogous liquids, materials or devices'. Poisoning trees and peoples' crops could well be considered a violation of the tenets of these two great pillars of international law, even before it was suspected that dioxin in Agent Orange caused cancer and birth defects. The American position was that the Geneva Protocol did not apply to herbicides and chemicals that were used domestically in the US, USSR and other countries to control unwanted vegetation. The United Nations disagreed though. In 1969, the General Assembly adopted a resolution that the Protocol applied to all weapons.

Was it a legitimate to lay waste nearly one-seventh of the area of the country of an ally – 5.5 million acres in all, more than the area of Wales, or use weapons whose long-term effects cannot be predicted? Ten years after spraying finished, some areas of jungle were covered with shrubby bamboo making reforestation difficult. In others, fire and erosion had turned the soil to rock where nothing will grow.

Around 36 per cent of the productive coastal mangrove forests were destroyed. This has caused silting that has destabilized the shore line, wiped out shellfish, driven several species to extinction and cut the production of local fisheries.

Added to that, 750,000 acres of land were scraped clean with massive Rome Plows – huge Caterpillar tractors fitted with a 2.5-ton plough blade and protected by 14 tons of armour plating. And large areas of forest were burned out with incendiaries.

It is also estimated that there are more than 20 million shell and bomb craters in the country, covering some 350,000 acres. As large as 40ft across and 20ft deep, these filled with rain-water and are a breeding ground for malaria and tropical dengue fever. In areas that saw heavy fighting, metal fragments and unexploded ordnance are so common that farmers dare not return to their fields. In forests too, many trees are filled with shards of metal making them susceptible to rot and impossible to mill. But war is a destructive business and there has been no serious suggestion that the use of shells and bombs be made illegal because of their *ecological* effects.

Was it legitimate to use crop destruction as a method of moving the civilian population out of villages they had occupied for generations? At first the US government stipulated that crop destruction should be confined to remote areas known to be occupied by VC and that only crops intended solely for the use of the enemy should be sprayed. However, Donald Hornig, science advisor to President Johnson, later admitted: 'It's all geared to moving people.'

Under international law, the destruction of food is only legal if it is solely for the use of the enemy or if the military advantage outweighs the harm it may cause civilians. Undoubtedly, crop destruction did harm the villagers, forcing them off the land. They were doubly hit because the VC would take what rice they needed regardless of the harvest. And it could be argued that the spraying gave the VC a military advantage. The resentment it caused among villagers gave them a good supply of new recruits.

Some American academics have proposed that the wilful and permanent destruction of the environment – ecocide – be considered a crime against humanity. In 1975, US President Gerald Ford signed Executive Order No. 11850 renouncing the first use of herbicides in war.

After a study of the residual effects of Operation Ranch Hand, the president of the American National Association of Science concluded: 'On balance, the untoward effects of the herbicide program on the health of the South Vietnamese people appear to have been smaller than one might have feared.'

NAS investigators said they failed to find any clear evidence of direct damage to human health from herbicides. But they did discover a consistent pattern of largely second-hand reports from Montagnards claiming that herbicides have occasionally caused acute or fatal respiratory problems in children.

Today – 20 years later – there are 32,000 outstanding disability claims filed by Vietnam veterans over the use of Agent Orange. So far the Veterans' Administration has granted none of them.

Agent Orange is still news – the front page of *Veteran*, December 1986.

THE HO CHI MINH TRAIL

1966

Late 1966: under intense US aerial bombardment, the communists are building their great supply route to the South through the mountains of Laos

For the Viet Cong and North Vietnamese Army, the failure of the world's greatest military nation to stifle the flow of traffic along the Ho Chi Minh Trail represented a triumph of human endurance over technology. Threading their way through rugged, mountainous country, infantry and motorized convoys braved unimaginable extremes of terrain and climate in their determination to reach the South. 'These forests and mountains are our homeland; our weapon,' stated one communist political leader. It was a sentiment the Americans could never truly comprehend – they saw only an inhospitable mountain range, covered with a dense blanket of rotting vegetation, from which the tentacles of communist infiltration reached out from the North, through Laos and Cambodia, and into South Vietnam.

Faced with intelligence reports that projected an estimated 90,000 infiltrators during 1966, the Pentagon saw no option but to continue its massive 'overkill' policy in a vain attempt to cut the

Left: Every means available was used to keep the vital supplies moving down the Ho Chi Minh Trail.

1966

Left: Despite continual bombardment from the air which left the roads pitted and cratered, the supplies kept on coming. Lorries were often camouflaged to help stop US reconnaisance planes spotting them. Below: By bicycles, by lorry and even by boat down the rivers in Laos, the communist forces lifeline had to be kept open.

communist supply lines. But round-the-clock B-52 bombing missions and jet fighter interdiction and strafing operations were obviously not working. Although a B-52 could unleash over 100 750lb bombs within 30 seconds, cutting a huge swathe through the target area, the estimated cost to the infiltrators of this devastating firepower was only one death to every 300 bombs.

Throughout a road system that covered some 10,000 miles, with arteries leading into critical base areas such as the A Shau Valley in the north, and War Zone C in the south, the men and women of Group 559 maintained an intricate overland logistic network that one day would become known as 'Hanoi's Road to Victory'. The Trail was not one single route or highway. It was a network of roads and narrow paths that zig-zagged through a long mountain corridor. Along the main arteries and tributaries lay thousands of 'rest spots', where communist troops could seek refuge from American bombing.

Groups of young 'pioneers', their morale reinforced by frequent visits from political cadres, stood ready to repair roads and tracks as soon as the last American bomb had fallen. Using radio communications, the supervisors of these teams kept in constant contact with one another, facilitating the never-ending flow of traffic along the Trail. Transit time in the early days was six months, but, by the mid-1960s, this had been reduced to a mere 12 weeks.

'I must not break'

Since most of North Vietnam's young males were drafted into the Army at 18, many of the supply convoys were made up of women. Travelling on foot, and carrying enough medicine and vitamin pills for one month, these convoys suffered a 10 per cent casualty rate from disease alone. The following extracts are taken from the diary of one of these women, Duong Thi Xuan Quy, during her three-month journey to the South:

'The boils on my back hurt me the whole of last night. Could neither sleep nor think clearly. Impossible to lie on my back and it was torture to lie on my side. Had to rock the hammock frequently to ease the pain. Haven't had a bath since Post 1. Will stay here till tomorrow morning and will cross the river at four...Have lost my appetite for several days now. Left my portion unfinished this morning. Never thought it could take so much effort to eat...I must not break down, not even with colic. I'd be left behind. Up at two in the morning. The moon is hidden by clouds. We crossed the pontoon bridges across the Sepon River. These pontoons will be dismantled before daybreak.'

Just as these pontoon bridges had to be dismantled so as not to present an easy target for American aircraft, the human convoys were often forced to build makeshift bamboo bridges across areas of sharp peaks and razor-backed ridges, where massive flooding during the rainy season had covered man-made trails with torrents of water. Weighed down with large, heavy rucksacks, Quy's convoy

NVA soldiers in Hanoi prepare to set-off down the Ho Chi Minh Trail. The bikes were a useful alternative when the going got rough.

1966

continued its tortuous journey, pausing to watch as an NVA unit glided past in the darkness:

'Catch up with a big infantry unit which crossed earlier in the night to avoid a jam on the bridge. The men are weighed down by equipment. There are extra rounds of ammunition to carry now that they are nearing the front. In the dim moonlight, youthful faces covered in sweat flit by. Laden with rifles, machine guns, grenades and backpacks, the soldiers move double-quick. They have travelled like this for three months and now they are nearing the front.'

Sprinting across Highway 9

At this point, the convoy began preparing for the following day's march. Rice-balls were cooked and stored in readiness – these would be supplemented by food from one of the hundreds of vegetable patches planted along the route. Snatching precious little sleep during the chilly night hours, Quy started out with the convoy early the next morning. Having crossed into Quang Tri Province from Laos, the convoy was about to cross Highway 9 – a strategic route that was watched closely by US forces:

'It's a scorcher, and there are no trees along the road. My skin is peeling and I'm tired out...I limped along and it was six o'clock when I crossed Highway 9...The road was not wide, but we had to sprint across it to evade the attention of enemy aircraft. It appeared suddenly in front of me, a curve blanched by the summer sun and strewn with boulders. It looked harmless enough though. Thus I set foot on Highway 9, a road which would long be remembered in the history of our heroic people'.

BUILDING THE TRAIL

In 1959, when the North Vietnamese politburo took the decision to support insurgency in the South, communications between the two parts of Vietnam were crude, comprising little more than mountain and jungle tracks, used for generations by local tribes. The first priority, therefore, was to improve this crude link and create a trail capable of sustaining a build-up in the South.

The process began with the first supply columns in 1959 (Group 559). At the end of each day's march, a small group was detached to set up a relay station. Camouflaged huts were built and caches of supplies established so that future columns of porters could be offered rest and refreshment at regular intervals on their journey south. As time went on, a few selected stations (about 12 in all) were improved and expanded to offer medical and stores facilities as well as rest areas. Many even grew their own crops to relieve the pressure on the supply chain.

It was around these relay stations that the Trail developed. Gangs of young men and women – known as Special Youth Shock Brigades – followed the existing tracks and either improved them or carved out new routes, some of which (after 1964) were capable of taking wheeled vehicles.

The work was arduous in the extreme, in some of the worst climatic and terrain conditions imaginable. In the Truong Son mountains, tracks had to be cut out of the rock, with flimsy bridges thrown across deep ravines or rushing mountain streams. In the valleys, jungle growth had to be hacked away using little more than shovels and machetes. Yet the work never ceased: because of the effects of climate and, after 1964, US airpower, constant repairs had to be carried out. In addition, the Trail was never a single track – by 1964 an elaborate network of routes, running roughly parallel with cross-links at various intervals, had begun to emerge.

At first, all the supplies were carried on foot or slung across heavily laden bicycles, but in 1965 the first Soviet and Chinese-supplied trucks were deployed. This led to a new programme of construction on the trail. Existing tracks had to be broadened and evened; special camouflaged vehicle parks, backed by repair and refuelling facilities, had to be built. The Shock Brigades provided the labour, supported by North Vietnamese engineers equipped with Soviet and Chinese road-building machinery. It was an enormous task, but the construction of the Trail was now entering a new and dynamic phase.

1966

The Ho Chi Minh trail

The Ho Chi Minh Trail was a myriad of tracks, roads and paths running through the mountains of Laos and Cambodia. While it remained open, communist forces could infiltrate into the South with ease

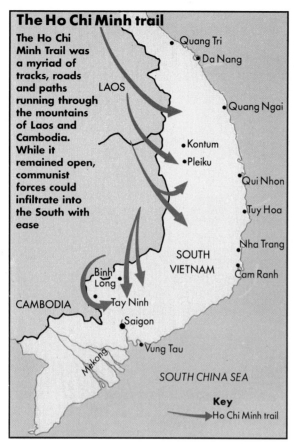

Quy's march south along the Ho Chi Minh Trail continued. Moving through countless staging posts, and diving for cover whenever an American aircraft was spotted high above the forest canopy, Quy was determined to reach her destination:

'Walking alone in the forest I was aware of how vulnerable I was. It was quiet on every side, nobody ahead, nobody behind, and I was all alone on a trail. Yet I felt confident, knowing my com-rades were near, that together we were marching to the front.'

Motorized supply columns began moving down the Trail in 1965 and, very soon, communist forces on the Truong Son Range had been reinforced immeasurably. Transport, engineer, anti-air-craft, communications, support and hospital units were all catered for. The trucks of each convoy, whatever front they were heading for, worked in relays–driving back and forth along one section of the Trail in an effort to reduce losses.

Running the gauntlet

Throughout the network of roads and trails, there was a series of control points guarded by NVA troops. Spaced at three-mile intervals along each route, these minor staging points enabled trucks, fuel, ammunition and food to be concealed from the prying eyes of US reconnaissance planes. Despite this careful planning, however, the trans-port vehicles still ran the gauntlet of American firepower. The imprint of tyres on a forest track, or a moving light at night, was enough to bring a shower of high explosives raining down on the Trail. But still the US was unable to stem the flow of revolutionary forces that was slowly engulfing the South. The following extract, translated from an original account by Do Chu, recounts one day's action for an anti-aircraft unit situated on the Trail:

'It was six in the morning, but the road was still covered in the mist. The drivers were backing their lorries to unload, apart from Lieu who had been held up by an engine fault. As the day broke, instead of hiding his lorry in the forest he decided to finish the last 20 kilometres in the open under cover of the mist...

'The first rays of the sun glanced off Lieu's broken windshield. Just at that moment an enemy jet flew past and turned to dive. Lieu

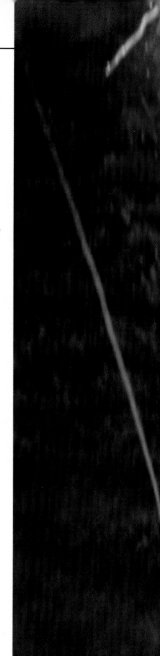

Above: An A1E Skyraider blasts a staging point. US planes attacked the supply lines any way they could. Left: But these raids did not always go unopposed. The NVA protected the Trail's railheads in North Vietnam with a barrage of machine-gun fire. Right: The Trail's radio controllers broadcast from stations protected in deep caves.

gripped his steering wheel and raced through the gears. He heard a blast behind him. "One miss," he thought, and braked. A blue flash and a bang in front of him. "Second miss!"

'Now he had to avoid the strafing. The enemy plane zoomed up and veered for a dive...Just at that moment, in the forest in front of Lieu, several anti-aircraft batteries went into action...Khoi's voice sounded in the command car: "More planes sighted. Battery One, ready yourself to attract enemy fire when our lorry enters the depot. Direction 12, two F-4s approaching. They've spotted their target!"

The enemy buzzed over again

'The battery commander adjusted his helmet and calmly ordered "Forward." The vehicle moved off, its camouflage shaking. After skirting the edge of the forest for a while the battery made for open ground. The enemy buzzed over again and again. Having escaped the most dangerous section of the road the lorry ran into a nearby forest.

'Their target lost, the enemy skimmed over the

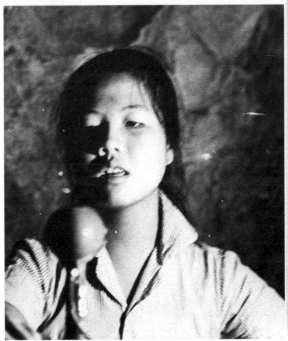

The Ho Chi Minh Trail was the lifeline of the communist campaign in the South. Along it travelled newly trained guerrillas, NVA main-force units and the supplies needed to sustain the war effort – supplies that ranged from food and weapons to medical equipment and revolutionary tracts.

Yet precise figures for the number of soldiers or tonnage of supplies moving along the Trail at any one time are difficult to gauge. North Vietnamese records are not available, while the habit of stockpiling supplies at key points meant that, far from flowing south in an endless stream, vast quantities remained static, awaiting future needs. Certainly in the early years (1959-64), the volume of traffic was dependent on variables such as the weather – more could be moved during the dry season (November-April) than the monsoon – and the demands of the VC guerrillas. In 1966 the US Secretary of Defense, Robert McNamara, estimated that the VC could maintain prevailing levels of violence on less than 60 tons of supplies (about 20 truck-loads) a year.

Regardless of the amount of traffic flowing along the Trail, however, the route had enormous strategic importance for the communists. It allowed them to build up forces and supplies for operations at times and places of their own choosing. Indeed, by 1966 the real threat posed by the Trail was not the flow of supplies to the VC, but the use made of it by the NVA in their war against US and ARVN units. According to US Intelligence estimates, some 10,000 NVA used the Trail in 1964 (the first year of main-force infiltration). This figure had increased to 36,000 by 1965, and 90,000 by 1966. Despite continued American attempts to destroy or at least block the traffic on the Trail, this figure continued to rise. By 1970 an estimated 10,000 tons of supplies would be threading their way along the Trail every week.

1966

Left: Deep ravines were crossed by makeshift bridges. Below: One US tactic was to bomb the rail lines from Hanoi and Haiphong to the beginning of the Ho Chi Minh Trail. This shot was taken from an A-7 Corsair flying from the carrier USS *Midway* as it drops six bombs, heavily damaging a span of the Phu Ly rail bridge.

This article is based on the personal accounts of Duong Thi Xuan Quy and Do Chu, two of the many thousands of people who travelled south along Hanoi's road to victory.

forest. The machine gun on the car began to fire. The first plane hurriedly zoomed up. Unaware of this, the second one dived. "Long distance, ready...fire!"

'A tremendous blast tore the latania leaves from the battery. The plane was hit and fell in a distant forest with a big explosion. "Direction 14, four F-4s sighted."

'Trung stood erect, one hand gripping the rail, the other his binoculars. Standing beside Trung, the battery commander ordered: "Reduce speed. Don't fire when they veer. Comrade Trung, watch the new planes. The first is preparing to dive!"

'Straining his eyes, Trung saw the planes coming from the east, using the sun for cover. "The first plane is diving...Fire."

'A volley compelled the enemy to fire his rocket across the road. But another plane dived, strafing the vehicle...Another flight of enemy planes passed over. Kilometres of road were plunged in smoke. Machine guns rattled. The fierce sounds of the battle seemed to echo in the distant forests.

'The battle raged on until midday. Once it was over, Khoi ran to the other batteries, his bare feet treading on the burning-hot road. An acrid smoke pervaded the area. This reminded Khoi of his first encounter with US pilots in Vinh Linh [just north of the Demilitarized Zone], one hot August day ...Today, he longed for the lagoons of his native land, the evening glow on the river banks and sand beaches, the boatman's songs in the clear nights. But all he could see was red fires, spreading through the forest and reaching to his heart.'

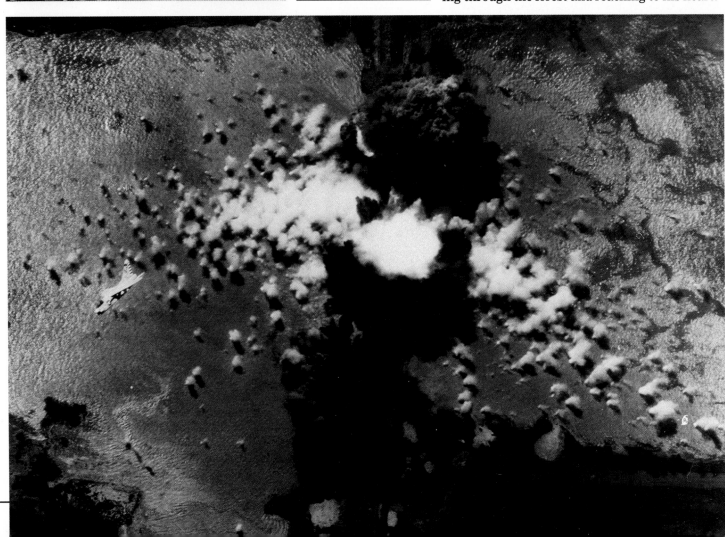

1966

GUARDING THE COAST

1966

Innocent fishing vessel – or VC junk smuggling arms and agents into the South? US coastal patrols had the dangerous task of stopping seaborne infiltration

Just how many arms and supplies the Viet Cong were getting from North Vietnam by seaborne infiltration by 1966 is anyone's guess. Up till then, the navy and junk forces of South Vietnam – some 300 vessels in all – were tasked with controlling coastal shipping. According to the figures they were doing a great job – in 1963, 136,000 vessels and 390,000 people were searched and six infiltrators captured; in 1964, 212,000 vessels and 880,000 people were searched and 11 infiltrators captured. In Saigon, the official line was that the Viet Cong weren't getting their material from the coast.

The trouble was that the Cong *were* getting

Previous Page: One of the many thousands of Vietnamese stopped on board a sampans explains the purpose of his journey to a US patrol boat. Below: Peering out on to the horizon, an American sailor surveys part of the 120,000 square miles of coastal waters covered by Operation Market Time.

their material – and they sure were getting a lot. At that time the Ho Chi Minh Trail was only a series of jungle footpaths. It took months to get down it, and a lot of those who tried it never made it into the South. So how in the hell *were* the Cong getting their supplies?

The US Military Assistance Command, Vietnam, got the answer on 16 February 1965 – by accident. Early that day, US Army Lieutenant James S. Bowers was piloting his UH-1 helicopter from Qui Nhon on the central coast to Tuy Hoa, 50 miles to the south. This was entrenched Viet Cong territory so Bowers kept a mile or so out to sea to minimise the danger from ground fire. Twenty miles north of Tuy Hoa he passed over Vung Ro Bay, in heavy duty Cong country. There he saw something that the South Vietnamese Navy and MACV said wasn't happening. A 130ft steel trawler lay close inshore and dozens of crates littered the beach. Bowers had caught the VC with their pants down.

The Battle of Vung Ro Bay

For the next three days Vung Ro Bay was not a good place to be. Bowers called in air strikes which, by 1200 hours, had reduced the trawler to a shattered hulk, keeled over on its port side. A follow-up South Vietnamese Navy/ARVN combined operation, which was supposed to capture any material not destroyed by the air strikes, was less successful. During the afternoon, troops from the ARVN's 23rd Division at Ty Hoa refused to board Vietnamese naval transports. There was no way they were going to Vung Ro Bay – that was Cong country!

So the South Vietnamese Navy went in alone. Over the next 48 hours, warships tried four times to enter the bay and each time were driven off by heavy automatic weapons fire. Air strike after air strike was called in and the bay area was brought under continuous, heavy naval gunfire. Finally, at 1100 hours on 19 February, the Vietnamese navy managed to get ARVN special forces ashore. There was no resistance – the only Cong left

around Vung Ro Bay were dead. They had pulled out before dark, but although they stayed less than six hours in the area, and although 72 hours had passed since Lieutenant Bowers had sighted the trawler, the ARVN still recovered more than 4000 rifles, sub-machine guns and light machine guns, several thousand cases of ammunition and large quantities of medical supplies.

Here was evidence that gave the lie to the South Vietnamese Navy's figures. Long before the Cong started using the Ho Chi Minh Trail in a big way, they had a route down the 1200-mile coastline of Vietnam. God only knows how much they had

Gulf of Thailand is hit by the southwest monsoon. Real seamanship is needed to keep small craft on station during these periods. Usually, the Vietnamese abandoned the effort and holed up on a friendly lee shore. Add to the weather the difficulties of maintenance and logistics, and the South Vietnamese Navy had a hell of a problem in even staying afloat.

Of course, it wasn't trying that hard. US naval advisors reported that units had no systematic method of operation. They spent days in aimless cruising, refused to close with craft within small-arms range of a hostile shore or carry out searches

MARKET TIME

Originally controlled by Task Force 71, and falling under the jurisdiction of the US Seventh Fleet, Operation Market Time passed directly to the command of General Westmoreland on 1 August 1965. Redesignated to Task Force 115 (TF115), Market Time became a key element in America's fight to interdict the flow of arms and supplies from North Vietnam along the southern coast.

From surveillance bases at Vung Tau, Qui Nhon, Da Nang, An Thoi and Nha Trang, Task Force 115 operated in nine coastal patrol areas – from the seventeenth parallel in the north, along the coast to the 'Brevie' line in the Gulf of Thailand. With Coast Guard cutters from Squadron One forming barrier patrols at both ends of the coast, each patrol area was assigned a destroyer escort or minesweeper. As the problems of patrolling this enormous waterway became apparent, TF 115's fleet was steadily increased; by late 1966, nearly 100 fast patrol craft, reinforced by 30 US Coast Guard cutters and nearly 500 armed Vietnamese junks, were patrolling the shoreline – stopping and searching any suspicious traffic (below).

As the war progressed, the tactics employed in Market Time became increasingly based on radar. Contact with a target would be established by picket destroyer, minesweeper or aircraft, and this position would be radioed to a Swift cutter or gunboat. With each vessel and plane working in tandem, the intention of the operation was to enforce a blockade on the infiltration of supplies into South Vietnam.

been bringing in – packing massive loads into 100-ton trawlers like the one sunk in Vung Ro Bay, or carrying smaller loads in the sampans and junks that plied up and down the coast. And in all their years of patrolling, the South Vietnamese Navy had not intercepted a single cargo!

Fighting against the elements

To be fair to the South Vietnamese, however, clamping down on seaborne infiltration was no easy business. It wasn't just the length of the coastline or the number of suspect vessels (at any one time, there were 50,000 sampans, junks and trawlers in South Vietnamese waters) that made the job hard. For four months, from November through February, South Vietnam's 1000-mile South China Sea coast is buffeted by the northeast monsoon; for another six months, from May through to October, the 200-mile coast along the

Above: Swift patrol boat crewmen prepare to let rip. Below right: Interrogation of suspects.

at night. And this was with US personnel on board. At other times – and this was most of the time – they supplemented their slender incomes by extorting funds from innocent traders and fishermen, or were easily bought off even if they managed to intercept VC craft. They were, in short, little more than, gun-shy pirates.

The Vung Ro Bay incident set alarm bells ringing from Saigon to Washington. Operation Market Time was the result – the largest inshore blockade operation undertaken by the US Navy since the American Civil War. Landlubbers might think that the blockade of even a 1200-mile, monsoon-buffeted coastline, much of which was under hostile control, would present few problems

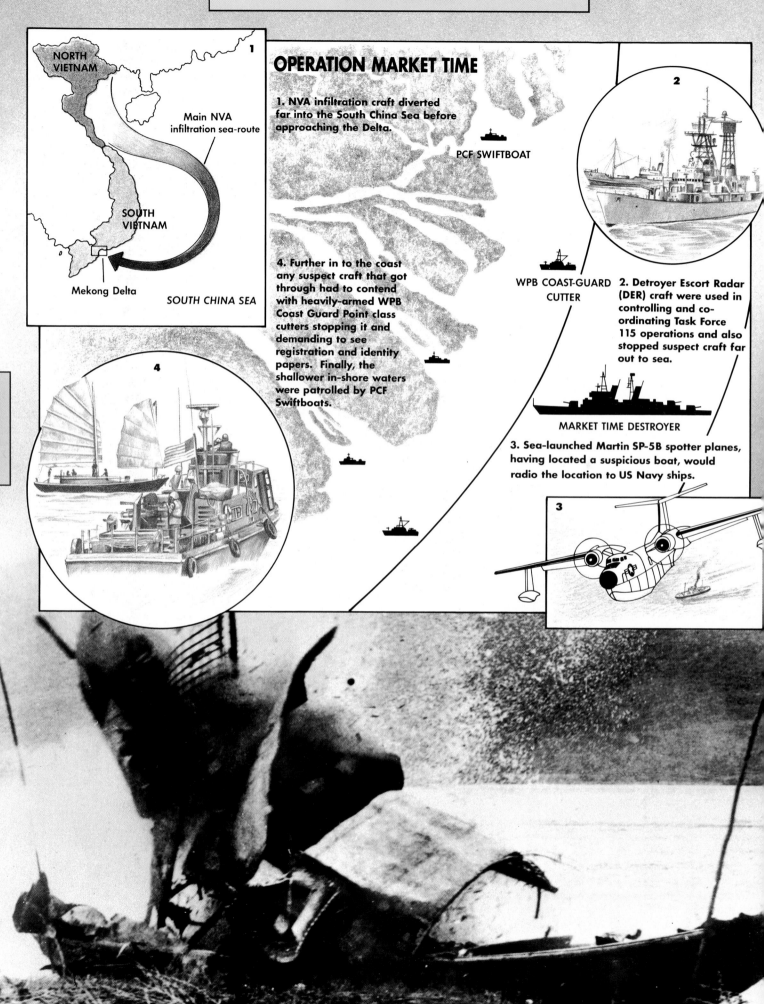

1966

NORTH VIETNAM

Main NVA infiltration sea-route

SOUTH VIETNAM

Mekong Delta

SOUTH CHINA SEA

OPERATION MARKET TIME

1. NVA infiltration craft diverted far into the South China Sea before approaching the Delta.

PCF SWIFTBOAT

WPB COAST-GUARD CUTTER

4. Further in to the coast any suspect craft that got through had to contend with heavily-armed WPB Coast Guard Point class cutters stopping it and demanding to see registration and identity papers. Finally, the shallower in-shore waters were patrolled by PCF Swiftboats.

2. Detroyer Escort Radar (DER) craft were used in controlling and co-ordinating Task Force 115 operations and also stopped suspect craft far out to sea.

MARKET TIME DESTROYER

3. Sea-launched Martin SP-5B spotter planes, having located a suspicious boat, would radio the location to US Navy ships.

to the most powerful navy in the world. But although the US Navy had hundreds of powerful warships in 1965, the problem was that none of them was designed for blockade duty. This requires ships that have both speed and all-weather endurance, as well as manoeuvrability, heavy surface armament, good communications, shallow draft and effective all-round radar. No one ship had all these capabilities in 1965. A few, like the Destroyer Escort Radar (DER), had excellent surveillance capability and a high level of weather endurance; but they were also slow, with a deep draft and relatively light armament. For closer inshore surveillance, point-class cutters of the US Coast Guard were used, with the Swift, a 50-ft aluminium-hulled boat adapted from commercial service, taking care of very shallow patrols.

By the time Market Time was fully underway in the summer of 1965, a new naval command, Task Force 115, had been established and Vietnamese coastal waters had been organised into nine operational areas, each about 120 miles in length and 40 miles wide. The key unit in each area was a DER, tasked with controlling the activities of all other units, as well as with the interception of suspect ocean-going vessels. DER surveillance was supplemented by maritime reconnaissance flights. Lockheed P3A Orions, operating from Sangley Point in the Philippines, patrolled the five northern areas, which covered 500 miles of coast from Vung Tau in the south to the 17th parallel. The four southern regions were patrolled by P2 Neptunes operating from Tan Son Nhut, with Martin P5 Marlin seaplanes covering the mouths of the Mekong Delta and the Gulf of Thailand coast.

A slow and harrowing task

For those on seaborne patrol, Market Time operations were characterised by a weird combination of tension and tedium. A vessel would be sighted and ordered to heave to. Then came the tension. Maybe this one was a Cong gun-runner – maybe at this moment a dozen AK-47s were trained on you. Hulls grated and a heavily armed boarding party would begin the search. It was no fun poking around the hold of an Asian fishing vessel – it was best done on an empty stomach. 999 times out of a 1000, nothing was found and the tension and tedium would produce exhaustion. Market Time commanders found that after about four days of around-the-clock patrolling, the efficiency of cutter and Swift crews began to decline quickly, so a regular system of rotation was introduced. In addition, devices were introduced to speed up searches. Metal detectors were found to be better for finding a cache of mortar bombs under a ton of fish than a man wading through them; lighted mirrors on flexible poles could illuminate nooks and crannies too small for heavily armed Americans to get into.

And when they did hit the jackpot, Market Time units found that their operation was every bit as dangerous as any patrol in Quang Tri or the Iron

Below Left: Having been loaded with explosive charges, a junk carrying food and supplies into the South is blown up by the US Navy. Below: A Lockheed AP-2H Neptune surveys two Vietnamese junks from the air. The key element of the US Navy's airborne patrol squadrons in Market Time, Neptunes carried two 0.50in machine guns in the dorsal turret, 16 127mm rockets and up to 3629kg of bombs, mines and depth charges.

Triangle. On the night of 14 February 1966, the crew of one Swift boat moved to intercept a sampan detected only 100yds from an enemy stronghold. But when the Swift closed in at speed, an immense explosion suddenly blew its aluminium hull apart, sinking the boat and killing four of the crew.

This was the pattern of Market Time operations. Week after week of patrolling and searching, always wondering if the next junk was the one, always alert to the possibility of ambush – suspense, monotony and a flash of action. Task Force 115 made its big actions and killings in 1965 and 1966, and afterwards the number of junks and trawlers taken with large cargoes declined rapidly. Very small cargoes may have got through in sampans, but by and large by the beginning of 1967 they were no longer trying to use the maritime infiltration route. Only at the height of the Tet Offensive in 1968, when the Cong were desperate for munitions, did they go back to using big trawlers. But by this time the US Navy was ready for them. The Cong soon learned that the seaborne route was effectively sealed up – but by then, of course, the Ho Chi Minh Trail was gearing up to operate at full throttle.

1966

EYE-WITNESS

The author, John Morris, served as an infantry squad leader in Nam. He was awarded the Bronze Star, Purple Heart and the Vietnamese Cross of Gallantry.

In the Nam you had a flak jacket, helmet and steel-plated boots. But was that enough?

BODY ARMOUR

Yea, though I walk through the valley of the shadow of death, I shall fear no evil – for I am the evilest sonofabitch in the valley' – Vietnam's version of Psalm 23. That's what was written on the front left panel of the flak jacket I was issued when I first hit the 5th Infantry Division repple-depple at Quang Tri in the Republic of Vietnam.

Like the rest of the olive drab nylon cover of the flak jacket, the words were bleached and faded from too many search and clears in the midday sun. And the letters were leached of their ball-

point blue by monsoon rain, river crossings, rice paddies and gallons of cold sweat.

I wondered whether my predecessor's message to Charlie had worked. It was only later, when I took a closer look, that I noticed the washed-out rust-coloured stains of dried blood smeared on the inside, stains which even the quartermaster's laundry unit could not remove.

The Speedy Four – Specialist Fourth Class – who issued it was a reedy-thin old timer, maybe 20, 21-years-old, who wore the yellowish tinge of hepatitis under his infantry tan – face, neck, arms – and a glaze in his eyes that I came to know as the 'thousand-yard stare'. I asked him if everyone wore flak jackets in the bush.

He looked sorta through me and said: 'Check that.' Meaning, yeah. 'And steel pots?'

He rapped the faded, camouflaged boonie hat on his head with his knuckles.

'Still all there, man,' he drawled. I gathered up my gear from the counter. 'You going back into the field, man?' I said. He slowly rocked his head from side to side. 'Not even, cherry,' he said, meaning no way. 'I'm so short I could trip on a dime.'

Protected from the waist up

Then he cocked his thumb and aimed his forefinger at me as I turned to walk away.

'You're Charlie's meat now boy,' he said. 'Five and wake up' – meaning in five days his tour would be over – 'and I'm in the World.'

Somewhere in the background, I heard the ARVN radio jock, broadcasting from downtown Saigon, sing out: 'Go-o-o-o-o-od morning, Vietnam!' Sure.

Like the rest of us bush rats, I got to know my flak jacket and steel helmet intimately during my 12-month tour. We wore them, sat on them, slept in them, wrote on them, sweated in them, cursed at them and, occasionally, thanked the people who made them for saving various parts of our anatomy.

Neither was really designed to stop an AK-47 round fired point-blank, but they did a pretty good job stopping shell blasts, rocket fragments, snake bites, fire-ant chomps, prickly thorns – unless they happened to get inside – and the odd bullet that had just about run out of gas. Maybe we weren't always the evilest SOBs in the valley, but Uncle Sam sure made the effort to see that we were the best protected – at least, from the waist up and the instep down.

Feet blown to pulp

In Vietnam, infantrymen still travelled on foot. Not out of choice, of course, but that's the way they'd find the VC and the NVA. The bad guys knew this all too well. And if he couldn't keep us out of his territory one way, he'd use another – like punji stakes, sharpened bamboo stakes dipped in human shit. Step on one of those, brother, and your foot would infect, swell up like a balloon and hurt like...well, like a sharpened bamboo stake

FLAK JACKETS

Every frontline soldier in Vietnam was issued with a flak jacket as part of his combat kit. Worn over the upper body, it was designed to give protection against small-arms fire, shrapnel, and flying debris.

Marines usually wore the 'Vest, Armored, M-1955'. Weighing just over 10lbs, this was made from a mixture of nylon and a special protective material known as 'Doron'. First manufactured in 1943 by the Dow Chemical Company, Doron was created by bonding together glass filaments under high pressure, using a resin called methacrylate. This produced a hard yet lightweight material which could withstand ballistic impact at very short range. Twenty-three separate Doron plates, fitted into the overlapping pockets of a sleeveless garment formed the M-1955, with layers of nylon to cushion the impact of a direct hit.

The Army's flak jacket was slightly different. Called 'Body Armor, Fragmentation Protective, Vest M69', it reflected the Army's preference for nylon-aluminium rather than Doron. Protection was built up by means of layers of ballistic nylon filler, sealed in a waterproof vinyl plastic casing. Weighing under 8lbs, it was more comfortable than the M-1955, especially in the heat and humidity of Vietnam, although in both cases the habit of wearing the flak jacket unzipped to keep cool undermined its value.

had been punched through your foot.

So Uncle Sam figured to even out the odds by putting metal plates in the soles of our jungle boots. 'Stomp on stake, hit the plate' was the theory. And it worked...sometimes. Looking back, it was a two-headed viper. Stomp on a .51 toe-popper cartridge booby trap and *kaa-BOOM*!!! That metal plate becomes so much shrapnel, shearing off toes and such. I never had the misfortune.

GIs who rumbled about the countryside in their M113A1 armoured personnel carriers, took one step up the ladder when it came to playing the moving target. At least we could dig a hole and get

in it. That was about the best body armour around – and cheap too. But the clankers faced two problems that boots, helmets and flak vests could not overcome: RPG rockets and landmines.

I saw the after effects of a PG-2 on a 113. That sucker just shaped-charged its way through the side and chopped the TC and his two M60 gunners – along with everything else inside – into coleslaw. Later, Sam experimented with packing foam on the outside of the hulls to cause premature detonation. That worked too, sometimes. But it was all part of the deal – you fired Charlie up and he, in turn, fired you up. Mines, though, weren't part of that contract. I watched it happen once, up near the Special Forces camp at Lang Vei. An ARVN M113 driver pulled off the main road and hit a landmine which must have been boosted. It nearly flipped the track. When the dust settled, we ran over and pulled the guy out of the hatch. The

Below: PFC Sam Hampton, a very lucky US Marine, points to the 0.50 calibre round that embedded itself in his helmet. Bottom: A helicopter crew in their flak jackets preparing for a mission. Opposite page: Toting an M79 grenade launcher, a member of the Riverine Force in the Delta wears a flak jacket.

1966

1966

Above: Body armour and helmets were useful – but not much protection against a direct hit to the face. This Marine has suffered a relatively light head wound – he will soon be on the plane home.

shield to protect him from smallarms fire and booby traps. All he had was his flak jacket and steel pot – his crewman's communications helmet wouldn't stop much more than the falling rain – sandbags piled all over the place and the fervent hope that luck would stay on his side for just one more day.

I guess you could say that luck was part of our combat survival kit, just like the Colt M – 'don't jam on me now, baby' – 16, the boots, the helmet and the vest. But there were a group of guys – the Wild Bunch – who were forever pinching Lady Luck's behind and walking away in the morning without so much as a 'Thank you kindly, ma'am'. These were the chopper jocks – the slick drivers, the guns and the dust-offs. They were warriors from above, the US Horse Cavalry reincarnated, jockeying UH-1 Hueys, AH-1G Cobras, OH-58 Scouts and OH-6 LOHs across our – and Charlie's – airspace. You got to know them by their call-signs: Black Widow, Cobra, Bounty Hunter, Blueghost, Gunslinger, Potato and, if it was your unlucky day, Dust-off.

Magic from the Rangers

Yeah, they were good all right. Flare that bird right into your hot LZ – green AK tracer, RPG rockets and .51 cal rounds ripping up the shrubbery – load on the wounded, kick out some ammo, then 30 minutes later come back and do it all over again. A lotta those guys didn't make it. Their OD bumblebees were fast, but they were Chuck's favourite target. And only Plexiglas and thin skin between them and the apocalypse.

Weight was their biggest problem. You couldn't pack a slick full of sandbags or armour plate and expect it to fly worth a damn. So they made do with what they had – which wasn't much. The pilots' ceramic armour seats would stop anything up to a .30 cal round. But it only covered their back, butt and part of their side. Up front, where it counted, they had to rely on chicken plates – a ceramic armour vest covering chest and stomach – and their trusty .45 or .38 dangling between their legs, for obvious reasons. And us riding in back, heading for a red-hot Charlie Alpha – combat assault – in Chuck's backyard? We'd be counting the butterflies doing drop kicks in our guts and sitting on our helmets.

But I guess the best form of body armour I ever ran across in Vietnam was worn by the stone-cold killers of Papa Company, 75th Rangers, working out of Quang Tri. Worn on the left shoulder, it was a semi-circular tab that spelt out the world 'Ranger'.

I got to talking to a tough old Ranger sergeant in from the bush one day, and he spelt it out pretty clearly. 'The tab keeps you cool when it's hot, warm when it's cold, dry when it's wet, and it protects you from every ballistic projectile known to mankind,' he said.

He grinned and winked, slung his CAR-15 over his shoulder and walked away. Hell, it was as good as anything else I'd ever heard about.

blast had turned his legs to something akin to jelly and had bounced him around so hard that every other bone in his body seemed – and probably was – broken.

In other parts of the country though, American clankers had gotten the word. Mines were beaucoup bad news, GI: Numbah Ten. Uncle was short on answers for this one, but the drivers weren't. Sandbags, my boy, and lots of them. Put extensions on the diesel pedals and two steering control levers, pack the driver's compartment with sand and sit topside on the hatch.

This was a trade off. Joe Driver lived to talk about the mine blast, but he didn't have the metal

THE COLT SEMI-AUTOMATIC

Those who mastered the recoil of the Colt semi-automatic pistol had 100 per cent stopping power at their fingertips

During the early years of the Twentieth Century, the US Army was equipped with a Colt 1900 pistol that fired a 0.38in cartridge. When US forces became engaged in counter-insurgency operations in the Philippines, however, the soldiers began to express dissatisfaction with the 0.38in cartridge. Against a determined enemy, it did not possess the stopping power necessary for close-range actions.

Colt had purchased four designs from Browning in 1896 and, when service trials for a new weapon were called for in 1907, Colt began work on a 0.45in calibre automatic gun. The result was the Military Model 1911, a watershed in the development of semi-automatic pistols. The US Army was so impressed with its performance that the M1911 was adopted for service use during World War I.

Combat experience during the Great War led to a number of modifications, including redesign of the grip, an improved manual safety catch and a new mainspring housing. The M1911A1 emerged from these adaptations as one of the most powerful and mechanically reliable handguns ever produced.

Whereas most contemporary pistols employed a receiver stop to arrest the backward motion of the receiver slide, the M1911A1 incorporated a more effective locking system base on interlocking lugs on the barrel and the slide. This enabled the spent case to be ejected and the loading cycle to continue with the minimum of error. By 1941, the M1911A1 was still a standard weapon in the US armed services. The Colt was not without its faults, however, and it had a love-hate relationship with some of the troops. Although the Colt gave 100 per cent stopping power in combat, it had a fierce twisting recoil that often unnerved those unused to handling such a powerful weapon. For many of the wartime troops, the hefty recoil of the Colt made accuracy difficult beyond ranges of 20yds.

Despite the introduction of the 7.62mm M1 Garand

A grunt goes into a tunnel hanging on to his Colt M1911A1.

carbine as a frontline weapon, the M1911A1 was used extensively during the Korean War, and remained the firm favourite of officers and Special Forces during the Vietnam war. Its performance was held in particular regard by the Tunnel Rats, men who understood the value of heavy firepower in small, confined spaces underground.

The usual cartridges for the Colt pistol were the 0.45in ball M1911, the blank M9 and the tracer M26. To these was added the High Density Shot M261, a round that was loaded with steel-shot projectiles and packed a heavy punch.

Although the last M1911A1 came off the production line as far back as 1942, soldiers continued to prefer the Colt over 9mm Parabellum cartridge pistols such as the Browning High Power GP 35. A recent survey revealed that, of the 418,000 M1911A1s still in the US armoury, every last one has been either overhauled extensively or rebuilt at least three times.

In the light of weapons trials held after the Vietnam war, a number of proposals were mooted for an improved pistol. Among these was a design that modified the M1911A1 to take a 9mm cartridge. This new service pistol will probably be known as the XM9. In the meantime, however, companies still produce spares and components for the M1911 series, knowing that the robust Colt semi-automatic will remain in faithful service for some time to come.

M1911A1 SEMI-AUTOMATIC

This profile of the Colt semi-automatic illustrates the backward motion of the receiver slide.

Calibre: 0.45in
Length: 128mm
Weight: 1.36kg
Feed: 127mm
Magazine: 7-round detachable box
System of operation: Recoil, semi-automatic
Muzzle velocity: 252 metres per second

THE BOB H

Left: The star of the show himself – Bob Hope jokes with the audience during his Christmas show. He took a show to Vietnam every year from 1966 to 1970.

Right: An MP tries to remain po-faced while the girls entertain the troops. A bevy of pretty girls was always on tap to tantalise the grunts.

Far right, top: Recon troops from the 1st Infantry Division observing the fun. The grenade rings attached to the hat were a common adornment.

Far right, centre: Anne Margret, film star turned singer displays a neat line in Sixties miniskirt and boots.

Far right, bottom: An enthusiastic response to the entertainment package from the troopers of the 1st Air Cavalry,

A Christmas gift for the grunts – girls, glamour and jokes. In sweltering heat far from home, the Bob Hope Show brought showbiz razzmatazz to the heart of the Nam on an annual round of glitter and tinsel

OPE SHOW

Past midnight at an outpost in the Delta. Suddenly whistles blow and mortar bombs rain down – Victor Charlie is attacking again. By the end of 1966, the Cong were well armed, and had devised deadly tactics

The comrades were like ghosts, an invisible enemy. They would watch the American helicopters circle the landing zone, but would not fire on them. Instead, they would hide themselves deep in the undergrowth. From there, they would watch the imperialist troops land and set off on their hunt. But some men and weapons would stay behind in the LZ.

As soon as the main body of imperialist troops had left, the comrades would swarm in. The Americans would be well-armed, but the Viet Cong would overwhelm them with their numbers. They would strip the bodies of their weapons and disappear back into the jungle.

'Our comrades felt no pity,' one Viet Cong explained. 'They knew they had to kill as many Americans as possible. We had been told to slaughter as many imperialist soldiers as we could

FIGHTING THE VC WAY

since, if the number of American dead mounted, the American people – who dislike this war – would overthrow their government.'

The Viet Cong did not fight to win and hold territory. Even less did they seek large-scale set-piece battles, in which the Americans could concentrate their firepower or use their mobility to reinforce at speed. Instead, the Viet Cong waged the 'war of the flea', thousands of hit-and-run attacks to bleed the enemy dry, exploiting to the maximum those vital weapons of the guerrilla, stealth and darkness.

The Americans said: 'The night belongs to Charlie.' And it was true. They would appear from nowhere, kill and vanish. But the one guiding principle of main-force Viet Cong tactics was to achieve an overwhelming superiority of numbers at the point of engagement: ten to one. In practice, however, a battalion of around 500 men would

Above: Preparing for action. Viet Cong officers were well trained in 'psyching up' their men – as the officer here is doing. Note the whistle around his neck, for maintaining communication and frightening the enemy during night attacks. This band is not a main-force unit – only the officer has an automatic weapon – but it is still capable of the kind of raid that destroyed the fuel dump shown left.

usually attack a US company of 100 to 120 men. Of course, numerical superiority was useless if the Americans could bring heavy firepower to bear. So the guerrillas always got in close, hugging the American positions, denying their enemy the chance to call in artillery fire or close air support.

When an engagement was limited to smallarms and infantry support weapons, the Americans had no superiority of armament. A Viet Cong soldier armed with the superb AK-47 was better equipped for a close-quarter infantry firefight than his US counterpart. And, by the end of 1966, the Viet Cong had no shortage of grenades, mortars, recoilless rifles or rocket launchers.

The Americans believed that the Viet Cong were careless of human life, that their leaders regarded men as expendable and that the guerrillas themselves were fanatics prepared to sacrifice themselves for their beliefs. They heard stories of guerrillas strapping grenades to their chests and hurling themselves as human bombs into American dug-outs, or of Viet Cong charging in waves straight into machine-gun fire, with strange grins on their faces as if drunk with fanaticism.

147

Indeed, the communist forces did use human wave tactics. It was a classic tactic of revolutionary war. A mass of infantrymen would approach as near to the enemy position as possible without being observed. They would then rush forward and overwhelm the defenders by sheer weight of numbers. But, in general, the Viet Cong soldier was no more keen to die than any dedicated and disciplined infantryman. And the tactics they employed showed a predominant concern to minimize casualties through meticulous planning, good intelligence, the exploitation of surprise in attack and a swift withdrawal from the scene of the action.

Slow preparation, quick attack

The Viet Cong fighting method was characterized as 'one slow, four quick'. The slow was all the painstaking preparation that they put into any operation: repeated reconnaissance of the target, the building of a scale model of the objective so that the men assigned to the mission would recognize every feature, rehearsals of the planned attack as part of training, and the placing of arms caches and food dumps in forward areas. The four 'quicks' followed when the operation actually began. First, there was the movement from the base area to the region of the objective, usually in small groups that would only reassemble just before

**Right: A Viet Cong assessment of how near they were to success in 1965, before the US ground forces moved in to arrest the slide.
Below: Well equipped VC main-force troops in Quang Tri Province. These men were well disciplined, and packed as much firepower as equivalent US grunts.**

they were to go into action. Then came the attack itself, where speed was the essence. The third 'quick' was the clearance of vital arms from the battlefield and the retrieval of the dead and wounded. Finally, there was withdrawal. This was always scrupulously prepared as part of the original plan and depended heavily on a detailed knowledge of the local terrain and the position of enemy forces.

Discipline and courage

An incoming intelligence report was the start of most main-force Viet Cong operations. The usual source of intelligence was the local guerrillas, Viet Cong part-timers who worked the land for a living but took time off to plant booby traps, carry out raids on weakly defended targets or reconnoitre US firebases and LZs. Reports would come in to the headquarters of a main-force Viet Cong regiment, indicating a number of potential targets. If the regimental commander liked the sound of one of these, he would send out some of his own reconnaissance personnel to contact the Viet Cong villagers and be taken on a guided tour of the objective. Then, if everything seemed right – the avenues of approach, assault and withdrawal all good – the operation would be authorized, a unit assigned and detailed planning begun.

Soon every man in the chosen Viet Cong unit would know the target like the back of his hand – every defensive installation, building, fuel store, weapon emplacement. And he would know exactly what he personally had to do, the route of advance, his part in the assault, the assembly

point after the fight and the various routes back to base. The Viet Cong soldier was not expected to show imagination or initiative. He was expected to learn his role by heart and carry it out with courage and immaculate discipline.

The objective would often be several days march from the Viet Cong base in the Highlands, or across the border from Laos or Cambodia. To remain unobserved during this advance was essential. The small columns of men would thread their way silently through the jungle, dropping to the ground at the sound of an aircraft. They carried twigs and leaves attached to wire frames on their backs that provided perfect camouflage once the men were flat on the ground.

Once out into populated farmlands, the guerrilla columns marched by night, guided by local guerrillas. In this way the Viet Cong could normally assemble a complete battalion or more near its target without the enemy suspecting their presence.

Attacking by night

The attack itself would began after dark. Sometimes, the Viet Cong would only bombard the objective with mortars, but if they were confident of their superior strength, an infantry assault went in. Again aided by the local guerrillas, the assault force would move up to positions just

Left: The back-up that gave the VC the mobility and logistic support that underpinned communist success. Here, women take the lead in ferrying supplies to VC units in the Delta. Below: Covered by a Soviet-designed 7.62mm RPD light machine gun, communist troops storm into the attack. Close-support weapons like the Degtyarev RPD supplemented the excellent short-range firepower of VC weapons such as the AK-47 assault rifle.

1966

outside the enemy's defensive perimeter. At zero-hour, a barrage of mortar and rocket fire would pound the target and then guerrillas would storm forward, pressing the fight to close quarters.

There was no question of the dedication and aggression of the Viet Cong soldiers in action. Wounded men fought on with smallarms and grenades as best they could, and courage in their struggle was commonplace. But as soon as it was felt that the tactical objectives had been achieved, the order would come to withdraw. The aim was to

deny the Americans time to react, and not to be caught by a counter-blow.

Clearing the battlefield was an important part of any operation. The Viet Cong were quite prepared to risk lives to retrieve dead bodies for proper burial, dragging them from the field by a wire tied to the ankle or by the leather thong many of them wore around their wrists. The weapons abandoned by their own dead or wounded and any enemy arms were gathered up, as other soldiers maintained covering fire. As the withdrawal began, a rearguard took up position to deter any pursuit.

Slipping away into darkness

The assembly point for the retreating force was usually set about 12 hours march from the scene of the action. On occasion, friendly local villages with a well-developed tunnel system offered an alternative, closer hiding place for at least some of the guerrillas. Local village guerrillas were always essential for guiding main-force units during a hurried withdrawal in a populated area, because only they knew how to avoid all the booby traps that littered the pathways. They also had the latest information on enemy patrols and could steer the soldiers clear of potential encounters which had to be avoided at all costs.

One they had reassembled, the Viet Cong would

Above: Veteran anti-French guerrilla Ho Nhet in conversation with young Viet Cong – just the men who could have led the raid that left shattered hulks on a US airstrip (below).

VC WEAPONS

Like most guerrilla armies, the VC started operations with inferior weapons. Some captured French – and even Japanese – rifles, and there were some machine guns still around. But most of these were past their best and ammunition was scarce. During the early years of the insurgency, from the late 1950s to about 1963, the VC's answer was to manufacture their own weapons, using whatever was available. Shotguns were constructed out of water-pipes, and single-shot pistols were put together using pipes, door-bolts and nails. These were extremely crude and were often more dangerous to the firer than the intended victim, but they could be used to capture more sophisticated weapons from the enemy. A favourite ploy was to build punji-stake traps, designed to incapacitate an enemy soldier long enough for a guerrilla to approach, fire his single-shot pistol at close range and escape quickly – with the victim's rifle. The home-made gun would then be passed down the line to another guerrilla, who would repeat the process.

There were limits to the success of such attacks, however. When the ARVN took steps to ensure that individual soldiers were protected by their colleagues, more dependable sources of supply had to be found. The key was the Ho Chi Minh Trail. And, as soon as a link had been forged with the North, more sophisticated Soviet and Chinese (Chincom) weapons could be delivered. These included machine guns, Simonov carbines and, after 1963, AK-47 Kalashnikov assault rifles. Later in their campaign, when the VC encountered enemy tanks and APCs, Chinese-manufactured 57mm and 75mm recoilless guns were also made available, together with mines and RPG-2 or -7 anti-tank and anti-emplacement grenade launchers. Once weapons like that were available, supplemented by captured US or ARVN equipment, the VC could begin to meet their enemy on more equal terms.

VC TACTICS IN ACTION

The Viet Cong were no weekend soldiers as the Americans found to their cost. Here suddenly they are caught up in stage three of the VC's 'one slow, four quick' strategy.

The US Special Forces camp at A Shau was set in the middle of VC territory, near Laos. Nevertheless, the opposing forces had adopted an uneasy policy of live and let live. This changed abruptly in 1966, when the Green Berets heard digging outside the wire. Then a white phosphorus shell signalled that co-existence was at an end.

All night the VC poured shells, mortar rounds and machine gun fire onto the camp. Morning brought the possibility of an allied air strike, but the VC's meticulous planning scored again and low cloud reduced the effect of the Phantom's attack.

Nightfall brought another heavy barrage. Creeping out from their carefully prepared trenches, the VC used Bangalore torpedoes to blast their way into the camp. Machine gun fire and Claymore mines cut down the first wave of VC, but sheer weight of numbers pushed the Americans into the northern corner.

Once again, daylight brought with it mist and low cloud. The Air Force mounted a rescue bid, even though it meant emerging low through the clouds into a hail of VC fire, losing six aircraft.

The Special Forces had fought courageously but had been defeated by careful preparation and weight of numbers in a classic Viet Cong assault.

Once again the night belongs to Charlie as Australian troops search vainly for the enemy.

either return to their base or be sent back into action in support of other comrades.

One aspect of Viet Cong operations that surprised the Americans was their highly efficient chain of command, right up to divisional level. This meant that, although most attacks were on a relatively small scale, the guerrillas were quite capable of mounting more complex operations involving co-ordinated action by different units or formations. For example, one unit would carry out an ambush and withdraw, and then a larger body of guerrillas would move into position to ambush the American force sent out in response to the first ambush. Similarly, if the Viet Cong wanted to conduct a more sustained siege of an American position, they were quite capable of giving battle in regimental strength.

By exploiting their strengths – intelligence, concealment, discipline and dedication – the Viet Cong were often able to force the Americans to fight at a disadvantage, despite their theoretical superiority in firepower and mobility. As long as the guerrillas were able to choose when and where to fight, they could bleed their enemy at will. The only answer for the Americans was to seize the initiative and impose their own style of warfare on Vietnam – if they could.

1966

Above: Suddenly the war seemed so far away. The salt water washed away the jungle rot and turned you back into flesh and blood again. There was beer, reefers and young, willing Vietnamese girls. But even on the beach, and in bed, there were dangers.
Opposite: For men who'd been bathed in blood and mud for months a smoke and a chat on Long Hai beach seemed like paradise.

REST AND

Sun, sand and surf and a few Vietnamese girls in scanty bikinis – but did official R&R go any way to actually meeting the needs of the ordinary grunt?

Everyone who served in the Nam was supposed to get a week's R&R out of country in a place of their own choice. The list was extensive: Singapore, Bangkok, Penang, Hong Kong, Hawaii, Taipei, Sydney and a few more should you be able to pull them. And late in 1966, the system was going full tilt. Most folks also got a three-day pass at an in-country beach resort. There was one at Vung Tau, Cam Ranh, Nha Trang, Qui Nhon, Chu Lai and Da Nang. A lot of outfits set up their own holiday camps within their general TAORs, places where small units could rotate for a little secure down time. Not that any place was really secure in a war where no front lines really existed. During the Tet Offensive of '68, even the mega base and airbase at Cam Ranh was hit. Mortars and rockets had a sneaky way of impacting where the high command least expected.

DID THE IMPACT OF R&R ON THE VIETNAMESE HELP LOSE THE WAR?

The US dollar lined many pockets, but freespending Americans alienated many hearts.

On R&R the American GIs squandered a large amount of money. This infusion of greenbacks produced a boom in the Vietnamese economy. Everybody had jobs. Vietnamese women found jobs as hootchgirls. Boys shined shoes. Bar owners, shopkeepers, waiters and taxi-drivers made small fortunes.

But though the Vietnamese people found employment, they often did not find themselves any better off. The American dollar brought with it 170 per cent inflation. And while the Vietnamese struggled with deprivation, they watched the Americans living in unattainable luxury. This caused untold resentment. Many Vietnamese believed that if the US government had not spent so profligately on amenities for the troops, more could be spent on the victims of the war.

The American's conspicuous consumption greatly offended Vietnamese sensibilities. While bar owners and shopkeepers were raking in the cash, they barely disguised the contempt they felt for the Americans. If the American's boisterous freespending was not bad enough, their indifference to local customs caused an even greater rift.

The Vietnamese puritanical courtship codes stood no chance with the randy GIs. Respectable Vietnamese women were shamelessly harassed.

The prostitution of so many Vietnamese women was seen as a national degradation. Stories circulated of mass outbreaks of impotence among Vietnamese males. They also believed the Americans brought 'shrinking bird disease'. This was said to cause the slow shrivelling of a Vietnamese man's genitals after sexual contact with a woman who had slept with an American.

The VC spread rumours in the villages about American soldiers capturing women and forcing them to become concubines. And American chaplains warned their men to refrain from playing around with Vietnamese women. This, they thought, gave the VC a strong motive for fighting. 'It is one thing to fight for political principles and another to fight to vindicate your manhood,' said one padre.

looking Da Nang Bay itself. Marine facilities had outgrown the gigantic air force base, so a complex – replete with airstrip and helicopter pads – was constructed by the Seabees just ashore, east of Da Nang city. The VC, however, continued to snipe at the facility from the inviolate grottoes.

The beach itself was an idyllic piece of paradise, if only the war hadn't been happening behind the rolling surf. It was five klicks of white sand, backed by gentle dunes dotted with scrub pine and palms. Before the Marines arrived in force, the press who hotelled downtown had daily jeeped across to the south side of a small fishing village. Here, at the 'Pink House', you could lap up fresh fish and frites, beer and soft drinks for only a few piasters. The joint had a minor line in massage, steam and cream, worked out in a couple of back rooms. ARVN troops would take their lucks into the pines on the dunes.

For the press, it was a clean place to work on your tan after covering an operation, considered insecure and therefore off-limits to the US military. However, when Viet Cong frogmen managed to blow the old French bridge across the Da Nang River, isolating Monkey Mountain, the Marines rebuilt it and placed a detachment on guard. China Beach was now secure, the Pink House thrived and boom-boom in the bushes became big business. Reeking of the boonies, whole platoons cruised the sands looking for something to pick up, the free beer coursing in their circuits. Others, too tired to look, passed out on the edge of the water.

The beach blossomed a concoction of umbrellas and furniture. Santa Monica and Coney Island minus the piers. Sea Stallions, 34s and Hueys

RECREATION

Rest and recreation, a tradition hatched during the Korean conflict, had become an established perk of serving in the US military, and a necessary boost to the troops' morale. Later, it was even dangled as a bait to bring in POWs. The small number of VC/NVA prisoners being taken alive was causing concern at all levels of the headquarter's structure. Sick of watching their buddies blown away and mutilated by an unseen enemy and his booby traps, grunts regularly topped anyone they took alive. Intelligence poured down the monsoon drain, thrown into thin air from the back doors of choppers. Division started handing orders down to battalion that they were to start bringing in live enemy. Battalions responded by offering whole companies the reward of in-country R&Rs when their POW counts improved.

China Beach in Da Nang was a Marine enclave stretching between the Buddhist grottoes of Marble Mountain, which Charlie sort of controlled, to the radar-dome topped Monkey Mountain over-

1966

Whether 'catching some rays' (above) or enjoying Saigon (right), off-duty GIs regarded R&R as 'heaven'. Far right: Passing the time of day with a taxi-driver. Below: Military personnel gather to swap tales of combat experience.

thudded along the surf line to rearm and refuel at the pads down the boardwalk. It was like taking a seat in a grandstand to watch young America.

As part of the humanitarian aid, the German Red Cross had docked a hospital ship to serve civilian casualties in Da Nang harbour. The buxom viking nurses were as penned up as the Marines. Their release to China Beach promoted a spectacle best enjoyed by the life-guards on the towers, who vainly blew their whistles as big, black machine gunners and whole squads took on the willing white flesh in the three-foot surf. The salt water really cured the itch of the jungle, the rot recycled back to flesh and blood. The main hazard was the high incidence rate of those off to see the corpsman for treatment of a dose of clap.

At the Aussie R&R camp between Long Hai and Vung Tau, another problem surfaced when a squaddie's penis was neatly sliced by a razor mounted on a cork inserted in a hooker's vagina. However, no-one met the the man or the woman, and the whole thing may have been another of those bizarre beer-born war stories heard wherever grunts take a boozy break from the hot stuff.

The military, both Australian and Vietnamese, kept their facilities on the Pacific side of the peninsula. Lobster from Cap St. Jacques was an Indochinese specialty, with the restaurants as well as the beach stalls serving the tastiest of delicacies. A more refined clientele, including Saigon's chic set, used the place en masse. US enlisted men, discouraged from the town, corralled on the beach. The 1st Royal Australian Regiment was based 10 klicks away in Nui Dat, with the logistics centred on the air field. Their patch of beach was under the flight path, a surf-boat standing off on shark patrol. Each Oz trooper got one tinny of beer for every day spent in the field, and platoons regularly rotated through the cleansing Pacific, passing out on the hot sands. Fronting as truck washes or coffee shops, illicit brothels, bars and massage parlours flourished outside the base gates.

Hairspray, pantyhose and liquor

Three days away from the tensions of combat were usually considered enough to clean up the hearts and minds of the average grunt. An enormous logistic exercise provided all the drug store mod cons to rear area troops, things which boonie bashers rarely saw. Coming in from the field, a unit issued with its MPC script (monopoly money used only on US posts) would hit the PX and then the bars and beach. The Vietnamese were only too happy to barter their services for hairspray, pantyhose, hi-fi and liquor. On the black market, the MPC traded at a deficit of 40 per cent to the green dollar.

Just up the coast at Nha Trang, was where the French had elected to build their villas along the beautiful bays of a tropical coastline. Nha Trang was the centre of the Special Forces and covert activities that had been installed along the front in the old French houses. They dumped their

Above: Hot sun and cold beers. Left: GIs from the 9th Division pose in a trishaw (rickshaw powered by a bike) at Ny Tho. R&R caused problems, however. 170 per cent inflation, prostitution, social disruption and cultural contamination all resulted from this process of 'Coca-colonisation'. Combat troops grew to resent the easy life experienced by the 'REMFs'. Corruption and bribery were rife, with materials such as medicines, clothing, gasoline and construction supplies being diverted from the war effort and into the pockets of profiteers.

discarded double agents in chains in the very same bay where the Volunteer Service Overseas (VSO) provided snorkelling and scuba activities for the grunts and officers. The roads leading out of town to the forward bases were wall to wall shanty truck washes. Nha Trang was never that expensive.

Chu Lai regularly hosted the Vietnam surfing championships on its golden sands. Automatic weapons were spotted to discourage sharks. Three days of booze, sex drugs and rock 'n' roll with no incoming were welcome any time, the next best thing to taking the big bird back to the world.

1966

OCTOBER 66: OPERATION ATTLEBORO

New arrivals in the Nam, the 196th Light Infantry took a real mauling from the experienced communist fighters of War Zone C

When the American troops went to Vietnam, many were straight from boot camp, where they had been taught to fight a very different kind of war. These cherries soon found themselves up against the battle-hardened veterans of the Viet Cong and NVA. The men of the 196th Light Infantry Brigade had been in-country less than a month before they found themselves tested to the limit in the biggest battle of the war so far.

The 196th Light Infantry were fresh. They'd only arrived in the Nam in late August 1966. After establishing a new base camp near Tay Ninh City and several weeks of acclimatization and local patrolling, they were gung-ho and ready to get at the enemy. They did so, at Operation Attleboro. It was to be a baptism of fire.

A good beginning

Attleboro is a town in Massachusetts near Fort Devens, the birthplace of the 196th Light Infantry Brigade. Like many of the designations for US operations, the codename Operation Attleboro, Phase II, is bland and unrevealing. But on the ground it was a bloody and savage battle – the first multi-battalion operation of the war.

In mid-October, the 196th took to the field for extended combat operations. Their aim was to find and destroy Viet Cong storage areas in parts of War Zone C that had received little attention until then. The area was home to the formidable VC 9th Division who shifted quickly on foot from Cambodian sanctuaries into the War Zone C base areas. From there they attacked targets in and near Saigon.

A single boot battalion headed for the boonies first, on 17 October. Its searching rifle companies soon hit pay dirt, finding sampans, ammunition, tunnels, documents and field hospitals. Over the weekend of 29-31 October, they unearthed more than 1000 tons of rice and 25 tons of salt. Giant Chinook helicopters were called in to fly out the food hoards.

Enemy resistance was light, mostly a few rounds of harassing smallarms fire. But reliable

Left: Plunging forward during Operation Attleboro. Inexperience cost the 196th dear during this operation, as many units walked into an ambush. Top: Close support from a 105mm howitzer. Above: Stopping to help the wounded. Right: General William DePuy, who took command of the operation in November.

Left: A halt for a conference during the advance into Indian country by men of the 1st Infantry. Caution paid dividends – as the 196th had found the hard way.

Right, below: Bringing in a captured enemy soldier. The VC fought Attleboro on their own terms, and their resistance surprised the Americans.

in the first bursts. In another half-hour, another six were killed, more were wounded and the medical supplies were dwindling. The company badly needed to move off the LZ into cover, but it was pinned down in the open in the intense heat.

After another 20 minutes, the company commander was killed and Company C's butcher bill was up to 10 KIA and 14 WIA. Bringing his supply officer to assume command of Company C, Meloy himself landed. He took over conduct of the battle.

From a stroll in the sun to search out rice caches, Operation Attleboro was transformed into a multi-battalion battle. For the men of the 196th fighting on the ground, the next three days were unrelieved hell. But the troops and their leaders were fresh and fought hard and well.

Company A landed and moved out towards the enemy positions, and soon came under intense enemy fire. One of the company, PFC Thomas Conners, dived for cover under a blown-down tree. 'What the hell an I doing here?', he thought. Up

intelligence suggested that the VC 9th Division, plus a regiment of North Vietnamese regulars, was in the vicinity. If they could be located and pounded into ground beef, it would be an opportunity to knock them out of the war for a while. On 1 November, Brigadier-General E. H. deSaussure was ordered to commit all three of his battalions to the operation, and he was also sent an infantry battalion from the 25th Division as reinforcement.

Trapped in the elephant grass

On the bright, sunny morning of 3 November, Major Guy S. Meloy and his 400 men went in by helicopter. The idea was for Meloy's battalion to set up blocking positions a few thousand yards north of the two other battalions just committed to the field. Those two battalions would beat the bush, forcing the enemy into Meloy's path. Then all four battalions would press inward.

The first part of the plan went OK. Meloy's Company B flew into the LZ in two lifts. At 0922 they reported the LZ cold – no contact – and Company B began moving out slowly to search the area. The helicopters then flew back to base to pick up Company C, who began to land at 1029 hours. But as the helicopters touched down all hell broke loose. Heavy automatic fire from the woodline blasted them as they unassed from the Hueys. Gunships and air strikes were called in, and the birds went back to pick up Company A as reinforcements.

Caught in the elephant grass of the now-hot LZ, Company C began to hurt. Six men were wounded

WAS BIG BEAUTIFUL?

Attleboro was the model for the large-scale operations of the next year, but did Westmoreland draw the right conclusions?

Attleboro was the largest US operation to date and the first real field test of a new concept of search and destroy. This new strategic corner-stone suggested that multi-battalion operations – rather than the mainly brigade-strength operations involving around 3000 men mounted so far – might provide the key to military victory. During Attleboro, 22,000 US and ARVN troops drove into the VC War Zone C in Tay Ninh Province.

Supported by B-52 air strikes and massive artillery fire support, Operation Attleboro lasted for 72 days from 14 September to 24 November 1966. Initiated by Brigadier-General Edward H. deSaussure's 196th Infantry Brigade (Light), Attleboro eventually drew in the 1st Infantry Division, the 3d Brigade of the 4th Infantry Division, the 173d Airborne Brigade, the 11th Armored Cavalry Regiment and ARVN formations. It apparently resulted in 1106 dead from the VC 9th Division.

But had Attleboro actually proved anything? It had not been without cost. The US forces had suffered 155 dead and over 800 wounded. It had begun with only sporadic contact by deSaussure's brigade, which had been searching for VC supply caches. In one located on 31 October there were documents. These indicated that the VC and NVA forces were nearby. US troops began a sweep through deeper forested areas, but it was the VC who initiated action by ambushing Company C of the 1st Battalion, 27th Infantry. The other US and ARVN units were then drawn in successively as the battalion, then the brigade, struggled for survival. Subsequently, it was concluded that deSaussure's men had cracked under the pressure of their first battle following their arrival in Vietnam in late August. DeSaussure was replaced by Brigadier-General Richard T. Knowles on 14 November. But, by then, the VC had characteristically begun to slip away and all contact was lost the following day. This was a pattern that was to be repeated again and again – it was always the communist forces who decided where and when they would fight. Major-General William E. DePuy, the commander of the 1st Infantry Division during Attleboro and an architect of 'search and destroy', took over the direction of operations from 6 November. After the war, he was to admit of Attleboro: 'We hit more dry holes than I thought we were going to hit. They were more elusive. They controlled the battle better. They were the ones who decided whether there would be a fight.'

It was not a lesson heeded at the time. The VC 9th Division escaped towards the Cambodian frontier to fight again.

ahead, the company's scout dog was hit and began howling in pain.

Conners' platoon was ordered forward again. He and his buddies crawled along the ground, keeping low and clambering over the dead and wounded in their way. In the wild firefight, officers and lead men were hit and downed and other men took up the lead. Conners' squad leader picked up an M60 machine gun and put it into action. When he was hit, Conners took over.

As night fell, the company coiled into a tight perimeter. Without Conners and his M60, they would have been goners. As the VC crawled about the perimeter in the darkness, he loosed off an occasional burst with the pig to keep them off.

Ambushed by the Cong

Two kilometres south of Meloy's life-or-death struggle, Lieutenant-Colonel Charles E. Weddle's battalion had started pressing northwards as per the plan, and when word of Meloy's heavy contact came through, deSaussure urged him to speed up.

For Lieutenant Bob Duffey, a platoon leader in Weddle's Company B, the going was tough. It was hard to hack through the vines and maintain proper security when he didn't even know where the VC positions were. His buddy, Lieutenant Perkins, made the mistake of putting his platoon onto two trails to make faster time. Bad move. The VC waited until Perkins' men were bunched up, then blasted off a Chinese Claymore mine. Thousands of steel fragments slashed outwards, cutting down 24 of Perkins' men, killing him and

several others.

From concealed positions in the ground and above in the trees, the VC veterans gradually pinned down Weddle's green battalion. In the searing heat of mid-afternoon, his men soon became dehydrated. But they fought on, shooting VC troops out of the trees and blasting them in their foxholes.

On 4 November, General deSaussure was given another battalion from the 25th. Its Company C attempted to thread through the thick underbrush to link up with Meloy, but the dug-in VC cut them off. The battalion commander, Lieutenant-Colonel William C. Barott, attempted to break through to his Company C. He was cut down and killed, and his remaining units were pinned down.

Near nightfall Weddle's Company C, under Captain James P. Thompson, began slogging through the zoo to reach the cut-off unit. Movement was slow in the thick second-growth jungle, and darkness found Thompson and his men still plodding forward quietly in the humid blackness. Suddenly, the darkness was shattered by the bright muzzle flashes and chattering of AK-47s and machine guns. Thompson's company had bumped into deep positions belonging to part of the NVA 273rd Regiment.

Thompson's grunts hurled themselves to the ground, returning the enemy fire with their own M16s and M60s, and throwing M26 hand grenades at the enemy muzzle flashes. Murderous enemy fire from all sides kept Thompson's company pinned within a tight perimeter. Throughout the night he moved from man to man, trying to

OPERATIONS AROUND SAIGON

A critical priority for US forces in 1966 was to secure the approach to Saigon from the north and west since the city lay only 30 miles from the Cambodian border and the VC sanctuaries beyond.

The idea was to place American formations in secure bases, then to sweep through the surrounding countryside finding, and killing, VC. In operations during January and February – such as Marauder, Crimp, Mastiff and Mallet – US troops moved out to sweep the VC from areas such as the Ho Bo and Boi Loi woods close to the Michelin Plantation. Things did not always work out as intended.

Crimp, for example, placed the 25th Infantry Division at Cu Chi, astride the strategic Route 1 – but right on top of a massive VC tunnel complex. The vigorous opposition encountered by US forces while sweeping through VC base areas suggested that they might easily be brought to battle. But further operations around Saigon such as Birmingham and Lexington conducted by the 1st Infantry Division in April, brought few significant contacts.

The 1st Infantry Division's (above) operation in Loc Ninh – El Paso I – in May only provoked the VC 9th Division into reaction against the succeeding El Paso II in June on ground of the VC's choosing. The tanks of the 1st Squadron, 4th Cavalry, were successfully ambushed by VC regiments at both Tau-O on 8 June and at Srok Dong on 30 June.

The VC 9th Division pulled back towards Cambodia but, in September, it moved into the Michelin Plantation once more. It was then that the 196th Infantry Brigade initiated Attleboro.

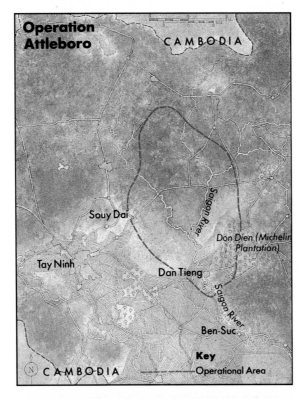

Operation Attleboro

CAMBODIA

Souy Dai

Saigon River

Don Dien (Michelin Plantation)

Tay Ninh

Dan Tieng

Saigon River

Ben-Suc

Key

N

CAMBODIA — Operational Area

Below: A Super Sabre blasts VC positions. The weight of airpower was not always sufficient, however, to root the communists out of their bunkers. Grunts had to go in where it hurt to clear an area.

keep them alert and confident of survival. Although they were surrounded, Meloy's men only 150yds away. It might as well have been on the moon as far as Thompson was concerned. He called down artillery support around his perimeter through the night. And when morning came, his company was still in good order and full of fight though much remained to be done.

The morning of Saturday, 5 November, found the NVA still attacking. Three mass attacks were pressed against Meloy's position in as many hours. All three battalions of the 196th fought their way towards Meloy's main force and the isolated survivors of Thompson's company.

Close to the main battle, men swung machetes and entrenching tools to cut the foliage in their way. They cursed the heat and the clinging undergrowth, and longed for cold water but dared do no more than sip from their depleted canteens. No-one knew when they would find water, or even if it could be flown in.

Silencing a bunker

Sergeant Lester Armstrong's platoon was leading the push from one direction when a VC machine-gun bunker pinned down the lead elements. From the flanks, six more VC poured AK-47 fire into the GIs. Armstrong's men tried to move against the enemy, but their M60 machine gunner became entangled in the vines and couldn't free himself as his buddies moved ahead.

The VC turned their weapons on the trapped gunner. Sergeant Armstrong rushed through the hot fire, grabbed the M60 and turned it on the six VC. He hosed them down with racking fire, killing all six. Enemy grenades arced toward him, but fell short. Fragments slashed open his arms. But he and another man charged the machine-gun bunker, killing its occupants and silencing the gun.

PFC Tom Conners continued to hold his position with the M60 against repeated VC attacks. But in mid-morning he was shot through the shoulder and spine, and someone else took over the hot machine gun.

As more air strikes and artillery pounded the VC and the NVA, their attacks dwindled and died away. By noon on 5 November, resupply and medevac helicopters made it in.

The conduct of the battle was then given to the 1st Infantry Division under Major-General William E. DePuy. He alerted two brigades that day and committed them to battle on 6 November. Over the next two weeks, the 1st Division continued the killing begun by the 196th, and their battle-weary battalions returned to Tay Ninh.

The VC fought tenaciously, inflicting severe casualties on the US units. Then, the survivors of the 9th VC Division melted away into the jungle and trudged back to its Cambodian sanctuaries.

For the 196th, this had been a bloody baptism of fire. Their inexperience at all levels had been exposed – deSaussure was actually relieved of his command. When they next met the enemy, the men of the 196th would be older and wiser.

INTO THE IRON TRIANGLE

1967

January 1967 – as the New Year opens, US forces smash into VC strongholds during Operation Cedar Falls, hoping to inflict the kind of losses that will stop the communist forces in their tracks, destroy their organization and at last provide a springboard for victory

Above: Assisted by an ARVN interpreter, an American officer questions villagers in the Iron Triangle. Moving into the VC stronghold once again, US ground forces had high hopes for Operation Cedar Falls.

1967

Left: As their CH-47 Chinook helicopter hovers overhead, a team of engineers from the 1st Infantry Division climb down a rope ladder carrying chain saws and explosives. Below: Their job is to hack out a landing zone in order that re-supply choppers can continue the huge logistical operation needed to sustain Cedar Falls.

At 0800 on 8 January 1967, the morning quiet of Ben Suc – a large and prosperous village less than 40 miles from Saigon – was suddenly broken by the roar of distant engines. Within seconds, the panic-stricken villagers could make out a swarm of 60 UH-1 helicopters – the greatest number that had ever been flown on one mission – swooping in at low level. Jumping the tree line before coming in low across the paddy-fields, the slicks flew into the centre of Ben Suc itself, throwing the village into a state of terror and confusion.

In less than 90 seconds, the choppers had deposited 420 battle-primed soldiers from the US 1st Infantry Division's 2d Brigade. The deafening clatter of the rotors made normal conversation impossible. Meanwhile, helicopters carrying loud hailers continued to circle the village, proclaiming in Vietnamese: 'Attention people of Ben Suc! You are surrounded by the Republic of Vietnam and Allied forces. Do not run away or you will be shot as VC. Stay in your homes and wait for further instructions.' The history of Ben Suc, which stretched back into the 18th century, was to end that day.

Zippo lighters flashed in the sun

The Americans met little resistance other than the sullen, hostile stares of the people grouped in the village centre. As gunships fired rocket salvoes into the surrounding jungle and jets screeched low overhead carrying their deadly cargo of napalm, interrogations began in the schoolhouse. Within two hours, ARVN interpreters had screened 6000 villagers from Ben Suc and its surrounding hamlets. After ruthless questioning they found 28 possible VC suspects. The evacuation began soon after.

First to be taken away were men between the age of 15 and 45. Herded into Chinook helicopters, they were flown directly to provincial police headquarters for further interrogation and then inducted into the South Vietnamese Army. The women, children and old men were bundled into an assortment of trucks, World War II tracked vehicles and transport helicopters, and taken to a hastily erected refugee camp at Phu Loi. In a camp that lacked proper wood, water or toilets, the relocated villagers were allotted an area of 10 square feet per family. As the people of Ben Suc shuffled towards the rows of makeshift red canopies, they glanced at the sign above the camp's entrance. With more than a touch of irony, it read: 'Welcome to the reception centre for refugees fleeing communism.'

Many of these villagers would never see their homes again. As the last civilian was moved out, every home, shop and restaurant was doused with petrol. Zippo lighters flashed in the sun as the soldiers set light to the thatched roofs. The charred remains were literally razed to the ground by M48 'tankdozers'. To complete the job a massive trench was dug in the town's centre. This was

filled with 10,000lbs of explosives and 1000 gallons of napalm, and ignited with a chemical fuse. Away from the village, bulldozer 'jungle-eaters' set about the task of levelling the terrain. Writing up their reports, the military commanders concluded that the first phase of Operation Cedar Falls had been an unqualified success.

A secure communist sanctuary

The purpose of Cedar Falls was to drive the Viet Cong out of their most important enclave in South Vietnam – the infamous Iron Triangle. Covering an area of 40 square miles, and bordered roughly by the Saigon River to the west, the Thi Tinh River to the east, and to the north by an imaginary line running from Ben Cat to Ben Suc, this communist stronghold was so secure that mention of the Iron Triangle instilled fear, caution and respect into US and ARVN forces. Ben Suc, the western tip of the Triangle, was seen as the key to Viet Cong control of the entire area; it was no secret that its people paid taxes to the VC, harboured their food and supplies and were themselves enlisted to fight.

Attempts to penetrate the Triangle had been made before. In late 1965, the 173d Airborne Brigade had tried and failed to sweep through this hostile sanctuary and, throughout 1966, B-52s had rained more than a million pounds of bombs on its rice paddies, marshes and forests in a vain attempt to quell VC activity. Neither strategy had any noticeable effect on the VC presence and, by the end of 1966, General Westmoreland was growing impatient. To drive the communists out of the area he needed to instigate the biggest operation of the war so far – an assault so devastating that it would uproot the very trees that sheltered the VC from American bombers. So ruthless that it would deny them even the civilian populace upon which their infrastructure was built. Once Cedar Falls was complete, the Iron Triangle was to be made a free strike zone – anything that moved would be bombed at will.

It was planned as a classic 'hammer and anvil' campaign. On 5 January, the 2d Brigade and 196th Light Infantry Brigade, reinforced by ARVN units, were positioned along the Saigon River leg of the Triangle. They were to form the anvil of the campaign – blocking the escape of enemy forces. The hammer blow was to be provided by units of the 1st Infantry Division crashing down from the east. After the 2d Brigade dealt with the sacking of Ben Suc on 8 January, at dawn the following day the 3d Brigade began a massive airmobile assault through the Than Dien

Below: Uprooted from their ancestral home during Cedar Falls, peasants eye their 'liberators' with guarded stares as rations are distributed.

forest to the east. Meanwhile, the 173d Airborne and 11th Armored Cavalry swept west from Ben Cat. Blocking positions on the southeast leg of the Triangle were covered by the 1st Battalion, 503d Infantry, and the 35th Ranger Battalion. Once the hammer started smashing its way from the north-east of the Triangle, air assaults and jungle-clearing operations would see to it that there was nowhere left for the VC to hide.

Where are the enemy?

To the frustration of US forces, however, it never worked out like that. Although Cedar Falls had been planned in an atmosphere of such secrecy that not even the commanding general of the South Vietnamese III Corps was notified until two days before the operation began, word had leaked out to the VC. Knowing that the best foil to any search and destroy operation was simply to pull out, avoid any conflict and wait, the VC commanders had wisely decided to withdraw. For Americans expecting to encounter heavy resistance, the eerie and frustrating experience of so many search

and destroy missions was now repeated on a massive scale – however hard they looked, the enemy was nowhere to be found.

For troops of the 173d Airborne and 11th Armored Cavalry, sweeping across the Triangle and flattening jungle and scrubland in their wake, it was a dispiriting experience. Occasionally, small VC squads would be discovered harvesting or protecting food supplies; but they rarely stayed to fight, instead melting back into the darkness of the forest. Evidence of recent VC presence was always easy to find but, for all the military muscle of this operation, not one major battle was fought during the entire 19 days of its duration. Apart from a number of small skirmishes, the VC had evaded the hammer's blow.

What successes there were came more from beneath the jungle floor – in the complex of tunnels that criss-crossed the Triangle like a subway network. One of the virtues of jungle clearance was that it laid tunnel entrances bare, exposing hidden VC and leading Americans to their supplies. As Lieutnant-Colonel J. Kiernan,

Right: A column of M113s and main battle tanks move into a blocking position just short of a heavily forested area. In the face of such firepower, the Viet Cong had done precisely what US commanders had thought would be impossible – they had simply vanished, leaving supplies and equipment behind them.

Right: Guns at the ready, American troops move through the Iron Triangle, fully expecting to encounter heavy Viet Cong resistance. Having relocated thousands of South Vietnamese peasants, thereby denying the guerrillas a secure infrastructure which they could exploit, the Americans were looking for a clean sweep. As was the case with so many other search and destroy operations, their hopes were dashed by communist stealth and determination.

1967

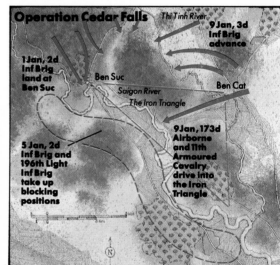

Operation Cedar Falls

1 Jan, 2d Inf Brig land at Ben Suc

Thi Tinh River

9 Jan, 3d Inf Brig advance

Ben Suc

Ben Cat

Saigon River
The Iron Triangle

5 Jan, 2d Inf Brig and 196th Light Inf Brig take up blocking positions

9 Jan, 173d Airborne and 11th Armoured Cavalry drive into the Iron Triangle

N

Above: While the 2d Infantry Brigade and the 196th Light Infantry Brigade move into position to form the 'anvil' of Operation Cedar Falls, a further four US formations prepare to flush out the Viet Cong from their Iron Triangle HQ.

commanding officer of the 1st Engineer Battalion and responsible for bulldozing the area around Ben Suc, recalled: 'I guess it was about 20 acres of scrub jungle...The place was so infested with tunnels that, as my dozers would knock over the stumps of trees, the VC would pop up from behind the dozers. We captured about...six or eight VC one morning. They just popped out of the tunnels and we picked them up.'

The job of scouring the tunnels themselves fell to the 1st Infantry's 242d Chemical Detachment – the fearless 'tunnel rats' who, of all US forces, were best equipped to fight the VC on their own terms.

THE SECRET STRATEGY

Did US planning in 1967 conceal a cynical plan to lay waste large expanses of the Vietamese countryside?

Early in 1967, a Combined Campaign Plan was agreed between the South Vietnamese high command and the US Military Assistance Command Vietnam (MACV), under General William Westmoreland. This confirmed a process that had been under way ever since the US had committed ground troops to Vietnam: henceforth, all offensive operations were to be conducted by US forces, while the ARVN was to restrict itself to looking after pacified areas.

The US commanders hoped that they could use 1967 to build on previous successes. In 1965, they had acted as a shield to protect the ARVN from collapse under pressure from the VC and NVA; in 1966, they had begun to undertake large-scale operations, such as Attleboro in September, which had struck deep into VC heartland, destroying supplies and rattling up what were, on paper, impressive 'body counts'. Now, the intention was to step up the large operations, exploiting the twin advantages of firepower and mobility.

Once an area had been chosen for a clearing operation, forces could be moved into blocking positions quickly by helicopter and large-scale search and destroy missions carried out, all behind a massive shield of air and artillery fire. The US high command hoped, no doubt, that these operations would wear down the enemy.

The question must be asked, however, whether the Americans really believed in the merits of this strategy. Body counts were clearly becoming increasingly unreal by 1967, with the most accurate indicator being the number of weapons collected from the dead bodies, a figure which was often ten times below the claimed number of enemy dead.

In addition, despite huge operations such as Cedar Falls and Junction City the guerrillas were back in business within a matter of weeks. Throughout this phase of the war, the Americans went to great lengths to clear areas, only to hand them back to the enemy soon afterwards.

The usual reason given for this is that despite the massive build up of forces, which had reached 380,000 by the beginning of 1967, Westmoreland never, in fact, had sufficient troops available to conduct offensive and holding operations simultaneously. As soon as one clearing operation was over, the units involved had to be rushed elsewhere, leaving the 'cleared' area to be policed by South Vietamese forces – who in general did a poor job.

This was certainly the major handicap that the US strategy laboured under; and together with the inflation of body count figures it would indicate that the US high command was going down a very unsuccessful road. But it may well be that there was another layer to US thinking – one that was never acknowledged but fits in with the methods actually used.

Villages would be surrounded, searched and levelled before the VC had time to disappear into tunnels or jungle hideouts; defoliants, napalm and high-explosive bombs would be used to denude the countryside; people and livestock would be moved out to more secure areas with speed. Any VC that survived would re-emerge to face a moonscape of devastation in which all the requirements of guerrilla warfare – people, food and shelter – had disappeared. The process of insurgency would then be effectively halted.

Rather than being handed over to the ARVN, many cleared areas were declared Secure Strike Zones (SSZs), within which any living soul was a legitimate target for air and artillery strikes. In such circumstances, renewed VC activity might be welcomed, for if no peasants were allowed into the SSZ, any reported movement was virtually bound to be the enemy. For example, operation Thayer II and Pershing early in 1967 in Binh Dinh Province resulted in the forcible depopulation of three fertile valleys that were strategically important.

But with hindsight, it is clear that the US high-command was failing to apply a coherent counter-insurgency strategy to the battlefield of South Vietnam, and was not facing up to basic problems. As the renowned theorist of war, Karl von Clausewitz, had said 150 years earlier: 'No-one starts a war, or rather no-one in his senses ought to do so, without being clear in his mind what he intends to achieve by that war and how he intends to conduct it.'

Were the American generals gradually creating their own battlefield, one from which hindrances to unrestricted firepower (such as the indigenous population) were being removed? And was this policy being carried out over fertile agricultural areas, destroying Vietnamese rural society? The US high command would deny such charges – but the questions must be asked.

Above: Laying waste to a village.

Moving through an area honeycombed with tunnels and passages, the tunnel rats – armed with silenced pistols to guard against ruptured eardrums – pursued their quarry never knowing what lay in wait behind the next corner. Left: Wearing a gas mask, a rat comes up for a breath of fresh air (left). Below: A dead VC is hauled out of his bunker in the dense bush of the Iron Triangle.

strategic enemy enclave had been decisively engaged and destroyed.'

In reality, however, it was the jungle terrain – or, at least, eight per cent of it – that had been cleared, and not the Viet Cong themselves. Rogers himself was to observe: 'It was not long before there was evidence of the enemy's return. Only two days after the termination of Cedar Falls, I was checking out the Iron Triangle by helicopter and saw many persons who appeared to be Viet Cong riding bicycles or wandering round on foot.' Rogers' observation pointed to a larger truth – the Viet Cong had pulled out of the Triangle as a temporary, tactical manoeuvre. Many tunnels had been destroyed, but even the tunnel rats had failed to grasp the size of the network. Beneath the village of Ben Suc, which had been burned, bulldozed and bombed, up to 1700m of tunnel networks remained intact. Villagers returned to live in their old bunkers, and Viet Cong set about rebuilding their lifeline to Cambodia.

As vegetation grew back over the flattened expanses of jungle, so the Iron Triangle quietly and stealthily returned to communist control. Later, during the Tet Offensive of 1968, the poisoned dagger pointed at the heart of Saigon would be unsheathed.

Armed only with pistols, torches and tear-gas, the rats crawled through almost 12 miles of tunnel during the operation, helping to unearth a massive cache of supplies. Over 7500 uniforms and 60,000 rounds of smallarms ammunition were captured, together with 3700 tons of rice – enough to feed an army of 13,000 VC for a year.

But the tunnel rats' most important find came on 18 January, when men of the 1/5th Infantry discovered a key tunnel complex west of the Saigon River. In what Lieutenant-General Jonathan Seaman, commander of II Field Force Vietnam, called 'the biggest intelligence breakthrough of the war', a treasure trove of thousands of VC secret documents was discovered. They revealed plans for future terrorist assaults, lists of sympathisers and finely detailed maps of Saigon and the Tan Son Nhut airbase. By a stroke of luck, the tunnel rats had struck upon the VC's underground headquarters for the Cu Chi district. After clearing it out, they filled the complex with CS gas, packed it with explosives and blew it to kingdom-come.

Unsheathing the dagger

Operation Cedar Falls was officially terminated on 26 January. Over 2700 acres of jungle had been cleared, 500 tunnels and 1100 bunkers lay destroyed, and 750 'confirmed enemy' dead were reported. The Iron Triangle was now, in the words of General Seaman, 'a military desert'. To prevent any rebuilding, anything that moved was to be considered fair game for American bombers. At the cost of 72 American lives, Lieutenant-General Bernard Rogers, the author of the US Army report on Operation Cedar Falls, could conclude that 'a

CHAPTER 33

AMERICAN GRAFFITI

Was the real truth about Vietnam the crude expletives grunts wrote on helmets and flak jackets?

TO REAlly WANT
TO LIVE, YOU MUS
AlMOST DIE!!!

"ARKANSAS
RAZORBACKS"

1967

Millions of words were written about the war – by journalists pro and anti, by generals in their reports, by politician hawk and dove, and by historians endlessly pouring over the minutia in the vain hope of making sense of it all. The grunts on the ground used a lot fewer words though. And they wrote them on the backs of their flak jackets, the sides of their helmets, the fronts of their tanks, the plating of their APCs.

Pithy or plaintive, vivid or vicious, these careless jottings expressed what the men who fought really thought about the war they weren't allowed to win.

'Fuck communism' and 'Fuck Vietnam' was the grunts' instinctive analysis of the politics of the war. 'Find the bastards, then pile it on' and 'Let's shoot them all and let God sort it out' was their appreciation of the tactics. And whoever this Uncle Ho was, he sure must be a bastard with burning ears. First off, he was a fag. And every motherfucker knew 'Ho Chi Minh ain't gonna win'.

One black soldier had, inexplicably, 'Gooks go home' written on the side of his helmet. Under it, he added poignantly 'Born by accident'. It left the impression that that was the way he was going to die too. Maybe he was just sore that they still wouldn't let nigras into 'The Viet Cong Hunting Club'.

Sinister shark's mouths appeared on the fronts of tanks, Phantoms, Hueys and hovercraft. Many crews christened their hardware. There was a gun called 'Abortion', an APC called 'Mr Clean', a tank called 'The Turtle'. One just had a line of crosses to show how many dinks it had killed – didn't say whether the dinks were theirs or ours.

The Marine lookout post at Con Thien dubbed itself the 'Dry Gulch Observatory' and had a sign that announced 'Performances at 1100 hours and 1700 hours featuring "The 85mm Guns"'. They didn't make the Bob Hope show. It was all part of the grim humour of the war.

The sick and the dead

The APC with 'Good grief' had been hit by a shaped charge. The pathos of Charlie Brown's wry epitaph was unfortunately lost on the men who died inside.

There were many versions of the grunt's prayer: 'Yeah, though I walked through the valley of the shadow of death, I shall fear no evil, cos I am the meanest sonovabitch in the valley.' Other grunts just announced that they were a 'Texas Hippie', a 'Soul Brother' or simply 'Number One'.

As the war progressed and the hopelessness of their situation set in, peace signs sprouted in the unlikeliest of places, along with marijuana leaves. But the last word on the war appeared on a sign stuck on the bullet-riddled carcasses of four dead Vietnamese left to rot on Route 13. It said, in Vietnamese: 'Viet Cong Meat – 300 piasters a kilo.'

169

THE MEN FROM THE NORTH

Hitting the trail south was the beginning of years of suffering and hardship for the men of the NVA. They weren't fanatics, but good, dependable soldiers determined to win the war

Captain Baldridge was on the other side of the hill when he heard the gun-fire. His first attempt to reach Lieutenant Darling by radio was unsuccessful. Then a voice crackled through on the company radio: 'November is hurt bad.' The radio operator, Spec 4 James Ellis, was using Darling's codename. It was his last transmission. All but one of the lieutenant's men were now dead.

Though seriously wounded, PFC Robert J. Bickel was able to crawl towards his platoon. But his cries for assistance drew not only the attention of his buddies, but also that of a small green-clad enemy soldier who emerged from behind a tree, levelled his AK-47 and shot him stone dead.

Captain Baldridge moved forward to the top of the hill. From there, he could hear the gooks laughing and shouting below. Lieutenant Darling and his men had been hit 30 or 40yds down from the perimeter. Three GIs had gone down to avenge PFC Bickel. They were in trouble. Having struck down Darling's men, the enemy did not fade. They turned their fire on these three soldiers, wounding all of them. Taking cover in a bomb crater, the wounded men exchanged fire until two of them ran out of ammunition and the third was about to expend his last magazine.

It was 1967, and these gooks were not the ordinary VC the Americans were so used to coming up against. These were NVA. And the North Vietnamese Army was not just an army like any other. It was particularly unlike the American Army. The difference started at the top. The leaders of the NVA were not essentially military men. They were political leaders, revolutionaries who had given their whole lives to the struggle for national independence. They wanted their army to be a revolutionary army, motivated by ideals of Marxist-Leninism and nationalism. To them, the political ideas in a soldier's head were as important for victory as the gun in his hand.

Opposite: The NVA did not have to rely on hit-and-run guerrilla tactics. They were disciplined enough to mount a First World War-style bayonet charge, going over the top from trenches. Above: The NVA brought with them heavy equipment, including Soviet-made 130mm field guns that could out range the Americans' 105mms. Right: Nguyen Cong Dam (right) was awarded the title 'Destroyed Yank, Intrepid Fighter First Class' for killing 15 American soldiers during an attack on Cun Viet in Quang Tri province.

The core of this revolutionary army was the cadre. Politically motivated, selfless, dedicated, tireless and incorruptible, the cadre member was supposed to be the ideal team-leader wherever he found himself, organizing and motivating the people around him to do whatever the Party wanted.

The military cadres – the officers in the army – were expected to have a correct grasp of the politics of the war and act with no thought of personal advantage. They were backed up by the political commissars attached to each unit. In the NVA, officers and commissars were equally political.

171

1967

Above: Everyone in the North followed the war in the newspapers and on wall posters. Wives and girlfriends of the soldiers searched avidly for news of their loved ones. Opposite top: New recruits march through the streets of Hanoi. There were no burning draft cards here. Opposite: Before they go south, the soldiers have one last shopping spree.

But the average conscript, a peasant farmer in his late teens, was in no sense a communist. The basic beliefs he would have imbibed from his village background were much more ancient – a mixture of Buddhism and Confucianism. But these did not bring him into any sort of conflict with the state. On the contrary, respect for authority was deeply ingrained in village life, where a man was always expected to subordinate his individual interests to the interests of his family. Ho Chi Minh was almost universally revered, and the authority of the Hanoi government was unquestioned. As for Marxist ideology, it was a familiar part of the background of life.

A lot of time was devoted to indoctrinating conscripts in North Vietnam, but much of it was water off a duck's back. An NVA soldier explained: 'When the political commissar gave his lecture...he was standing up there talking, and we were down here pinching one another, smoking cigarettes and fooling around.' Yet the basic message sank in: the revolution had brought independence to one half of Vietnam, the other half still had to be liberated from the yoke of American

imperialism. Once the US bombing of North Vietnam had begun, the NVA recruit took little persuading that there was an enemy who had to be fought. To the ordinary North Vietnamese citizen, the bombing seemed an outrageous act of aggression. It stilled any doubts of the justice of going south to support 'the people's struggle' there.

Never seeing home again

But that is not to say that the NVA soldier was keen to go to South Vietnam. Some deserted when their unit was ordered south, and had to be retrieved from their villages. Most felt apprehension, as well they might, given the high chance of their never seeing their home or loved ones again. But the commissars and officers worked tirelessly to convince the men of the importance of their mission in the South and to raise morale.

The men needed all the morale they could muster to survive the journey down the Ho Chi Minh Trail. Like his southern equivalent in the Viet Cong, the North Vietnamese soldier had lived a frugal existence, light on material comfort and heavy on strenuous labour. But the journey down the Trail was often a nightmare beyond anything he had previously experienced. Each day's march began at half-past-three in the morning and was halted only at the approach of night, with only a short break for lunch.

Malaria was the killer

Carrying an 80lb pack through jungle and over mountains was an arduous routine, even without the snakes, the leeches and the mosquitoes. Rations were rice, a little salt meat or fish, condensed milk, sugar and tea. As long as a man stayed fit, the routine was bearable, but a blister or a twisted ankle could make it agony. Worst of all was malaria. It is reckoned that more than one in ten NVA soldiers died on the Trail, and it was malaria that killed most of them. Enemy air strikes were by comparison a minor worry for the troops.

When men got sick, they not unnaturally asked to be sent back home. But no permission to turn back was ever given. If a soldier was incapacitated, he was left at one of the way stations along the Trail and would join another unit going southwards when he recuperated. Otherwise, the soldier struggled on, aided by his 'comrades' in the three-man cell to which every NVA – and every VC – soldier belonged. These three stayed together, supporting and keeping an eye on each other.

By the time they arrived in the South, the NVA troops were exhausted and demoralized. They had to be given time to recover before being sent into combat. They also had to cope with the discovery that, rather than joining a popular uprising, they found themselves hiding in the jungle to avoid pitched battles with American forces.

When NVA soldiers did come into contact with the South Vietnamese, the experience could be disillusioning. Taught to see himself as a liberator, the NVA soldier expected a hero's welcome. He didn't get it. The southern peasants regarded the Northerners as clumsy and stupid, and overcharged them mercilessly if they tried to buy supplies. Even the Viet Cong were at times uncomfortable allies. The guerrillas and the NVA could trade insults, based on differences of accent or habits, and even the officers often failed to co-operate smoothly – chiefly because the Viet Cong cadres resented newly arrived Northerners assuming control of the struggle.

COMMUNIST WAR AIMS

The North Vietnamese leadership had one overriding aim in its support for insurgency in the South – the reunification of Vietnam under communist control. For the members of the Hanoi Politburo, including Giap (above), the revolution had begun in the 1930s. And despite success against the French in 1954, it would always be incomplete while the country was split along the 17th Parallel.

The question of whether the North had wider war aims has been debated since the early 1960s. It now seems likely that the Hanoi Politburo was bent on pursuing some of the long-term goals that had preoccupied Vietnamese rulers since the middle ages: asserting independence from China and maintaining regional dominance over Laos and the Khmer people of Cambodia. Certainly, since 1975, Laos has had no independent political existence, and Vietnam has fought wars against Cambodia and China.

Before the US main force intervention in 1965, the communists seemed close to success. As the US build-up continued, however, the prospect of immediate victory began to recede, and the objective became to defeat the Americans. To this end, the Hanoi leadership portrayed themselves on the world stage as a peace-loving government bullied by the world's greatest military power. Fortunately for them, the excesses of American military might lent weight to this claim.

As the routine of training got underway, the NVA troops' morale improved. Homesickness remained a constant problem, not unnaturally. Letters took around four months to arrive from the North and even this slow mail service was unreliable. It was a tenuous link with family left behind. NVA troops spent much of their time talking about sweethearts they'd left in the North. Most carried faded pictures of girlfriends they would not see again for years.

Apart from home news, the monotony of jungle

Below: An NVA Captain – he would remove his insignia before going South. There, rank was denoted by the number of Biros in his top pocket.

life might be broken by a visit from an entertainment troupe, performing revolutionary songs and 'improving' plays. There were art classes teaching the boring identikit style of socialist realism. Troops would be expected to write ideological essays under the watchful eye of the political commissar. The troops played volleyball and very occasionally enjoyed a glass of a rice vodka. There would be a sing-song of socialist songs every evening and they would listen to the radio. The BBC World Service was a particular favourite. But the companionship of comrades in the three-man cell was the best defence against low spirits.

The Americans were alien invaders

Once in combat, however, the North Vietnamese were outstanding soldiers. Their American enemies found them tenacious, disciplined and courageous. In practice, Hanoi's 'revolutionary army' really worked.

Although they had no choice but to fight, the NVA was powerfully motivated. This was because endless political sermons sank in, and partly because the Vietnamese are extremely nationalistic. The men knew why they were fighting and had faith in their leaders.

And, unlike the American soldier, the North Vietnamese trooper felt he had the whole of society behind him. Civilians too believed wholeheartedly in the war and believed that they would win. The soldier knew that the folks back home were fighting and suffering just as he was, under the American aerial onslaught. The South may have been surprisingly strange to the northerner, but still he was persuaded that it was his country, and the Americans were alien invaders. This gave him an immense moral advantage over his enemy.

But perhaps most important was the soldier's relationship to his officers. Significantly, no insignia of rank were worn in the NVA. An officer enjoyed few privileges and little separated him from his men. A high proportion showed outstanding commitment to their task. There were no reports of fragging in the NVA.

As the Hanoi leadership dictated, a clear sense of purpose and duty was transmitted down to the ordinary soldier by his officers and political commissar. And this sense of purpose held up against the demoralizing weight of hunger, homesickness and military set-backs. A soldier will fight, and if necessary lay down his life, as long as he does not feel his sacrifice is in vain.

He was never a wall-eyed fanatic, even when he had three wounded American soldiers pinned down in a bomb crater, as Captain Baldridge's men were to discover. As the NVA soldiers closed in on the helpless wounded men, Captain Baldridge called down a mortar barrage. A salvo of 60mm mortar rounds erupted in front of the crater. The NVA withdrew and the Americans made it back to the company perimeter. For them the battle, and probably the war, was over. For the NVA, the struggle would never cease.

WAR OF ATTRITION

Did the politburo decide to buy victory with blood?

The method of warfare practised by Vo Nguyen Giap, the de facto commander of the communist forces, was based on the theories of Mao Tse-tung, developed some 30 years before in China. Mao had set up a model in three stages. First of all, communist cadres would infiltrate a remote rural area and persuade the local population that the revolution was worthy of support.

The second stage was to organize guerrilla bands, which would attack government forces, using hit-and-run tactics. The government troops would be extended to cover lines of communication and key population centres, unable to control the revolt because the guerrillas had the support of the population.

The third stage would come when the government troops were over-extended to the point of collapse. The guerrillas could then come out into open warfare, and sweep to victory. In 1965, the VC had been in the middle of the second phase.

Giap's response to US intervention had been characteristically cautious. He had seen that American firepower and mobility could win the day in engagements like that of the Ia Drang Valley in November 1965. During 1967, he tested US forces and US willpower. NVA main-force units were to move down the Ho Chi Minh Trail in ever-increasing numbers. These were used for two strategic purposes. The first was to see how the Americans would respond to their presence. The second was to inflict casualties in a war of attrition. The young NVA soldiers were live meat going into the mincer – killing Americans in the process. By early 1967 Giap knew he could not win a sudden victory. But he could show the American public that however high Westmoreland raised the stakes, the Vietnamese peasant army would continue to kill young Americans.

KALASHNIKOV AT WAR

In the hands of the VC and NVA, the AK-47 assault rifle proved itself the final arbiter of many ambushes and firefights

Rated by many weapons experts as the best smallarm ever produced, the AK-47 assault rifle was developed by the Soviet Union in the aftermath of World War II. The Red Army had always placed a high priority on firepower, equipping many of its units with sub- and heavy machine guns, but in the German family of assault rifles – the MP43, 44 and StuG44 – the Soviets knew they had found what they were looking for. The high command soon recognised the potential of weapons which, although capable of delivering rapid firepower, were more accurate than sub-machine guns.

Sacrificing longer range for sheer volume of fire, and basing his design around the 7.62mm round that the Germans had used to such great effect, Mikhail Kalashnikov employed the talents of captured German designers in his quest for a weapon suited to the type of close-quarter combat that now dominated modern infantry warfare. The result of his work was the Avtomat Kalashnikov, Model 1947.

In almost every respect, the AK-47 was an exceptional assault rifle. The lack of undue vibration when firing on fully automatic enabled the rifle to shoot accurately up to ranges of 300m, and it could be field-stripped without special equipment since there were few moving parts in its gas-operated firing.

Despite the inherent weaknesses of mass production, the AK-47 was a very robust and reliable weapon. Much of the credit for this must go to the use of good-quality steel pressings and wooden furniture that could absorb any amount of hard use and mishandling.

Often described as a 'peasant's weapon' on account of it being a hall-mark of communist-supplied forces around the world, the AK-47 could be fired on one of two settings – automatic and single shot. However, the fact that the first setting was automatic reflects the underlying philosophy that the Soviets thought it preferable to fire on fully automatic.

A plethora of sub-variants sprang from the original design and, for the most part, the communist forces in Vietnam used the Chinese version of the AK-47, designated the Type 56-1. Unlike the Soviet version, the Type 56 had a permanent folding bayonet underneath the muzzle, but a chrome-lined barrel was standard. The latter greatly extended the life span of the weapon.

The AK-47 was perfectly suited to the nature of the war in Vietnam, and the VC and NVA exploited this weapon to the full in countless firefights and ambushes. Massive US artillery and aerial firepower often proved impotent in a conflict where success or failure depended heavily on close-quarter infantry battles. And for many US soldiers, the distinctive 'clack' of the safety catch being taken off the AK-47 was the only warning they had of enemy presence in the area.

Above: Capable of sustained heavy firepower, the AK-47 became the hallmark of communist forces in Southeast Asia.

AK-47 KALASHNIKOV ASSAULT RIFLE

Length: 880mm
Weight: 4.3kg
Calibre: 7.62mm
Operation: Gas
Feed: 30-round box
Sights: 800 m
Muzzle velocity: 717 m per second
Cyclic rate of fire: 600 rounds per minute

BEFORE AND AFTER

Phan Thi Kim Phuc was just nine when the pagoda she was hiding in was hit by napalm. Her clothes were set on fire. The image of the naked child running from her devastated village was captured on film by Nguyen Kong (Nick) Ut. The photograph he took was reprinted around the world and won him a Pulitzer prize. The girl, Phuc, now lives in Ho Chi Minh City — formerly Saigon — and remembers the incident vividly. She ran for over half a mile before being taken to hospital. Her left arm, her neck and her back all suffered burns and she was in a coma for six months. She was in hospital for 18 months at the time and her treatment was only completed years later when she went to a plastic surgeon in West Germany. Phuc, who is now a pharmacist, still suffers from headaches. She has since visited America where she was treated as a celebrity by the US television networks.

The Vietnam war gave the world some of the most striking — and horrifying — images ever captured by the camera. Yet the moments frozen on film were just single instants within lives that carried on after the war was over. Here are the compelling stories of just three of those people.

French photographer Catherine Leroy captured this picture of Vernon Mike desperately feeling for the heartbeat of a dead friend on Hill 881. Fifteen years later, in 1982, she tracked him down in Prescott, Arizona. He was then 35, had been married three times and was father to several children, one of whom is 15. After the picture on Hill 881 was taken, Mike himself was hit and paralyzed in both legs; he still can only walk with the aid of a stick. His veteran's pension and the small saddler's workshop he has installed in his home brings him in just enough to live, and he is able to indulge his passion for motorbikes. The scars that the Vietnam war was to leave were deep. It is impossible to tell how Vernon Mike's life would have turned out if he had not fought, but many veterans blame the war for the stunted lives they've lived afterwards.

South Vietnam's police chief Nguyen Van Ngoc Loan became notorious after being pictured administering summary justice to a Viet Cong suspect. The photographer Eddie Adams — who won a Pulitzer Prize for this picture — later

discovered that the victim had murdered a police major who was one of Loan's best friends and knifed his entire family. There seems little doubt about the truth of this story. Eight years later, Loan was managing a pizza parlour in Burke, a Washington suburb. Many other prominent South Vietnamese citizens now live in the US, including Prime Minister Ky who now runs a liquor store in Los Angeles. Meanwhile, the unfortunate Viet Cong suspect has earned an eerie immortality.

GETTING DRAFTED

Unpopular, unfair and racially prejudiced? The draft system was how the USA got over two million men into uniform and ready for action

'**B**oy, did I make a mistake coming here.' These were the words running through my mind over and over in July of 1967 at steamy Fort Dix, New Jersey. There I was – 22 years old, 35lbs overweight, two months out of college and a draftee in the US Army waging a physical and emotional struggle to make it through eight weeks of basic training.

It didn't exactly help that the drill instructors (DIs) singled out draftees for particular harassment. Our basic training company consisted of a mixture: guys who'd enlisted in the regular army for three years in order to assure themselves of a job (usually of the non-combat variety); guys who took their chances with the draft's two-year, no-job assurance lottery; and a group of National Guardsmen, undergoing six months of active duty training, who would be returning to civilian life and their six-year National Guard commitment of two-week 'summer camps' and 'meetings' every other weekend.

Learn the spirit of the bayonet

'Leepson, you'd better learn how to fire that weapon,' my platoon sergeant would bark at me on the rifle range as I continually failed to make even a semblance of a tight shot group. 'You're going to be fighting the Cong,' he'd yell, 'not like Jones over here who's headed back home to his honey in Texas'. Or: 'Leepson, you'd better learn the spirit of the bayonet because you're going to Tigerland [the jungle-like infantry training centre in Louisiana] to learn how to kill Gooks, not like Smith over here who's next stop is auto mechanics school in Fort Jackson.'

'What am I doing here?' I wondered as the pounds – and my brain cells – melted away under the hot New Jersey sun.

I was one of the 1,766,910 men who were drafted during the Vietnam war era – from August 1964, when Congress passed the Gulf of Tonkin Resolution giving President Johnson the authority to send in large numbers of troops, to December 1972, the month before the draft ended.

I'd been exempt from the draft for four years following my registration at age 18 with the Elizabeth, New Jersey draft board – one of thousands of local boards staffed by citizen volunteers who chose which young men to draft into the armed forces. The local boards worked with requirements set by the Selective Service System.

I had a student deferment. About a month before I was due to graduate from George Washington University, I received a letter from my local draft board. I was to be reclassified upon graduation. I would then be I-A, top of the list. This was the big one – I knew that the chances were extremely good that I'd soon be going from my college campus to the war zone in Vietnam.

I had several options. I could have joined the Army, Air Force or Navy for three years and gotten a guaranteed non-combat job. 'There ain't no VC in submarines,' the saying went. I could have gotten an exemption by taking a job teaching high school, getting married, or joining the Peace Corps or going on to graduate school. I could have joined the National Guard or the Reserve. I could have declared myself a conscientious objector, pretended I was mentally unstable or homosexual. As a last resort, I could have gone into exile abroad or underground at home. I decided to take my chances with the draft.

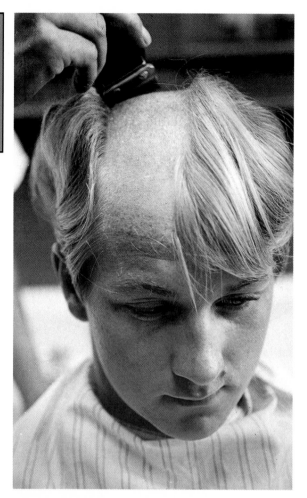

EYE-WITNESS
Marc Leepson was drafted into the US Army on 20 June 1967 and assigned to a personnel company near Qui Nhon.

Some draftees went to extreme lengths to avoid service – one faked a stomach ulcer by consuming a pint of his own blood and then vomiting in the examining room. For others, however, a close crop was the army's way of welcoming its new recruits (right). Men then had the opportunity to meet their new 'buddies' (below). From there, the DI took over (left).

DRAFT CATEGORIES

How you were classified by your draft local board was vital to the future of any young man. The main classifications were:

I-A Available for military service.

I-A-O Conscientious objector available for non-combatant military service only.

I-C Member of the armed forces of the United States, the Coast and Geodetic Survey, or the Public Health Service.

I-D Member of reserve component or student taking military training.

I-O Conscientious objector available for civilian work contributing to the maintenance of the national health, safety or interest.

I-S Student deferred by statute (high school).

I-W Conscientious objector performing civilian work contributing to the maintenance of the national health, safety or interest.

I-Y Registrant available for military service, but qualified for military service only in the event of war or national emergency.

II-A Registrant deferred because of civilian occupation (except agriculture or activity in study).

II-C Registrant deferred because of agricultural occupation.

II-S Registrant deferred because of activity in study.

III-A Registrant with a child or children; registrant deferred by reason of extreme hardship to dependants.

IV-A Registrant who has completed service; sole surviving son.

IV-B Official deferred by law.

IV-C Alien.

IV-D Minister of religion or divinity student.

IV-F Registrant not qualified for any military service.

V-A Registrant over the age of liability for military service.

Left: Destined to see combat in the hills and rice paddies of I Corps, draftees get a taste for mud and hard slog during Marine Corps basic training.

Left: Moving on to the rifle range, raw recruits are shown how to zero sights by a senior instructor. In 1969, a Pentagon survey showed that the death rate among draftees was almost twice that of regulars.

Left: Drill instructors continue their efforts to raise the pain threshold of new recruits. The inequalities inherent in the draft system meant that most draftees came from a working-class background and had little or no education beyond high school. These people were sitting ducks for the draft boards.

'Are you sure you know what you're doing?' That's what the clerk at the local Washington DC draft board asked me on 20 June 1967, my 22nd birthday. I was about to sign a document authorizing my local board to draft me as soon as possible. I had decided that it was better to get the two years over with rather than wait for Uncle Sam to get me. I signed the form. The letter came a week later. I was to report to the Elizabeth draft board at eight in the morning a week hence, where a bus would take me and a group of fellow inductees to the big Armed Forces Examining and Entrance Station in nearby Newark. I was to pack a small bag with toiletries and a change of clothes.

My mother drove me to the draft board. I boarded the bus at eight o'clock. Six hours later I'd passed my physical and had taken an oath swearing my allegiance to flag and country. I was then Private E-1 Leepson, service number US 51979277.

Haircuts, uniforms and inoculation

I joined a busload of fellow draftees for the 90-minute drive to the US Army Infantry Training Center at Fort Dix. We were given military haircuts, uniforms, numerous inoculations, and, after a series of military lectures, we all underwent a battery of aptitude and intelligence tests. At one point I was ushered into a room with a couple of dozen others. An officer told us we'd scored highly on our tests and were therefore eligible to go to officer's candidate school. All we had to do was sign up for an additional year. I said no thanks. Later, I was given the chance to get a guaranteed non-combat enlisted man's job if I'd say yes to a three-year commitment. I said no.

After four days of processing, a group of 200 of us were bused across the sprawling base to our basic training company for eight weeks of what promised to be drill instructor-induced torture. I was assigned to Company A, 3d Battalion, 5th Combat Training Brigade.

As it turned out, only the first couple of weeks were hellish. Once I got into physical shape, the forced marches, the running and the endless drilling were easier to bear. And once I figured out that the DIs' yelling and harassment was a lot of sound and fury signifying almost nothing, my mental burden eased considerably – I learned the spirit of the bayonet, the manual of arms, the rudiments of the M14 rifle and lots of other things. After eight weeks it was time to graduate – to go on to eight more weeks of training in a specific area, something the army called advanced individual training (AIT).

We trainees, as our DIs called us, began getting our orders two days before graduation. My orders came down one night after evening formation. 'Leepson, Smith, Jones, Wilson. Report to Building C for orders,' our DI commanded. The four of us kept up a stream of falsely cheerful banter as we walked off to find out what fate held for us. I was clinging to the hope, voiced once by a friendly DI, that maybe, possibly, I would be lucky enough to

1967

go to artillery AIT. Or, better yet, if the gods were with me, MP school. We'd heard that the day before, a college grad draftee in the first platoon had gotten orders for MP school. I was praying for anything but Fort Polk and the dreaded IIB, the infantryman's MOS (military occupational speciality).

My buddies and I entered Building C, took our seats and waited as graduating trainees from other companies filed in. Then a clerk, a dyspeptic Spec. 4 (a rank that is the same pay grade as a corporal, but carries no authority to issue orders) came into the room. 'Men, I'll be passing out your 201 files,' he announced. 'They contain all your official military records, including your orders. Do not open them until Sergeant Barnes says so.'

They were going to Tigerland

The Spec. 4 handed out the manila folders. We opened them immediately. I saw several pages of mimeographed orders with lots of coded numbers and letters. Then I saw my name on one page. It was underlined in red pencil. This is what it said: 'USATC ENGR FT LEONARD WOOD MO FOR TNG IN MOS 70A10, LEEPSON MARC N.' In plain English: US Army Training Centre, Engineering, Fort Leonard Wood, Missouri, for training in MOS 70A10. I knew what 'MOS' meant, but had no idea what 70A10 stood for. All I'd ever heard of was IIB. As the clerk passed by my seat, I looked up and asked him in a quavering

Above: A chance to write home. According to US authorities, draft policy not only provided manpower for the armed services, it also enabled them to rehabilitate what MacNamara called the 'subterranean poor'. Far from being given valuable new skills, however, those who failed to score at least 31 per cent in the written test were almost certain to be sent into combat. Even men who obviously had no aptitude for combat were given a rifle and sent to Vietnam (right).

Left: Having completed their basic infantry training, new recruits board a plane at Travis Air Force base, heading for Vietnam. Four out of six of these men are black, and could well be the victims of Robert McNamara's 'Project 100,000' – a blatant attempt to pluck underprivileged youths from the streets of America and place them onto the battlefields of a country half a world away.

voice, 'What's 70A10?' I'll never forget his exact words: 'Same as me, clerk.'

But that couldn't be, I thought. Draftees weren't supposed to get to go to clerk school. You had to enlist for that. At least that's what the recruiting sergeant told one of the guys in our outfit who'd joined with a guarantee to get into clerk school. I looked back down at the orders. MOS 70A10, it said. Same as me, the clerk said.

I was going to clerk school. As I pondered this shocking, unexpected turn of events, my mind reeled. It was as if the the sword of Damocles had been lifted from above my head – a death sentence commuted. I looked around in a daze. My three buddies were silent. Then I caught the drift of what had happened to them. They got Tigerland. I immediately retreated into silence.

We left the building and headed back to the company. My buddies talked philosophically about their bad luck. I minimised my good fortune. But once back in the barracks I couldn't hold back any more – I actually jumped up and down and shouted my good news. I called my girlfriend, then my parents. There were tears of joy on both ends of the line, as I recall.

'Combat, clerk typists!'

The next eight weeks of clerk school at Fort 'Lost in the woods' in the Ozark Mountains, were a breeze compared to basic. Our company was made up of about half draftees and half enlistees. Nearly all the drafted guys, like myself, were college grads. We had much more time off than we did during basic. At times, the atmosphere was more like a fraternity house than an army unit.

Our battalion commander was a physical training nut, though. That meant we were constantly doing PT and running long distances before dawn, between classes and in the evenings. I remember one of our marching songs. 'We are typists!' the sergeant would shout. 'Combat, clerk typists!' we'd reply.

Besides running everywhere, our days were filled with classroom instruction on the finer arts of military paperwork. Then, eight weeks later, on 14 November 1967, my newly minted Army clerk buddies and I got our orders. All 200 of us were to report on 13 December to the US Army Replacement Station at the Oakland Army Base in California. From there we were to be assigned to the US Army, Republic of Vietnam, 90th AG Replacement Battalion at Long Binh Post in South Vietnam.

I was one of the lucky ones. I wound up serving my year in Vietnam in a clerical job at the 527th Personnel Services Company in fairly quiet Qui Nhon. We had to pull a lot of guard duty and dodge some sniper fire and an occasional satchel charge, but that was the worst of it.

Oh, I also found out why the army didn't send me to Tigerland. One day, while I was going through my 201 file, I noticed that I'd made a high clerical score and a low infantry score. It was as simple as that.

AN UNFAIR DRAFT?

With US forces now heavily embroiled in combat, the growing number of body bags arriving home prompted some Americans to look long and hard at a draft system that seemed to discriminate between rich and poor

During the Vietnam war, 26,800,000 young American males were eligible for military service under the selective service legislation of 1948. Of these, 8,720,000 volunteered for service and 2,215,000 were drafted. This left 15,980,000 men who never set foot in Vietnam. But, contrary to common belief, only 3.5 per cent of these – little over 570,000 men – were technically 'draft dodgers'. Whether they avoided the call-up by failing to register, or by moving residence abroad, is of little significance compared with the 15,410,000 men who were disqualified or obtained deferment or exemption from military service.

There were those who lodged conscientious objections. Marriage and even self-mutilation were also employed to sidestep the draft, but enrolling for college or graduate education was by far the most popular method used to frustrate the draft boards.

Only 23 per cent of college students were drafted and just 45 per cent of high school graduates. As students were generally the offspring of the more affluent sectors of American society, it soon became clear that the burden of US commitment to Vietnam was being shouldered by the under-privileged.

The inequality of the draft system was exemplified by Robert McNamara's infamous 'Project 100,000'. Initiated in 1966, this was a blatant attempt to use the armed forces as a dumping ground for those of low intelligence.

In the face of mounting protest, some attempt was made to remedy the obvious inequalities in the draft system. Graduate deferment was abolished in 1967, and a random lottery draft was introduced in December 1969. Other exemptions, such as that for college students, had been phased out by 1971. But it was too late to make the draft system equitable – the Nixon administration was forced to introduce a voluntary system of enlistment in January 1973.

1967

DOG FIGHT OVER NORTH VIETNAM

Taking heavy losses over the North, the USAF decided to launch Operation Bolo, and unleash the Wolfpack – the F-4E Phantoms of 8th Fighter Tactical Wing

1967

Above: Robin Olds paints another red star on the side of his Phantom. Left: Sparrow air-to-air missiles ready to be loaded onto the Phantom strike force. Previous page: The instrument lights of the F-4C cast an eerie glow onto the face of the Phantom pilot (main picture). Phantom pilots give the V- sign after two MiG kills.

E arly in the morning of 2 January 1967, Colonel Robin Olds lined up his Phantom with the centre strips on the runway at Ubon Royal Thai Air Force Base and got ready to kick some ass. After signalling to his wingman, he released his brakes and turned both throttles to full afterburner. As he roared down the runway and up into the sky, dozens more Phantoms taxied forward for take-off. The 8th Tactical Fighter Wing – the Wolfpack – was about to leave its lair.

The aim of their operation, codenamed 'Bolo', was to take on the North Vietnamese MiG fighter jets in a head-to-head engagement. For too long now, the Soviet-made MiGs had been a dangerous and versatile threat to American bombers flying over the North. The fighter jocks felt that red tape restrictions were stopping them from hitting back with air strikes on North Vietnamese airfields, leaving enemy fighters free to feint air attacks against incoming US bombers, forcing them to jettison their bombs before running back to base. For the Americans, the time seemed ripe to teach the enemy a lesson. Operation Bolo was planned to catch the North Vietnamese unawares. Fifty-six F-4 Phantoms from the 8th Tactical Fighter Wing (TFW) were to fly into the North, using F-105 Thunderchief radio call-signs, communications, approach routes, refuelling tankers and altitudes. To the enemy, it would appear that a F-105 Rolling Thunder strike force was on its way. They were in for a surprise.

Blocking the MiGs' escape route

The East Force of F-4s from the 366th TFW were tasked with covering two of the airfields and blocking the MiGs' escape route to the North. The West Force, comprising the Wolfpack, would arrive in the area in flights of four Phantoms with five minutes between each flight. It was no easy mission – they would be facing the new MiG-21 Fishbed, with its Atoll air-to-air missiles and superior manoeuvrability.

On the day, things began according to plan and, despite the poor weather, the MiGs took off to intercept the bombers after they had crossed into North Vietnam. Having risen to the bait, the MiGs suddenly found themselves running head-on into a pack of Phantoms. At the head was the legendary Robin Olds. He describes the action:

'At the onset of the battle, the MiGs popped up out of the clouds. Unfortunately, the first one to pop through came up at my six o'clock position. I think this was more by chance than design. As it turned out, within the next few moments, many others popped out of the clouds in varying positions around the clock.

'This one was just lucky. He was called out by the second flight that had entered the area, they were looking down on my flight and saw the MiG-21 appear. I broke left, turning just hard enough to throw off his deflection, waiting for my three and four men to slice in on him. At the same time I saw another MiG pop out of the clouds in a wide turn about my 11 o'clock position, a mile and a half away. I went after him as he disappeared into the clouds.

'I let him have two Sidewinders'

'I'd seen another pop out in my ten o'clock position, going from my right to left; in other words, just about across the circle from me. When the first MiG I fired at disappeared, I slammed full afterburner and pulled in hard to gain position on this second MiG. I pulled the nose up high about 45 degrees, inside his circle. Mind you, he was turning around to the left, so I pulled the nose up high and rolled to the right. This is known as a vector roll. I got up on top of him and, half upside down, hung there and waited for him to complete more of his turn and timed it so that, as I continued to roll down behind him, I'd be about 20 degrees angle off and about 4500 to 5000ft behind him. That's exactly what happened. Frankly, I'm not sure he ever saw me. When I got down low and behind, and he was outlined by the sun against a brilliant sky, I let him have two Sidewinder missiles, one of which hit and blew his right wing off.'

The tactics which Olds Flight had encountered were directed by the North Vietnamese ground controllers. The plan was that two MiGs would attack him from different directions, forcing the F-4s to turn in from the rear encounter and putting the MiGs in position for a tail-on attack.

Within minutes, however, the crews of Olds 02 and 03 had both scored kills and the second wave of Phantoms – Ford Flight – had arrived to join battle. Although James did not get a Mig for himself, he observed the MiG kills and noted the enemy tactic of double attacks from the front and rear. He describes his part of the battle:

'At approximately 1504 hours, my flight was attacked by three MiGs, two from 10 o'clock high and one, simultaneously, from six o'clock low. I didn't see the MiG at six o'clock at first, as I'd already started to counter the attack of the two closing from the front quarter. My rear-seat pilot called me, very urgently, stating that a Mig was closing in and within missile range on my number three and four aircraft. I was a bit hesitant to break off the attack I had already started on the other two MiGs, as I had just seen Olds flight pass underneath us a few seconds before and I had a fleeting thought that this was what my rear seater was seeing. However, I quickly rolled from a left bank to a steep right and observed the low MiG as called. I called a hard right break for 03 and 04. As they executed, the MiG broke left for some strange reason and, for a split second, was canopy to canopy with me. I could clearly see the pilot and the bright Red Star markings.

'I immediately started a barrel roll to gain separation for attack and fired one Sidewinder. As he accelerated rapidly and broke harder left, my missile missed, but he broke into the flight path of my number two aircraft, flown by Captain Everett T. Raspberry. I called Captain Raspberry and told him to press the attack as the two aircraft that I had initially engaged had now swung around into

Above: Major Tran Hanh, a pilot of the Vietnam People's Air Force, pictured after shooting down an F105-D Thunderchief. Left: Colonel Chappie James, leader of Ford Flight, the second wave of Phantoms.

AIR STRATEGY 1967

In 1967, the USAF's bombing still had not stopped the flow of supplies and troops south. So it was decided to step up the bombing of the North, but the first aim was to crush any air resistance by taking out the North Vietnamese Air Force and its Soviet-made MiGs. On 2 January, Operation Bolo began. A force of F-4C Phantoms used new electronic jamming pods and simulated F-105 Thunderchiefs on a bombing mission. They engaged and destroyed seven MiGs without loss. Four days later F-4Cs lured more MiGs into combat by imitating an unarmed reconnaissance mission.

After a six-day truce, the way was clear to move Operation Rolling Thunder into Phase V. Attacks were authorized on new targets – the airfields at Kep, Kien An and Hoa Loc, the Phuc Yen air base and the military facilities around Hanoi and along the Chinese border. All these had previously been off limits. Again the US were escalating the war.

During these attacks 52 enemy planes were shot down, but the USAF suffered heavy losses. 11 F-105s and nine F-4s were shot down by MiGs, and 17 F-105s and three F-4s were taken out by SAMs. In all, that year, 294 USAF aircraft were lost to enemy action and there were 87 operational losses.

Again the F-105 Thunderchiefs – or Thuds – bore the brunt of the fighting and 113 were lost, but they made 22.5 of the 59 MiG kills claimed by the USAF.

A new Phantom, the F-4D, was introduced at the end of May. The AGM-62A Walleye TV-guided missile was first used on 24 August. And the AIM-4 Falcon air-to-air missile scored its first kill on 26 October.

But again, raising the stakes in the war did the Americans little good. The USSR simply replaced the planes lost and the NVNAF's pilot training programme continued to supply replacements. Nor had the escalated bombing any noticeable effect on the North's ability or willingness to fight.

1967

THE WOLFPACK MAKES ANOTHER KILL

3. Since the target is turning at speed, Olds makes a full Vector Roll to maintain his advantage.

2. Olds' path is crossed by second MiG. Olds applies afterburner in order to latch onto target.

4. Having closed on his target, Olds downs it with Sidewinder missiles.

F-4 PHANTOM OF THE 8TH. TACTICAL FIGHTER WING (CODENAME: THE WOLFPACK) PILOTED BY COLONEL OLDS.

1. Col. Olds chases first enemy MiG-21 Fishbed, fires, but misses. MiG escapes into clouds.

range, head-on. I had a good missile growl and fired two AIM-9s in rapid succession at them. I immediately rolled over to realign in fighting wing position on my number two, Captain Raspberry. It was during this manoeuvre that I saw an F-4, which was Olds' lead, blast the wing off an another MiG in another fight in progress a few miles from us.

'I continued down with Captain Raspberry and I remember thinking he was getting a little inside optimum missile parameters. He then executed a rolling manoeuvre, placing him in perfect position. Captain Raspberry fired one AIM-9 which impacted the tail section of the MiG-21. The MiG pitched up violently, then started into a slow, almost flat, spin. I followed in down to cloud top level and observed it burst into flames and disappear into the clouds.'

As Olds and Ford flights got low on fuel and left, the third Phantom pack – Rambler Flight – led by Captain John B. Stone, arrived. Major Phillip P. Combies, the back-seater of Rambler 04 recalls:

'We were flying at 16,000ft sea level and 540 knots true air speed. Shortly after completing the turn to the northwest, we spotted a flight of four MiG 21s in loose formation, two o'clock low at approximately six to eight miles. One or two miles behind were two more MiGs, making a total of six observed. Due to their position "Ahead of the beam", I wondered now if they were being vectored against us or possibly against Olds or Ford Flight, who were initiating their egress from the area.

'We outflew and outfought them'

'As the MiGs crossed in front of Stone, he started in on them, breaking left and down. This caused the flight to slide to the right and I, as 04, wound up higher and right from the remainder of the flight. I went "burner" and held minimum burner throughout the initial engagement. The MiGs broke left and our flight began the engagement.

'My pilot secured, by foresight, a full system lock-on on one of the MiGs. I don't think I pulled over four Gs at any time during the whole battle. Using the Navy tactic of disregarding the steering dot, I pulled lead on the MiG using the reticle. When I felt I was where I wanted to be, I pulled the trigger, released, pulled again, and held. I didn't even see the first Sparrow.

'However, I saw the second from launch to impact. We were about one mile behind the MiG, in a left turn, at approximately 12,000ft at the time of launch. The second Sparrow impacted in the tailpipe area followed by a large orange ball of fire and chute sighting.'

Captain Stone and aircraft 02 both scored kills, bringing enemy losses to seven, nearly half the Vietnamese operational inventory. If the weather had been better, enabling more of the 14 flights of F-4s to engage the enemy, the losses would have been higher. However, the skies were clear of MiGs for the next few months. As Colonel Olds told newsmen afterwards: 'We outflew, outshot and outfought them'.

LOOKING FOR HEROES

Did American public opinion glorify the air war superstars at the expense of the grunts on the ground?

It was one of the many ironies of the Vietnam war that, while US actions on the ground came under mounting public criticism, with soldiers being vilified and abused for their part in an 'immoral war', many of the pilots and crewmen of the air campaign were hailed as heroes in the best traditions of 'honourable' combat. Their operations, particularly over the North, may have been condemned, but personalities such as Robin Olds or Randy Cunningham benefited from the full star treatment. Their photographs appeared on the front cover of mass-circulation magazines and their exploits were described in glowing terms, free from the normal hostility of the press.

In retrospect, this is not difficult to understand. Air operations still took place largely out of the public eye – unlike the ground war, fought under the probing lens of the television camera – so their flaws, disasters and horrors could be glossed over in favour of glorification. In addition, both the aviators and their machines seemed to represent a much 'cleaner', more acceptable image of modern war, made even more impressive by a dependence on technology that seemed to epitomise the superiority of the all-American way of life.

The pilots were invariably better educated and more photogenic than the men on the ground, and their arena of war was not sullied by steamy jungles, booby traps or frightened peasants. After all, it was argued, anyone could tote an M16 or use his Zippo to torch a peasant shack in Vietnam, but it took real brains to fly an F-4 or F-105, dodging the SAMs and manoeuvring to destroy enemy MiGs in one-to-one combat. So it was small wonder, that in a war depressingly devoid of episodes to catch the pride of the American people, the exploits of men whose traditions of combat did not seem to be compromised or depreciated by Vietnam should be exploited to the full.

To the North Vietnamese, though, they were not heroes, they were war criminals.

Left: Colonel Dean Macho, one of the Phantom commanders involved in operations over the North. Opposite above: The air war superstars go into action in their Phantoms, as seen by the much-maligned grunts on the ground.

COL. DEAN MACHO
MAG 12 C.O.

1967

TARGET: VIET

Largest operation of the war to date, Junction City saw the US trying to take out the VC central command apparatus using airborne troops and bringing tanks into the thick of the action

PFC William D. Kuhl was bubbling with nervous excitement. Over the roar of the C-130's engines he was saying: 'My mother is going to be prouder of me than I am of myself.' The rest of the 2d Battalion of the 503d Airborne began checking their equipment. Each was strapped into more than 100lbs of gear – main chutes and reserves, ammo and weapons, radios and grenades, Claymore mines and anti-tank rockets. 'Today we're not just read-

Left: Sitting astride a Sheridan light tank, troops of the 11th Armored Cavalry move towards their jumping-off point. Below left: A brief time-out for men of the 'Big Red One'. Right: An armoured column drives into the horseshoe, attempting to trap the VC.

Americans were growing tired of this hit and run, counter-insurgency war. They wanted to fight a proper war, a conventional war – the type of war they could be certain of winning. So, this time, the hammer that would crush the VC against the airborne troops' anvil would not be infantry, but armour.

The 845 parachutists made their jump and, apart from a few strained ankles, suffered no injuries. Once their defensive positions were established, the armoured divisions swept in.

CONG HQ

ing history – we're making it,' he said. Then he began singing the paratroopers' song: 'Glory, glory what a helluva way to die.' The rest of his buddies fell quiet and curled up inside. The drop zone was approaching and they wondered whether the B-52 strike earlier had really knocked out the VC's anti-aircraft 50-calibres. They were about to make the first – and only – parachute assault in Vietnam. America was upping the stakes again.

The dateline was 22 February 1967 and 249 helicopters were airlifting the equivalent of eight battalions to close the north end of a giant, inverted horseshoe cordon. Westmoreland was determined that, this time, in Operation Junction City, the VC would not be allowed to slip way.

Something else would be different too. The

There was some contact with VC at Prek Klok and Suoi Tre. Then, on 19 March, Lieutenant-Colonel Sidney S. Haszard's 3d Squadron, 5th Cavalry – the 'Black Knights' – moved on Ap Bau Bang.

The Black Knights had arrived in the Nam on 2 February to act as divisional reconnaissance for the 9th Infantry Division. Their task was to keep open the strategically vital Route 13. At 1150 hours on the 19th, the squadron's A Troop, under Captain Raoul H. Alcala, was deployed to secure a fire support base located in flat terrain 1500yds north of the hamlet of Ap Bau Bang on Route 13. A rubber plantation lay to the south with woods to the north and west of the position. Immediately east of the highway was a unused railway line with more woods beyond. The vicinity was a known location for VC, and a trail used by them

OPERATION JUNCTION CITY

Junction City was designed to penetrate War Zone C, engage the VC 9th Division and destroy COSVN and other bases. Armour would be involved in an effort to trap and drive the VC into a blocking cordon. It was also preceded by deception operations. Gadsden, during 2-20 February, placed the 25th Infantry Division around Lo Go to the west of the operational area and Tucson, during 14-17 February, brought two brigades of the 1st Infantry Division to the east around Binh Long. Phase One of Junction City began on 22 February with both divisions and the 173d Airborne Brigade creating a horseshoe blocking position into which the 2d Brigade, 25th Infantry Division, and the 11th Armored Cavalry Regiment drove from the south next day. Phase Two began on 18 March with a shift eastwards by the 1st Infantry Division variously supported by the 11th Armored Cavalry, the 173d Airborne and 1st Brigade, 9th Infantry Division. An unplanned Phase Three followed on 16 April when units under 25th Division control continued the search until the operation ended on 14 May. Contact was limited to five occasions when major VC assaults were repulsed – at Prek Klok on 28 February and 10 March; Ap Bau Bang on 19 March; Suoi Tre on 21 March and Ap Gu on 1 April. Compared to 282 US dead and 1576 wounded, an estimated 2728 VC were killed and 34 captured while 139 defected. Materials taken included 810 tons of rice, 600 weapons and 500,000 pages of documents. But, although hit hard, the VC 9th Division was not destroyed and COSVN was never found. It proved impossible to keep US units other than Special Forces permanently in the area as intended, and an airfield constructed at Katum was simply left unsecured. Deploying 22 US battalions had achieved little. The VC were soon back.

1967

DID COSVN EXIST?

Or was it a projection of the American need to fight a conventional war?

The Central Committee of the People's Revolutionary Party – the purely communist organization existing alongside the supposedly non-communist National Liberation Front in South Vietnam – was commonly referred to as the Central Office of South Vietnam (COSVN). In reality, it was not separate from the Central Committee of the NLF nor independent from Hanoi, but it did serve as a co-ordinating headquarters for communist military and political activity in the South. Consequently, many Americans envisaged COSVN as a miniature Pentagon when, at most, it consisted of a handful of senior communist commanders and staff officers and represented a highly mobile forward command post capable of moving location frequently and rapidly. While Operation Junction City, aimed at its supposed location in Tay Ninh Province, uncovered what was assumed to be COSVN's public information office – complete with 120 reels of motion picture film, its military affairs section, and the printing presses of its propaganda and cultural indoctrination section, it failed to capture anything resembling COSVN itself.

Essentially a shadow flitting from hamlet to hamlet, COSVN had simply moved beyond reach into Cambodia. Subsequently, the US incursion into Cambodia in May 1970 also failed to locate COSVN, and the organization remained a mystery to the end. What is more, there are some who believe that COSVN was never ever more than a co-ordinating office in Hanoi.

had been identified in the woods 2800yds to the north – there had been an earlier battle at Ap Bau Bang in November 1965 when 2d Battalion, 2d Infantry had repulsed the VC 272d and 273d Regiments.

Alcala's command consisted of 129 men with six M48A3 tanks, 20 M113 APCs and ACAVs and three 4.2in mortar carriers. First-Lieutenant Roger A. Festa's 1st Platoon was placed on the west of the perimeter and Second-Lieutenant Hiram M. Wolfe's 3d platoon on the east, while First-Lieute-

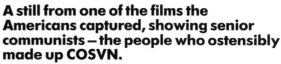

A still from one of the films the Americans captured, showing senior communists – the people who ostensibly made up COSVN.

nant Harlan E. Short's 2d Platoon was to move out of the perimeter at 1800 hours to establish an ambush on the trail to the north. The perimeter was not wired and, instead of being dug in, the tanks and tracks were arranged in circle 'wagon train' fashion.

Mass VC attacks developed

At 2250 hours, cattle were heard being driven across the highway 150yds northeast of the camp and, almost at once, that part of the perimeter was raked by fire from a 50-calibre wheel-mounted machine gun on the railway embankment. Spec. 4 Eugene W. Stevens caught the VC position in his tank searchlight and the machine gun was soon silenced. Wolfe fired on the woods beyond the railway but drew no response. Infra-red scans also failed to detect VC. Then suddenly, at 0030 hours on 20 March, there was an eruption of fire from the west as mortar rounds, rockets and rifle grenades rained down. Festa's track was hit together with two other M113s and two tanks. And, within 20 minutes of the opening barrage, massed VC attacks developed from the south and southwest with diversionary attacks from the northeast.

Alcala requested fire support and at 0050 hours he asked Haszard for a reaction force to be readied if needed. The 3d Platoon, C Troop, 5 klicks to the south along Route 13, and the 1st Platoon, B Troop, 8 klicks to the north, were warned to be ready for action. Haszard also authorized Alcala to withdraw Short's exposed ambush team back

into the perimeter.

Artillery support was laid on from Lai Khe with two airborne observers helping to direct fire on the flashes of VC mortars 1500yds west of the perimeter. Almost 3000 artillery rounds were fired in support during the next six hours.

A Spooky Flareship, armed with miniguns, and a fire team of gunships were also called in, and aircraft delivered over 29 tons of high explosives. But, despite this intense fire support, the VC closed on the south west of the perimeter and

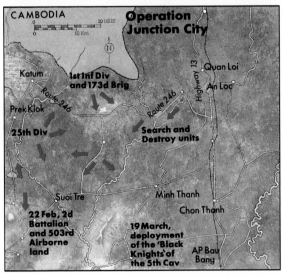

Above left: Part of the VC ammunition captured during Operation Junction City. Far left: The men of Battery C, 2d Battalion, 32d Artillery, load a round into a 175mm gun, giving artillery support during Operation Junction City. Above: Troops take cover as armour slews across the track and pours fire into suspected enemy positions.

forced Festa's men to 'button down'.

It was then that Staff Sergeant Dorren heard an urgent voice from Track 10: 'They are swarming over my track. Dust me with canister.' Dorren hesitated but the appeal came again: 'My people are down, shoot.' Several rounds of 90mm canister fired directly at the track blew the VC away. Dorren did the same for Staff Sergeant Ramos-Rasario's Track 11, and other tanks also fired canister at point-blank range.

When they ran out of canister, high explosive rounds set on delayed-action fuses were fired into the ground to create a ricochet that exploded overhead and showered the VC with fragments. Track 10 burst into flames from a direct mortar hit and two others were also hit. When a track was disabled, the VC would try to remove its arma-

ment while the American priority was to evacuate the crew. Festa and Spec. 4 Albelardo Penedo dismounted under fire to rescue one crew. Then Wolfe's track was hit and his crew had to be evacuated to the medical clearing tent.

Gaps were appearing in the perimeter as vehicles were put out of action, but tanks and tracks were still able to move backwards and forwards – sometimes as much as 20yds – confronting and scattering the attacking groups of VC. But the perimeter had contracted by 0115 hours, Short's platoon fought its way in under heavy fire to plug some of the gaps.

Firing by searchlight

Haszard now ordered the relieving platoons into action. The 3d Platoon, C Troop, arrived at 0127 hours and Alcala ordered it to sweep 1500yds to the south before circling into the southeast of the perimeter. Haszard himself followed up the platoon, but his track was disabled and he had to leap out to attach a tow-line to a tank sent to assist. The 1st Platoon, B Troop, swept around the entire perimeter when it arrived shortly afterwards, guns firing continuously in the beams of searchlights and headlights. The perimeter expanded once more at 0220 hours to accommodate all the new arrivals, and another massed VC attack at 0300 hours was repulsed easily. When VC fire slackened at 0330 hours, the opportunity was taken to evacuate 26 of the more seriously wounded and to re-supply with ammunition.

For the next four hours, under brilliant illumination, a series of 87 sorties with fire support cleared an area of 800yds around the perimeter. Artillery swept the northwest, west and southeast, with aircraft running north to south along

The Vietnam war involved long periods of boredom, or fatigue (right), punctuated by short periods of intense activity. Below: Waiting for medical evacuation.

the highway before switching to running east to west along the southern perimeter. Under illumination, the VC could be seen massing yet again in the south at 0450 hours. But their final assault was crushed by artillery, cluster bombs and napalm followed by 500lb bombs. By 0700 hours the VC had retreated.

The value of fire support

The cavalry had suffered three dead and 63 wounded in the battle for the fire base, while the attackers – identified as the 2d and 3d Battalions, VC 273d Regiment – left 227 bodies on the battlefield and three were taken prisoner.

As in the other engagements when the VC had lost heavily against sustained US firepower, this action seemed to confirm the value of fire support. The tanks had proved their worth. But more significant was that once again the action had been initiated by the VC. The 366,000 artillery rounds and 3235 tons of bombs expended during Junction City worked out at several tons of ordnance for each VC killed.

1967

WINNING HEARTS AND MINDS

Although new plans to win the peasants over were introduced in 1967, it was the gun that still ruled in the countryside of South Vietnam

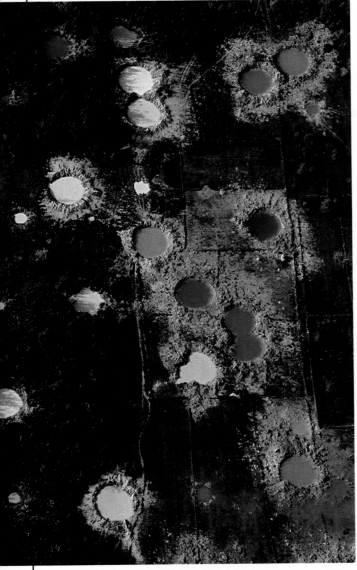

Previous page: 'Pacification' was open to a number of interpretations by the ground troops. It could mean herding villagers into refugee camps (opposite), bombing their fields and homes (left) or individual acts of human kindness (below left).

In June 1967, the 1st Brigade of the 101st Airborne Division went in to clear the Song Ve valley. The 8465 inhabitants were simply told they had to leave the homes and villages that their families had inhabited for centuries. They were told they could take only what they could carry. The plan was to move their 1149 animals with them, but the ARVN soldiers charged with herding them found this duty degrading and began slaughtering the animals instead. Crops were also burned, but the brigade commander, Major-General S.H. Matheson, still felt able to refer to Song Ve as the formation's largest 'civil affairs' project to date and 'an overwhelming success and a model for future operations'. It was certainly the latter.

The military textbooks say that WHAM – winning hearts and minds – is the very essence of pacification and true counter-insurgency. But to the US Army, this was merely the other war, the

TO BUILD OR DESTROY?

Pacification aimed to improve the lot of the villager. Why did it fail?

South Vietnam was an artificial creation of the Geneva agreements of 1954 and was intended to be temporary. It simply was not a nation. There were substantial racial minorities such as the Montagnards and ethnic Khmers, and there were religious divisions between Buddhists, Catholics and other religions. Formerly powerful sects like the Hoa Hao and Cao Dai were not altogether broken by Diem's government and society was further fragmented by the enormous gulf between the urban and rural dweller. The growth of political factions made the state vulnerable and there was no unifying commitment to a national identity. Only the family unit and rural village communities retained any strength and continuity.

But rather than build on family and village as a means of creating wider national unity in the face of communist insurgency, the American and South Vietnamese pacification programmes struck at these local institutions. Large scale resettlement under the Strategic Hamlets Program and its successors – there were supposedly 12,750 such hamlets incorporated in the Hamlet Evaluation System in 1967 – forcibly moved families from their villages and their homes.

The aim was to move the people into new villages which would be surrounded by barbed wire and patrolled by troops. This would prevent communist infiltration. In return, the people would be given plenty of food. Many saw this form of control of the populace as little short of the concentration camp. And for the ancestor-worshipping Vietnamese, the forced move from their family graves and their ancestral fields was a particularly hard wrench. It also resulted in much land being taken out of cultivation.

To add insult to injury, villagers were often required to construct the defences of their new hamlets without payment of any sort. In many cases the material benefits promised by the move were not forthcoming. And those resettled invariably became resentful and unco-operative. People contented and secure in their own environment would have provided a better defence against subversion. Frequently, too, the population was not given adequate protection against guerrilla intimidation and many villagers were forced to flee their new homes not by the VC but by the US reliance upon indiscriminate firepower.

The fact that there were at least 1.2 million persons classified as refugees in the country between December 1965 and June 1967 and possibly 3.5 million people were refugees at one time or another between 1964 and 1969 emphasizes the failure of pacification on the ground. What's more, pacification did offer any real expectation of ending the corruption of the South Vietnamese administration or of giving genuine social, economic or political reforms likely to create a broad popular base for government.

HISTORY OF PACIFICATION

In May 1967, pacification really got underway as a co-ordinated programme when South Vietnam's Revolutionary Development Program was combined with the US Office of Civil Operations to form Civil Operations and Revolutionary Development Support.

It had long been recognized that counter-insurgency could be fought by protecting the population against the guerrillas and giving them positive reasons for supporting a government – the redress of social, economic or political grievances, for example. The French had tried it against the Viet Minh. The Americans used it in the Philippines and the Caribbean, and 'civic action' had been promoted by American advisors in Greece, the Philippines and Latin America during the 1940s and 1950s.

The Diem government began a half-hearted pacification campaign in 1956, but the first significant scheme was the construction of fortified villages – or 'agrovilles' – on strategic highways in April 1959. Population resettlement was then continued in the form of the Strategic Hamlet Program. A variety of projects were implemented in subsequent years, such as the Chieu Hoi – 'Open Arms' – Program in 1963 offering amnesty to VC defectors, and the Hop Tac – 'Co-operation' – Program in September 1964 to ensure maximum co-ordination of effort in seven provinces adjacent to Saigon.

Strategic hamlets stuttered after Diem's death but were revived as New Life Hamlets in January 1964. Hop Tac was overtaken in 1966 by a national Revolutionary Development Program – referred to by Saigon as Rural Construction – based on civic action cadres developed as People's Action Teams in 1965. CORDS gave new impetus to pacification, leading to such programs as the Hamlet Evaluation System and the morally questionable Phoenix Program.

one that was best left to the ARVN and to civilian agencies. Even the Army's Special Forces, trained in the art of winning the confidence of villagers, were soon diverted from pacification to the big unit war. Only the US Marine Corps, with its tradition of civic action in the Caribbean and Central America in the 1920s and 1930s, seemed fully to understand the necessity of winning the population over to the South Vietnamese government. Most Americans simply thought of the villagers as gooks and did not understand their basic human aspirations. For the Americans it was a case of 'grab 'em by the balls and their hearts and minds will follow'.

In Operations Thayer II and Pershing, for example, the 1st Cavalry Division (Airmobile) and a brigade of the 25th Infantry Division aimed to pacify the coastal Binh Dinh Province. This followed earlier operations in the same area which had resulted in 85 new refugee camps with an estimated population of 129,202, as well as an undetermined number of refugees squatting along Route 1.

The new operations were considered a great success. The body count was 1757 – even though this had been accomplished only by the expenditure of 136,769 artillery rounds, 5105 rounds of naval gunfire, 3078 bombs dropped during 171 B-52 sorties and 2.5 million pounds of explosives, including 500,000lb of napalm and 35,000lb of CS gas dropped by other aircraft.

Short-duration, high-impact

Though the object of Thayer II and Pershing had nominally been pacification, this largely consisted of daily medical visitations to refugee camps and a number of concerts which the Cav characterized as being 'short-duration, high-impact' pacification. At the same time, the division resettled the inhabitants of the Kim Son and Soui Ca valleys, while two ARVN battalions also forcibly resettled 5200 people from the An Lao valley. Excluding those moved from An Lao, some 12,000 people were said to have moved 'voluntarily', but only 560 families from Kim Son and Soui Ca and 1886 individuals from the An Lao could officially be found places. The South Vietnamese Air Force then began to destroy the crops in the valleys, to deny supplies to the VC and to ensure that the inhabitants could not return.

Left: Despite individual Americans' best efforts, the children always suffered. Below: Slowly, the pity of it all began to eat into the troops' morale.

The Cav was able to report that 80 per cent of the population in the operational area was free from VC influence – although it was admitted that this did not necessarily imply they were under government control. In fact, the VC were even able to infiltrate the refugee camps and the one at Berin Sac was actually considered unsafe for government visitors.

While Binh Dinh Province was certainly one of the least affected during the Tet Offensive of early 1968, curtailing the influence of the VC there had only been achieved by forcibly removing the population who did not flee to escape the destructive nature of the operations. The valleys had then been turned into free fire zones.

It is hardly surprising that Army debriefing reports placed so little emphasis on the contribution to pacification. In a 31-page report by Lieutenant-General F.C. Weyland, for example, covering operations in II Field Force between March 1966 and August 1968, only four paragraphs were devoted to pacification.

Revolutionary Development

In so far as pacification was practised, it was largely implemented by the ARVN. But the ARVN had also been trained for conventional war and had as little interest in pacification as the US Army, though it agreed to commit 60 per cent of its battalions to Revolutionary Development operations from October 1966. Little use was made of the Regional Forces and Popular Forces even though long-term local security would depend on them. They were poorly armed and treated with disdain by the ARVN.

The real potential of the 'Ruff-Puffs' was only recognized by the US Marines, who began forming Combined Action Platoons (CAPs) consisting of 15 Marines and 34 PFs in the Phu Bai area in late 1965. By 1966 there were 57 CAPs. By 1967 there were 79, tasked with attacking the political infrastructure of the local VC, protecting the government infrastructure and local population, collecting intelligence and training more PFs. MACV, however, was unimpressed with this 'oil spot' technique and the project remained limited through the wider commitment of the Marines to the defence of the northern provinces against direct NVA infiltration.

The efforts of the civilian agencies were no better directed or conceived. The Chieu Hoi – 'Open Arms' – Program was said to have resulted in 75,000 communist defectors to the government by 1967. But there was a suspicion that many of these Hoi Chanh, or ralliers, were seeking only temporary respite from the conflict before slipping back to the VC. And there were those out for simple monetary gain with little or no connection to the insurgents. Once again, it was the US Marines who really made good use of genuine ralliers by forming groups of 'Kit Carson Scouts' in October 1966. In any case, individual operations were often disappointing. The 9,768,000 air-dropped leaflets and 102 hours of aerial loudspeaker

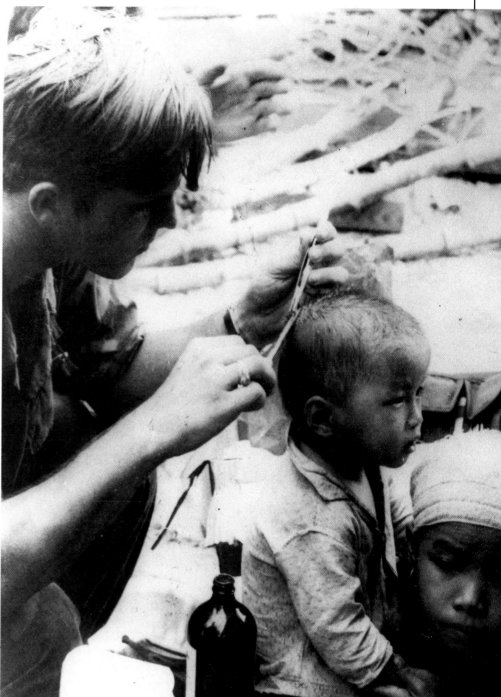

broadcasting brought in only 139 defectors.

An even greater failure was resettlement. Developing from the 1959 scheme of moving the population into secure 'agrovilles', the Strategic Hamlet Program began in January 1962 with Operation Sunrise in three locations around Vinh Long in Binh Duong. The idea was influenced by the success of the 'New Villages' created by the British during the Malayan Emergency (1948-1960) and partly sold to President Diem by Sir Robert Thompson, who headed a British Advisory Mission to South Vietnam from 1961 to 1965. It envisaged government cadres preparing the people for resettlement in secure areas and then moving with them to help them to reorientate.

Bouquet of barbed wire

In practice, the creation of strategic hamlets became an end in itself, hence the apocryphal phrase: 'If you stand long enough down there, they'll throw a piece of barbed wire round you and call you a strategic hamlet.'

By September 1962, it was claimed that 3225 hamlets had been established. By July 1963, in a gross perversion of the original concept now aimed more at extending the political control of the Diem brothers over the countryside rather than winning hearts and minds, there were 7200 with a total population of 8,732,000. But they could not be adequately defended and the government's showpiece strategic hamlet at Ben Truong was burnt down by the VC in August 1963.

In February 1966, the Americans insisted on the more dynamic name of Revolutionary De-

Above left: Security meant living behind barbed wire. Above: It also meant medical treatment and good food.

velopment for the existing Rural Construction Program. The South Vietnamese government complied. They announced that Xay Dung Nong Thon – Rural Construction – would now be translated into English as Revolutionary Development.

By 1967 it was claimed that 67 per cent of the population was 'secure' compared to 42 per cent three years earlier, although it is small wonder that US Defense Secretary Robert McNamara concluded in October 1966 that progress in pacification was actually going backwards. Even the new efforts in a co-ordinated campaign to win hearts and minds in 1967 could not seriously affect this conclusion.

1967

FIREBASES

You're moving up a hillside in the jungle, sweating through every pore, and liable to come under fire at any moment. It's good to know that you've got a firebase in support, able to crash down 105mm rounds within seconds of a call on the radio net

It's a hot, steamy Vietnamese afternoon, temperature 98 degrees fahrenheit, humidity 90 per cent. The 120 troopers of Charlie Company, 3/21st Infantry are humping the boonies, stepping cautiously through scrub brush eight klicks southwest of Fire Support Base West. The company is spread out in platoon combat formation, ready for action. They have been in the bush for 10 days now, methodically working the jungled countryside to keep the enemy off balance. Some days they have patrolled in daylight, checking for signs of enemy activity. At others, they have laid up during the day, hidden from enemy view, with the CO and his platoon leaders moving the men into ambush positions along trails and streams after dark, and then spending the night waiting for Victor Charlie or the NVA.

This afternoon, the CO is shifting Charlie Company from its lay-up position towards the ambush site; the men will trudge to about one mile from the planned site in daylight. Only after full darkness (about 2030 hours tonight) will they slip silently into the selected ambush positions.

This method works well for Charlie Company. In the past 10 days, they have sprung three night ambushes, killed 16 of the enemy and captured several AK-47 rifles and documents. Against this, they have lost two of their own men KIA with four more wounded and evacuated. In two more days, they'll be choppered out of the bush to FSB West for five days on the hill, guarding the firebase. Some grunts say the bush is better, days on the firebase are a grind, endured then checked off one at a time from your calendar.

Nobody in Charlie Company's point squad is thinking of calendars right now. Up front, the point man carries his M16 rifle at the ready. His grip is relaxed, but his finger is on the trigger and the safety is clicked off.

Suddenly he stops and sniffs on the light breeze. His non-smoker's nose has picked up the pungent odour of the Cambodian cigarettes smoked by the enemy troops. He swings his M16 in the direction of the smoke, squeezes off two five-round bursts, shouts: 'Dinks in the bush!' and flops to the ground, where he continues firing into the undergrowth.

Behind him, the squad members spray 5.56mm rounds from their own M16s into the brush, trying to gain fire superiority over an enemy they haven't yet seen. But he's in there somewhere, and where exactly soon becomes clear. From the right

front, 20 yards away in a tree line, comes the high-pitched stutter of AK-47 assault rifles playing counterpoint to the chattering M16s.

From dead ahead, an enemy 7.62mm machine gun adds its heavy rattle, hitting the last man in the point squad, who's been slow to hit the dirt. He jerks and falls, clutching his gut and screaming: 'I'm hit! I'm hit!' His buddies hear his screams and aim forward, laying down fire while the corpsman rushes over to begin first aid. The men shrug off their heavy rucksacks, revealing dark sweaty patches on their jungle fatigues. Another man is hit, then another, the medic does what he can, ripping their own field dressings off their harnesses and pressing them over the wounds. Meanwhile the platoon leader radios the contact and his situation to the company commander.

Fifty yards behind the first platoon, the CO, Captain Jones, estimates the situation: AK-47s and a machine gun mean at least a platoon, maybe a company in that tree line. Maybe bunkers in the bank. He'll develop the contact, lay on artillery and mortar fire, and see if the dinks hang in there. The thought process takes only a second or two. His two other platoon leaders are manoeuvring their men right and left of the first platoon, adding their guns. But the enemy fire is picking up too, so it's time to call for artillery and mortar support and hope their heavy weight will blast those gooks in their holes.

Next to him stands the forward observer (FO) from Battery B, 3/82nd Artillery. He's been walking with Charlie Company for three months, and

Opposite: Once an area of the jungle was cleared, the 105mm howitzers were airlifted in by sky crane. Below: With the firebase established, operational units could go out into the surrounding area. On search and destroy, they would sweep through the countryside until they made contact with the enemy. Then they would radio back the map reference and call down an artillery barrage.

1967

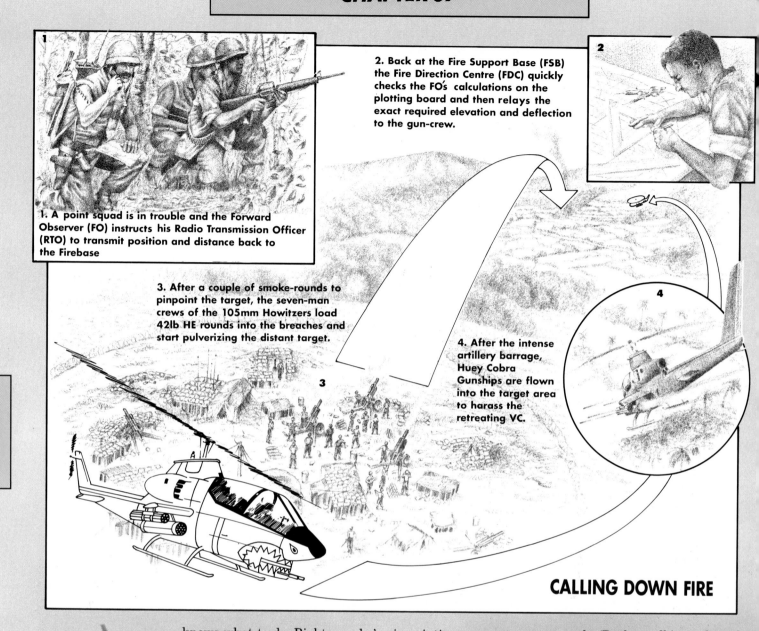

1. A point squad is in trouble and the Forward Observer (FO) instructs his Radio Transmission Officer (RTO) to transmit position and distance back to the Firebase

2. Back at the Fire Support Base (FSB) the Fire Direction Centre (FDC) quickly checks the FO's calculations on the plotting board and then relays the exact required elevation and deflection to the gun-crew.

3. After a couple of smoke-rounds to pinpoint the target, the seven-man crews of the 105mm Howitzers load 42lb HE rounds into the breaches and start pulverizing the distant target.

4. After the intense artillery barrage, Huey Cobra Gunships are flown into the target area to harass the retreating VC.

1967

CALLING DOWN FIRE

knows what to do. Right now he's pin-pointing their position on the map and checking the pre-planned locations for fire missions to cover their route that he arranged earlier in the day. One of the concentrations, labelled BC202, marks a trail junction about 800 metres ahead.

Captain Jones tells the FO 'I want a battery three rounds on that tree line, right now.' 'Roger, sir,' replies the FO. The FO lieutenant's radio operator squeezes the 'Push to talk' switch on the handset of his Prick-25 (AN/PRC-25) radio. He alerts the Fire Direction Centre (FDC) at FSB West to stand by. The FO looks up form his map, calculations finished.

'Fire mission!' orders the lieutenant, and the RTO relays the instructions which come quickly from the FO, in a familiar format.

'Troops in contact. From BC202 drop 500.

Enemy in tree line. HE fuse, superquick and delay. One round, will adjust.' On FSB West, the men dozing in the FDC bunker hear the 'Fire mission' crackle over the radio loudspeaker mounted on a 12 by 12 timber and spring to the alert. One man grabs the radio handset and relays the alarm to the guns. Another picks up his pencil and slaps the clear plastic fan of the plotting board onto the clear acetate covering the map of the area. He picks out concentration BC202, checks the planned calculations for that spot, and begins to radio firing data to the guns.

They're hot in the FDC bunker, but not as hot as Charlie Company are out in the bush. AK-47 bursts are ripping up the leaves and dirt all around the first platoon and M16s chatter back as the point squad lays down return fire. The platoon leader yells for the M60s to swing to his right and set up a base of fire.

The six 105mm howitzers of Bravo Battery, 3/82nd Artillery, shimmer in the hot afternoon sun behind their sandbag parapets. The crews are slumped in whatever shade they can create, then the radio from the FDC blares out: 'Battery adjust.' The men quit whatever they're doing and run for the guns. Three men can fire a 105 if need be, but it's a lot easier when all seven men in the section are present: the gunner, assistant gunner, loader, two ammo bearers, radio man and section chief.

Number Six is the base gun: the fire-direction centre radios the deflection and elevation and tells the crew to load one smoke round. The gunner lays the deflection and elevation on his sight, then peers through it, aligns the crosshairs with the red and white striped stake to his front, and spins the elevating wheel to level his sight bubbles.

When clearance is given, Number Six gun fires, smoke belches from its muzzle and the round soars through the sky towards Charlie Company, eight kilometres distant. A new smoke round is slammed into the breech, ready for the next adjustment. 'On the way,' yells the section chief, and the radioman relays this to the FDC, who in turn transmits it to the FO with Charlie Company in the thick of the action. The FO watches to his front for the burst, which is announced by a puff of bright white phosphorus smoke, followed by a 'pop' sound. The first round is 100 metres high, right above the tree line, but about 200 metres to the right of where he wants it. He radios a correction to the FDC: 'Left 200, repeat range.' The FDC recalculates, and sends the corrected data to Number Six. The gunner re-lays his howitzer, the section chief yells 'fire'.

Meanwhile, the crews of Bravo Battery's other

Below left: This is an M102 105mm howitzer, the newer lighter version of the M2 which was introduced in Vietnam during a war where guns were often transported by helicopter. It is in action on a new firebase. Earth revetments have been bulldozed but the sand bags have not yet been put in place.

DID FIREPOWER BACK FIRE?

America had the firepower – a military machine that was backed by some of the most sophisticated technology in the world. But why, against a much smaller foe, was it ineffective?

Throughout the Vietnam war, the Americans depended on mobility and firepower to engage and destroy a less sophisticated enemy. Military wisdom of the time argued that if the enemy could be located and held in place by ground units, calling in artillery and air power would guarantee his destruction at minimum cost.

This was an attractive proposition, particularly in a war in which human casualties had a political backlash back home, but it did have its weaknesses. The first was that the enemy, knowing the terrain like the back of his hand, had the chance to evade a firepower trap.

A more serious problem was that, in a country where the terrain was difficult, navigation was always a problem. Although experienced ground units could call in artillery support surprisingly quickly, relayed grid references were not always accurate. If the Americans got it right, the results could be devastatingly effective, but the enemy often shifted position or melted away during the time it took to correct firing errors. Time after time, huge bombardments would be lifted to reveal a battle-scarred landscape but little sign of the VC or NVA the barrage had been intended for. As an NVA commander said at the time 'the American infantryman has only a minor role because firepower is relied on to destroy the enemy … However, the Americans have not taken into account our capacity to resist bombing by going underground.'

Finally, in the 'Village War', firepower was notoriously indiscriminate. No-one has yet invented an artillery shell that can differentiate between insurgents and civilians, and although efforts were made by the Americans to avoid calling in artillery fire on innocent villages, some collateral damage was inevitable. Specified strike (or free fire) zones were often seen as the answer, clearing villagers from an area and regarding anyone found in it as enemy forces, but the forcible removal of civilians invariably led to resentment and distrust. In such circumstances, firepower alone was not subtle enough to deal with the problem. The US military machine never really appreciated this fact.

FSB WEST

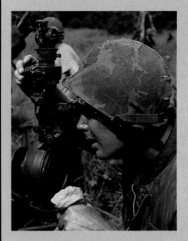

For thousands of years, the hill was another knob in the Annamite Chain overlooking the Que Son valley. Its elevation, 452 metres above sea level, meant it was simply called Hill 452. In November 1967, the operations officer of the 196th Light Infantry Brigade selected Hill 452 to become a fire support base, and, since it was the farthest west in the brigade's area of operations, he named it 'Fire Support Base West'.

First, helicopters flew in to drop off the artillery survey teams who picked the sites for six 105mm howitzers. From the same Hueys, an infantry company alighted to provide security and assess possible threats to the base. While the surveyors worked, they thrashed the bush downhill, clearing fields of fire and spotting ambush and infiltration routes.

Next morning, Chinook heavy lift helicopters brought howitzers, crews, and 200 rounds of ammunition for each gun. Using C-4 plastic explosive, crews blasted holes for bunkers and gun positions into the side of the hill. Others unloaded bales of sandbags from the constant stream of incoming helicopters and began digging up dirt to fill them.

From that day until the US withdrew, life at FSB West (above) was a constant effort in three directions: to be ready to deliver fire immediately to support the grunts in the bush, to improve the quality of life on the hill, and to make it impregnable from enemy attack.

Left: A 105mm howitzer is airlifted into a firebase on top of a 1700ft hill near the Laotian border. Everything for these remote firebases had to be airlifted in and out. But gradually this muddle of guns, ammunition and other equipment became home for the gunners. Below: Shorter range cover was provided by mortars. Here a series of American mortar pits bombard nearby VC positions.

five guns are shifting the trails of their 105s to align them with Number Six, and laying the firing data on their sights. The FDC has told the whole battery to ready three high-explosive rounds for firing. The ammo bearers are laying out the 42lb 105mm rounds and inserting fuzes into the noses.

The FDC orders two types of fuzes as the FO requested: superquick and delay. The rounds with superquick fuzes explode immediately on hitting the first tree branches, spraying thousands of steel shards on the enemy troops down below, whereas those with delayed fuzes pass through the trees without exploding, then burst after they have penetrated a few inches into the ground. This sprays deadly steel horizontally and upwards. It will turn an area into a slaughter-house.

In contact with enemy automatic fire, and with grenades bursting nearby, the FO crouches, waiting for the second marking round. It's burst is dead over the enemy positions. 'Damn good,' he yells, 'battery, three rounds.' And the RTO relays it to the FDC.

A burst of grey, red and green

The six howitzers are standing ready, loaded with HE, when the radio crackles out: 'Battery fire.' They boom out as one. 'On the way' is sent to the FO, and he begins counting the 28 seconds for the impact of the first six rounds. In the pits, the gun crews scramble in a well-rehearsed drill to reload, relay the guns, and fire six rounds again, and again. In seconds, 18 high explosive rounds are en route to an appointment in the tree line.

At the fight, the men of Charlie Company are holding their own. Most of them are about 50-100 metres from the tree line, yelling, firing and hugging the ground all at the same time. Suddenly the trees in front explode in a burst of grey, red and green as the first six rounds explode with a single CRRRUMMMP. Within seconds, the second six slam into the enemy, followed by the third six.

The FO yells: 'On target, give me battery six rounds!' Charlie Company's troops are cheering now, and increase the volume of their fire. Back at the firebase, the crews race with each other, sweating and straining to load and fire six more rounds. In the tree line, 36 more HE rounds slam into the enemy, devastating trees and slashing into flesh, forcing the enemy commander to order a withdrawal before his unit is ground away. As the enemy fire slackens, Charlie Company's Captain Jones calls for helicopter gunships and orders his men to assault the position. His riflemen, grenadiers and machine gunners pick up and move along, firing, chanting and screaming obscenities.

Two things made the difference between victory and disaster for Charlie Company this afternoon: the point man's keen nose and the swift, accurate fire of the howitzers on FSB West. Eight klicks away, the gun crews will clean the guns, return to their bunkers and wait, another fire mission has been completed.

GUARDING THE FIREBASE

The M101A1 Light Howitzer provided battlefield flexibility for US gunners in the rough terrain of Vietnam

Above: The 105mm could be towed, but in Vietnam it was usually airlifted.

Developed from the mortar family of weapons, the howitzer is a very different beast to the artillery field gun. Whereas the latter fires in the low register only (low barrel elevation), the short-barreled howitzer is used primarily in the upper register. By elevating the barrel up to 45 degrees, it can project its shell onto the target in a curved trajectory with great accuracy. This en-until 1939 that an American-made equivalent—the M2A1 105mm Light Howitzer—rolled off the drawing board and onto the production lines. The US Army, having had a huge stock of French 75mm howitzers following World War I, had been slow to develop its own light howitzer, but the M2A1 was destined to become one of the most widely used weapons of World War II.

sive and anti-tank. The M101s were deployed in their thousands during the Vietnam war and proved ideal fire-support weapons when dug in around the perimeter of a firebase. The howitzer remains in US Army service.

Served by a seven-man crew, the howitzer is designed to be towed by a six-by-six truck. It has an initial rate of fire of eight rounds per minute which

105MM LIGHT HOWITZER M101A1

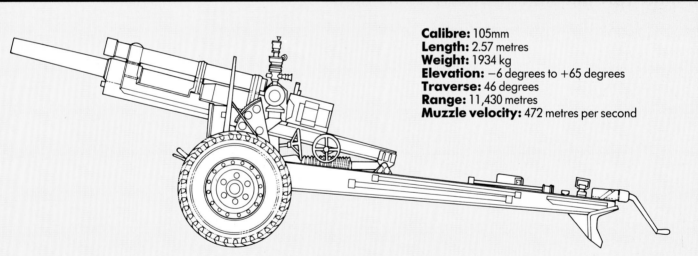

Calibre: 105mm
Length: 2.57 metres
Weight: 1934 kg
Elevation: −6 degrees to +65 degrees
Traverse: 46 degrees
Range: 11,430 metres
Muzzle velocity: 472 metres per second

ables the gunner to engage targets that are obscured by geographical features such as hills. A further advantage of the howitzer is its ability to accommodate variable charges. These two factors provide the howitzer with a great deal of flexibility, allowing it to be used in the front lines of battle, well forward of the field gun.

Western armies have favoured light howitzers with a field gun capability since the later stages of World War I, but it was not

It fired 13 types of ammunition. Although there is nothing revolutionary about its design, this weapon has become the yardstick by which the performance of all other US artillery designs is measured.

Production of the M2A1 continued until 1953, when its designation was changed to 105mm Light Howitzer M101A1. This weapon was capable of firing 20 different types of ammunition, including anti-personnel, high explo-

decreases steadily to the sustained rate of 100 rounds per hour.

The howitzer has a split-trail design with the gun assembly mounted in such a way that the centre of balance is slightly forward of the horizontal sliding breech. Although the two-ton M101A1 is heavy for its calibre, this weight does give the weapon the benefit of extra strength—the barrel and carriage can stand up to heavy use and still maintain a steady rate of fire.

Above: The 105mm in action.

FIGHTING WITH THE HILL TRIBESMEN

1967

They called them 'cidgees' – the hill tribesmen recruited to help fight the VC in the mountain wilderness of central Vietnam

EYE-WITNESS

Much of this article was supplied by Colonel Rod Paschall, who served with US Special Forces unit, Green Berets, during the CIDG programme.

Opposite: Montagnards preparing for action. Right: A cidgee guards the gate of his camp. Liberally festooned with bamboo spikes, the primitive defences guarded against surprise attack.

Lang Vei Special Forces Camp, 0315, 7 May 1967. After a mortar barrage, NVA sappers push bangalore torpedoes into the barbed-wire entanglement surrounding the base. Given accurate information by VC infiltrators who had posed as recruits, the attackers made straight for the Special Forces command bunker and wiped it out, before pulling back with only light casualties.

This assault on Lang Vei was just the latest episode in the bloody war in the hills that had been mounting in intensity since the Special Forces had gone into the Central Highlands in the early 1960s. It was a war that had initially gone well for the Americans, but which was proving difficult and costly as time went on.

As Colonel Rod Paschall, in on the scheme from the very start, described it: 'The idea was Mao in reverse. In other words, we would arm the people so they could resist the Viet Cong. Mao had said that the guerrilla was the fish and the people were the water. Well, the VC were going to have a hell of a time swimming in our pond – if the people of South Vietnam would fight.

'Our mission was to organize, train, and equip the Montagnard tribes of the Republic of South Vietnam. These hill tribesmen comprised only about a million of South Vietnam's population of 18 million. But it was where the Montagnards lived that mattered, not their numbers. First, they occupied more than half of Vietnam's countryside, the Vietnamese preferring the Delta and coastal lowlands where rice was easily cultivated. Second, the hill tribesmen dominated the high plateau region of South Vietnam and that area was the prime strategic target of the communists. Dominate the Central Highlands and you can cut South Vietnam in two.'

This struggle, fought in lonely forest outposts, with American training teams moving silently along hill trails with bands of tribesmen who had barely moved out of the stone age, was a unique aspect of the Vietnam war. Rod Paschall describes how the system worked: 'The Mnong

WERE THE CIDGEES WASTED?

The idea was to involve the ethnic minorities and keep them loyal to Saigon. If the 'cidgees' could have been woven into the American military effort against the Viet Cong guerrillas, the programme might just have worked. But did ancient racial rivalries doom this strategy to failure?

The CIDG programme appeared to offer Saigon the opportunity to win the support of the Montagnards, who lived in the central highlands, as well as other minority groups such as the Khmers in the west and the Chinese Nungs of Cholon city. These ethnic minorities all lived in strategically important areas and were traditionally hostile to the Vietnamese. The programme began promisingly in Darlac Province (December 1961), with the area being declared secure within a year.

At its peak, the programme in its various guises involved 80,000 men in 80 major camps. However, problems arose from both the dilution of the original concept, and Saigon's failure to recognize wider minority asperations. Dilution was a result of the programme's control passing from the CIA to MACV, for MACV was only interested in the contribution the 'cidgees' could make to a big unit war. Thus, although 11,250 cidgees were involved in the Border Surveillance Program by July 1964, they were spread so thinly along the frontiers that they were largely ineffective in stopping infiltration at a time when most VC recruitment was from within South Vietnam.

CIDG units had a high rate of contact with the enemy, but their true value was as local security units, and removing them from their villages virtually turned them into mercenaries. An even greater problem arose as US Special Forces were themselves diverted to other roles, and control of the cidgees was increasingly turned over to South Vietnamese Special Forces (LLDBs). Tension between the Montagnards and the LLDBs built up – over 70 LLDB members were killed in mutinies in four CIDG camps in September 1964, and there were further incidents in 1965. The South Vietnamese were simply unable to gain the same trust and loyalty as the Green Berets, and eventually, at the end of 1970, the CIDG programme was closed down, with 15 camps converting to Regional Force battalions and 19 to Border Rangers.

weapons. Additionally, we would teach some first aid methods and some patrol techniques. I would also supply a few armed men to protect the village during the training if it were necessary. At the conclusion of the training, a radio would be installed in the village and, if the VC conducted an attack, my strike force would respond to a plea for assistance. All of the 20 villages of the district responded favourably to my offer.

'The strike force was a company-sized organization of about 10 men who volunteered to become full-time soldiers. They had to move to my base camp and, unlike the village defenders, the "strikers" were paid a monthly wage.

'Mike' quick-reaction units

In 1965, a profound change came over CIDG operations when the first 'Mike' forces were established. Essentially, these were strike forces that were removed from their immediate village context, and used as quick-reaction units. This was part of the general introduction of US ground troops, and the development of the conflict into a large-scale struggle.

The CIDG units now found themselves engaged in a far more deadly struggle. NVA troops were being sent south in greater numbers, and, because the CIDG groups were a considerable obstacle on their infiltration routes, the NVA pressed home their attacks with considerable resolution, as this description of an attack on Plei Mei camp illustrates:

'The attack was led by NVA sappers carrying satchel charges and bangalore torpedoes, followed by clustered infantry firing assault rifles from the hip. The assault pioneers rammed pipe sections filled with explosives through the barrier wire and blasted it apart in a series of detonations that rocked the camp. Streams of tracer bullets etched red lines across the blackness close to the ground as bunkered machine guns furiously pumped grazing fire into the tangle of barbed wire and struggling soldiers. Tribal riflemen and Special Forces sergeants fired weapons so rapidly that the barrels glowed. Onrushing North Vietnamese infantry staggered and fell in writhing agony as they were pitched into the upchurned dirt.

'The northwestern bunker shuddered under a direct 57mm recoilless rifle hit at 0600, which partially destroyed the structure. Dazed and bloodied defenders, wounded by shell fragments and splinters, reinforced sagging timbers and hauled more ammunition boxes to the smoking machine guns. Two hours later, daylight aerial firepower forced the assailants back into the surrounding jungle. They dug emplacements around the camp within smallarms range and locked it under siege.'

This large-scale action was typical of how the war in the hills was escalating into something the original CIDG programme had not been intended to cope with. Of course, the cidgees were given greater weight of firepower than before; and they gained other benefits from the association with

Above: A Green Beret gives tactical instruction to a group of hillmen armed with M-1 carbines. Left: Coming into a CIDG camp at Ban Me Thout on the Darlac plateau. Air support for isolated camps was essential in 1967, when the NVA began putting them under severe pressure. Opposite top: A Green Beret and a Khmer mercenary on operations at the base of Nui Coto, seven miles from their camp at Ba Xoui. Opposite: The Special Forces who worked with the cidgees often wore non-regulation headgear.

village chief of Doun Don Bak had already agreed to have 12 to 15 of his youths trained and armed by my team, and that was our first task. After a brief but successful defence of the village from a VC attack, we settled down to our plan of providing a village defence system.

'This system consisted of two parts: the strike force and the village defenders. All together, it was called the Civilian Irregular Defense Group programme. The village defenders were recruited by purely voluntary means. The way it worked was that I would take a patrol out and visit an outlying village. I would sit down with the village chief and, conversing in French, I would tell him that if he would agree to defend his village against the VC, I would supply arms and training to a dozen or so of the village men. The training would only take 10 days and would consist of a firing course and a few classes on the maintenance of

THE CIDGS

In January 1967, project Gamma saw self-contained intelligence-gathering hunter-killer groups composed of both Green Berets and 'indigs' operating on VC infiltration routes along the frontiers.

This was the high point of the Civilian Irregular Defense Group (CIDG) Program. The CIDGs, which were composed of Montagnards and other ethnic minority groups, at first came under the juristriction of the Central Intelligence Agency.

The first group was raised in December 1961 by Captain Ronald Shackleton's Special Forces A-Team from Rhade tribesmen around Buon Enao in Darlac Province, and the experiment proved to be a great success. Yet the US Special Forces personnel remained essentially advisors – the CIDG was commanded in the field by the Luong Dac Biet (LLDB) – the South Vietnamese Special Forces – until 1966.

Tribesmen were either trained as hamlet militia or Camp Strike Force units, and by 1963 there were 18,000 strike force and 43,000 militia under US command. The CIA handed over control of the CIDG programme to MACV on 1 July 1963, and this led to a more aggressive role which began with the Border Surveillance Program of October 1963.

From October 1964, quick reaction Mike Force – later Mobile Strike Force – elements were also raised and eventually numbered 11,000 men in 34 companies. Mike Forces manned the 'Greek alphabet projects' of Delta (May 1964), Omega and Sigma (September 1966), and Gamma (January 1967).

These operations, which could employ as many as 16 recce teams, each comprising two Green Berets and 4 indigs, 12 Roadrunner teams disguised as Viet Cong, and maybe an infantry battalion in support, were reasonably effective in curbing VC infiltration.

the Americans. Colonel Rod Paschall again:

'Our Special Forces medical capability was a vital element of the programme. Each team had two medics who had been trained for over a year and were up to emergency surgery, disease diagnosis, elementary dentistry, child delivery and a wide range of treatment requirements.

'Mao turned on his ear'

'My two medics were soon running 90 out-patients per day and running a primitive jungle hospital with five or six bed patients. The hospital was a great source of intelligence since it pulled in patients from other tribes and distant villages. It was also a source of high morale since our village defenders and strike force soldiers knew that they had a good chance to survive a wound if hit.'

As CIDG operations extended during 1966 and 1967, however, problems began to emerge. The tribesmen were very useful for reconnaissance and cross-border operations, but were not necessarily natural soldiers. As Colonel Paschall explains: 'Training the Montagnards posed a number of problems for us. While the village chiefs and some of the older members of the tribe spoke French, most of the young men did not. That meant that my sergeants had to use one or two interpreters for most of the instruction. Second, we quickly learned that the hill tribesmen were not very good at field craft. For example, we had to teach them not to use trails and constantly caution them to cover their tracks in areas of soft footing. Then too, they were very unfamiliar with movement at night. All this took a lot of time and effort.'

The CIDGs would soon become marginal to the war as a whole, for a war of attrition, as practised by both the US high command and the communist leadership, left small bands of hillmen as just a few more pawns to be sacrificed.

Later, the full tragedy of the Montagnards would begin to unfold as they were irretrievably identified with the losing side. It was a sad end to a scheme that had begun so promisingly, and had, as Colonel Paschall experienced, been based on 'the great sense of cameraderie, friendship and warm relations between the mountain people and the Americans. We did not just get along well together, we flourished. The hill tribesmen had a great sense of humour, an admirable dignity and a well developed code of honour. They were fun to be with. Our association was based on mutual respect and mutual needs. We had put our faith in them and they had trusted us. Mao had been turned on his ear.'

1967

Left: Directing traffic on an aircraft carrier's deck is never the safest of jobs. But it was no more dangerous in the Gulf of Tonkin than in San Francisco Bay. Right: These two presents for Ho were going to make a hole in Hanoi. On board the USS *Constellation*, there was little fear of being attacked.

CARRIER WA

It was hot on the huge metal deck – twice the size of a ball park – in the South China Sea. You didn't feel the swell, not on a birdfarm that size. And you'd hardly know there was a war on. The bombs, the missiles, it could all have been an exercise. Except when someone came back all shot up.

Right: The deck crew attach the catapult to a Skyhawk ready for take-off.

Right: The bombs had to be loaded and armed before they could do damage. Below right: Even on a hot carrier you could be cool — the only dangers were from the sun in your eyes, the roar in your ears or if you happened to stray into the path of a jet. Bottom right: The catapult jock wears a light blue shirt. The colours deck crew wear indicate their function in a noisy environment where communication is by hand signal.

FARE

1967

WAR IN THE VILLAGES

They had paid a heavy price for a single sniper shot fired at the American soldiers after entering the village.

Millions of Americans watched the 'Battle of Cam Ne' on the CBS evening news. They heard reporter Morley Safer state that the Marines had been ordered to burn down the village if they received any enemy fire, although there was no 'enemy' left in Cam Ne to suffer the consequences. 'If there were Viet Cong in the hamlets,' he reported, 'they were long gone.' The village had undoubtedly been under enemy control, but as so often in the Vietnam war, it was the villagers themselves who had suffered.

The fate of Cam Ne may not have been typical of American actions in Vietnam, but the frightening dilemma it posed – to US soldiers and Vietnamese villagers alike – certainly was. By the time the Americans arrived in 1965, over 60 per cent of South Vietnam's village population was under the leadership of National Liberation Front

Caught between VC pressure and US firepower, the villagers of South Vietnam were the inevitable losers in the war

Above: Corporal Lindy R. Hall of the 3d Platoon, Company K, 3d Battalion, 3d Marines, sets fire to a Vietnamese hut during Operation Prairie III. Right: The destruction of a schoolhouse was just one of the duties of a US Marine in Vietnam. It may have been a VC meeting place once, but now it was certainly a communist propaganda victory.

AGI calmly flicked his Zippo lighter and raised it above his head. The flame touched the straw roof of a Vietnamese village hut and within seconds the roof burst into a firey inferno, turning a home into a burnt-out charcoal shell. Screaming in fear and impotent distress, the people of Cam Ne could do nothing but stand and watch as 150 of their huts suffered the same fate.

cadres and guerrillas. But in few cases was this control very obvious. Robert Komer, who took over the American aid programme in Vietnam in 1967, said that the Viet Cong 'shared all the concern of the people in their area and so they were really protected by the people and by their information. They were not separate from the people.' As in Cam Ne, the VC often left before the Americans arrived and few GIs could tell whether an enemy or victim lurked behind the hostile stare of a Vietnamese villager. As General Greene, Commander of the US Marine Corps, acknowledged: 'You could kill every Viet Cong and Vietnamese soldier and still lose the war.'

The NLF had answers for all

The history of My Thuy Phuong, a poor farming village seven miles southwest of Hue, illustrates General Greene's comment. Larger than Cam Ne, My Thuy Phuong was typical of many South Vietnamese villages. Most of its 7600 people lived – as they still do – from rice farming, and the NLF had been at work since the 1950s building a slow but powerful pattern of influence.

'The Liberation had answers for all of the most

Below: The villagers were always caught in the middle. While they went about their business and tried to live their lives as normally as possible, they were open to attack from either side.

important problems that we all knew' said one peasant. 'They had an answer about land reform, which was that they would give land to the poor people. They had an answer about high taxes. They said that the Liberation would spend the taxes only for the people, and would collect them without corruption. They also said that they would help the poor, and this was something else that made them popular, because many people in the village were very poor.'

With promises of a better life, the NLF worked hard in group study sessions and informal meetings to teach the people about the history of revolution both in Vietnam and the rest of the world, encouraging them to think and co-operate as a community. There were self-criticism meetings, where the peasants would be asked to admit to moments when they had put their own needs above those of the revolution, and lessons in praising great heroes of the revolution – Ho Chi Minh above all. One peasant recalled:

'Many of the [Front] cadres respected and loved Ho Chi Minh very much. A few of them said they had met Ho, and some carried his photograph with them. They all said they admired Ho Chi Minh for

1967

leading the struggle, and admired him because of his bravery, and because he was in the highest position in the communist organisation.' Facing this level of indoctrination – common in villages throughout Vietnam – the Americans were never going to have an easy job in drawing the peasants over to the government side.

More importantly, the Viet Cong repeated one central message to the people of My Thuy Phuong in leaflets, broadcasts and study sessions: 'Unite The People, Oppose The Americans, Save The Nation.' Before they had even seen an American, the peasants were sure of what they represented. As one Vietnamese remarked:

'We often heard the communists tell us about America. They said America was an imperialist country. They said America was destroying our fatherland. They said everyone must unite to fight the American army. Well, I'd say that almost everyone agreed with them. I did.'

The struggle for the 'hearts and minds' of the people of My Thuy Phuong began after the US Marines arrived at nearby Phu Bai in April 1965 and immediately sent a Combined Action Platoon of 30 ARVN soldiers and 15 Marines to barracks in the centre of the town. For peaceful farming villagers preparing for their spring rice harvest, the war had now come truly to their own door-steps. A villager recalls: 'When the American Marines came, everyone began to worry more and more. We could see the war getting bigger and bigger and we worried about heavy fighting coming into our home.'

WERE FIRE ZONES EFFECTIVE?

One favourite American strategy was to change the environment the war was fought in. They reckoned if there were areas where they could kill anything that moved they would win the war. Were they right?

The creation of 'free fire zones', within which US and allied forces could strike targets without worrying about the social or political consequences, was one of the most controversial aspects of the search and destroy strategy of the 1960s. In purely military terms, it made a lot of sense. If ground forces could sweep through a VC-infested area, destroying villages and removing ordinary civilians to 'safe' refugee centres, what remained should contain nothing except the enemy or his hard-core supporters. Any signs of activity within the zone would therefore indicate enemy movement which, if attacked using artillery or air power, would seriously disrupt the VC.

Unfortunately for the Americans, the concept was never that neat. The very name 'free fire zone' conjured up images of indiscriminate destruction, and even when MACV Directive 95-2 of 20 December 1965 changed it to 'specified strike zone' (SSZ), many people remained unconvinced. In addition, of course, the idea of firing huge amounts of explosives into a region of a supposedly 'friendly' country seemed to go against the declared aim of helping the South Vietnamese to achieve settled, popular government. The forcible removal of villagers from settlements which had been their homes for generations led to deep resentment, undermining many of the advantages of 'pacification'. After all, as US civilian advisors grew weary of pointing out to the military, it was not much use building up a pro-government infrastructure if, virtually without warning, an area became an SSZ and the people were forced to become refugees. Nor was this all, for many people simply refused to move or drifted back to their homes as soon as an opportunity arose, presenting the Americans with the problem of populated SSZs. In the end, the concept presented political problems which far outweighed its purely military advantages.

Five guerrillas summarily executed

As they continued about their daily work, the villagers knew that the American and ARVN soldiers were after the very men who they had supported in daily meetings. Within days their fears were realized when three of the communist leaders and five guerrillas were summarily rooted out and executed. The power of the gun soon began to have a persuasive force of its own and, out of fear and vulnerability, the villagers started to withdraw their support from the communists. The Viet Cong knew now that they had to fight back quickly and effectively. In spite of their grass roots support, the NLF leaders knew that many in the village, especially the richer landowners, continued to back the government. While political cadres doubled their efforts in whipping up anti-American feelings, the Viet Cong began sniping and ambushing the CAP camp. Booby traps were laid throughout the village and peasants were given the chance to show their real commitment to the revolution. Villagers were told that no-one could be neutral any longer. To support the Viet Cong, or avoid them and face recriminations brought the same risks.

For the people of My Thuy Phuong – like many of the peasants of South Vietnam – this was their

Above: Somebody was going to die and you were going to leave. Below: VC were sometimes thrown from helicopters.

most traumatic time. Every man, woman and child was a potential target for an American bullet and every day brought harassment, intimidation or worse. The complex programmes of American pacification were destined to have little success here, and US Marines made few efforts to win the villagers' confidence. One peasant recalls:

'The American soldiers went by in their trucks and shot as many water buffalo as they could. They liked to see the animals fall, I think. They killed so many that after a few years we felt that to have water buffalo was dangerous. One time a boy was hit in the leg when an American soldier tried to kill the water buffalo he was sitting on.'

Roaring along the main highway without stopping for pedestrians or cyclists, the trucks were disruption enough, although one peasant woman will never forget a more brutal result of the US presence: 'I was walking along the road with my son who was wearing a hat. There was a string to hold the hat to his chin. One of the American soldiers grabbed the hat and pulled my son up and under the wheels of the truck. The truck stopped, but it was too late.'

The soldiers said they were VC

As the Viet Cong stepped up a programme of assassinations and ambushes, the village turned into a battleground. Villagers were stopped and searched by CAP soldiers on a regular basis and the rattle of sniper fire echoed through the nights. A village councilman remembers: 'One night there was frightful shooting, so much of it, out in the ricefields. When we got up the next day, we saw the Americans and the soldiers bringing in two bodies, carrying them in a raincoat. We knew the dead men. But the soldiers said they were VC.'

Late in 1967 the VC launched a major attack on the CAP compound. With only two or three losses, the guerrillas killed a number of American and South Vietnamese soldiers before being driven off. The attack had failed to oust the enemy soldiers altogether, but it gave a massive boost to the morale of the village. A student recalls that 'the people were very happy after they saw how brave the Liberation Front guerrillas could be in such an attack against the Americans.' If VC support in the village had been vulnerable until this point, it was suddenly fortified by this display of strength. Beyond the propaganda, the villagers wanted above all to support – and be supported by – the strongest side. From then on, they had few doubts that this side was the communists.

The pattern of the war in My Thuy Phuong was repeated in varying degrees in villages throughout South Vietnam. Medical and economic aid was given to many villagers to induce their support for the government cause, but as Lieutenant-Colonel David Marshall argued: 'We needed 50 years to do what we wanted to do in Vietnam. We had to change the Vietnamese national character, and that would take three generations.'

VILLAGE AID

In addition to the resettlement programme, pacification also embraced a variety of civic action activities designed to involve local people in government and to improve their social, economic and educational environment. A 59-strong South Vietnamese Revolutionary Development cadre would typically have 34 members establishing village defences and militia, while others would provide a census/grievance unit to undertake a full survey of inhabitants and to listen to their complaints, a civil affairs squad to organise hamlet government, and an economic development unit. Ninety-eight separate tasks were laid down for such cadres.

Indications of the scope of US participation are provided by 1967 statistics which show that Americans distributed 572,121 cakes of soap, gave personal hygiene classes to 212,372 persons, cut the hair of 69,652 and bathed 7555 children. In 1969 Americans constructed 1253 schools, 175 hospitals, 153 market places, 263 churches, 422 dispensaries, 598 bridges, 7099 houses and 3154 kilometres of road. US Marine bands attempted to create a 'county fair' atmosphere of entertainment which, combined with the administrative duties in their TAOR and the protection of rice harvesters in 'Golden Fleece' operations, attempted to portray a positive side to the US presence. Unfortunately, all this still represented less than 10 per cent of US resources devoted to pacification.

CHAPTER 42

FOOD AND RATIONS

If you liked lima beans you were lucky – if you liked food that tasted good, then C-rations weren't for you

Everyone hated rations – and no one would eat them unless they had to. I've seen guys so wasted that you'd think they would eat anything and be eager for it. But they'd still be chewing screw-faced on their C-rations, only eating them because they needed energy to keep going while they searched for Charlie out in the boonies.

Nobody not on a tour of the zoo would eat them, though I heard one time of a USAF unit who were made to eat C-rations once a week. Whether this was supposed to give the fliers more of a feel for the grunts on the ground or because the commissary office got a load cheap I don't know. Either way, the fighter jocks must have hated it.

C-rations came in cases. In most platoons each man had a first pick, then a second and a third in turn, so everyone got a fair chance. Then the trading would start. The guys would get down to it – swapping ham and eggs for tuna, franks and beans for stew.

Beans and motherfuckers

I was lucky. I liked ham and lima beans. Everybody else hated them – we called them beans and motherfuckers. What's more I hated turkey and chicken. I'd eaten raw birds on survival training and couldn't stand the taste of fowl. So I had plenty to trade with.

You'd break open the packs and distribute the things around your pack and pockets. In each pack there'd be some crackers, which would usually be eaten for breakfast, and a spread – peanut butter, jam or cheese. Cake or chocolate was a great favourite because it gave you instant energy. In a little tin, there'd be bread or date pudding. And sometimes there'd be a tin of fruit. The guys dug for the juice. Peaches were number one. A guy would kill for a can of peaches – literally. Little things like a can of fruit assumed a great importance in the Nam.

Also in the pack would be a book of matches, a can opener, a plastic spoon, toilet tissue and a pack of coffee or cocoa. A can was used as a coffee pot. The cocoa was mixed with peanut butter to make fudge. Later, marijuana was added. Early in the war there was no problem with drugs out on patrol. Anyone unreliable, who might get you killed, was dealt with out in the zoo. You hear a lot about fraggings, but ordinary grunts got wasted too. If you were going to be a danger out there in the jungle, the solution was simple. You didn't come back. Or if you did, it was in a body bag.

1967

Another can was used as a stove. You were supposed to get a heat tab with each pack, but usually you didn't and a bit of C-4 plastic explosive was used instead. It didn't explode, but you had to stay upwind of it. One toke of the smoke given off by one of those babies and you'd blow half your brain cells.

In the heat of the Nam you'd need a lot of water. Some guys would put Koolade in it to cover the taste of the purification tablet. Problem was that the Koolade made you even thirstier, and cut down the effectiveness of the purifying tab. Next stop dysentry.

Grape juice was a favourite also. But it gave you the shits, and the only cure for that was to trade all your C-rats for peanut butter and crackers which set in your stomach like quick-drying cement. As many of us regulars used to say: 'Between the grape juice and the peanut butter you were regular.'

Grunts preferred Lurp rations when they could get them. These were lightweight dehydrated pre-cooked meals that came in packs rather than tins. The idea first came from some guy on Okinawa. Guys going on Long Range Patrols didn't want to carry heavy tins, and he noticed the orientals could carry more food because it was dried and lighter. From that point good old American know-how took over and some boffin – I guess in the space programme – figured out freeze drying. There was beef stew, chilli and six other real tasty meals plus crackers and dried fruit. Then all you had to do was add water to the stuff and hey presto – instant chow.

Waterbuffalo steaks – a US beef

The problem that no-one had figured was that there wasn't a lot of good water in Vietnam. That meant, though you saved weight on the Lurp rations, you had to carry an extra six or seven pints of water to rehydrate them. Occasionally guys would kill a waterbuffalo and cook steaks. But this made the brass sore because the government had to compensate the owner, although I don't think it paid out that often.

All units would swap food. Our platoon would often trade with the Australians for a change until they too got issued C-rations later in the war. No-one swapped with the Koreans though, and although C-rations were often sold to the Vietnamese on the black market, no-one – but no-one – ate Vietnamese food either. That was for the gooks, not Uncle Sam's boys.

Some of the real hardened Lurps got into that rotting fish sauce, nuoc mam, though. In every Vietnamese village there'd be a huge pot. It was so strong you could smell it miles away. You could tell Charlie was near from the smell of nuoc mam on their breath, just like they could detect us from the smell of our soap and aftershave. Sentry dogs would go mad when they caught its scent. It was enough to turn your stomach. But once you got used to it you could eat anything if you smothered it with nuoc mam.

Opposite: C-rations were okay if they were hot. But eaten cold they were greasy with a thick layer of fat. Above right: Hot food was sometimes flown in. Other than at firebases under siege, hot meals were prepared by Army cooks. Here the grunts are getting turkey for Thanksgiving. Centre right: Guys would often mix all their C-rats up into one big stew, just to make a change. Another trick was to slightly burn the meatballs, then smother them in Tabasco. That way they tasted almost like food. Below right: Two packs of C-rations a day did not contain enough calories to keep you going. Lurp rations had even less. After a couple of days on patrol your energy was drained. But then you'd carry extra ammo rather than extra food.

THE KOREANS

With their own version of karate, and without many scruples, the Koreans imposed their iron control over Dinh Binh Province

In February 1967, a large force of NVA made the fatal error of engaging a company of Koreans at close quarters. In the bloodbath that followed they lost 243 KIA and were forced into a chaotic withdrawal. That was the first major collision between North Vietnamese and Korean forces. It would be a good while before there was another.

The first Korean troops had arrived in-country way back in February 1965, and although they were officially assigned to non-combat duties, they first came under fire on 3 April. By this time, there were 200 ROKs in-country, and their numbers would eventually rise until there were 44,829 superbly trained Koreans stationed in Vietnam. Most of them were in II Corps, on the central coastal plain around Qui Nhon and Nha Trang. Binh Dinh Province was somewhat hidden from the mainstream of the war, and the Koreans there were reduced to a sideshow – but an effective one.

Besides the American effort, South Korea's was the second largest fighting force in Vietnam, and the last out, leaving in March 1973. The US had withdrawn its last ground personnel by 1972. The South Korean President, Chung Hee Park, proudly explained that fighting in the Nam 'would not only solidify our national security, but also contribute towards strengthening the anti-communist front of the Free World'. They had vivid memories of their own vicious fight against the communists just over a decade previously to remind them what commitment meant, and it made them fanatics.

Left: Fresh from their own war, the Koreans did not believe you could re-educate communists.

Korean area of responsibility

During their stay in Vietnam, the Koreans established tight control over the areas they were allotted, by their ruthlessly effective methods of counter-insurgency, which did not endear them to the local population

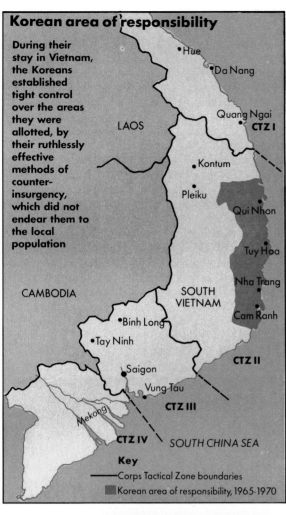

LAOS

• Hue
• Da Nang

• Quang Ngai
CTZ I

• Kontum

• Pleiku

Qui Nhon

CAMBODIA

SOUTH VIETNAM

Tuy Hoa

Nha Trang

Cam Ranh

• Binh Long

• Tay Ninh

CTZ II

Saigon

Vung Tau

CTZ III

Mekong

CTZ IV   SOUTH CHINA SEA

Key
— Corps Tactical Zone boundaries
■ Korean area of responsibility, 1965-1970

British photographer Tim Page started his photographic career in Vietnam at the age of 18. In 1967 he spent some time with the ROKs at Hui An, I Corps, and in Binh Dinh Province, II Corps.

Above right: Men of Tiger Division practise Taikwondo, the Korean form of karate. Below: Memories of their own struggle against communism made the Koreans tough but resourceful fighters.

It was surprising to walk into the officers' mess at the ROK Blue Dragon Brigade and, prior to being seated, hear a very fierce sounding, totally unintelligible grace. The only words I could understand were, Westmoreland, America, and Viet Cong. An escort officer explained that the prayer was to give the Dragons and their allies strength to kill VC. The detached Marine brigade based at Hui An, near Quang Ngai in I Corps, was a model of military propriety. Their camp was enhanced by the debris of war: shell casings lined the gravelled walkways, flattened C-ration cartons shingled and lined buildings, and ammo cases became hootches. There was no scrap of litter anywhere, and they had even planted flower beds and Kentucky blue grass borders. Lurking

1967

sentries, spotlessly turned out even in the worst conditions, would snap to attention as I slouched past. My escort told me it was a greeting, though every evening at the Taikwondo exercise they screamed it before they bisected a brick with bare head or hand. Every trooper was trained in this deadly form of karate.

For three days I had been photographing the ROKs performing med-caps, civic action and routine patrolling, but I missed any hard-core

Left: The Koreans did not have to exaggerate their body counts. They did not fight shy of killing civilians either. Below: ROK troops advance through the morning mists in search of VC and NVA. Opposite: The ROKs were known for their brutal interrogation techniques.

action – though we had been sniped at and the company commander had ordered his men to Zippo the hamlet where the shots had come from. When they took fire in supposedly secure areas, they often gave impromptu Taikwondo demonstrations on the offending housing. Their Tactical Area of Responsibility (TAOR) was secure and we rode about in an open jeep, watching grunts helping the locals harvest and thresh the rice crop, dispensing first aid in hamlets, and rebuilding a Buddhist shrine damaged by American shelling. Later on we watched a team of instructors teaching karate to high-school girls in Quang Ngai, before we drove the 20 klicks back to base, at night, without incident.

My batman woke me before five. The same unit I had patrolled with the day before had gotten hit in a night laager in a cemetery. I rode a beat up H-34 out to the battle. We dropped in a combat spiral from 1500 feet into a tight defensive perimeter around an ancient Viet cemetery, with

foxholes dug into the graves. A few wide-eyed, dishevelled Korean Marines ran up to the bird and threw in a body wrapped in a poncho. Two walking wounded followed. Everywhere there were bodies, most in black pyjamas, some in green NVA uniforms. I stopped counting after 50, that was just inside the perimeter, and they were still bringing in the kills from the bamboo tree line. I found the Marines I had buddied up with, and they told me the story.

They knew they were going to be hit – maybe it takes an Asian to know what another Asian is going to do – so their ambush patrols were some way out. They had gone unarmed except for garottes and knives, and the first VC hadn't known what had zapped them. The ambush patrols pulled back, booby-trapping the KIAs, arming the trip wires and calling artillery onto the tree line 50 metres away. Some of the bodies hardly had a scratch on them. I flipped one over to get the already gone belt buckle, the neck flopped like a broken doll, the sergeant giggled and made hand-chopping signs.

The Koreans did not have to exaggerate their

THE KOREANS AT WAR

ROK forces fought hard, but did they fight fair?

In general terms, Korean fighting methods were identical to those of the Americans. Using the same basic weapons and tactical doctrines, ROK units were expected to carry out village searches, ambushes and cordon operations, contributing to the general strategy of search and destroy. But there were differences of detail. On the positive side, most ROK actions involved more careful planning than those of their allies, with greater fire discipline and better co-ordination of sub-units. During village searches, ROK soldiers would subject the settlement to a series of detailed sweeps while interrogating subjects on the spot. By comparison, American units tended to favour a single sweep followed by a removal of all civilians for screening. Such a painstaking approach certainly paid dividends in terms of weapons seizure and reduced VC activity in ROK areas. But ROK soldiers were renowned for carrying out brutal interrogations and for silent killing techniques involving the garotte or karate. This struck fear into the hearts of the enemy, but it went far beyond the norm of Western warfare.

1967

body counts for the computers in the Pentagon: in that one action they had 85 confirmed VC, whilst taking three of their own KIA and 10 wounded. The trees around the cemetery were splattered with bits of once-human beings, and blood trails ran everywhere. The ROKs guessed at another century. Another company unit of 150 men working up on the Cambodian border with the US 4th Infantry Division got ambushed by the NVA 101st Regiment. When the action was finished,

I ended up spending over a week with the Tigers after I met a couple of signal corps photographers from the 1st Cav. The Tigers were operating out of Bong Son, from their home base at Ninh Binh, north of Nha Trang. The 1st Cav had won the area in Operation Masher/White Wing, then the ROKs had secured it. It was the NVA/VC granary of Central Vietnam. On small French plantation roads the Koreans set up market zones, and allowed peasants from pacified and hostile areas

the NVA withdrew, leaving 182 KIA – the ROKs had seven. Captured VC documents showed the respect they were treated with, stipulating 'contact with the Koreans is to be avoided at all costs unless a victory is 100 per cent certain'. Lieutenant-General Chae, who ran the Capitol Division, the famous Tiger unit, did not exaggerate when he stated 'where the ROKs are, it is 100 per cent secured'. In Binh Dinh Province they were fired on from a hamlet and a unit was ordered to sweep through. The next day, a US naval officer entered the hamlet and found scores of dead civilians, including the bodies of the hamlet chief, his wife and children. They had been tied to stakes and disembowelled. A survivor claimed that an ROK officer had said: 'Leave this place and tell people what happened.'

to trade freely under the watchful eyes of an alert platoon and eager beaver med-cap unit. Although controversial, this policy brought in a lot of intelligence, prompting one attached US advisor to say he suspected 'they stay awake all night to think up new ways to do things around here'. They even learnt a bastardized version of the Vietnamese language, freed themselves of unnecessary interpreters, and discovered a lot of their assigned ARVN translators were deep cover VC. They took them out and executed them. Korean intelligence was hard and new.

After a rare chopper assault ferrying in two companies (rare because the US could ill afford choppers for their seconded allies), the Tigers flushed out a dozen VC suspects while I was with them. The suspects were wizened old men, too old

THE ROK

As a country with a recent history of fighting communism, it was perhaps inevitable that the Republic of Korea should take an active interest in the affairs of Vietnam. By 1967 there were 47,829 Korean soldiers in the country, many of whom had been there far longer than their American comrades. Indeed, as early as 1954 President Syngman Rhee had offered to send troops to support the French in their fight against the Viet Minh. On that occasion, the offer was rejected, but 10 years later, as the South Vietnamese faced disaster, the situation changed. In August 1964 a small ROK liaison team travelled to Saigon, followed in February 1966 by a so-called 'dove' unit of engineers, medical personnel and advisors, skilled in the art of winning over the population.

These troops were under strict instructions not to become involved in a shooting war but when, a few weeks later, the United States cast around for allies to help their efforts in Vietnam, the South Koreans were quick to respond. In September 1965, elements of the Capital ('Tiger') Division began to arrive, taking responsibility for securing strategic highways and port facilities in the central coastal provinces. In October, the ROK Marine Corps' 2nd ('Blue Dragon') Brigade was deployed to Hui An, and a year later the 9th ('White Horse') Division occupied a base at Ninh Hoa, north of the installation at Cam Ranh Bay.

At the end of 1966, the Korean area of operations was large, covering the key provinces of Ninh Thuan and Binh Dinh, including Highways 1 and 19. Within this area, ROK units provided port security, kept the highways open and actively assumed the offensive against the VC. Search and destroy operations, as well as a policy of close contact with the local people, soon produced results, creating some of the best controlled areas in the South. The Koreans remained in Vietnam until March 1973.

1967

for military service, probably VC sympathizer farmers. However, the LZ had been hot with sniper rounds. Terrified women and children were flushed from the corn breaks claiming 'no VC', but everywhere we found fighting holes and bunkers.

As the company CO took a couple of suspects aside to get some updated information, the US forward artillery observer and his radioman drifted off. In bad Vietnamese, the captain barked questions at the cringing suspect. I hardly saw his hands move, and the VC was doubled over, a vivid mark on his neck. Still no answer. Next time, I saw

Below: White Horse Division troops prepare a free fire zone at Bang Son. Bottom: Not all the Koreans were skilled at winning hearts and minds.

loans. The Koreans also cleaned up to the tune of $650 million for military procurements. The ARVN wore Korean-manufactured uniforms. In Saigon, it was possible to order a refrigerator or air-con unit from a Korean black market middle man before it even hit the docks in Canh Hoi or Cam Ranh. They could guarantee delivery of nearly anything at a knock down price, and it was transported down their secured roads. To demonstrate to the locals the progress they had made since their own war, they would point to the labels on the goods: 'Made in Korea'.

the hand move and heard the forearm break. I snapped a frame on my camera which no-one saw. Writhing now, but still not talking, he was led over to kneel on the edge of one of the fighting holes. The CO backed up a couple of paces, brought up his M-2 carbine and, with great pantomime, jacked one up the spout and snicked the safety off. At 15 yards he put a burst of automatic fire a millimetre to the side of the VC's head. I missed that frame because another Korean had finally spotted the camera, bringing his M16 to bear on my midriff, grunting 'no photo'. I slumped off to join the Americans while the VC spilled his story. Minutes later, when I was taking a leak, he was led down the hill by three ROKs. There was a single pistol shot and the troopers plodded back alone. The ROKs did not believe you could re-educate a communist.

South Korea's devotion was not cheap: the US paid the $1 billion of their budget from 1965-70, besides another $150 million in development

THE FIREFIGHT EXPERIENCE

What does it feel like to come under fire? No-one can predict how they'll react when a firefight starts

Take a walk in the jungle. Hands sweating against the plastic of an M16 rifle stock, you listen to the blood pumping through your temples. Safety off, you're moving through the trail with eyes and gun working as one. The split-second it takes to align the barrel with a shadow flitting through the jungle is a split-second too long. Where your eyes go, the gun follows. Toe-poppers, Claymore-type mines and punji stakes – who's next for the meat grinder?

221

Above: The enemy may not be visible until it is too late. Left: You could relax and smoke, but you never let go of your gun. Opposite top: You were most vulnerable crossing a river or (opposite) in an area that had been defoliated. Previous page: The safest place, of course, was behind an M60.

Where's Mr Charles hiding tonight? Darkness doesn't make the job any easier but, after days spent waiting for contact, things had to loosen up sometime – as illustrated by the experience of one Vet:

'You're sitting out there in the dark. You been out there every God damn night for a month and you ain't seen the first VC. Where in the hell are they? We'd decide to go buy a few and import them. You sit and sit and sit. You're supposed to be real quiet and serious because you really don't know when it's going to happen. But it's been a long time, so you figure, what the hell – *brrrippp.* Somebody'd let out a fart that'd blow your God damn socks off. Everybody'd start laughing.'

But then it's time to start moving again, and hair-trigger tension slowly eases itself out of the back seat and works its way back into your gut. Every member of the platoon deals with this in his own way:

'You're back at it again, hunting humans. I hope one shows up man. I'm going to blow that mother-fucker to kingdom-come. If the world could only see me now. This is bad news out here and I am bad. We are armed to the teeth. If I could get back to the States with my platoon intact, I could take over the world. Somebody fuck with me, just somebody fuck with me. Come and get me.'

But when the shit hits the fan, it's like the earth is screaming. The suspense of the last few days erupts into violence as enemy fire pours in from both sides of the trail. Then the hunter becomes the hunted and all thoughts of taking on the world as a warrior king give way to chaos as the calls for fire support come up over the radio net.

'You certainly ain't John Wayne'

'When they came to get you – holy shit. I can't even talk on the radio to call in the fire mission. I'm calling in the fire mission. At last I'm calling in the fire mission. But I'm warbling like a kid going through puberty. You swallow slowly and force yourself to say the co-ordinates. Everything hits slow motion, like you're in your own movie. You try to be cool, calm and collected, and you are ...kind of. You certainly ain't John Wayne.

'Where's it coming from? Who's getting hit? I don't want to die. You can see everything that's happening in immediate terms – life-and-death terms.'

There's no call for heroics in 99 per cent of the firefights, but the fear can give way to frenzied excitement when things go right and support arrives as you requested. Whether it's the fire-birds roaring overhead, or artillery booming on up there from the rear, you know your prayers hit the spot:

'You call in a fire mission real good, you get your field of fire right, deploy your men so that you can outflank them and stand up and walk right through them – it's thrilling. It's so real. Talk about getting high, this is beyond drugs – ultrareality.'

Sometimes, just sometimes, the pieces fit

together like some macabre jigsaw puzzle and, like First-Lieutenant Archie Biggers, you find yourself sensing victory among the carnage all around:

'While we were following this trail through the jungle, the point man came running back. He was all heated up. He said: "I think we got a tank up there." I told him: "I don't have time for no games." The enemy had no tanks in the South.

'Then the trail started converging into a really well-camouflaged road...Then I saw the muzzle of this gun. It was as big as anything we had. And all hell broke open. It was like the sun was screaming....

'The snipers had just got Joe'
'In front of us was a reinforced platoon and two artillery pieces all dug into about 30 serious bunkers. And we were in trouble in the rear, because a squad of snipers had slipped in between us and the rest of Charlie Company. All the NVA needed to do to finish us off was to set up mortars on either side.

'Someone told me the snipers had just got Joe. He was my platoon sergeant.

'That did it. I passed the word to call in napalm at Danger Close, 50 metres off our position. Then I

ARTILLERY SUPPORT

The absence of fixed front lines in Vietnam meant that bases had to be set up to give artillery firepower for large-scale infantry attacks, and to give those pinned down in firefights some heavy suppresive fire they could call on. Every combat brigade in Vietnam was supported by two battalions of field artillery, one of which provided direct fire support to operational ('manoeuvre') units while the other provided augmenting fire or general area protection. Each field artillery battalion comprised three light batteries (each of six 105mm or 155mm howitzers), and the usual procedure in the field was to use one of these to support each manoeuvre battalion in the combat brigade. Heavier artillery – 175mm and 8in howitzers – were kept at divisional level.

Close liaison between the manoeuvre battalion and its supporting battery was essential, especially in a combat environment where front lines were non-existent and enemy attacks could be expected at any time, from any direction. The construction of firebases, situated to give support throughout a battalion's area of operations, was the normal tactic, with artillery officers accompanying patrols or larger formations.

If the enemy attacked the firebase, direct fire – in which the gunners could see their targets – would be necessary, using special munitions such as the XM546 Beehive round, designed to explode into a shower of small metal darts. Even more effective was a technique known as 'Killer Junior', in which time-fuzed projectiles were set to burst about 10 metres off the ground.

Above: After the firefight, there was the cost to be counted. Here a member of Bravo Company, 2/18th, 1st Division, wounded during heavy fighting about three miles from the Cambodia border during Operation Junction City II, receives medical attention. Some of his buddies are beyond help. Left: And then there were the dead. These are dead NVA soldiers, killed during a firefight in the Michelin plantation. No body bags for them. They would be tossed in a mass grave or doused with petrol and burnt.

turned to go after the snipers. And I heard this loud crash. I was thrown to the ground. A grenade had exploded and the shrapnel had torn into my left arm.

'The Phantoms were doing a number. It felt like an earthquake was coming. The ground was just a-rumbling. Smoke was everywhere, and then the grass caught fire. The napalm explosions had knocked two of my men down who were at the point, but the NVA were running everywhere. The flames were up around my waist. That's when I yelled, "Charge. Kill the gooks. Kill the motherfuckers."

'The ridge was ours'

'We kept shooting until everything was empty. Then we picked up the guns they dropped and fired them. I brought three down with my .45. In a matter of minutes, the ridge was ours.

More often that not, however, each firefight followed the same pattern – stalemate. Hours, days, maybe even weeks of patrolling through thick undergrowth never knowing if death was going to scythe you down around the next corner. What does a bullet in the gut feel like? But even when action breaks loose and the sun explodes it's often all over within minutes:

'You got 20 guys over there shooting at you and 20 or 30 guys over here, shooting back at them. We're calling in artillery fire. They're calling in artillery fire. Somebody decides, "Okay, I've had enough." Then that's over. But there was no ground taken. Nobody won anything or moved their lines.'

A guerrilla war, not a war of fronts but plenty of body bags for the medevacs to take out. After the battle, there's an eerie emptiness that crawls out of the jungle:

'All of a sudden that's over with. It's something everyone talks about to mark the days. A point of reference...Then you go back to the mind-numbing routine. You're a zombie again.

'It get's dark, you occupy the high ground. You set up the perimeter...No big deal...But then the sun would go down and I could feel my stomach sinking. There goes the light. There goes one of your senses, the most important one. Life stops ...The only technology you have is death: M16s – black plastic rifles – grenades, pocket bombs, Claymores, M-79s, M60s, mortars, flak jackets, jungle boots, C-4 plastic explosive, radios and jet planes to drop the napalm. That was the only technology happening.

Back in the World

'You think about people back in the World walking around downtown, going out to get a beer. You'd be staring into the dark so hard, you'd have to reach up and touch your eyes to make sure they were still open...

'You know it's going to be the same tomorrow as it was today...only maybe it might be worse. It won't be any better. We had a saying about how bad a thing could be: As bad as a day in the Nam.'

DEFENDING THE FRONTIER

The US Marines were walking into real trouble when they moved into Con Thien on the DMZ and tried to force out the NVA mainforce units that wanted it for themselves

It was barren, like something out of a World War I movie, or the dark side of the moon. It was cratered, shell-holed, bombed flat. And it was haunted. You just knew there were bad things out there. This was the Trace, the beginnings of 'McNamara's Line'.

It was 700yds of nothing, a haunted place. Try to cross it, to retrieve bodies say, and the NVA would hurl everything they had at you – rockets, mortars, machine guns, even CS gas when it didn't blow back in their faces.

This was the situation along the northern edge of 'Leatherneck Square' – the northernmost region of South Vietnam that the Marines had been ordered to hold against NVA infiltration from the north. The Green Berets with their CIDG forces had already tried to hold the line but their bases had been repeatedly overrun. Though the American forces were – publicly at least – restrained from entering the so-called five-mile De-Militarized Zone which straddled the border between North and South Vietnam, the other side of the Trace.

The North Vietnamese did not respect the DMZ, though. They massed their troops there ready to strike at the line of hill forts that guarded this wild frontier. The American defenders had no need to use binoculars to spot the NVA. They could run patrols up to 70yds from their columns – less than the length of a football field away. Closer than that and there would be trouble.

In the summer of 1967, the Marines moved in to

During the summer of 1967 the bitter and heavy fighting around Con Thien, on the edge of the DMZ, made a mockery of its benign title 'The Hill of Angels'. Left: Unloading desperately needed supplies from a Boeing CH-46 helicopter (top), whilst (bottom) an M60 machine-gun crew watch out for infiltrating NVA patrols. Right: A 105mm Howitzer is unloaded from a chopper. Previous Page: An advance patrol (top) fights it out while weary GIs (bottom) snatch a rest before being sent back into the conflict.

the Special forces camp to start filling sandbags, creosote bunker timbers and string barbed wire to make up the McNamara Line. The NVA were determined to smash the Line before it became too strong. And where they decided to attack was Con Thien.

Outpost to invasion

The Marine strong point at Con Thien was 14 miles inland and two miles south of the DMZ. It marked the northwest corner of leatherneck square and overlooked the NVA's major infiltration route. If the NVA took this outpost they would overlook the vast US logistics complex at Dong Ha and would open the way for an invasion of Quang Tri province by the 35,000 NVA troops massed north of the DMZ.

Before work on the McNamara Line could begin the Marines had to secure their position. So on 2

then swarmed in to finish off the job. An airstrike was called in to nape them at 50yds. Instead they were roasted at 20, but who's complaining. It was enough to halt the assault.

Helicopter gunships and four tanks from Con Thien forced the enemy back and Company D secured a landing zone. Another company was then flown in from Dong Ha.

The tanks forced their way on up the road to Company B where Sergeant Burns, the acting commander, was asked where the rest of his company was. He replied: 'Sir, this is the company, or what's left of it.'

The wounded were loaded into the tanks and, under heavy artillery fire, began to pull back. Two of the tanks hit mines which slowed their withdrawal. Back at the LZ, the wounded were being pulverized by a devastating artillery and mortar barrage. Medics and stretcher bearers were added

July two companies set out to sweep an arc around north of the Trace from the east. 1200yds north of the Trace, still well outside the DMZ, Company B came under sniper fire. As they pushed forward the fire intensified. They tried to outflank the NVA, only to find themselves forced back into a position where they were taking fire from the front and both flanks. Casualties mounted.

Company A moved up to help, but tripped two Claymore mines and casualties became so heavy that they could not fight and move at the same time.

Mortar fire dispersed Company B. Many of the Marines were forced into the open by flamethrowers and were cut down by artillery fire. The NVA

to the casualties.

The commander directing the defence of the LZ was hit and around 50 survivors began to walk back to Con Thien across the Trace. The commanders at Con Thien spotted them crossing the wasteland and a truck, a jeep, an ambulance and two helicopters raced out to rescue them. Many were in danger of bleeding to death, but despite heavy artillery fire all were rescued.

A day and a half without water

Mid-afternoon three more relief companies were flown in to the battle north of the Trace. They staged a twilight attack, while the battle-weary companies fell back on the LZ and Con Thien.

WAR ON THE DMZ

At the beginning of 1967, the 3d Marine Division was based around Phu Bai and the 1st Marine Division divided between Da Nang and Chu Lai. Their task was to defend the northern provinces of South Vietnam against communist infiltration. In April, the 1st Marines were relieved of their duties in the south of this area by the Army's Task Force Oregon and moved north, closer to the DMZ.

The Marines occupied a series of combat bases along Route 9 – Khe Sanh, the Rockpile, Camp Carroll, Cam Lo and Dong Ha – designed to impede NVA infiltration through the DMZ and, as 1967 progressed, most of the fighting took place along or close to this line. On 16 March, men from Company B, 9th Marine Regiment, were ambushed near Hill 861, close to Khe Sanh. This led to a bitter campaign known as 'The Hill Fights', which was to last until 13 May. By then, Hills 861, 881 South and 881 North had been seized and garrisoned by the Marines.

At the same time, the Marines were ordered to set up the first, experimental stretch of the McNamara Line, centred on the forward base of Con Thien. As they began to clear the area preparatory to the creation of a 'fence' of surveillance devices, the NVA concentrated against them. The 'Siege of Con Thien' was to last until 4 October, involving hard fighting, significant casualties and, in late May, a Marine/ARVN sweep and clear operation – Hickory – into the southern part of the DMZ as far as the Ben Hai river. This was supported by amphibious landings by elements of the Special Landing Forces of the Seventh Fleet, but it did little to curtail NVA activity. By the end of the year, Marine Intelligence was beginning to monitor the build-up which would culminate in renewed attacks on Khe Sanh in 1968.

1967

WAS THE DMZ DE-MILITARIZED?

The so-called De-Militarized Zone between North and South was an open invitation to NVA infiltrators.

Under the 1954 Geneva agreements there was to be an inviolable five mile-wide buffer zone which straddled the 17th parallel. During 1967, defense analysts, pro-war politicians and bar-room hawks suggested that the United States should have occupied this De-Militarized Zone to frustrate North Vietnamese infiltration and, later, large scale incursions. In fact, in 1965 and 1966 serious consideration was given to occupying the DMZ and the neighbouring area of Laos with three of four US divisions. These would block NVA infiltration from well prepared positions. At one stage it was even suggested that an International Force might assume this role. But all such ideas were rejected.

In operational terms, establishing a permanent static line across the DMZ would have required enormous logistic effort and tied down US forces in positions where they could be bombarded constantly from the North. As it was, the US Marines opposed the construction of the 'McNamara Line', which began in April 1967, because similarly it would have tied down a large amount of manpower, artillery and aerial support. Their own fire bases along Route 9 to the immediate south of the zone were frequently under long-range attack. And it is by no means clear that infiltration could have been stopped even by occupying parts of Laos since the insurgent trail would probably have been diverted further west.

The political consequences of occupying the DMZ or any part of Laos or North Vietnam were equally daunting. It was felt that this would invite Chinese military intervention as during the Korean War.

Nevertheless, in July 1966, the Joint Chiefs of Staff did authorize the bombardment of the DMZ and limited incursions up to the 17th parallel provided no public disclosure was made. Return fire across the DMZ was authorized in December 1966 and pre-emptive fire, including air-strikes, from February 1967.

In May 1967, Operation Hickory cleared 13,000 people from the DMZ and its immediate vicinity to facilitate unrestricted bombing of NVA positions. But even these drastic measures had little effect.

Only 27 men of Company B walked out of the action.

Enemy mortars were then zeroed in on the LZ and supply helicopters could not land. During the continuing action the relief companies had to go without water for a day and a half. Some 3000 NVA troops moved in on the position but artillery and airstrikes held them at bay.

More NVA troops were engaged south of Con Thien. A reconnaissance patrol was sent out to see where the NVA were crossing the Ben Hai River, violating the DMZ. An aerial observer spotted a large force closing in on the patrol. Asked how big the force was, the observer radioed back: 'I'd hate to tell you.'

Tattered flesh where a hand had been

Marine battalions to the east of Con Thien came under heavy, accurate artillery fire with about 1500 rounds hitting their position. The reconnaissance patrol was surrounded. They were pinned down with mortar and smallarms fire. Then the NVA got close enough to hurl hand grenades into their position. Lance Corporal James L. Stuckey tried picking them up and throwing them back. Minutes later, only tattered flesh remained where his hand had been.

Next morning, by some woodsman's instinct, Major Woodring ordered the reconnaissance patrol back. Thirty minutes later NVA were blasting the hell out of their old position.

Meanwhile the battalions to the east of Con Thien continued to take much of the punishment. The NVA 90th Regiment were getting close

enough to hurl fuzed blocks of TNT into their positions, but at immense cost. Hundreds of bodies covered the battlefield, some half buried, others in pieces, all surrounded by battered equipment and spent ammunition.

On 8 July, the Marines found an NVA bunker system to the south-west of Con Thien. After an airstrike was called and the bunkers were cleared, NVA ground activity was cut to the planting of mines and harassing fire. 159 Marines were dead and 345 wounded. The Marines claimed to have captured two NVA and killed 1290 – the main accounting system among the badly mutilated bodies was counting the canteens left on the battlefield.

Worse though, the NVA had brought in heavy artillery support for the first time and, dug in over the border, their 152mm howitzers – which could out range any field artillery the Americans had – continued to pound Con Thien and Dong Ha during the lull.

They stepped up their activities for propaganda effect as the South Vietnamese elections scheduled for 3 September approached. On election day alone 41 artillery rounds pounded into Dong Ha, destroying the ammunition store, the bulk fuel farm and damaging 17 helicopters.

Con Thien was also a prime NVA target. Perched on top of the Hill of Angels, it was only large enough to accommodate one reinforcement battalion. Still, during September, it took at least 200 rounds of incoming a day. And on 25 September, 1200 rounds pounded the bunkers there.

Under cover of these artillery and rocket attacks NVA ground activity increased. On 4 September Marines came under attack a mile south of Con Thien and had to be relieved by tanks. Fourteen Marines were killed in a similar action three days later.

On 10 September, they encountered what seemed to be the entire 812th NVA Regiment four miles south-west of Con Thien. The NVA reportedly attacked in US Marine Corps flak jackets and helmets. A Marine flame tank was destroyed by a rocket-propelled grenade and a gun tank was put out of action. Thirty-four Marines were killed and 192 were wounded.

On the offensive again

On 13 September, the NVA attacked Con Thien itself but were forced to withdraw. An all-out attack was expected and two more Marine battalions were moved up. The attack did not materialize but the NVA bombarded all three battalions with savage artillery and mortar attacks for the next seven days.

The Marines went on the offensive again and soon patrols found themselves fighting at close quarters with the 90th NVA Regiment. They called in tanks, but after 96 hours of rain the tanks could not reach the scene of the action.

As the weather deteriorated, the struggle for Con Thien became an artillery battle. During 19-27 September more than 3000 mortar, artillery

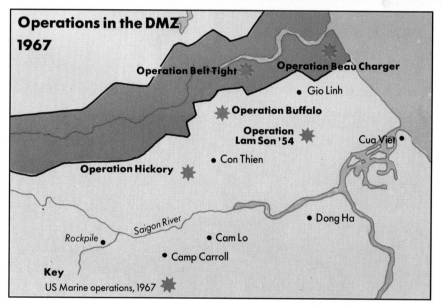

Operations in the DMZ 1967

Operation Belt Tight

Operation Beau Charger

Gio Linh

Operation Buffalo

Operation Lam Son '54

Cua Viet

Operation Hickory

Con Thien

Dong Ha

Saigon River

Rockpile

Cam Lo

Camp Carroll

Key
US Marine operations, 1967

Above: Enemy-laid Claymore mines took a very heavy toll on reconnaissance patrols whilst the unending NVA artillery barrage (right) hampered the rescue of the wounded and also slowed down any attempts at re-supply.

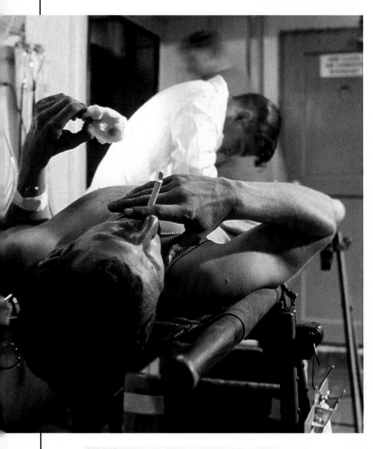

On 2 July, 1967, Companies A and B of the 9th Marines came under intense and lethal enemy fire on three sides. Claymores, snipers, artillery and flame-throwers all took their toll. By the end of the day, only 27 men of Company B survived. Below: The dead being ferried out piled high on a Marine tank. Left: One of the lucky ones – a wounded survivor taking a welcome drag as field surgeons get to work.

and rocket rounds blasted the hill fort. The Americans retaliated with one of the greatest concentrations of firepower in support of a single division in the history of the war. Artillery units fired 12,577 rounds at enemy positions. The Seventh Fleet contributed another 6148 rounds.

NVA activity did die down, but this bombardment did not deter them completely. Marine patrols repeatedly found bunker and trench complexes around the perimeter of Con Thien. Even when these were destroyed they were quickly rebuilt.

In the meatgrinder

There was no escape from the depressing drizzle and the mud. And there was the constant danger of artillery, rocket and mortar fire. Shell shock – the World War I condition unknown in the rest of Vietnam – was not uncommon at Con Thien. And duty on and around the drab Hill of Angels was referred to by the Marines as taking their turn 'in the barrel' or, more grimly, 'in the meatgrinder'.

At Con Thien the Americans began to fight the conventional war they had long craved. It was not the fast moving action of World War II, but rather the slow bloody attrition of World War I. But this time the Americans were not fresh off the boat and eager for victory. They were pounded into the mud.

THE ARMALITE M16 ASSAULT RIFLE

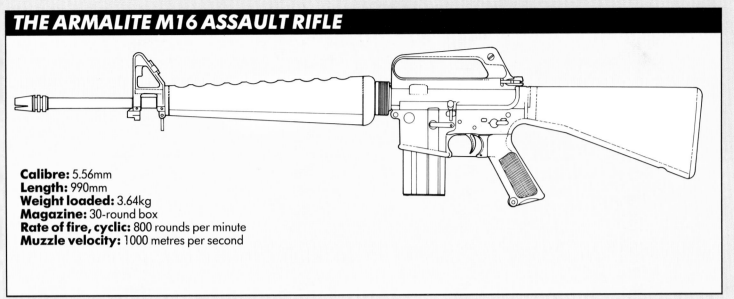

Calibre: 5.56mm
Length: 990mm
Weight loaded: 3.64kg
Magazine: 30-round box
Rate of fire, cyclic: 800 rounds per minute
Muzzle velocity: 1000 metres per second

THE M16 ARMALITE ASSAULT RIFLE

Compact, and firing a high-velocity bullet, the M16 overcame teething problems and evolved into a formidable weapon

The M16 rifle which became standard issue with the US forces in Vietnam, and which is still used by NATO forces today, is a direct descendant of the Armalite AR-10. This rifle was designed in 1953 by Eugene Stoner as a replacement for the M1 carbine then in service with the US armed forces. The AR-10, however, was rejected by the army in favour of the M14, the main complaint being that it was too light to fire the standard NATO 7.62mm bullet. The AR-10 was tested by several other Western countries but did not find any buyers.

In the late 1950s the US military increasingly adopted the Soviet tactic of sacrificing accuracy in favour of lighter weapons with a faster rate of fire. This saw the AR-10 redesigned to fire the new lighter 5.56mm ammunition and the result was the AR-15 which went into production in 1959. It was bought first by the US Air Force, and later by the Army to replace the heavy and awkward M14. It was renamed the M16. Soon after this, production was switched to the Colt Firearms Corporation. Colt supplied the army with 85,000 M16s in 1963 and a further 200,000 over the next three years

The M16 possessed a rapid rate of fire, and a high muzzle velocity. This meant that in a close-range firefight the bullets would hit their target at supersonic speed and turn internal organs into a bloody mush. It also possessed an 'in line' recoil feature which reduced the tendency of the barrel to jar sideways or climb upwards when firing on automatic. The compact nature of the M16 made it an easy weapon to carry into combat.

However, in spite of these advantages there were major teething problems with the M16. Firstly, the spring in the magazine was weak and filling it with the capacity 30 rounds could lead to a jam. Troops soon learnt by experience that loading only 27 or 28 bullets into the magazine rather than filling it helped solve that. The big problem, however, lay with the gun's firing mechanism. To keep the gun light, the M16 was designed with neither a piston nor a bolt handle. Instead, the hammer was operated by gas pressure.

This meant that the gun – especially the chamber and gas tubes – had to be kept very clean. The mud and dust of Vietnam's battlefields made this task difficult enough. To make matters worse, the slow-burning ball powder ammunition was notorious for leaving calcium carbonate deposits in the gas tube. When this happened, the gun jammed instantly, often in the middle of a firefight. Since the M16 did not possess a bolt handle, it was almost impossible to clear the barrel in combat – especially as many soldiers were not issued with proper cleaning kits. The only way the gun could be unjammed was by ramming a cleaning rod.

This unreliability assumed almost legendary proportions, caused a congressional enquiry and cost many lives before the problem was finally solved by redesigning the gun with an easy-to-clean chrome chamber and issuing troops with cleaning kits.

With the problems ironed out, the M16 proved itself to be a reliable and hard hitting weapon. Indeed, over 4 million have been produced to date and the M16 is now in such widespread use with so many of the western armed services that it could almost be described as NATO's equivalent of the Kalashnikov.

Above: A Marine puts his M16 to the test.

DEFECTORS FROM THE VC

They called them 'Kit Carson Scouts' – deserters from the Viet Cong who helped the US forces. But what were their motives? And would a grunt ever trust a former member of the Viet Cong?

Distrusted by his new comrades, and hated by his old ones, the average VC defector, and especially a Kit Carson Scout (below), was recruited through the Chieu Hoi Program. Massive propaganda drops from light aircraft (top right) included incentives such as safe-conduct passes (bottom right) issued by the South Vietnamese Government.

It is doubtful whether the average ex-VC Kit Carson Scout guiding American troops through 'Indian country' in 1967 had the slightest idea that his namesake had scouted against real Indians thousands of miles away. Indeed, he would more likely be pondering on how he would spend the paisters he was being paid for betraying his former comrades, or perhaps worrying that the nervous and untrusting grunt walking behind him might misinterpret one of his actions and put a bullet in his back. Any Kit Carson Scout with a sense of irony might smile at finding himself crawling through the claustrophobic stench of a VC tunnel complex in the company of American tunnel rats: the same type of tunnel complex had helped to convince him to give up his previous troglodyte existence and 'rally' to the government cause. For the most part, however, the Kit Carson Scout thought about the same thing most participants in the war thought about – survival.

The Kit Carson Scouts were an offshoot of the Chieu Hoi (open arms) amnesty programme

1967

THE CHIEU HOI PROGRAM

It would be wrong to imagine that the VC consisted entirely of dedicated revolutionaries, intent on freeing South Vietnam from the influence of the 'American Imperialists' and imposing a communist regime. A proportion must have felt that way, but significant numbers of VC recruits were just ordinary peasants, persuaded by communist propaganda or intimidated by threats to themselves or their families to join a revolution they neither fully supported nor completely understood. In such circumstances, their morale was constantly at risk, posing a problem for their leaders and presenting an opportunity to their enemies.

Morale was affected by a variety of factors. The most obvious was that it was no fun being a guerrilla. You had to be a dedicated believer in the cause to put up with the physical hardships involved, including lack of food, spartan living, constant movement across difficult terrain and restricted contact with families or friends. When this was added to ceaseless indoctrination, a lack of entertainment and rigid security, it did not take much to persuade a waiverer to search for escape.

This was where the government came in, for if they could offer attractive incentives — money, better food, more regular leave and contact with families — the waiverer might turn himself in, weakening the guerrillas, providing intelligence and, if persuaded to join the government forces, offering unrivalled expertise in guerrilla techniques.

The Saigon government initiatea such a 'package' of incentives in 1963 through the Chieu Hoi amnesty programme, using leaflets, free passes, rewards and airborne or ground-based loudspeakers to tempt the waiverers to change sides. Some success was achieved — by the end of 1967 over 75,000 communists had taken full advantage and defected, their morale as guerrillas effectively shattered by the combination of harsh conditions and government promises.

which had begun in 1962. Under this, former members of the Viet Cong could turn themselves in – often by presenting an air-dropped pamphlet bearing the South Vietnamese flag on one side and a promise of safe conduct on the other – and receive good treatment at a government 're-education centre'. Throughout the war the Chieu Hoi programme was controversial. Its opponents claimed that many VC used it as a way to infiltrate the South, or simply exploited R&R by being well fed and sheltered by the government before rejoining their comrades back in the jungle. The supporters of Chieu Hoi argued that many defectors provided good intelligence and that the programme was good 'psy' war — worrying the VC cadre about the possibility of defections. Both views of Chieu Hoi held some validity: there were infiltrators, but there were also many real turncoats.

An atmosphere of distrust

The Kit Carson Scouts were formed during the summer of 1966 from experienced and promising VC who had been encouraged to defect by Chieu Hoi. The Scouts were used to help counter the inexperience of US troops, caused by a combination of poor jungle training and a one-year tour of duty. The latter meant that experienced jungle fighters were constantly leaving to be replaced by FNG's (Frigging New Guys). Kit Carson Scouts functioned much as the old Indian scouts had on the American frontier and the 'Turned Terrorists' had in Britain's Malayan campaign of the early

1950s. They would lend their jungle experience and specialised knowledge of the enemy to that of the allied forces. Although they were often viewed with a distrust based on the assumption they might still be VC, the Kit Carson Scouts proved to be very effective and, with a few exceptions, loyal.

Their reasons for coming over varied from disillusionment with the communist cause, to conflict with a superior, or simply a desire for better pay and living conditions. Certainly the high pay they received for service with the Americans went a long way towards keeping them loyal. The quick death meted out to any Kit Carson Scouts suspected of disloyalty to their new masters no doubt helped as well. Initially, the Scouts were employed chiefly with the US Marines in I Corps, but before long they were also assisting Army units. They were used in locating enemy personnel, weapons and supply caches, in spotting booby traps or ambushes, and, more subtly, helping US troops understand how the VC

1967

destroy VC tunnels and bunkers. Certain Special Forces projects also made use of Kit Carsons. The 'roadrunner' teams, composed of indigenous tribesmen dressed as VC or NVA, operated along communist trail networks and made use of the Scouts' experience to keep up on the enemy's methods and equipment. Whether he was working with the roadrunners or elsewhere, the Scout proved invaluable at luring VC into ambushes, and many were successful in getting others to rally to the government cause.

Ironically, the very reason many Scouts came over to the government side proved to be their undoing. The desire to be with his family often prompted a former VC to avail himself of the Chieu Hoi programme and come over. Also, once in the Kit Carson Scouts he would have the money to give his family a better standard of living. However, visits to the family would have to be as clandestine as possible, for Kit Carson Scouts and their families were prime targets for assassination, mutilation and murder by the VC, who wanted to make examples of them to discourage others from contemplating changing sides. As with turncoats through history the Kit Carson Scout often found himself mistrusted by his new comrades and hated by his old ones.

Left to their fate

The Kit Carson Scouts were phased out around 1971 when the US ground commitment ebbed, though many were incorporated into South Vietnamese units. As the fall of South Vietnam approached, many former Scouts no doubt realised that they were not only fighting for the South's survival, but for their own lives as well. It was doubtful whether the communists would deal kindly with those who betrayed them to join the 'puppets' of the South. After the fall of South Vietnam, former Kit Carson Scouts found themselves in the same position as former members of the National Police, the PRUs, and certain others who would be singled out for execution. Few ex-Kit Carson Scouts could have survived in Vietnam unless they joined one of the guerrilla organisations fighting against the present government, or unless they remained Viet Cong even while infiltrating the Scouts. Although most were left to their fate, a limited number of Kit Carson Scouts probably made it out of South Vietnam during the hectic final days of the war, or even after the fall, especially those with good contacts within the US 'spook shops'.

Throughout the history of warfare, turncoats have rarely been treated with respect. They have been distrusted, yet used whenever possible to further the ends of those employing them. The Kit Carson Scouts were no different. Their skills certainly saved a lot of American lives and, on an individual level, some Kit Carson Scouts became very close to the Americans they worked with – especially among the tunnel rats. Today, however, the Kit Carson Scouts remain only a footnote to a long and nasty war.

Top left: A would-be Scout is put through a rigorous interrogation. US officials were mindful that many volunteers were in actual fact VC infiltrators on intelligence missions. Many Scouts were used to persuade others to join the government cause, by demonstrating the incentives offered (bottom left). But this often disclosed their identity to their former masters.

thought and operated. Since many of the Scouts had lived in VC tunnel complexes before their defection, they were in special demand to work with US 'tunnel rats'. Most VC tunnels were constructed along similar patterns, and the Scouts could predict with a high degree of accuracy where booby traps might be located, where important documents might be stored. Whenever possible, they would try to coax VC out of the tunnels. Although tunnel rats might initially be wary of the Scout assigned to them, once he had proved himself, the Kit Carson Scout often became an accepted part of their outfit.

Kit Carson Scouts proved especially valuable in guiding patrols around Khe Sanh, and some were present at that base during the long siege of January-April 1968. Other Scouts worked with the Royal Thai forces, helping them find and

Below: A captured member of the VC (in disguise) is made to point out former comrades to members of the 27th Infantry 'Wolfhounds'. If he wanted to stay alive, a man such as this had little option but to change sides. After the programme was ended, former Scouts (right) faced a bleak future, pondering the likely revenge to be meted out to them once the Americans had left.

1967

SENSORS AND

Sci-fi ideas and new technology – all designed to sniff out the human animal

In 1967, the war in Vietnam had become an episode of Star Trek. The military commanders in Saigon believed that if they showed the courage and fortitude of Captain James T. Kirk, they'd win through in the end. Washington believed in the superior technology of Science Officer Spock. And the grunt on the ground believed that, at the end of a year, he'd be beamed up by Scotty. Meanwhile Laos had turned into the Twilight Zone.

In Laos, there were private armies, backed by the CIA. Defoliants rained from the sky. Government agents dealt in drugs. Secret bombing mis-

Bombing raids on the Ho Chi Minh Trail (right, centre) by planes such as the A7 Corsair (above) were acting on information supplied by the sensor devices dropped all over the Trail. These included the PSID (right) and were

sions pulverized a country still supposedly at peace. Clean-cut Green Berets fought alongside opium-smoking warlords. Medieval princes collaborated with modern-day Marxists. Stone-age tribesmen were armed with the latest 20th-century weapons. And strange space-aged probes fell from the heavens. Long ago, Laos had given up its place in the real world.

The reason this backward country had been propelled into another dimension was the Ho Chi Minh Trail. From the beginning the Americans knew they must close this communist supply line. The problem was that Laos remained stubbornly neutral. After all, the Laotians were split into three factions – rightists backed by the Americans, the communist Pathet Lao and a neutralist faction. Any overt ground operations on their territory by the Americans would simply widen the theatre of the war.

Aerial interdiction, science fiction

So the US Air Force and the US Navy started secret bombing missions, or aerial interdiction as they called it. This, of course, was against international law. And it was a direct contravention of the American Constitution. But then, in Laos, only the rules of science fiction applied.

Unfortunately, as the Ho Chi Minh Trail was more a network of footpaths than a two-lane blacktop, the US planes had a problem finding anything useful to drop their bombs on. They tried using reconnaissance planes, but they could not see through the jungle canopy. So the Ranch Hands were sent in to defoliate the trees, but the paths soon changed and the undergrowth quickly grew back. And anyway, it was easy enough for the North Vietnamese to move by night.

Covert ground reconnaissance was used: road watch teams drawn from Major General Vang Pao's CIA-sponsored private army of Meo tribesmen, and US Special Forces who undertook Shining Brass reconnaissance sorties into Laos from South Vietnam. The primitive Meo tribesmen's

SURVEILLANCE

loaded (far right) into planes such as PV-2 Neptunes, seen here (top right), dropping Adsids. Neptunes were used because of their navigational aids. But as enemy AAA defences along the Trail grew, faster F4 Phantoms had to be deployed.

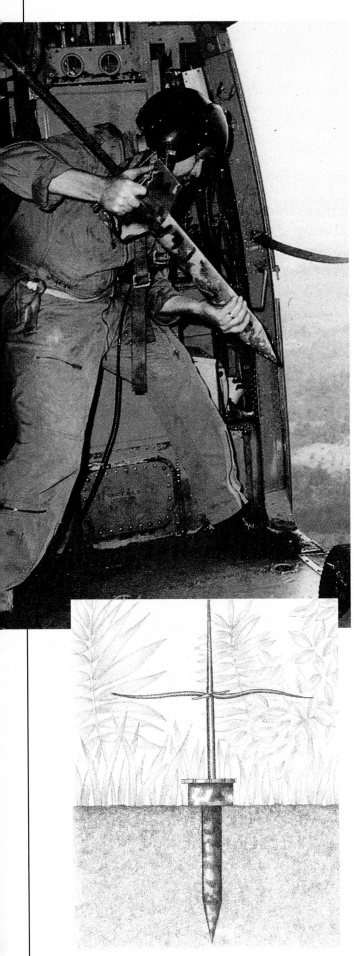

information was unreliable though. And North Vietnamese soon became very adept at hunting down the Green Berets' 12-man A Teams.

One science fiction answer proposed by US defence scientists was the use of electronic sensors instead. These were manufactured by the Pentagon's obscure Defense Communications Planning Group, at the behest of the shadowy think tank known only as the Institute of Defense Analysis.

The sensors were designed to be air-dropped from helicopters or planes and were called Spikebuoy, Acoubuoy, Adsid and Acousid. Spikebuoy and Acoubuoy used sonar technology modified for land use. When Spikebuoy fell from a plane, it was designed to hit the ground hard enough to bury the body of the device, leaving only the aerial protruding. Acoubuoy had a parachute which slowed its fall and hung the unit up in the jungle canopy. Both were battery powered and tuned to respond to particular sound frequencies – those made by men or trucks. The devices would transmit signals which would be picked up by an aircraft circling above.

Smashed to bits

The 3ft long and 6in diameter Adsid – air-delivered seismic intruder detector – was the most widely used unit. Like Spikebuoy, it was a free fall device which buried itself in the ground. Its antenna was 4ft long and shaped like a jungle plant and its onboard radio transmitter was pre-set to transmit when it detected seismic vibrations. Adsid had a battery life of between 30 and 45 days.

The Acousid detected both sound and seismic vibrations and later a device was introduced that detected the ignition systems of truck engines. Seeding the trail with these detectors began during the mid-1967 when the USAF's 20th Helicopter Squadron began launching Helosids – helicopter-delivered seismic detectors – from its Sikorsky CH-3C. This was not a great success as the sensors were often smashed to bits when they hit the ground.

On 15 November 1967, the US Navy arrived at Nakhon Phanom in Thailand with OP-2E Neptune aeroplanes specifically modified for the sensor dropping. But when the squadron went into action on the 25th, they were little more successful than the CH-3Cs. As the Neptunes were originally designed for hunting submarines and dropping sensors at sea, they flew low and slow, presenting ideal targets for the NVA anti-aircraft gunners on the trail.

More successful were the F-4D Phantoms of the USAF's 25th Tactical Fighter Squadron who took over in late June 1968. Equipped with the sophisticated Loran-D navigation system, these aircraft could place the sensors accurately and evade the worst of the North Vietnamese defences. Where to drop the sensors was decided after intelligence from aerial photography, observation flights, the interrogation of prisoners and ground reconnaissance was evaluated. They were deployed in straight lines running diagonally

Left: An airman prepares to launch a Spikebuoy sensor from a CH-3E helicopter. The Spikebuoy, like the Adsid (bottom left) was designed to bury itself in the ground, with only its antenna showing. All the information that they transmitted was picked up by Beech Bonanza light planes and relayed to high-flying Lockheed C-121 Warning Star reconnaissance aircraft (top right). Below: A GI out on patrol, searching for enemy presence with a 'people-sniffer' attached to the muzzle of his M16.

across active routes or in box patterns around truck parks or rest areas. Once the sensors were in place, the data was transmitted to a Lockheed EC-121R Warning Star from thc USAF's 553d Reconnaissance Wing circling above. They relayed it to the top-secret Infiltration Surveillance Center at Nakhon Phanom.

The problem with this arrangement was that while the Warning Star had the internal volume to carry the necessary electronics and the endurance to remain on station for extended periods, it was just as vulnerable to enemy fire as the Navy's Neptunes. So, under the Pave Eagle programme, the USAF introduced the QU 22 derivative of the Beech Bonanza light plane. This was unmanned and acted as an intermediate relay, passing the data on to the Warning Stars who operated out of range of the NVA's anti-aircraft guns.

At the heart of the operation was the Infiltration Surveillance Center at Nakhon Phanom in Thailand run by the USAF's Task Force Alpha. Known locally as the Dutch Mill after its windmill-shape main antenna, the ISC used two IBM 360-65 computers to process the incoming data. The centre then ordered immediate air strikes against targets they'd identified. They also planned future missions. By calculating the speed and direction of travel of a particular convoy detected one night, they could estimate with reasonable accuracy where it would be the following night.

The trail surveillance operation Igloo White cost a massive $725 million between 1967 and

1971. As one US Air Force officer put it: 'Every fourth bush on the Ho Chi Minh Trail had an antenna in it.' But it must be seen as a failure.

It is not known what counter measures the NVA took against this surveillance. But for all their electronic intelligence, the Americans could not stop the flow of men and equipment south. Maybe the devices they used weren't sophisticated enough. Maybe the sort of technology that worked in the sterile conditions of the moon could not cope with the real world. Maybe you couldn't fight a war with machines instead of men. Or maybe the goodies did not always triumph over the baddies and even rules of science fiction did not apply.

Some of the planes called in to bomb the Ho Chi Minh Trail came from the USS Enterprise whose five-year mission had boldly brought it to the South China sea. But Laos was the Twilight Zone – and no one ever returned control of the set.

PEOPLE SNIFFERS

Although the acoustic and seismic surveillance devices of 1967 did not work well, still the scientists went on trying. Clifton Berry was operations officer with the 196th (Light Infantry) Brigade and was tasked with testing the new devices they came up with.

'In early 1968, the brigade chemical officer returned from Chu Lai to the forward command post with great news. A new electrochemical device had arrived from the Stateside laboratories, and we were to test it. Called the XM2 (modified E63) airborne personnel detector, it was an infantryman's dream. The device was said to detect enemy troops, even those hidden in the jungle. Already nicknamed People Sniffer, this sensor had undergone field trials in the States. The concept was simple. Human sweat and body wastes, both liquid and solid, give off minute particles into the atmosphere. Since the air in Vietnam was relatively free of pollutants, even tiny concentrations of human waste could be detected.

'Mounted on a Huey helicopter, the People Sniffer patrol would scout large areas. When it detected exudations from people, such as the ammonia from urine, the indicator needle would jump. Then the pilot would simply fly upwind toward the source, find the enemy and call in the location.

'It was an ingenious idea and we were ready for the tryout. Up went the chemical officer in the specially-rigged helicopter, flying a pre-arranged search pattern. He quickly found that the sniffer reacted. The trouble was, there were too many people and animals around and the waste from women, children and old men gave the same readings as those from troops.

'Out in the fields, the rivers of urine from thousands of water buffalo overrode any indication from human insurgents. And in heavy jungle, wild animal waste also triggered the sensors. Almost anywhere we flew, the needles jumped, indicating something was there. But what?

'The People Sniffer sniffed too well. We ODed on false alarms. There were too many to cope. So we sent it back — another gadget that seemed ideal but didn't work out in practice.'

ELECTRONICS AT WAR

Electronic warfare first came into its own during World War II. Radar was an invaluable aid to the RAF during the Battle of Britain, while during the bombing offensive over Germany later in the war there was a constant struggle to gain technological advantage.

At sea, too, electronics were crucial. The Battle of the Atlantic was won in large part because Asdic enabled escort vessels to locate German U-Boats underwater, while aircraft provided with radar sets were able to detect U-Boats on the surface at night.

During the Vietnam war, however, the US took the concept of electronic warfare to a new level, hoping that sheer technological ingenuity could supplant the need for troops on the ground.

The Vietnam war accelerated electrical-optical systems such as the laser and night vision devices. Early laser devices had quite low energy outputs and so were used in missile and bomb guidance. The drawback was that cloud, smoke or haze would diffuse or deflect the laser beams, limiting their effectiveness under war conditions – or even when the weather was bad. Where the war-generated development was successsful was in the vast array of electronic systems for command, control and communications (C3) that has become a vital part of the modern battlefield.

But whereas it had been possible to destroy sufficient submarines in the Atlantic to inflict unacceptable losses during World War II, stopping the flow of men down the Ho Chi Minh Trail was a totally different ball game. The US failure marked a triumph of man over machine.

DEATH OF AN AMERICAN

EYE-WITNESS

Costas Manos, a photographer for the Magnum agency, was driving down a back road in Mount Pleasant, SC, when he passed a funeral. He stopped and captured the tragedy of another victim of Vietnam on film.

Left: Tears are no consolation to Ethel Scott, the dead soldier's aunt. Above right: Harold T. Edmondson Senior holds Harold Jr's young brother. Will he lose another son to this senseless violence? Right: The open invitation to the funeral. Below right: The flag, which never gave him a fair shake, is folded. Far right top: The pall bearers' heavy duty. Will it be their turn next? Far right bottom: The grandparents — were these the equal rights they'd spent their whole lives waiting for?

PFC Harold T. Edmondson Jr, 19. Killed in South Vietnam. Buried in South Carolina

Funeral Services

for the Late

Harold T. Edmondson, Jr.

— AT —

EBENEZER A.M.E. CHURCH

44 NASSAU STREET
CHARLESTON, SOUTH CAROLINA

Dr. B. J. FINKLEA, Pastor

MONDAY, FEBRUARY 14, 1966

AT 2:00 O'CLOCK P.M.

— Interment —

ZION A.M.E. CEMETERY

12-Mile, Mt. Pleasant, South Carolina

Wainwright Printers

THE AUSTRALIAN COMMITMENT

Australian troops had experience of fighting communist guerrillas in Malaya, and they brought to Vietnam skills that added a new edge to the anti-communist forces operating there against the VC

Major Peter Badcoe of Australian Army Training Team, Vietnam, was supposed to have been on leave in Okinawa the day he died in 1967, but he had managed to wangle his way out of it. He had met his mate, Major Ross Buchan, at Hue airfield as planned, but said that because of the illness of an advisor he was not coming on leave. Instead he was taking over as duty officer. Buchan shrugged. This was not untypical of Badcoe. He did not mix much and, unusually for an Aussie, did not drink or smoke.

Back in 1962, during his first visit to Vietnam, he'd been delayed in Saigon for two days by engine trouble. But instead of having a root and a toot around sin city, he joined an ARVN operation in the Mekong Delta. His justification was that he 'wanted to get the feel of a guerrilla war in a basically hostile population'.

After saying cheerio to Buchan, Badcoe went back to sector headquarters and began combing through the radio messages. He quickly learned that there was a firefight in progress less than eight miles away.

He grabbed his equipment and checked his rifle and ammunition. He jumped in a jeep and collected Sergeant Alberto Alvarado, his assistant and radio operator. Together they sped towards the village of An Thuan.

Bullets sliced the air around him

There, they found the ARVN preparing for a second attack. Badcoe and Alvarado joined the leading cavalry vehicles and led the charge towards the enemy positions. As they reached a cemetery some 250yds from the communist forces, the fire became heavy. Further advance was met with machine-gun, rifle, mortar and recoilless rifle fire.

Badcoe and Alvarado left their vehicle and moved out in front of the infantry to lead their assault. But the fire was so intense the ARVN troops were forced to retreat. Undeterred, with bullets slicing the air around him, Badcoe moved through the ranks of soldiers, who were now hugging the ground, rallying them for a fresh assault.

After an artillery barrage, Badcoe led another charge with Alvarado close behind. The ground was flat and open. Fire was coming from the front as well as the flanks – but Badcoe pushed forward

Above: Major Peter Badcoe. Far left: Escorted by a phalanx of APCs, the 1st Ranger Battalion moves into Bien Hoa Province as a prelude to taking on the enemy in his jungle haunts (left). Constant vigilance, and machines that pumped gas into the tunnels (below), was needed to prise the VC from their lair.

1967

1967

setting an example for the company to follow.

They were stopped again by a hail of fire, but Badcoe refused to fall back. He had spotted an enemy machine-gun post and headed straight for it. In the midst of heavy, well-aimed fire, he took cover in the knee-high rice. Suddenly, Badcoe rose with a grenade in his hand. Alvarado pulled him down as bullets whistled overhead.

Not to be stopped, Badcoe crawled further. He rose again and was immediately hit by the Viet Cong machine gunner. Alvarado was hit in the leg in a vain attempt to recover his body.

Those who knew Badcoe were not surprised when they heard of his death. An artillery officer by training, he had always preferred the daring

**Below:
Australians add one more Viet Cong to their body count. It was rumoured that the men from Oz considered only a 300yd trail of blood as a legitimate claim for enemy wounded.**

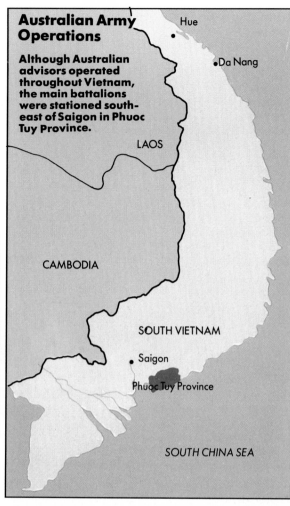

Australian Army Operations

Although Australian advisors operated throughout Vietnam, the main battalions were stationed south-east of Saigon in Phuoc Tuy Province.

PHUOC TUY PROVINCE

Between June 1966 and November 1971, Australian forces conducted their own counter-insurgency (COIN) campaign in Phuoc Tuy Province, to the southeast of Saigon in III Corps. An area of about 150,000 square miles, Phuoc Tuy comprised a central plain, bordered to the west by the 'impenetrable' Rung Sat Special Zone, to the north and east by VC-dominated hills and to the south by the sea. It was a known centre of VC activity.

The first task confronting the Australian force, a two- (later three-) battalion group, was to dominate the central plain. This was achieved by occupying a prominent hill feature known as Nui Dat, close to Binh Ba in the middle of the province, and constructing a fire-base for US 8in and Australian 105mm howitzers. Their range protected infantry patrolling out to about 17,000 yards (beyond which Australian SAS operations took place), and it was during this phase of the campaign that one of the few pitched battles occurred. On 18 August 1966, D Company of the 6th Royal Australian Regiment clashed with elements of the VC 275th Regiment at Long Tan, inflicting heavy casualties.

Success at Long Tan allowed the Australians to concentrate on COIN within the artillery zone. Many of the techniques – the resettlement of villagers in secure areas, civic action ('hearts and minds') and the raising of local forces loyal to Saigon – were based on those perfected by Commonwealth troops in Malaya between 1948 and 1960, and concentrated on splitting the insurgents from their local support. Some mistakes were made – for example the construction of a mine barrier south of Dat Do merely allowed the VC to lift the mines for their own use – and there were never enough Australian troops to dominate the whole of the province while simultaneously protecting the people. But a remarkable degree of pacification was achieved. Unfortunately, when the Australians withdrew in late 1971, the VC quickly regained the upper hand.

infantry-style raid to sitting behind the guns. And his boundless enthusiasm for action was regarded with sympathetic tolerance.

In 1966, for example, within a week of beginning his second tour in Vietnam, Badcoe had been out on a clearing operation with a company of regional force militia when they were stopped by a VC bunker. After an unsuccessful attempt to silence the enemy with rifle fire and grenades, the company commander requested air support. But Badcoe replied that it would not be necessary for just five men in a bunker.

Instead, he got two jerricans of petrol from a jeep in the rear and made for the bunker, whose occupants were by this time concentrating their

fire against him. After a final dash from the blind side, Badcoe emptied the jerricans over the bunker. He ignited the petrol with a phosphorus grenade. The bunker silenced, the company moved forward.

The Badcoe legend quickly began to grow, but it wasn't until 1967 that the exploits that led to his Victoria Cross – awarded posthumously – began. On the hot afternoon of 23 February, Badcoe was with a company of Ruff-Puffs, assisted by Captain James Custar of the US Marines. They were crossing a dry paddy field looking for VC. Captain Clement and Sergeant George Thomas of the US Army were leading another platoon 600yds to the flank.

AUSSIES IN THE NAM

In July 1962, the Australian government sent 30 advisors to South Vietnam, beginning 10 years of Australian involvement in the Vietnam war.

The number of advisors continued to rise steadily, and in 1965 1400 combat troops were committed to the conflict. On its arrival in Vietnam, this contingent was welcomed by none other than General Westmoreland himself (above). Over the next two and a half years this force was expanded until it peaked in December 1967 with 7672 Aussies in the Nam.

The ground forces were mainly concerned with carrying out routine search and destroy operations in Phuoc Tuy Province, southeast of Saigon. As a result they saw few large-scale operations until 1968, when Australian forces helped defend US bases at Binh Hoa and Long Binh.

On an individual level, there were numerous examples of bravery, with 4 Victoria Crosses and over 50 other medals awarded.

Back home in Australia, however, the war was even less popular with the public than it was in America. It provoked protest, controversy and impassioned debate, the effect of which far outweighed the size of the Australian commitment.

Between July 1962 and December 1972, (when the last advisors were withdrawn) 46,852 Australians served in Vietnam. The final count was 496 killed and 2398 wounded, and the whole adventure cost the Australian government somewhere in the region of $A500 million.

Below: Australian troops close in on a VC enclave. Right: To the rear, medics patch up a wounded colleague. Only very rarely did the Aussies wear helmets into action, and they usually tore the insignia from their uniforms as a precaution against maltreatment of captured officers.

1967

Badcoe and Custar heard rifle fire, and over the radio came the message that Thomas was in trouble and Clement had been hit. Next they heard a machine gun. Badcoe left Custar with the Ruff-Puffs and began to jog towards the sound of the firing, across the open paddy field which was being raked by fire.

Reaching the beleaguered platoon, Badcoe found that Clement had been hit going to the aid of one of his men, and Thomas had been hit trying to reach him. The platoon had withdrawn to a small rise, but the increasing intensity of the VC's fire suggested they were in company strength and about to attack.

Badcoe rallied his small force and led them straight towards the enemy position. Dodging the automatic fire, Badcoe charged a machine gun post with his rifle and shot the crew.

As the platoon took heart and continued the attack, Badcoe evaded small arms fire to retrieve Clement's body and rescue the wounded Thomas.

Two weeks later, the district headquarters of Quang Dien was attacked by two battalions of VC. Badcoe – 25 klicks away in Hue – headed for the action. On the way his jeep careered off the road, killing his assistant, a US captain. Badcoe left the vehicle and hitched a ride with a Vietnamese company commander.

At Quang Dien, Badcoe found the headquarters surrounded on three sides by the VC. Quickly he formed the relieving company into three platoons and led them in a mad dash across open, fire-raked ground to a position where they outflanked the enemy. From there, Badcoe led a fierce assault against the main body of enemy troops and forced the VC to withdraw.

These two actions and his fatal attack on the machine-gun post at An Thuan earned Badcoe the Victoria Cross. His memorial service in Hue was the largest for any allied soldier. Colonel Arch Hamblen Jr., deputy senior advisor in I Corps, said of him: 'He was courageous to an infinite degree – almost fearless, I should think.'

Above left: Riding high on an armoured personnel carrier. Below: Following a successful search and destroy operation, Australian Rangers board a flotilla of Hueys bound for base.

SHOULD AUSTRALIA HAVE FOUGHT?

Apart from the US and South Vietnam, other countries lent their support to the war effort. Should they have got involved?

Although the US and South Vietnamese forces bore the brunt of the fighting in Vietnam, they were not alone. One in eight allied troops were there in response to President Johnson's 'More Flags' campaign which attempted to get as many other countries as possible involved in Vietnam so that the war could then be presented as a free world effort to stop the spread of communism in Southeast Asia.

Many countries lent their support, mainly in the form of medical supplies. Britain sent a printing press for the Saigon government's propaganda machine. The Swiss sent microscopes for Saigon University. Morocco sent 10,000 cans of sardines! But only seven countries – Australia, New Zealand, South Korea, Thailand, The Philippines, The Republic of China (Taiwan) and Spain – sent men.

The biggest contingent was the Koreans, who numbered 48,000 in 1967. But they did not come cheap. America had to agree to modernize the Korean armed forces and grant Korea several lucrative military contracts – making the ARVN's uniforms, for example.

The now disgraced President Marcos of the Philippines sent 2000 troops in 1966. In return, the Americans turned a blind eye as he turned his country into a virtual dictatorship.

If South Vietnam fell, nearby Thailand would almost certainly be threatened by the spread of communism in the area. As well as sending 11,568 troops, the Thais allowed B52s, Phantoms and reconnaissance aircraft – along with the Infiltration Surveillance Center – on their soil.

The Republic of China which, like Korea, had its own beef against communism and its own reasons for keeping in with the US, sent 31 men. Franco's Fascist Spain sent a 13-man medical team. And there are rumours that members of the British SAS had some covert involvement in Vietnam.

The peak Australian strength was 7672 and New Zealand's 552. Both governments felt they had good reason to fight. They had seen communist insurgency in Malaya and were convinced that it would spread further south if Vietnam fell.

But in both countries anti-war feeling – especially among the young who risked being drafted – ran high. They discounted the domino theory and pointed out that the insurgency in Malaya had been halted with relative ease.

1967

A giant electronic fence hacked through mountain and jungle – was this the answer to communist infiltration into South Vietnam?

THE McNAMARA LINE

US Secretary of Defense Robert McNamara (right) was appalled by the rising cost in men and machines caused by the largely ineffective standard military options. By building an impassable barrier south of the DMZ he hoped to free American units (below) tied up in preventing NVA infiltration. Construction of the Line was well under way by September, 1967. Right: Using a rock-drill to dig fence-post holes Bottom right: Sweating GIs working to set up a fire-base along the barrier.

Innocuous looking bed-bugs, wired up so that they could, literally, bug enemy troop movements; kamikaze pigeons, loaded up with explosives and trained to dive-bomb truck convoys; even monitoring devices disguised as dog-shit. What part did these strange devices, straight out of James Bond, have to do with the blood and guts reality of the killing fields of Vietnam? And why were M, Q and Dr No discussing them in a girls' school in Massachusetts?

On 7 September 1967, Secretary of Defense Robert McNamara announced that an impassable barrier was being created along the southern edge of the DMZ in Vietnam, extending up to the southern dogleg of Laos to cover the Ho Chi Minh Trail. It was to be composed of stretches of barbed wire, sensor devices, mines and chemical weapons, interspersed at intervals with well-defined and defoliated free-fire zone corridors.

Initial press reaction was favourable, and possible names being bandied about for the barrier included: McNamara's Wall, De Fence, The Strip, McNamara's Fairway, The Electronic Fence. Finally general consensus settled on The McNa-

The idea of creating a physical barrier to prevent the movement of enemy forces or supplies is nothing new. The Romans who built Hadrian's Wall used it, as did the French who constructed the Maginot Line in the 1930s, but more recently it has become closely associated with counter-insurgency, particularly campaigns in which the insurgents depend on outside sources of support. Prevent contact between the guerrillas and the outsiders, and the guerrillas will be decisively weakened, even to the point of defeat.

Examples of success were provided by the French in the 1950s. During their war against the Viet Minh in Indochina (1946-54), they constructed a barrier of interlocking blockhouses around the key cities of Hanoi and Haiphong – the De Lattre Line – and although this was occasionally breached, it did provide protection as well as a reasonably secure base from which to mount more mobile operations. More impressive (and relevant to the American dilemma on the DMZ in the 1960s) was the Morice Line, built by the French along the Tunisian border during the war in Algeria (1954-62). At the time, this was seen as a miracle of modern technology, comprising an electrified fence, minefields and mobile reaction forces. By April 1958, only seven months after completion of the Line, it was reckoned that 85 per cent of guerrillas who tried to breach the barrier were being killed or captured.

With such effectiveness on record, it was perhaps natural for the Americans to try a similar approach on the DMZ in Vietnam, and although the McNamara Line was never completed, its principles of sensors and reaction fire were sound. Since Vietnam, other armed forces have also adopted the idea, notably the Sultan of Oman's (under British leadership) in the Dhofar War (1970-75), where the Hornbeam, Hammer and Damarvand Lines gradually isolated the Marxist rebels from their support bases in neighbouring South Yemen.

mara Line. But if the journalists had known the outlandish story behind the scheme, they would have been incredulous.

During the summer of 1966, the cloistered halls of Dana Hall, a quiet, secluded Prep school for girls in Wellesley, Massachussetts, was the leafy, sun-dappled and tranquil setting for an intensive series of seminars and study groups. But the subjects discussed were not the usual 3Rs of innocent childhood, but the killing machines of war. It had also been the unlikely forum for some of the most bizarre discussions ever conducted during the course of the war.

Jason and the Argonauts

Attending the seminars was a group of top academic scientists known as the 'Jasons' – after Jason and the Argonauts who also took a mythological trip into uncharted territory. They had gathered at the behest of McNamara, who was responding to a memo he had received earlier from Robert Fisher of Harvard Law School. Fisher had suggested building a physical barrier, 10 miles wide and 160 miles long, designed to stop NVA infiltration. Neither Admiral Sharp (Commander in Chief, Pacific) nor General Westmoreland thought that it would solve any problems, but the Secretary of Defense determined to pursue the matter.

The first report out of Dana Hall estimated that the whole thing could be set up 'a year or so from

1967

M107 175mm self-propelled gun located in supporting fire-base

THE McNAMARA LINE

CH-54 Tarhe Sky-Crane ferrying in supplies

Watch-tower to spot NVA units infiltrating through the DMZ

C130 Defoliation plane working to create defoliated zones either side of the barrier.

SeaBee unit, assisted by an M48 tank complete with dozer-blade, constructing the main barrier. This barrier included barbed wire, mines, watchtowers, search-lights and a whole range of seismic sensor devices.

SCHEMATIC PLAN OF PROPOSED BARRIER

NORTH VIETNAM

LAOS

DMZ

MAIN PHYSICAL BARRIER

SUPPORTING FIREBASES

SOUTH VIETNAM

SOUTH CHINA SEA

go-ahead', and could be refined as new technology emerged.

Among the most definite proposals was for an area about 12 miles wide and 60 miles long, cleared of people and sown liberally with a wide variety of small but lethal mines. These included 'gravel' mines, which were 3in square packets of cloth-covered explosive designed to detonate, with devastating results, when stepped upon or run over by a vehicle. There were also 'button bomblets', tiny devices no bigger than an aspirin which, when triggered by enemy activity, would, as well as possibly blowing off a few toes, make a noise that would be picked up by acoustic sensors. These were to be monitored by special patrol aircraft flying low over the barrier area. They would call in air strikes, in which Cluster bombs, designed to shower baseball-size bomblets around the target, would be used. The Jasons estimated that, to be effective, an annual commitment of 240 million gravel mines, 300 million 'button bomblets' and 120,000 Clusters would be needed. Add to this the need for more than 100 patrol and mine dropping aircraft, as well as the on-going requirement for new research, and the total cost would be a staggering one billion dollars. The scheme was nothing if not ambitious.

Unfortunately, it was also not totally foolproof as these bombs could be triggered by animals as well as humans, and stories abound of gunships and air-strikes being called down on some hapless water-buffalo.

Bed-bugs and dog shit

Some of the other ideas which emerged were totally bizarre. One whizz-kid came up with a proposal for using live bed-bugs. Having noticed that the hopefully friendly neighbourhood bed-bug stayed dormant until a human body came near, upon which it would get wildly excited at the prospect of a meal, the plan was simple: glue the bed-bugs to electrodes, distribute them over the DMZ. Rumour has it that the idea was actually tried out, but either the bugs did not take to the jungle or the glue melted. In any event, the experiment failed.

Another equally optimistic idea was the proposal to train pigeons, loaded with explosives, to land on enemy trucks, detonating on touchdown. But it soon became apparent that no pigeon could be trained to differentiate between a communist and a non-communist truck.

An attempt was made to disguise a monitor as a pile of dog shit (Turdsid), but this was quickly dropped after an Air-Cav commander pointed out, not too subtly, that while a bear might shit in the woods, there was no evidence that dogs had done so in the Vietnam jungle.

Even so, some of these monitoring devices were so good that conversations in the combat zone could be monitored. One of these, played to a Congressional Sub-Committee in 1970, clearly relayed Vietnamese voices, followed by the sound of axes being used to chop down the tree in which

Left: A Russian-made NVA 130mm gun used to shell Line installations. They had a greater range than the US 105mm gun, and their lightweight base made them more manoeuverable. These factors helped make them a constant threat to US forces working to construct the Line. Bottom: US troops involved in a typical fire-fight with NVA infiltrators. Below: Snipers working between the DMZ and the Line.

the device was snagged. The recording ended with a crash followed by screams as the tree fell on the men below.

Backed by new munitions such as the wide area anti-personnel mines and 'Daisy Cutters', all of which produced enormous destruction over vast swathes of territory, the acoustic devices clearly enhanced the potential of the projected barrier and successful experiments were being carried out, both in Florida and Vietnam, by mid-1967. By this time a 600 yard strip had already been cleared from the sea to about 10 miles inland – the Trace – just south of the DMZ.

Unfortunately, it soon became obvious that, since neither flank – the sea to the east and Laos to the west – could be made totally secure, NVA units and supply convoys could literally by-pass the barrier. At the same time, the actual construction of the barrier was made extremely hazardous under enemy's mortar, artillery and rocket fire. Field-commanders regarded it as yet another piece of hi-tech wizardry designed to prevent set-piece battles which were the only real way to win the war. By early 1968, despite Pentagon announcements that part of the Line was set up and working, press reports began to doubt its efficiency, and when this coincided with an obvious NVA build-up around Khe Sanh, to the south of the barrier, the whole affair was discredited.

1967

1967

For the average white middle class American man and his wife sitting at home in 1967, life had become a confusing and frightening dream. In his newspaper, the opinion polls showed that the great mass of the American people stood solidly behind the war effort in Vietnam. On the front page the official pronouncements were optimistic: the enemy was being hurt, 'our boys' were doing a great job, the war was going to be won – and soon. Yet the syndicated columnists pointed to gaping cracks in this reassuring facade. And the editorial pages suggest that, behind the scenes, even worse fissures were opening up, threatening to bring the whole edifice of US policy crashing down about President Johnson's ears.

Other strange things were happening in America at this time, according to the fat newspaper that landed on the stoop every morning. Since the Beat Generation of the 1950s, there had been a growing underground or counter culture. Their children, and the children of their friends, were rejecting the values they had been brought up with.

In the summer of 1967 it burst upon the front pages of America, and the world, as a youth revolution. In their tens of thousands, young people responded to the call of a Harvard professor – and LSD adocate – Timothy Leary to 'turn on, tune in and drop out': to turn on to hallucinogenic drugs and free love, tune in to flower power and a life of idleness and drop out of school, college or business. This was the summer of love. And for Mr and Mrs Middle America, their son growing his hair long and wearing beads and their daughter practising free love while high on pot was their worst nightmare made flesh.

But in the summer of 1967, another white

THE WAR AT HOME

Above: This area of Detroit's 12th Street black ghetto has not been hit by a B52 airstrike. Even Rolling Thunder did not reach this far north. It has been burned down during the July riots which bordered on an insurrection and brought the 82d Airborne Division to the streets of America. After action in the Pentagon parking lot, they were sent to Vietnam.

Love Ins, Human Be Ins, Make Love Not War, Black Power. Hippy slogans became mixed with urban racial violence as opposition to the war gathered momentum in 1967

American nightmare, perhaps even more potent, was being acted out in the streets and on the nightly newscasts. The blacks of the depressed ghettos of Newark and Detroit rioted with unprecedented violence. It was almost an uprising. In Detroit, troops who could have been fighting the Viet Cong were instead sent in to counter American snipers and arsonists as the cities burned. On the TV, pictures of the old non-violent leaders of black protest, men such as Martin Luther King, were replaced by armed Black Panthers, the Black Muslim Elijah Muhammad and by the revolutionary separatist Malcolm X – all of them intent on violent change.

Black riots and flower power

Neither the black riots nor the flower power movement were initially related to the war in Vietnam. But the link was soon made by the draft dodgers and their anti-war friends. The black radicals wanted nothing to do with 'the white man's war' while hippy daughters were happy with the simplistic slogan: 'Make Love Not War'. And in the so-called underground press left around the house, parents began to realize that, for their children, the anti-war movement was seen as inextricably bound up with a wider revolt against the military industrial complex upon which all the evils of US domestic and foreign policy were blamed.

Veterans Against the War

Since 1965, Students for a Democratic Society had been organizing 'teach-ins' at college, where prominent intellectuals lined up to explain their opposition to the war. Their names made impressive reading – novelist Norman Mailer, baby expert Dr Benjamin Spock, world-renowned linguistics professor Naom Chomsky – but it was not until 1967 that these articulate anti-war spokesmen began to appear on TV. Even on the nightly Johnny Carson show, where many mouthed 'my country right or wrong', other celebrity guests openly declared their opposition to government policy. Johnny, of course, never said what he thought – but the platform was there for those who wanted to use it.

Under the leadership of such men as pacifist David Dellinger – who in 1966 had become the first of many American radicals to visit Hanoi – and Jerry Rubin, later founder of the Yippies (Youth International Party), the anti-war movement spread into a broad coalition of all the disparate elements most despised by traditionalist White Anglo-Saxon Protestant (WASP) Americans – Black Muslims, white intellectuals, flower children, film stars, respectable but left-wing Democrats, provocative anarchists. They had only one thing in common, a conviction that the war had to be stopped. Increasingly, they were joined by Vietnam veterans, who formed their own organization, Vietnam Veterans Against the War. In every anti-war demonstration, their mutilated limbs added a powerful wordless pro-

Above: Sheriffs drag a demonstrator away. The police attacked hundreds of University of Colorado students with gas and batons. Right: American youth was divided. Demonstrators and troops: the same age, different uniforms. But in 1967, the phoney war was coming to an end. Here empty taunts confront empty guns.

1967

test to the crude slogan: 'Hey, hey, LBJ, how many kids did you kill today?'

The 1967 anti-war campaign climaxed on 21 October, when about 50,000 demonstrators marched on the Pentagon. In a televised show down, they faced 10,000 army troops and National Guardsmen drawn up to defend the building. The soldiers had rifles but no ammunition, but they were authorized to break up the demonstration by force. At first all was peaceful. Young people stepped forward to put flowers in the soldiers' gun-barrels. The attentions of another group of demonstrators were devoted to a mystical attempt to *levitate* the Pentagon. But eventually the demonstration was broken up with considerable brutality. Norman Mailer and many of this army of the night were arrested. Rioting erupted, continuing sporadically and violently, like a guerrilla action, for two days. Coverage of the 82d Airborne's action on the Potomac was interspersed with the 1st Air Cavalry's action at Dak To on the nightly news. The war may not have made it to the Pentagon's back door, but it had gotten as far as the parking lot – too close for comfort for the military technocrats.

'Mr and Mrs Middle America'

The immediate effect of the march on the Pentagon, though, was to confirm Mr and Mrs Middle America in their support of the war. Violence on the streets won few friends. President Johnson could rest secure in the knowledge that voters backed his war policy, even if the anti-war demonstrators included members of his own Democrat Party. The media had started to become more critical, and in Congress, a few Democrats had begun to express doubts about the war, including Senate Foreign Relations Committee chairman William Fulbright, Robert Kennedy and Eugene McCarthy. But these as yet posed no real threat to the president's authority. For the time being his

WHY THE HAWK BECAME A DOVE

In 1967, the war's chief architect, Robert McNamara, began to change his mind.

Secretary of Defense in both the Kennedy and Johnson administrations Robert McNamara was one of the most relentless advocates of the war. It had been McNamara who had presented evidence of North Vietnamese aggression to Congress after the Gulf of Tonkin Incident in 1964. He backed the National Security Council's approval for retaliatory air strikes in February 1965 and supported Westmoreland's demands for more troops. But by 1967 McNamara was growing steadily more disheartened with the lack of progress. The bombing campaign against the North was a failure. Millions of tons of bombs were being dropped but they were having no marked impact upon infiltration into the South, the North's economy or Hanoi's commitment. After his eighth trip to South Vietnam, in October 1966 – his first in almost a year – McNamara showed the first signs that his resolve was weakening. In a memorandum to Johnson on 14 October, McNamara suggested 'stabilising' the bombing campaign, limiting further troop increases and giving far greater emphasis to pacification and the promotion of genuine reform by Saigon. The concept of a technological barrier – the McNamara Line – as an alternative to bombing to prevent infiltration was accepted, but his other views found little support outside the State Department that handled foreign policy.

By March 1967 McNamara's retreat from the war was in full cry. He suggested limiting bombing to staging areas and infiltration routes. And in August 1967 he voiced his new views before the Preparedness Subcommittee of the Senate Armed Services Committee, which strongly favoured escalating the bombing campaign. McNamara was also associated with the so-called San Antonio Formula peace proposal, later rejected by Hanoi, suggesting a bombing halt in exchange for genuine negotiations.

McNamara's Draft Presidental Memorandum of 17 November 1967, which recommended curtailment rather than escalation of the war, marked the final break with Johnson's hard line on the war. Johnson believed that McNamara had fallen under the influence of Robert Kennedy and was near to a nervous breakdown. It was agreed that McNamara should leave the administration after a suitable interval and on 29 February 1968 he left to become president of the World Bank.

Robert McNamara was a graduate of Harvard Business School and was fundamentally a pragmatist. And, in the way of 1960s business school graduates, he analysed problems dispassionately and followed the conclusions no matter where they led. In May 1967, the Defense Department's Systems Analysis Office showed that the communist forces had control over their losses by controlling the pace of the action – the number, the size and the intensity of combat engagements. 'The VC and NVA started the shooting in over 90 per cent of company-sized firefights,' the report said. 'Over 80 per cent began with a well-organized enemy attack. Since their losses rise – as in the first quarter of 1967 – and fall – as they have done since – with their choice of whether or not to fight, they can probably hold their losses to about 2000 a week regardless of our force levels. If...their strategy is to wait us out, they will control their losses to a level low enough to be sustained indefinitely, but high enough to tempt us to increase our forces to the point of US public rejection of the war.'

Given the anti-war feeling on the street, this analysis led McNamara to the conclusion that America could not win, so de-escalation and ultimate withdrawal was inevitable.

McNamara the dove wrote the epitaph of McNamara the hawk in a letter to Johnson in 1967: 'The picture of the world's greatest superpower killing or seriously injuring 1000 non-combatants a week, while trying to pound a tiny backward nation into submission on an issue whose merits are hotly disputed is not a pretty one.' It could have come straight from an anti-war pamphlet.

bedrock supporters were loyal and backing for him was as strong as ever at the church social, the supermarket checkout and in the country club.

Still, there was a mounting pressure on Johnson from abroad. Wherever he went, anti-war demonstrators dogged his footsteps. There were violent demonstrations against the war in London, Berlin, Tokyo and Paris. When Johnson visited Australia in December 1967, the authorities were barely able to guarantee his physical safety. The venerable British philosopher Bertrand Russell gave his financial backing to a War Crimes Tribunal in Stockholm. But then, what did foreigners know about keeping the Free World free?

Governments also, of allies like Britain, were increasingly concerned that America should withdraw from Vietnam. Only the French among the NATO countries openly opposed US policy. But other western governments felt the Vietnam war was diverting arms and money from more essential strategic areas, and that America was dragging them into a diplomatic quagmire by demanding their support. They'd been kicked enough by Uncle Sam for fighting their colonial wars and they weren't about to help him out with his own imperial designs.

In a meeting with US Defense Secretary Robert

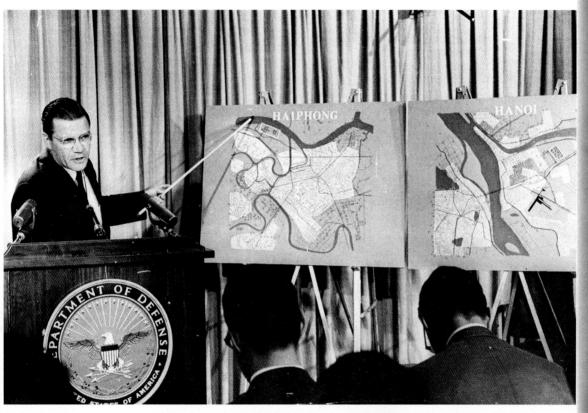

Above: In June, McNamara briefs the press corps on the bombing of the Hanoi and Haiphong oil depots. Already his faith in the war is waning. A month later, Westmoreland will supply the straw that breaks the camel's back. Right: Lifelong pacificist Bertrand Russell backed a Swedish tribunal to try the US for war crimes.

CALENDAR OF DISSENT

18-26 Jan: Violent anti-war demos mark the visit of South Vietnamese President Ky to Australia and New Zealand.
30 Jan: US Court of Appeal rules unanimously that local draft boards cannot punish registrants who publicly protest the war and draft by reclassifying them 1-A.
31 Jan: 2000 clergy march in Washington demanding an end to bombing of North Vietnam.
8 Feb: Start of three-day 'Fast for Peace' by Christians and Jews.
25 Mar: Martin Luther King leads 5000 demonstrators in Chicago, and says the war is a 'blasphemy against all that America stands for.'
15 Apr: 100,000 march in NYC and 20,000 in San Francisco.
2 May: International Tribunal on War Crimes in Stockholm accuses US of aggression.
10 May: Teach-ins held at over 80 colleges across the US.
8 Aug: US Court of Military Appeals upholds court martial and sentence of one-year hard labour on soldier found guilty of anti-war demonstrating.
21 Oct: Nation-wide demos end with 125 arrests in Oakland.
23 Oct: 10,000 troops ring the Pentagon against a peaceful march and vigil by over 50,000 protestors. The demo ends in brutality. Similar demos held in Japan and Western Europe.
14 Nov: Violent clashes in NYC.
19 Dec: 268 arrests in Oakland.

1967

On the weekend of 16-17 April 1967, 125,000 anti-war demonstrators turned up in New York. They came from all over the country. Another 55,000 were also gathering in San Francisco in this 'Spring Mobilization to End the War in Vietnam'.

In Central Park, the psychedelic pot left participants in kooky costumes and painted faces carried signs which read: 'Draft beer, not boys'; 'I don't give a damn for Uncle Sam' and 'No Viet Cong ever called me nigger'. There were Vietniks, peaceniks, Trotskyites, potskyites, Sioux Indians, civil rights activists, taoists, Maoists and those who followed Lennon rather than Lenin. Draft cards were burned. The cops did not stop them.

Outside the UN building, mounted policemen protected the protesters from rightwing groups who supported the war.

'What do we want?' the cry went up.
'Peace!'
'When?'
'Now!'
'Why?'
A dead silence was followed by one shrill female 'Because'.

Martin Luther King delivered a statement to the UN accusing the US of violating the charter. Anti-white militant Stokely Carmichael branded McNamara a racist and Johnson a buffoon. Dr Spock spoke too. Journalists concluded that the antics of the painted protesters might prolong the war.

Meanwhile President Johnson was opening the 1967 baseball season at Washington's DC Stadium. He pitched three balls into the diamond. But the cries of 'Strike!' meant nothing more sinister than a waist-high pitch right over the plate.

Yet, despite the outward confidence of the President and his administration, the times they were a-changing. Within six months a national poll would reveal that only 44 per cent of Americans backed the war (61 per cent had supported their government at the time of the Gulf of Tonkin Resolution). And before the year was out McNamara would quit.

McNamara in July 1967, General Westmoreland suggested that, if he was given all the troops he wanted and allowed to strike into Cambodia, Laos and North Vietnam, the war *might* be won in two years. But an invasion of North Vietnam would escalate the conflict unpredictably and quite possibly bring no advantage on the battlefield, the administration felt. And giving Westmoreland a blank cheque for troop numbers would have involved a massive extension of the draft. Yet if he was not given what he wanted, Westmoreland reckoned winning the war would take at least five years. This was equally unacceptable to the administration, which wanted the boys home by next Christmas. Faced with this impasse, McNamara offered his resignation in November 1967. Only to save the impression of unity did he agree to stay on until the following February.

The rot sets in
The defection of one of the main architects of the war did not break the faith of Johnson's administration that the war was just. But eventually they

Above: This year Detroit, next year Vietnam. Nam or Newark, it was all the same. For dreams were not enough. Nor were equal rights, or integration. In 1967, Mr and Mrs Middle America discovered that America's blacks wanted power. The American dream – and Martin Luther King's – was turning into a nightmare.

would have to face a choice: the war could not be won without escalation; if they would not escalate the conflict, then they must choose withdrawal.

As 1967 ended, the support for the war still held firm. Anti-war demonstrations, black riots and hippy cultural subversion gave Mr and Mrs Middle America the feeling that things were falling apart. Although draft refusals or evasions remained of manageable proportions and draftees still marched off to Nam ready to fight for their country, the rot had set in. Each night, they would listen to the names of those killed that day in Vietnam being read out after the 11 o'clock news and they would wonder whether that last name was the name of the boy who used to live down the block, wonder when their boy would flunk a grade and lose his student deferment. Still their friends' sons were out there, doing their bit – but hadn't told what's his name's eighteen-year-old just lost a foot? Soon, as more friends were collecting more coffins from the airport, they would begin to realize what McNamara already knew – that America was not winning the war. And their disillusionment, the effect of anti-war propaganda, black radicalism and widespread drug abuse would begin to spread from the States to the Nam itself.

THE BROWN WATER NAVY

In the Mekong Delta, the Mobile Riverine Force hit hard and fast. But then Charlie wised up to its routine. The Zippos and Monitors never knew what lay around the next corner.

1967

The Mekong was bad, real bad. Try hoisting the Stars and Stripes on the VC-infested land of the delta and you were likely to get a bullet for breakfast and an RPG for lunch. The Navy guys up along the coast had their own moving picture show called Operation Market Time, but shoring up infiltration routes in the brown waters of the delta demanded a different approach. The Navy had already assumed the role of policeman in the inland waterways, swamps and rice paddies of the delta during Operation Game Warden, but what it really needed was a mobile combat unit with enough firepower to patrol, engage and wipe

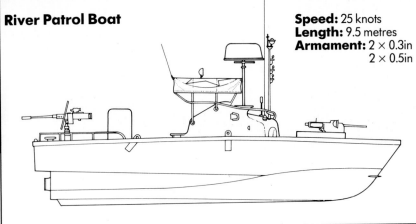

River Patrol Boat

Speed: 25 knots
Length: 9.5 metres
Armament: 2 × 0.3in
2 × 0.5in

Previous page: A Mobile Riverine Force assault squadron ploughs towards its floating barracks ship after a search and destroy operation in the Mekong. Top left: Toting a 0.3in machine gun at the stern, a river patrol boat hugs the shoreline on the lookout for VC. Centre left: Getting ready with the blooper, the M79 grenade launcher. Bottom left: the dual-mounted 81mm mortar and 0.5in machine gun that added firepower to the Swift's high speed.

out known VC sanctuaries. MACV wanted a force of lethal water babies, and came up with the Mobile Riverine Force (MRF).

Becoming operational in June 1967, the MRF was a twin-headed shark that brought together the grunts of the 2d Brigade, 9th Infantry Division, and the riverine craft of the Navy's Task Force 117. Once again, Uncle Sam had looked at the state of play and married technology to Joe Grunt in an effort call the shots.

The backroom boys got to work on a fleet of postwar landing craft and spawned a new type of weaponry – tailor-made for taking on Chuck in the Mekong. Armoured Troop Carriers (ATCs) with steel slats to take the beef out of recoilless-rifle rounds; Monitors and Command Control Boats (CCBs) for co-ordinating assaults; Zippos for turning on the heat, not forgetting the trusty Swifts and river patrol boats (PBRs). Add helicopter pads to some of the craft, and equip each and every one with a factory of weapons ranging from the ubiquitous 0.5in machine gun to the 40mm cannon and 81mm mortar, and you're left with a pack of sharks that can do more than just bite your legs off.

The arrival of the Assault Support Patrol Boats (ASPB) added still more firepower to the MRF's inventory, and provided a razor sharp cutting edge during the ambushes, patrols, reconnaissance and escort missions that were part of everyday life for the grunts and sailors down in the

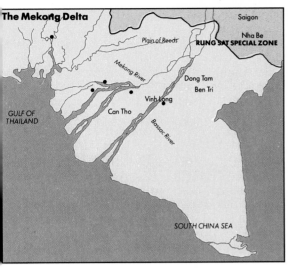

The Mekong Delta

Saigon
Nha Be
RUNG SAT SPECIAL ZONE
Plain of Reeds
Mekong River
Dong Tam
Ben Tri
GULF OF THAILAND
Can Tho
Vinh Long
Bassac River
SOUTH CHINA SEA

delta.

Complete with a heavy-duty battalion of 105mm howitzers based on mobile barges, the MRF plied the waters of the delta. Two self-propelled barracks ships (APBs) provided floating base facilities and accommodation for the grunts when they came back from an op. Each ship was usually moored no more than 30 miles from the zone of operations, and had berths for 800 men, with space for a further 600 at a tight squeeze.

The operations themselves usually followed the same pattern. The heavily armed ASPBs would take on the role of point as the column of boats ploughed through the water, with minesweepers on both flanks. Next came the river assault squadron's naval commander in his CCB. A Monitor was usually the next craft in line, ready to unleash sustained firepower into the bushes on the river banks if any incoming was received. Then came a force of three ATCs carrying the battalion's first company.

The Zippo's tongue of flame

A man's first time on one of these search and destroy operations was an unreal trip into fantasyland. Instead of being surrounded by a jungle envelope that would close in without remorse, he was listening to the sound of the bow wave and the constant throb of engines. But whether he's toting a grenade launcher or standing behind the protective cupola of a 40mm cannon, he's still wondering where the first shot is going to come from. Pretty soon, however, he remembers his training at the Coronado naval base in California and slips into the groove.

On the run-in to the target zone each company is assigned its own section of the river bank, usually at intervals of 150 to 300yds. Time for the Monitors and ASPBs to unleash the suppressive fire, possibly supported by a tongue of flame leaping into the bush from the Zippo. Into the undergrowth go the troops, trained to sweep the area, hit hard and fast, and then re-embark on the waiting craft. With this mobility and firepower at its fingertips, the MRF launched a series of operations in the Mekong Delta and Rung Sat Special Zone that reduced the infiltration of communist

RIVERINE OPERATIONS 1965-1967

Prior to 1965, operations against the VC in the Mekong Delta were the responsibility of the South Vietnamese forces. However, from December 1965 onwards they devolved to the US Navy's River Patrol Force (Task Force 116).

One of the earliest operations mounted by the RPF was Game Warden, which deployed river patrol boats and experimental hovercraft to prevent VC use of the waterways. It was run parallel to Operation Market Time, begun in March 1965 by Task Force 71 (later 115), and was designed to cut off NVA seaborne infiltration.

However, by mid-1966 it had become clear that more had to be done to challenge VC control of the delta and the coastal mangrove swamps of the Rung Sat Special Zone, southeast of Saigon. Between August 1966 and November 1967, therefore, 17 million cubic tons of silt were dredged in order to create a base on the My Tho river for a new Mekong Delta Mobile Afloat Force (MDMAF).

The Mobile Riverine Force (MRF), as the MDMAF became known, comprised a naval component (Task Force 117) harnessed to the 2d Brigade of the 9th Infantry Division, now designated as a riverine unit. After the experimental Operation River Raider in the Upper Tau shipping channel and the Rung Sat from 16 February to 20 March 1967, the MRF began intensive operations from its Dong Tam HQ on the My Tho river.

The Coronado operations (I to XI) from June 1967 onwards, concentrated on Long An and Dinh Tuong Provinces in the Mekong, with special attention to the Rung Sat Special Zone. Initially, the VC attempted to stand and fight against the MRF hammer and anvil tactics, but the sheer scale of the MRF operations accounted for over 1000 VC during the last six months of 1967.

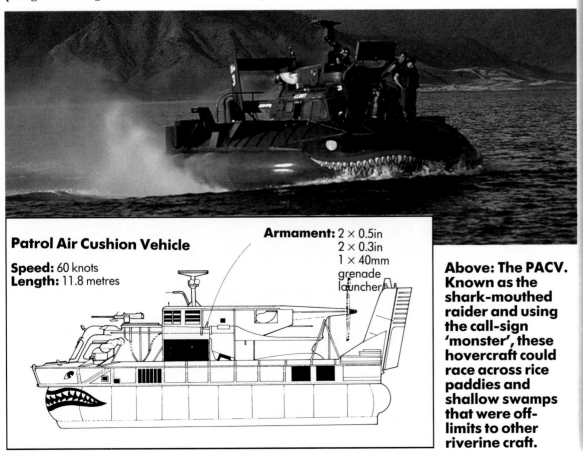

Patrol Air Cushion Vehicle

Speed: 60 knots
Length: 11.8 metres

Armament: 2 × 0.5in
2 × 0.3in
1 × 40mm grenade launcher

Above: The PACV. Known as the shark-mouthed raider and using the call-sign 'monster', these hovercraft could race across rice paddies and shallow swamps that were off-limits to other riverine craft.

Left: Zeroing in with a twin 50 calibre. This heavy-duty weapon was only part of the Assault Support Patrol Boat's armoury. It was supplemented by two grenade launchers, a 20mm cannon and an 81mm mortar. The craft's hull was made of steel, while the superstructure was made of aluminium to save on weight and increase speed.

1967

Command Control Boat

Length: 17.5 metres
Armament: 1 × 40mm
2 × 40mm grenade launcher
1 × 81mm mortar
2 × 0.5in

Right: Converted from one of the MRF's Monitors, a Zippo uses its flamethrower to burn away the riverside foliage, denying the VC cover from which to launch an ambush.

supplies to a trickle. But sometimes it didn't quite go as planned. By late 1967 the VC had wised up to the MRF's tactics and had a few surprises of their own.

In the dim moonlight of 15 September '67, the men of the 3d Battalion, 60th Infantry, clambered down the side of their barracks ship and jumped into the assault craft below. It was 0415 hours.

The murmur of voices and the scrape of weapons against the steel ship penetrated the damp night air as the grunts awaited their briefing. Only 24 hours since their last op, but Lieutenant-Colonel Doty's men were on the move again.

Learning from Intelligence that the VC 263d Battalion had set up camp along the Rach Ba Rai river, Colonel Bert David, the commander of the 2d Brigade, had planned an all-out attack. Doty's battalion would form blocking positions while other riverine force units advanced from the south and east. Good plan, except when you realise that, to get to its objective, the battalion would have to sail past the suspected enemy position.

As he looked down from his command helicopter, Doty watched as the naval convoy transporting the 3d Battalion moved out in the classic riverine force column formation. Navy crews manned the guns as the boats churned through the swift-flowing waters of the Mekong river and into the Rach Ba Rai tributary. Having experienced the dull run up to operations of this kind, the riflemen inside the ATCs slept soundly. Three hours later, and everything was still quiet. Helmets off, flak jackets unzipped, some of the men lay on the troop compartment asleep; others rested against the bulkheads, smoking and talking low.

Bang on 0730 the crash of an exploding RPG

split the morning calm. Seconds later, radios burst into action when one of the minesweepers reported being breeched by an underwater explosion. Other boats came over the network to report incoming. The unmistakable rip of AK-47 assault rifles vied with the measured roar of machine guns. As boat after boat entered the jaws of the ambush, more troops and sailors fell prey to enemy fire. New to the Green Machine, a young grunt had failed to watch out for unfriendly RPGs headed in his direction. Dead meat for the body bags.

The combined guns, cannon and mortars of the MRF unit let loose, but rockets and recoilless-rifle rounds kept pouring in and automatic fire continued to beat against the hulls. No-one had yet spotted a single VC – only muzzle flashes. Soldiers took over the guns of fallen sailors and others climbed, crawled or ran to firing positions.

Circling above, Doty saw two rockets explode on the side of his staff's CCB – the steel slats absorbed most of the blast, but a few more direct hits like that and the boat would be a dead duck.

Within 10 minutes of the ambush being sprung

Where Zippos were unavailable, the grunts improvised in true Indian-country style (right). This guy is using a longbow to send a flaming arrow into a fortified VC bunker.

1967

RIVER TASK FORCE

The concept of riverine forces was not new to Southeast Asia. During the Indochina War of 1946-54, French forces created the Dinassauts, combat organizations designed to operate in the hostile environment of Vietnam's waterways. These employed a variety of modified landing craft in the fire support and stop-and-search roles.

When the first South Vietnamese Naval units were established in 1955, their River Assault Groups (RAGs) took over the discarded French equipment. By 1964, the RAGs possessed over 200 craft.

But it was the American attempt to control VC infiltration in the delta that saw the largest expansion to date of riverine forces when, after June 1967, the Mobile Riverine Force became operational. Reviving a strategy used during the American Civil War, when Union Army forces operated Navy gunboats on the Ohio, Mississippi and other inland waterways, US Army troops were given special training, including combat operations in the Rung Sat Special Zone and at the Coronado Naval base in California.

The US Army element of the Mobile Riverine Force comprised the 2d Brigade, 9th Infantry Division. This included the 3d and 4th Battalions, 47th Infantry; the 3rd Battalion, 60th Infantry; and the 105mm howitzers of the 3d Battalion, 39th Artillery. This task force was often combined with units drawn from the South Vietnamese Marine Corps.

By the end of 1968, the objectives of Market Time, Game Warden and the MRF along the coast and in the Mekong Delta had largely been achieved. But now there was a new problem. Thwarted in the delta, the VC began to exploit a new infiltration route – across the Cambodian border. To counter this, Market Time, Game Warden and MRF units were welded into a combined force under the codename 'Sealords'.

Above: Un-assing from the Navy riverine craft, men of the 2d Brigade, 9th Infantry Division, set out on routine patrol in the delta. Other times, it was not quite so routine. Emerging from dense undergrowth to await pick-up (right), the exhausted, mud-spattered men of the MRF know that the VC could open up any second.

1967

Soaked by the spray as the Swift guns her engines, a grunt uses his M60 for reconnaissance by fire (left). Below: If the MRF required support, Naval helicopter units known as the 'Seawolves' were never far away.

the convoy was going nowhere but sideways. Monitors and ASPBs careered from bank to bank, laying down fire in an attempt to let the convoy break through the killing zone and land the 2d Battalion on its objective – 'White Beach' – a few thousand yards up the narrow channel. But the force was pinned down over a one-mile gauntlet of fire.

Running the gauntlet

Artillery from a support base to the northeast was called in to some effect, but it needed a direct hit from something as big as a 155mm to knock out the bunkers. Two boats did make it to White Beach, however. A platoon led by Captain Davis hit the shore and sent out the message 'I have one element ashore now, waiting for the rest.' Doty's hands were tied. Mobile Riverine Force procedure demanded that troop carriers be preceded by minesweepers. With most of his sweeper crews either killed or wounded he was unable to push the rest of his unit forward. Responding to his superior's order to withdraw, Doty had no option but to tell Davis to re-embark and run the gauntlet in reverse.

The grunts ran in twos and threes back to the ATC and clambered aboard. The boat captain shifted into reverse, brought the bow around and gunned the engines to full speed. Incredibly, the boat navigated the mile-long ambush site taking only one direct hit.

A Helicopter Landing Deck Medical Aid Boat (HLDMAB), stationed down river, began ministering to the wounded as boats made their way back from the inferno up river. Once the choppers had departed with their cargo, sailors and grunts got to work. Damaged guns were

Left: Coming across a hamlet known to be harbouring VC sympathisers and supplies, MRF troops on a search and destroy operation lay waste to the huts. Combined with the regular patrolling of the Mekong's network of waterways, stopping and searching any suspicious traffic, these tactics proved highly effective. Exhaustion sets in (far right top), but armament is always to hand.

replaced, weapons reloaded and fires put out. After calling up replacement Monitors and mine-sweepers from the second assault force to the rear, the Navy was ready to try again as soon as the 2d Battalion had reorganised itself.

Artillery units were instructed to 'walk fire' up both banks of the river as the boats advanced, and Huey gunships and Phantoms now entered the fight – spraying machine-gun fire and dropping napalm onto the VC. Several boats took direct hits but the battalion reached White Beach under the umbrella of air and artillery support. Three companies dashed ashore 150yds apart and began the hunt – the plan had changed; the battalion would now push south instead of taking up a blocking position. The dense foliage not only hindered visibility, however, it also prevented the heavy weapons on the riverine craft from opening up.

The slow advance continued all afternoon, with the battalion forced to take cover when the VC came on strong. The hot afternoon was drawing to an end and Doty became worried that his men might have to face the night disorganized. He ordered the setting up of a semi-circular defensive position. Captain Davis, the senior company commander, took charge and kept his men on 50 per cent alert.

Next morning, as patrols of converging battalions from the north, south and east established contact and closed the trap, it became clear that Charlie had melted away. Over 250 enemy bunkers and 79 bodies were uncovered. US casualties were seven killed and 123 wounded. Just another day in the delta.

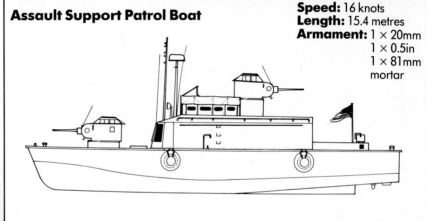

Assault Support Patrol Boat

Speed: 16 knots
Length: 15.4 metres
Armament: 1 × 20mm
1 × 0.5in
1 × 81mm
mortar

1967

Below: A flotilla of Monitors, River Patrol Boats, CCBs and troop carriers ply the snake-like channels of the Mekong, in a never ending battle to stem the tide of communist manpower and supplies flowing through the region.

1967

FORWARD AIR CONTROLLER

EYE-WITNESS

The author, Major Robert Mikesh (above), was a B-57 pilot with the 8th Bomb Squadron before being assigned to Vietnam as a Forward Air Controller. For his part in the incident described, Mikesh was awarded the Distinguished Flying Cross.

When the going got tough, the call went up for fire from the sky. The FACs would pick out the hotspots and send down an inferno.

Very slowly, very carefully, the Marine laid down the binoculars that he had been using to observe the jungle at the bottom of the ridge. He drew his rifle towards him and in a quiet, but urgent voice alerted his buddies with the cry 'Gooks'. As he chambered a round and started to adjust his sights, the squad radioman tuned into the Tactical Air Control Airborne (TACAIR) frequency and put out a call for help.

Under the rules of engagement used in Southeast Asia, bombs could not be dropped in South Vietnam and certain areas of Laos without a Forward Air Controller (FAC) to control the strike. It was the responsibility of the FAC in his slow, low-flying plane to locate the target, identify it to the attack aircraft, and ensure they dropped their ordnance in the correct place.

At the very start of the war the usual mount for the FAC had been the ageing, single-engined 0-1 Cessna Bird Dog. It was in use in each of the four Corps Tactical Zones, but there were problems with its use in the northernmost part of South Vietnam. Here, the rugged and mountainous terrain meant that an engine failure was usually fatal for the pilot. A new plane, preferably with two engines, was needed. This problem was solved by the arrival of the 0-2A Cessna.

The first 0-2A Cessna was delivered to the 20th Tactical Air Support Squadron at Da Nang on 2 July 1967 and, although pilots missed the all-round visibility of their old Bird Dogs, they were extremely pleased with the increased performance and ease of control of the 0-2A. There were, however, the odd problems now and then that needed rectifying. On 13 October 1967 Major Robert Mikesh was asked to carry out a routine check flight on an 0-2A which had just had its tachometer replaced. The war usually quietened down as the afternoon heat built up, and Major Mikesh was grateful for the chance to get in the air and cool off:

Big one-seven was a negative

'It was late afternoon when the airplane was ready and I left the gravel runway inside the walled city of Hue at 1630 hours, on what should have been an uneventful 15 or 20 minute flight. Checking in with "Big Control", our "Victor" Direct Air Support Centre for this northern sector, I gave them my time off and intentions as was the normal procedure. The usual unconcerned "Roger" came back. I went on about my business in checking the airplane over, drinking in the refreshing air and beautiful landscape that was taking on a deeper green as the late afternoon sun sank lower on the horizon.

'The tranquility of the flight was suddenly pierced by the voice of a desperate radio operator calling for assistance. Using the callsign "Mongoose" he was transmitting in the blind for any "Big" aircraft, our FAC callsign to respond. I recognised the 'Mongoose' callsign as a Marine reconnaissance squad north of Hue and heard "Big one-seven" answer. The Marines were under intense enemy fire and needed immediate air support. However, "Big one-seven" had already been on visual reconnaissance for three hours and reported that he was on his way home and could not help due to lack of fuel. He had heard me report in after take-off and asked if I could help out. I had only a partial load of fuel, and there were only seven smoke rockets left over from the previous mission. I could do very little, but no-one else was in the air.

The Marines were established in a look-out position on a high ridge where they could visually monitor the surrounding area. Apparently, the VC were getting tired of having the Marines report on their ground movements and calling in air and artillery strikes against them. They decided to take the Marines' position and eliminate

them. Judging by the continually rising pitch of my ground contact's voice, the situation was getting desperate.

'As I proceeded towards the co-ordinates, I called "Big Control" and asked for air support aircraft, hoping to have fighters on station by the time I got to the Marine position. So far, things were going routinely. "Big Control" gave me the call-sign of a flight of F-4s and the frequency on which to call them. I made contact, but only to learn that they were heading north, to provide air cover for one of their comrades who had gone down north of the DMZ. I called "Big Control" for another set of fighters and was told a flight would be on hand shortly.

'By now, I was passing across the top of the ridge where the Marines were in a lot of trouble. They confirmed that they saw me and let off a smoke flare to mark their position. The VC were on the north slope, but I could see little action at first. They hid themselves along the bank as soon as they heard my engines. Their gunfire on the Marines' positions continued, and the controller said that they were now within grenade-throwing distance. Something had to be done right now.

'The second set of fighters came on my frequency, but just then, they too were diverted to the north to provide air cover for the recovery of the downed pilot. The situation below was critical, and would end within moments without immediate air support.

"Big Control" recognised this urgency, but the only air available was the ground alert aircraft at Da Nang. They were to be scrambled immediately, but by the time they could arrive the battle might be over.

Providing an essential link between attack aircraft such as the A-4 Skyhawks (far left), and beleaguered ground units (below), was the unenviable task of Forward Air Controllers such as Major Robert Mikesh. During his support of the Marine reconnaissance squad north of Hue, Mikesh had entered the fray without his flak jacket – a 'must' item of FAC personal equipment on any mission. What had been intended as a simple, functional flight check had culminated in a desperate struggle for survival.

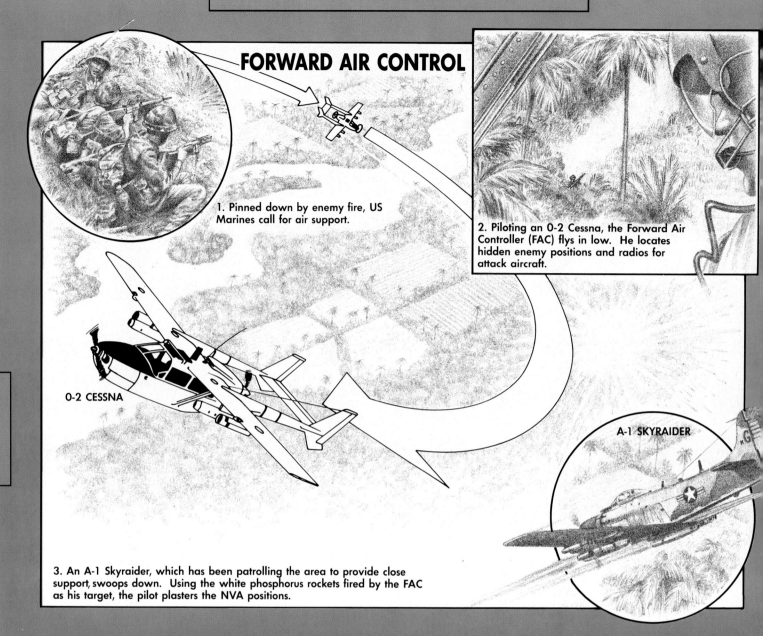

FORWARD AIR CONTROL

1. Pinned down by enemy fire, US Marines call for air support.

2. Piloting an O-2 Cessna, the Forward Air Controller (FAC) flys in low. He locates hidden enemy positions and radios for attack aircraft.

O-2 CESSNA

A-1 SKYRAIDER

3. An A-1 Skyraider, which has been patrolling the area to provide close support, swoops down. Using the white phosphorus rockets fired by the FAC as his target, the pilot plasters the NVA positions.

One of the most important advantages enjoyed by conventional forces in a counter-insurgency campaign is control of the air. Below: Flying an O-2 Cessna over South Vietnam, an FAC exploits this advantage.

'There was no alternative now but to make attack passes on the advancing VC, even though this was just a lightly armed FAC airplane. Perhaps this would be enough to pin the enemy down until air support arrived. I rolled in and lined up a dive on the area of the north slope where I was told the VC were located. I fired off one smoke rocket and watched it hit the ground as I banked away and pulled off. The Marine radio operator reported with excitement that my hit was "Right on". Little damage can be caused by a smoke rocket because they have little explosive impact, but when fired at you, it can be disconcerting. The splattering of burning white phosphorus which causes the marking smoke is dangerous enough. The ground controller gave me corrections for the

next attack, and I rolled in and fired one more rocket. This could not continue for long for now I was down to only five rockets and there was still no sign of fighter support.

'The next pass was dry, trying to conserve what rockets I had left, yet making an attempt to slow the advance of the enemy. This seemed to cause them to keep their heads down, since they held their shelter for the possibility that I might fire off a rocket at them at each pass. As the shadows deepened, I was aware that the VC were firing at me with hand-held weapons as I made each pass. It was like flash cameras at half time in a football stadium.

'Keep 'em coming'

'By now, I was having to make two dry passes for every time I let off a rocket. As each one hit into an enemy position, I was cheered on by the Marine radio operator. This was probably more for his morale, since smoke rockets are not going to stop an enemy for long, and the Viet Cong knew it. But it slowed them and although my seven rockets were now gone, I was not going to let the enemy know that. I kept making random passes and jinking during each dive in an effort to avoid being hit by their ground fire.

'To my surprise and great relief, a flight of Marine A-4 Skyhawks came on station and reported in, much sooner than the expected Air Force Phantoms. I described the location of the ridgeline to them and they immediately located it and spotted the remains of the smoke that lingered along the slope of the rise. With this recognition I cleared them to drop their bombs under the top of the ridge. Their 500-pounders hit their mark

and brought a favourable response from the radioman. He reported that they all had their hearing impaired by the nearby blasts but "Keep 'em coming".

'After the Skyhawks' second pass, a line of Hueys came into view and began snaking from the south side of the ridge to the Marine position. I was off to the side, and away from the attack line of the A-4s as they prepared for another pass. This put me in a good position to watch the rapid extraction of the Marines as it took place. With the Skyhawks laying their ordnance on three sides of the area around the Marines, the first Huey made its approach. The helicopter hardly paused, with its skids not even touching the ground, as the Marines jumped on board and were whisked away. The second, and those that followed, did the same until all were safely off the ridge. It was all over in seconds and they were now on their way to the Marble Mountain base without loss.

'It was nearly dark by now, yet there was enough light to identify features on the ground. The Skyhawks continued the attack until all their ordnance was expended, then turned for home. By now, I had bade them farewell, for I was very low on fuel after this 40-minute bout with the Viet Cong. The enemy had successfully neutralised the look-out post by having caused the Marines to leave, but now they were at the mercy of the 500-pounders from above.

'Returning to my base with not enough fuel left to go elsewhere, I made my last landing at the Hue Citadel Airport, gliding across the protective wall that encircled this ancient city, over the moat and onto the 2400ft gravel runway that had no lights. With this, I had had enough for one day.'

CHAPTER 53

1

The army gave them badges that they should have been proud of, but the troops in Vietnam decided that they should make their own. They were every bit as good as the real thing, of course. They were embroidered in an idle moment, run up by a backstreet tailor in Saigon or manufactured from metal salvaged from beer cans. But tin or cloth, the gruesome designs were often inspired by a freezer full of Milwaukee's finest.

They had symbols, unit designations and mottos, just like the army's official insignia. And they fulfilled the same function. They marked the wearer out as a member of a special group – even if they were those who thought they were mushrooms as they were 'kept in the dark and raised on horseshit' – rather than the anonymous 'organization'.

'We kill for peace'

Peace signs abounded, especially later in the war, along with insignia depicting marijuana leaves and joints. But the most common symbol was the death's head, including one with a bullet hole in it weeping a tear of blood. After all, killing and being killed was what it was all about – a sentiment summed up in the well-known ironical Special Forces motto: 'We kill for peace.' Others boasted: 'We who do not die' and 'We deal in death.' Or promised: 'Instant' or 'Sudden death.' Meanwhile the devil parachutes from the skies.

Unofficial badges celebrated units' nicknames. The Thud pilots who flew missions over North

BEER CAN

They gave you badges and told you, you belonged to something. They gave you insignia and told you, you got rank. I tell you the whole thing was rank. So we made our own. They were nothing the shitkickers back home would recognize.

7

1 Locally made Radio Research – that's army security; 2 Pocket patch for chopper pilots; 3 RT Mike Force badge; 4 Strategic Air Command out of Anderson AFB, Guam; 5 An example of unauthorized insignia worn inside the beret by MACV/SOG personnel; 6 MACV/SOG wings; 7 RT Rhode Island; 8 RT Adder; 9 USMC 1st Recon; 10 Thunderchief pilots.

Vietnam called themselves the River Rats. The 7th Transportation Division called themselves the Orient Express. And the B-52 bomber pilots flying out of Anderson Air Force Base on Guam called themselves the Black Barons. Their unoffical insignia showed the mailed fists of the Strategic Air Command crushing the letters VC. The red represents North Vietnam, the green represents the South.

Assassins and outcasts

Race was another theme. Many badges bore the legend: 'Injuneers' and 'Injun scouts'. Then there were the Apaches, the Comancheroes and Geronimo, while the herd's insignia showed two arms – one black, one white – bound together making the clenched fist black power salute. The herd were those guys whose helmets described themselves as 'two shades of soul' and promised 'togetherness'.

There were the 'Angels from Hell', the 'High Angle Hell', 'Low Level Hell' and 'From Heaven to Hell'. Others proclaimed themselves to be 'avengers', 'assassins', 'outcasts' and 'silent and deadly'.

There were eagles, wildcats, sword-flailing cartoon cats, well-armed spiders, parachuting frogs, stampeding horses, battling buffaloes, mules, lip-licking foxes, bears, rattlesnakes, alligators. Death comes from above, below, steathily from behind. And everywhere there was the skull – winged skulls, parachuting skulls, gun-toting skulls, jawless skulls, sword-pierced skulls, arrow-shot skulls and skulls with Vietnamese coolies' hats on them.

INSIGNIA

WHY I JOINED THE VC

What induced a simple peasant to stop tilling the land, take up arms, and fight for the Viet Cong?

EYE-WITNESS

The author is a member of the Vietnamese expatriate community in London, England, and does not wish to be identified.

My name is Lam. It means wood or forest. My father gave me the name. He was a peasant who worked the land, just like his father before him. I did too, before I joined the Viet Cong in 1967.

I was 16 when the Americans first came to our village. It was the planting season and I was in the fields when I heard the chop chop of the helicopter. At that time, I think it was 1966, things were still quiet. The Viet Cong moved freely through the area in the night, passing like black ghosts. They took nothing, talked only to the village elders and we kept our doors shut.

Because our village was peaceful, the Americans came openly and kept their guns out of sight. But they came with the province chief and one of the tax collectors, who acted as interpreter. We had nothing to fear and were curious to see these big strangers with their white skins turning red under the sun, so we gathered in the dusty village square.

'We are your friends,' they said. 'We have brought food, a machine to make electricity, building material for your houses. We will help you grow more food with special fast growing rice.'

They promised us a lorry to take our goods to market, a doctor to visit each month who would give medicines. All this, for free.

But the province chief was not a local and spoke with a funny accent. We hated and despised the tax collectors when they had walked round the village and talked to the village chief and the elders. They left as suddenly as they came. Later that evening, my parents spoke together while I listened.

'Because we are poor and they are rich, they think they can buy us,' said my mother.

'Everyone here is poor, but we are not stupid. We remember the French before these Americans, and they wanted the same thing.'

My father, who worked hard all his life in the fields, said: 'I don't want all these things. I only want what I worked for. All this land we break our backs for belongs to the landlord and after the tax man has taken his cut, there's hardly anything left.'

We fought to escape the land

My village was in the middle of Vietnam where the soil is poor. But because everyone was poor, we helped each other. Believe me, it was the only way to survive and the village had been there for generations. That is why the great fighters, like Ho Chi Minh and General Giap, came from my province, Nghe Thinh. We were so desperately poor, we fought almost as an escape from the land.

The village doesn't exist any more, so the name would mean nothing to you. It was destroyed by the Americans, rebuilt and then destroyed by them again. After that it was called a free-fire zone. Then they said that with the village dead, there was no reason for anyone to go there, not even to visit our ancestors' graves.

I realized later that those first Americans were not soldiers but worked with the army and the government. I remember they wore sun-glasses so you could not see their eyes – how can you trust anyone without seeing their eyes? And that tax collector, he came every season, no matter how small the harvest, for his due.

So we didn't trust the Americans and hated the people they worked with. The province chief would take a young man and say he was a communist and put him in prison. The village had to pay to get him back. And these were the very people who were supposed to look after us.

But the Viet Cong would come and tell us that the land belonged to us by right and that when they were in power, it would come to us. Some of them were farmers during the day and Viet Cong at night, going to each village, talking to people like us. Some of the older boys joined.

The next year, the American soldiers began their patrols. They came in helicopters, walked all

Opposite: The VC may not all have been communists, but they were certainly dedicated fighters. Above: US attempts to win villagers' hearts and minds was often the best recruitment drive the VC could wish for. Right: Americans found themselves fighting legions of women trained in the art of guerrilla warfare.

1967

Above: The VC won much of their equipment in ambushes. Here they strip an ARVN truck looking for the spoils of victory. Note their motley collection of equipment. One VC wears a pith helmet, another a bush hat, another a Japanese World War II helmet. Left: Communist forces scramble over a downed American helicopter, scavenging for weapons that can be used against the imperialist aggressor. There would already be a good deal of jubilation in this unit, with members looking forward to a cash bonus for shooting down a helicopter. Opposite: As the war continued, the communist forces became better equipped.

The Mekong Delta, extending south and west from Saigon to the Cambodian border and Gulf of Thailand, is ideal guerrilla terrain. Covering about 1500 square miles, it comprises a flat alluvial plain created by the Mekong river and its tributaries. Much of the land surface is covered with rice paddies – it is the main rice-producing area of Vietnam – but the key feature is its myriad of waterways. Cross-country communications are poor – in the 1960s, the only road was Route 4, linking Saigon to Ca Mau. Any military forces traversing the region had to stick to existing roads or tracks, especially during the annual monsoon (May to October), when rice paddies are flooded and incapable of supporting tracked or wheeled vehicles. Even during the dry season (November to March), many areas are covered in deep mud, making tactical movement difficult. The existence of ditches, high banks, swamps, marshes and forests provided guerrillas with ample defensive locations.

Similarly, the high density of population (about 200 people per square mile in 1967) made the task of controlling the region using firepower very difficult – especially when the population sided with the guerrillas.

By 1967, the Mekong was a VC stronghold. The long-established links between guerrillas and the people, plus the existence of supply routes from Cambodia or along the coast, meant that communist roots were deep. According to US intelligence estimates, 82,545 VC were operating in the area by 1967, comprising 19,270 combat troops, 1290 support troops, 50,765 part-time guerrillas and 11,220 political activists. Organized into three regimental headquarters, 28 battalions, 69 separate companies and 11 separate platoons, they occupied positions throughout the Delta, from the Plain of Reeds in the north to the U Minh Forest in the far south-west. Destroying their grip would clearly be a major task – and yet the US forces had no choice but to attempt it.

day and then left by helicopter. They never got to know the land, they went along the exposed paths beside the fields and the woods. It was only a matter of time before the VC ambushed them.

It took place just outside a neighbouring hamlet. There was a burst of gunfire, then it sounded like all hell let loose. We heard it all. Soon, we heard jets overhead. We were terrified. The jets screamed down low and even from a couple of miles away, we heard the terrible explosions. I knew some of my friends were beneath the bombs. They only had their rifles and the tunnels to save their lives. We saw helicopters with red crosses go over, so we knew the ambush had succeeded. But I knew there would soon be reprisals.

My parents told me I had to leave because, at my age, they would take me as a Viet Cong suspect. That night, some Viet Cong main-force troops passed by, stopping only to collect some rice. But this time I left with them, together with my friends Troung and Chau who also had to leave the village. The village was the only thing I knew, but there was no hope for me if I stayed.

COMMUNIST OPERATIONS, 1967

Throughout 1967, as the full weight of US commitment was brought to bear, communist units in South Vietnam were forced to adopt a more reactive role. Infiltration and subversion still took place, especially in areas less strongly defended by the ARVN, but in the key areas of confrontation – the northern provinces, the Central Highlands and the approaches to Saigon – NVA and VC formations followed a policy of absorbing US attacks, inflicting casualties as part of a strategy of attrition and pulling back as soon as the pressure became too great.

This inevitably led to losses. In the area around Saigon, for example, the VC 9th Division, backed by elements of the NVA, was badly mauled during Operation Junction City. Although the communists had mounted effective ambushes at Prek Klok and Ap Bau Bang in March, US firepower had inflicted heavy casualties. As a result, the VC pulled back to sanctuaries in Cambodia.

The picture was the same elsewhere in the Central Highlands. The NVA 1st and 10th Divisions made life difficult for US forces as the latter pushed into the western enclaves during Operations Sam Houston and Francis Marion. But by December, the NVA 32nd and 66th Regiments had virtually ceased to exist. Even in the northern provinces, where infiltration was a major aim, the establishment of US Marine defences south of the DMZ effectively blocked communist movement. Further south, the NVA 2nd and 3rd Divisions found the going hard.

But this did not mean that the communists were close to defeat. On the contrary, their willingness to accept casualties and to revert to guerrilla operations under pressure showed that they were continuing to oppose the Americans. Furthermore, by the end of the year, Giap had recognised that he would have to match his enemy in terms of commitment and was already building up his forces for the Tet Offensive.

We moved quickly out of the area, knowing it would be crawling with American soldiers for the next few days. We moved into the jungle, that dark, green, awful mystery which was to be our home and our graveyard. We were peasants and didn't live in the jungle, where there are snakes, insects whose bites sting for days, and where you caught malaria. If you were strong and lucky you survived, but almost everyone was weakened.

We moved from camp to camp in the jungle, passing through friendly villages for food, news and to keep contact with the people. We depended on them, so we treated them decently. We were just like them, really, except we carried guns. The Americans would go back to their bases each day and sooner or later they'd go home. But we lived there, it was our country and every day we survived we were winning the war.

It was hard being away from home, away from my friends and family. I heard that after the ambush, the Americans came and burned down the village and moved everyone away while they built a new one with barricades and barbed wire and defensive positions. Then they let people go back but kept government troops there to hold it. It was things they did like offering us what we did not want and rebuilding something they had destroyed in the first place that showed how simple minded the Americans were. As if we could forget what they had done so easily. They could be generous to us if they wished but at the same time they could destroy whole villages and kill so many so quickly.

Americans were slow and clumsy

Because we were weaker than the Americans, not even as well armed as the North Vietnamese soldiers, we had to be patient and use our intelligence. We laid traps, ambushes, using simple but deadly weapons – sticks smeared with excrement, arrows tripped off by the unwary soldier. His automatic rifle and grenades would keep us in firepower for weeks.

The Americans were well armed but slow and clumsy. They had firepower that we feared so we stayed hidden and out of range. They were like elephants, especially when moving through the jungle. We moved in cells of three, lightly armed but travelling silently and quickly. If we wounded or killed only one of theirs and lived to fight another day, it was a victory. Like the drop of water that wears away the stone, we would wear away the American Army.

I fought side by side with Troung and Chau who were like brothers to me. We looked after each other and shared our food. We used to joke that we

Left: The Viet Cong interrogate a captured ARVN soldier. He is questioned in front of the villagers so that they can benefit from any political lessons there are to be learned. Below: In a brief respite from their struggle, VC soldiers relax over a glass of the lethal local rice wine – drunk hot it's like supercharged saké. Decorating the wall behind them is a home-made National Liberation Front flag.

thought life was hard at home, but that life in the Viet Cong was 10 times worse. We went hungry for days sometimes, and Chau would remind us that we used to complain that we ate rice gruel with fish sauce when we were small. A bowl of rice gruel with fish sauce would have been a feast in the jungle. We would kill and eat almost anything – snake, monkey, rat and birds.

Our intelligence officers said the Americans enjoyed steaks, beer and ice cream back at base, but that the war was only part time for them. We were carrying the war on our backs wherever we went, gun or no gun. Unlike them, we had few medicines and no hospitals when we were wounded or ill. We used whatever traditional medicines we knew, but gunshot wounds and shrapnel were terrifying and usually nothing could be done for those with such injuries.

As the war deepened, and the Americans used more and more firepower, we moved further into hostile terrain and away from villages where we could find food and rest. We even moved underground to try to escape the napalm and the B-52 raids, living for days without sunlight while they passed overhead.

I don't really know how we kept going all those years. There was nothing to do but fight and carry on fighting once the decision was made. The American soldiers were the lucky ones. They would fly home thousands of miles away when their duty finished. We had nothing but the land, our land. If we gave up we would have nothing. Maybe, in our hearts of hearts, we hated them.

SHORT TIME

When a man got close to going home, he was in no mood to play bush tag with a bunch of guerrillas or NVA

He was a drunk buck sergeant from Charlie Company, 75th Rangers, balanced – sort of, anyway – on a small, round table in the smoke-filled hovel we called the Tuy Hoa NCO club. His beefy paw was wrapped around a large glass filled with something potent and evil looking, spilling some on the floor, some on himself, and occasionally splashing some into his mouth.

'SHO-O-O-O-O-O-RT!' he bellowed, his 6-

EYE-WITNESS

The author, John Morris, served seven years in the US Army and reached the rank of infantry squad leader during the Vietnam war.

foot-5 frame challenging anyone to say he wasn't.

The club manager, a sergeant first class who'd seen it all before, strolled over to the towering sweat-and-booze drenched short-timer who was threatening to destroy – as they'd say in Army-ese – one table, round, for the use in dingy NCO clubs only.

'Git offen my table, sarge,' the chunky manager's voice carried over the raucous din of NCOs drinking the place dry, his head craned backward to stare at the behemoth weaving atop the table. 'Git offen afor I pull ya off'.

Silence, the type you hear just before a tornado levels your house, grabbed hold of the club. Every eye in the house was glued to centre stage.

The drunk Ranger went stock still, like he'd just eyed a booby-trap trip wire. His face and eyes turned cold and hard, muscles in his neck and arms bunched and corded. Then, like a balloon bursting, his laughter rocked off the walls and the stubby body of the club manager.

'Sheeeit, y'all. Ah'm too short fer this shit.' He took another half-gallon swallow from his glass and dumped the rest on top of the SFC standing

275

1967

Previous page: A grunt's helmet saves him the trouble of counting off the months. Left: Dreaming of home, a Budweiser and a dry cigarette. Short-timers were men near the end of their one-year tour of duty. Those Stateside city lights might only be a few days away, and no-one was going to play hero when the World was that close.

Above: Goofing-off in a bunker, hoping to see those days fly by. Right: Often worn on boots in case of mutilation during combat, dog-tags were a constant reminder that death and injury were no respecters of short-timers. The smallest lapse could mean dead meat.

below. 'A Wake-up, gennlemen. A Wake-up 'n' ah'm going' home!' His glassy eyes started to roll back in his head, and he let loose with a resounding wet belch. 'Ah'm so short that whales shit on me…'

He threw his arms up and pulled off a perfect back dive, the floor breaking his fall.

It was my last night in Tuy Hoa, too, so I knew how he felt. After 12 months of heat and dust, wet and mud, leeches and mosquitoes, disease, rice paddies and mountains, bad food, endless patrols, rotten feet, and playing bush tag with a bunch of VC and NVA trying to blow your ass away, it was time to go home.

That final nail in the coffin

Like most everyone else, my genuine short-timer warm-and-fuzzy feeling kicked in about 30 days before that last drunken night in Tuy Hoa-by-the-sea. You'd get the feelings earlier, of course, but they were like a pregnant woman's false labour: the pangs and twinges and certainty that your

time had come – but it hadn't. Then you'd get depressed. Unlike a woman's due date, which is guesswork at best, your DEROS (Date Eligible to Return from Overseas) was as fixed as the final nail that could seal your coffin shut if you missed it. Women get over-anxious if they're late delivering; troops would go absolutely bat-shit if anything kept them a second over that magic day.

After all, one more minute in the Nam was one more minute they could kill you.

'Short-timer' wasn't just a term for a guy on his way back to the World. It was a state of mind, a presence that seemed to build inside a grunt. At first no one would notice. Joe Grunt just did his job, the same way he'd been doing it for the last 11 months. But then, during the smoke breaks or patrol halts, you begin to see it. A kind of endless summer stare where you'd know he's not seeing

jungle or feeling the rain or smelling rotting dead things. He's on a beach back home, or driving his car with the top down along Main Street, or cuddling up with his girl in front of the fire.

We'd all do that, of course, but not quite in the same way. To the rest of us 'long-timers', it was a mythical, fantasyland dream, too far in the future to even dare to hope it would come true. But to a short-timer, fantasy steadily became reality, and the reality of the here and now – Vietnam – fast faded into a bad dream. And that was dangerous.

With 10 days left in-country, Specialist Fourth Class Short-timer was day-dreaming about home when his squad walked around the right side of a fallen tree. He walked around the left, kicked a trip-wire, and set off a booby-trapped 105mm howitzer round. He got lucky. He only lost a chunk of his right leg and his right arm from the elbow down. Two squad members were killed by the blast and two others so mangled that they might as well have been.

Watch that calendar fill up

I know it happened, because it took place in my platoon about a month after I'd gone home. I saw Short-timer some years later and we talked about it. Not a night went by that he didn't dream about that log.

Many units established a short-timer policy for just that reason. Commanders knew that grunts tended to screw the cat one way or another when their calendars started filling up. This was especially true with single-digit midgets – grunts with less than 10 days to go. When there was any kind of a slot open in the rear – be it assistant armourer or supplyman, or even cook's helper – pragmatic COs would try to ease their short-timers out of the bush.

That's if he could, or wanted to. Sometimes there just weren't enough grunts to go around, so Mister Short would sweat and shake his way down to his last day in the bush before flying out. Or, if the boss was a hard-ass, or just too stupid to think about it, it was up to the platoon to take care of the situation.

That 'care' manifested itself in a number of ways, some good and some bad. Short-timers were never put on point (the lead man in the patrol), or even given the drag (the last man in the patrol).

TOUR OF DUTY

Every individual experience of the Nam was different, but there were certain benchmarks. Generally, men would have enjoyed 30 days' leave prior to reporting to a West Coast air terminal for a civilian flight to Da Nang or Saigon. Processed and orientated by the 22d Replacement Battalion at Cam Ranh Bay or the 90th Replacement Battalion at Long Binh, they might undergo a further week's training before posting to unit. Near the middle of the tour, which was 12 months for all enlisted men – volunteers, draftees and lifers alike – there would be five days' out-country R&R. Then came the 'Freedom Bird' flight home when a man reached his DEROS (Date Eligible to Return from Overseas).

The burden of combat was undecidedly unequal in Vietnam. In the Korean War, there had been a similar rotation policy but with the crucial difference that those serving in support units stayed longer than those in combat units. In the Nam, only 22.2 per cent served in combat arms and, because of the 'circular' nature of the war, combat troops returned constantly to base camps shared with rear echelon 'immunes' – men who served their time in some comfort at little risk.

Another problem was the 'hump', whereby units might lose large numbers of experienced soldiers simultaneously. It became practice to transfer men arbitrarily to achieve a more acceptable rate of attrition, but this damaged unit cohesion. Moreover, the 12-month tour also meant that, while a man might reach a plateau of moderate or dutiful commitment between months two and 10, and maximum combat efficiency in months nine and 10, he would become increasingly less willing to take risks thereafter as his DEROS approached.

Left: The blood, fear and stench of the battlefield left far behind them, grunts relax in Annie's bar in Saigon, each man counting off the days until his DEROS. The eagerly-awaited release date made men extremely unpredictable and reduced their effectiveness towards the end of their tours. Woe betide any officer who made a 'short' exceed his tour by even one day. Fuelled partly by a mistaken belief in their own invincibility, burnt-out short-timers could be as much a danger to their buddies as to themselves. Alternatively, they simply refused to fight. Below: Dreaming of home, and determined to get there without need of a body bag.

They were kept away from high profile targets like RTOs (Radio Telephone Operators) and machine-gunners. They were kept off of ambushes and LP/OPs (Listening Post/Observation Post). They weren't sent in to clear huts or caves or tunnels. In essence, they weren't entrusted with any duty other than keeping themselves alive – and making sure they didn't kill anyone else in the process.

On the other hand, many infantrymen, being a superstitious lot, tended to shy away from a short-timer who just last week had been best of friends. The reasoning here was that Short must have just about used up all of his luck to make it this far in the war. That meant he was due for a bullet, grenade, RPG-2 rocket, mortar bomb, terminal VD, snake bite, sun stroke or contagious bad breath. No-one wanted to be around when any of that happened.

And no one really wanted to be around a short-timer when the shit hit the fan, either. Fire and movement into an NVA platoon position? Last month Short won a Bronze Star for taking out a machine-gun nest single-handed. Today, with a week left in-country, that big old tree he's hiding behind looks mighty comforting.

'C'mon, man! You gotta cover my ass. We gotta move up!'

'Not even, bro'. No way I'm goin' out there.'

'Godammit! We need your gun!'

Slow, resolute shake of the head. 'Uh-uh. I'm too short for this shit.'

Then again, being short hit different people in different ways. Some guys curled up inside themselves, cut themselves off from Vietnam and everything in it, and just went through the motions until they hit Camp Alpha, the out-processing centre down Saigon-way. In others, you couldn't tell if they had three months or three days left in-country. They'd take their share of dirty and dangerous jobs, talk about this-and-that like everyone else, then one day they'd be gone. Just hop on the ol' re-supply bird with a last wave to the boys, then vanish.

And then there were the burn-outs. Just the opposite of the typical short-timer who was looking for a cool skate to ride out his last days.

Burn-outs thought they were invincible. 'Luck? Sheeit, man. Luck ain't got nothing to do with it. Them bastards had all year to kiss my ass and they missed. I'm gonna get me a few more 'fore I go home!'

Burn-outs got angry and wanted revenge before they left. 'Hot damn! Gooks 'bushed my people last night and sent old Billy to the promised land. They better start flying or they're gonna start dying'!'

And burn-outs had a death wish. They'd seen too many friends die in nameless firefights and ambushes, and wondered why that bullet with their own name on it never found them. It was the supreme guilt trip – survivor's guilt. Why one's left alive when the other one's dead. This kind of mind warp sent grunts charging into ambushes and across no-man's-land during fire fights. It sent chopper pilots into unsecured hot LZs when just another few minutes would have stabilized control on the ground. And it sent a lot of them into bars and whorehouses, looking for a terminal fight.

But burn-outs, as a rule, were a rare and endangered breed. You'd often see them extend their tours by another six months, or volunteer to come back after a month or two in the States. They were playing Russian roulette, Vietnam style – but they just didn't know it.

Catching the Freedom Bird

That drunk Ranger sergeant and I flew out together from Tuy Hoa to Saigon the next day on a C-130, two short-timers headed for home. I felt worse than he looked, which put us both near the terminal hangover stage. We shouted a bit of conversation over the roar of the engines, but there wasn't that much to say. We were both on our way out, so being a short-timer wasn't as impressive or important as it had been a few days before.

We hung around Camp Alpha for the next couple of days, waiting to be manifested on a flight back to the World. The place was full of short-timers just like us, but by then it didn't mean anything. No one looked at us with envy or jealousy, or treated us with kid gloves; no one got drunk and shouted 'SHO-O-O-O-RT!' or bothered with short-time calendars anymore.

That glow or presence or whatever it was that had made us special and different back in our old units was gone. We were now just another bunch of grunts waiting for the Freedom Bird to wing us home.

Right: Nothing lifts the load from a man's shoulders like the thought of catching the big bird back to the World. Left: The 'thousand-yard stare'.

TOURS FOR OFFICERS AND MEN

Shorter tours and lower casualty rates among the officers increased the grievances of Joe Grunt

Adding to the 'turbulence' created by the rotation policy for enlisted men was the fact that officers served only six months in combat commands. It had been anticipated that the war would be short and, as there had been no combat commands since Korea, the military authorities determined to provide maximum opportunities in the US Army's long-term interests. Less convincingly, it was also argued that it would prevent 'burnout' in officers facing the strain of combat command responsibilities. Unfortunately, this policy proved immensely disruptive both to unit cohesion, and to officer integrity.

For enlisted men, it meant constant exposure to new and less experienced officers – one enlisted man had five different platoon and four different company commanders during his tour. It also encouraged 'ticket punching', with officers using their period of command to achieve demonstrable results at the cost of their temporary charges' lives.

The proportional increase of officers within the US Army from 9 per cent (1 officer per 15 men) in Korea to 15 per cent (1 officer per 6 men) in Vietnam also added to the pressures, since more officers were chasing fewer commands and a successful tour was a sure guarantee of promotion. The fact that more officers were seen to be safe in the rear echelon could only contribute to distrust on the part of the enlisted men – especially when statistics bore out the suspicion that officers were suffering substantially fewer casualties – in relation to their numbers.

1967

LIFE IN THE NORTH

While American planes flew overhead and news filtered through of their comrades fighting in the South, the North Vietnamese people went on about their business with the same quiet courage as Londoners under the Blitz. The hardships they endured created a common bond and a sense of purpose that withstood all American attempts to shatter it.

Clockwise from right: A young Vietnamese girl watches for American planes; even the farmers carry guns; business as usual in the industrial sectors; bridges were prime American targets – this one is being repaired yet again; bombed houses would have to be rebuilt; even in Haiphong harbour you had to keep your eyes peeled for US warplanes.

Above left: Despite the bombing, meals had to be prepared and eaten, crops had to be planted and harvested, and (above, far left) dams still had to be built by the glorious workers of the revolution.

1967

As dawn was breaking over the small Vietnamese village inside the Mekong Delta, the girl was worried. The headman of the village had not yet woken. True, he had been very tired the night before, but in a couple of hours he had to attend an important meeting some miles away, to co-ordinate a major strike against the Yankee invader. Well, at least he'd enjoyed an undisturbed sleep. The girl had been on guard duty during the night and knew that nothing suspicious had happened.

She would have to wake him, she decided, and approached the door of his hut. His sleeping form did not stir as she called his name softly, so she went inside and bent over him, about to shake him by the shoulder.

She froze. His stomach had been cut open, and his severed liver lay next to the ugly gash. A piece of it had been roughly bitten off. She realized in sorrow that this meant that he could not now enter Nirvana intact. She knew what she would find even before she looked at his face. It had been roughly decorated with broad stripes of green paint. The 'Green Faced Men' had paid a visit during the night.

The above account may be apocryphal, but it is fairly typical of the stories told by the Viet Cong about the Green Faced Men, their name for the most ruthless, efficient and feared detachment of the American forces – the US Navy SEALS.

In 1962 President Kennedy had ordered the setting up of the SEALs as an elite group. Their title was an acronym for the various elements in which they waged their own brutal form of guerrilla warfare: SEa, Air or Land.

The SEALs were commissioned as a unit with the aim of greatly expanding the role and capabilities of the already-existing combat swimmer force, the Navy's underwater demolition teams (UDTs).

SEALs were primarily forward infiltration teams. These were small units – usually less than seven men, sometimes as few as three. Each member was a specialist in a specific area. There

US NAVY SEALS

was the 'wheel', the officer-in-charge; a couple of swimmer scouts; and the 'powder train', or explosives expert, backed up by a 'rigger', who led the powder train to and from the objective and supervized the laying of charges. There was also a radio operator and a heavy-weapons man, who carried the lightweight Stoner sub-machine gun.

SEALs carried an assortment of basic weaponry. Among their most favoured items was a shotgun which was 'choked' to throw 4-buck (buckshot) at a horizontal, and gave a nice wide spray when fired. It also made a hell of a mess of whoever

The special ops personnel of the SEALs were the toughest hombres in the delta

'Cam' cream liberally applied, a SEAL (above) is ready to indulge in one of his unit's favourite pastimes – 'kicking ass and taking names' in the swamp warfare of the Mekong.

got in the way. Another favourite was the Navy K-bar knive. It had a 7-9in blade, and was sharp enough to shave with. Not that the SEALs bothered with their personal appearance much.

They also had a wide assortment of transport vehicles, depending on the situation. There was the Mike boat, a heavily-armed riverine patrol craft. Or, for travelling narrow waterways, they used Boston Whalers, 16ft glass-fibre boats with a very narrow draft and 85hp outboard engines. This made them very fast – useful if you had to leave an area suddenly after doing a number. There was also the IBS (Inflatable Boat, Small) for submarine drops and, when the area was inaccessible by any other means (such as dense swampland), they'd just de-ass from low-flying choppers. Not with parachutes, though. If they

were feeling lazy they'd abseil down, otherwise they'd just jump. The SEALs would go anywhere, do anything. The more dangerous the location or the dirtier the job, the more they liked it.

When the SEALs started arriving in Vietnam in 1966, they were initially used for intelligence-gathering operations – setting up observation posts in the Delta to help chart the VC water and trail network. Once they had identified a route or base, they took it out. A very important early

Besides their 'Sat Cong' (kill communists) missions in the heart of enemy-held territory, the special ops personnel of the SEAL teams also spearheaded routine reconnaissance by fire operations (below).

CLANDESTINE FORCES IN VIETNAM

The US Navy SEALs had one of the most fearsome reputations of all the US forces committed to Vietnam. Closely modelled on the British Special Boat Squadron (SBS), their missions ranged from information gathering to assassinations. The co-operation between the SEALs and the Vietnamese Provisional Reconnaissance Units (PRUs) was the most striking and successful aspect of the US Special Forces' programme of raising Civilian Irregular Defence Groups (CIDGs).

As early as May 1964 the CIDGs provided 'indigs' for Project Delta, which saw the birth of the Long Range Reconnaissance Patrols (LRRPs). Like the other 'Greek Alphabet' projects – Sigma, Omega and Gamma – Delta conducted covert operations which, on occasions, went beyond South Vietnam's borders.

The Military Assistance Command Vietnam-Studies and Observation Group (MACV-SOG) was a joint service unconventional warfare task force operating throughout Southeast Asia. At its peak, SOG had 2000 Americans and 8000 indigs under its command, tasked with cross-border operations, the rescue of American POWs, agent infiltration and psychological warfare. In all these areas the SEALs excelled.

SOG operated inside North Vietnam as early as February 1964, in Laos from September 1965 and in Cambodia from May 1967. In November 1967, three separate commands were established at Kontum, Da Nang and Ban Me Thuot. Each deployed Spike Recon Teams (RTs), Hatchet Forces and Search-Location-and-Annihilation Mission companies (SLAMs). Typically, the RT, comprising three Americans and nine indigs, laid ambushes and prepared the ground for the five Americans and up to 300 indigs of each Hatchet Force and the as yet still classified SLAMs, who acted as a cutting edge.

operation was Charlestown, in December 1966, during which the SEALs captured documents indicating the locations of VC wells throughout the Rung Sat Special Zone just south of Saigon. Using their demolition skills the SEALs blew these wells and deprived the VC of most of their fresh water, forcing them to spend valuable time searching for fresh supplies.

In September 1967, during Operation Crimson Tide, the SEALs acted as scouts and pointmen for a large operation aimed at destroying enemy strongpoints in the Delta. Bold Dragon III was a similar operation in March 1968, during which the SEALs blew up enemy bunkers on Tanh Ding Island and destroyed a VC arms factory.

Once infiltrated into a specific area, the SEALs

On board a riverine patrol craft (above), the SEALs run through their assault plan. After the lead elements of the team have waded ashore (top right), the craft noses up to the bank under the protection of a 180 degree defence (right).

Left: Watching and waiting for action. During operations, the SEALs usually maintained complete silence – communicating with hand signals and relying on long hours of operational experience to gauge how each member of the team would react when contact was made.

would allow no more contact between them and other US forces until the end of their mission. The reason for this was that they tended to distrust the re-supply networks, which were apt to make to much noise and give away the SEALs' position. Instead they evolved a system of 'silence and reliance'. They hardly ever spoke amongst themselves whilst in action: when you've worked with a buddy for some time you don't need to talk to know exactly what the other guy is thinking. You relied on his intuitive understanding of your needs. If he failed you, you'd end up dead. Or in a VC POW camp, which was probably worse.

'You can become a bush'

Moving through irrigation ditches in the Delta, wading in water up to their chests (SEALs often travelled barefoot, so as not to leave tell-tale bootmarks), they would set up observation and listening posts throughout the area.

Left: SEALs prepare a welcoming committee after discovering a VC booby trap along the trail. Above: A typical SEAL team.

Once they had a fix on the enemy, they'd set up an ambush and rig a few Claymore mines along the likely escape routes from the fire-zone, to catch any VC lucky enough to get out alive. Then the SEALs would just lie in wait. For hours at a time. No movement, no sound. They had the knack of blending completely into the background. As one ex-SEAL explained: 'It's incredible to explain what you can become, the illusion that you can present to people. You can become a bush, a log, if

285

1967

Above: Trained for operations by sea, air and land, SEALs abseil from a Huey during a reconnaissance mission. Vietnam was an unconventional war that demanded unconventional methods. Kitted out in their tiger-stripes and packing heavy-duty hardware, the SEALs were about as unconventional as you could get.

THE HUSH PUPPY

Among the special weapons with which the US Navy SEALs were equipped in Vietnam probably the most fascinating was the Smith and Wesson Mark 22, Model O, 9mm pistol, also known as the 'Hush Puppy.' It acquired this nickname because of its intended function of killing enemy guard dogs. Naturally it was put to other uses as well.

The 'Hush Puppy' was developed by Smith and Wesson specifically for the SEALs and was based on the Model 39 automatic pistol. It was equipped with a five-inch threaded barrel to which could be screwed a suppressor (silencer) developed by the Naval Ordinance Lab in Washington. To make the weapon even quieter, the slide could be locked, thereby keeping the mechanism closed and silent while firing.

Since the 9mm round is normally supersonic, and therefore creates an audible sonic-crack in flight, a subsonic round had to be specially developed for the Mark 22 to eliminate this tell-tale sound. The Super Val cartridge corporation, a leading developer of extra-lethal loads for pistols, was given a contract by the US Navy to develop special ammunition for the Hush Puppy. The result was a green-tipped Parabellum projectile which, at 10.2 grams (150 grains) was substantially heavier than the standard 9mm bullet. It also had a reduced muzzle velocity of 274 metres per second. Furthermore, it was equipped with special caps and plugs which permitted it to be carried underwater. The ammunition was packed in boxes holding 22 rounds and a spare insert for the suppressor. Each of these inserts would last about 30 rounds before needing to be replaced. (With supersonic rounds a suppressor would only last for about six rounds.)

The Hush Puppy was never intended to be used as a SEALs primary armament, and so only about 100-200 of them were acquired by the Navy.

MARK 22, MODEL 0 SILENCED PISTOL

Calibre: 9mm
Overall length: 320mm
Weight: 0.963kg

you just concentrate hard enough on being that. They told us in our training that you could become a master of illusion if you believe enough in the illusion. And it works. I couldn't believe it. Also the power of your eyes, not to look directly at something but to look off to the side of it. You wouldn't concentrate your focus because if you look at something too long, it'll look back at you, and you don't want them to turn around and see you there.'

Tough with a capital 'T'

Often the SEALs worked in tandem with Provincial Reconnaissance Units (PRUs), which included all types of tough mercenaries from VC turncoats to convicted felons. Men who had nothing to lose. Among the missions that SEALs and PRUs worked together on was the ambushing and killing of VC tax-collectors, especially in the Rung Sat Special Zone – the aptly named 'Forest of Assassins' south of Saigon. Strangely, the SEALs often seemed to claim that the tax-money the collector was carrying had been destroyed during the fire-fight. But then no-one wanted to argue with a SEAL too much.

Other jobs involved locating and destroying arms and food dumps. (It was the PRU's job to bring back hard evidence of a successful operation, either in the form of weapons or, in the case of 'wet jobs' – assassinations – ears). Sometimes SEALs had to hit guys right inside their huts, often with the families there at the time. To help their getaway, they'd rig up a frag-grenade on a tripwire across the door. While making tracks away from the target, they'd hear the crump of the grenade going off.

SEAL missions were numerous and varied. They helped select and train the Vietnamese version of the SEALs, the LDNN (Lin Dei Nugel Nghai). The US SEALs conducted many operations alongside the LDNN during the latter stages of the US involvement in Vietnam, including many raids into VC POW camps in the Delta to free prisoners. It was also rumoured that they

Inserted into 'Indian country' after rumours were heard of a large Viet Cong bunker network in the Mekong war zone, SEALs monitored VC movements before moving in to clear the complex. Explosive charges were then laid (left). Having retired to a waiting patrol boat, the team was able to watch the fruit of its labours as the complex disintegrated into a ball of smoke (below).

regularly used to visit Haiphong harbour, the main port in North Vietnam for importing weapons and supplies from Russia and China. Using explosives, they opened narrow rivers to help the passage of naval vessels. They were even used to recover the bodies of downed US aircrews from underwater. But, whether they were mounting operations against the VC or were using their underwater skills to provide port security for US ships, such as laying charges to remove underwater obstacles, they always remained true to their personal motto: Sat Cong – kill communists.

Off-duty, SEALs didn't let up. They had little respect for non-SEALs, officers or enlisted, and, after a few beers to loosen up, they'd prowl around causing mayhem. One of their favourite games was to tear off the underwear from frogmen in bars, and leave it hanging from the overhead fans, blowing in the breeze. Frogmen weren't supposed to wear underwear, SEALs claimed.

But, as one ex-SEAL put it: 'I'd create havoc, and they would say, "SEALs are supposed to be crazy. Leave him alone. He's going to die tomorrow". And I think our attitude was "If you fuck with us, we'll blow you away". But then again, you know, it was a business, and the business was terrorism.'

THE M63 STONER

The M63 system, designed to fulfil several roles, was a favourite of the hard-hitting SEAL teams

The Stoner M63A1 weapons system was a revolutionary concept that failed to gain general acceptance within the US Army. However, its unique features were picked up by the US Navy SEALs who felt that the weapon's adaptability made it perfect for the specialised role that they performed.

The weapon was designed by Eugene Stoner – the designer of the M16 rifle. The M63, however, was based on an entirely different concept to the assault rifle. It had one basic mechanism onto which various barrels, stocks and magazines could be mounted. It could therefore be used as an assault rifle, a submachine gun and, when mounted on a tripod, as a light or medium machine gun.

The M63 worked by gas, which operated a rotating bolt and helped keep the gun's weight remarkably light for so sophisticated a weapon.

It was usually belt-fed from a plastic magazine, although the size of the magazine could vary tremendously. The SEALs would normally use the weapon with a 150-round box magazine. This gave them a light weapon capable of laying down sustained bursts of continuous fire.

The Stoner could also use a 20-round clip or 90-round drum and could be adapted to continuous belt feed for use as a medium machine gun.

Nevertheless, there were some problems with the Stoner system. Like the M16, it was gas fed and thus required a great deal of maintenance. This was a fact more relevant to the average grunt than the special ops personnel of SEAL teams, however. The M63 was a complicated weapon and needed specialised care.

Above: The US Navy SEALs are the only unit to use the Stoner. Provided the weapon is kept clean, it packs a hefty punch in close-quarters combat.

THE STONER M63A1 WEAPONS SYSTEM

Calibre: 5.56mm
Weight: 4.39kg
Type: Multi-purpose machine gun
Magazine: Variable, 20-round clip to 150-round box
Range: 800 metres
Rate of fire: Cyclic, 660 rounds per minute
Muzzle velocity: 1000 metres per second

THE TAKING OF HILL 875

When the 173d Airborne met the NVA at Dak To, veteran war correspondent Peter Arnett was there to record their torment

Surrounded by body bags in the battle-scarred landscape of Dak To, a paratrooper surveys the grim scene. Not until the fourth day of fighting could an LZ be secured and the dead flown out.

'Hill 875, Wednesday, 22 November 1967. War painted the living and the dead the same grey pallor on Hill 875. For 50 hours (starting Sunday) the most brutal fighting of the Vietnam war ebbed and flowed across this jungle hill-top and by Wednesday was still not over.

'Death picked its victims at random and broke and twisted their bodies.

'At times the only way to tell who was alive and who was dead amongst the exhausted men was to watch when the enemy mortars crashed in. The living rushed unashamedly to the tiny bunkers dug into the red clay of the hilltop. The wounded squirmed toward the shelter of trees that had been blasted to the ground.

'Only the dead, propped up in bunkers, where they had died in direct mortar hits, or face down in the dust, where they had fallen to bullets, didn't move.

'The 2d Battalion (503d Infantry) of the 173d

Airborne Brigade that first ascended this remote hill in the western sector of the Dak To battle-ground, nearly died.

'Of the 16 officers who led their men across the ridge line of Hill 875 on Sunday, eight were killed and the other eight wounded. Of the 13 battalion medics, 11 died.

'The days and nights of fighting, the waits for a reinforcing column that inched across the ridges, the stench of the dead and moans of the wounded etched deep lines in the young faces of the para-troopers who clung to the hill.

'Some of the wounded cracked under the strain. "It's a goddamn shame that they haven't got us out of here", gasped one paratroop sergeant with tears in his eyes early afternoon Tuesday. He had been lying on the hill for 50 hours with a painful groin wound. All around him lay scores of other wound-ed. You could see who had lain there the longest. Blood had clotted their bandages, they had ceased moaning, their eyes were glazed.

'The bandages of those hit in the recent mortar barrages were still wet with blood. These wound-ed still squirmed with pain.

A foul play of war

'The most seriously hurt were stretched on a carpet of leaves next to a helicopter landing zone that lay between towering trees. These casualties were wrapped in bloody poncho liners to protect against the night chill. The North Vietnamese forward positions began just 45m along the ridge. Each helicopter that came in drew heavy mortar and automatic weapons fire.

'One helicopter made it and carried out five seriously wounded [on] Sunday and ten other ships were disabled in trying.

'"The wounded can see the choppers trying to get in. They know they are not being left to die", a young officer, himself wounded, said.

'Yet some did die as their blood seeped away into the clay of Hill 875. Some of these were the men blasted by a 500-pound bomb dropped by mistake from an American plane late Sunday during an air strike on the nearby enemy bunkers. [Forty-two] men were killed in that explosion, "a foul play of war" one survivor said bitterly.

'When another landing zone was being cut below the crest of the hill late Tuesday and evacuations of the wounded began, it was found that others had died in the last hours of waiting. Whether this was from shock, thirst, or just plain giving up, none of the medics knew.

'The battalion took its first wounded midday Sunday as it crested Hill 875, one of the hundreds of knolls that dot the ridges in the Dak To fighting

Above left: Even fortifed foxholes offered precious little protection to the men dug in on Hill 875. As soon as they broke cover, the NVA would unleash a torrent of fire. Left: The fatigue begins to show. Right: But the fight goes on.

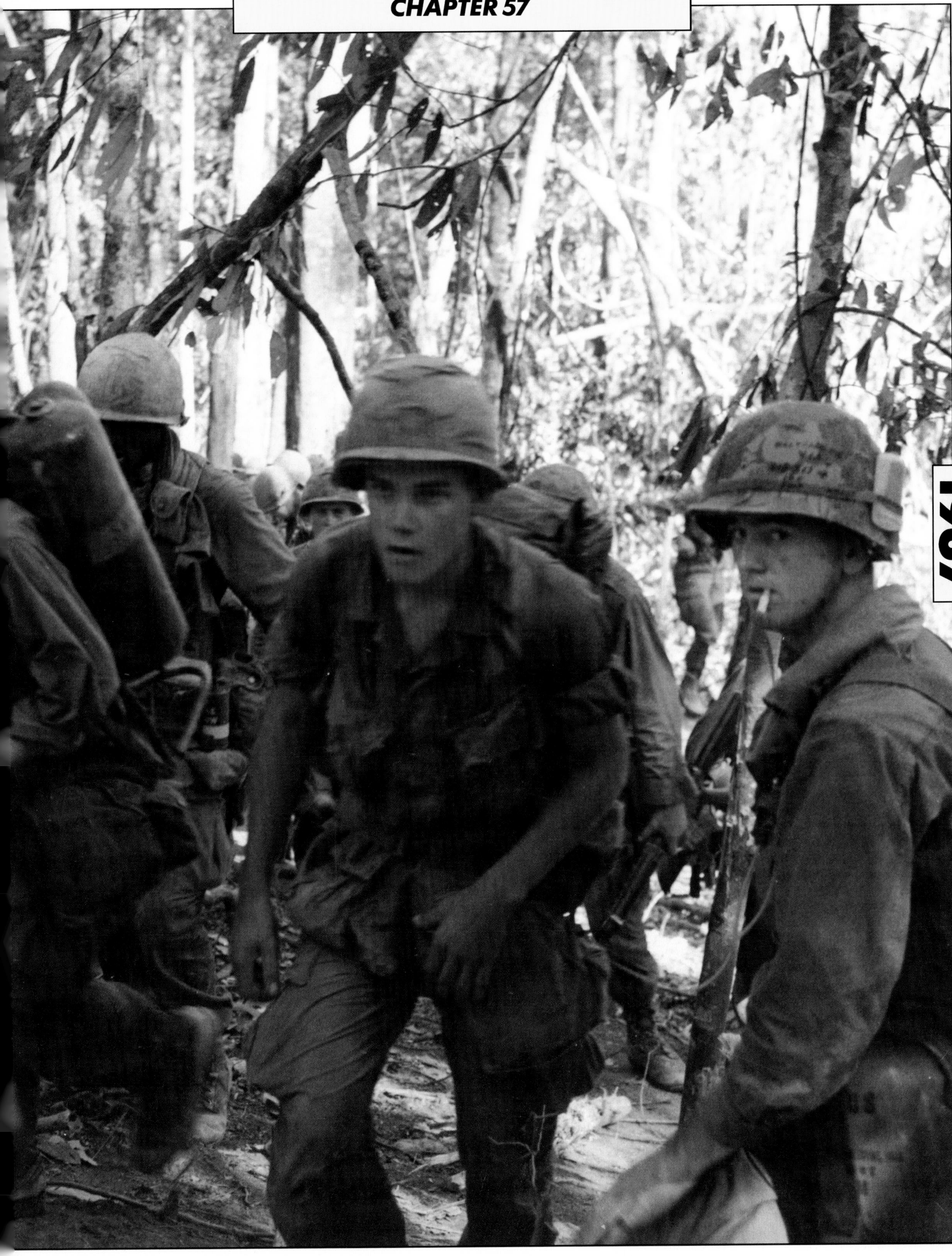

region on the Cambodian-Laos border. All weekend, as the paratroopers moved along the jungle hills, enemy base camps were uncovered.

'The biggest was on 875 and Company D lost several men in the first encounter with the bunkers.

'Company A moved back down the hill to cut a landing zone and was chopped to pieces by a North Vietnamese flanking attack. The remnants managed to flee back to the crest of the hill while a paratrooper propped his [machine] gun on the trail and kept firing at the advancing enemy troops, ignoring orders that he retreat with the others.

"You can keep gunning them down, but sooner or later when there are enough of them they'll get to you," commented Specialist 4 James Kelley, from Fort Myers, Florida, who saw the machine gunner go down after killing an estimated 17 communist troops.

Bodies lay spread-eagled

'Company D, hearing the roar of battle below them, returned to the crest of the hill and established a 50m perimeter "because we figured we were surrounded by a regiment," one officer said.

'As the battalion was regrouping late in the afternoon for another crack at the bunker system, the [American] bomb came in at tree-top level, the burst smashing shrapnel into those below. The bomb crippled the battalion, killing many of the wounded who were strung along the ground under the trees.

'From then on until the reinforcing battalion arrived the following night, the paratroopers on

Right: Stepping off the Huey into a hot LZ that is close to boiling point, the Airborne troopers of the 173d dive for protective cover – what little there is (below left). The paras knew it was not going to be easy, but no-one told them just how well entrenched the NVA bunkers and spider holes at Dak To really were. Below centre: M16s pointed uphill, the men get ready to move against an unseen enemy. Below, far right: For men on point, the hunters became the hunted.

ACTIONS IN THE CENTRAL HIGHLANDS, 1967

In early January 1967, the US 4th Infantry Division moved into the western area of the Central Highlands, determined to engage the NVA 1st and 10th Divisions. Operation Sam Houston began immediately, with US units clearing the plains of Pleiku and Kontum Provinces, preparatory to more sustained campaigns west of the Nam Sathay river.

The 2d Brigade of the 4th Division crossed the river in mid-February, entering some of the most difficult terrain imaginable. Mist-shrouded valleys, covered in dense jungle, were overshadowed by rugged mountains; daylight temperatures soared above 105 degrees and water was scarce; artillery and air support was virtually impossible to organize. Joined by the 1st Brigade, helicoptered into Plei Djereng, the 4th Division pushed slowly westwards, hoping to trap the NVA close to the Cambodian border. Instead, they suffered constant ambush in ideal guerrilla terrain. By mid-March, both brigades had been forced to pull back east of the Se Sanh river; Sam Houston ended officially on 5 April.

Operation Francis Marion began immediately, taking advantage of the summer monsoon. The 4th Division now concentrated in the flat rolling hills of western Pleiku, south of the Se Sanh river, guarding the border against NVA infiltration. It was a campaign that was to continue until 12 October, by which time the division, having suffered continuous ambush, was close to exhaustion.

By October, it was clear that the NVA were concentrating further north, in western Kontum. US forces, including the 173d Airborne Brigade, moved to counter this in Operations Greeley and MacArthur. They fought in Kontum, Pleiku and Phu Bon Provinces in late October and throughout November. MacArthur culminated in the major battle of Dak To and, when it ended in late November, the NVA had been forced back across the Cambodian border.

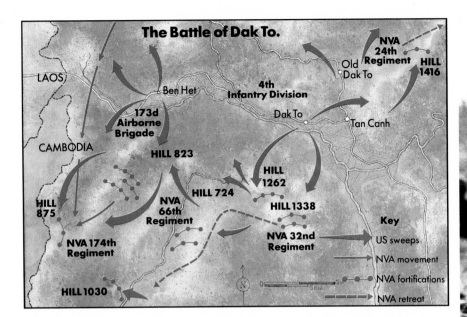

The Battle of Dak To.

LAOS
CAMBODIA
Ben Het
4th Infantry Division
Dak To
Old Dak To
Tan Canh
NVA 24th Regiment
HILL 1416
173d Airborne Brigade
HILL 823
HILL 875
NVA 66th Regiment
HILL 724
HILL 1262
HILL 1338
NVA 174th Regiment
NVA 32nd Regiment
HILL 1030

Key
US sweeps
NVA movement
NVA fortifications
NVA retreat

1967

the hill desperately dug in. Only one medic was able to work on the numerous wounded, and the enemy kept fighting off the rescue helicopters.

'The relief battalion, the 4th of the 503d, linked into the tiny perimeter on 875 Monday night. The moonlit scene was macabre. Bodies of the dead lay spread-eagled across the ground, the wounded whimpered.

'The survivors of the battalion, hungry and thirsty, rushed up eagerly to get food and water only to learn that the relief battalion had brought enough supplies for one day and had already consumed them.

'Monday night was sleepless but uneventful. On Tuesday the North Vietnamese struck with fury. From positions just 100m away, they began pounding the American perimeter with 82mm

Right: During a lull in the fighting, corpsmen work desperately to save the life of one of their buddies. Other casualties had to be brought in under heavy fire (below). Far right: The agony of war.

mortars. The first rounds slapped in at daybreak, killing three paratroopers in a foxhole and wounding 17 others on the line.

'Then, for the rest of the day, the communists methodically worked over the hill, pumping rounds in five or six at a time, rewounding those who lay bleeding in the open and tearing through bunkers. The plop of the rounds as they left the enemy tubes gave the paratroopers only seconds to dash for cover.

He kissed the rosary

'The foxholes got deeper as the day wore on. Foxhole after foxhole took hits. A dog handler and his German shepherd died together. Men who were joking with you and offering cigarettes would be writhing on the ground wounded and pleading for water minutes later. There was no water for them or anyone else.

'Crouched in one bunker, Private First Class Angel Flores, 20, of New York City, said, "if we were dead like those out there we wouldn't have to worry about this stuff coming in." He fingered the plastic rosary around his neck and kissed it reverently as the rounds blasted on the ground outside.

"Does that do you any good?" a buddy asked him. "Well I'm still alive," Flores said. His buddy replied, "Don't you know that the chaplain that gave you that was killed on Sunday?"

'The day's pounding steadily reduced the platoon commanded by First Lieutenant Bryan Mac-

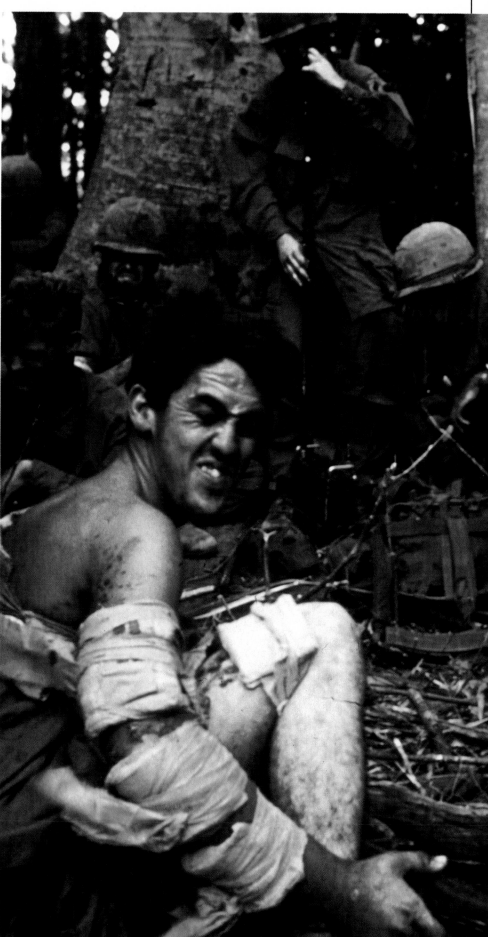

Donough, 25, from Fort Lee, Virginia. He started out Sunday with 27 men. He had nine left midday Tuesday. "If the Viets keep this up, there'll be none left by evening," he said. The enemy positions seemed impervious to constant American air strikes. Napalm fireballs exploded on the bunkers 25m away. The earth shook with heavy bombs.

"We've tried 750-pounders, napalm, and everything else, but air can't do it. It's going to take man power to get those positions," MacDonough said.

'By late afternoon Wednesday a new landing zone was cut beneath the hill. The enemy mortars searched for it but the helicopters came in anyway. A line of wounded trudged down the hill and by evening 140 of them had been evacuated.

The final rout?

'The arrival of the helicopters, and food, water, and ammunition, seemed to put new life into the paratroopers. They talked eagerly of a final assault on the enemy bunkers.

'As darkness was falling flame throwers were brought up. The first stubborn bunker yielded and the final rout was beginning.

'The paratroopers were at last on the way to gaining the ridge line which they had set out to take three days earlier. The deserved every inch of it.'

The 'final' attack with which Arnett closed his report was not, as it turned out, the end. Thrown back that afternoon, the 4th Battalion, 503d Infantry, succeeded only the following morning, Thanksgiving Day, in taking Hill 875.

REPORTING THE WAR

Grab a pen and notepad and head out for the combat zone. But remember to stay close to a phone and meet the deadline

Vietnam was not the place to learn to become a journalist – especially for a woman. But when the syndicated wire service UPI posted my husband, Nat, to Saigon, I decided to tag along. I had a job as researcher on the New York Times and I was extremely excited at the prospect of getting out of the Big Apple and into the war.

But UPI told Nat that Saigon was not for wives. 'What am I supposed to do for the 18 months he's away?' I asked. 'Do what other wives do, and stay in New York or Bangkok,' they told me. But I followed Nat out to Saigon six weeks later, even though UPI refused to pay my fare.

Down to earth

Landing in Vietnam, even as a non-combatant, was something of a shock. One moment you were an ordinary passenger on a civilian aircraft, next you were in a war. Tan Son Nhut, which then ranked among the half dozen busiest airports in the world, was an uncompromising landscape of sandbags, barbed wire, figures in camouflage, Hueys, big-bellied C-130 transports, Phantoms and Air Force 707s bringing men to war and taking them out again. There was heat, noise and dust.

Nat picked me up in a UPI jeep – one of three dilapidated vehicles the bureau rented and the journalists systematically smashed up. The bureau was run from an old French town house. The newsroom was in a gloomy garage. The

photographers hung out in a hot little room in the rear. The drinking-water tank periodically yielded up dead rats, but most of the journalists found consolation next door in the Melody. It was a bar cum brothel where the beer was cold and the girls hot and mercenary.

Within a couple of weeks, we were posted up-country to Da Nang. I wanted to try my hand at writing some features for UPI and acquired my Vietnamese and American press credentials from the two separate headquarters in the city. The Americans gave journalists the rank of major. In case of capture, the VC were supposed to treat us like officers – we wondered whether this meant torture in the hope of extracting officer-level information as well.

A plague of mosquitoes

We had seats on a C-130 leaving for Da Nang at 8am, which meant arriving at Tan Son Nhut an hour and a half earlier. To book seats on military flights, journalists rang the press office, but these flights always entailed the long bouts of the apparently senseless waiting the ordinary soldier

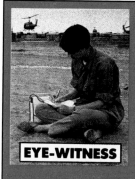

EYE-WITNESS

The author, Helen Gibson (above), covered the Vietnam war as a stringer with United Press International. Her assignments ranged from Da Nang, to the Mekong.

Left: Just when the grunts thought they were on their own, a barrage of media men and cameras would show up, hoping to beam the war into the homes of millions of Americans. Many of the troops simply couldn't understand why reporters risked life and limb just to send a story down the wire. Right: Another news team makes its deadline. Television and newspaper coverage of the war – with all its thirst for action – came in for stiff criticism after the war, with Westmoreland claiming that the press, not the military, lost Vietnam.

THE YELLOW PRESS?

Did open reporting during Vietnam feed the anti-war movement?

The United States has a long tradition of press freedom. It is enshrined in the Constitution and regarded as a mainstay of the democratic system. One of the results has been the development of a powerful press lobby, intent on seeking out the dark corners of government and exposing them to the public. During times of war, the right of investigation has been curtailed in the interests of security, but Vietnam was different. As successive administrations pointed out, no formal declaration of war had been made, so the media felt no moral or security constraints against its coverage of the conflict or its management.

The results were dramatic. Press coverage of the fighting in Vietnam spared no detail, however horrific, while portable cameras brought the war to American TV screens in all its gory drama, night after night. At the same time, investigative journalists in Washington probed the administration of the war, exposing its weaknesses and its contradictions. The publication of the supposedly secret Pentagon Papers in 1971, for example, not only highlighted the absurdities of government policy but also, on occasion, its unconstitutional nature.

All this was grist to the mill so far as anti-war protesters were concerned. Their leaders were acutely aware that if they argued against the war from a base of ignorance, they exposed themselves to charges of unsubstantiated prejudice. Open reporting gave them the knowledge and evidence they needed to make their case convincing. And, as more and more Americans absorbed the full horror of modern war from their newspapers or TV screens, they too began to doubt the validity of government policy. There can be no doubt that the protesters occasionally simplified or exaggerated their case, but as their basic message about the stupidity and waste of the war was increasingly reinforced by the brutal images the media presented, the government's position became less and less viable.

Without a formal declaration of war – and the censorship that would impose – the media had no choice but to chase good stories. After all, the American media had almost universally supported the war to start with. It was only as the death toll mounted, little progress was made and other responsible opinion turned against the war, that it began to change its mind.

had to endure. Old hands learnt other tricks, like cadging lifts in the luxurious little jets which carried VIPS and generals.

This was my first experience of a troop plane. Its insides had been scooped out and the belly filled with rows of webbing seats back-to-back. A little light filtered in, prison-like. The gloom, combined with the exposed pipes, made it feel like sitting inside a gutted whale. And for added surrealist effect, cold air was turned on from time to time which would wreathe the men in a ghostly white mist. On the two-hour journey, the only toilet was an uncurtained urinal in plain view of scores of soldiers. I suffered in silence.

In Da Nang, the press lived in a Marine compound. The men slept in the offices which doubled as dormitories. The few women shared a room over a drain. It had no air conditioning and was plagued with mosquitoes. The first week, the camp was hit by rockets aimed at the fuel storage dump. Amid mind-numbing explosions, Nat came running across the compound carrying a helmet and flak jacket for me. Marines were grabbing M16s and running in all directions, I was sure we would be overrun. But by the early hours all was calm again.

We made trips further north to red, dusty Dong Ha Marine camp. Nat covered various stories and I called them through to Saigon. Telephoning copy into the bureau was one of the major headaches in Vietnam. It took endless patience as you were patched, military installation to military installation, down the country. Then, just as you'd get through to Saigon after maybe an hour or two, a colonel would come on the line with an urgent message and you'd be back at square one.

Five O'Clock Follies

Being a woman helped. I learnt the names of all the operators on the Da Nang exchange and managed to wheedle extra-quick service out of them. This was so effective that our chief rival, the wire service Associated Press (AP), had to bring in their own female telephone operator. For the news agencies, seconds counted as gold in the continual race to get the story out first. The competition was so fierce that verbal fights sometimes broke out over the phones between agency reporters.

When we returned to Saigon, I had to find an apartment. It took a while as I had only a sketchy city map, no help and no idea of where to look. And I was terrified that the pedicab driver might bike

Above left: A United Press International (UPI) correspondent earns the respect of combat troops by risking life and limb to get a story on the front line. Right: A military commander faces the press. Armed with their plastic accreditation cards, journalists could go anywhere in Vietnam – hunting in packs and probing for holes in the official version of events.

me off into the Chinese quarter, a notorious VC stronghold. Three journalists were killed there that year, driving through in a jeep. And a UPI stringer was killed by a VC sniper on a nearby street, standing next to a UPI radio reporter fresh in from the States. The experience shook him for months. Eventually we found two rooms in a secure part of the city, opposite the US ambassador's residence. UPI began to let me cover the 'Five O'Clock Follies', as the daily military press briefings were known. Then I was given my first assignment – the simple job of covering a general's visit to the huge US base at Long Binh. As the general walked down the parade ground followed by a clutch of officers, an AP reporter rushed out and stopped the group dead in their tracks. I was aghast at his daring. The general talked, and the AP man scribbled in his notebook. But I decided I couldn't go over and listen in as it was the AP man's interview. The next morning, the log which compared the number of newspapers that used UPI copy as against AP's read 'Long Binh general 0-9'.

On my next assignment, another general's visit, I shadowed the AP man so doggedly that I almost ended up in the toilet with him – and I interviewed the general as he disappeared into a cubicle. No matter that it was pouring with rain, that my writing ran in rivers of blue and the general's aides had to rush to cover him with a poncho. I was much more scared of the bureau chief than of any four-star general.

A crazy Loach pilot

After that, I covered all kinds of stories. I flew on a night Spooky gunship mission, with a forward air controller calling in bombers, on a bombing mission with the 33rd Vietnamese Air Force Wing in propeller-driven A-1 Skyraiders, and with a madman in a tiny egg-shaped Loach helicopter who kept grenades in a bag under his seat for throwing into enemy bunkers. I rode with Vietnamese river patrols, covered appalling stories in orphanages and was lowered onto a destroyer off the coast of North Vietnam. The moment my feet hit the deck, everything on the USS *Blandy* packed up. The

compass went berserk, the engines stopped for 12 hours as we drifted nearer and nearer the enemy coast, and a rating dropped a can of white paint on the pristine grey deck. The sailors muttered that it was bad luck to have a woman on board ship, but they still treated me like a queen.

I rode elephants with Special Forces and Montagnard tribesmen and covered the premiere of John Wayne's film *The Green Berets* at the Green Berets' headquarters in Nha Trang. I learnt to parachute with 300 Vietnamese airborne recruits and stayed at a Vietnamese airborne outpost in Ben Soi woods – 500 men had dug in along a prime infiltration route into Tay Ninh, 60 miles northwest of Saigon, and were expecting a ground attack. We took incoming that night which killed one man and injured 10 others.

Notepads in the delta

On another occasion, I went on patrol with paramilitary police forces in the Mekong Delta. We waded ashore from the boat looking for a VC camp. Half the party continued on foot while I joined the other half poling down a narrow, booby-trapped creek. The party on land tripped mines guarding the camp and a sergeant on the US advisory team was killed – he was a career army man in his late forties with only a few weeks in-country to go. Two Vietnamese were killed too, but the camp was found deserted.

Although we could never claim to have shared the hardships and horrors that many soldiers endured, it was hard to adjust to the outside world again after leaving Vietnam. Nothing outside seemed worth writing about. I may have been a cub reporter, but I had already achieved the ultimate in journalism – I had reported a war.

THE MEDIA AT WAR

The Vietnam war was the most reported conflict in the history of warfare, turning a small Southeast Asian country into a hotbed of journalism.

In 1964, a full year before the Marines landed at Da Nang, there were already 40 American and foreign news media representatives in Saigon alone. By early 1967, with Operation Cedar Falls in full swing, media representation in South Vietnam had grown to staggering proportions. There were over 420 of them, including support personnel, wives and husbands. They arrived in Vietnam from 22 nations across the globe, with approximately 180 Americans among them. Of this total, however, there were usually only 40 US reporters and photographers out in the field with combat troops at any one time.

Many of the war correspondents such as Michael Herr (*Esquire*), Dan Rather (*CBS*) and Peter Arnett (*Associated Press*) shared the dangers that confronted the frontline units, and acquired a somewhat macabre reputation among the soldiers for their willingness to do so. Sixteen American journalists lost their lives while covering the war, and media representatives are among the 42 US civilians still unaccounted for in Southeast Asia. Above: As journalists fire in their questions, General Weyland does his best to answer them.

Above: It may only be a training exercise, but the leader of this NVA platoon is urging his men on with a battle cry that Ho Chi Minh would be proud of. This particular 'Hero Unit' has claimed to have shot down six American planes with its infantry weapons.

INTO ACTION WITH THE NVA

Try to pin down the NVA – you might as well try and get blood from a stone

As the Vietnam war dragged on, the US Army looked more and more like a flat-footed heavyweight boxer, cut around the eyes and lurching blindly after an opponent too nimble to be caught, mostly punching thin air and beginning to take some fairly tough blows to the body, too. Yet in theory the Americans had not just the greater weight of firepower, but superior mobility as well.

Anyone could understand that small units of

Viet Cong guerrillas would be hard to pin down, but once the North Vietnamese Army (NVA) was appearing in strength to give combat as regular army against regular army, especially in the northern provinces, how did it manage so often to outwit and outmanoeuvre its imperialist enemy?

The NVA commanders knew that if they fought on the Americans' terms, they would surely lose any encounter. Their first priority was to ensure they fought on their own terms at all times. Even when the Americans went looking for the NVA, it was almost invariably the NVA who found them.

NVA fire discipline

Alert and always ready to move at a moment's notice, the NVA were rarely taken by surprise. When a US force set out to sweep a remote area thick with NVA troops, their arrival would be anything but secretive, advertised by massive helicopter movements and prepping by artillery and aircraft. This left the NVA with a choice: stand or run. If they fancied their chances, the NVA would stay. If not, they would split into small units and swiftly evacuate the area – ready to return the moment the Americans departed.

Often, however, the NVA would hold their ground. They might decide to provide a hot reception at the LZs. Here, preparation was normally the NVA's strongest suit. They would have reconnoitred the whole area, identifying likely LZs, and positioning mortars, light machine guns and other weaponry around them. As the helicopters came in, the concealed NVA would maintain total fire discipline until the order came to open up. The volume of fire against incoming US troops could be staggering.

Alternatively, the North Vietnamese would wait for a company to push out from the LZ. There would follow a classic pattern of events repeated over and over again in the protracted war. At some point, the US troops would walk into a carefully prepared ambush. They were looking for the enemy, but the first they saw of him was a hail of fire from hidden positions, command-controlled mines exploding everywhere like an artillery barrage, and mortar fire pouring in. Every man would get flat on the ground and stay there. At that point, the NVA had completely triumphed over the Americans' supposed superior mobility.

A key element in NVA tactics at this stage was to ensure that they were far too close to the Americans for artillery or aircraft to be called in to give support. The American units in the field could call in an awesome array of firepower, from Cobra gunships and napalm strikes to B-52 bombing missions and artillery. The closer the NVA could move in on their enemy, the safer they were. Some US units were even forced to call down fire on their own positions to hit at the NVA.

Death was part of battle

Fighting so close to the enemy demanded special qualities, of course. It required steadiness and discipline. Men had to trust implicitly those fighting alongside them, knowing they would not break. The average NVA company had to be very cohesive to withstand the strains of deliberately choosing combat so close to an enemy with superior firepower. The soldiers had to trust their officers too – that the orders they were given were right, and had to be obeyed; something that became a big problem for the American army later on, when men did not trust their officers. And finally, fighting at such deliberately close ranges demanded an acceptance of casualties. Death was part of battle – you could not escape that reality. Sacrifice was essential. Many on the American side, so it seemed, wanted a battlefield from which death was removed.

Once they had the Americans pinned down near an LZ, the NVA would manoeuvre behind them, cutting off their line of withdrawal. This ensured them tactical control of the whole US operation.

GIAP

According to his own account, Vo Nguyen Giap was born in An Xa in Quang Binh Province, just north of the 17th Parallel, in 1912. In 1933 he enrolled for a law degree at Hanoi University, and during this period he met Ngo Dinh Diem, who was later to become a bitter enemy. However, political activism forced Giap into exile in China in 1939, his wife dying in a French jail two years later.

In China he met Ho Chi Minh and was one of the founders of the Viet Minh in May 1941, before returning to Vietnam to organize political subversion and embryonic military units. He organized the first 'armed propaganda team' – the nucleus of the NVA – in December 1944, and was named as Commander-in-Chief and Minister of Interior in Ho's revolutionary government in 1945. His skill at logistics and meticulous planning brought victory over the French at Dien Bien Phu in 1954, after which he became Minister of Defence and a member of the North Vietnamese Politburo.

Critics of Giap say that his normal caution was offset by an occasional recklessness. As evidence of this they point to his switch from guerrilla to conventional war against the French in the Red River Delta in 1951, and his repeat of this against the South in the 1968 Tet Offensive and the 1972 Spring Offensive. In terms of conventional warfare, both were massive military and tactical defeats for Giap. The question must be asked, though, whether the political and strategic gains that resulted from these offensives, not least the crushing effect that Tet had on US morale, were not major considerations of Giap's when he planned them.

After 1972 Giap was eclipsed by his protege, Van Tien Dung, who led Hanoi's forces to final victory in 1975. Ironically, Giap's return to an advocacy of prolonged political struggle as a response to the threat posed to the unified Vietnam by Pol Pot's Kampuchea in 1977/8 led to his being dropped as Minister of Defence in 1980, and from the Politburo in the following year.

Right: The US had the firepower, but the warriors of the North had the determination. Undeterred by the American 'scorched earth policy', a mortar team works out range and trajectory before sending another round crashing into US troop concentrations on Route 9 in Quang Tri Province.

Instead of seeking out and destroying the North Vietnamese as they had intended, the Americans found themselves devoting all their efforts to getting their own men out of a trap. The NVA were quite happy to soak up reinforcements sent in to relieve the encircled company, until the advantage of manpower and firepower seemed to be turning against them. At that point, the NVA force would split into small units and filter away from the battlefield. The US might try their own encircling move, using helicopters to land men in the rear, but blocking the NVA was like collecting water in a sieve. They would slip away through any gap in the US line – a 10m break would be enough in heavy jungle – and reassemble later at a pre-arranged spot.

True guerrilla tactics

These were the tactics of turning defence into attack. For actual offensive operations, the NVA had two main methods. One was small-scale raiding – true guerrilla tactics, in fact. A small unit would launch an attack on a US base by night and disappear before morning, after inflicting what damage they could. But increasingly, as the war went on, and especially near the DMZ where their supply lines were shortest and places of refuge most readily available, the NVA turned to larger scale co-ordinated attacks. The aim of these was to achieve the maximum political and psychological impact, rather than straightforward military objectives. The North Vietnamese knew they could not defeat the Americans in direct military conflict. But they were sure that they could win the war, because the Americans' will to fight would crack under pressure. Major attacks on firebases and prolonged sieges of US forces were means of applying that pressure.

Achieving the local superiority in mobility and firepower that they needed was, perhaps paradoxically, more difficult for the NVA in a scrupulously planned attack than in an improvised defensive operation. A US firebase, the most common object of attack, was a fearsomely defended position. Whenever the NVA tried to overrun a firebase with a mass assault, their losses were very heavy, and the objective rarely achieved. But siege proved a powerful tactic.

The NVA were expert at moving large bodies of men into position unobserved. They knew that once the American position came under fire, the whole weight of US firepower would be directed

'Anywhere, any place, any time.' That might just have well been the catch-phrase of the NVA – at least, that's how the ordinary American trooper saw it. The North Vietnamese were convinced that their's was a just war, and that American resolve would eventually falter. Below: Where once sat a plough harness, now sits a machine-gun base. Below right: No sign of the NVA.

NVA AMBUSH

1. US troops are watched closely by NVA scouts as they leave a supposedly safe LZ on a search and destroy mission.

2. The main NVA ambush party, armed with AK-47s and RPD light machine guns, lies in wait deeper in the jungle.

3. The ambush is triggered by a lead man in the platoon stepping on a buried 105mm shell. Immediately, the NVA pour in heavy fire, keeping close to the Americans to prevent them calling up air and artillery strikes. Meanwhile, other elements try to encircle the platoon.

4. The NVA withdraw in the face of overwhelming US firepower, removing their dead and wounded.

1967

protuding, fixed so they would hit a US target when fired. During a siege, a North Vietnamese would run quickly from his dug-out, drop a mortar bomb into the tube and leap back under cover as the weapon fired. US counter-fire against the mortar position would have little or no effect. The NVA infantry also used free-flight rockets – not very accurate but good enough against a target like a US base –and the 75mm wheeled, recoilless rifle. But near the DMZ, the NVA was also able to offer its infantry true artillery support. Batteries located across the border could hammer the American position under siege. The favourite NVA gun, the Soviet M46 130mm, had a range of around 27,000m, greater than that of its US counterparts, so it could be used without fear of counterbattery fire. The NVA also countered the air threat by dispersing the artillery, but fire was still concentrated, being co-ordinated from a central command post linked to all the guns by wire telephone.

'Time will defeat the enemy'

The crucial point about a siege, from the NVA point of view, was that they held the initiative almost totally. If the Americans sent in reinforcements by land, ambushes could be mounted and secondary sieges begun. If relief was flown in, the fresh forces were in their turn besieged. The NVA really could not lose – as long as they maintained the siege the psychological effect on the Americans was massive. A siege became a focus of American anxiety, showing US troops on the defensive in a hostile country and taking losses. But whenever the NVA thought that their own losses were too heavy, they could simply lift the siege and disappear into the jungle. The Americans were left with no sense of victory, only thoughts of survival. From the NVA's viewpoint, the ideal end to a siege might have been the overrunning of the US forces and their annihilation. But a prolonged siege followed by withdrawal served their purpose almost as well.

NVA losses during any single action are difficult to ascertain – but were often very heavy. On many occasions the Americans were the first to pull out of a contact, ruling out an accurate body count of enemy KIA (Killed In Action). And, whenever possible, the NVA would take their dead comrades with them as they melted into the jungle after a firefight.

What made the NVA approach to war so different to that of the US forces was their appreciation of the political and psychological aspects of warfare. For the NVA, even the details of tactics in the field related to the overriding political objective of bringing mounting pressure to bear on the Americans without necessarily winning any decisive military engagement. 'Only time will defeat the enemy,' Ho Chi Minh wrote. The North Vietnamese were convinced they only had to keep fighting on their own terms to keep the strategic initiative, and that in doing so, they would eventually win the war.

against the besieging force. So the North Vietnamese dug themselves into strong, deep trenches that would survive all but a direct hit from a shell or bomb. Once they were in position and entrenched, they were hard to flush out.

During a siege, the NVA demonstrated just how much firepower they could concentrate on a target. First there were stand-off infantry weapons. The 60mm and 107mm mortars were especially effective, since the NVA always reconnoitred any objective minutely before an engagement and planned the targets of each mortar and the firing angles required. Mortars were even dug into the ground, with only the tip of the barrel

Top: Digging in. NVA siege tactics may have seemed costly failures (above), but the effect they had on the American will to fight was enormous. NVA tactics were causing US willpower to crack open at the seams.

NVA ANTI-ARMOUR ROCKETS

Light, accurate and with a range of 500 metres, the RPG-7 was used to devastating effect against US armour

RPG-7

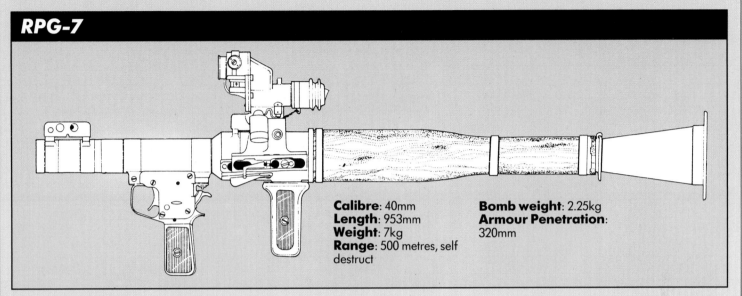

Calibre: 40mm
Length: 953mm
Weight: 7kg
Range: 500 metres, self destruct

Bomb weight: 2.25kg
Armour Penetration: 320mm

The NVA and Viet Cong used several types of rocket-propelled grenade launchers (RPGs) during the course of the Vietnam war, including the Chinese Type 56 and the Czech P-27. But the weapon that most often found its way into the communist arsenal was the Soviet-designed RPG-7.

Shoulder-fired and therefore man-portable, the RPG-7 was a direct descendant of the German World War II Panzerfaust anti-tank weapon. The Russians copied the basic German design and came up with with the RPG-2 (Chincom Type 56) – a weapon that saw extensive service in Vietnam with both the Viet Cong and the North Vietnamese Army.

The RPG-7 (Type 69) was the successor to the RPG-2. This new weapon was more effective than its predecessor, possessing both greater penetration and improved range. Although the RPG-2 had an effective range of around 150 metres against armoured vehicles and was capable of penetrating 220mm of armour, its effectiveness declined rapidly beyond this point. The RPG-7, on the other hand, was able to penetrate armour at a maximum effective range of 500 metres. Used against the thin armour of American M113s, the RPG-7 could be devastating.

The principle behind all rocket-propelled grenade launchers used during the war was broadly similar, but with the RPG-7 it was slightly more advanced.

The grenades were percussion-fired: a cardboard cylinder containing the propellant was screwed into the missile which was then inserted into the muzzle of the launcher. To fire the weapon, the communist soldier simply had to take aim and squeeze the trigger. At a pre-set distance from the launcher, the missile's rocket motor would ignite to thrust it towards its target at high speed and low trajectory.

Earlier versions had been prone to inaccuracy, but the RPG-7's basic design had eliminated this problem. The grenades had four knife-like fins that opened out as soon as the projectile got clear of the launch tube. These, along with smaller fins at the rear, rotated the missile in flight and added to its stability.

The RPG-7 did have its flaws, however. Chief among these was its piezoelectric fuzing system. This fuze was intended to produce an electric current that detonated the explosive charge when it was crushed against the target. However, in order for this to happen, the missile had to hit a reasonably solid target. The Americans exploited this and neutralized the force of many grenades by the simple expedient of erecting wire mesh around possible targets. This would absorb the missile's impact and short out the fuze.

Above: An NVA prepares to fire his RPG-7. Much of the weapon was covered in wood, which, together with the conical blast shield, protected the firer from excessive heat during the grenade launch.

HANOI HILTON

Denied basic rights as laid down by the Geneva Conventions, American prisoners of war in Hanoi found themselves tortured, starved and used as tools of propaganda by the North. But somehow life went on – it had to.

Left: US POWs gaze out from a cramped cell. But many more endured the hell of solitary confinement, often for months at a time, being kept inside 'tiger cages' with scarcely room to stand. Above: Contemptlating a bleak future.

Top right: Some lucky POWs were able to get much needed exercise by performing light duties, such as laundry. But for many more, vicious torture was the norm. Right: An open door seems to promise freedom, but it is only an illusion.

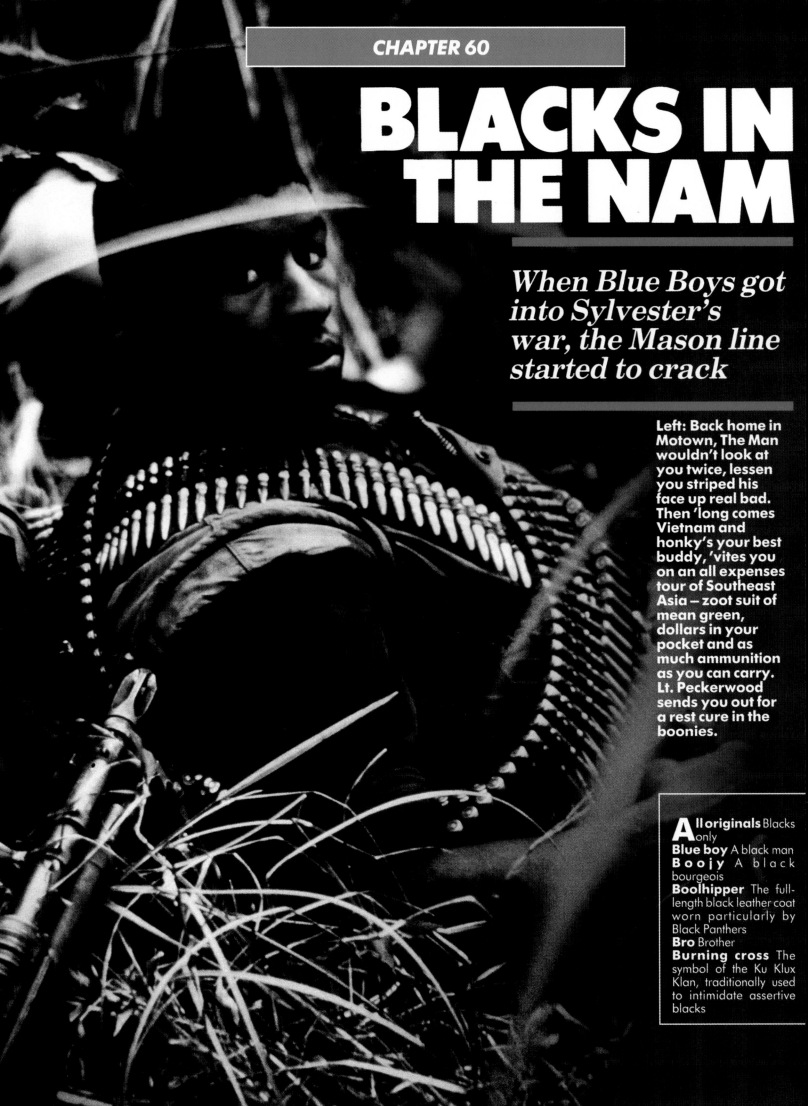

BLACKS IN THE NAM

When Blue Boys got into Sylvester's war, the Mason line started to crack

Left: Back home in Motown, The Man wouldn't look at you twice, lessen you striped his face up real bad. Then 'long comes Vietnam and honky's your best buddy, 'vites you on an all expenses tour of Southeast Asia – zoot suit of mean green, dollars in your pocket and as much ammunition as you can carry. Lt. Peckerwood sends you out for a rest cure in the boonies.

All originals Blacks only
Blue boy A black man
Boojy A black bourgeois
Boolhipper The full-length black leather coat worn particularly by Black Panthers
Bro Brother
Burning cross The symbol of the Ku Klux Klan, traditionally used to intimidate assertive blacks

In the Kim Son Valley, Captain Lewis, a handsome, conscientious officer in the Air Cav, flicked his Zippo.

'Please don't film this,' he told the TV cameraman. 'Officially, you see, we're not allowed to burn down these huts.' Just another American atrocity, you may say. But Captain Lewis was a black from Alabama, the home of the burning cross and strange fruit. Niggers who'd overstepped the Jim Crow laws there were summarily lynched. Captain Lewis had been a victim himself. The day before he was due to go to Nam, he was in a phone booth in Montgomery, Ala, calling his wife and was shot in the back by a Klansman.

Until 1967, there weren't any 'blacks' in the Nam. There were coloureds and Negroes, and other much worse names. But no blacks. For generations, the sons and daughters of former slaves had shunned the word, just as they had shunned the heavy African features of the 'Oxford' black – so-called after the shoe polish. Drug stores in Harlem sold hair straightener and skin lightener. Black was bad, it was everything you did not want to be. 'If money was black,' said prison intellectual Eldridge Cleaver, 'I wouldn't want none of it.'

Not a skin colour, a state of mind

It was only the year before – in 1966 – that civil rights activist Stokely Carmichael had first talked of 'black power'. Suddenly black was beautiful. The next year, Number One Soul Brother James Brown would proclaim: 'Say it Loud, I'm Black and Proud.' Black wasn't the colour of your skin, it was a state of your mind. And in 1967, blacks who were proudly, consciously black were first trickling through into Vietnam.

To Joe Blow, Muhammad Elijah Razzamatazz or LeRoï X, the black draftee, Vietnam was not just his first experience of an alien country and of war – it was also the first time he had ever mixed on anything like equal terms with the white man. First assigned to his platoon, he would talk only to the other bloods, and on the flight up to the combat zone they'd be as stiffly segregated as a Mississipi meeting house. Anyone crossing the Mason Line

Above: 'Carry the pig, boy' – we got second-class jobs and second-class treatment, but first-class death. Man with the scythe, he don't discriminate.

would feel the draft.

Joe Blow would say: 'In the States, even in the rear in Nam, blacks and whites fought each other. But out in the field, man, we were just a force of unity and harmony...Charlie had a tendency to make you unify in a hurry.' This was the democracy of the foxhole. Once in the boonies with a patrol of four blacks, two spics and three honkies, racial harmony was no abstract concept. Once Charlie starting kicking ass, your anger, your common sense told you, you needed everybody, that means

Clip side of the big moist The other side of the ocean
Cuffee A black, from the African word
Flatbacker A prostitute
Feel the draft Experience racial prejudice
Honky A white person
Jackie Robinson The first black to make his presence felt in any particular area of American life

Jim Crow Enforced segregation, after the Negro minstrel character
John Henry A hardworking black person
Klansman A member of the fanatical southern white racist organization the Ku Klux Klan
The Man A white man in authority
Mason Line The demarcation line between a black area and a white

area, after the Mason-Dixon line which separated Pennsylvania from Maryland, that is the free states from the slave states
Mister Charlie The white man
Nigger A black person – used affectionately by blacks, offensively by whites
Ofay A white, from foe in pig latin
Peckerwood A white

man
Rednecks Rural southern whites, white trash
Scoffing fishheads and scrambling for the gills Eating poor food
Soul food Traditional black American food – Chitlins (pig's tripe), corn bread, blackeyed peas, candied yams, scrambled pork brains, backbone and dumplings, grits, cracklin' biscuits,

fried catfish, cow pea and ham bone soup
Spic A Puerto Rican
Storyville sawbones An overworked underqualified ghetto doctor
Strange fruit The body of a lynched black which has been left hanging from a tree
Sylvester A white man
Tan town A black ghetto
Trashing Deprecating

EVERYBODY. One bull-nosed son-of-a-bitch could get you all killed. Even rednecks from the Deep South found themselves buddies with the black boys they despised back home. White boy would tell a brother: 'I hate niggers, but you's okay.' Week later, blue boy would be giving Peckerwood the kiss of life after his jaw got shot away. For the US, this was the first two-tone army that had ever gone into combat. Previously, 'Negroes' had been restricted to their own separate units – under white officers – and mostly kept away from combat duties. The Marines admitted no blacks at all until World War II. Sergeant-Major Edgar A. Huff, the Jackie Robinson of the leathernecks, used to get arrested for impersonating a Marine. 'Ain't no damn nigger Marines,' the MPs would tell him as they chucked him in the slammer.

But by the 1960s, the armed forces were ahead of the rest of America in integration. 'Only one colour we recognize, that's olive drab', was the official army line. Ofay officers would still lay it on you but hard. The cuffees would join up just to escape the ghetto though. And they'd re-enlist in The Man's army – there wasn't much for a John Henry outside. When Vietnam brought the draft, over two-thirds of the brothers didn't make it 1A. They flunked on faith and fitness – sixth grade schooling, Storyville sawbones and scoffing fishheads and scrambling for the gills did not a soldier make.

In the end, the army reckons, in the Nam, blacks were found in the same proportion as they were in

BLACK POWER

The growing call for 'black power' in the United States coincided with the war in Vietnam and, inevitably, was fuelled by it. By the mid-1960s, the constitutional battle for equal rights had been won. But the majority of blacks found themselves no better off. Discrimination made it difficult for them to get jobs and lack of money prevented them from moving out of the deprived ghettos of the northern cities. Worse, Lyndon Johnson's promise of the 'Great Society' was becoming nothing more than a joke. The funds that were to have supported its welfare programmes and improve the appalling living standards of the great majority of blacks were being dropped on Hanoi in the form of bombs. Understandably many young blacks turned to

the Nation of Islam – aka the Black Muslims – who preached that the white man was the devil and the need for a separate black state, and the Black Panthers who advocated the violent overthrow of the white-dominated establishment. Under this heated rhetoric, the ghettos exploded – as it was widely felt by even middle-class blacks that they were no longer obliged to obey laws that so flagrantly favoured whites. These riots were brutally put down by the army and the National Guard.

A spread of disenchantment to Vietnam was unavoidable, given the high proportion of blacks in combat units, and rumours of subversion were rife. However, by 1969, even in the Marines – the last wing of the armed forces to be integrated – the clen-

ched-fist black power salute was permitted on informal occasions and other symbols of black pride were accommodated, including a modified 'Afro' haircut. Despite a lack of discrimination in combat, many blacks preferred their own company back at base or on R&R, forming their own clubs and listening to their own music. This did little to ease the tension. At the same time, news of events in America including, in April 1968, the death of Martin Luther King, merely reinforced existing distrust. The situation was certainly ripe for subversion. But even in the US, racial turmoil never resulted in urban terrorism. In the Nam, black and white alike discovered that the only discrimination in a foxhole was between the living and the dead.

the whole population Stateside – round one in ten. But when it came to combat, it was tan town. By 1967, almost one in four of the US soldiers at the sharp end of the action were black. To the boojies in The World railing against the white man's war, this was 'unfair commitment to combat'. To the bloods in the boonies, it was genocide.

Still, on the clip side of the big moist, the brothers got the chance to prove they were real men and real Americans. Say 'Fuck you' to a racist drill sergeant, you'd get seven days for disrespect. Once out of the brig, they put you in recon, the toughest unit. Others took tough assignments for the extra bucks – $55 more a month as a paratrooper was a lot of dough to a brother from the ghetto or the rural South. Some airborne companies were 60 per cent bloods getting their jollies jumping out of airplanes. And you'd better believe it, it was less likely for a black to have the juice to pull a safe post at base and less likely for him to have the book-learning for a desk job.

So the brothers were out in the swamps and paddies and jungle and still got shit. Mister Charlie didn't go through no ceremony neither. Sylvester'd say: 'Here boy, you carry the motherfucking pig.' Still the trooper would walk point – didn't want to put his life in another man's hands, didn't want to get killed so that the sons of white America could cruise through college or serve their tours in air-conditioned offices, shacking up with some good-looking gook in downtown

Above: Stay cool, hophead. There ain't no action getting your ass shot off holding the line, bro. If Bronco Jim and Handkerchief Head say no-no to go-go, best slew a brew on the base that's ace. Right: 'Nobody knows the trouble I've seen, Nobody knows my sorrow.' The holy roller who penned that tune must have been to the place.

Saigon. But for a brother who'd been treated like shit all his life Stateside, it was a chance to learn pride, black pride – and to show he was a meaner motherfucker than any John Wayne.

Back at base it was a different story. The walls of latrines were scrawled with racist graffiti: 'I'd prefer a gook to a nigger' was number one. When a black patrol leader was featured on the cover of *Time* magazine, he woke up to find a Ku Klux Klan cross burning outside his tent. Fights erupted between black and white. Sometimes guns were used. After 1968, this would all get much worse. In July 1969, there would be a race riot in Lejeune Marine camp, in North Carolina.

Bopping in a boolhipper

Men who had been like blood brothers in combat didn't suddenly cease to be buddies when they were behind the lines. But blacks and whites did not tend to hang out together. It was a matter of taste. Blacks didn't dig the redneck's hillbilly music. Whitey didn't wanna hear no funky soul.

In Saigon the brothers stuck to 'Soulsville', the bars and brothels of Khanh Hoi. The white equivalent, Tu Do, wasn't exactly off limits, but the looks you got in those Tu Do bars – man, they hurt more than a Claymore.

Soulsville was where it was at. It was all originals. A man could bop in a boolhipper or rap with a brother over a plate of soul food. Even the flatbackers there were blacker, dark-skinned Cambodian girls, or daughters of Senegalese soldiers brought to Vietnam by the French. In Soulsville, to the sounds of sweet soul music, for a moment a bro could feel free of whitey and the war.

After Captain Lewis got shot in the phone booth, the army promoted him to commander of an almost exclusively white company. But black officers were rarer than a holy roller in a gin joint – just over three per cent in the army, less than one per cent in the Marines. And medals and stripes came easier to whites.

There were blacks in high places – Major-General Beauregard Brown III made head of MACV logistics – but they were few and far between.

Black soldiers were targeted by Viet Cong propaganda. Brothers were called on to 'fight their true enemies, those who called them niggers'. And from the States the same call came from black radicals: Vietnam was a racist war.

By 1968, every incoming plane brought bros who got down with the Panthers or the Black Muslims.

They knew where it was at. They knew they were there to kill and be killed. About ready to die, most of them, and do first-class dying. But in assignments and promotions and awards, they were second-class citizens. That created a special brand of bitterness.

Yet it could be the soul brothers were used to suffering. There is no trashing the performance of black troops. No question, they earned their black badge of courage. Sergeant-Major Huff, for exam-

AN UNFAIR COMMITMENT?

Was putting blacks in the front line one way the white establishment cleared the ghettos and got rid of radical blacks?

In the mid-1960s, blacks made up about 11 per cent of the population of the United States. The armed forces reflected this statistic fairly accurately. In 1966, 12.6 per cent of enlisted men in the army were black. In the air force, the figure was 10.2 per cent and in the navy 5 per cent. And, theoretically, equal opportunities existed for specialised training and promotion.

Yet the fact remains that, between 1965 and 1967, some 23 per cent of Americans killed in Vietnam were black, fuelling accusations that Uncle Sam was using his black recruits as cannon fodder. In the prevailing atmosphere of struggle for civil rights and militant black power in the United States, such an obvious discrepancy between enlistments and combat deaths reinforced a widespread belief that the blacks were being deliberately wiped out in this white man's war.

But was this a cynical white man's ploy or just a reflection of the realities of life in the US at the time? Because of institutionalized prejudice and a history of underprivilege, many blacks received only a rudimentary education. The result was that fewer passed the pre-induction tests devised by the armed services to identify those recruits best suited for specialized training. Consequently, a disproportionate number of blacks found themselves in combat units, where the need for specialized training was less. By 1967, 20 per cent of combat troops were black and in some elite units such as airborne infantry, which bore the brunt of the fighting, this figure rose to 45 per cent. Black casualties were sure to rise. Injustice breeds injustice and this unfair commitment to battle was a reflection of unfair treatment at home.

ple, always took care of his men, both black and white. When one of his radio operators had been hit by the VC and was lying out 50 yards in front of his platoon, pinned down by enemy fire, Huff ran across the open ground and ended up crawling on his knees with grenade fragments in his arm, his helmet dented by enemy bullets. But he got to the radio operator and the man was saved. Sergeant-Major Huff was black. The RTO was a white boy. Huff knew he might get killed.

'He was my man,' said Huff. 'That's what mattered.'

Left: For blue boys, the Nam was a way out of tan town. Right: So? I ain't no jew boy. Right below: Hell no, they just wasted us. Below: To play *America* you need the black and white keys.

CHAPTER 61

Push Uncle Sam too far and you'd end up in the glass house. Leroy Thompson takes a look inside a military prison, a place where murderers and drug-takers rubbed shoulders

STOCKADE

Compared to Vietnamese jails with their 'tiger cages' – cells so small that their inhabitants, usually political prisoners, could not even stand up – the US military stockades in Vietnam were model penal institutions. But even compared to life on a remote firebase under siege, they were bad news.

War brings out the best in some men and the worst in others, and murderers, rapists, thieves, junkies, black marketeers and deserters accumulated in the stockade, where they were guarded by the meanest sons-of-bitches. One MP lieutenant who had drawn stockade duty related the story of an American soldier who had freaked out on drugs as they were processing him. He had tried to climb the fence of the stockade compound. A ROK – Republic of Korea – sentry at a Korean compound across the road heard the junkie's screams, saw him climbing and shot him, just as he would have shot an escaping Korean. The MP officer felt no pity. On the contrary, he applauded the ROK's

Below left: A GI is frisked by an MP; next stop: the 'LBJ Ranch'. Right top: One of the most common offences committed by rear echelon US troops was involvement in the black market. Right centre: Getting high to forget the pain. A high proportion of prisoners were found guilty of drug offences. The use of drugs by GIs was a major headache in Vietnam.

firm hand in dealing with the problem.

Another bit of ROK rough justice made the rounds. It was about a black marketeer found stealing from the ROK supplies. They cut his hands off and strung them around his neck with a sign saying: 'Don't steal from the ROKs!'

The American Uniform Code of Military Justice which all US troops came under didn't normally include such draconian punishments, but it did lay out tough penalties for courts-martial offences.

Black marketeering and drugs probably accounted for the largest numbers of courts martial in Vietnam. In 1967, for example, there were 427 courts martial for drug offences and about 500 for black marketeering.

While awaiting trial, defendants would usually be incarcerated in stockades in Vietnam. The most famous of these was the Long Binh Stockade, known to the troops as the Long Binh Jail or 'LBJ Ranch'.

The US stockades in Vietnam were run on much the same lines as the old French Foreign Legion disciplinary units in Indochina. Hours were long and the physical exertion was arduous, though certain serious crimes might rate close confinement. But once a soldier was actually convicted he was normally returned to the USA to serve his sentence – if his offence was serious enough, it would land him in Leavenworth, the military's maximum security prison in Kansas.

For certain infractions at divisional or lower levels, a soldier might be confined to barracks in Vietnam, then returned to duty without receiving a bad-conduct discharge. In these situations, confinement often resembled the less appealing aspects of basic training – lots of marching, physical training and KP duty. Most of the soldiers who had screwed up were glad of the chance to wipe the slate clean with sweat and return to their unit.

Probably the best comment on the regime of stockades in Vietnam is the fact that I heard of no soldier who considered committing some crime so that he could avoid combat by going to jail. In fact, REMFs – rear-echelon troops – tended to end up in the stockade more often than combat troops. This was part because they had more opportunity to get into trouble, and part because combat commanders often cut their troops a bit more slack. They realized that aggressiveness was a plus for a combat soldier and that wrecking a local bar was more likely to indicate a need to let off steam than a threat to the fabric of the US armed forces. Besides, the morality of life and death becomes somewhat distorted in combat – especially in a war like Vietnam.

The stockade regime was harsh. Right: the riot act is read to GIs protesting at the killing of a fellow prisoner. They were later charged with mutiny and given prison sentences of up to 15 years.

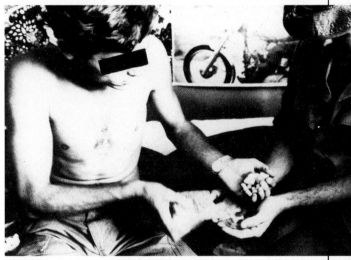

In September 1969, Senior Specialist 4 Doug Miller, an experienced bushman, led a small, six-man team on a five-day training mission deep inside enemy territory. But this was no ordinary training mission.

When it hit the target area, in the hills above the Bong Son plain in Binh Dinh Province, the team decamped quickly from the Huey helicopter. It consisted of Miller, his experienced assistant PFC Foster, a radio man, a medic and two scouts. They were heavily armed, hefting M16 rifles, M26 hand-grenades, Claymore anti-personnel mines, .45 pistols and long killing knives. All this hardware weighed a man down, so they had dispensed with inessentials such as flak jackets and steel helmets, substituting instead bandanas and floppy hats. They also carried coloured smoke grenades, for bringing choppers to the landing zone.

The area was definite 'Indian country', ideal for breaking in new men and with a near-certain potential for encountering enemy troops. Miller's team infiltrated it quickly, setting up a concealed observation post. Straight off the bat, they zeroed in on a three-man VC scouting party. 'We set up a hasty ambush and waited all that day and part of

Left: Relaxing with the funny pages between patrols. But long-range reconnaissance was a serious business. The use of specialized squads for LRRP duty has a long history in the US Army. In Vietnam, LRRP tasks included the gathering of information, the taking of prisoners and the ambushing of VC trails. Lurps also often took on the highly demanding — and extremely dangerous — task of walking point for patrols.

LONG RANGE

You had to be special to be a Lurp in the Nam. They were loners, trained for survival. No-one, but no-one, messed with the recon teams

the next', Miller reports, 'but it was a bust.' So on the third day he moved his team down a ridge line to the lower ground. They came to a well-used trail by a river.

Miller was worried that his men would make too much noise, since they were still green. But they slipped quickly into the groove, moving silently through the tall elephant grass. Miller deployed them up in a classic ambush formation. They set up the deadly Claymore mines and waited.

The wait soon paid off. Two women in green

NVA uniforms and a boy carrying a rifle were spotted weaving their way along the trail. Miller recalls: 'I let them go by because I knew they were decoys, and the men were probably behind them.' He was right. Moments later, nine armed men in distinctive green uniforms suddenly appeared in the open.

As Specialist 4 Johnny Howard, one of the new scouts, remembers, 'It was too good to be true. They bunched up right in the kill zone. I detonated the Claymores, killing three immediately.' His buddies opened up with their M16s at the enemy.

It was all over in seconds. When the smoke had

RECONNAISSANCE

cleared, five NVA bodies littered the trail. Four AK-47 assault rifles and several rucksacks lay strewn about. The rest of the enemy had fled. Doug Miller's team returned to base with a rich haul of captured documents and weapons, and no casualties. Not bad for a training mission.

A special breed of man

These men were training to be 'Lurps', the colloquial nickname given to members of the Long Range Reconnaissance Patrols (LRRPs), which had been founded in 1964. Lurps tended to be

volunteers, a unique breed of men. A man who signed up for Lurp duty knew what was required of him and possessed the special skills that were needed for this type of work: fieldcraft, survival techniques, and a psychological preference for working in a small, self-sufficient group.

There were plenty of volunteers. Not only because the work on offer was exciting, and the sort that appealed to loners, but also because you knew that the man beside you thought and acted just like you. He wouldn't let you down. This was essential, since on the sort of mission the Lurps

Above left: The company commander gives the landing-site brief to the team leader. Above: Taking it easy. Lurps generally never bothered with helmets or flak jackets.

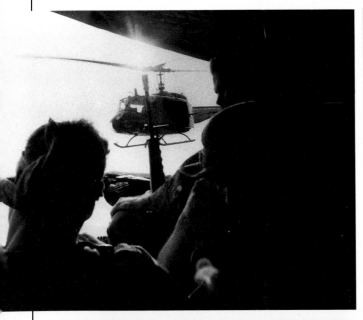

WHY US INTELLIGENCE WAS NOT ABLE TO SUPPLY INFANTRY COMMANDERS WITH TACTICAL INTELLIGENCE.

The means of collecting intelligence in Vietnam were highly sophisticated, the quality of the advanced communications and surveillance technology far exceeding that of any other previous conflict. Yet the Intelligence services proved incapable of supplying field commanders with the required information. The reasons for this failure are complex.

The MACV Combined Intelligence Center received some three million pages of captured documents every month, of which ten per cent were usually regarded as of sufficient value to be translated. By the beginning of 1967, half a ton of reports based on this one source were being printed every day. This was in addition to any intelligence processed by the other components under the command of MACV's Assistant Chief of Staff for Intelligence (MACV J-2), such as the Combined Military Interrogation Center, the Combined Material Exploitation Center or the Combined Document Exploitation Center. Yet what might be termed as direct human sources – information from agents, prisoners or defectors, as well as that provided from captured documents – provided only 20 per cent of the information collected by MACV. The other 80 per cent was provided by electronic means ranging from signals intercepts to ground sensors and aerial reconnaissance.

But this sheer volume of intelligence and the huge demands generated by the need for a full appreciation of its value was also a problem. There were simply too many agencies attempting to collect intelligence – in one province there were no less than 15 different bodies performing the same intelligence functions simultaneously – and little attempt was made to create a unified system for their control and co-ordination. Moreover, so much information was being provided that it could not be transmitted in time to units at lower levels.

Exacerbating the difficulty of providing units with the kind of hard contact or tactical intelligence they required, was the reluctance of MACV to pass on to them

Left: Operating a control console at Long Binh. The growth of 'hot lines' and excessive use of high-priority codes hopelessly overloaded the intelligence system.

information gained from sophisticated electronic sources on the grounds of its sensitivity. But in any case, there was an over-reliance upon signals intelligence which could be manipulated by the enemy. Even at the lowest levels, there was little real comprehension of the most valuable intelligence required in an insurgency situation – that on the political infrastructure of the enemy – since the army's standard manual, 'Combat Intelligence', had been written with conventional warfare in mind. There was also the tendency to reduce all to statistics.

It was not surprising, therefore, that tactical intelligence was either not forthcoming or arrived too late to be of any value in the field. Operation Cedar Falls in January 1967 was actually initiated as a result of a sustained intelligence effort – Operation Rendezvous – but still failed to generate any major contact with the VC. More often than not, it was American Intelligence that was caught by surprise. Even when Intelligence did provide accurate assessments, however, as was the case prior to the Tet Offensive of January 1968 and the NVA Spring Offensive of March 1972, military commanders were often reluctant to act on them.

The irony of the US failure to make full and proper use of the intelligence material they gathered was further compounded by the fact that their carelessness in transmitting messages and their failure to use secure codes in transmissions fed the communists' own highly efficient intelligence network with much valuable information.

pulled – primarily information-gathering, but also taking prisoners or ambushing well-used NVA trails – you tended to be stuck right out there on a limb, far from any help when the shit came down.

The record for longest service in LRRP or Ranger (as the Lurps were later re-designated) units has to go to Staff Sergeant Patrick 'Tad' Tadina of the 173d Airborne Brigade. He spent a record 60 months on continuous Lurp duty, from mid-1965 through to October 1970. An ex-paratrooper with

the 82d Airborne Division, Tad was assigned to the 1st Infantry Division in Nam and helped form their LRRP unit, seeing his first Vietnam combat with them in War Zone C. After a year he extended his tour and rejoined a paratroop unit, the 173d Airborne.

Tad was born in Hawaii. He was short, fit and well-knit. His Hawaiian heritage gave him an appearance that was more Oriental than Caucasian. He used this to good effect in his five years of long-range patrolling in enemy territory. Most paratroopers wore their hair close-cropped. Tad, however, let his black locks grow some six inches. His hair, small size and dark complexion all helped to confuse the enemy. Also, in approved Lurp fashion, he wore a red bandana and a captured NVA floppy hat. This tended to confuse the enemy further, as did the fact he carried a captured AK-47 instead of an M16. But then Tad needed all the help he could get, since he always walked point in the jungles and forests, which some might regard as just plain dumb.

The situation was a mother

But Tad got results. In constant patrols in the bush he led more than 200 different GIs on missions. Every man that he led in combat returned alive, an extraordinary record. At the same time he personally killed 111 enemy troops in close-combat encounters. He was wounded three times and received 12 medals for heroism, including two Silver Stars and five Bronze Stars.

He recalls one of his closest calls with death. As usual he was walking point, and suddenly found himself in the middle of an NVA ambush: 'They were very well camouflaged. One gook leaned out from his cover and stared at me. It was obvious they thought I was NVA too. The only thing I could do was spray a 30-round burst into them.' The enemy's delay and Tad's quick reaction allowed his team to escape. He took two rounds through the calves, but managed to get away with his men.

On several patrols, the NVA even called out

Above: A corporal of the 1st Recon Battalion cradles his 'Blooper' M79 grenade-launcher. Note the tape over the barrel to keep out dirt. Right: Briefing platoon leaders. Opposite page. A typical Lurp mission (top to bottom): Setting out in the Hueys at sunrise; relaxing on the flight; un-assing at the LZ.

1967

Below: Being extracted from the pick-up zone (PZ) by 'Jacob's ladder'. Lurp missions were generally carried out in extremely hostile enemy territory, miles from any support. Access was frequently difficult, but speed of response by back-up units was essential if the mission was to succeed and the Lurps' lives saved. Below right: Sacking out after a mission. Lurps tended to be loners, and very self-sufficient.

greetings to Tad just before he cut them to ribbons with his AK-47.

Lurp patrols operated from some 10 to 40 miles out from base camp, frequently well beyond the range of any supporting artillery fire. Being only five or six men alone in enemy-held areas, Lurps soon learnt to rely heavily on each other's skills, steadfastness and courage. If a man got wounded or killed, he knew his buddies would not leave him whatever the danger to themselves.

Extracting a wounded Lurp was a tough proposition. After all, if he were wounded, the enemy had a fix on their position. Any medevac chopper flying in to pull them out was dead meat if the enemy couldn't be pinned down fast, or preferably killed, either by grenades, gunships or airstrikes. In bad weather or at night, the situation was even more of a mother.

'We had to get him out'

One such night evacuation was especially ingenious. In the autumn of 1970, Captain James Lawton, commanding Company N, of the 75th Rangers, had a team out in the mountains of Binh Dinh Province. At dusk the team got into a firefight with a small NVA unit. One of the Rangers was gutshot, one of the worst possible wounds. As night fell, the team moved to a pick-up zone (PZ) and radioed for medical help.

It was a tough mission. The PZ was in mountains which were pitch-black, heavily jungled and 2800ft high. The coastal plain along that region is narrow and the hills rise steeply from it in jagged steps. To make matters worse, a light fog floated around the hills back of the coast. The attempt to rescue one man could be disastrous to 10 others if the chopper crashed. But, as Captain Lawton

pointed out: 'The soldier had a gut wound. He'd bleed to death before daylight. It was a typical small Ranger team – six men. The crying and moaning of the wounded man would bring the enemy in on them before daylight. We had to get him out.' He could have added that the Lurps always stuck together and never let a buddy down.

Lawton set out a scheme he had used in other night extractions. He recalls how he explained it to Brigadier General Elmer Ochs, the 173d's commander, and the chopper pilot:

'I had an exact fix on the PZ, and we planned the best route to it from our base at LZ English. We'd have the artillery fire flares at fixed locations and elevations along the route of flight. My operations officer would be at the artillery fire-direction centre, in radio contact with me. He would fire the flares on my command and we would simply fly to each flare in succession, staying clear of the mountains and heading to the PZ. Once we were near it, the team would talk us in.'

Lawton and the chopper crew launched into the darkness. Going flat out, the pilot flew on instruments while penetrating the fog layers. From inside the helicopter Lawton called for the succession of flares to be fired, and the pilot homed in on their bright, eerie glare illuminating the scene like a movie. Suddenly they were over the PZ. The enemy was taken totally by surprise, finding the air filled with the banshee whirr of the rotor blades. Before the NVA could collect their wits and react, the Lurp team was talking the chopper in to a safe landing. As Lawton recalls with a big grin: 'The extraction went off great!' Indeed it had. The return flight was uneventful and the wounded Ranger lived. Not a bad end for a routine Lurp mission.

77 DAYS AT KHE SANH

Lights go out in the movie theatre and the ammo explodes sky-high. As NVA move towards the perimeter, this is no 'Paradise Hawaiian Style'

On the morning of Saturday 10 January 1968 the US Marines at the Khe Sanh combat base checked out the newly posted chit of paper advertising the feature films scheduled for showing over the next week. Looking down the list of forthcoming attractions, they saw that for this particular evening 'Paradise Hawaiian Style' – starring Elvis Presley – was billed for screening in the six separate movie facilities scattered around the huge base area. Further down the list came 'Murderer's Row', 'Beau Geste' and 'Gunsmoke'. These entertainments, flown in specially from the States, relieved some of the boredom and drudgery of life on this isolated outpost of American presence in Vietnam. But while the grunts looked forward to taking in a movie, the base commander, Colonel David E. Lownds, had more important things on his mind.

In the base radio room Lownds listened intently to the flow of incoming reports from Captain Bill Dabney, the commanding officer of one of the Marine companies tasked with holding the outlying hills around the main base. Dabney and the men of India Company had run into a battalion of North Vietnamese soldiers while patrolling on Hill 881 North and were now engaged in a tough firefight. In Lownds' mind the long awaited offensive against the Khe Sanh base had begun.

Paradise Hawaiian Style?

The hill outposts and the combat base were immediately put on full alert. Artillerymen busied themselves with their 105 and 155mm guns, barbed wire defences were checked and strengthened, and extra trip flares and Claymore mines were laid along the perimeter defences. As evening fell, Marines cleared their weapons with short bursts of fire, checked their ammunition and kept as calm as they could. 'Paradise Hawaiian Style' came off the bill and the Officers' Club was closed until further notice.

The giant Marine base at Khe Sanh was situated on a small plateau in the far north of South Vietnam, just 15 miles to the south of the Demilitarized Zone. Sitting squarely overlooking Route 9 – the main through road from Laos to the important cities of Quang Tri and Hue – Khe Sanh had become something of an obsession with General Westmoreland.

Before the war, it was reputedly one of the most beautiful places on earth. Heavily wooded mountains and rolling hills, separated by green and misty valleys, surrounded the little village of Khe Sanh, situated on the edge of the unspoiled plateau.

By 1966, however, it was a different story. Under pressure from Westmoreland, who was deeply concerned about NVA activity in the northern provinces, the Marines had moved on Khe Sanh in force. Huge bulldozers carved out an extension to the old French airstrip, which was carpeted with metal planking, while engineers

and construction workers set about putting up all the facilities for a new combat base.

The arrival of the Marine garrison also brought the war to Khe Sanh. In the spring and summer of 1967 the Marines met the NVA in a number of pitched battles in the hills around the plateau and the new combat base was further reinforced. By January 1968 there were 6000 Marines at Khe Sanh, but they were not alone.

Incoming intelligence reports indicated that in early January large-scale North Vietnamese forces had crossed into South Vietnam and taken up positions in the strip of country between Route 9 and the DMZ. Out in Laos on the Ho Chi Minh Trail, hidden sensors sown by the Air Force went into a frenzy of electronic activity as the volume of traffic intensified. During October 1967 they reported the movement of just over a thousand trucks around Khe Sanh; the figure for December was nearly six and a half thousand. There seemed little doubt about what the North Vietnamese had in mind for Khe Sanh.

In mid-January the North Vietnamese gunners had began to lob the odd shell into the combat base. The Marines now wore their flak jackets at all times, just in case, but everyone knew Charlie's gunners were just finding their ranges. Marine howitzers dished out H&I – harassment and interdiction fire – to keep the NVA on their toes, but targets were very difficult to identify. The weather around Khe Sahn was a bitch for the arty men. Dense fog and low cloud enshrouded the hills, making it impossible for airborne observers to adjust the Marines' gunfire onto the enemy's artillery. To send out forward observation teams to spot for the Marine guns in the enemy-infested area around the base would be like handing them their death warrants as they walked out the gate. Most of the target information they got came from the electronic sensors seeded around Khe Sanh. But it was pretty thin information on which to calculate co-ordinated fire, and the gunners never knew if they hit anything or not. Frustrating.

But on 20 January the ball began to roll. While Captain Dabney was on Hill 881S, a North Vietnamese lieutenant had strolled up to the main base waving a white flag. To his somewhat astounded Marine interrogators he gave the whole plan for the NVA attack. The first assaults would go in at half past twelve that night, aimed at the hills and the main base. Having crushed the Marines, the NVA divisions would then pour eastwards and overrun the cities of Quang Tri and

Previous page: For the umpteenth time that day the cry goes up: 'Incoming!' The only thing to do in Khe Sanh was keep your head down. Below: You could always watch the fireworks. Day one: the Marines' ammo dump was hit by an NVA rocket and 1500 tons of high explosive went sky-high. It was a pretty sight, unless you were close, or until you began to wonder where your next shell was coming from.

1968

1968

WAS THE GENERAL RIGHT?

Did General Westmoreland see the siege of Khe Sanh as an opportunity to rewrite history and eradicate the memory of the French disaster at Dien Bien Phu?

Khe Sanh was one of the most controversial battles of the war. From the President downwards, the US public was obsessed with Khe Sanh, especially with the parallels drawn by commentators who compared it to the French nightmare at Dien Bien Phu 14 years earlier. There, isolated in an inaccessible valley in a corner of Vietnam close to the Laotian frontier, dominated by Viet Minh artillery, over 10,000 French troops had been overwhelmed in a 56-day siege that lasted from 13 March to 7 May 1954. The fall of Dien Bien Phu signalled the final French defeat in Indochina.

Khe Sanh, with its French-built airstrip, appeared similar to the base at Dien Bien Phu, and former French officers were reportedly flown to Saigon to share their experiences with the Americans. After all, Khe Sanh had been established as a major base in 1967 astride a major infiltration route from Laos, and, like Dien Bien Phu, it could be utilized as a staging post for possible operations inside Laos. General Westmoreland argued that its abandonment would open up Quang Tri province to the NVA, enabling them to outflank US forces on the DMZ and threaten the coastal cities and populous lowlands. However, there were many who believed that occupying remote areas merely diverted resources to the defence of worthless terrain and disagreed with Westmoreland's interpretation that the siege was a vain NVA attempt to re-create Dien Bien Phu. Like the French before him, he desperately sought a decisive set-piece battle.

More perceptive observers than Westmoreland believed that the siege served a wider communist strategy: it diverted 30,000 US troops away from the cities that were to be the main targets of the Tet Offensive.

Hue. But was this lieutenant a plant, a devious ploy on the part of the North Vietnamese to spook the Marines? Lownds decided he had nothing to lose by believing him – fortunately.

As predicted by the deserter, the NVA hit Hill 861 with a barrage of heavy rocket, mortar and machine-gun fire exactly on schedule and a fierce battle for possession of the hill began. Five hours later the Khe Sanh base itself came under fire. Several hundred 122mm rockets, each one weighing more than 100lbs, screeched into the Marine positions on the base, followed by a massive bombardment of artillery and heavy-mortar rounds. As luck would have it, one of the first rockets to crash into the base found its way into a large bunker at the eastern end of the perimeter and detonated. The explosion that followed was like nothing even the most battle-hardened Marine had ever seen. The Khe Sanh plateau lit up like a giant phosphorus flare as 1500 tons of ammunition went sky-high. Helicopters parked on the airstrip were scattered like bowling pins, tents and buildings dematerialized and a terrible rain of shells of every type and description fell back to earth all around the base. Some detonated on impact, others 'cooked off' in the intense fires. Aviation fuel and oil supplies ignited in the heat and all the while more and more enemy rockets and shells pounded into the base.

The morning of the 21st found Khe Sanh a total shambles. Fires continued to burn around the base and everywhere the ground was a mass of debris from the ammunition dump explosion. Dud shells, hunks of shrapnel, bits and pieces from the blown out buildings lay everywhere. A black, choking smoke caught in the throats of the Marines as they tried to get the base back on a war footing. Their efforts were hampered by random shells fired by the enemy and they were tired, dirty and just a little shell shocked. It was something they were going to have to get used to.

For the rest of January the NVA kept up the pressure on the base and the hill outposts, but there was absolutely no question of the Americans relinquishing the position. After all Westmoreland's rhetoric on the importance of Khe Sanh, the image on every TV screen in America of Marines retreating to Route 9 with their tails between their legs was something not worth contemplating.

Heroism, ads and Dr Kildare

Harrowing reports of life in the bunkers appeared nightly on American TV, front-page stories in the nation's press told of determination to hold out. Tales of heroism were slotted between the ads and Dr Kildare. But in the trenches and bunkers of Khe Sanh itself the Marines were more interested in staying alive. For everyone on the base, officer and grunt alike, the conditions of the siege were a living hell. The only thing they had to be thankful for was the weight of firepower they could call up to stop them being overrun by the much-dreaded human-wave assaults they knew the NVA capable of making. Day after day they watched fighter-bombers and the heavy B-52s pounding

the hills around the base or heading out towards the NVA staging areas and long-range artillery platforms in Laos. Westmoreland had christened the aerial support of Khe Sanh Operation Niagara. Inside the base itself, the Marines were well protected with batteries of 105 and 155mm arty and plenty of heavy mortars. The 16 huge 175s over at the Camp Carroll and Rockpile firebases to the northeast could be brought to bear when they were needed. But continuous gunfire, both incoming and outgoing, the scream of low-flying jets and the thunder of their bombs didn't do much for the men's sleeping habits. It didn't seem to have any effect on the rats though.

By the first week in February, living conditions at Khe Sanh bordered on the unbearable. Huge piles of garbage smouldered around the base, the Marines' excrement was doused in black oil and burned in oil drums. The stench was appalling.

Running sores and ugly infections

In the bunkers where they slept, the Marines had to endure the nauseating stink of other men's sweat and urine. In these underground shelters, with incoming shells plastering the earth above them, the Marines were plagued by rats scuttling across their legs, pouncing from the rafters onto their chests as they slept. They wrapped themselves tightly in their ponchos at night, their faces covered, to avoid being bitten by their unwelcome bedmates. Some did get bitten, and developed running sores and ugly infections. Some smeared their toes with peanut butter to attract the rats, get a bad bite, and get the hell out of Khe Sanh.

On some days, over 1000 rounds of enemy fire would hit the base while well-placed snipers harassed Marines lugging timber out in the open.

ORDER OF BATTLE AT KHE SANH

The 1st Battalion, 26th Marines, arrived at Khe Sanh on 13 May 1967. The 3d Battalion, 26th Marines, arrived a month later and, by 1968, the 1st Battalion, 13th Marines, was emplaced with three batteries of 105mm howitzers, one each of 155mm howitzers and 4.2in mortars and seven batteries of 175mm guns: a total of 46 artillery pieces. With the build-up of communist forces becoming apparent to the north, the 2d Battalion, 26th Marines, arrived at Khe Sanh on 16 January 1968.

As the siege developed, the 1st Battalion, 9th Marines, was flown in on 22 January. Either from a South Vietnamese desire to make a political gesture, or because Westmoreland insisted that they be seen to participate (the record is conflicting) the ARVN 37th Ranger Battalion was also flown in on 27 January. This brought the total garrison to some 6000 men.

Ranged around Khe Sanh were four NVA divisions supported by two artillery regiments with 130mm and 152mm artillery pieces and two armoured units. The NVA 324B Division was identified as being located around Dong Ha, and the 325C Division – previously encountered by the Marines during the 1967 hill fighting to the west of Khe Sanh – was also present in strength. The 320th Division was to the east, close to Camp Carroll and the Rockpile. By mid-January, it was clear that the elite Hanoi Guard formation, the 304th Division, which had won a formidable reputation at Dien Bien Phu, was moving east towards the base from Laos. There are no precise numbers available, but it is generally accepted that between 15-20,000 men from the 304th and 325C divisions were committed to the siege of Khe Sanh.

Left: 1602 NVA bodies were left on the battlefield – Westmoreland reckoned that they lost between 10,000 and 15,000 men in all. Of the 6000 Marines at Khe Sanh, only 205 lost their lives. The guy with his helmet off, Mike Mielichan, survived. He is still in the Marine Corps, now as a captain, and is serving as a helicopter pilot in England.

STOPPED BY A BULLET

'It is night again, and the sky is burning with slowly dropping magnesium flares. Heaps of equipment are on fire. terrifying in their jagged black massiveness, burning prehistoric shapes like the tail of a C-130 sticking straight up in the air, dead metal showing through the grey-black smoke. God, if it can do that to metal, what will it do to me? And then something very near me is smouldering, just above my head, the damp canvas coverings on the sandbags lining the top of a slit trench. It is a small trench, and a lot of us have gotten into it in a hurry. At the end farthest from me there is a young guy who has been hit in the throat, and he is making the sounds a baby will make when he is trying to work up the breath for a good scream. We were on the ground when those rounds came, and a Marine near the trench had been splattered badly across the legs and groin. I sort of took him into the trench with me. It was so crowded I couldn't help leaning on him a little, and he kept saying, "You motherfucker, you cocksucker," until someone told him that I wasn't a grunt but a reporter. Then he started to say, very quietly, "Be careful, Mister. Please be careful." He'd been wounded before, and he knew how it would hurt in a few minutes. Far up the road that skirted the TOC [tactical operations centre] was a dump where they burned the gear and uniforms that nobody needed any more. On top of the pile I saw a flak jacket so torn apart that no-one would ever want it again. On the back, its owner had listed the months that he had served in Vietnam. *March, April, May* (each month written out in a tentative, spidery hand), *June, July, August, September, Octobler, Novembler, December, Janurary, Feburary,* the list ending right there like a clock stopped by a bullet.'

From 'Despatches' by Michael Herr, freelance journalist, Khe Sanh

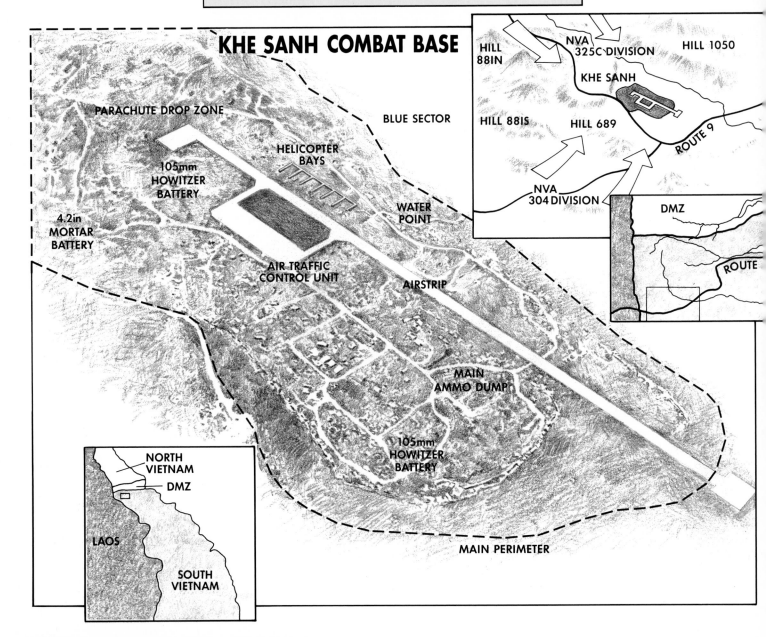

KHE SANH COMBAT BASE

NVA 325C DIVISION

HILL 88IN

HILL 1050

KHE SANH

HILL 88IS

HILL 689

ROUTE 9

NVA 304 DIVISION

DMZ

ROUTE

PARACHUTE DROP ZONE

BLUE SECTOR

HELICOPTER BAYS

105mm HOWITZER BATTERY

4.2in MORTAR BATTERY

WATER POINT

AIR TRAFFIC CONTROL UNIT

AIRSTRIP

MAIN AMMO DUMP

105mm HOWITZER BATTERY

NORTH VIETNAM

DMZ

LAOS

SOUTH VIETNAM

MAIN PERIMETER

Left: Living conditions pretty soon bordered on the unbearable. The ground was littered with spent shell cases, discarded equipment, mouldy canvas and half-consumed C-rations festering in blasted trenches. This Marine is trying to maintain a veneer of civilization by washing his face in his helmet.

On 23 February, Lieutenant Jacques led 29 men from Bravo Company to locate an NVA mortar position that was hammering the base with uncanny accuracy. Charging across open ground, Bravo was driven to the ground by a sheet of rifle fire. Outflanked and outgunned, only four men made it the 200m back to the combat base perimeter. The long-awaited massed infantry assault on the Khe Sanh combat base would never really materialize. But the Marines weren't to know that at the time. NVA units probed the defences, dug trenches that snaked their way towards the perimeter fences, and put the fear of God into the defenders. But only the odd small-scale attack was launched. After a unit of NVA assaulted the east end of the base and were beaten back by ARVN Rangers, enemy infantry never again threatened the base. But the shelling continued for a further five weeks. It was four weeks before the Marines could retrieve their dead. Four weeks living with the knowledge that 25 of their buddies lay dead outside the perimeter.

THE M-46 130MM GUN-HOWITZER

Calibre: 130mm
Weight: (travelling): 8450kg
　　　　　(firing) : 7700kg
Length: 11.73 metres
Height: 2.55 metres
Width: 2.45 metres
Elevation: +45/-2.5
Crew: Nine
Muzzle velocity: 930 metres per second
Max range: 27,150 metres

GUN-HOWITZER FIREPOWER

The mobile M-46 artillery piece was so effective that the US often called in B-52 strikes just to silence one gun

The most effective piece in the NVA's heavy armoury was, without doubt, the PRC Type 59 130mm gun-howitzer. This weapon was a Chinese copy of the Soviet M-46, first seen in public during the 1954 May Day military parade. The M-46 was developed from a naval gun and adapted for field use by fitting it to a two-wheeled split-trail carriage.

Although the weapon that saw service with the NVA was a copy of the Soviet-built weapon, it had several distinctive features. The gun had a long, thin barrel ending in a pepperpot muzzle brake. This was very useful to the NVA as it cut down on muzzle flash and made the weapon harder for the Americans to pinpoint.

The M-46 is built with a manually-operated, horizontal, sliding breech block, while the recoil system consists of a hydropneumatic recuperator – which has a distinctive

front-end collar support – above, and a hydraulic buffer below the barrel. This is located just in front of a rearward angled winged gunshield.

It is a very mobile piece and, although the barrel is almost 25ft, it can be detached and transported on the carriage. This design made it possible to transport the M-46 along narrow jungle trails – once again making it very difficult for US aircraft to find and destroy. Indeed, the Americans had such problems locating NVA artillery units that there were cases of B-52 strikes being called upon to destroy a single gun.

The M-46 requires a nine-man team for optimum efficiency and can be ready for action within four minutes. Once set

up, it is then possible for an experienced team to fire at a rate of six rounds a minute. This high level of firepower and mobility was vital for the NVA whose gunners often had only a limited period in which to inflict as much damage as possible upon the US or ARVN forces before an airstrike would be called down on them.

The M-46 can fire a variety of ammunition including high explosive, fragmentation and armour-piercing capped tracer. Indeed, the M-46 was so accurate that it was very effective when used as an anti-tank weapon at short range,

and many people who were on the receiving end of an M-46 barrage considered the artillery piece superior to anything the Americans had in Vietnam.

The NVA did not have large numbers of the piece until later in the war, but they were put to good use around the Khe Sanh combat base in 1968 and played a major role in both the invasion of Laos and the 1972 Easter Offensive.

Perhaps a measure of the weapon's quality is that 30 years after it first appeared, the M-46 is still used by more than 30 countries throughout the world.

Above: The M-46 gun-howitzer complete with its distinctive muzzle brake.

Four F-100 Super Sabres hugged their own shadows on a flat roof of cloud, circling while their pilots absorbed instructions. Captain Don Hewlitt stared at the grey soup and twisted his face into the look of a tolerant visitor to a madhouse. It was his third combat mission of the day and Hewlitt knew an NVA artillery position lay beneath the grey-white crud clinging to one of the ubiquitous hillsides, although there was no logical way he could know since not even the hill was visible.

'No problem,' Hewlitt thought out loud. He knew that it could be a hell of a lot worse: he could be one of the Marines on the ground, ringed by two elite NVA divisions, pounded by artillery around the clock. Those Marines were real heroes, sitting there on the low ground, and just taking everything that was thrown at them.

Flying blind

Hewlitt was flight leader. He was the first to roll in. He aimed his F-100 down into the murk, where criss-crossing NVA bullets sought out the sound of the airplane. Having been given an update from a flying command post nearby, Hewlitt now used instinct and dead reckoning to proceed with the little-publicized and little-rewarded task of delivering his bombs. 'No problem,' he repeated. 'Just forget every rule you ever learned that was supposed to save your ass while flying, ignore even the most basic precautions, and forge right ahead.'

Hewlitt's approach to these missions was simple: 'Take fifteen tons of stovepipe-powered airplane, brimming with bombs, and fly the doggoned thing right where the enemy's gunfire is strongest. Locate your target with guesswork and guts. Fly straight down into the soup, blind, where hilltops rise to a thousand feet. Go straight in against the bastards and hope you don't collide with a ridgeline going in and out.'

Hewlitt's description was typical. From Air Force and Marine bases in South Vietnam and

AIR SUPPORT

While the fighter-bombers roared in from cloud-level, the B-52s cruised over Khe Sanh and delivered their version of the 'Whispering Death'

from Navy carriers at Dixie Station, men were taking the same risks.

They called it Niagara. Whoever handed out the codenames in Saigon must have visualized a waterfall of aerial ordnance flooding down to drown out the NVA around Khe Sanh. The air support effort to relieve Khe Sanh did, in fact, involve a tremendous downpour of death. With a C-130 command post, codenamed Hillsborough, calling the plays 24 hours a day, Niagara involved high-altitude radar bombing missions by B-52s and close support by up to 350 fighter-bombers of the Air Force, Navy and Marine Corps. The air activity was so frenetic that daisy chains were set up over the heaviest NVA concentrations.

In a daisy chain, 'hot' bomb runs were carried out in relays, warplanes stacked up in a pattern above the enemy's criss-crossing gunfire, each pilot waiting his turn to go in. Hewlitt had written home 'It's a little like the traffic pattern at O'Hare [Chicago International Airport] on a foggy day.'

Rarely had American airmen fought in such numbers in weather so poor. In January 1968 when the Tet Offensive was unleashed and the siege of Khe Sanh became serious, the area was covered by low clouds every morning, hiding some of the NVA and keeping visibility down to a mile with a ceiling of 1000 to 1500 feet. Conditions improved briefly at mid-day but many of the airmen never noticed. Many kept flying around the clock, landing to re-load, catching a quick breather, and taking off again.

Khe Sanh had become a political symbol, so it

Left: The view from a B-52 cockpit. Using sensors installed along the DMZ and reconnaissance flights to pin-point targets, the B-52 Stratofortress bombers, or 'BUFFs' (Big Ugly Fat Fuckers) as they were known, deposited a staggering 110,000 tons of bombs around the Khe Sanh combat base perimeter during the gruelling 77-day siege. Right: A napalm bomb explodes amongst enemy positions. Below: An NVA artillery emplacement on the Khe Sanh perimeter is bombed by an A-1 Skyraider. The gun managed to fire only two salvoes before it was destroyed.

scarcely mattered that the two NVA divisions with formidable back-up forces had encircled the Marines on a piece of real estate that was virtually useless. On his 26 December 1967 Christmas visit to Cam Ranh Bay, President Lyndon Johnson, mindful that the troops at the base were already threatened by an NVA build-up, had asked if airpower alone could support the defenders of the outpost in the event of an attack. General William Momyer, 7th Air Force chief and top airman in Vietnam, had assured Johnson that it could be done. Momyer's first step – ignoring Marine sensibilities with his usual directness – was to get General Westmoreland to grant him operational control over Marine fixed-wing aircraft involved in the effort.

This was done on 18 January 1968. The Marines, fiercely proud of their own air arm and its close tie to their ground force, had envisaged supporting the immediate area around Khe Sanh

329

THE WHISPERING DEATH

Between June 1965 and August 1973, B-52 Stratofortress bombers of the US Strategic Air Command (SAC) flew more than 126,000 sorties in support of ground units in Southeast Asia. Stationed on the central Pacific island of Guam and, from April 1967, at U-Tapao in Thailand, these giant aircraft – each capable of delivering up to 54,000lbs of bombs in a single mission – operated at high altitude, depositing their deadly loads by radar through the thickest cloud. To the NVA and VC troops on the receiving end, they were known by the ominous nickname 'the Whispering Death', since the first the enemy knew about the presence of the bombers was the whistling of the bombs.

These raids, carried out under the codename Arc Light, began on 18 June 1965 with the bombing of VC base areas north of Saigon. This mission created an immediate storm of controversy, with many claiming that it was akin to 'swatting flies with sledgehammers', since it had cost a staggering $20 million. Two B-52s had collided during this mission, further fuelling the controversy. Anti-war factions criticized the raids on the basis that they led to indiscriminate civilian casualties.

But, as the US high command argued, America had no option but to take advantage of the crushing firepower that high-altitude bombers could deliver. By November 1965, the B-52s were operating close to the Cambodian border, interdicting enemy supply lines. By March the following year they were involved in raids north of the DMZ, bombing the strategic Mu Gia Pass – a 'choke point' on the Ho Chi Minh Trail just inside North Vietnam. By then, SAC had deployed ground-based radar, known as 'Combat Skyspot', which allowed a controller to guide the bombers towards their targets and even tell the pilot when to release his bombs. Accuracy was impressive.

During the siege of Khe Sanh in early 1968, another new technique was introduced. Called 'Bugle Note', it involved a stream of B-52s flying from Guam – a 12-hour round trip – and appearing over the Marine base at regular intervals of less than 90 minutes. These raids were instrumental in breaking up enemy concentrations before they could launch attacks on the combat base.

By 1972, the bombers were hitting targets in Cambodia (Operation Menu), Laos (Operation Good Look) and, in December, were even released over Hanoi (Operation Linebacker II). The Arc Light bombing missions continued as required until after the last US ground units had been withdrawn from Southeast Asia.

Top left: Checking a catapult cable prior to a launch from an aircraft carrier. Above: A US jet streaks away as its bombs detonate among the entrenched NVA positions around Khe Sanh. After the siege, Westmoreland paid tribute to the aircrews: 'Without question, the amount of firepower put on that piece of real estate exceeded anything that had ever been seen before...the enemy was hurt, his back was broken, by airpower.'

OPERATION NIAGARA

By the beginning of 1968, it was obvious that the NVA were massing their forces in the northern provinces close to the DMZ. Accordingly, on 5 January, Westmoreland convened a top-level meeting to consider possible responses. Out of this emerged a contingency plan codenamed Niagara. As soon as the communists attacked, they would be met by a hail of artillery and air strikes, the momentum of which would not falter until the danger was passed.

The operation was divided into two phases. Niagara I, which began immediately, concentrated on building up a comprehensive intelligence picture of the enemy, identifying targets and earmarking the forces needed to destroy them. Niagara II was essentially the total commitment of such forces as soon as the enemy took the offensive. When the attacks on Khe Sanh began on 21 January, Niagara II was triggered.

Within 24 hours, over 600 tactical airstrikes, carried out by Air Force, Navy and Marine squadrons, (below) had been ordered. B-52s, flying from Guam and Thailand, carried out 49 of these strikes. The effects were devastating: pre-located enemy bunkers, trenches and tunnel networks were shattered, storage areas were hit and attacking NVA units destroyed. Nor was this an isolated response: by the end of the siege in April, 24,000 tactical and 2700 B-52 strikes had been called in. At night, AC-47 gunships maintained the pressure, while by day the raids were continued, often in poor weather, using 'Combat Skyspot' guidance radar.

directly with their A-4, A-6, F-4 and F-8 aircraft, needing no other help. Although under Army control the Marines continued to provide air support, while their own Huey and Cobra helicopters (these *not* under Momyer's control) pulled off some dramatic rescues when pilots went down near the embattled base.

From the start, it had been planned to use B-52 bombers to help relieve pressure on the base. Momyer had insisted that the Stratofortresses could bomb safely within 1000ft of the Marines, though 3000ft was set as a minimum range. It was felt that Arc Light strikes, as the B-52 missions were called, could prevent the North Vietnamese from moving new divisions into the surrounding hills.

Identifying refugees

When a B-52 dropped its lethal cargo of 108 high-explosive 500-lb bombs, anything within the impact area was certain to be pulverized. The sheer noise of an Arc Light exploding nearby was enough to break ear-drums. A B-52 bomb run left craters over a vast area, making it look much like the surface of the moon. Throughout the war, it was charged that B-52 missions rarely actually hit anything, and that they were as likely to hit friend as foe, but at Khe Sanh the big bombers

were effective. By covering the outer ring of the air support area, they markedly slowed down the NVA's efforts to reinforce.

B-52 crews were relatively safe over the besieged base. Fighter-bomber pilots faced greater risks. But perhaps the most difficult job of all was carried out by Marine and Air Force Forward Air Controllers (FACs) who often had to make instant decisions, based solely on their observations from light planes, as to which targets should be attacked and when. Numerous refugees were on the move in the trails around Khe Sanh. While dodging ferocious enemy gunfire, the intrepid FAC had to distinguish NVA troopers from genuine refugees. The 'Combat Skyspot' technique of combining radar and computer, enabling a ground operator to tell a pilot when to drop his bombs, helped to compensate for the execrable weather around Khe Sanh.

By the time the siege of Khe Sanh was broken on 14 April 1968, pilots of B-52s, fighters, FAC aircraft and airborne command posts had made a major contribution, their own courage as great as that of the men who flew cargo aircraft in to make supply drops at the base. Incredibly, despite the bad weather and enemy gunfire, the only tactical aircraft lost were one A-4 Skyhawk, one F-4 Phantom and 17 Marine helicopters.

1968

Lownds said keep the high ground. Captain Dabney and his 400 Marines obliged

The sniper was well-concealed on a hill about 400yds to the north, the only ground high enough and close enough to our positions on Hill 881 South to offer a vantage point for effective rifle fire. He had been there about a week. He fired rarely, when visibility was good and a clear target was offered, but he was deadly. With a total of perhaps 20 rounds, he had killed two of my Marines and wounded half-a-dozen others. Even a napalm storm failed to silence him. He had my stretcher-bearers pinned down at a time when I had some serious medevacing to get on with.

He was careful, but not quite careful enough. On a still afternoon, a machine gunner spotted a slight movement in a bush. A recoilless rifle, our primary mid-range anti-tank gun, was zeroed in on his spider hole and a 106mm high-explosive plastic round was sent crashing through the bush.

EYE-WITNESS

The author, William H. Dabney, was a captain in the US Marine Corps during the Vietnam war. At Khe Sanh, he commanded India Company, 3d Battalion, 26th Marines.

Main picture: Under constant threat of mortar and smallarms fire, a Marine scouts for enemy troops on the moonscape that was once Hill 881. His buddy lies dead beside him, one of the Grim Reaper's many casualties in the hills around Khe Sanh. Right: Taking the high ground.

The NVA nest became a crater, and its former occupant a formless pulp.

Another sniper sprang up from nowhere to take his place. He too got a 106. The sniping continued for 10 days – this time from a different part of the hill. Again the crew wrestled their 106 around the rough slopes. While the gunner and spotter picked their mark, a young private crawled towards me. Crouched in his foxhole, he had been watching this particular sniper for the past week. The guy had fired about as many rounds as his predecessors, but hadn't hit a damned thing. The private suggested that we leave him be for the time being. If we blew him away, the North Vietnamese might replace him with someone who shot straight. This idea made sense, and the 106 was moved back. My men even started waving 'Maggies' drawers' at him – a red cloth that we used to signal a miss on the rifle range. Then we figured he might be faking us and we quit the taunts. He stayed there for the whole of the battle – about two months – fired regularly, and never hit a man.

The spectre of Dien Bien Phu

Hill 881 South (881S) was one of several high hills overlooking Khe Sanh combat base that came under heavy NVA attack. We'd all feared a repeat of the French disaster at Dien Bien Phu, and vowed there was no way heavy enemy artillery was going to get a foothold in the hills around us. For covering North Vietnamese routes of advance onto the base, none of the high ground was more critical, nor more exposed, than 881S, a steep-

DABNEY'S HILL

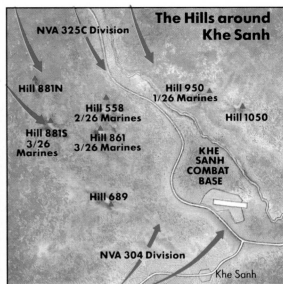

The Hills around Khe Sanh

NVA 325C Division

Hill 881N

Hill 950
1/26 Marines

Hill 558
2/26 Marines

Hill 1050

Hill 881S
3/26 Marines

Hill 861
3/26 Marines

KHE SANH COMBAT BASE

Hill 689

NVA 304 Division

Khe Sanh

slopes during the past couple of days, but I was worried about a possible NVA build up to the north. I took India Company out on recce as dawn broke on the 20th, but the two lead platoons ran into serious trouble. They were pinned down on both flanks and only a classic infantry assault by Lieutenant Brindley's platoon took the heat off us – for a short time at least. Brindley caught a fatal bullet just as he reached the crest, and now the NVA skirmish line charged up the rear slope. Napalm sent them packing, but it fell so close that several soldiers had their eyebrows singed. By now we'd located the enemy positions and India brought heavy fire to bear. The two platoons made it back to rejoin Mike on 881S.

sided hill rising 500yds from its surrounding valleys, some five miles west of the base. The Marines had finally seized it a year back in a long and bloody fight that had left its slopes devoid of vegetation, packed with craters and littered with collapsed bunkers where the remains of North Vietnamese soldiers were still entombed.

A Marine 'daisy-chain'

Those of us occupying the surrounding hills had to rely on paradrops for supplies – sending anyone down the slopes was only inviting a skirmish with the NVA. Besides, by occupying fixed positions we could make everything around us a free-fire zone. Each of the hills was occupied by a company-sized Marine unit of, or attached to, the 26th Marine Regiment that had overall responsibility for the defence of Khe Sanh. I knew that Hill 881S was going to be the big problem – being the most distant, it would be difficult to reinforce. On 20 January I had some 400 Marines under my command: Company I ('India'), and two platoons and the headquarters of Company M ('Mike') of the 3d Battalion. For heavy stuff, I had a section of 81mm mortars, two 106mm recoilless rifles and three 105mm howitzers.

We'd carried out aggressive patrolling along the

STARS AND STRIPES

'The flag is battered, heads are bloody, but the "colors" still sound on Hill 881S.' This extract from the *Times-Herald* of February 1968 stands as testimony to the courage of the US Marines who went through 77 days of hell at Khe Sanh. The flag-raising ceremony was one of the ways Captain William H. Dabney rallied the morale of his company and showed how the beleaguered troops were responding to the North Vietnamese Army's relentless attacks.

Each morning, a bullet-torn Stars and Stripes would be hoisted up an improvised mast under full view of the enemy. The muted tones of a bugle would then remind the Marines that Hill 881S remained in American hands. Renowned through the ranks as a fine leader of men, and gifted with a flair for the unorthodox, Captain Dabney would urge his embattled Marines to stand bolt upright until the last note was sounded, despite the fact that enemy guns were trained on them every moment.

This ceremony took place in spite of the fact that it was prohibited for the American flag to be raised over South Vietnamese territory.

The Marines argued that since it was their blood alone that bought the hills around Khe Sanh, it was Old Glory that belonged there.

Above left: Marines move along the slit trench earthworks at the crest of a hill outpost. Top right: Around Hill 881S, all but a few isolated patches of bush were flattened. Right: Ten months previously, the Marines had taken the high ground in a series of bitter firefights.

The NVA were not going to give up. Two hours past midnight they tried to storm several of the base's outlying positions. Hill 881S got off lightly, but my mortarmen set their hot tubes at near-maximum range and laid down support for the embattled Marines on Hill 861 to the north. They let loose nearly 700 rounds. Their two mortar tubes got so hot that the propellant ignited as the rounds slid down the tubes, causing the bombs to go unpredictably astray, and the tubes had to be cooled. The Marines used their precious water first, but soon exhausted that – together with a meagre cache of canned fruit juice. Finally, they formed a Marine daisy chain to piss on the tubes. The fire mission continued until, with the coming of dawn, we were no longer needed. The smell was unpleasant, but the job was done.

No end in sight

The NVA knew they were up against alert and well-emplaced defenders – India had seen to that – so they tried to force us off the hill by cutting off our resupply. 120mm mortar rounds started crowding into our hilltop landing zones, with horrible consequences. On the 22nd, a medevac chopper carrying more than 20 of my wounded men was obliterated. By early February, the combined effects of enemy mortars and anti-

1968

aircraft fire had cost India and Mike dear. Including men shot by snipers, the casualty rate was over 50 per cent with no end in sight. We were down to one-quart canteen of water a day.

The noise was constant

What saved us was the 'Super Gaggle' ground resupply operation – without that we'd have been lost for sure. Kept in ammunition, food and water, we were strong enough to deter the NVA from launching a full-scale assault on 881S. There was the occasional attempt to probe the outer perimeter, but a Marine could always toss a hand grenade down the hill far better than an NVA soldier could throw one up it.

As the weather improved, so our air support grew more intense. By March the action was winding down. Captain Harry Jenkins (commanding Mike Company) and I acted as the conductors of an orchestra. With radios as our batons we orchestrated the unlimited and instantly available artillery and aircraft ordnance upon any movement, or sound, or smell or hunch. The noise was constant. What had been a green rolling plateau three months earlier now looked more like the surface of the moon, with long series of overlapping craters and blasted stumps where before there had been lush forests. All but the NVA diehards simply melted away. An incident that took place on 1 April shows why.

Just as the relieving forces were arriving, two naked North Vietnamese soldiers ran up to our

Below: Moving, watching, waiting, Marines advance through terrain laid waste by constant artillery, air and mortar strikes. While the Marines held the crests, the lower slopes often swarmed with North Vietnamese.

wire in broad daylight, waving propaganda leaflets to indicate surrender. One was shot in the back by his comrades, and the other went to ground outside the wire until a Marine, under our covering fire, crawled across and led him to the safety of the trench. He was an impressive man, almost six foot tall, healthy looking, and of imposing physique. We began to question him, but were interrupted by his amazing transformation as a Marine jet passed overhead. He literally lost complete control of himself – his muscles, his eyes, even his bowels – and fell in a quivering heap to the bottom of the trench. The man had been psychologically destroyed by the awesome pounding from the air he and his comrades had been subjected to.

Right: Spent cartridges fly as a grunt puts his M16 to work. Throughout the long siege of Hill 881S, the Marines were inspired by Dabney's leadership and his flair for the unorthodox. On one occasion, when the captain made a request for supplies to be sent from HQ, his requisition read: 'Need saxophone and trombone to fill out Trench Foot Trio. Technicians for this position available this position.'

1968

KEEPING THE HIGH GROUND

Did the US get it right by occupying outlying hills around Khe Sanh?

Everyone knew that, in 1954, the French at Dien Bien Phu had made the fundamental mistake of allowing the enemy to dominate the high ground around their positions in a deep valley. In spite of the criticism levelled at them, however, the embattled Marines followed precisely the right defensive strategy at Khe Sanh.

Initially, US Special Forces had occupied the area in 1962. But after they moved to Lang Vei, it was not until an NVA presence was identified in October 1966 that American forces returned. Although perched on a plateau, Khe Sanh was commanded by surrounding high ground. Numbered according to their height (in metres), Hills 1015, 950, 558, 881 North and 881 South lay to the north and northwest, while Hill 689 lay to the west. In particular, the crests of 861 and 881S, some 5000m apart, formed a protective barrier across the natural approach route from the Laotian border.

At first, the base on Hill 881S was held only by a single Marine company. But, after an ambush of a platoon returning from 861 on 16 March 1967, the battle developed into a prolonged series of 'hill fights' during which a more substantial and permanent Marine presence was established on the vital crests. 861 was cleared by the 2d Battalion, 26th Marines, on 28 April 1967, and 881S by the regiment's 3d Battalion on 2 May – but only after sustained and bitter fighting. 881N was the last to be cleared, on 5 May.

As a result of this fighting by the Marines back in 1967, Khe Sanh was well defended when the NVA launched its first major assault by attempting to storm 861 on the night of 20/21 January 1968. Both 861 and 881S became the scene of frequent NVA mass assaults. With artillery and supporting aircraft able to deliver massive firepower with pinpoint accuracy against NVA concentrations, however, it was not necessary for the Marines to manoeuvre away from their fixed positions overlooking the base. The Marines had done their homework.

1968

BATTLEWAGON

The USS New Jersey sat on the gun line in the South China Sea and supported Marine actions with 16in shells and rockets. A World War II vet, she was mothballed after Korea, then redrafted to Vietnam in 1968. In 120 days on the gun line, she pounded the Nam with 20,579 shells.

BATTLEWAGON

Far left: On board ship they plotted the co-ordinates of targets from information supplied by forward observers miles inland. Accuracy was vital if they were to smash the unseen enemy and not their own men.
Left: It's hot below decks on a ship in the tropics — but not as hot as where this little mother, a 5in rocket, is going to land.

Left: USS *New Jersey* was re-supplied by her own Seasprite helicopter so she could sit out in the ocean pounding Charlie almost indefinitely. She delivered 5688 16in rounds and 14,891in rounds to Vietnam. And in 1982, she gave more of the same to the Lebanon.
Right: The boys in the mud of bases near the DMZ could draw some comfort from the artillery support they got from these floating firebases in the South China sea. The *New Jersey's* 16in guns could hurl shells weighing over a ton some 25 miles.

THE FALL OF LANG VEI

1968

When you operate from a Special Forces camp, guerrilla warfare is the name of the game. You're not expecting tanks

J ust past midnight on 7 February the observation post at Lang Vei was suddenly lit up by a descending trip flare. As a startled Sergeant Nikolas Fragas squinted his eyes at the blinding flash the surprise was complete. There, behind two North Vietnamese calmly cutting the perimeter fence, idled two olive green hulks – tanks! Jolted back into gear by the sight of the NVA troops keeling over shot dead, Fragas radioed his detachment commander, 'We have tanks in our wire!' If the 24-year-old assistant medical specialist's voice sounded a little shrill then it was understandable – two North Vietnamese tanks were about to run

him down, something which had never before happened to an American serviceman in South Vietnam. The NVA were deploying armour for the first time.

It was only days after the opening of the Tet Offensive had rocked the length of South Vietnam and this small Special Forces base had been expecting trouble – but not in the form of these green monsters. The day before, 50 rounds of enemy heavy artillery fire had streaked in, cratering the camp, shredding two bunkers and giving the corpsmen a couple of wounded to work on. There had followed an ominous pattern of triggered trip flares and strange rumbling noises. The guys had put these down to the base's clanking old

A Montagnard keeps watch from behind a curtain of barbed wire. Allied forces stationed at the Lang Vei Special Forces camp faced a grim struggle for survival the night that NVA tanks overran the perimeter fence.

340

END OF THE CIDGS

On 12 May 1968 the CIDG camp at Kham Duc, on the Laotian border in I Corps Tactical Zone, was overrun by elements of the 2nd NVA Division. US Special Forces Detachment A-105 was decimated and a relieving force from the Americal Division suffered heavy casualties as an airborne evacuation degenerated into a panic-stricken rout. Kham Duc was the last of the CIDG outposts on the northwestern border of South Vietnam to fall.

This disaster, coming so soon after the loss of Lang Vei, posed serious questions about the future of the CIDG concept. When it had been introduced in 1962, it had catered for a specific low-level need – border surveillance – but by 1968 the nature of the war had changed. CIDG detachments were now too isolated and vulnerable to survive an NVA main-force attack.

A number of other factors reinforced this view. By 1968, the 5th Special Forces Group, responsible for providing CIDG advisers, was running short of experienced manpower: only 10 per cent of replacements reporting for duty in Vietnam had previous battle experience, and almost 25 per cent were not even qualified for Special Forces work.

This situation led to a gradual breakdown in the relationship between CIDG and US personnel, leading to incidents of poor combat performance and indiscipline.

All of this was noted by Westmoreland's successor as MACV commander, General Creighton W. Abrams. Appointed in June 1968, he introduced a policy of Vietnamization, part of which was directed at the CIDG programme. But few of the mountain tribes who made up the CIDG groups trusted their new ARVN masters, and consequently made little effort to maintain their specialist skills. Special Force commitment was deliberately reduced until, in March 1971, the 5th Special Forces Group left Vietnam. The rot that had set in at Lang Vei and Kham Duc had finally destroyed the CIDG experiment.

generator, but now the true sources of the row were horribly visible.

Secluded in heavily wooded, craggy countryside, 35 kilometres south of the Demilitarised Zone and eight kilometres southwest of the Marine stronghold at Khe Sanh, Lang Vei had been set up to deal with communist forces on their own terms. Serving as a base for recon missions along the Ho Chi Minh Trail and clandestine guerrilla ops over the border, it was no custommade defensive position.

Drifting ribbons of tracer

With its 22 Green Berets and 400 irregs, Lang Vei was in a delicate position. There were now around 40,000 NVA troops converging on the Khe Sanh area, and the only thing that made the US command think Lang Vei could be held was the Marine heavy artillery at Khe Sanh and the fighter-bombers at Da Nang. As the night exploded with drifting ribbons of tracer and blasts of automatic weapon fire, the defenders at Lang Vei were praying to God that this firepower would enter stage right when the show really got going.

Ploughing relentlessly through the base's array of barbed wire and Claymore anti-personnel mines, the NVA armour smashed inside the perimeter. As the tanks shattered the darkness with their tracer fire and spotlights, Fragas could make out two infantry platoons following in their

LEFT WITHOUT SUPPORT?

With such massed firepower at his disposal, can Colonel David Lownds be accused of failing to support the defenders of Lang Vei?

When NVA tanks rumbled towards Lang Vei early on 7 February, the commander of Special Forces Detachment A-101, Captain Frank C. Willoughby, should have been in a position to call for support from a variety of sources. At Khe Sanh, Camp Carroll and the Rockpile there were 16 175mm, 16 155mm and 18 105mm guns, already pre-registered onto targets around Lang Vei. In the air, Forward Air Controllers were available to call down Marine and US Air Force ground attack fighters. If all else failed, a contingency plan existed for two rifle companies of Colonel Lownds' 26th Marine Regiment at Khe Sanh to move on foot or by helicopter to relieve the isolated camp.

As the NVA attack materialised, Willoughby tried to trigger all available responses. So far as artillery and air support was concerned, he encountered few problems, but when he radioed the 26th Marines, his request for infantry reinforcements was refused. This failure to respond was later criticized, implying that Lownds' Marines had sat back and waited, sacrificing the Special Forces camp in the interests of their own security.

This is an unfair charge to lay at Lownds' door, however, since he really had little choice. Khe Sanh was besieged, and on the night of 6/7 February was under NVA artillery and mortar fire. As the attack on Lang Vei had all the appearance of being a feint, designed to weaken Khe Sanh by drawing elements of Lownds' force away from the combat base, any commitment of reinforcements to Willoughby could have been disastrous. It is well known that Lownds was worried by the reports of tanks being deployed at Lang Vei – he knew that his men were not equipped for anti-armour operations. In addition, the fact that the attack on the Special Forces base took place under cover of darkness prevented Lownds from sending in the helicopters. Indeed, it was not until early afternoon on the 7th that any were made available. Once cleared to fly, however, the choppers were immediately sent in to evacuate the survivors from Lang Vei.

Left: An aerial reconnaissance photograph clearly shows abandoned NVA tanks. The US defeat at Lang Vei went against the usual pattern of the war. An NVA force possessing superior firepower had attacked what was in effect a US guerrilla force and defeated it. Opposite centre: GIs survey the remains of a PT-76. Opposite top: Lieutenant-Colonel Daniel F. Schungel presents an interim Bronze Star Medal for Valor to Sergeant Allen for his part in the defence of Lang Vei.

wake, using the armour as their protection and their battering ram. Blasted awake, the defenders desperately sought to halt these gatecrashers. Though only lightly armoured, the Soviet-designed PT-76s shrugged off this smallarms fire and rumbled on.

As two PT-76s crashed into the southeast corner of the base, Sergeant James Holt swung round with one of the base's pair of 106mm recoilless rifles. Making sure of his aim with an illuminating round he was able to knock out both tanks from less than 350m. As the crews, including three women, bailed out of the burning death traps, a third PT-76 came veering around its stricken predecessors and set about destroying three bunkers. Coolly traversing the gun, Holt fired again and scored a third direct hit. Just as well – it was his last round. Then, hot on the trail of the three destroyed PT-76s, came another two green monsters. The abandoned 106mm was blown to kingdom come.

Spooky gives support

While the battle raged above, Captain Frank C. Willoughby, commander of Special Forces Detachment A-101, down in the operations centre bunker, had been radioing for artillery support from the Marine base at Khe Sanh. Fifteen minutes after the fight had begun, the first rounds came crashing down just outside the perimeter fence. Willoughby relayed target corrections to the Marines, directing volley after volley at what was apparently the enemy's main effort. Ten minutes later this assault was augmented by a Spooky gunship, a flareship and an Air Force forward air controller.

Despite this, the North Vietnamese troops pushed on, exploiting their tanks' close-in firepower. As the defending troops vainly attempted to halt these clanking bolts from the blue with smallarms, grenades and ineffectual light assault weapons, the PT-76s overran the southeast corner of the base, directing fire inward. This tactic was duplicated on the other side of the camp with a further three tanks bulldozing through and overrunning the bewildered defending forces.

As the Lang Vei defenders grappled desperately with their invaders, the inevitable happened. At 0245 a tank rolled through the inner perimeter, swivelled its turret and began shelling the emergency medical bunker. Almost simultaneously a second tank penetrated Lang Vei's beleaguered inner sanctum, took out a mortar position and moved inexorably towards the camp's nerve centre. Willoughby's command centre now lay like a peanut waiting to be shelled by a caterpillar-tracked nutcracker.

Surprisingly, a stay of execution was forced. Up until now, ad hoc 'tank-killer' teams organised by Lieutenant-Colonel Daniel F. Schungel, who was visiting the base, had merely irritated the tank crews. But now, with an abrupt change in fortunes, Schungel ran forward and deposited two grenades under the belly of one of the tanks.

Seconds later, a LAW rocket slammed into the tank's rear. The tank's hatch creaked open but only flames emerged. Demoralised by this belated display of tank-cracking finesse, the crew of the second PT-76 crawled out of their stalled vehicle and were picked off one by one. Schungel slipped into the darkness.

Assault on the bunker

Regardless of the loss of these two tanks, the North Vietnamese were now virtually in possession of the base. That's not to say that Lang Vei's defenders had given up. Isolated in the depths of the command bunker but still defiant were Willoughby, Fragas, six other Green Berets, the South Vietnamese camp commander and 25 irregulars. The NVA began their attempts to winkle out the bunker's occupants. They first tried to crush the bunker by driving a tank over it and then started to blast the interior with explosives, grenades, tear gas and smallarms fire. Mostly wounded, nauseous and short of breath, the defenders assumed that destruction was imminent and began to destroy valuable documents. Then a voice called down the stairwell in Vietnamese: 'We are going to blow up the bunker, so give up now.'

After a brief, but frantic discussion, the South Vietnamese dashed outside, only to be met with a hail of machine-gun fire. This left only the eight Americans, six of whom were wounded, determined to hold on to the bitter end.

But if the Green Berets were determined, the NVA were equally persistent. Just then, billowing clouds of dust and a collapsing wall signalled a successful digging operation. The NVA had broken into the bunker. Just when it seemed that this resolute, last-ditch defence was about to collapse, help was on its way. Setting out from the original Lang Vei camp, one kilometre to the east, were three Americans, Sergeants Eugene Ashley and Richard Allen and Specialist Joel Johnson, together with some 100 armed Laotians.

After radioing the FAC for some strafing runs over the camp, the would-be rescue force moved gingerly towards the camp from the east. They were met with machine-gun and mortar fire and forced back, calling for further airstrikes. Peppering their assaults with airborne fire, they attempted two more pushes before sending runners back to the old camp for a 51mm recoilless rifle and trying one more time. This added firepower allowed them to penetrate the bunker line before they were repulsed yet again. Then an enemy artillery round killed Ashley and Johnson and put paid to any further rescue missions.

In the command bunker, Willoughby knew that their chances of salvation were fading. Time was running late and they had been without food and water for over 18 hours. The young Green Beret commander knew that their situation was desperate and acted accordingly. He radioed for all available airstrikes, hoping to escape in the ensuing confusion. As plane after plane zoomed in, unleashing its ordnance, the daylight-startled

survivors, protected by numerous dummy runs, tiptoed out into the battle-scarred camp. The bombardment had obviously done its job – the group slunk out of the base hindered only by fire from one bunker.

When this battered band reached the old camp they found Colonel Schungel shrugging off three wounds and attempting to organise a slightly belated evacuation force. Willoughby told him not to bother. Instead, the FAC was radioed once more, bringing a final hail of fire down on the camp.

With over 200 of Lang Vei's original complement killed or missing, the brief and bloody battle of Lang Vei was over.

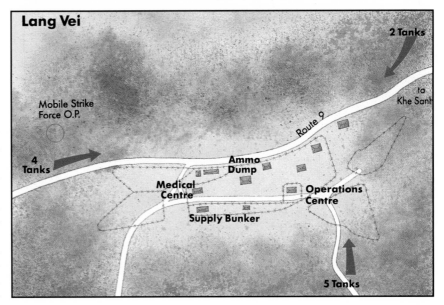

Lang Vei

Mobile Strike Force O.P.

Route 9

to Khe Sanh

2 Tanks

4 Tanks

Ammo Dump

Medical Centre

Supply Bunker

Operations Centre

5 Tanks

1968

EYE-WITNESS

Colonel Thomas M. Sumner saw action in World War II and served nine years as a test pilot before his tour in Vietnam.

The 'Herk' and Provider pilots flying into Khe Sanh diced with death as they braved a gauntlet of fire.

Right top: Marines work desperately to unhook a loaded pallet from a hovering Sea Knight helicopter.

Around 0530 hours on the morning of 21 January 1968 the first enemy shells and rockets began exploding among the trucks, bunkers and helicopters at the Khe Sanh combat base. Minutes later the earth started to shake as the 1500 tons of ammunition at the base dump began to explode. Six helicopters were destroyed or damaged and shell craters reduced the length of the runway almost by half.

AIR SUPPLY

Right bottom: Parachutes billowing, a supply drop lands at the Khe Sanh combat base. Damage to the airstrip early on in the siege made landings by the heavier transport planes both difficult and dangerous. But supplies, especially ammunition, were of prime importance.

As four North Vietnamese Army regiments closed in on Khe Sanh the defenders' only means of supply was by air. The intention had been for B-52 bombers and tactical support aircraft to keep the besiegers busy while twin-engined C-123 Providers and four-engined C-130s carried out re-supply. But with the runway reduced to 2000ft by the destruction of the ammo dump, only the C-123s could land. Although they could be turned around in just three minutes, they were restricted to five tons of cargo, a third of the capacity of a C-130. A difficult job had been made nearly impossible. So the Marines rolled up their sleeves, and by the end of January, frantic repair work on the cratered runway had enabled the C-130s to touch down. One of the 'Herk' pilots who braved the torrent of enemy fire was Colonel Thomas M. Sumner:

'The runway was about 3700ft in length and was laid out on sloping ground, steep enough to require all take-offs to be downhill and all land-

ings to be uphill. So the North Vietnamese always knew where our touch-down point would be, where the lift-off point would be and, of course, where the off-load location was. With this bit of intelligence they were able to aim their weapons accurately at these critical areas, which ensured you would be shot at and most likely hit during any mission to Khe Sanh. The only question would be, to what degree?

Stopped on the runway

'The operation required the C-130s to spend minimum time on the ground. There was an off-load ramp area located adjacent to the runway, and one at the end opposite from the touch-down point. So the procedure was to turn off the runway after the landing roll out, taxi quickly to the ramp, drop the tailgate, unlock the pallets with their loads, keep the airplane moving so that the inertia caused the pallets to roll out of the cargo compartment onto the ramp, close the tailgate, continue to the departure end of the runway and take off. By following this procedure the time spent on the ground was only a few minutes and we could usually get in and out before the enemy gunners could cause serious damage to the airplane. Although we almost always got hit someplace. They would shoot at us during the flare out, during the off load and just as we lifted off, but since we were moving the damage was less than if we'd been a sitting duck.

'I made about 20 trips into Khe Sanh during this period, was hit numerous times, but got away with just minor battle damage each time. There was one trip though that I remember very well because it was one in which I did not get one single hit, but by all odds should have been blown to pieces.

1968

1968

RESUPPLYING KHE SANH

1. At beleaguered Khe Sanh, Marines watch for an approaching re-supply aircraft.

2. In the surrounding hills, NVA gunners prepare to plaster the airstrip as the plane comes in.

3. As the shells rain down, the C-130 Hercules minimises the risk of being hit by flying in at five feet and 130 mph to deliver its cargo by LAPES (Low Altitude Parachute Extraction System).

4. Still under sporadic artillery fire, the Marines rush to bring in the supplies before they are destroyed and clear the runway for another drop.

During the off-load phase of the mission one of the cargo pallets became jammed in the guidance rails as it was rolling out of the cargo compartment. We had to stop the airplane to allow the load master to work the pallet free. The jam was bad and the load master was unable to loosen it quickly, so we sat there with our engines running while he did his best to set the pallet moving again. After we had been stopped for about a minute the NVA gunners began firing rockets with considerable accuracy. To make matters worse, one of the engines had a nacelle overheat light come on full. Some warning systems in some airplanes are notorious for giving false warnings, but not that

Aerial re-supply was vital to the survival of Khe Sanh and its surrounding hill strongpoints. Supplies were delivered to Khe Sanh by aircraft landing on the runway, parachute drop and parachute extraction.

Both landing and parachute drop had their disadvantages – the C-130 Hercules, for example, was very heavy, and vulnerable on the ground to rocket and mortar fire. After one was lost on 11 February and others damaged, they were withdrawn from landing operations. The C-7A Caribou was unable to carry sufficiently large loads, so it was the C-123 Provider that became the mainstay of the landing operation. These spent less time on the ground than the C-130, but three Providers were still lost.

Dropping supplies by parachute could be inaccurate, and exposed Marines to hostile fire when retrieving wayward pallets. After 2 March, when one Marine was killed when a 2000lb load fell on his bunker, loads were mainly delivered either by LAPES (Low Altitude Parachute Extraction System), with pallets being dragged by parachute out of a low-flying aircraft, or by GPES (Ground Proximity Extraction System). In the latter, a ground arresting wire pulled the pallet straight out of the approaching aircraft.

In all, there were 273 landings by C-130s, 179 by C-123s and eight by C-7As. There were 496 parachute drops by C-130s, 105 by C-123s and 57 extractions from C-130s. Using these methods, the aircraft delivered 12,400 tons of cargo to the base. The hill positions were supplied by USMC Boeing Vertol CH-46 Sea Knight helicopters – direct from Dong Ha. The Super Gaggle operation, once perfected, allowed 12 helicopters to drop 3000 lbs each from nets slung underneath – all in the space of 30 seconds. These operations took place three times a day, with mortars, artillery, gunships and A-4 Skyhawks providing cover. Seventeen helicopters were lost during these missions.

system in the C-130s. It was famous for its reliability in giving true warnings.

'A three-engine take-off from that strip was impossible. There was not enough runway and we didn't want to get out of the airplane and become guests of the local Marine Corps. While the shelling was getting closer and closer, with huge chunks of debris flying all around us, my flight engineer and I discussed the overheat problem. The co-pilot's instinctive reaction to the crisis was shut the engine down, but his training to always take his lead from the pilot prevailed. The engineer and I figured that the prop was still in a reverse pitch angle, even though the throttle was in a forward pitch position giving us a reverse air flow. Always a problem if the prop control was even slightly out of adjustment. The solution was simple: advance the throttle real gentle and put the prop in forward pitch, directing the air flow from front to rear instead of the other way around.

If a prop is left in reverse pitch very long, the air flow through the engine nacelle is reduced to the point where the overheat light can be triggered. The load master finally got the pallet free and we moved forward to release the rest of the load, closed the tailgate, continued to taxi to the take-off position and proceeded to roll. Meanwhile, the NVA gunners were still giving it all they had.

A lucky escape

'We were in the off-load position and had stopped for about five minutes, drawing heavy rocket fire. Two helicopters parked on a ramp next to us were hit and chopper parts were flying all around us. We could see direct hits being made on the ground in near proximity, the explosions being very audible. The bottom line to the episode is they never touched us. There was not one single hole in the aircraft, which was just beyond my belief. I guess it was our day to beat the odds.'

Left: A C-130 Hercules completes a supply drop. The cargo is being pulled out of the hold by parachute. Above: As explosions rock the earth around it, a transport prepares to take off – a plane could be turned around in three minutes. Right: One that didn't make it.

Top: Marines and pallets of cargo spill from a US Air Force C-123 Provider. Above: GIs work to extinguish the flames of a blazing C-130 hit by smallarms and mortar fire. Three of its five-man crew were killed. Left: The burnt-out hull of a helicopter bears mute testimony to the bravery of the men involved in the re-supply operation.

Soon the risks to the valuable C-130s led to their being limited to cargo delivery by parachute or the Low Altitude Parachute Extraction System (LAPES). Using LAPES, the C-130 would fly down the runway at just five feet and 130 knots. Trailing from the open unloading door would be a parachute reefed to a diameter of 48 inches. As the runway approached, the reefing line would be broken and the parachute would open to its full diameter of 28ft, dragging the load out of the aircraft and onto the runway. Care had to be taken though. One load master cut loose a faulty parachute, only to see the load fall out of the door, slide 1500yds, hit a bunker and kill a Marine.

Some aircrews paid the price for their dedication. Three C-123s and two C-130s were lost during the siege. One of the Hercules was a Marine KC-130, carrying fuel bladders, which caught fire and crashed on approach. The other downed C-130 belonged to Sumner's unit. He remembers it like it was yesterday:

Reduced to air-drops

'One of my squadron's crews had a bad accident at Khe Sanh. They were attempting to make an aerial delivery of a load of canisters by parachute. Landing at the field had become so hazardous that it was decided to make only air deliveries. The idea was to fly down to within about 150 to 200ft and release the load onto the runway. Then the ground troops would retrieve the canisters during a lull in the enemy firing. This operation was successfully accomplished many times. There was a ground-controlled approach (GCA) unit at the field operated by the Marines that the pilots relied on as their eyes and ears to guide aircraft down to a minimum ceiling of 200ft. At this point, the pilot would decide whether to proceed with a safe landing, or level off and make an aerial delivery onto the runway if the place was hot with incoming.

'On the day of the accident, the pilot had a weather report in front of him that seemed to give the all-clear. But someone had goofed. In fact, the ceiling and visibility were zero. The crew descended via GCA towards the minimum but then flew right on into the ground without levelling off as they were supposed to. The aircraft hit hard, catching fire with all but one of the crew members perishing. The cockpit split apart right at the pilot's window. He just managed to get out through the opening even though he had a broken arm, dislocated shoulder and blood pouring from his cut face.

'He was lucky to be alive, as were most of us who flew at Khe Sanh. He was eventually returned to flying status and completed his combat tour. Why he hadn't levelled off at minimum no-one knows. He couldn't even recall passing through the 200ft ceiling. Fatigue may well have been a factor, even though the official investigation ruled it out. All of them in that C-130 had experienced yet another long, tough day – and I'm sure they were dog tired by the time they made that approach.'

When a Marine holds out for 77 days in one of the most God-forsaken places on earth, the last thing he wants is a relief force coming his way with the intention of rescuing him

It was 'not a relief in the sense of a rescue...but relief in the sense of re-opening ground contact and eliminating the enemy with mobile operations'. That's what the man himself, General William C. Westmoreland, said. And it was no bullshit. Two days before Operation Pegasus even began, the Marines in Khe Sanh had begun their first offensive action. Bravo Company were going out to extract a terrible revenge for the ambush on Lieutenant Jacques that had left those 25 men lying dead outside the wire for more than a month. Their unreclaimed bodies rotting right in front of the face of the Marines was the worst sort of canker on the Corps' cocksureness.

OPERATION PEGASUS

1968

Below: The Air Cavalry fly the flag on Hill Timothy as they set up a firebase on their way to Khe Sanh. At this point, the NVA made serious efforts to halt the relief forces.

Since those men had first gone down, the mood of the Bravo leathernecks had been dark. Over 50 of them had been killed and 135 wounded by incoming, but few of the survivors had even seen Mr Charles. The talk was they'd poison Marine morale if they weren't allowed to settle the score.

For a whole month, the action had been planned down to the last detail. A moving double box of artillery, mortar and fighter support would protect the Marines every inch of the way to the target. At 0800 on 30 March, the men of Bravo Company climbed out of their bunkers and moved forward under cover of a thick fog. Just 75m ahead of them and to both sides, volleys of artillery shells threw up a rolling tidal wave of red earth. Four 106mm recoilless rifles poured fire onto the NVA's positions. The Marines fixed bayonets.

As they approached the enemy's bunker line,

the rolling artillery fire stopped, forming a curtain to cut the NVA off from reinforcements. But then the Marines' luck faltered. The fog lifted and enemy mortar fire began pouring in. One of the first rounds hit the command group, killing the radio man and the forward observers. Captain Pipes took a fragment which lodged in his chest two inches from his heart. It would take more than that to put him down though. Still standing, he urged his men forward.

The Marines were as mad as hell

Bravo Marines swarmed into the enemy trenches, pinning down the defenders with automatic fire while others fried them with flame throwers, grenades and satchel charges. The slaughter went on for three hours until the NVA trenches became a smoking tomb for 115 enemy dead. The dead Marines of the lost patrol were recovered – their wallets, watches, rings and dog tags still in place – and the honour of the Corps had been vindicated in battle.

But that did not mean they were not still sore. The Marines were as mad as hell. They'd never wanted to defend Khe Sanh in the first place, then they'd been criticized for not doing it right. Westmoreland had used it as an excuse to put an Army general in control of the Corps and put their air wing under Air Force command. And now, when the enemy had been squelched into the mud, some goddamn mythical flying horse was supposed to come and rescue them.

At every planning meeting for Pegasus, Marine Commander General Robert E. Cushman Jr made his position clear: 'I want no implication of a rescue or breaking the siege by outside forces.'

But Army officers had been shocked by the Marines' leadership and tactics. Westy's new army commander, Lieutenant-General William B. Rosson, generously suggested that the Marines had not prepared their troops sufficiently for this kind of war.

Rats, rubble and rubbish

Lieutenant-General John J. Tolson, the 1st Air Cav's commander, who flew into the beleaguered base to discuss Pegasus, was a little more forthright about the Marines and their morale. He said Khe Sanh was 'the most depressing and demoralizing place I have ever visited. It was a very distressing sight, completely unpoliced, strewn with rubble, duds and damaged equipment, and with troops living a life more similar to rats than human beings.'

Everybody knew what was going to happen next. The US Marine Corps was going to be humiliated in front of the world.

On 1 April, when the 1st Air Cav made their much-publicized leap-frog to new landing zones halfway down Route 9, it was a charade. General Tolson knew there would be no resistance. He had read the intelligence reports. There were no NVA there, but there were plenty of cameramen and reporters.

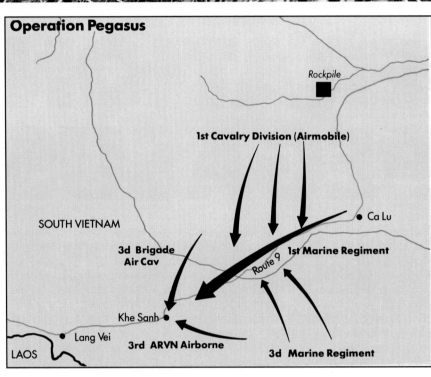

Operation Pegasus

Once the photocall was over, the Air Cav trundled calmly on down the road. Army, Navy and Marine engineer units went ahead to make repairs. They reconstructed over three miles of road, rebuilt four bridges and constructed 12 by-passes.

That is not to say the advance down Route 9 went entirely unopposed. As the Air Cav leapfrogged nearer to Khe Sanh, landing zones came under artillery and rocket fire. The NVA tried to retake the strategic Hill 471, only to be cut down by a tremendous artillery barrage and air support. They held the 2d Battalion of the 7th Cavalry for a day, and staged a final action at an old French fort halfway between the besieged base and the village of Khe Sanh. Fresh troops were brought in and resistance crumbled. General Tolson could hardly wait to put his division to more useful work.

Brave smiles from the Marines

When the Air Cav reached the village of Khe Sanh itself, they found rubble, bodies and craters the size of houses. The coffee plantations on the rolling green hills outside had been pounded into orangy-red moon dust. Before the siege, the Khe Sanh area had been described as a beautiful haven where the forests were full of game and the streams full of trout. Now there were no trees, no game, no trout and no streams. Khe Sanh had become a moonscape.

On 8 April, the Air Cav completed their sweep of Route 9 and met up with Marines from the besieged base. The leathernecks put on brave smiles for the TV cameras, but most shrugged indifferently. And, to add insult to the Marines' injury,

HILL TIMOTHY

'Helicopters of all shapes and sizes were buzzing around when I arrived at "Stud", the main landing zone along Route 9 in the A Shau Valley. I was there with Larry Burrows, the *LIFE* magazine photographer, and through his good contacts we got attached to the 2d Battalion of the 7th Air Cav.

Larry and myself took off in a command helicopter in order to be among the first to land on Hill Timothy. The area had been shelled and strafed prior to our landing, but a gentle breeze blowing through the elephant grass lent a tranquil air to the place – until I looked out over the hills and saw the destruction caused by constant bombing and artillery.

'We flew back to Stud that night, but returned the following morning. We learned that the adjoining hill, "Tom", had been hit and everywhere we looked we saw men dig-ging in. Larry and myself dug a hole near the command bunker. Giant flying cranes were bringing in 155mm artillery pieces and radar equipment was being erected on some high ground. It was early evening and, in true Air Cav tradition, hot food had been flown in.

'It was while I was filling my mess tin that the first rocket came in. The incoming continued throughout the night, with our arty returning the compliment. Dawn was damp and misty as the helicopters came in to evacuate the wounded. Larry and I dug deeper – heavy casualties on a hill below us meant we were not able to continue our journey towards Khe Sanh. The noise of incoming and outgoing continued through the night, with the wounded and body bags being medevaced out at first light.

'Later that morning we took off for Hill 471, with the Khe Sanh combat base looming in the distance. The perimeter fence was only yards from the crest of the hill, and NVA bodies lay all around. The Cav's first job was cover the bodies with earth to keep the smell from rising. We were also supposed to dig new holes. I started, but immediately stopped when my spade hit a dead body.

'After a quiet night, men began warming their breakfast on heat blocks while a patrol moved off in the direction of Khe Sanh town. Waiting for pick-up, I sat talking to a sergeant while watching a B-52 strike in the distance. It was from him that I learned of Martin Luther King's assassination. He'd heard it on his portable radio and remarked "there's nowhere safe in this fucking world".'

Terry Fincher – combat photographer, Operation Pegasus.

Opposite page above: More reinforcements arrive at Hill Timothy, ready to take over the fight against the NVA forces blocking Operation Pegasus. Opposite page below: Looking towards the base at Khe Sanh from Hill Timothy. Above left: War photographers at the front – Terry Fincher (left) and Larry Burrows (right) after a night under fire.

RELIEVING KHE SANH

The move to relieve Khe Sanh began at 0800 hours on 1 April 1968. Codenamed Pegasus, it involved men of the 2d Battalion, 1st Marines, and the 2d Battalion 3d Marines, advancing along both sides of Route 9 to the west of Ca Lu. Meanwhile, troopers of the 1st Air Cav conducted heliborne assaults to clear the surrounding hills. In line with normal policy, artillery and air support was lavish.

At first, the operation ran surprisingly smoothly. Late on 1 April, the 3d Brigade of the Air Cav conducted a set-piece airmobile assault to occupy LZs to the north and south of Route 9, about half way between Ca Lu and Khe Sanh. At the same time, Marines pushed forward on the ground, clearing the road for repair gangs of engineers and Seabees who followed.

After a brief period of consolidation, the 2d Brigade repeated the process, setting up further LZs even closer to the embattled base. On 4 April, men of the 1st Battalion, 9th Marines, were able to take Hill 471, overlooking the Khe Sanh valley. At first, it appeared that the NVA had just melted away.

However, on 5 April, elements of the NVA 66th Regiment tried to recapture Hill 471 and were repulsed only after a pitched battle with the Marines, the latter having to take full advantage of their air and artillery support. Similar contacts were made on 6 April by men of the 5th Cavalry south of Khe Sanh – this position was taken by the unit's 2d Battalion after a solid day's fighting. On the 8th, an ARVN unit further south had to fight hard to survive. By then, however, contact with the Khe Sanh defenders had been re-established and, as the engineers cleared the road to the base, the siege was at last lifted.

A UNITED MILITARY FRONT?

Did the siege of Khe Sanh reveal deficiencies in the American chain of military command?

The apparent significance of the battle around Khe Sanh placed the American command system under strain in both Vietnam and Washington. On 9 February, Westmoreland's deputy, Creighton Abrams, was dispatched hurriedly north to Phu Bai to establish MACV Forward. This body was given responsibility for co-ordinating both the relief operation and the battle for Hue. On 10 March, MACV Forward was replaced by Provisional Corps Vietnam (later XXIV Corps) under Lieutenant General William B. Rosson, and Abrams returned to Saigon.

But the conduct of the siege had brought great dissatisfaction with the present command arrangements to the surface. Concerning the co-ordination of air support, Westmoreland wanted the tactical direction of all Air Force and Marine aviation elements vested in the 7th Air Force commander, General William Momyer – reporting directly to MACV. Yet the III Marine Amphibious Force was determined to retain full control of its own air wing over Khe Sanh and took its objections all the way to the Joint Chiefs of Staff in Washington. The JCS supported Westmoreland, however, and Momyer was given nominal control over fixed-wing missions on 8 March (though this was not fully implemented until 1 April). In turn, the JCS was subjected to enormous pressure from President Johnson, who was haunted by the spectre of Dien Bien Phu.

Johnson had a model of Khe Sanh constructed in the White House basement and demanded daily reports in minute detail from the JCS and from Westmoreland, the latter being forced to sleep in his Combat Operations Center for almost two months. Johnson even went so far as to demand an unprecedented declaration – 'signed in blood' – from the entire JCS that Khe Sanh would be held.

In the aftermath of Khe Sanh, the US military congratulated itself on having held onto this isolated outpost. By April 1968, no-one doubted that NVA forces in the northern provinces had been badly mauled. But Khe Sanh was not hailed as a major victory in the United States. General Giap's army may have lost heavily, but he had exposed the underlying fragility of American firepower. Ultimately, US public opinion would see Khe Sanh as a victory for the communists.

it was the lead elements of an ARVN airborne battalion which finally reached Khe Sanh in company force.

By then they did not even need relieving. On 9 April the incoming stopped. And a week later, the NVA up in the hills decided to call it a day and the siege was over.

Under New Management

But worse was still to come for the Marines. Soon plucky young troopers from the Air Cav were nailing up signs on the Marines' bunkers saying: 'Khe Sanh – Under New Management, Delta CO 2/7 Cav.'

Then, two months later, the Marine garrison at Khe Sanh was demolished and its ammunition and stores were moved back to the now secure

Left: An Air Cav trooper prepares to go into action during Operation Pegasus, festooned with M60 ammunition and grimly contemplating the fighting to come. Right: The real end at Khe Sanh. The base is destroyed in June as the last grunts are pulled out, leaving the US public to wonder just why so many lives had been put at risk during the 77-day siege.

Route 9 – the line the Marines' had wanted to hold in the first place. It was left to the Five o'Clock Follies in Saigon to explain to the press why, if Khe Sanh had been so damn vital, it was now being abandoned.

But General Westmoreland could stand on the White House lawn in Washington and proudly proclaim: Victory at Khe Sanh. It was to be his last great battle. Two months later, he was rotated home.

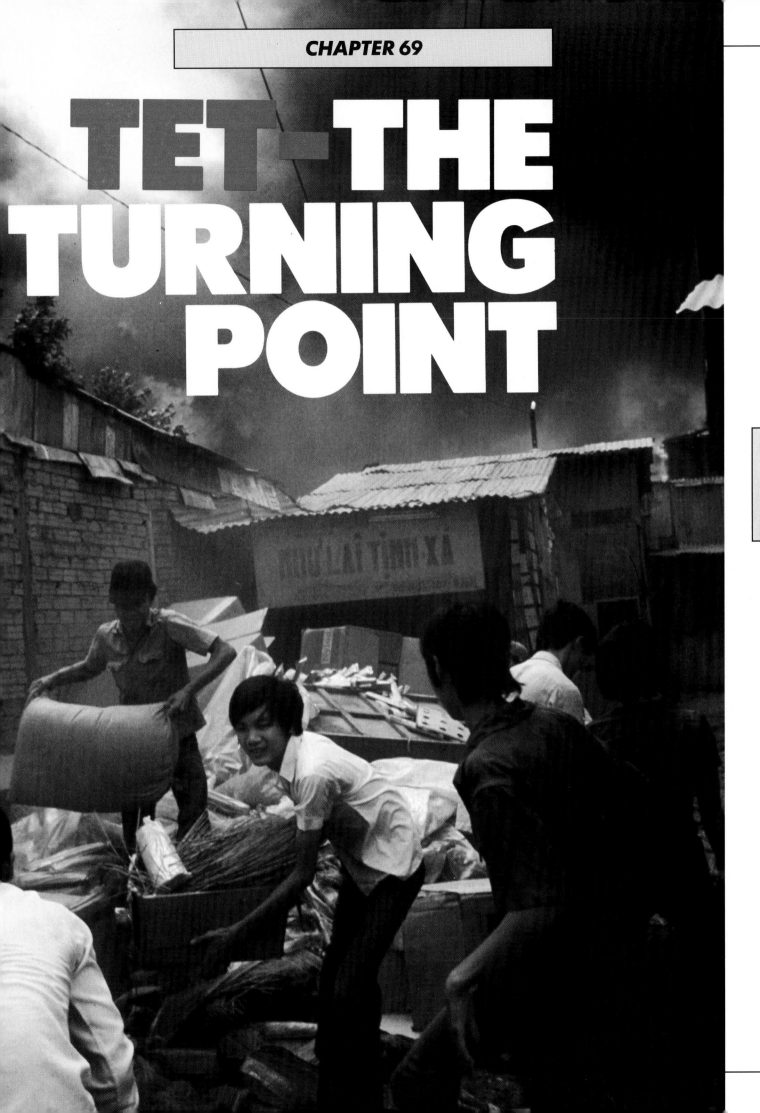

TET—THE TURNING POINT

1968

By January 1968 the Americans had been in-country for almost three years, so why was Tet such a stunning surprise?

Previous page: Saving possessions from the fires that rage around Saigon. Below: A dead VC sniper is hauled from a building in the Cholon district. Below right: ARVN soldiers rest in the aftermath of battle.

Things at 'Foggy Bottom' were usually quiet during Tet. At the lunar new year the people in Vietnam would stop fighting and start partying with their family and friends, and things on the Southeast Asia desk in the basement of the State Department in Washington, DC, would slow to a crawl.

Most of the guys would take off skiing in Vermont and New Hampshire and only a skeleton staff would be left on the desk. To the Vietnamese on both sides of the DMZ, Tet was a time of temporary peace, usually marked by a ceasefire that was scrupulously observed. So State Department stringers in-country would have little but a good hangover to report. 1968 seemed no different. As the holiday approached in late January, the communist-run NLF in the South announced the

usual ceasefire, the Saigon government did the same and the country looked forward to the celebrations. So the desk ran down its operations as usual.

But things were not as they seemed. Around six months earlier, Foggy Bottom had begun to receive intelligence reports hinting that Hanoi was planning a major military offensive inside South Vietnam. But although they may have suspected that large-scale surprise attacks would be launched the information was far too sketchy.

In any case, this soft intelligence was blitzed out on 21 January by the hard news that NVA main-force divisions had laid siege to Khe Sanh. On the desk, some suspected that this might be a ploy to get Westmoreland to concentrate his attention – and his reserves – on the northern border. And Westy, of course, obliged. He seemed convinced in his own mind that Khe Sanh was the beginning of a major NVA attempt to breach the US-held perimeter. This didn't mean that he ignored the possibility of attacks elsewhere.

Too little too late

For weeks, the desk had been monitoring US Military Intelligence reports on a build-up of communist strength. The army had even captured documents giving details of a forthcoming offensive. But nothing coming across the desk in Foggy Bottom indicated its scope, motive or precise date.

Then it happened. Around the time the day

team were heading home, they got reports of sporadic fighting. Before dawn on 30 January Vietnamese time, communist soldiers, mixing with the peasants coming into Ban Me Thuot, Kontum, Hoi An, Da Nang, Qui Nhon and Pleiku started attacking government buildings and military posts with mortars, rockets and small-arms fire. Westmoreland responded by placing all US forces in the South on full alert. He warned President Thieu of the danger and Thieu agreed to cancel ARVN leave – though how he intended to get his troops away from the Tet festivities and back into barracks he did not specify.

At first these attacks seemed like they might be the suspected offensive and they lulled the Army

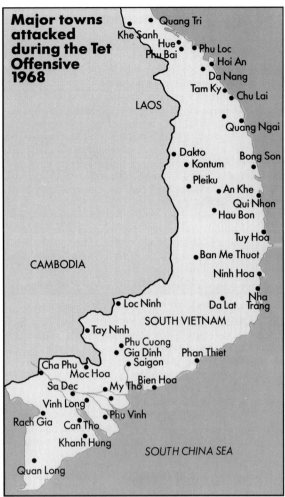

Major towns attacked during the Tet Offensive 1968

Quang Tri
Khe Sanh
Hue
Phu Bai
Phu Loc
Hoi An
Da Nang
Tam Ky
Chu Lai
LAOS
Quang Ngai
Dakto
Kontum
Bong Son
Pleiku
An Khe
Qui Nhon
Hau Bon
Tuy Hoa
CAMBODIA
Ban Me Thuot
Ninh Hoa
Da Lat
Nha Trang
Loc Ninh
SOUTH VIETNAM
Tay Ninh
Phu Cuong
Gia Dinh
Phan Thiet
Cha Phu
Saigon
Moc Hoa
Bien Hoa
Sa Dec
My Tho
Vinh Long
Phu Vinh
Rach Gia
Can Tho
Khanh Hung
SOUTH CHINA SEA
Quan Long

into a false sense of security. After all, the attacks were hardly overwhelming. Most of the infiltrators had been rounded up or killed by late on the 30th and it was a relief to realize that the feared offensive could be so easily contained. After a long night, some of the guys on the desk went home.

An explosion of violence

No sooner had they got back to their Georgetown brownstones or their suburban homesteads across the Potomac in Virginia than they were called back to the office. During the night of 30/31 January, towns the length and breadth of Vietnam had exploded into violence. The scale of the offensive was staggering. Telexes poured in. By 1 February, Saigon had been hit, along with 36 of 44 provincial capitals, five of six autonomous cities and 64 of 242 district capitals. More than 84,000 communist fighters had emerged, apparently from nowhere.

In Saigon, which until then had been spared the worst effects of the war, specially trained VC sappers, drawn from the locally raised C-10 City Battalion, stole taxis to approach key installations. They surprised sentries who were distracted by the firework displays celebrating Tet. At the ARVN Joint General Staff Command, Gate 5 was attacked with satchel charges and rockets at 0200 hours. Further assaults on Gate 4, carried

PLANNING AND SCOPE OF TET

The decision to mount an all-out military offensive against the South was taken by communist leaders in Hanoi as early as July 1967. In that month, senior North Vietnamese diplomats were recalled from around the world to attend a top-level conference, chaired by Ho Chi Minh and General Vo Nguyen Giap. It was decided to organize a series of simultaneous attacks inside South Vietnam. The intention was to put so much pressure on the ARVN that it – and the government of South Vietnam would collapse.

Preparations began immediately. Contact with the NLF in the South ensured that VC units were made available to carry out the attacks, and supplies and weapons started to move down the Ho Chi Minh Trail to ensure maximum impact. At the same time, an elaborate deception plan was put into effect.

NVA divisions marched against US firebases at Loc Ninh and Khe Sanh, creating an American preoccupation with border security and persuading Westmoreland to move forces away from the cities before the attacks took place. Diplomats and politicians in the North began to offer new terms for peace negotiations, diverting the attention of President Johnson at a crucial time.

Finally, the decision was taken to mount the offensive over the Tet (lunar new year) period in late January 1968 – a time when ARVN soldiers would be on holiday leave and the cities crammed with celebrating civilians, providing ideal cover for VC infiltrators.

By mid-January, up to 84,000 VC and NVA troops were moving into position, while NVA divisions laying siege to Khe Sanh diverted US attention. South Vietnam was about to explode into unprecedented violence.

1968

MOTIVES AND MACHINATIONS

There has been much debate regarding the motives of the Hanoi Politburo for launching the Tet Offensive, but how much do we really know?

In the years since the Tet Offensive, analysts and generals of all persuasions have given their account of the motives of the communist leadership. Western commentators seem to take it as axiomatic that the Hanoi Politburo aimed to influence US public opinion against the war – but Giap himself has claimed that this consideration had little effect on communist planning. There is a further point of debate as to whether Hanoi believed it was losing the war and felt it had to act quickly and decisively, or whether it was over-confident, and thought that a single stroke could give it complete victory.

We will almost certainly never have any definitive answers to these questions: the discussions of the Politburo are a closed book. Nevertheless, there are some considerations that were undoubtedly important. The first is that, although Tet and Khe Sanh involved the risk of defeat (and of heavy losses), the possible gains were enormous. If either had succeeded – if Khe Sanh had fallen or the ARVN collapsed – then the war would have been won. And even in defeat, Tet could hold advantages for the future.

Merely by entering the cities in force, the VC and NVA would demonstrate to the population of South Vietnam the fragility of government control. The fact that there was selective assassination of government officials in Hue reinforces the interpretation that Tet served as a powerful warning to the South Vietnamese people of where the power really lay. The possibility of affecting US public opinion must obviously have been discussed by Hanoi; but it was really the opinion of the people in the South that counted.

Finally, there are often claims that a 'failure' in Tet, resulting in heavy casualties among VC cadres, might well suit Hanoi's plans, in that a potentially independent, and perhaps difficult to manage, southern-based force would have been eliminated. But again, whether this was an important motive will never be known for sure.

Left: General Giap listens intently as two of his field commanders brief him on the latest preparations for the Tet Offensive. Giap had already given notice of his intention to bleed the US dry in a war of attrition, but the sheer scale of Tet was an indication that he was prepared to take the war into a new phase – in which attrition rates would be higher, and decisive victory for the communists possible. Bottom left: Members of the Viet Cong stand in proud pose shortly before the launch of Tet.

out by men of the VC 1st and 2nd Battalions, breached the defences. Similar attacks on the Independence Palace, the National Broadcasting Station, the Vietnamese Navy's headquarters and the Korean and Filipino embassies met with some success, adding to the confusion and stretching the city defences to the limits.

Death flashed across the ether

Then the US embassy in Thong Nhat Boulevard was hit! Two Marine sentries were killed and the rest of the Guard Detachment forced to retire behind the heavy doors of the main chancery building. American reinforcements were rushed in, but fighting continued throughout the night. By dawn, Saigon time, all 19 VC infiltrators had been killed or captured, which gave the guys at Foggy Bottom some cause for elation as they went off duty that evening.

But once they got home their elation soon turned to gloom as they watched the TV news. Far from applauding the speed and effectiveness of the response, newscasters were deeply shocked by the apparent ease with which the enemy had penetrated to the heart of Saigon. All the assurances of eventual victory evaporated as images of death and destruction filled their TV screens.

Saigon districts in VC hands

Back on the desk they were getting reports that, by dawn on 31 January, most of western and southern Saigon, including the whole of the Cholon district, was in VC hands, and reports of attacks on Long Binh, Bien Hoa and even the international airport at Tan Son Nhut were being received. And although ARVN and US counterattacks succeeded in restoring control, often in a matter of hours, the guys at Foggy Bottom knew this was no longer relevant. It was the images on the TV screens of America that counted. These ranged from airstrikes on areas of Saigon to the summary execution of a captured VC by South Vietnam's police chief.

Incoming intelligence reports said that the situation was no different in areas beyond Saigon. Although NVA and VC attacks on towns throughout the country were contained, the fighting was severe and the levels of destruction high.

Nowhere was this more apparent than in Hue, the old imperial capital of Vietnam. ARVN defenders were overwhelmed, and Marine reinforcements entered a nightmare of urban fighting, suffering heavy casualties as they advanced, house by house. Pinned down beneath the walls of the Citadel, it was to take them until 25 February to re-occupy the city. By then it had virtually ceased to exist. Airstrikes had destroyed the historic buildings and the population had been forced to flee.

The attacks all followed the same basic pattern: behind a screen of mortar bombs, VC sappers moved in to link up with cadres that had already infiltrated. This spearhead made at once for key centres – radio stations, barracks – while larger

forces moved in later. Well coordinated, these attacks often left the VC deeply entrenched, and hard to dig out.

By early March, action at the Southeast Asia desk had slowed. The last of the towns had been cleared of enemy troops. The Pentagon was elated. In purely military terms, no-one doubted that the allies had inflicted enormous casualties. As early as February, Westmoreland had been claiming 37,000 communist dead and the final figure may have been as high as 50,000. But over 2000 US and some 11,000 ARVN had been killed, thousands of refugees had been added to the seemingly endless list of civilian misery, and the devastation of cities and towns had been enormous.

In spite of Westmoreland's claim that the VC had been severely hurt by the offensive, the communist forces were ready to strike again by the summer, in a second wave of attacks known as 'mini-Tet'. While smaller in scope than the January offensive, mini-Tet demonstrated yet again that after three years of US involvement, the towns of South Vietnam were still vulnerable to the communist.

Any debate about victors and vanquished in the aftermath of Tet cannot obscure this essential point. After years of confident oratory from Johnson and Westmoreland, Tet was irrefutable evidence that the war was far from being won. Within a year, the US political and military leadership would change radically, and with these new leaders came a new approach to the war. Tet had been the turning point.

Right top: Sheltering behind a pile of rubble, Viet Cong prepare to attack. Right centre: As fires rage an armoured personnel carrier inches through Saigon's devastated streets. Below: Tet was a severe shock to the Americans, who had believed that the communists were incapable of mounting such a blow. Even so, the Stars and Stripes continued to fly — for the time being at least.

BATTLE FOR SAIGON

The allies had to fight like demons when VC suicide squads hit Saigon

Left: An ARVN soldier dashes for shelter. Below: The dead bodies of three American GIs. Their Vietnamese drivers had turned traitor, leaving the US troops to their grisly fate.

When the Viet Cong broke cover and attacked, everyone thought that the gunfire was just the sound of bangers being let off, fireworks to celebrate the Year of the Monkey. But the fact that the noise went on so long persuaded us that there really was fighting in the streets. At first nobody imagined that it was possible. Not here, right inside the capital. Then, once the sound of smallarms became unmistakable, everyone thought it was a palace coup. It was Ky finally moving against President Thieu. But we were wrong again. (In fact, as it turned out, Thieu was not even in Saigon but in My Tho, about 60 kilometres away.)

In 1968, I was back in Saigon. I had been back for two years now, after working out in the provinces. I had been a civilian administrator for the Saigon government, first in Ben Tre, then in Bien Hoa.

It was the end of January and we were looking forward to celebrating Tet, the Vietnamese New Year. The war seemed very distant. Everyone was war-weary and almost all the soldiers were on leave.

Tet falls at the nicest time of the year, during our winter, which means that the weather is very cool and mild. Tet is a special time, a bit like your Christmas. Everything is closed, no-one goes to work, families get together and everyone is very generous. All we thought of was escaping from the wretched war. Everywhere there was a holiday mood. At the time there had been talk about palace plots being hatched by Ky, President Thieu's deputy, and all sorts of rumours about a possible coup d'etat. But all grudges are traditionally laid aside during Tet; fights are abandoned and the usual endless conspiracies are absent from conversations. But when the fighting broke out, the rumours sprang to mind instantly.

Smuggled in coffins

What we did not know was that for months the Viet Cong had been infiltrating arm caches into the city. They came in dribs and drabs: rifles, machine guns, grenades, explosives and ammunition. Some weapons had even been smuggled into Saigon inside coffins. And then the unarmed fighters had entered the town, and filled up the hotels. And waited. People travel from town to

1968

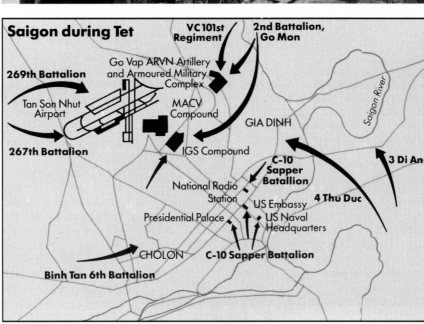

Saigon during Tet

- VC 101st Regiment
- 2nd Battalion, Go Mon
- 269th Battalion
- Go Vap ARVN Artillery and Armoured Military Complex
- Tan Son Nhut Airport
- MACV Compound
- GIA DINH
- Saigon River
- 267th Battalion
- IGS Compound
- C-10 Sapper Batallion
- 3 Di An
- National Radio Station
- US Embassy
- 4 Thu Duc
- Presidential Palace
- US Naval Headquarters
- CHOLON
- C-10 Sapper Battalion
- Binh Tan 6th Battalion

The planning and preparation for the Tet Offensive went back many months – to July 1967. Giap had decided to put American resilience to the test and, throughout the length and breadth of South Vietnam, Viet Cong guerrillas began to sharpen their combat edge (left). For Giap, whether Saigon fell or was held by the Americans was immaterial in the short term. Either way, the offensive would demonstrate Hanoi's belief that the communists, and not the US, would be the eventual victors.

1968

town for Tet, staying near their family for the holiday. So no-one thought it strange that the hotels were filled with people from the countryside.

So it was that in the early hours of 31 January the Viet Cong hit their first target, the Presidential Palace. They then struck at all the other main public buildings, including the radio station. They hijacked cars to get themselves around town. They even attacked the American embassy later that same morning, just before three o'clock.

I had been playing poker with friends until two in the morning, quite unaware of what was about to take place. I even drove home right past National Broadcasting Station.

There was no warning

All over the country, similar attacks were taking place in every major city. In Saigon itself they even managed to sweep into the Chinese quarter of Cholon before the government forces counter-attacked.

The six-storey embassy building that towered over much of central Saigon had been a constant reminder of the US presence, and a symbol of its prestige and power. The Americans felt so safe on this little patch of US soil more than 10,000 miles from home that they only had a handful of Marines on guard.

There was no warning. A sapper squad of 19 Viet Cong blasted its way through the outer wall and was all set to storm into the building itself, armed with mortars and grenades.

But the Viet Cong only managed to get as far as the compound before their leaders were all gunned down by the guards. With their commanders gone, the other guerrillas wandered aimlessly around the embassy grounds until they were forced to take cover when the US reinforcements arrived. It was that close.

A picture of hell

But it still took six hours for the Marines to win back total control of the compound. The scene afterwards was like a picture of hell. Embassy staff, covered in blood, were being treated by doctors. Humble clerks had changed their pens for guns. There were dead bodies everywhere – some American, but mostly Viet Cong. They lay in heaps on the lawn, staining the green grass red with their blood. They were draped across the concrete flowerpots, among the peaceful palms. Chunks of stone and concrete were strewn about, and the once beautiful white walls of the embassy were now full of bullet holes. You could read the shock on the American faces. Their haven of peace had been violated. For the first couple of days, the US troops were ordered to stay in their barracks, but when they were finally asked to intervene, they moved in with a vengeance. For the first time the Americans armed government troops with M16 automatic rifles. Then they used all their terrible firepower to win back ground seized by the Viet Cong. Wherever there were concentrations of

THE SOUTH WINS THROUGH

Viet Cong leaders had promised their men victory, beginning with the toppling of the South Vietnamese government. But Thieu was not dislodged from power and the ARVN fought like demons. Why?

Two of the objectives of the Tet Offensive had been to encourage a popular rising against the South Vietnamese government and to bring about its collapse. The scale of the communist effort, it was hoped, would weaken government at both local and national levels, while the ARVN would be subjected to such intense military pressure that it would disintegrate under the strain. However, the anticipated popular rising did not occur and both the ARVN and the Saigon government survived the challenge.

In part, their survival can be attributed to the fact that VC and NVA strength was too diluted. While assaults on five autonomous cities, 36 provincial capitals and 64 district capitals were impressive evidence of the communists' ability to strike at will throughout the South, they actually weakened their ability to hold any territory gained. The communists were therefore speedily evicted from all but Saigon and Hue. A more important factor in the Southern government's survival, however, was the brutality with which the communists imposed their temporary control. Although many of the estimated 14,000 civilians killed, 24,000 wounded and 800,000 homeless were obviously victims of the US and ARVN response to Tet, VC and NVA atrocities and terrorism won Hanoi few converts among the South Vietnamese people. There was also general outrage at the violation of such a special and significant occasion as Tet, while ARVN troops were seemingly galvanised by the reality of fighting in defence of their own homes. Certainly, not only was the Thieu government now confident enough of its own people to introduce a bill for general mobilisation – implemented on 19 June – but the ARVN was also swollen by a substantial increase in voluntary enlistment. It did not necessarily mean that Tet had made the South Vietnamese love their government more, but it did suggest that they preferred President Thieu to Ho Chi Minh.

guerrillas, the Marines just levelled the place.

The Viet Cong had been hoping for a public uprising in support of their action. But they did not realize that people were afraid of them. And they also did not expect the Americans simply to blast everything, right in the middle of the city. It was the first time that anyone had seen helicopters hovering over the roofs of the city, firing rockets right into rows of houses. If anything worked against the Viet Cong, it was these helicopters armed with rockets. Whole streets were set ablaze and many civilians were killed alongside the Viet Cong.

It was not only civilians who were killed by the Americans. A school filled with government soldiers was mistakenly attacked by US helicopters and, although there was a scandal, nothing ever came of their deaths. I was told that there was a lot of indiscriminate killing going on.

No longer safe

While the fighting raged, whole areas of Saigon were cordoned off. The Americans would think nothing of sending in a recoilless rifle mounted on a jeep and firing rounds straight into houses where the Viet Cong were holding out. A fire would start and blaze away for half a street. These were people's homes, where they lived, but all that was left were burnt-out hulks.

These people had nowhere to go. They put up makeshift shelters, made little shacks out of packing cases, or went into big drainage pipes left above ground. Somehow a sort of shanty town

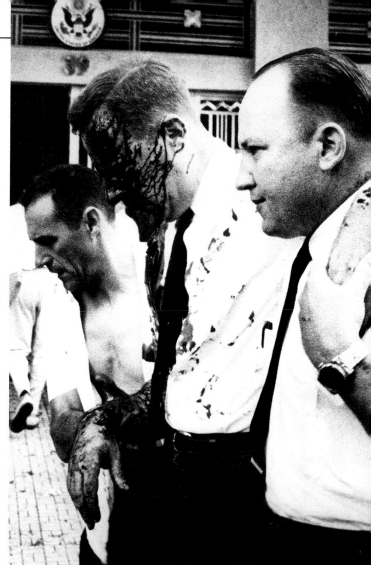

The aftermath. Far left: Felled only yards short of the embassy building itself, a VC guerrilla lies dead in a tangled mass of shrubs. Right: Visibly shocked by the extent of his wounds and the fact that US soil has been violated, an embassy official is led out of the building. Below: Marines and Military Police had regained control of the compound, but at what cost to US morale?

grew up, peopled by thousands of innocent victims that had been caught up in the fighting.

Throughout the fighting there was a curfew, imposed by the Military Police. People stayed well out of sight and out of the cross-fire. The war had well and truly come to Saigon, a place where life had seemed relatively peaceful. Before, the war had been fought out in the countryside and, though everyone knew someone who was fighting, life in the capital had seemed safe.

I was staying in the Gia Dinh district at the time and had planned to return to Ben Tre just before the attack. But my travelling companion changed his mind at the last minute and so we stayed in Saigon. It was just as well as it turned out because Ben Tre was heavily attacked and it was two weeks before anyone there could move again. The market was totally destroyed and a new one had to be built.

The hoped-for mass desertion from the ranks of the ARVN failed to appear, and the civilian population refused to take to the streets in support of the offensive. Instead, the army regrouped and fought back alongside the Americans, gradually gaining ground around Saigon and the other cities. The massive firepower wore down the isolated pockets of resistance, though at great cost to both sides.

Death lists and mass graves

In the ancient capital of Hue in the north, when the nationalist forces regained the Citadel, they found mass graves of government supporters who had been killed by the Viet Cong. They must have been on death lists, or perhaps some old scores had been settled. But in other provincial towns, as much destruction had been caused by rooting out the Viet Cong as by the Viet Cong themselves. According to a US spokesman: 'It became necessary to destroy the town [Ben Tre] in order to save it.'

After it was clear that the nationalist forces had won, there was elation in the air. The North would never win now. The government had fought instead of throwing down its weapons, and once again the Americans had been solid allies. Their military might had saved the day. The Viet Cong had thrown in everything they had, and had still lost. Their strength was sapped, their weapons

Left: Two ARVN soldiers, a Marine and a trooper, display a mixture of pain and anger during the clearing of communist forces from the outskirts of Saigon. Bottom left: Even when the whirlwind of violence had subsided, troops had to be on the alert for snipers concealed in windows high above the streets. Above right: Surrounded by dead VC, ARVN soldiers reflect on a battle that they believed had ended in complete failure for the communists.

gone, their main units destroyed, their organization in ruins.

It had been a military victory for the government and its major ally. The South Vietnamese felt proud of their army and the way it had stood the test of battle. But although it was seen as a victory by the South Vietnamese people, the US public thought differently. They had seen their own embassy penetrated, and that was something they could never forget.

Below: Fires rage in Cholon as the ARVN continues its efforts to flush out remaining VC from the Chinese district of Saigon.

THE ALLIED REACTION

At the beginning of Saigon's 48-hour truce at 1800 on 29 January, many ARVN personnel had gone on leave and were beyond recall when communist attacks began the next day. Although American troops were not on leave, MACV had transferred responsibility for Saigon's security to the South Vietnamese, and, apart from the United States Marine Corps, Saigon Guard Detachment, the only major US unit in the capital was the Military Police 716th Battalion.

The ARVN presence was mainly limited to the 5th Ranger Group, although two airborne battalions were fortuitously nearby – transportation difficulties had delayed their departure north to I Corps Tactical Zone. Nevertheless, there was considerable panic when VC attacks erupted in the early hours of 31 January. One American officer, plotting the assaults on a map in MACV headquarters in Saigon itself, likened them to a pin-ball machine suddenly lighting up.

MACV hastily assembled a scratch, 'MACV Tigers' defence company, while Americans trapped in other parts of the city holed up and fired at anything that moved, including hapless military policemen summoned to their rescue. So few staff could reach MACV that many of its functions were assumed by US Army Vietnam (USARV) at Long Binh.

A ruling that key personnel had to billet close to Tan Son Nhut airbase enabled Air Force headquarters to function, but the fighting prevented any aircraft taking off from Bien Hoa for 48 hours. Despite the confusion, not least among reporters outside the US embassy, the Americans had five battalions in Saigon by the evening of the 31st, and the ARVN 15 battalions by 3 February.

ESCAPING THE WAR

1968

If you didn't want to go to the Nam, there were two possible alternatives. Either try to wangle a deferment, or skip across the border and begin the life of an exile

EYE-WITNESS

The author, David Vandivier (above left, with his father), was due for call up in 1969 but avoided the draft. He now works as a freelance writer.

Left: At a 1968 Democratic party gathering, two anti-war protesters make contrasting gestures; a defiant fist and a peace sign. By this time the draft avoidance movement was digging in its heels. Right: Singing songs around a pile of burning draft files, Milwaukee anti-war protesters make a graphic anti-draft statement. Fourteen arrests followed.

One night in 1968, my dad came into the room my brothers and I shared and sat down on a bed. He had been drinking. We were leaning out the window of our tenement block in Spanish Harlem, smoking a joint and listening to *Sergeant Pepper's*. The old man pulled the plug on the record player. 'We're leaving the country,' he said. John, my elder brother, had been sent his draft notification and in less than a year my ass would be on the line also. 'I haven't raised you boys in this shithole to get your asses shot off eight thousand miles away. You'd better start saying your goodbyes.' He pushed the plug back into the socket and the record player started up again – 'She's Leaving Home'. Holy shit, talk about: 'We sacrificed most of our lives.'

My father was a Hoosier, a shit kicker from Indiana. He was a World War II veteran and a blue collar worker – not exactly the stuff pinko pacifists are made of. But he knew the war was wrong. He was one of Patton's men and thought we had no business stirring up shit in other people's countries.

On the way home from the war he'd met my mother in New York. She was Polish and lived in the block where I'd been raised the whole of her life. He quit the plains of the Midwest and moved into the Bronx.

No love in the heart of the city

He worked as an elevator mechanic and drank hard. He was a good man, looked after his family. In 1967 he had finally bought himself a little piece of land out in the Catskills. Now, because of the war, he was selling up and moving to Canada.

The summer of 1968 was not a good time to be living in New York City. In the Bronx where I lived, all hell was breaking loose. The race riots in Harlem had come up as far as 139th street and my family lived on 155th street. Some nights I'd go to bed to the sound of gun shots and car gas tanks exploding. It was one hell of a lullaby.

The Vietnam war had switched into high gear. Kids from the neighbourhood were disappearing wholesale, reappearing six weeks later with a funny haircut and a uniform. Six weeks basic training at Fort Dix in New Jersey, home for two weeks leave, then the chance of a lifetime – an all expenses paid trip to Southeast Asia, courtesy of Uncle Sam, with guns and ammunition provided in case you fancied skeet shooting.

The local draft board was taking everyone. If you had two arms, two legs and you were warm, you were Grade A soldier material. Up in the leafy suburbs like Scarsdale, kids were getting deferments – physical deferments, student deferments, any damn deferment money could buy. But down in my neighbourhood where everybody was on welfare or hiding from the man there weren't many deferments about. Uncle Sam was emptying out the ghettos like so many trash cans into the jungles of Vietnam.

As the summer cooled, the riots were over and life was settling back to what passed for normal in the Bronx. The mailman delivered a letter to our apartment. It made my brother an offer he couldn't refuse. Lyndon Baines Johnson, the mad Texas schoolteacher turned president, wanted him to come and play soldiers for the good old U.S. of A. John was being drafted.

My father made the arrangements. My brother and I said goodbye to our girlfriends. Then early one morning we all got in the car and headed for the North.

Over the Peace bridge

We crossed the border into Canada at the Peace bridge in Niagara Falls. It was a cold, October morning and the roar of the Falls and the wet spray made it look like a scene from a B movie. Even though I had just spent 14 hours in a car with four other adults, a dog and a cat, this was pretty impressive stuff. As I stood there in the mist, I couldn't help wondering: 'What the hell comes next?' I was 17 and leaving the only country I'd ever known.

A couple of hours up the road we decided this town looked as good as any. It was a little place called Guelph – population 60,000 – and it had a

1968

1968

AVOIDING THE DRAFT

Why, during the early stages of the Vietnam war, did the American public have little or no sympathy for the draft dodgers?

Attitudes to those who try, by fair means or foul, to avoid being drafted into war will vary according to the public's perception of the conflict. During World War II, for example, the allied countries believed their fight against Germany was *jus bellum*, conforming to the principles laid down by the theory of Just War. As a result of this, draft avoiders during this war were widely condemned.

During the early period of US commitment to Vietnam in the mid-1960s, the attitude of the American people was broadly similar. Draft avoidance was roundly criticized as unpatriotic or criminal. This was understandable for a generation that had grown up before or during World War II. Memories of total war and the sacrifices needed to fight it left little sympathy for 'pampered offspring' who seemed to delight in denigrating the establishment or belittling its efforts to defend the cause of freedom in Southeast Asia.

Contempt of draft dodgers was made even more apparent by the fact that the public at large displayed neither interest nor concern about the inherent inequalities of the draft system. The weighting of the system in favour of white, middle-class, educated Americans may not have been immediately apparent, but the systematic persecution of minority groups such as the Jehovah's Witnesses – many of whom were tried and imprisoned when they refused to recognize the draft laws – should have led to an outcry.

Such a passive acceptance of government policy began to falter after 1968, however, when public attitudes towards the war became more critical. Awkward questions began to be asked. Families, particularly from the more affluent sectors of society, began to help their sons to avoid military service. Various methods were used – paying for their son to continue his education beyond high school, exploiting the reports of medical or legal experts or by helping their offspring to escape beyond the borders of the US.

As the 1960s ended, and the public saw the US withdrawal getting under way, draft avoidance merged with demands for disengagement. It became more respectable; seen as a legitimate form of protest. Doctors and lawyers were more willing to issue certificates to ensure their client wasn't the last GI to die in Southeast Asia.

By the early 1970s, public opinion had shifted away from condemnation towards a more liberal attitude. The change in atmosphere was sufficient to allow President Ford to introduce his clemency programme less than 18 months after the end of the American commitment to Vietnam. By 1977, President Jimmy Carter was able to introduce a blanket amnesty for all draft offenders without causing a major public outcry. By that time most Americans just wanted to forget the Vietnam war and the divisions it had created in their society.

movie theatre. That was a big plus. All the time, I was thinking: 'Christ, here we are, a thousand miles from nowhere. No friends, no relatives, no jobs, not even a place to call home, all because we didn't want to go shoot someone in their own country who didn't do anything to us anyway.'

We booked into a motel. Every window overlooked a cemetery.

Lonely town

That first winter was one of the coldest that southern Ontario had in years. We left the motel after six weeks and moved into a house. Jobs were gotten and schools gone to, but I was still high on culture shock. I would be walking down the street and all of a sudden I would come over all dizzy. Here I was in small town Canada after being on the streets of New York all my life. There weren't any blacks or hispanics! Just a lotta people staring.

I did a lot of staring too, and a bit of fighting. If you were from New York City, the average Canunck figured you were pretty tough. But they didn't understand you could be bad without even lifting a finger. It scared a lot of people off at first. It was real lonely, like being in outer space. Both my brother and I got married real soon but my marriage did not last. I was just a kid.

On the outskirts of Guelph, there was a university and I started hanging out there a lot. It was a bit more cosmopolitan and there was a folk scene going with a bunch of hippies. And there were drugs.

The news wasn't good

I ran into quite a few Americans on the run from the draft. Most of the guys who had come up from the States were alone. They were scared and doing far too many drugs. Most had been cut off from their parents who branded them cowards and traitors.

Being so close to the border we got to watch American TV. Draft dodgers were always on the news and the news wasn't good. On the US side of

Left: Six American draft dodgers living in Stockholm are interviewed by an English TV team. Above right: For servicemen who failed to dodge the draft, desertion made an effective substitute. These four Marines disappeared on R&R in Tokyo and resurfaced in Moscow.

the border there was a computerized watch list. Most draft dodgers were on it and if you got caught going back, you went straight to the military prison. So there it was, fuck it, I couldn't go back.

Homesickness and harassment

I was in worst trouble. My brother had broken the military code by dodging the draft – but I had committed a serious Federal offence by not registering. The Royal Canadian Mounted Police warned me not even to go near the US embassy in case they tried to arrest me.

My father went back occasionally. He'd get drunk and homesick and would drive over the border, but even his family would not talk to him. And because he had Canadian plates he was marked. He would often be arrested on some trumped up charge. The local sheriff had lost a son in the Nam.

Nam in the living room

The Canadian people, with a few notable exceptions, never accepted us. And the TV brought the horrors of the war and the unrest at home into our lives daily, in living colour. Here we were, the ones that wouldn't go. Were we heroes or villains? In truth we were neither. In me and my brother's case, we were just plain scared – and angry. John and I proceeded to 'turn on and drop out'. But we couldn't tune in because I think that part of our heads was broken. Cut off from his friends, his

family and the country he'd fought for, my father drank himself into a dense fog.

As I understand it now, after all these years, we had not dodged the war at all. We had gone to our own Vietnam. We too were in an alien country separated from our country and everything we knew. We were strangers in a strange land. The difference was that people weren't shooting at us. Not real bullets, just bullshit.

Amnesty international

My brother got pardoned under Jimmy Carter's amnesty. My legal problems took longer to sort out. I can go back now, but I had to take Canadian citizenship. The Americans wouldn't give me a passport. The Statue of Liberty has an inscription that reads: 'Send me your tired and weary...your huddled masses...' Bullshit! I was born there, but I couldn't go back for over 10 years. I live in England now. This is the third country I have lived in and I don't feel I really belong in any of them.

My dad died about six years back of pneumonia, in Canada, and he's buried in the cemetery not 200yds from the motel where we spent our first nights. He always said the cold in Canada would kill him. It did, long and slow

He saved my life at the expense of his own. It was a high price to pay. Looking back I sometimes wonder whether it was all worth it. I think my father knew the answer to that one. I wish I did.

DRAFT AVOIDANCE

On 16 September 1974, President Gerald Ford signed an executive order establishing a clemency programme for all Vietnam-era draft offenders. According to figures compiled by the Departments of Defense and Justice, apparent draft dodgers (including deferments) numbered over 570,000, of whom 209,517 were actually accused of dodging by the government. Of those accused, 8750 were convicted of draft offences. The majority of the cases, however, were dropped under Ford's clemency programme.

Offenders ranged from men who had been arrested and imprisoned for their crimes, to those who had fled to countries such as Canada or Sweden and were still living in self-imposed exile. Included in these figures were those who had simply ignored the draft and, through bureaucratic mismanagement, had never been brought to justice.

When presented with the prospect of being drafted, the potential avoider had a number of options open to him. He could dodge or delay his registration with his local board, but this was unlikely to succeed on its own – there were just too many ways a man could be traced. More effective was to find some legitimate excuse for deferment or low draft grading, the most popular being marriage, education or health. Student deferments were common – anyone in full-time education beyond his registration date had his call-up delayed until completion of his course – but draft boards could monitor student progress, cancelling their decision to defer if marks were low. Medical deferments had a more permanent effect, and it was not unknown for potential avoiders to indulge in self-mutilation to ensure success. Religious belief was another possibility, leading to conscientious-objector status and deferment to non-combat duties. Jehovah's Witnesses and Black Muslims refused to serve at all, however, and 3250 conscientious objectors went to prison.

In the ruins of Hue, the Marines fought a desperate battle to regain the Old City

It was 31 January 1968 and Hue, the most important city in the northern provinces of South Vietnam, was fast asleep, caught in those small hours between the games of the night and the work of the day. The former capital of Annam was resting. Movement was restricted to the occasional cyclist wending his solitary way along the banks of the Perfume River, beneath the walls enclos-

FIGHTING FOR THE CITADEL

ing the Old City that housed the majority of the 100,000 population and countless more refugees. Suddenly the silence was brutally shattered as incoming mortar rounds ripped apart the delicate fabric of the night, and rockets tore gaping holes in the facades of the beautiful old French colonial houses. Wholesale death, in the form of the Tet Offensive, had begun to visit the Imperial City.

Above: The VC show the flag on top of Hue's ancient Citadel. Left: The Marines had to fight street by street to take back the city.

Hue was largely unprepared. Everyone had guessed that an offensive of some sort was coming. But no-one had expected its scale and intensity. The city had so far escaped large-scale fighting, despite being situated less than 50km south of the DMZ. The US military presence was minimal, restricted to a handful of advisors.

However, the small ARVN force that was in Hue that fateful morning was the elite 'Black Panther' company, assigned to Brigadier-General Ngo Quang Trong's 1st Division. They fought like demons, managing to slow the advance of the two NVA infantry battalions. But they were hopelessly outnumbered, and it was not long before the enemy controlled almost all of Hue. The Viet Cong flag, gold stars on red and blue, was flying triumphantly over the ancient Imperial Palace.

An afternoon of street fighting

The nearest US Marine base was at Phu Bai, some 12 klicks to the south. There, Brigadier-General Foster Lahue, a veteran of World War II and Korea, was in command of the Marines of the seriously weakened Task Force X-Ray, comprising barely more than three understrength battalions, when it should have included two whole regiments. A mere 4000 men to defend Phu Bai, Route 1 – the key north-south land communications route from Hue to Da Nang – and all the western approaches to Hue.

Charlie was swarming like lice all over the place, Task Force X-Ray was already under mortar-fire itself, and now it was expected to go into

THE BATTLE FOR HUE

When the communist attack on Hue began at 0340 hours on 31 January, the American soldiers in the MACV Compound in the New City, although taken by surprise, managed to fight off the 804th Battalion, NVA 4th Regiment, and hold their position. However, in the Old City, the elite ARVN 'Hac Bo' (Black Panthers) Recondo Company was not so fortunate. Faced with the combined strength of the 800th and 802nd Battalions, NVA 6th Regiment, along with the VC 12th Sapper Battalion, it was forced back to the ARVN 1st Division HQ. The NVA 806th and 810th Battalions then took up blocking positions north and south of Hue respectively.

Although early attempts by elements of the 1st and 5th Marines to enter the city failed, counter-attacks began in earnest in the Old City on 1 February, and in the New City three days later, when three more Marine rifle companies joined the battle. To the west of the city, the 3d Brigade, 1st Air Cavalry, prevented the infiltration of three fresh NVA regiments.

Although 'Ontos' – tracked vehicles mounting batteries of six 106mm recoilless rifles – proved effective, a reluctance to use heavy weapons in the ancient city forced the Marines to put up their own covering fire as they fought from house to house.

However, when supporting fire from naval gunships was authorized on 5 February, and artillery and air support on 7 February, the course of the battle changed dramatically.

The US barrage was immense, with 5191 naval rounds, 18,091 artillery rounds and 290,877lb of aerial ordnance being expended.

The New City was cleared by 9 February and the use of 250lb 'Snakeye' bombs and 500lb napalm canisters enabled the ARVN and the 1st Battalion, 5th Marines, to breach the Citadel walls on 22 February. Hue was declared secure three days later, at a cost of 3228 Allied casualties, including 357 ARVN and 142 Marine dead. The NVA lost 4601 dead and 45 captured.

1968

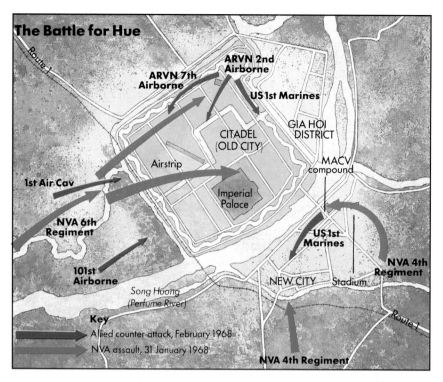

The Battle for Hue

ARVN 7th Airborne

ARVN 2nd Airborne

US 1st Marines

CITADEL (OLD CITY)

GIA HOI DISTRICT

Airstrip

MACV compound

1st Air Cav

Imperial Palace

NVA 6th Regiment

101st Airborne

US 1st Marines

NVA 4th Regiment

Song Huong (Perfume River)

NEW CITY   Stadium

Route 1

Key

Allied counter-attack, February 1968

NVA assault, 31 January 1968

NVA 4th Regiment

group of the 1st Battalion, together with Company G, 2d Battalion, 5th Marines, a tank platoon and some engineers. On the way out of base Gravel stopped his jeep and called out to Lieutenant Richard Lyons, 'Do you want to go into Hue City for an afternoon of street fighting?' Lyons, the battalion chaplain and a man not above loosing off with an M16 to cover his buddies in the field, willingly climbed aboard. Gravel had had no time to formulate a plan, so he just bellowed 'Get on the trucks' to his men, and they were soon barrelling along Route 1.

Gravel's small force managed to punch a way through the NVA screen, extricate Alpha Company and, although under fire from the enemy elements within Hue, it crossed the bridge over the Phu Cam canal and entered the MACV compound just before 1500 hours.

Having got this far, Gravel was ordered to try to make contact with Truong's ARVN units, who were holding out in the northern corner of the Old City. His men moved over the fire-swept Nguyen Hoang bridge, but without any heavy support – the tanks were unable to follow because of their vulnerability in close-quarters urban fighting – they found themselves facing far more enemy firepower than they could cope with. Gravel pulled back with his wounded.

A toe-hold, then a foothold
The next day he tried again to force a way through to Truong's headquarters, only to meet renewed resistance from the NVA troops digging in within the walls of the Old City.

But all the time more and more Marine forces

Hue as well. But SOMETHING sure as hell had to be done. So Lahue sent Company A, 1st Battalion, 1st Marines, towards Hue to recce the situation on Route 1 and to try to link up with the beleaguered MACV compound inside the New City. But Company A quickly ran into trouble. It was pinned down by an NVA ambush with barely half the distance to Hue covered. So Lahue sent out Lieutenant-Colonel Marcus Gravel, with his command

In street fighting death can come from any direction. Below: Marines take cover from sniper fire behind an M48 tank.

were arriving, under the command of such renowned shit-kickers as Colonel Stanley Hughes, the regimental commander of the 1st Marines, and Lieutenant-Colonel Ernest Cheatham, whom many described as 'the finest Marine officer they had served with, ever.' Slowly, but surely, the Marines began to secure a toe-hold, then a foothold, in the maze-like streets of the Old City.

But it was a bitch. Most of the Marines at Hue were short-term enlistees, who expected to have to fight the VC in the countryside where they could call upon their enormous resources of firepower and had the great advantage of superior mobility. Now, however, they faced a different kind of warfare: close-quarters, almost hand-to-hand combat with movement confined to swift dashes across fire-swept streets, dodging from one scrap of cover to another, with enemy snipers liable to pick off anyone careless enough to show himself. The beleaguered grunts, pinned down in the rubble, cursed the lack of heavy fire support. It was rumoured to have something to do with protecting civilians, or restricting damage to buildings. That was a joke: your buddies getting blown to pieces because some lousy gook temple might get scratched. Hearts and minds, right?

But these boys were first and foremost Marines,

Right top: Elements of the 1st Air Cav move down Highway 1 on 22 February to reinforce the Marines. Shortly after passing this road marker they were ambushed. Right middle: The Marines don gas masks as tear gas is used to flush a sniper out of a house. Right bottom: The civilians, as always, came off worst. Many were killed in their homes by artillery and bombs. Others were killed by VC death squads.

1968

COMMUNIST ATROCITIES IN HUE

With the grisly discovery of mass graves in the aftermath of Hue, can Hanoi be accused of cold-blooded murder?

On 4 February – five days after communist forces had occupied most of Hue – Radio Hanoi ominously announced that they had 'rounded up and punished dozens of cruel agents'. When Hue was finally cleared on 25 February, it became apparent that there had been a calculated purge of the inhabitants. A captured Viet Cong document revealed that the communist forces estimated they had eliminated 1892 administrative personnel, 38 policemen and 70 'tyrants'. In the following 18 months 2800 bodies were discovered in mass graves. These were located in jungle clearings, river beds and coastal salt flats. Many of those who had been taken away for execution had been buried alive in these mass graves, while many others had been viciously mutilated.

Those who opposed American involvement, and others, blamed American airpower and the ARVN; later they attributed the deaths to the actions of frustrated NVA troops in retreat. This hardly squared with the communist propaganda at the time. As late as September 1969, Radio Hanoi ridiculed the continuing search for the bodies of 'hooligan lackeys who had owed blood debts'. A retreating army bent on revenge was hardly likely to have carried its victims so far from the city. In fact, death squads had come armed with blacklists of civil servants, teachers and religious leaders, and had executed them after perfunctory courts-martial. A second purge struck at other community leaders, intellectuals and those connected to US forces, while a third eliminated any witnesses of the earlier killings. Among the dead were Stephen Miller of the US Information Service, three German doctors and two French missionaries.

Terror was a common feature of Hanoi's strategy of intimidation, but that which was practised routinely in the countryside generally went unreported. What had happened in Hue was different, both in terms of its sheer scale and the publicity accorded it. President Nixon said these were a prelude of what would happen in South Vietnam if the communists ever took power. But soon barbarism would flourish on both sides.

and Gravel was proud to see that their natural fear came second to the regimental traditions. Certain scenes would always live in his memory, such as that of young Jim Soukup (1st Battalion), who had drawn a big bulls-eye on the back of his flak jacket, with the defiant inscription: 'Try your luck, Charlie!' Or Lieutenant Allen W. Courtney, a genial Texan who, ignoring his own horrendous wounds, gave single-handed covering fire during the evacuation of some shot-up buddies. He wouldn't leave his post, so Gravel ordered him to the base-hospital in language he reckoned the Texan would understand: 'Be out of town before dark.'

It was slow going, but Gravel's men pushed on. On 6 February, the prison, hospital and provincial headquarters were recaptured, and by the 9th the Marines controlled the New City. Three days later, they deployed in the Old City. There the bitter, bloody battle continued.

The battle in Hue during those long February days was unlike anything experienced in the

Nam. The VC holed up in the city were not going to just slip away to fight another day. They had been ordered to hold on till the bitter end, and they would have to be winkled out, house by house, bunker by bunker. The Marines had to fight their way in and take out the defenders one by one.

Prising out the enemy

The enemy had strongpoints everywhere. Snipers crouched in the upper stories of buildings or in small spider-holes, just waiting for some poor bastard unlucky – or stupid – enough to show his head, while machine-gun nests were set up on the ground. Mortars, dug in to avoid detection, covered the approach routes. As if all this wasn't enough, it was the monsoon season. The glowering skies and murky, fetid atmosphere made any close air-support virtually impossible. For the Marines, the days spent fighting in Hue under these grey, leaden skies assumed a kind of routine. They would force their way forward during the day, struggling to prise the enemy out of their concealed defences, bringing up what support weapons they could and then hope to catch a hot meal at night. And all the time the NVA and VC launched local counter-attacks, and crept about stealthily at night, laying hidden booby traps. But the Marines endured stoically, even managing a

Above left: Black humour spread through the ranks after the battle for Hue. Here, Sergeant F.A. Thomas takes a spin in a Merc. Above: Sergeant P.L. Thompson sits on the throne of the old Imperial Palace in the city. Below: The Marines mourn their dead in time-honoured fashion.

sort of black humour, like the kids who were overheard singing: 'We gotta get out of this place, if it's the last thing we ever do!' And they took casualties. Gravel would never forget the boy waiting to be medevaced out, who was asked by a reporter: 'How many times have you been wounded?' The kid answered deadpan: 'Today?'

Crouching behind walls, setting up as much covering fire as they could, the Marines inched forward, haggard with fatigue. 21 February saw the Imperial Palace recaptured and finally, on the night of the 25th, the battle of Hue was officially terminated. It had lasted 26 days.

THE KICKLESS CANNON

Portable and versatile, the recoilless rifle was the US infantry's own artillery.

The recoilless rifle is a relatively large calibre weapon which has a high velocity of fire, light weight and flexibility – a readily available extra kick for the grunt on the ground.

In contrast to the normal artillery round, the gas-propelled recoilless rifle shell is perforated with dozens of holes and does not fit snugly into the gun's breech. When the gun is fired, a portion of the propellant gas is diverted out through the breech of the gun. The remaining gas fires the projectile out of the barrel. Thus, a flaming, rocket-like blast from the breech produces a force to balance exactly the recoil created by the shell.

Recoilless rifles were designed to be carried primarily by infantry soldiers. However, both the M40A1 and the M67 types were rarely lugged about. The 90mm M67 was usually left at base for perimeter defence and the 106mm M40 was most commonly used mounted on a jeep.

The M67, a single-shot, breech-loaded weapon, was intended for use against armoured fighting vehicles (AFVs) but was also effective against bunkers. It could be fired from the shoulder or used as a ground-based weapon and was effective at a maximum range of 400 metres.

The 106mm M40 – in fact a 105mm gun, designated 106 to avoid confusion with the 105mm M27 recoilless rifle – could fire high explosive as well as normal anti-armour rounds, and provided the infantry with something resembling integral artillery. The M40 was sighted by a 0.5in calibre rifle bolted to its barrel. The rifle fired a special phosphorus tracer bullet which, upon hitting the target, exploded with an easily visible white puff. The M40 round could then follow the smaller calibre rifle shot onto the target. A disadvantage of the spotting shots, however, was that they could give away the position of the gun.

As well as its primary roles against AFVs and hardened positions, the M40 could also be used against infantry assaults, a role facilitated by the XM546 Beehive round. These shells were packed with over 8000 arrow-like 'flechettes' – two-inch metal darts—which, when released, fanned out to halt massed enemy attacks.

To produce a highly mobile tank destroyer, six M40s were mounted on top of a T165 tracked vehicle, creating the M50 Ontos. The M40 almost achieved another even more bizarre role when it was auditioned for use in the AC-130H Spectre gunship version of the Hercules. However, it was abandoned in favour of a 105mm howitzer.

Below: An M40 106mm recoilless rifle is set up in a schoolroom during the battle for Hue. It was a vital weapon in house-to-house fighting, bringing heavy firepower down to street level.

M40A1 106mm RECOILLESS RIFLE

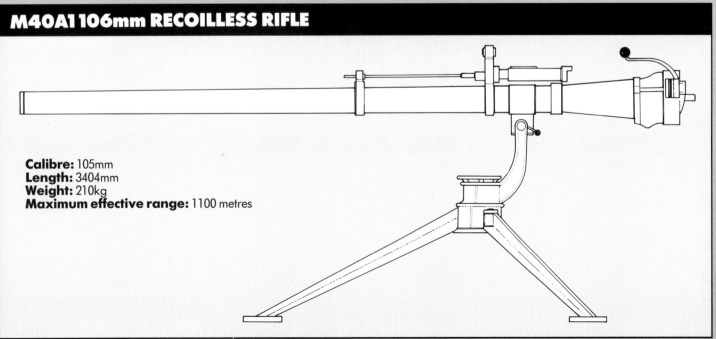

Calibre: 105mm
Length: 3404mm
Weight: 210kg
Maximum effective range: 1100 metres

Images frozen in time. From a grenade being hurled during the thick of the fighting, to a surreal scene of two Marines seemingly unaffected by the bitter struggle for the Imperial City. As the Marines inched through Hue, photographer Don McCullin captured the heat, dust and fear of the battle, together with the overwhelming sense of cameraderie and loyalty that rises to the surface when men face death around the next corner.

HUE

EYE-WITNESS

Don McCullin, a British photographer, has covered wars from Northern Ireland to the Middle East. Intent on examining the human tragedy of war, his photos captured the horror of Vietnam. He was wounded in Cambodia in 1970.

Above left: Dashing through the battered streets of Hue, a helmetless Marine lets fly with a grenade. **Left:** Stumbling through bullet-riddled corrugated iron, three Marines drag an agonized buddy to safety. **Right:** Looking up from his precarious shelter, a grunt casts an apprehensive glance skywards, as a shell bursts over the wall.

THE IMPACT OF TET

As images of Tet flashed across the ether, US public opinion – from the bars to West Point – was in turmoil

I will never forget Tet. While I didn't carry a rifle during the Battle of Hue, or sink in fear when the American embassy in Saigon was stormed, nor squat helplessly in a foxhole in Khe Sanh, I remember Tet because of what it did to my belief in my country and its leaders.

The story of Tet is really a story about two nations. It's the story of America before Tet, and the story of America after Tet. Tet is the division in our history, the yawning maw that gave us humility, that broke our youth. Our leaders say: we are such a young nation, with such great dreams. But that's not true anymore, and it hasn't been true since Tet.

You would have had to live in America in the 1960s, have grown up in the rich farm country of the nation's upper Midwest, to really understand what I am about to tell you.

I grew up in a small paper-mill town in Wisconsin, the centre of a farming community of hard-working second-generation Scandinavian Protestants who attended church every Sunday. Patriotism was an article of faith.

Our heroes were Joe McCarthy, the man who baited communists during the 1950s (he was a neighbour) and Douglas MacArthur, the hero of World War II, the state's favourite son. My mother's fondest wish was that I attend West Point, following in the footsteps of Dwight Eisenhower. In 1960 Richard Nixon came to town during his campaign for president, and swept the votes in our district. When ultra-conservative Barry Goldwater lost the election of 1964 we were stunned into silence.

In 1966, at the age of 15, I was sent off to military school, an environment as conservative, as close-minded and self-assured as any in the world.

My friends and I actually loved military school, loved the deep, almost ineffable camaraderie, the long grey lines of young men marching in unison, the easy loyalty. It was a difficult but disciplined life, a mini-utopia, where rules were easily understood, where limits and traditions were real things, as if you could reach out and touch them.

Today, just across the river from where I live is the long dark caliper of the Vietnam Veterans Memorial. Some of my classmates are on that wall.

During my first year, my class was shown a movie about counter-insurgency. I remember the movie vividly, perhaps because it was when I first sensed that things weren't quite right in Southeast Asia. In the movie, a communist guerrilla comes into a Vietnamese village and extorts rice from the village elders. When they refuse to turn over the rice the communists make an example of one of them through execution. The rice is taken, the young men forced into the guerrilla army. Then the Americans arrive, tall men in green with floppy hats, smiling with confidence and 'know-how'.

The Americans are good guys: they inoculate the children, build a school, bring in food, help in the harvest and listen respectfully as the village elders tell them their problems. At the end of the movie the Americans ask the villagers for volunteers for the South Vietnamese Army. All the young men volunteer to fight the communists; their mothers smile with pride as they walk off into the jungle.

How could the Viet Cong ever win?, my classmates asked. It was suicide. Why did they fight? My classmates and I were the truest reflection of the movie. Americans were boy scouts with M16s, ambassadors of freedom with a clip of ammo and a candy bar. We meant well, and thought that when the Viet Cong realized this they would lay down their weapons and join us.

The seeds of doubt

But the war dragged on, through my first year in military school and then the second. I should mention that for all our discipline and loyalty, our regimentation and love of tradition, our school was intellectually vibrant. Nothing was kept from us, there was no censorship. While the pressure to conform was palpable, these pressures were suspended at the classroom door. Once in the classroom, the distinctions of rank – distinctions that otherwise dictated our every move – ceased to have meaning. It helped that rank was predicated on grades, as well as on 'military bearing', because that meant that the highest ranking cadets were

Below: For others like this student-dominated section of the Woodstock generation staging an anti-war 'moratorium', the war was a corrupt, immoral fusion of bullying, feeding of the arms industry and wasted life. After Tet it was also unwinnable. Theirs was an attitude increasingly reflected throughout America after the shock of Tet.

1968

EYE-WITNESS

The author, Mark Perry was at military school during the Tet Offensive. He is now Senior Editor of *VETERAN*, the monthly newspaper of The Vietnam Veterans of America.

Left: The events of Tet cut a divide across the American nation. For some, like these determined, blue collar 'hardhats', demonstrating in support of the war and their interpretation of the American dream, the conflict was a valiant struggle against communism.

no dummies. And so the seeds of doubt were sewn from the top down. By the autumn of 1968, my senior year, when I was promoted to one of the top officer positions, the faith of the cadet corps in Vietnam, in American military tradition, was being slowly but certainly undermined.

Rank has its privileges. My senior year was a cornucopia of freedom. For the first time in my years at military school I was allowed off campus at weekends. Throughout the autumn of 1967, senior officers had roared off in cars to meet girls and go to bars. The entertainment of choice was 60 miles away from our military world, on the campus of the University of Wisconsin at the state capital in Madison, with its 54,000 students and a vibrant bar life. But by the autumn of 1968 the University of Wisconsin had changed.

The students were continually organizing rallies and protest marches against the war. The

ANCHORMAN OR AXEMAN?

After Tet shocked America, just how big a part did news anchorman, Walter Cronkite, play in polarising public opposition to the war in Vietnam?

By 1968, Walter Cronkite, who had joined Columbia Broadcasting System (CBS) 18 years earlier, was one of the most respected and influential anchormen on network television. According to one politician, Cronkite could change the way thousands of Americans voted 'by a mere inflection of his deep baritone voice, or by a lifting of his well-known bushy eyebrows'. From 1965 to 1968 Cronkite had adopted an even-handed approach to the reporting of the war, reflecting a general caution on the part of the major networks not to present the war and the Johnson Administration in an unfavourable light on national television. But even by October 1967, attitudes were changing. On the 7th, Cronkite introduced a news item that showed a young American soldier cutting off the ear of a dead VC.

When the storm of the Tet Offensive broke in early 1968, middle America and Cronkite were shocked into action. As the VC attempted to blast their way into the US embassy in Saigon in the early hours of 31 January local time, the news reached America just before the evening news bulletins were to be transmitted. Confused initial reports suggested the embassy had been occupied and Cronkite reputedly exploded: 'What the hell is going on? I thought we were winning this war.'

The veteran newsman flew out to Saigon – his first visit since 1965 – to assess the situation. On 27 February, in a rare personal report on CBS, he announced that it was 'more certain than ever that the bloody experience of Vietnam is to end in stalemate'. Cronkite saw only only one solution to the morass in which America was now firmly embroiled – negotiations with Hanoi. President Johnson, watching the broadcast in the White House, turned to his press secretary and remarked: 'if I've lost Walter, I've lost Mr Average Citizen'.

But Cronkite was reflecting rather than guiding public opinion. On 20 February the Senate Foreign Relations Committee had begun televised hearings questioning the necessity of the war, while two days later, MACV had announced the highest ever weekly total of 543 US combat deaths. For Johnson, even worse was to follow. On 12 March the virtually unknown Senator Eugene McCarthy, standing as a peace candidate, won 42 per cent of the poll in the New Hampshire primary. In this, a battle to find the Democratic candidate for New Hampshire in the forthcoming presidential elections, McCarthy had polled only 300 votes less than Johnson himself.

A more prominent peace candidate, Senator Robert Kennedy, entered the race for the presidential nomination four days later. On 18 March, 139 Congressmen – including 41 Democrats – sponsored a resolution demanding an immediate congressional review of Johnson's Vietnam policy. The president's popularity dipped from an approval rating of 48 per cent to one of 36 per cent. On 31 March he bowed out of the presidential race altogether. Cronkite – 'the most trusted man in America' – had put the final nail in Johnson's coffin.

university itself, and the conservative city surrounding it, was in turmoil. During one rally, police swung clubs at demonstrators. That night the head of the Madison police appeared on television to denounce the demonstrators as 'instigators who are not from Wisconsin'.

By November 1967, just two months before Tet, it was apparent that the once united and tradition-bound cadet corps of which I was a proud officer had become viciously divided over our Vietnam commitment. It was the unstated subject in every class, the topic of choice at the periphery of every conversation.

In December three senior cadets were caught with marijuana in their rooms and suspended. It was an unheard-of event, an unprecedented and thundering act of rebellion in our school's history.

Above left: During the Vietnam war, Walter Cronkite, the veteran CBS anchorman, was effectively the voice of Middle America. When he declared the war to be 'mired in stalemate', it was a blow to Lyndon Johnson's morale.

The perpetrators went silently, but sullenly, from the school, while the rest of us assessed the uprising. Always and everywhere among us the rude possibility of cadet violence seemed to waver like sheets of heat. Only months before, during the last day of our junior year, a group of us had 'trashed' the room of a particularly well-hated senior, shredding to nothingness his every possession.

Post Tet depression

Veterans of that conflict tell those of us who never went to war that violence was real in Vietnam, and never felt here at home. But they are wrong. Vietnam gripped us like a great fear, the feeling Goliath had before falling to earth. I think now that the frustration of our commitment, the knowledge even of our certain defeat, was somehow known to us then.

But Tet was the crowning blow. During the last week of January 1968 our obsessive thinking about the war was given a breather. In Vietnam, American troops 'stood down' from their constant tussle with the enemy. Even in our military school, the debates of the previous months which divided us reached an impasse. As if exhaustion had set in. But on 31 January the Tet Offensive revived our disagreements and finally, inevitably, made every man – boy really – rethink the war.

Television war

For us the most traumatic event was the takeover of the American embassy. For seniors, whose freedoms included a nightly two-hour after-dinner stint before the television, the flickering image of William Westmoreland standing in a group of aides, deciding what to tell the press in the wake of the embassy attack, was the most vivid piece of evidence that our war was lost.

On 2 February, just one day after the embassy attack – when it became plain that Hue had been captured by the Viet Cong – a fistfight broke out in front of the television. A group of seniors, wedded to our commitment in the war, fought gallantly for the right (believe it or not) to change the channel

fight to the death in downtown Hue, watched in stuttering and terrified amazement as a South Vietnamese officer blew the brains out of a suspected Viet Cong irregular.

Our time before the CBS evening news became a death watch. The CBS evening news was more than required viewing. It was our window on a nation that was changing before our eyes.

But the greatest change took place on the evening of 27 February 1968. Hue was liberated. Our graduated fellow-cadets were safe, at least for a time. South Vietnam had survived, but our faith in the war, from that evening on, was destroyed forever.

Walter Cronkite, the CBS newsman, was something of a hero to all of us. Trusted, professional, fatherly, we listened and compared notes on what he had said as if it were sport. On the evening of 27 February, he gave us his long hoped-for assessment of the war.

'Who won and who lost in the great Tet Offensive?' he asked from behind his desk in New York. He paused, and then said: 'I'm not sure.' There was nervous movement throughout the room, and hisses from the pro-war cadet element. 'We won', someone suddenly yelled from the back, and then fell abruptly silent.

'It seems now more certain than ever that the bloody experience of Vietnam is to end in a

The television coverage of the war had a profound effect on opinion in the US. One of the most notorious and powerful TV sequences back home in 1968 was this apparently summary execution of a recently captured VC suspect. Below far left: the suspect is dragged forward by ARVN troops, unaware of his brutal fate.

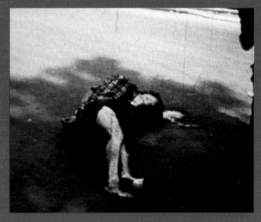

from a news report on Vietnam to a situation comedy. Bad news was propaganda, they said. Some of us fought back, and the news report, with its unremitting menu of bad news, stayed on the air.

At our dinners, during that first week of Tet, as we stood to attention behind our seats, the long roll of dead from graduated classes was read, and greeted, in solemn tones. For us, the Tet Offensive had brought the war home – into our rooms, into our school, into our corps. Something had changed in America, and we knew it. Oddly, but perhaps understandably, the riots and demonstrations had suddenly ceased during February, as will often happen to a nation that is faced with the spectre of its own tragedy. We looked on in horror as thousands of American troops were caught in a

stalemate,' Cronkite continued. 'To say that we are closer to victory today is to believe, in the face of the evidence, the optimists who have been wrong in the past...it is increasingly clear to this reporter that the only rational way out then will be to negotiate, not as victors but as an honorable people who lived up to their pledge to defend democracy, and did the best they could.' And then Cronkite signed off: 'This is Walter Cronkite,' he said, staring at the camera, 'Good night.'

We've lost, I remember thinking. We might have been wrong, or right, had good intentions or bad, but we lost. More than anything else, it is this defeat that amazes me still. A group of 'little men in black pyjamas running in the rain' – as one returning graduate told us – defeated the greatest military power in the world.

Above centre: Blasted through the temple from point blank range, he slumps to the street. Above right: Perhaps already forgotten by his killer, a frail form spills his blood onto dust and shadows. These were images that the armchair viewers Stateside would never forget.

As the Phantom pilot approaches the target, he pushes the stick forward, aligns the pipper on the ridgeline and presses the red 'pickle' button. Above: Earth flies and explosions flare as another mission strikes home. With the two 750lb bombs released the Phantom leaps up, the pilot powering it away from the target, weaving and twisting as he goes, to escape from enemy fire.

PHANTOM MISSION

As tongues of red-orange fire stab back from your Phantom's afterburners, you level out, head for the SAM envelope and wait for the target

EYE-WITNESS

This article has been compiled by Robert F. Dorr from interviews with the officers of 469th Tactical Fighter Squadron.

Right: Tail fin shattered, this Phantom was lucky to make it home after a close encounter with an SA2 Guideline SAM.

The time is oh-dark-thirty. A flashlight beam burns your eyes as you're shaken awake in your narrow billet at Korat, Thailand. The missions were fragged last night – targets are assigned in what's known as a frag order – so you already know where you're going this morning, an NVA supply dump just across the border in Laos, the country where we don't admit flying, as yet.

Shower, shave, grapple with the clawing heat even in pitch darkness and stride into squadron ops for a weather brief. Scattered clouds, light winds. The Intel brief follows. Ground fire? Moderate to heavy. You'll be in the SAM envelope. No MiGs expected.

You're a member of the 469th Tactical Fighter Squadron, commanded by Lieutenant-Colonel Edward Hillding and occupying a sizeable corner of the revetment area at Korat, an airfield bombarded, in turn, by searing heat and drenching thunderstorms. The squadron is part of the 388th Tactical Fighter Wing, under Colonel Paul P. Douglas, the World War II ace who flies a Phantom called The Arkansas Traveler. Your outfit has just gotten the model E Phantom. 'We do the job with Es,' reads a sign at base operations. It is longer, heavier, with different fuel capacity and different radar. Above all, the F-4E has an internal gun, a 20-mm 'Gatling gun' M61Al cannon with 640 rounds, designed to even the odds against the MiG in a close-quarters fight. The 469th is a high-spirited outfit. Against regulations, and in defiance of high muckety mucks such as TAC chief General William Momyer, the 469th has painted shark's teeth on the Phantoms' noses. Even the squadron's Jeep has shark's teeth. A little thing, but it helps morale.

Loading the shark's bite

Today you're front-seat pilot of Gunshot Two in a flight of four F-4E Phantoms. Your back-seat weapons systems officer, that's a WSO or whizzo, is Captain Gilbert Murray. Briefings finished, you wave optimistically towards Gunshot Flight leader, Major Thomas E. Sanridge and follow him out the door. A faint hint of pink hangs along the pre-dawn horizon as you pre-flight the Phantom and climb aboard.

Sanridge pulls out of his revetment and heads for the taxi strip, red-green formation lights winking in the semi-darkness. You shut the canopy, check Murray on the intercom, release brakes and follow. Today, you're carrying six 750lb bombs with fuze extenders, long poles that protrude from the front of the bombs and cause them to explode inches above the ground. Your Phantom also carries an electronic counter-measures pod, designed to foul Hanoi's radar, three AIM-7 Sparrow radar-guided missiles and four AIM-9 Sidewinder infra-red missiles. But, in all, your Phantom and its warload weigh less than 60,000lb.

After take-off, you climb out, tuck in the wheels, and ease the stick forward, breaking out of low

FAST-JET TRAINING

In the 1960s, anyone wishing to become a pilot in the USAF (above) had first to be trained as an officer. High-school graduates could attend a four-year course at the USAF Academy in Colorado Springs, at the end of which they would receive a commission and a Bachelor of Science degree. Those attending college or university could join the Air Force Reserve Officer Training Corps (AFROTC), which maintained over 170 campus facilities nationwide, or could wait until after graduation and then apply for a three-month Officer Training School (OTS) course at Lackland Air Force Base, Texas.

Those wishing to go on to pilot training would then attend a 53-week course at one of 10 training bases throughout the country (this course was reduced to 48 weeks in 1971). After a short period of ground tuition, the potential pilot would receive 30 (later reduced to 16) hours basic training in a Cessna T-41 single-engine light aircraft. If deemed suitable for fast-jet training, he would follow this up with 90 hours in a North American T-28 or Cessna T-37 and 120 hours in the supersonic Northrop T-38. At the end of this training cycle, he would move on to the aircraft of his allotted role – fighter-bomber, attack, interceptor or bomber. During the period of the Vietnam war, the USAF faced a shortage of fast-jet pilots, but expansion of Air Training Command (ATC) facilities and a policy of 'weeding-out' pilots from non-flying administrative posts gradually solved the problem. Between 1965 and 1973, a total of 33,000 pilots were trained, the majority for fast-jet roles.

1968

cloud cover and into a brightening sky. Gunshot Three and Four are seconds behind you. Sandrige calls, 'Gunshot, go mission frequency.' Your back-seater shifts channels on the UHF radio. The flight of four Phantoms turns into a shallow bank, bearing northeast towards Laos.

Your long, bent-wing Phantom, propelled through the air by two monstrous J79 engines, bursts upward into full daylight as the sun rises ahead to your right. While you handle the flight controls, your back-seater navigates and monitors aircraft systems. Gunshot Flight is now approaching the target area at 500mph.

Below, the terrain becomes more mountainous, its slick green canopy intermittently shrouded with cotton-wool murk that hangs in ravines and valleys. Sanridge is a helmeted silhouette in the lead Phantom, a little above and 30ft to your left. His voice has unmistakable authority. 'Clean 'em up, green 'em up, start your music,' meaning clean your aircraft by levelling all control surfaces, flip the bomb safety switches to green and turn on your ECM 'music'.

Sanridge again: 'Gunshot Flight, set 'em hot.'

Murray rattles off a checklist. You respond. Bomb arming switch? 'Bombs armed.' Intervalometer? That's the device which spaces the release of your 750lb packages for Ho Chi Minh. 'Intervalometer set.' Station Selector? 'Bombs, all.' Master arm switch? The tight, face-chafing oxygen masks lends a confined, rubbery quality to your voices.

Sanridge is eyeing the target, the NVA dump hidden beneath greenery up a valley ahead.

No curtain rises, no trumpet sounds, to signal that you're in Laos. Sanridge talks to Hillsborough, an ABCCC (AirBorne Command and Control Centre) about the target. 'They're on the northeast ridge, the one with two peaks.' Hillsborough is a C-130 with special communications gear. Some of the target information comes from reconnaissance flights. Some from a top-secret Air Force outfit called the Ravens which is operating small spotter aircraft from inside Laos despite all official denials.

SAMs on the trail

Never mind how the target was spotted, they know you're coming. They're shooting at you. Garden-hose streams of red-orange puff balls describe a shallow arc in the sky, floating towards you. Those come from smallarms and machine guns. In a moment, there's a furious stream of bigger, faster tracers flying in criss-cross pattern from 37mm and 57mm cannons. A single hit from one of those will transform your Phantom into twisted wreckage. Meanwhile, your RHAWS (Radar Homing and Warning System) tells you that SAM missile sites across the border in North Vietnam are stalking you.

'Gunshot Flight, let's roll in and take 'em out.' 'Two,' you acknowledge.

It's cramped inside the Phantom canopy. Sweat puddles on the lip of your oxygen mask. Murray asks you something about the bomb run. 'Shut the fuck up!' you snap over the intercom.

You check your air speed, dive angle, drift. Your aiming point is a bald spot on the ridgeline ahead.

Below left: Major Roy S. Dickey, a MIG-killer from the 388th Tactical Fighter Wing gives a broad grin after completing his 100th combat mission over North Vietnam. Below centre: Scrambling into their Phantom, a crew sets off on yet another mission. Below right: A pair of F-4Es, loaded with 750lb bombs with fuze extenders, Sparrows and jettisonable fuel tanks, wait their turn for refuelling by a KC-135 tanker.

CHAPTER 74

THUNDER STOPS ROLLING

Operation Rolling Thunder raged over North Vietnam for more than three years. When it was all over, the US had spent billions of dollars and lost 922 aircraft – but what, if anything, had been achieved?

On 31 October 1968 President Johnson ordered all air, naval and artillery attacks on North Vietnam to cease at 0800 hours (Washington time) the following day, as part of his policy of 'de-escalating the war and moving seriously towards peace'. In return for Johnson's concession, the North Vietnamese agreed to enter into more meaningful peace discussions in Paris.

Johnson's executive order marked the end of Operation Rolling Thunder, begun as a series of selected airstrikes on the North in March 1965. The objectives of the operation had been laid down as improving the morale of the South Vietnamese, reducing the flow of men and supplies from the North and 'imposing a penalty' on Hanoi for its continued support of insurgency in the South. After three years and nine months of gradually escalating strikes, during which over 300,000 aircraft sorties had been flown and nearly half a ton of explosives dropped on the North every minute, none of these aims had been achieved.

South Vietnamese morale had improved, but it was impossible to say if this was as a direct result of Rolling Thunder. As the Tet Offensive had shown, the North Vietnamese delivery of supplies down the Ho Chi Minh Trail had increased dramatically, while the communist main-force strength south of the DMZ was estimated to have grown by 75 per cent. Despite Hanoi's agreement to conduct peace talks in Paris, North Vietnamese resolve had been hardened rather than shattered by the air attacks. In addition, increasing disgust over the bombing tactics led to a growing loss of US domestic support for the war.

Thus, although significant material damage had been inflicted on the North, Rolling Thunder was widely judged to have been a failure. Raids against the North were not to take place again until 1972, by which time new technology and a new president would combine to make them infinitely more effective.

Sanridge's Phantom is already rolling in, gunfire swirling around him. Funny. From your base in Thailand you've flown 67 missions in Vietnam plus a dozen more 'unmentionables' in Laos. You've gotten hit three times. You've seen a buddy get blown to bits in mid-air. Yet you've never met a Vietnamese face to face, friend or foe.

'Sorry,' you say to your back-seater. You're always snapping at him. Then apologizing. 'We're going in.'

'We're hit, we're hit!'

You bring the Phantom in and drop the bombs. There's a sudden pitch upward when the 750-pounders break free. You bring the Phantom's nose up through the horizon and ignite both afterburners to put the Phantom into a weaving, twisting flight to escape from all the anonymous men with guns down there who are trying to kill you. ThuuuuuNNNNKKKK!

'We're hit, we're hit,' Murray utters. The Phantom trembles. You look for a fire warning light. No light. Hydraulics okay. The Phantom seems steady in your grasp, but that doesn't mean it isn't disintegrating on you.

'There's a fracture on the canopy behind your head,' Murray tells you. 'Looks like something struck the glass and careered off.'

'Okay. We'll assume no critical systems damage.'

'Uh, Roger. Hey, look! They're getting secondaries over there!'

Gunshot Three and Four have dropped their 750-pounders and a gigantic wall of fire rises at

1968

out after dropping their bombs.

'SAMs. Up ahead. Two o'clock, low.' They say you can elude a SAM easily enough if you can see it coming. When you're flying closer to the SAM sites, the red ink-smudge from the SAM sustainer booster gives you plenty of warning. But here there is no warning except for the blurred image of telephone poles flying around you. They're aimed at the Phantoms behind you. Gunshot Three racks around in a tight, gut-wrenching turn and evades one SAM, then another. Gunshot Four also out-turns a missile, which explodes harmlessly in the distance. But then another SAM races up at Four's tail and this time he can't evade. Looking over your shoulder, you see the Phantom devoured by an expanding yellow flash.

'Four's hit. Four's hit!'

'Not quite.' The voice of the pilot in Gunshot Four is a surprise but he is gasping for breath. You look back to see his Phantom emerging from the explosion, seemingly intact except that its tail has been blown to pieces. 'That was a near miss, guys. But I've lost rudder. Hydraulics are shot to hell.' Will they have to eject over Laos where the Jolly Greens can't get them?

Limping back to base

'I think we can divert to NKP,' Four says hopefully. 'Do it,' snaps Sanridge. The airfield at Nakhon Phanom – called NKP or Naked Fanny – was not built to accommodate Phantoms and its runway is perilously short, but it's much closer than Korat.

For the moment though, you are less concerned with Gunshot Four than with your own battle damage. You follow Sanridge, while his back-seater looks you over trying to assess the damage. Something has been hit besides your canopy. A pencil-thin stream of smoke is jetting back from the Phantom.

In formation with Gunshot Lead, you descend toward Korat with no serious problems.

'I got carried away,' Murray admits.

'I'm sorry too. You were a great help. Really.'

'Think that hit damaged our landing gear?'

'Knock on wood.'

'You've got a good clear, Gunshot Two,' confirms Sanridge. The runway rushes up to meet you.

'Good landing,' Murray says as the tyres screech. You raise the canopy and taxi in to the revetment, your crewchief quickly raises a ladder and scrambles up to meet you. It's all very cheery. You survived another hit. You're smiling. You expect the crewchief to smile back. Instead, he turns ashen as he takes your helmet. 'Oh, my God, sir.'

'What? What's the problem?'

'My God, my God.'

Your helmet is full of blood. The red-brown liquid slops around inside, like soup in a bowl.

A chip of glass from the damaged canopy has inscribed a small cut on the back of your neck, below the helmet line. You've been bleeding ever since. The cure: a Band-aid.

Above: Their carnivorous decorations glaring, a line of 388th Tactical Fighter Wing F-4Es are loaded up for another sortie into SAM Alley. Armourers scurry around the aircraft checking electrical continuity and preparing armaments. Soon the Phantoms will rush down the runway in pairs, fire stabbing back from the afterburners, shattering the air. Left: In the clear blue Vietnamese sky, a Phantom makes rendezvous with a KC-135 tanker and laps up fuel like a thirsty child.

least a thousand yards into the air.

'That's the biggest goddamned secondary fire I've ever seen. It must be an ammo dump. It's...'

'Murray. I gotta tell you again. Shut the fuck up.'

This is no joke. Again and again, it's been beaten into you. 'Clutter' in your earphones can prevent you from hearing a vital message. Now, while you're upbraiding your back-seater, the ABCCC is calling to warn that SAMs have been fired.

From across the border inside North Vietnam, several Soviet SA-2 Guideline missiles have come shooting upward at a shallow angle, directed by radar towards Gunshot Flight. With Sanridge ahead, you're already turning to clear the target area. But Gunshot Three and Four are just pulling

The fighting on Hamburger Hill was not the heaviest in Vietnam – and casualties weren't all that high. But after this battle, US troops never again initiated large-scale actions

On the morning of 11 May 1969 Company B, 3d Battalion, 187th Infantry part of the 101st Airborne, moved cautiously up the north slope of Hill 937. It was a routine search-and-locate exercise. They knew the enemy were in there somewhere.

Suddenly the undergrowth around them erupted in a red-hot storm of machine-gun fire which poured out of hidden bunkers, cutting down those men who were fractionally slower in hitting the deck. Their buddies returned fire with M16s and light anti-tank weapons, before retreating a safe distance back down the hill with the wounded. Company B had located the enemy, and in force. Now all it had to do was fix his position and get air support to prep the shit out of him.

HAMBURGER HILL

borne. Their mission, codenamed Apache Snow, was to stop the NVA and Viet Cong infiltrating from the Ho Chi Minh Trail and into the 30-mile-long natural funnel of the A Shau valley near the Laotian border in northwest South Vietnam. The valley consists of rolling terrain covered by eight-foot-high elephant grass. It is protected by a rim of triple-canopied hills, one of which was Hill 937 – the number corresponding to its height in metres. It was a rugged, densely-forested peak, covered with lush, green vegetation and spiked bamboo. The Vietnamese knew it as Dong Ap Bia. Soon the world would know it as 'Hamburger Hill.'

The commander of 3d Battalion was Lieutenant-Colonel Weldon Honeycutt, codename 'Blackjack', a shit-kicker who often liked nothing better than walking point. He was a good officer, and respected by his men. He had just one fault. He tended to go by the book, to obey command orders unquestioningly. By the end of the battle for Hamburger Hill, that trait would leave him with a price on his head.

Carnage and retreat

All through that first afternoon and night bombs and shells rained down on the NVA positions. The following morning – 12 May – most of the GIs reckoned that if there were any gooks left on those slopes they wouldn't be in much of a state to fight. They couldn't have been more wrong.

The troopers quickly ran, as Spec 4 Jimmy Spears recalled, 'into garbage': rocket grenades, automatic fire, lethal Claymore mines dangling

Sure enough, within minutes the fire support base at Ta Bat opened up and shells howled over the heads of the grunts before churning up the slope above. Next, USAF jets screamed through the smoke, unleashing incendiary and high explosive bombs on top of the hidden NVA bunkers.

When the bombardment ceased, it should have been a simple job to mop up. But when Company B next moved up the hill they found themselves still on the receiving end of withering enemy fire. There was nothing else for it but to retreat, call up the flyboys again and get them to really cream those bunkers. But good.

Company B, along with Companies A, C and D, made up 3d Battalion, 187th Infantry which, with 1st Battalion, 506th Infantry and 2d Battalion, 501st Infantry, made up 3d Brigade, 101st Air-

Previous page: A descent into hell, as troopers un-ass from a chopper at the LZ. Above: An NVA rocket explodes directly behind a paratrooper of the 101st Airborne, wounding him seriously. One other trooper was killed by the blast. Above right: Pondering on the futility of it all.

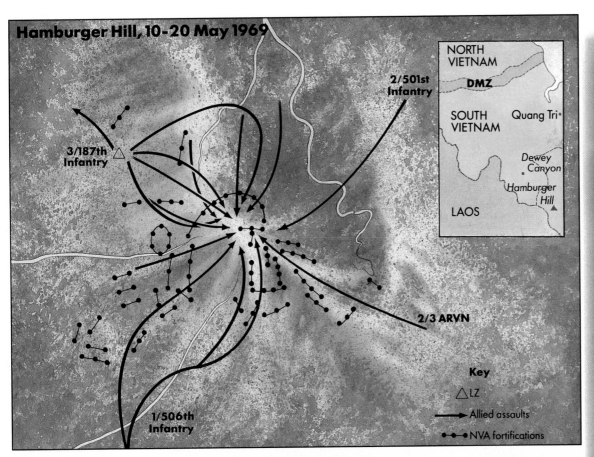

Hamburger Hill, 10-20 May 1969

2/501st Infantry

3/187th Infantry

2/3 ARVN

1/506th Infantry

NORTH VIETNAM

DMZ

SOUTH VIETNAM

Quang Tri

Dewey Canyon

Hamburger Hill

LAOS

Key

△ LZ

→ Allied assaults

•—•—• NVA fortifications

Right: Drenched and in pain, a wounded grunt hangs on while he waits to be medevaced out from the base camp at Hamburger Hill. The thunderstorm of 18 May was just one of the many cruel tricks that fate played on the luckless paratroopers of the 101st Airborne, during a battle that was to earn a grisly notoriety.

THE A SHAU VALLEY CAMPAIGN

In the immediate aftermath of the 1968 Tet Offensive, General Westmoreland decided to commit forces to the A Shau valley, one of the least hospitable regions of South Vietnam, close to the Laotian border in Thua Thien Province. Convinced that this had been a major staging area for Tet, he was determined to clear the valley once and for all.

The subsequent operation, codenamed Delaware, did not, however, achieve its aim. As troopers of the 1st Cavalry Division (Airmobile), backed by the ARVN, helicoptered deep into the valley on 19 April, they encountered heavy anti-aircraft fire but little ground opposition. A second operation (Somerset Plain) took place in August, when men of the 101st Airborne Division swept along the valley floor. But once again the NVA declined to stand and fight. Supply caches were discovered and anti-aircraft guns captured, but the NVA melted away without offering battle. Somerset Plain ended on 19 August.

By early 1969, MACV Intelligence was beginning to monitor renewed NVA activity in the valley, and on 1 March the 101st Airborne was recommitted, this time in Operation Massachusetts Striker. Firebases were set up along the edge of the A Shau and the 101st used helicopters to occupy key locations. Again, supply dumps were uncovered but little contact with the enemy was made.

Thus, when a fourth operation (Apache Snow) began in early May, the men of the 101st, joined by elements of the 9th Marines and 3d ARVN Regiment, imagined that the pattern of insertion, search and extraction would be repeated. The fact that it was not and that the NVA decided to fight, denying Ap Bia mountain (Hamburger Hill) to the Americans for about 10 days, therefore came as something of a surprise. This was compounded when, despite heavy US casualties, Hamburger Hill was abandoned and Apache Snow called off in early June. The A Shau had not been cleared.

A NEW TEAM – A NEW BALL GAME?

When it became clear that Richard Nixon would be the next president to walk into the Oval Office, political analysts predicted a change in strategy.

I shall not seek, and will not accept, the nomination of my party for another term as your president.' Johnson's war would soon be over. In July 1968, three months after LBJ dropped his bombshell, General Westmoreland was appointed Chief of Staff of the Army. There was now a new man at the helm of MACV, General Creighton Abrams. Up until early 1968 the role of US main-force units had seemed fairly straightforward – to 'hold the ring' around South Vietnam. But now, in the light of the Tet Offensive, it was clear that an urgent reassessment of US strategy was required.

Johnson had refused to run for the presidency on the grounds that he wanted to 'rise above partisan divisions' and devote himself to the pursuit of an honourable peace. During the last weeks of 1968 the successful candidate, Richard Milhous Nixon, waited in the wings. Recognizing that Vietnam could not be won by force of arms alone, and believing that the Soviet Union and China were disposed towards the North Vietnamese entering constructive peace negotiations, Nixon had decided on a more flexible policy to the war. Inaugurated on 20 January 1969, he set about organizing a team of advisers to implement this strategy – a marrying together of American troop withdrawals and diplomacy into a package that was intended to gain peace with honour. In came Henry Kissinger as National Security Adviser, a master of diplomatic intrigue. The new Secretary of Defense, Melvin Laird, was given the task of working with Abrams to implement the programme of troop withdrawals and combining this with the gradual handing over of the prosecution of the war to the ARVN – a policy known as 'Vietnamization'. Where Johnson and Westmoreland had been portrayed as floundering in their attempts to find a solution to the war, Nixon and his team seemed set to bring the conflict into a new phase. As the first units withdrew from Vietnam in July 1969, the nature of the war did indeed begin to change.

1969

Brothers in arms. Left: Oblivious to the mud and the rain, a trooper works desperately to keep a badly wounded buddy alive. Above: Helping hands assist the wounded at the battered base camp. The casualties sustained by the men of the 101st Airborne during the 10-day battle for Hamburger Hill were the result of having to attack well-entrenched NVA positions while enjoying minimal cover.

from bushes and trees. It was carnage, and the troops were forced to retreat once again. Company B set about preparing a new landing zone to evacuate the steadily increasing numbers of wounded. Once again, air support was requested; once again, air strikes and artillery relentlessly pounded the enemy positions throughout the day and night. But the nightmare was only just beginning.

The assault just fell apart

The problems were twofold. The first was the way the enemy – the 7th and 8th Battalions of the NVA 29th Regiment – had set up their fortifications. These, built flush to the ground and concealed by deep vegetation, were not only practically indestructible, they were also designed in such a way that their fire mutually converged and interlocked, covering every approach up the mountainside. The other problem was that all the cover on Hill 937 was steadily and surely being destroyed by the air support bombardments. To the men of the 187th it was rapidly becoming very clear that if they were going to keep on attacking up those slopes, it wasn't a question of if they were going to die, but when.

But attack they did, for day after fruitless day. And the casualties mounted. On 13 May it was

again the turn of Company B, along with Company C, to attempt the scarred and blistered mountain. The attack lasted just 30 minutes before it was repulsed, ripped apart by rocket and heavy automatic weapons fire. The grunts took another 37 casualties. The next day saw Companies B,C and D going up the hill separately, on different lines of advance. For the men of Company B, it was the third time they had walked forward into enemy fire since the action started.

This time the attack broke down when the commander of Company C, which was in the lead, was wounded, and his radio silenced. Company C pulled back, and the rest of the assault just fell apart.

Another retreat, another bombardment, another night listening, waiting for the dawn and a bullet with your name on it. But it was beginning to look as if nothing was going to shift those gooks. The whole thing was beginning to resemble some ghastly dance with death.

The morning of 15 May saw the 187th reinforced by the other elements of 3d Brigade, along with a battalion of the ARVN 3rd Regiment. But this did not mean any respite for the thinned-out ranks of Company B. Together with Company A they moved off, desperately searching for any scrap of cover that remained on the bomb-ravaged

Above: Supporting a wounded comrade, two paratroopers eagerly search the skies for a medevac chopper. If nothing else, the bloody battle for Hamburger Hill proved that, when the chips were down, the men of the 101st Airborne would stick to the job, despite being demoralized and pushed to the brink of mutiny.

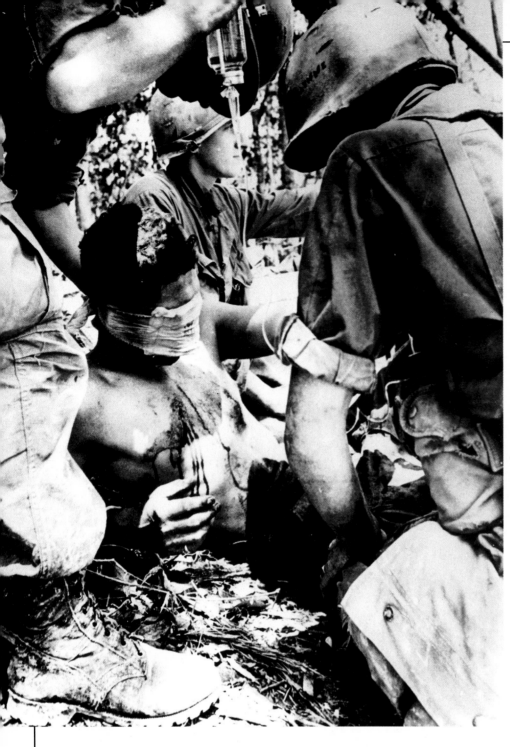

Later that afternoon Honeycutt's battalion HQ was hit by enemy RPGs that wounded Honeycutt – his third wound of the battle. He refused the offer of evacuation. Quite a few of his men wouldn't have minded if Blackjack had had to be evacuated – in a bodybag if necessary.

17 May was a rest day. A non-stop bombardment – supplemented by CS tear gas – was kept up against the enemy installations for the next 36 hours, and the troops were issued with extra-heavy flak jackets. Not only were these almost unbearable to wear in the suffocating heat, but they were about a week late.

They had been attacking Hill 937 for a full week now. Each day they had thrown more troops in, more firepower, and it did no good – 18 May saw a frontal assault by two full battalions, the 3/187th and the 1/506th. Spurred by desperation and rage, the grunts stormed the NVA positions and clawed their way up to the summit. Once again fate took a hand. A sudden thunderstorm drenched the hill, deluging the attackers, and visibility fell to zero. But even worse was the fact that the repeated bombardments of the slope had reduced its surface to a barren, chewed-up dust heap. The rains turned this in an instant into liquefied mud, and the desperate men couldn't keep their footing. Suddenly they found themselves bombarded by grenades, as well as mines being detonated by the enemy within his own perimeter. Yet another retreat was ordered.

Resigned to death

The senselessness of the situation they found themselves in, combined with the general low level of morale and purpose experienced in recent months, was producing a near-mutinous attitude amongst the pitiful remnants of the 187th. One GI recalls: 'There were lots of people in Bravo Company who were going to refuse to go up again. There'd been low morale, but never before so low – because we felt it was all so senseless.' Or as one wounded man snarled: 'That damned Blackjack won't stop until he kills every damn one of us.'

So when 20 May dawned, there was a resigned fatalism pervading the atmosphere. But the tide had turned. The allies mounted a combined attack by all four battalions. Once again they reached the summit. The fighting from bunker to bunker was so intense that air support was useless. This time though there was to be no retreat. The men of the 187th ended the day in control of what was left of Hamburger Hill.

Colonel Honeycutt could not praise his troops enough. 'I love every one of them. My boys were really doing their jobs.'

Nearly 80 GIs had lost their lives during those long days in hell, and five times that number were wounded. After the hill had been secured and the bunker complexes searched and destroyed, allied forces abandoned the peak. On a piece of cardboard, pinned to a tree along with a black 101st neckerchief, an unknown GI left the scrawled message: 'Hamburger Hill. Was it worth it?'

Medics tend a trooper who has been wounded in the face by a hand grenade. Pictures such as these called into question US military strategy in Vietnam. Senator Edward Kennedy pointed out that Hamburger Hill had no strategic value, and called the attack 'senseless and irresponsible.'

slopes. With divisional helicopters covering their advance with constant rocket salvoes into the enemy positions, the men inched forward. It was slow and painful going, not least because the previous night the VC had rigged up Claymores throughout their defences. But gradually the bunkers fell, one by one.

Slaughtered by their own gunship

Suddenly, the crest of Hill 937 could be seen, and the surviving GIs were already tasting victory when complete disaster struck. A helicopter gunship bore down on Company B, strung out over the exposed hillside, and just let rip with its rockets and machine guns. Bodies fell everywhere, and the mutilated screamed where they lay. After everything, after all the shit they had taken for the past five days, some idiot scores an own goal. Give the man a big hand.

On the morning of 16 March 1968, three companies of the 11th Infantry Brigade, Americal Division, launched a search and destroy operation in the My Son area. Company C's target was the VC 48th Battalion which intelligence believed was based in the hamlet marked on US military maps as My Lai-4. The Americans began by launching a heliborne assault.

There was no resistance at the landing zone, so Captain Ernest L. Medina sent his 1st and 2d Platoons into the village. Seeing the Americans approaching, some villagers began to flee and were gunned down. The 2d Platoon swept through the northern half of My Lai-4, hurling grenades into hootches and killing anyone who came out. They raped and murdered village girls, rounded up civilians and shot them.

After half an hour, Medina ordered the 2d Platoon on to the hamlet of Binh Tay, where they gang-raped several more girls before rounding up 10 to 20 women and children and killing them.

Slaughter of the innocents

Meanwhile, the 1st Platoon, under Lieutenant William L. Calley Jr, swept through the south of My Lai-4 shooting anyone who tried to escape, bayoneting others, raping women, shooting livestock and destroying crops and houses. Survivors were rounded up and herded into a drainage ditch. There Lieutenant Calley opened fire on the defenceless villagers. He commanded his men to join in. They emptied clip after clip into the tangle of human flesh until all the bodies lay motionless. Then, miraculously, a two-year-old child crawled out of the carnage, crying. Calley pushed him back and shot him.

Half-an-hour later, the 3d Platoon moved in to mop up. They shot wounded villagers to put them out of their misery, burned houses, killed the remaining livestock, shot anyone trying to escape and rounded up a group of women and children and sprayed them with M16 bullets.

Altogether between 172 and 347 people died – all of them unarmed old men, women or children. Captain Medina reported a body count of 90 VC, no civilians. The divisional press officer announced 128 enemy killed, 13 suspects detained and three weapons captured! It was just another ordinary day in Vietnam.

The problem was that two pressmen – combat photographer Ronald Haeberle and army reporter Jay Roberts – had been assigned to Calley's platoon. They had witnessed appalling carnage. A woman had been hit by such ferocious, continuous fire that bone flew off chip by chip. Another woman was shot and her dead baby opened up by an M16, another baby slashed with a bayonet. A GI who had finished raping a girl then put his M16 into her vagina and pulled the trigger. An old man was thrown in a well and given a grenade – his choice: to drown or blow himself up. A child escaping from the carnage was brought down with

MY LAI

In September 1969, Lieutenant William Calley was charged with horrific war crimes, and the US public could hardly believe what it was hearing. For was Calley's crime just the tip of the iceberg?

1969

THE RIGHT STUFF?

In war, soldiers must depend on their officers for leadership. But did the US military establishment fail to staff its formations with men of a sufficiently high calibre during the Vietnam war?

Between 1965 and 1968, in an effort to meet the demand of Vietnam, there was an expansion of the US Army from a strength of 950,000 to one of 1,550,000. This expansion created particular problems since the army was already top heavy with officers. By 1972 there was one officer for every 5.7 men, representing almost a 100 per cent increase on the proportion of officers in 1945, and an increase of 59.9 per cent on 1965 levels. Compounding this problem were the rotation policy, which limited an officer's service to six months in a combat command, and the refusal of Washington to call on the army's reserves or National Guard. Consequently, there was a constant demand for new officers and NCOs at a time when anti-war feeling in the United States was severely curtailing recruitment.

Only 7 per cent of officers in Vietnam in 1967 were West Point graduates, the balance being sought from the Reserve Officers Training Corps (ROTC) on 268 university and college campuses. However, enrolment in the ROTC Program declined rapidly from 232,000 in 1965 to 216,000 by 1967. By 1972 it was as low as 73,000. Many of those who were joining the army were leaving after two or three combat tours, declining the opportunity to stay on for a long-term career. As a result, the army had to turn to its own Officer Candidate Schools (OCSs), which drew mainly on those of lower social and educational quality.

Lieutenant William Calley, for example, was an OCS product. Even his own defence counsel commented that Calley would never have been commissioned in the army were it not for the pressing need for officers during the war. In a sense, therefore, it was not so much the training but the quality of those trained that contributed to declining leadership in the army, although the nature of officer training did lean towards producing a modern manager rather than the gladiatorial leaders of the past. In the case of NCOs, however, the alarming decline in quality did stem to a large extent from the hasty 'Shake 'n' Bake' courses, which attempted to turn privates into sergeants of three or four stripes in just 21 weeks. Even then there were not sufficient numbers of NCOs, and many squads were led by Spec 4s. The inevitable result of this situation was inexperienced and permissive leadership amongst junior officers and NCOs. Subsequently, in the light of the Vietnam war, the army began to emphasize the need for more training in 'leadership ethics'.

a single shot. And Warrant Officer Hugh C. Thompson, the pilot of a small observation helicopter circling the village, began dropping smoke flares to mark wounded civilians so they could be medevaced out. He was horrified to see American soldiers follow the smoke and shoot the civilian casualties.

Gradually, the news leaked out. The men of Company C proudly proclaimed their great victory at My Lai. The VC distributed pamphlets denouncing it as an atrocity. And the army half-heartedly investigated rumours of a massacre that had even spread up the chain of command, but decided that there was no basis for investigation. One soldier, Ronald Ridenhour, also heard the rumour of a massacre and took an interest. He met men from Company C, including the most prominent abstainer from the atrocity, Michael Bernhardt. As their DEROS approached, their euphoria over their great victory was cooling and many of them were wondering how they were going to live with what they had done when they returned to The World. They knew that there was no action they could take without inviting murder charges, but they were willing to talk to Ridenhour.

He compiled their evidence, but felt if he took it to the army, they would stage a cursory investigation, resulting in another whitewash. However, when he returned home after his tour of duty he found he still could not forget what he had heard. So he wrote a letter outlining his evidence and sent out 30 copies to prominent politicians.

Congressman Morris Udall of Arizona pressed the army to send investigators to interview Ridenhour. Six months later and, nearly 18 months after the massacre, Lieutenant Calley was charged with murder.

He couldn't even read a map

Calley was an ordinary guy. An insurance appraiser in San Francisco, he was driving back to his native Miami where he'd been drafted when he ran out of money in Albuquerque. So he enlisted right there.

He took basic training at Fort Bliss, Texas, went to clerical school at Fort Lewis, Washington, and then went to officer candidate school at Fort Benning, Georgia, where he did little to distinguish himself. He graduated without even being able to read a map properly. Before leaving, he was asked to deliver a three-minute speech on 'Vietnam Our Host'. He recalled saying that American troops should not insult or assault women and that they should be polite, but the rest he was foggy on.

This sketchy training was not enough to prepare him for that moral vacuum called Vietnam. He found himself unable to control his own men and incapable of resisting the mounting pressure from superiors for a 'body count'.

The trouble was that he and his men could not find any VC. He has described how a prostitute he went with showed communist leanings and this

Previous page: Heliborne assault. Left: Calley arrives to testify. He is flanked by his military counsel (left) and his information officer. Above right: The newspapers break the story to the world.

worried him: should he have shot her? But out in the paddy fields he could find no one. His inept efforts at ambush were noisy enough to alert the enemy miles away. And on patrol his men were always getting shot at.

Patrolling near My Son in February, Calley's radioman was shot. For three days the company tried to penetrate My Son but were driven back. Two men were killed by booby traps. Another was hit by sniper fire. The patrol blundered into a nest of booby traps, but when they extricated themselves unscathed, two more men were cut down by sniper fire.

Severed limbs flew through the air

On their next assignment they were heading for the rendezvous point when an explosion tore through the early morning stillness and a man screamed. There was another explosion and another scream. Then another explosion and another and another and another.

They had stumbled into a minefield and, as men rushed forward to aid their wounded buddies, there were more and more explosions. Severed limbs flew through the air, medics crawled from body to body and always more explosions. It went on for almost two hours, leaving 32 men killed or wounded.

On 4 March the company was mortared and most of the men's personal possessions were destroyed. Ten days later, two days before the assault on My Lai, four men – including one of the company's last experienced NCOs – were blown to bits by a booby trap. In 32 days, Company C – whose field strength was 90 to 100 – suffered 42 casualties and had scarcely seen the enemy.

Calley had seen atrocities committed by the VC too. One night, the VC had captured one of his men and they heard him screaming all night, seven klicks away. Calley thought the VC had ampli-

MY LAI

In a wider operation carried out by Task Force Barker (under Lieutenant-Colonel F. Barker), Charlie Company of the 1/20th Infantry, Americal Division, went to clear Lai-4, a sub hamlet in Son Tinh district, Quang Ngai Province.

Commanded by Captain Ernest L. Medina under the direction of Lieutenant-Colonel O. K. Henderson and Major-General S. W. Koster, Charlie Company was moving on a known location of the VC 48th Battalion; heavy opposition was expected and no warning was to be given.

It was anticipated that civilians would have evacuated the area, and Medina left little doubt in his men's minds that their mission was to destroy VC. When the choppers touched down at 0730 on 16 March there was confusion over whether they were being fired on: no fire was actually received. In clearing the hamlet, at least two large groups of civilians were killed in cold blood. Only three known VC were among a total variously estimated at between 172 and 347 dead. Contributing factors were the universal 'gook syndrome', the expectation of losses and the inexperience and permissive attitude of officers.

Medina's report of 90 VC dead and only one American casualty (self-inflicted) should have aroused suspicion and both Barker and Henderson had flown low enough to have known that something was amiss. Koster knew that at least 28 civilians had died, but also chose not to press for investigation.

The attempt to conceal what had happened succeeded until an ex-GI turned reporter, Ronald Ridenhour, began in April 1969 to investigate allegations of a massacre at 'Pinkville'. This led to the establishment of the Peers Inquiry in November 1969 which eventually named 30 individuals as guilty of omission of duty or commission of an offence. Of 16 charged, only five were court martialled, and only Lieutenant William L. Calley was found guilty.

children grew up they'd be VC, like their fathers. And where were all the men? A village full of kids and no men? Their fathers must be VC.

Anyway, was what he had done any worse than dropping 500lb bombs on them or frying them with napalm? The atomic bomb had killed women and children in Hiroshima, hadn't it? And what were these damn Yankees getting so worked up about? He had done nothing worse than General Sherman in his march to the sea during the Civil War. The wisdom of the time was: 'The only way to end the war in Vietnam was to put *all* the dinks in boats and take them out to sea, kill all the North Vietnamese…then sink the boats.'

Calley arranged sewing lessons

Like many American servicemen, Calley eventually stopped believing in the war. He came round to thinking that to argue that communism had to be stopped in Vietnam, before it spread to

Left: Chairman L. Mendel (centre) of the House Armed Services Committee, who on 12 December 1969 ordered an in-depth investigation of the massacre, to be conducted by Senator F. Goward Herbert (right). On the left is Senator Leslie Arends, a leading Republican on the committee.

1969

fiers, but they didn't. They had skinned the GI alive, leaving only his face, then soaked him in salty water and torn his penis off. Calley had also seen a village chief broken in spirit when the VC delivered an earthenware jar containing what looked like stewed tomatoes to his door one morning. There were fragments of bone in it, and hair, and lumps of floating flesh. It was his son.

He'd seen GIs shoot down civilians for fun or target practise. He'd heard of helicopter gunships hired out for human turkey shoots and bored GIs going 'squirrel hunting' in civilian areas. He'd seen US soldiers casually fire on each other for no reason at all and heard of CS gas grenades being tossed into officers' hootches.

Duty above conscience

But within all this meaningless violence, Calley knew he had a mission. The US government had sent him to Vietnam for a reason. He was there, he believed, to stop communism. He did not know exactly what communism was, only that it was bad.

'I look at communism the same way a southerner looks at a Negro,' he said in an interview. 'As for me, killing those men in My Lai didn't haunt me. I didn't – I couldn't kill for the pleasure of it. We weren't in My Lai to kill human beings, really. We were there to kill ideology that is carried by – I don't know – pawns, blobs, pieces of flesh. And I wasn't in My Lai to destroy intelligent men. I was there to destroy an intangible idea.'

He even wished, humanely, he could shoot the philosophy part out of people's heads. Besides, it wasn't even really him doing it. 'Personally, I didn't kill any Vietnamese that day, I mean personally. I represented the United States of America. My country.' And Calley believed that he should put his duty to his country above his own conscience. He wasn't even worried about killing the aged, the women, the children. He'd heard of mamasans throwing grenades, children laying mines, girls carrying AK-47s. Besides, when the

THE TIP OF THE ICEBERG?

In a war of no fronts, where men saw their success or failure measured by the body count, civilian casualties were perhaps inevitable. But did US soldiers perpetrate war crimes that went unreported?

Although there was clearly much brutality during the Vietnam war, the American record was, given the circumstances, probably no worse than that of many other armies. In many areas, they found themselves fighting amongst a hostile population where civilians and guerrillas were virtually indistinguishable. Mines and booby traps caused continual casualties, with no indication of who had laid them; nothing could be more tempting than to take random revenge in villages almost certainly inhabited by VC sympathisers if not by actual part-time combatants. Some officers were only too willing to accept civilian dead as VC to boost body counts.

The United States recognized the Hague and Geneva conventions on the conduct of war, and imposed Rules of Engagement (ROE) through its own Uniform Code of Military Justice (UCMJ) and repeated MACV directives. Unfortunately, however, not enough was done to promulgate the laws of war at lower levels. The average soldier failed to achieve a basic familiarity with them. A mechanism existed for reporting atrocities through superiors but, until March 1966, only those inflicted on Americans by VC. Even when extended to cover all atrocities, there was still the difficulty that officers themselves might be implicated or reluctant to acknowledge their own lack of control over subordinates.

After October 1970, in the light of the revelations concerning My Lai, subordinates could report on their superiors and all procedures were generally tightened up. Even so, the failure to guard against the possibility of cover ups probably ensured that many cases went unreported. As it was, 79 per cent of all allegations of war crimes made against army personnel occurred only after the news of My Lai. Furthermore, in 1971 it was adjudged constitutionally impossible to prosecute former servicemen who had since left the army.

Vietnam was a media war, however, and major atrocities could not be concealed with groups such as the International War Crimes Tribunal in Stockholm and the domestic US war crimes 'industry' eager to expose any failings by American servicemen. Excluding My Lai, 241 war crimes allegations were made against army personnel between 1965 and 1975, of which 78 cases were substantiated. In some 36 cases involving 61 individuals, convictions were brought against the accused. In all, 201 army personnel were convicted of serious offences against civilians. Ninety Marines were also found guilty of such offenses, although Marine data does not distinguish between crimes committed during combat and those committed 'off duty'.

Thailand, Indonesia, Australia and finally the US, was like a man coming round to your house to murder his wife because he did not want blood stains on his carpet at home – and murdering your wife into the bargain.

He knew that it was the VC who were winning the hearts and minds of the Vietnamese people. After My Lai he became an S-5, an officer who bought pigs for peasant farmers, arranged sewing lesson for prostitutes and took children to hospital. But he began to realize that even his best efforts were wasted. The Vietnamese people did not want his help. They did not care about democracy or totalitarianism, capitalism or communism. They just wanted to be left alone.

'I was like a boy scout'

Calley's trial split the country. Those for the war protested that he was only doing his duty. Those against the war said that Calley was a scapegoat, massacres like My Lai were happening every day and it was Johnson, McNamara and Westmoreland who should be in the dock. But 80 per cent of those polled were against his conviction.

The jury went out on 16 March 1971, the third anniversary of the massacre at My Lai, and deliberated for two weeks. They found him guilty of murdering at least 22 civilians. He was sentenced to life imprisonment with hard labour. On review this was reduced to 20 years, then 10 years. He was finally paroled on 19 November 1974 after serving 3½ years under house arrest – less than two months for each murder he was found guilty of and less than four days for each of the civilians killed at My Lai.

Charges of premeditated murder and commanding an unlawful act – homicide – against his superior, Captain Ernest Medina, were reduced to involuntary manslaughter for failing to exercise proper control over his men. Not convinced that Medina actually knew what his men were doing inside My Lai-4, the jury acquitted him.

Charges – including one of the Nuremberg charges of violating the laws and customs of war – were brought against 12 other officers and men. Only five others were tried. None was found guilty.

A dozen officers – including Calley's divisional commander Major-General Samuel W. Koster – were charged with participation in the cover-up. None was found guilty.

Calley himself believes that he was no worse than most, and better than many, of the officers and men who served in Vietnam.

'I was like a boy scout, and I went by *The Boy Scout Handbook.*'

He believes that he did his duty to God and country, that he was trustworthy, loyal, helpful, friendly, courteous, kind, obedient, cheerful, thrifty, brave, clean and reverent. And still there were 347 civilians dead in My Lai-4. One hundred were slaughtered in a ditch. One of them was a two-year-old child.

Below: Helpless villagers cowering in terror. For those at My Lai, there was to be no mercy. The revelations of what happened there shocked the world. For the US public, the effect was traumatic. While most people thought Calley had been made a scapegoat, the discovery that such indiscriminate slaughter could be carried out by American troops was a cause for deep shame, and helped fuel the growing disillusionment with US involvement in the Vietnam war.

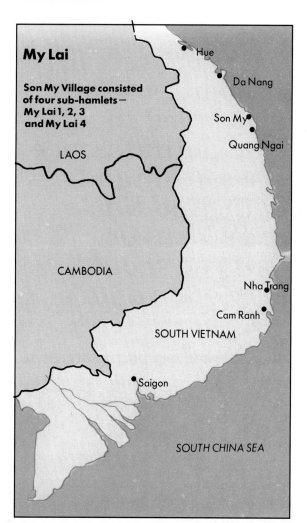

My Lai

Son My Village consisted of four sub-hamlets — My Lai 1, 2, 3 and My Lai 4

LAOS

CAMBODIA

SOUTH VIETNAM

Hue

Da Nang

Son My

Quang Ngai

Nha Trang

Cam Ranh

Saigon

SOUTH CHINA SEA

1969

When you were in the boonies, what you carried could mean the difference between life and death. And Uncle Sam's ideas on what you should carry often didn't make much sense

GRUNT KIT

'**S**hit!'...pant, wheeze, gasp...'This goddam hill's killing me'...sweat, strain, cramp...'Don't know if my legs can take it'...eye-blurring agony...'I'm carrying too much crap!'...stumble, trip...THUD! 'Medic! We've got a man down here!'

Everyone had to learn the hard way. It usually took only one trip to Vietnam's bush to figure out what infantrymen have known for centuries: the less stuff you carry, the better off you are.

And that really became a problem because Uncle Sam had his ideas of what you needed to carry to fight a war and, of course, Private Snuffy had his own ideas of what the job required.

About the only thing the two agreed upon was that grunts needed a weapon and bullets to shoot. After that, it was anybody's game.

Take, for instance, something as simple as headgear. Sam designed the steel pot, and figured that if it worked in World War II and Korea then it was good enough for Vietnam too. Well, weren't under artillery barrages or bombing raids much of the time, so the steel pot became just that much extra weight to lug around. Enter the soft-cover, boonie-hat, head band, head scarf, US Cavalry broad-brimmed hat, Aussie slouch hat, or just no hat at all. Many units demanded that grunts wear the steel pot as standard equipment in the field, and just as many combat troops wouldn't leave base

camp without one. Uncle Sam figured that everyone should wear it, and all of the time.

And Sam was probably right, but tell that to a bunch of grunts 15 days into a busted search and destroy mission where the temperature's hitting 105 and the most dangerous item flying around is a mosquito. Amazing how many helmets went missing in Vietnam.

Carry that weight

Webbing or LBE (load bearing equipment) was another area in which the powers that be and Private Snuffy found reason for conflict. In basic training troops were taught to wear the basic harness (pistol belt and suspenders), a butt pack, two canteens, two ammo pouches and field dressing pack. Nothing so unmilitary as a knife on the harness was allowed.

Try wearing that get up in a nasty little firefight. When you ran out of ammo you could always throw your butt pack at Charlie.

Although it varied from unit to unit, grunts I worked with tended to look like walking ammo bunkers. Four, and sometimes six, ammo pouches festooned the pistol belt, with a pair of crossed bandoliers hanging off one's chest, occasionally a few more slung over the shoulder. That didn't take into consideration the 200-400 boxed rounds sitting in the pack, or the spare belts for the M60 hanging around necks. What space was left on the pistol belt went to canteens, with the field dressing and knife hanging upside down on the harness for easy access. (Though not on the firing-shoulder side. After all, one has to put the rifle butt somewhere when shooting.)

Of course, bullets weren't the only killers in Snuffy's arsenal. Grenades – frags, willy-pete, CS gas and smoke – were stuffed into pockets of jungle fatigue pants as well as hung off ammo pouches and harness hooks and straps. ('It's getting heavy, sarge.' 'Shit, son, we ain't even started yet!')

Was that enough to send Snuffy off to war? Not even, GI. We've got to add just a few more mission-essential items on top of the steel pot, flak jacket, LBE, M16, the million or so rounds, grenades and knife to make your life pure misery – instead of just miserable. And since we've run out of space, here's a pack.

Left: On patrol in War Zone C. This grunt is wearing a steel pot helmet and carrying canteens, his M16, extra ammo for the 'Pig' and a large machete in his pack. Right: The 2d Battalion, 1st Air Cav, prepare for a long day in the boonies. If those packs seem heavy now, just wait until later.

1969

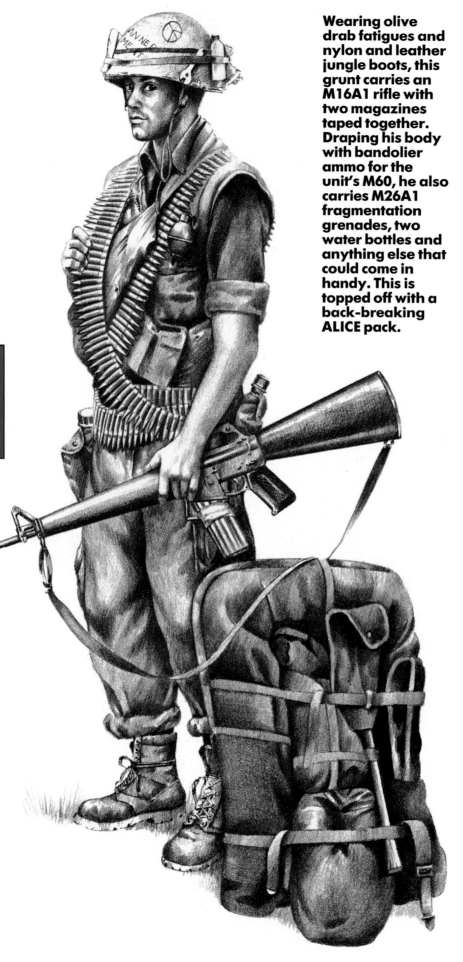

Wearing olive drab fatigues and nylon and leather jungle boots, this grunt carries an M16A1 rifle with two magazines taped together. Draping his body with bandolier ammo for the unit's M60, he also carries M26A1 fragmentation grenades, two water bottles and anything else that could come in handy. This is topped off with a back-breaking ALICE pack.

The good old ALICE (All-purpose Lightweight Individual Carrying Equipment – Uncle Sam's military name for 'pack') backpack, with its metal frame, was guaranteed to leave permanent grooves in your back within the first kilometre. ('Dad, what are those marks on your back?' 'Got 'em in the war, son. VC ALICE pack jumped me from behind.') The Alice pack is why God created C-ration packing boxes; they fitted quite neatly into the space between frame and back, saving the latter for better things.

Into or onto this olive-drab monster went Claymore mines and more grenades, trip flares, spare radio batteries (and if you're the lucky one, the radio itself), spare ammo for the machine gun, extra water, C-rations, heat tabs, rope and/or pull cord (for flipping booby-trapped bodies), spare socks, rifle cleaning kit, bug juice, poncho and liner and perhaps wet weather jacket and pants, extra field dressings, cigarettes, toilet articles, a book or two, entrenching tool, machete, and perhaps a LAW (light anti-tank weapon) or two. Forty or 50lbs? No sweat, GI. Sling on your LBE, heave Aunt Alice on your back, wrap a towel around your neck to soak up the sweat, port your M16 and it's off and stumbling into Charlie's backyard barbeque.

Experience as the teacher

One other item bears brief mention, as it was the finest and most widely-carried piece of equipment ever developed by Uncle Sam. It was small, durable, lightweight, cheap (thereby going against strict Army equipment procurement doctrine), functional and nearly indestructible. Everyone carried two or three, and if you lost one Uncle Sam gave you a free replacement. This truly magic piece of Army hardware was called the P-38 or, in civilian terms, a can opener. When one eats nothing but canned C-rations as a steady diet the P-38 becomes as integral to field gear as rounds are to the M16.

The battle between Private Snuffy and Uncle Sam over field kit never really resolved itself, although a pattern was easy enough to discern: the more combat a unit engaged in, the more likely it was that the type of gear carried to the bush was determined by an individual grunt rather than higher headquarters. Conversely, the closer to base camp a unit stayed, the more likely you were to see pressed jungle fatigues, shined boots, steel pots and trainee-type webbing. Needless to say, grunts really did prefer the bush to base camp.

As in most every war, lessons learned were generally passed down from generation to generation of Vietnam fighters. The prime axiom, 'Use the book as a guide and experience as the teacher,' held true, even to the most basic concept of field kit. And if there wasn't anyone around to extend that bit of wisdom and sort you out, then instant experience would.

Trip, stumble...THUD!

THE M79 BLOOPER

Where hand grenades and artillery couldn't go, the M79 provided the perfect punch

riflemen to form a squad, the launcher could be used without ranging up to 150 metres. At longer distances it was necessary to know how far away the target was because of the round's unusually high trajectory. A large flip up sight was situated about half way down the barrel with a rudimentary leaf foresight fixed at the end of the barrel. The rear sight was calibrated up to 375 metres in 25 metre intervals.

To use the weapon effectively the gunner needed to be encumbered by as little extra weight as possible. He therefore generally carried only a pistol as additional personal armament.

In the final years of the war, the M79 was superseded by the M203 40mm grenade launcher. This weapon was designed to be fitted to the M16 rifle so the gunner could take a normal part in the firefight using the rifle until he was needed to fire his grenades.

M79 40mm GRENADE LAUNCHER

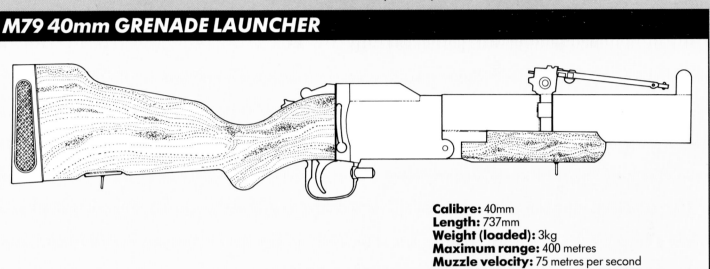

Calibre: 40mm
Length: 737mm
Weight (loaded): 3kg
Maximum range: 400 metres
Muzzle velocity: 75 metres per second

Making its debut in the Vietnam war, the US Army's M79 grenade launcher or 'Bloop gun' was a completely new infantry weapon without an equivalent in any other armed force.

Resembling a sawn-off shotgun, the grenade launcher was designed as a close-support weapon for the infantry. It plugged the gap in firepower between the maximum throwing distance of the hand grenade and the lowest range of supporting mortars, an area between 50 and 300 metres.

The M79 was a single-shot, shoulder-fired weapon which broke open for loading into the breech. It fired a spherical grenade which, although just 40mm in diameter, nevertheless had a kill radius of five metres.

The grenades were stabilised in flight by fins and by spin imparted by grooves in the rifled barrel. The shell travelled with a muzzle velocity of only 75 metres per second (com-

pared to around 800 metres per second for a machine gun) and a trained man could direct a grenade through a house window from 150 metres.

As the grenade spiralled through the air, the rotation caused weights in the fuze mechanism to arm the grenade when it had flown 30 metres, after which the grenade would detonate on impact. Thus, the warhead could not be accidentally detonated through a fall or bump or being struck by a bullet. The minimum range also prevented the launcher from placing himself in the grenade's fragmentation radius.

For close range use the Army developed two shells for the M79, one containing buckshot and the other containing 45 dart-like 'flechettes'. The launcher could also fire airburst projectiles, smoke grenades, flares and CS gas-grenades.

Generally operated with two M79 grenadiers joining with eight M16

The grenadier's standard equipment — M79 and flak jacket.

THE COLLAPSE OF MORALE

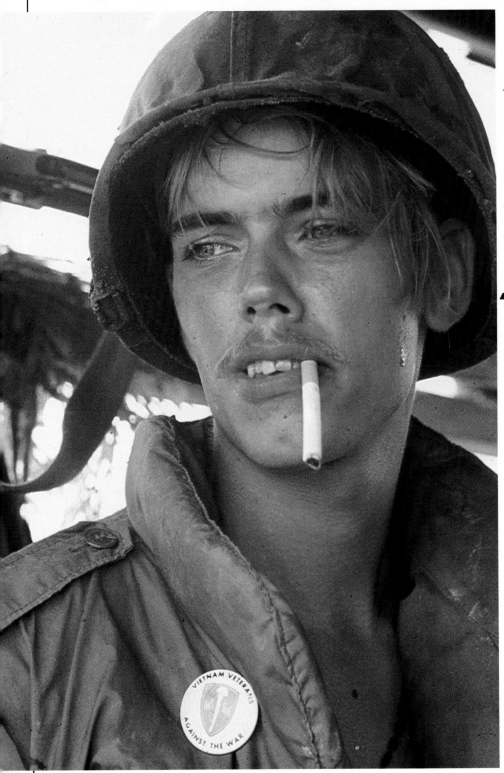

Grunts had fought hard, and taken what was thrown at them. But who wanted to be the last man to die in Nam?

'I remember 20 July 1969. I sat in my hooch and watched a satellite relay of the astronauts landing on the moon and saw Neil Armstrong's first step on the surface. When I heard that fucking bullshit-nonsense phrase, 'One small step for man, a giant leap for mankind', I was so angry. I thought to myself, 'Come here and step with me for a day, motherfucker!'

As the war limped on towards a new decade, this Nam-weary Marine was speaking for every front-line, mud-caked, leech-bitten, VC-taunted grunt throughout the length of this ravaged country.

Fighting, killing and fear

For the young Americans arriving in Vietnam in 1969, this war had rapidly decreasing credibility. By the end of the year, Americans would have been fighting longer in Vietnam than they did in World War II, and there was no end in sight – the spectacle of Charlie running riot during Tet had destroyed any notion of imminent US victory. By 1968, Nixon had decided that the war could not be won solely by force of arms. Now this belief was surfacing in speeches calling for 'days and even years of patient and prolonged diplomacy'. For the grunt on the ground, this could only mean wasting more time and lives in a war that was to be determined not in the paddyfields of Nam but in the air over Hanoi and in the corridors of power.

In the mind of every US combatant, the validity of the war was being challenged. Troop withdrawals began in June, the anti-war movement gained the support of more respected figures every day and the TV no longer reported victories, just endless footage of bloody, stubborn fighting.

More and more soldiers began to wonder why they were there. Afterwards, 60 per cent of post-'67 combat veterans, troops who were draftees rather than the professionals of 1965, would admit that either they were against the war or simply didn't know why they were fighting.

As the conflict dragged on, morale sank, self-preservation became the order of the day. The motto of the moment echoed everywhere: 'Don't be the last GI to die in Nam.'

A year after Tet, the routine of fighting and killing, fear and boredom and watching friends being shipped home in body bags continued. But Westmoreland's 'search and destroy' tactics gave way to guerrilla warfare – endless jungle patrols, ambush and counter-ambush. Marine Lieutenant James Webb sweated through this composite of booby traps, greenery and paranoia:

'I was not prepared for the continual primitiveness; I carried my pack – it had a poncho, a toothbrush, letter-writing gear and that was it...We moved every three days, didn't take a bath for months...We ate C-rations continually and virtually every single person in my unit got either ring worm, hook worm, dysentery or malaria, and some of us had them all.'

Slogging through the jungle, fighting a war you couldn't care less about, soon produced reluctant troops. And some of the reluctants saw mutiny as the only way out.

Rebels with a refusal clause

In 1969 more and more men simply refused to fight. In the next year the number of 'wilful refusals' would rise sharply and even the elite 1st Air Cav would notch up 35 combat refusals over the next 12 months. And these were only the reported cases. There were many more instances where a little ingenuity avoided both combat and a confrontation with superiors. Tim O'Brien, infantryman and later prize-winning novelist, unashamedly applied just this ingenuity: 'At night we were supposed to send out ambushes; so sometimes we did, other times we did not.' When they didn't, O'Brien's officers radioed false grid co-ordinates to the artillery who would blast the hell out of the empty jungle where the non-existent ambush team had 'seen' communists. 'Phoney ambushes were good for morale,' concludes O'Brien. At worst, combat refusal meant a prison sentence and a dishonourable discharge; combat could, and often did, mean death or permanent disability.

There was one other, more hazardous, route out of combat – desertion.

Getting out

Up to 1968, the desertion rate among American troops in Vietnam had been lower than for previous wars. But from 1969 onwards, desertion increased fourfold. And it didn't just take place in Vietnam – the mere chance of being sent Namward was increasing desertion world-wide. In Saigon, Tokyo and Hong Kong, soldiers on R&R were disappearing, to resurface in Canada or Sweden. There was a vast number of underground GI newspapers around to help the would-be deserter. Many of these splashed anti-war sentiments on every page and either operated an escape route themselves, or gave contacts for one. The dispi-

Far left: The badge says it all. A soldier makes his feelings clear. Below: Combat readiness with the 1st Air Cav.

EARLY US TROOP WITHDRAWALS

In effect, US disengagement from Vietnam began in April 1968 when Johnson's Secretary of Defense, Clark Clifford, had rejected demands by Westmoreland and the JCS for 206,000 men to be added to the army world-wide. Clark also initiated 'Vietnamization', although the word was first coined by his successor in the Nixon administration, Melvin Laird.

The process accelerated greatly once Nixon became president in January 1969. Pulling out ground forces would satisfy US public opinion, reduce expenditure and enable the draft to be phased out.

Following discussions with President Thieu on the Pacific island of Midway, Nixon announced on 8 June 1969 that 25,000 men would be withdrawn by 31 August. The 'Nixon Doctrine', proclaimed on Guam on 25 July, emphasized the policy of Vietnamization, and further withdrawals were announced on 16 September (35,000 men) and 15 December (50,000).

However, Nixon was careful not to commit himself to total withdrawal, since the pace at which Vietnamization could be accomplished was dependent upon balancing domestic opinion against both communist activity and ARVN capability. Moreover, Nixon had inherited the Paris peace talks and was determined to maintain pressure on Hanoi through airpower.

MACV was wary of withdrawal but Laird insisted on daily statistics and Westmoreland's successor, General Creighton Abrams, drew up a 'glide path' of 14 incremental stages of withdrawal up to November 1972.

In the first phase, from 1 July to 31 August 1969, the promised 25,000 men – primarily the 9th Infantry Division – were withdrawn, while the 3d Brigade, 82d Airborne Division and the USMC 3d Division comprised most of the 40,500 men withdrawn in the second increment between 18 September and 15 December. By the end of 1969, 51,670 men had left Vietnam.

1969

rited, near anarchic state of the US Army was felt everywhere. Ernest Hemingway's advice still rang true – anyone pondering the glamour of war should: 'Ask the infantry, ask the dead'. One infantryman shows why:

'You could shoot him in the head'

'We had a sense that we were no longer the GI who had to march, who had to salute. That was shit. We didn't have to salute nobody. We dressed the way we wanted to dress. If I wanted to wear a boony hat, I wore one. If I wanted one sleeve up and one sleeve down then I did it. If I didn't want to shave I didn't. Nobody fucked with nobody in the field. An officer knew that if he messed with you, in a firefight you could shoot him in the head. That was the standard procedure in any infantry unit. Anybody tells you differently, he's shitting you. If you mess with my partner as an NCO or something like that, in the unwritten code there, I had the right to blow your brains out.'

Mutiny and the bounty

This breakdown in discipline soon gave the military a new word – fragging. The word originated from the murder of officers with fragmentation grenades, but soon came to cover any method of doing away with your superiors.

The easiest way to deal with an officer who made life difficult, or wanted his men to take unnecessary risks, was to get rid of him in the field. Company scout Mike Beaman recalls, 'We were aware that officers were being fragged and the officers knew it too.'

Fragging usually followed two patterns. The first came in three stages and gave the targeted officer a chance to change his ways. First a smoke grenade was thrown into his hooch and, if that didn't convince him, it was followed by a CS gas grenade. As one GI said, 'When they put the gas on you, yeah, you know they mean you no good.' If this final warning wasn't heeded, death in battle

could come from any direction.

A 'bounty' fragging would arrive with no warning. Here money was offered for the removal of an officer. The underground newspaper *GI Says*, went as far as offering a $10,000 dollar reward for the death of Lieutenant-Colonel Weldon Honeycutt, the man responsible for the attack on Hamburger Hill. One ex-Marine tells how he contributed to a bounty on a hated sergeant in the 3d Marine Division:

'The first man with a witness in a firefight who blew his ass away with a round across his eyeballs, would get $1000. I personally offered approximately $25 for his head.'

Charles Anderson, another Marine, remembers an incident which, he stresses, 'did not occur in my particular company'. Some of Anderson's buddies were being given a hard time by a gung-ho sergeant, an old professional who was hot on spit and polish. One day the company was caught in a communist ambush. 'When they found the sergeant there were more holes in his back than in his front.'

Flare ups and fraggings

Fragging made officers reluctant to enter situations that could lead to major incidents. But under the conditions of constant fear, officer-men confrontations sometimes flared up over nothing. Captain James Hickey, a gunship pilot, was queuing in a PX. Without thinking, he referred to the soldier who pushed in ahead of him as 'boy'. The man was black and began to accuse Hickey of racism, threatening to 'blow him away'. Trying to calm the situation, Hickey left, but the man followed. Once outside, he hit the captain several times.

The officers were often pitifully inexperienced. These green young men could lead their men into an ambush or drive them up the wall through misreading a map. As one NCO describes:

'With rations for only one day's patrol we stayed in the bush for three days and three nights, simply because we were lost. This gentleman wouldn't listen to anyone. I know for a fact that we crossed the same river three times and I made every attempt to indicate that to him, but of course I had no jurisdiction as to which way we should go.'

Sometimes an incompetent officer could be saved from a bullet in the back if his superiors noticed his incompetence and removed him. Captain Smith was one such officer who, through sheer stupidity and needless casualties, lost the respect of his men. He very nearly lost his life: 'The lieutenants gracefully avoided him. He was openly ridiculed by the men. There was half-serious talk about him being a marked man. The black soldiers hated him, saying it was only a matter of time before someone chucked a grenade into his foxhole. We were all careful not to sleep near Captain Smith.'

Smith was moved soon after – but many other officers received the grenade before the recall.

Left: A disruptive sentiment on a disruptive-pattern helmet? **Right:** These battle-weary troops from the 1st Air Cav had just staged a 'combat refusal' at the PACE firebase. **Below:** The symbol of peace and the bullets of war clash on the chest of this 61st Infantry Division trooper. **Below right:** After the ultimate holiday – 365 days of sun, shells and shrapnel – just where do you go next?

FRAGGING

It is a fact of war that soldiers often take the opportunity of battle to murder or disable unpopular or feared NCOs and officers. What was unusual about Vietnam was the sheer scale of 'fragging', and the fact that a recognized system for its operation was developed.

The official totals cover a four-year period, from 1969 – when the phenomenon became so widespread that it could no longer remain unnoticed among battlefield casualties – until 1972. They originate from Congressional hearings on the subject. There were: 239 incidents in 1969, 383 in 1970, 333 in 1971 and 58 in 1972. A total of 1013 fraggings in four years, of which 86 died; roughly 3 per cent of the 3269 officer deaths in Vietnam between 1961 and 1972. These figures are only of deaths from grenades and can only be approximate as they omit figures for rifle and automatic-weapons fire and knifings.

As with all statistics originating in Vietnam, these figures are highly debatable – the Judge Advocate General's Corps estimated that only 10 per cent of fragging attempts resulted in the offender coming to trial.

The only figures available for combat mutinies, identified by the euphemism 'combat refusal', are the official Army statistics on 'Insubordination, mutiny and other acts involving wilful refusal to perform a lawful order'. Convictions for such offences were 82 in 1968, 117 in 1969 and 131 in 1970. The figures for 1971 (the year of the mutiny at the PACE firebase) and 1972 are not provided.

Figures for world-wide AWOLs and desertion indicate a clear increase as the Vietnam war progressed. In 1967, these were low at 78 AWOL per 1000 enlisted monthly strength. And there were only 21 per 1000 desertions. This increased to 112.3 per 1000 AWOL and 42.4 per 1000 desertions in 1969. By 1971, these figures were standing at 177 per 1000 and 74 per 1000 respectively, and by 1973 the Marines were suffering 234 per 1000 AWOL.

AMERASIANS:

CHILDREN OF THE WAR

Estimates vary, but there were probably about 35,000 children born to Vietnamese women of American fathers. Scorned and discriminated against, most Amerasian children were abandoned when the US pulled out. The Vietnamese themselves called these Amerasian war babies the 'dust of life'. Many became beggars, others survived in orphanages – a tragic legacy of war

Left: Abandoned by her American father, scorned by her homeland as the 'dust of life', nine-year-old Binh is one more orphaned relic of the war's culture clash.

Below: A product of black America and bloodied Vietnam, Le Thi Ut now learns arithmetic under the gaze of Ho Chi Minh and the red flag of communism.

Left: For American troops, forming a relationship with a Vietnamese girl was fraught with problems. One GI's girlfriend told him that 'seeing you makes me a prostitute in the eyes of my country.' Below left: Le Thi Lien with a photograph of her American father. He left in 1970. Below: Distinguished by the pale skin of his GI pop, Cuanh lives and works with his grandparents.

FORCE REMAGEN

In spite of it all, when the US Army was given a real task to fulfill, it responded magnificently – even when that task involved taking tanks over ravines and moving an armoured column into the NVA heartland without any ground supply

Above: Lurching their slab-sided battlewagon to a halt, the crew of an M113 APC emerge and await supplies from the sky, their only lifeline. Far right: Crunching along a prime Vietnamese arterial road, M48s lead the armoured column onwards. Right: A tanker maintains radio contact as a force of M113s and M48s races through billowing smoke and a battle-deadened landscape.

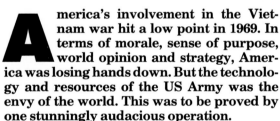

America's involvement in the Vietnam war hit a low point in 1969. In terms of morale, sense of purpose, world opinion and strategy, America was losing hands down. But the technology and resources of the US Army was the envy of the world. This was to be proved by one stunningly audacious operation.

On 14 March 1969 Lieutenant-Colonel Carmen P. Milia, commander of the 1st Battalion, 77th Armored Regiment, was ordered to report to Lieutenant-General Richard G. Stilwell, commander of XXIV Corps in Quang Tri Province. Since arriving in the province nine months earlier, the crews of Milia's tanks and Armoured Fighting Vehicles (AFVs) had been kicking their heels, restricted to infantry support. But this was about to change.

Milia was ordered to form an armoured task force, take it westwards along Route 9 to Khe Sanh, and from there conduct a reconnaissance-in-force along the Laotian border. Milia left the interview excited and exhilarated; he later described the task as 'challenging'. Others described it as 'impossible'.

Problems abounded. For a start, the terrain was extremely difficult. Route 9 was basically a single-track road – badly in need of repair – which followed the Quang Tri river westward through jungle-clad gorges, climbing 430m to the Khe Sanh plateau. Landslides had washed away whole

sections and what nature hadn't destroyed NVA sappers had. Along the entire route not a single culvert or bridge remained intact. Moreover, since the 3d Marine Division's evacuation of the Khe Sanh plateau in July 1968, this was virtually a no-go area for the allied forces.

Testing the tanks

So why had Stilwell given such a difficult task to an armoured force? The two stated objectives, protecting the allies' northern flank and disrupting the enemy's logistical system, were better suited to the infantry or air cavalry. Stilwell's motives were more complex. He wanted to test claims that the most effective employment of armoured units was not in an infantry support role, but as an independent strike force operating without land lines of communication: supplied only by helicopters.

Many XXIV Corps officers predicted disaster. Even if armour made it to the plateau, they argued, it would be defeated by maintenance and supply problems. But Milia was undaunted. During the Korean War he had operated tanks in mountains higher and more rugged than any in Vietnam. He also had impressive technical qualifications, including a degree in engineering. Since arriving in Vietnam, Milia had spent many long hours trying to streamline the notoriously inefficient logistical systems within armoured units. He solved the problem for his own battalion by converting one of his mechanized infantry units, Company D, into a logistical support company. Although this reduced overall firepower, it meant that extra fuel and spares would always be on hand. In the forthcoming operation Company D was to play a vital role.

Chinook shuttle service

Only 72 hours after leaving Stilwell, Milia had put together an integrated multi-role task force. Its teeth lay in the M48 Patton tanks and the M113 APCs of the mechanized infantry of the 1st Battalion. These were supported by batteries of self-propelled guns and mortars – 105mm M108s, twin 40mm M42s, and M106 4.2in mortars. Maintenance, engineering and construction were the province of two giant M60 Armored Vehicle Launcher Bridges (AVLBs), platoons of M88 recovery vehicles, M728 combat engineer vehicles and D7E bulldozers. Logistics would continue to be the responsibility of Captain Emerson Addington's Company D, whose M113s were to be restocked each day by a CH-47 Chinook shuttle service. Apart from that, Milia declined aerial support. If the operation did succeed it would be the armour, not the air cavalry, which would claim the credit. Task Force Remagen comprised

1500 men and 86 tracked vehicles of 10 different types, a force which Milia estimated would require at least 13 Chinook loads of supplies each day, and virtually round the clock maintenance. Men, as well as systems and machines, would be tested to the limit.

Slow progress

The advance was methodical. At dawn on 17 March the M113s of 1st Battalion's scout platoon, accompanied by AVLBs and bulldozers, rolled out of Ca Lu westward on Route 9. At first the land was relatively flat. The scout platoon reconnoitered every potential ambush site and swept the road for mines, providing protection for the bulldozers clearing obstructions, and the engineers replacing culverts. By dusk the foot of the escarpment had been reached. Milia moved his M108s, M106s and a company of mechanized infantry forward and established a firebase. At dawn the next day the force continued its advance.

The going gets tough

The going rapidly deteriorated. Route 9 followed a deep gorge in the wall of the escarpment, climbing at a 45 degree gradient via a series of hairpin bends. This was 'Ambush Alley', notorious since

THE MILITARY-INDUSTRIAL COMPLEX

Huge profits were possible through the Vietnam war. Is there any truth in the theory that the military-industrial complex was merely a self-perpetuating, war-mongering monster?

America's dependence on technology to fight the war in Vietnam clearly suited those firms which manufactured the appropriate weapons. Huge profits were to be made from war-related contracts – by 1972, for example, over $10 billion had been made available just to replace aircraft losses in Vietnam – and, in the right circumstances, enormous funds could be extracted from the government to pursue research into new or more effective technological devices. As many of the companies involved had close ties with the administration and the Pentagon, they were ideally placed to influence decisions and ensure the adoption of new ideas, however bizarre. Small wonder, therefore, that this military-industrial complex was blamed for creating false hopes which only served to fuel unworkable strategies. To many commentators, the influence of weapons-producing companies was evil, perpetuating a hopeless war and tempting the military to adopt ever more destructive responses to enemy attack.

There is an element of truth in all this. Just to cite one example among many, the promises made in 1966-67 about the effectiveness of sensors undoubtedly helped to persuade McNamara to press ahead with his 'Line' of static firebases south of the DMZ, even though the Marines were advocating a more mobile strategy. But the military-industrial complex argument can be taken too far. Indeed, there is doubt whether it had a substantial impact on the prosecution of the war. In 1965, when US main force commitment began, many firms were just not interested in the war, arguing that if it turned out to be as short as people were saying, any investment in war-production would be a waste, diverting resources from a 'consumer boom' that virtually guaranteed long-term profit. In this sense, the effect on strategy was less clear-cut, although it may have helped to force the military to recognise the limitations of the Vietnam conflict. If the military-industrial complex is not fully mobilized, the war will, by definition, be restricted.

Above far left: Hovering like some mechanical dragonfly, a CH-64 Skycrane supplies grateful grunts with their logistical lifeblood. Above left: Suspended feet above the ground, an H-46 Sea Knight delivers its load. Above: As his buddy dons shades, as if wishing for a healthier climate, one soldier sits astride a tin can and cracks open a tin of beer. Left: Amidst the gloom of a Vietnamese forest, an M551 Sheridan reconnaissance tank straddles the road and waits.

CIVILIAN CONTRACTORS

The rapid expansion of US forces in Vietnam after March 1965 imposed substantial strains on existing support services, and it soon became apparent that the Army alone could not cope. Civilian firms were already being used to supplement the Army's efforts. In May 1966 the process was regularized with the creation of the US Army Procurement Agency, Vietnam, charged with negotiating and administering all civilian contracts.

Civilian companies provided a wealth of services, ranging from air movement of servicemen to and from Vietnam to laundering their jungle fatigues, but the really big contracts were awarded in three distinct areas. By far the largest was for repair and utilities, through which civilian firms constructed and maintained base camp facilities, as well as providing repair teams to look after installed equipment such as generators and refrigerators.

The second was for electrical power, essential as South Vietnam lacked the generating capacity to satisfy the enormous demands of US forces. As early as March 1966 the Vinnell Corporation converted 11 oil-tankers, sailing them to Vietnam with generators on board.

The third contract area concerned fuel distribution. Here, the Army was lucky in that three big oil companies – Esso, Shell and Caltex – already had refinery facilities in Saigon, and they were contracted to provide petroleum products throughout South Vietnam. More difficult was transportation, and civilian trucking companies such as Equipment Inc, Philco Ford and the Korean Han Jin outfit had to be specially contracted. The Alaskan Barge and Transport Company helped by providing coastal barges and tugs.

All of this was expensive – in 1968-69 the Procurement Agency awarded contracts worth half a billion dollars – and involved the employment of more than 50,000 civilians inside the war zone. Without it, however, the US military effort in-country would have been impossible to sustain.

the siege of Khe Sanh a year earlier. The bulldozers, followed by the massive AVLBs, crawled forward, pushing rock-slides before them. To the right was a sheer cliff while to the left was the gorge, hundreds of metres deep. At several points the road was not wide enough to take the tracks of the AVLBs until bulldozers had gouged at the cliff face. Three hundred metres up and two kilometres from the rim of the plateau, the biggest obstacle lay in wait. Here the river gorge swung abruptly to the north. Route 9, however, continued westwards across the deep and swiftly flowing river. Or it would have done, if the bridge had not been completely destroyed by NVA sappers. The platoon was tense, watching as the AVLB edged its own bridge forward. Suddenly wild cheering erupted as the bridge reached the far side with just a metre to spare. Now the only worry was the NVA.

Before him lay a moonscape

By twilight on 18 March, Lieutenant Goldsmith, the commander of the scout platoon, had reached the edge of the plateau. Behind him lay 'one of the most beautiful valleys in Vietnam'. Before him lay a moonscape. The ground, honeycombed by B-52 strikes, was still devoid of vegetation – mines, unexploded bombs, fortifications, barbed wire and rotting parachutes were everywhere.

With the route to the rim of the plateau now

secure, the bulk of Task Force Remagen rolled forward at 0800 hours on 19 March. Anticipating ambush and mechanical breakdown, Milia arranged his order of march so that similar weight-class vehicles travelled together. If one vehicle was disabled the other could push or pull it out of trouble. However, thanks to careful preparation, the advance went without incident. The Task Force moved into the ruins of Khe Sanh at 1300 hours. During the afternoon Milia moved his covering forces up onto the plateau and shortly before dusk the AVLB picked up its bridge from the Quang Tri River crossing. Lines of communication were now severed. Task Force Remagen was deep in hostile country, totally dependent on aerial resupply.

Bulldozing the jungle

NVA and VC forces on the plateau, taken completely by surprise by the sudden appearance of massed enemy armour, fled westwards across the Xe Pon river into Laos, aiming for the safety of the Co Roc mountains. Milia's inclination was to follow and bring the NVA to battle. Instead he was ordered to push south across country parallel to the Xe Pon and interdict traffic on the NVA-controlled Route 926.

The 20km advance to Route 926 through heavy jungle, constantly observed and harassed by fire from the Co Roc mountains, was the most testing part of the operation. Bulldozers a tore a path for the

heavy equipment while the tanks and M113s smashed through independently.

End of experiment

Route 926 was finally reached five days later on 26 March. For the next four days Task Force Remagen conducted extensive search and destroy operations, covering approximately 100 sq km. But the enemy contacts they made were few and far between. On 30 March the task force withdrew back along the Xe Pon river to Khe Sanh.

A tribute to Milia's maintenance and logistical system was that although the Task Force continued to operate independently of land lines of communication in extremely rugged terrain, not a single vehicle had to be abandoned because of breakdown. Though 50 of his 86 vehicles suffered major mechanical faults, replacement parts were usually available within two hours.

Nor did logistics restrict Milia's operational concept. During the 43-day operation, an average of 15 Chinook flights per day brought in more than 1000 tons of supplies. Apart from major mechanical components, Task Force Remagen received more than 80,000 gallons of fuel, 18,000 artillery rounds and 225,000 rounds of smallarms ammunition.

Though in a purely military sense Task Force Remagen achieved little – only 73 enemy were killed during the entire operation – as an experiment in proving a theory it was a resounding success. Some have claimed it was irrelevant to the war but, in terms of what could be achieved by American technology and know-how, it had been an object lesson to the world.

1969

Above: Rain, radios and red earth. Two grunts huddle in their ponchos as the weather turns nasty.

US LOGISTICS

Throughout the period of main force commitment to Vietnam, virtually all supply needs had to be imported from the United States, a distance of about 16,000 kilometres. The size of the operation was staggering: between 1965 and 1969 alone, something like 22 million tons of dry cargo and 14 million tons of bulk petroleum were moved across the Pacific, almost all in merchant ships. Arriving at ports such as Saigon, Qui Nhon or the specially constructed facility at Cam Ranh Bay, the supplies were then sorted, stored and distributed, creating a logistics 'pipeline' of enormous complexity, made worse by the existence of parallel supply lines for both the USAF and Marines.

The movement of supplies in South Vietnam was co-ordinated, initially in Saigon and then (after 1969) at Long Binh, by the US Army's 1st Logistical Command. Activated in April 1965, it faced formidable problems. The existing supply infrastructure in Vietnam was poor – ports lacked deep-water berths, warehouse facilities were virtually non-existent and roads and railways were only rudimentary and prone to guerrilla attack. It took about 18 months to produce a workable system. During that time, new ports were opened up, warehouses were built and the process of supply requisition was computerized. At the same time, an elaborate in-country distribution network was created.

Initially, the network used coastal and river transportation, but this proved inadequate as the size of US (and allied) ground force commitment increased. Some priority supplies could be moved by air, although the small aircraft and helicopter fleet available to the army precluded a heavy dependence. Instead, rail and road facilities had to be used, the latter proving by far the more effective. By 1968, army and contract truck companies were shifting nearly a million tons of supplies a month, moving into all areas of Vietnam in protected convoys. It was a vital lifeline.

Left: An attractive 'cable-drum' table forms the centrepiece in this view of a firebase 105mm gun position. The shells, wood and the ephemera of war littering the site give a chaotic appearance to what was in fact a highly organized and meticulously executed operation.

Ken Sams is now working on a book about underground newspapers and his Vietnam war experiences.

Neither government propaganda nor an anti-war tract, the Grunt Free Press aimed to give the grunts a humourous look at a nasty war

It was in 1969 that *Grunt*, the glossy magazine that I had been publishing for the troops in the Nam, went hippie and became the *Grunt Free Press*. The art became psychedelic, the articles more far out, the nudes more explicit, the humour blacker and the editorial tone more anti-regulation army.

I had been in my third year as Chief, Air Force CHECO (Contemporary Historical Evaluation of Combat Operations) in Vietnam when I first came up with the idea of an unofficial mag for the grunts. It was 1967. The war needed a laugh. I needed one too. My idyllic French colonial lifestyle in Saigon was beginning to disintegrate. The city was overcrowded with US troops, civilians and carpetbaggers from all over the East. The battleground was getting crowded too – NVA pouring in down the Ho Chi Minh Trail, US divisions flying in from The World. More guns. More planes. More bombs. More operations.

Poems, limericks and nudes

General Westmoreland was being suckered into a big Dien Bien Phu-style shoot-out at Khe Sanh. The Cong were infiltrating Saigon in preparation for Tet. And I was in my Tan Son Nhut office grinding out official Air Force reports which were slowly convincing me that the only way we could win the war was if we could devise the sort of bomb which, if dropped in the middle of Yankee Stadium, would kill only the Italians in the crowd.

I needed something to balance the heavy Air Force bombing stuff I was writing. A couple of cartoon and humour books I had written the previous year were selling quite well on *Stars and Stripes* bookstalls throughout the Nam, so I decided to put out a magazine. I called it *Grunt* and, instead of burning myself out after work in the Saigon bars, decided I'd burn the midnight oil laying out cartoons, poems, graffiti, nudes, in magazine format, just as *Playboy's* Hugh Hefner would have done. I aimed it at grunts and gave them something they could identify with. I paid a couple of the moonlighting *Stars and Stripes* staff to handle printing and distribution.

Printed in Tokyo, the magazine contained 50 pages of non-violent fun stuff. There were Viet-

Far left: Typical covers of *Grunt* and *Grunt Free Press*. Main picture: One of Tran Dinh Thuc's distinctive psychedelic centre-folds. Note the peace symbol. Left: Writings and drawings were often contributed by the troops themselves. Above, a cartoon feature that regularly adorned the fold-out inner cover.

413

namese girls in sexy poses, girls who I suppose have since done time in post-war VC re-education camps: 'You posed like this in *Grunt* magazine. Slap. Slap.' We had a cartoon showing Marines landing on the beach at Da Nang among bikini-clad girls. The caption read: 'You sure this is where we're supposed to assault?' There was an advice column. *Question*: 'I'm a nice guy. How do I meet a Vietnamese girl outside of bars?' *Answer*: 'Just tell the girl to meet you outside a bar.' A photo of VC radio newscasters had a caption which read: 'Our attack on the Cholon PX resulted in the capture of 28,000 tons of rice, thereby denying the Americans enough food to feed a division for a year.' And there were limericks: 'There was a Marine from Da Nang. Who met a young girl in Nha Trang. He had quite a shock when he looked at his clock. It was too late to cure what she brang.'

That kind of stuff. Nothing sensational. Nothing radical. But still I was on tricky ground. Even though I never neglected my official duties, there were spooks planted in my office. They ransacked my apartment and seduced the live-in maid, looking for something to pin on me.

Nobody was allowed to die

In February 1968, 10,000 copies of *Grunt* had hit the news stands. It was a success. All copies sold in short order. Grunts started sending poems, drawings and photos. Artists came round offering their services. I had no difficulty putting out an issue a month and, by the third issue, *Grunt* was selling 30,000 copies. It was not making me any money, but then I wasn't in it for money.

For me, *Grunt* was therapy. No matter what I wrote in my official reports I couldn't get across what I knew to be true. You could bomb North Vietnam back to the Stone Age, even nuke it, but that wouldn't get rid of the VC sniper on the end of the Tan Son Nhut runway who could well be working by day as a barber for US troops; or the VC bar girls teasing secrets out of grunts or the mamasans pushing hard drugs in the barracks. My underground brief as publisher of *Grunt* was to write about anything in the war that struck me as funny – and that included the war itself. CHECO, balanced by *Grunt*, kept me sane.

In 1969, I visited my hippie son in London. When I came back, I switched from a slick format to a cheap paper tabloid like the underground papers back in The World. The *Grunt Free Press* was then printed in Saigon by a moonlighting Vietnamese Air Force officer who had access to a US AID printing press. In *Grunt Free Press*, nobody was ever allowed to die – not in stories, cartoons or pictures. Even a VC, if he captured one, would get a laugh or two out of the magazine. That's the kind of publication I wanted it to be. After a day writing about bombing North Vietnam, Laos, Cambodia and the 'short round' bombing of friendlies, including grunts, it was a relief to get back to my penthouse and sketch out a cartoon showing a US bomb on the Ho Chi Minh Trail ticking away 2ft from a terrified Cong – a jack-in-

I DON'T RELATE TO THIS ENVIRONMENT

Grunt Free Press relied on a mix of cartoons and pin-ups (left and opposite page). The paper showed both sides, US and Vietnamese, in a humorous light, and often used other comic book heroes, such as Alfred E. Newman of 'Mad' (below).

"WHAT--ME WORRY?"

TRUTH OR PROPAGANDA?

When the average serviceman in Vietnam wanted to know how the war was going, he picked up the army's official newspaper. But did he glean the truth from his reading?

Service newspapers were nothing new. During World War I, semi-official and unofficial trench newspapers such as *The Wipers Times* flourished in the British Army, while officially authorized service newspapers multiplied in all theatres during World War II. The British Army Newspaper Unit produced *Union Jack*, while American forces were served by such publications as *Yank*, which was available worldwide by 1945, and *Roundup* in the China-India-Burma theatre. US forces in the Mediterranean had a daily *Stars and Stripes*, which also appeared in weekly versions elsewhere. The latter remained the chief official service newspaper after 1945 and reported closely on the war in Southeast Asia. Indeed, on the very first day of its post-World War II publication (3 October 1945), it reported on an impending clash between French troops and the Viet Minh. Among its headlines were '2 Americans Killed by Saigon Terrorists' (the first US casualties, 1959); 'Viet Victory Near' (a US general's prediction, 1963); '3PT Boats Attack American Warship' (Gulf of Tonkin incident, 1964); and 'Pullout of 25,000 Ordered by Nixon' (1969).

This is little doubt, however, that *Stars and Stripes* reflected the official version of the war and was generally sympathetic to the administration of the time. A complaint common among many of the servicemen, newspaper and wire service correspondents was that the magazine was heavily censored before it hit the battlefields of South Vietnam. It was not surprising, therefore, that underground newspapers proliferated during the Vietnam war, purporting to tell the real truth of combat.

Although there were at least 245 unofficial underground newspapers circulated in Vietnam between 1967 and 1972, few went beyond a single issue and their readership was severely limited. As a result, servicemen's main source of news remained *Stars and Stripes* – with all the possibilities for news manipulation associated with an official publication.

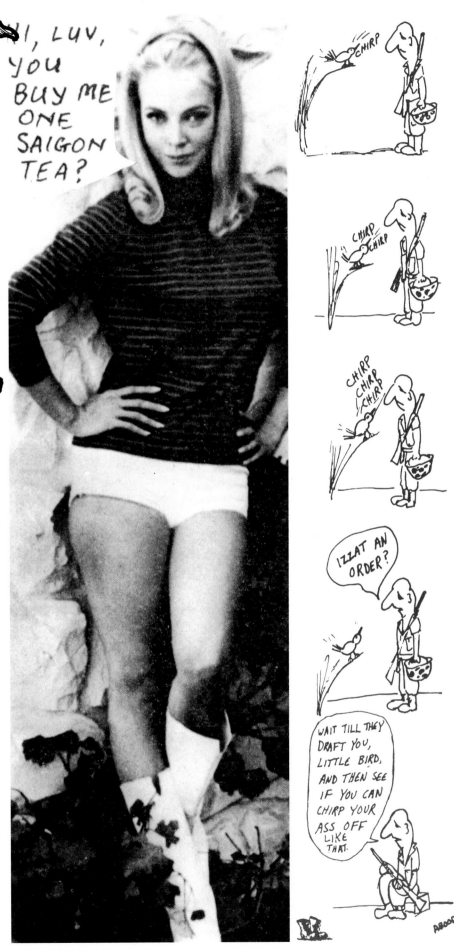

se *Americans and their damned superior air!'*

the-box pops out holding a sign: 'April Fool!'

But apart from gags, what do you put in a magazine for all those GIs on one-year tours in a country best described by Vietnam's most common graffiti: 'IHTFP' – I Hate This Fucking Place?

They tried to draft the artist

First, there were nude photos which I got from a Tokyo photo agency at a dollar a time. Oriental tit and bum stuff mainly. Roundeyes I left to *Playboy*. Grunts had one week's R&R in their year in Nam. Except for a few straight arrows – guys faithful to wives and girl-friends – they weren't going to spend it checking out the temple scene in Bangkok or Hong Kong. They'd be bedding Asian girls.

Sex wasn't reserved for R&R. They encountered Asian girls in local bars and magic fingers massage parlours, not to mention those ubiquitous 'car wash' places where any grunt in a vehicle could pull over and get a complete service.

Every centre-fold of *Grunt Free Press* was a double-page psychedelic poster done by far-out artists, just like the ones on college kids' walls back home. Most had a peace theme. Many had the peace sign and mysterious messages in psychedelic calligraphy. All had a nude.

These posters hung everywhere. The most popular were the work of Tran Dinh Thuc, a Vietnamese student who revealed strong 'peacenik' leanings in his *Grunt Free Press* drawings and came to the attention of Vietnamese authorities who decided to draft him. When the word got out, grunts arranged for him to be smuggled aboard a plane to Darwin.

...AND IF WE'RE NOT BACK IN 2 HOURS, BETTER START WINNING HEARTS & MINDS.

Whether deriding the policies of the US military (left), or seeing the funny side of the ever-present dangers (below and bottom), *Grunt Free Press* struck a responsive chord in GIs who were disillusioned with magazines such as *Stars and Stripes*, which toed the official line and failed to reflect the true feelings of the men on the front line.

GRUNT OF THE MONTH

Below: In order to ensure that it represented the views of the troops, *Grunt Free Press* went out of its way to solicit contributions from the ordinary GI.

IF YOU CAN WRITE YOR NAME YOU CAN WRITE FOR GRUNT FREE PRESS. SEND CONTRIBUTIONS TO: BOX 1164 REDLANDS, CAL. 92373

HEY BUDDY COULD YOU LEND ME A HAND, PLEASE?

TOILET

Lifers versus draftees was another hot subject. Young draftees, many right off college campuses, did not like gung-ho career soldiers. Grunt graffiti summed it up: 'This is a war of the unwilling led by the unqualified dying for the ungrateful.'

Then there was the conflict between black and white troops. This became so touchy that when Martin Luther King was assassinated, Armed Forces TV screened nothing but his picture for three whole days. On the cover of *Grunt Free Press*, we carried a drawing of a black and a white grunt in one pair of trousers punching each other. Whitey is saying: 'Hey, what are we fighting for, anyhow?' Blackie was saying: 'I don't know. I forgot.' Shortly after, a brother sent me the 'Soul Brother Dictionary' which we published. It said of blue-eyed soul, for example: 'He's white, but he's groovy-mellow, got a taste of soul. There ain't too many blue-eyed souls over here.'

Grunt Free Press could also look behind the lines. We investigated crooked NCO club stewards, the khaki mafia and the real mafia, Indian money-changers, smugglers, crooked contractors, surplus arms dealers, dope pushers: all the crooks who had been milking over US$20 million annually out of Vietnam. We looked at the totally corrupt Vietnamese government where a man could become a province chief by getting his wife to lose $45,000 at poker to the wife of the top boss.

Vietnamese rock and roll

During the last year of *Grunt Free Press*, the magazine became popular with Saigon students. There were times when up to 100 students would come across to my penthouse and dance to the latest Beatles and Stones records sent by my son in London. As I came to know these kids, I printed their thoughts – things like: 'Before you started bombing the North, there were no North Vietnamese down here... When you are no longer here, they have no excuse to be here either...'

I did a photographic feature about a 100 per cent hippie Vietnamese rock and roll band – long hair, beads, peace symbols and all – who were wowing the grunts at a club on Plantation Road outside Tan Son Nhut airbase. They were called CBC, a Vietnamese codename for peace. Partly as a result of the *Grunt Free Press*, they drew a sizeable following among young Vietnamese who formed the closest thing you could find to a hippie-style peace movement in Saigon. Two months after the story appeared, a bomb went off under the bandstand of a club where they were playing. The girl singer lost a leg. That spelled the end of Vietnamese rock and roll, and nipped Saigon's flower-power movement in the bud.

Despite efforts by a powerful underworld syndicate in Nam to take it over, and attempts by MACV to ban it, I was able to keep *Grunt Free Press* going until I retired in 1971.

Today, nearly two decades later, I'm convinced that the answer to why we lost the war in Vietnam is more likely to be found in my comic stories and cartoons than in all my reports for CHECO.

VIETNAMIZATION

'In the final analysis it is their war. They are the ones who have to win or lose it.' So said President John F. Kennedy in 1963. And yet it took six years for the US to inaugurate a policy called 'Vietnamization'. And even then, there were well founded suspicions that this policy was merely a cynical attempt to use Vietnamese blood because the number of US casualties was becoming a strain on the US political system.

Vietnamization began as a concept late in the Johnson Administration. By the final months of 1967, Johnson was becoming dissatisfied with General Westmoreland's continual requests for more troops. He told one of his aides that the military high command in Vietnam were 'going to have to live with what they got...and waste some of their valuable time training Viets.' Westmoreland's deputy, General Creighton Abrams, was therefore tasked with spending time trying to improve ARVN performance.

A fresh approach

Meanwhile, the failure of pacification programmes in the villages of South Vietnam led to a rethinking of the structure of US management of the pacification effort. In May 1967 a new organization – Civil Operations and Revolutionary Development Support (CORDS) – came into being. This was an integral part of the military structure, but was initially headed by a civilian (Robert Komer) and included personnel from intelligence-gathering units such as the CIA. The idea was that more accurate processing of intelligence and more focus on attacking the political structure of the VC in the villages might bring results that were clearly not being achieved by ARVN pacification or big battles on the frontiers.

Neither of these two new approaches – more emphasis on the ARVN and more attention to low-level intelligence and pacification programmes – had made much headway by the time the Tet Offensive took place in January/February 1968. But Tet discredited William Westmoreland's concept of a 'big-unit' war primarily waged by US forces: and so a new approach was necessary. By the beginning of 1969, there was a new leader in the White House (Richard Nixon) who wanted to wind down US ground force commitment. In Vietnam itself, Creighton Abrams had succeeded Westmoreland in summer 1968.

The result of this change in policy and leadership was that Vietnamization became the key to a change in the nature of the war. Abrams was a more subtle military thinker than Westmore-

It seemed a good idea to let the ARVN fight their own war. But would the soldiers of the South be able to take on the might of the Viet Cong and North Vietnamese?

Above left: A man with an unwelcome inheritance: one well worn war.

land. Under him, pacification in the villages and the implementation of schemes such as the Phoenix Program became central to the anti-communist effort. Meanwhile, Nixon was playing a complicated international game in which Vietnam was merely a part. He was looking for better relations with China, and a restructuring of the world power balance. The simple verities and plans of Johnson and Westmoreland were superseded by more complex and cynical schemes.

Expanding the ARVN

From 1969 to 1971, US combat deaths went down while ARVN deaths stayed about the same, at around 21-22,000 per year. This figure was about twice as high as the figure for the years before 1968. The strength of the ARVN also rose dramatically. A full-scale mobilization during the summer of 1968 was followed by wide recruitment into Regional Forces and Popular Forces. In 1968, force levels reached 820,000 men, but by 1972 there were over one million men in arms – about half in the regular army and the other half in part-time forces.

A critical part of preparing the ARVN to take on the major burden of the fighting lay in upgrading its equipment. Before 1968, most ARVN soldiers had been armed with the M1, a World War II-vintage rifle that was heavy and cumbersome. But by April 1969, the lighter M16, capable of automatic fire and a reasonable match for the AK47-type weapons used by the communist forces, was the standard weapon of all regular ARVN units. By February 1970, almost the whole of the Regional and Popular Forces had M16s as well.

Holiday in Cambodia

The ARVN had taken on the vast majority of offensive operations against the communists by the middle of 1970, as US force levels fell dramatically. And there were signs that the much-maligned 'dinks' were proving able to maintain this burden. In April and May 1970, they performed well in incursions into Cambodian territory, and proved able to carry out far more operations than they had previously managed. In 1970 and 1971, the South Vietnamese military carried out three times as many large operations as during the 1966-67 period.

There were still many problems, however. The biggest single weakness that faced the ARVN lay in the quality of its officers. These tended to come from the formally-educated town dwellers, who

While the slicks that ferried them in dust off and hurry out of range of ground fire, troops of the 33rd ARVN Rangers scour the grass for enemy troops on the Plain of Reeds. American advisers who worked with ARVN soldiers agreed that the quality of an ARVN unit was in direct proportion to that of its leader. Ranger commanders were usually of excellent quality.

1970

TERRORISM IN THE NAME OF PEACE?

The Phoenix Program was instigated as a means of gathering information. But was its prime role one of counter-terrorism and political assassination?

The Phoenix Program grew out of American attempts to find an effective way of defeating the Viet Cong after it had become clear that relying on overwhelming firepower was not sufficient. It was only one element in the general 'pacification' effort that had got under way in late 1967 under the direction of Robert Komer, the Deputy to the Commander of MACV and Director of CORDS (Civil Operations and Revolutionary Development Support). Komer had calculated that the Viet Cong controlled 60 per cent of the countryside and he saw the need for a new set of rural policies: 'We realistically concluded that no one of these plans – relatively inefficient and wasteful in a corrupt Vietnamese wartime context – could in itself be decisive. But together they could hope to have a major cumulative effect.'

Komer recommended a joint MACV and CIA programme, called ICEX (Intelligence Co-ordination and Exploitation). It was designed to improve the gathering of information from the villages by unifying all of the agencies previously responsible for such work: the CIA, US Military Intelligence, the South Vietnamese Central Intelligence Organization, Special Branch and National Police. By July 1968 the South Vietnamese government had formally assumed responsibility for the programme. In theory, American advisers were to be phased out by January 1969. However, there were still 600 American military and 50 civilian advisers on the Phoenix staff in 1971 and they remained until the main US withdrawal in 1972.

The aim of the programme was to identify the estimated 70,000 members of the Viet Cong infrastructure – the VC political leaders. Phoenix offices were set up at district and provincial levels. Information on individuals and families was collected from all possible sources and then collated. The South Vietnamese government could then use this information to identify and arrest suspects who, at the behest of a Provincial Security Committee, would either be held in a detention centre, or tried by a military court.

However, this administrative set-up was only part of the picture. Phoenix was essentially a programme of counter-terrorism. According to congressional testimony by Komer's successor, William Colby, between 1968 and 1971 about 17,000 Viet Cong sought amnesty, 28,000 were captured and some 20,000 killed. By February 1972 this last figure had risen to 24,800. The high number of suspects killed and the frequency of involvement of Special Forces-trained Provincial Reconnaissance Units (PRUs) – who registered a high number of kills – led to claims that Phoenix was a CIA-run programme of slaughter. People involved in Phoenix operations have themselves claimed that indiscriminate killing was common. Frank Snepp, a senior CIA operative, claimed that: [as] the prisons came to overflowing...the hit teams became impatient and instead of bringing the sources in, they began killing them.'

The fact that the Viet Cong carried out acts of terror as a part of their own strategy – executing an estimated 36,725 village officials and South Vietnamese civil servants in the period 1957-1972 – justified the use of counter-terrorism to many. It is also true that many Americans did their utmost to prevent murders. William Colby ordered: 'If any American sees anyone being assassinated he's to object and he is to report it to me.' Despite this, Phoenix began to become an unchecked 'hit' list, and there were even allegations that President Thieu was using it to eliminate political opponents.

One of the greatest problems lay with the dubious nature of much of the intelligence gathered by Phoenix. The Saigon government was not popular with the peasantry, and the peasants were wary of committing themselves to a government that was not sure of victory. This led to a reliance on information supplied by unreliable sources – suspects who had been tortured and informers who would supply names in return for cash. Misinformation often led to the innocent suffering along with the guilty.

The Phoenix Program was vicious. But it was certainly proved to be more effective than a reliance on free fire zones and high explosives in combatting a guerrilla enemy.

had little in common with the villagers who formed the majority of the rank and file. Promotion was due to political favour rather than proven combat efficiency (from 1966 to 1968, less than two per cent of promotions were cited as due to success in action) and when US advisers tried to have incompetent or corrupt officers removed, they found it well-nigh impossible to make any headway. These problems were compounded in the period 1968-71 by the rapid expansion of South Vietnam's armed forces. Despite rapid promotions and crash courses, qualified combat leaders were hard to find. So, although there was expansion of numbers, quality did not necessarily expand to keep up.

Technology gap

A further difficulty lay in the nature of the up-grading of equipment. On one level, the ARVN was being expected to fight like a US Army – but it was not getting quite the level of sophisticated machines it needed for this. An ARVN unit, for example, could expect only one third of the machine guns a US unit would be provided with. But a further problem was that even if the ARVN had been given the weaponry to make it fully comparable, the technological back-up to maintain and use such weapons to their full capacity would have been lacking. One US senior officer put it succinctly:

'I don't see leaving sophisticated helicopters

Below left: This ARVN interrogator's smiling face belies his occupation. Right: ARVN Special Forces prepare to leave the combat zone. Below right: An ARVN soldier relieves his dead buddy of his boots. Bottom right: In front of a Northrop F-5, VNAF airmen assemble aircraft flown in in kit form.

and continuing to replace them. Oh no. That would be like dropping them into the Pacific Ocean.'

The ARVN also failed to make any real attempt to reach the hearts and minds of the villagers it was supposed to protect. A study in 1969 found that ARVN soldiers upset the civilian population in almost half of all hamlets. In Vinh Binh Province, one particularly notorious battalion stole cattle which it then removed on barges for sale elsewhere. And while this well organized corruption was rare, the scale of bribery and corruption was admitted to be high in general.

Barbed wire diplomacy

Perhaps most worrying for the future was the fact that in large-scale population transfers, where an attempt was made to root out VC influence in an area for good, the ARVN often made little or no attempt to look after the civilians involved. As one US study put it: 'Putting the people behind barbed wire against their will is not the first step to earning loyalty and support, especially if there is no concentrated effort at political education and village development.'

The final indication of ARVN weakness lay in the number of desertions. In 1970, there were well over 100,000 soldiers who slipped away, who failed to report back after leave or who defected to the other side. This total – one tenth of the effective strength – was enormous, and represented a problem that only time could cure. And time was something the ARVN simply did not have.

Despite these glaring faults, however, the ARVN was in no way losing the war in 1970. Government statistics were obviously going to look on the optimistic side, but it is clear that the number of attacks by communist units – whether individual assassinations or larger attacks on

ARVN SPECIAL FORCES

With ARVN units such as the 25th Division turning in statistics like 100 enemy contacts in 100,000 combat operations, the South Vietnamese army suffered from a poor reputation – many in the American military doubted their ability to take over as Vietnamization came into full swing.

However, not all ARVN units performed poorly – when good leadership was combined with motivated troops, as it often was with the Marines, Airborne and Rangers, the ARVN were as good as any forces in the world.

Ranger battalions were not found in the ARVN until the 1960 conversion of the Special Action Companies. By 1965, elite units still only totalled 17,000, five per cent of total RVNAF (Republic of Viet Nam Armed Forces) manpower. This situation was improved as Vietnamization proceeded: in 1970 as US Special Forces were beginning to withdraw, the Joint General Staff approved the conversion of the best of the CIDGs (Civilian Irregular Defense Groups) into ARVN Ranger border defence battalions. 14,534 CIDGs were converted, adding 37 battalions to the ARVN Ranger strength which now stood at 57 battalions. Seven Ranger group control headquarters were created, one of which took part in the 1971 Lam Son 719 raid into Laos, seeing particularly heavy fighting there.

The conversion of the CIDGs meant the end of the Vietnamese LLDB (Luc Luong Dac Biet) Special Forces, who were technically in charge of CIDG operations. The best LLDB personnel were absorbed into the Strategic Technical Directorate.

By 1974, the ARVN Rangers were reorganized into 15 groups, each with three Ranger battalions. Stationed mainly along the Cambodian, Laotian border, each corps kept one Ranger group in reserve as a fact reaction force.

fortified positions – began to fall during the year, a trend that accelerated during 1971. The monthly average of assaults was 318 in 1969, 295 in 1970 and 187 in 1971. Again by 1971, the areas of fighting had become more clearly defined, and insurgency confined largely to 10 provinces. This area contained one quarter of the total population, and so the problem was still very large – but it was nothing like as bad as it had been in the mid-1960s when US intervention was needed to prevent collapse of both army and state. Perhaps the most significant index of improving conditions was that more than one million refugees were able to return to their homes.

Part of the reason for the better showing of the ARVN lay in weaknesses within the communist camp. The Tet Offensive had resulted in serious losses among the more experienced leaders of the VC, and this loss of able commanders was to make

Left: ARVN Rangers carry a wounded comrade during fighting at Bien Hoa. Right: Corruption was widespread among the armed forces: wary of photographic evidence, as he illegally sells off government rice, an ARVN captain points at the photographer. Below: ARVN forces hold the line.

THE RIGHT STRATEGY?

Could the co-ordinated programmes put in motion under General Abrams have won the war, or did US troop withdrawals from Vietnam invalidate any chance of success they may have had?

By the middle of 1970, a series of co-ordinated policies was being implemented in South Vietnam. They were designed to wrest the initiative from the communists in the villages and among the rural population, and although there were problems, and final success was not in sight, they were having a fair degree of success. The basis of the programmes was a recognition of the needs of the peasantry. In 1969, more local democracy was introduced, so that by 1970 most villages had their own council that directed local affairs and, many years too late, a fundamental land reform was at last introduced in March 1970. 'Land to the Tiller', as the law was known, gave many peasants what they prized most – ownership of the plot that they farmed. Special rural development teams went out to help organize village life.

Backing up these reforms was the Phoenix Program – heavily criticized as a thinly disguised cover for assassination squads, but, nevertheless, an attempt to target guerrillas in a way that had been impossible for 'search and destroy' missions. The government even took the step of allowing villagers to form their own 'Self Defense Force'.

All this was carrying on while the US commitment was being phased out, and the ARVN was expanding in numbers and capability. During 1970 and 1971, guerrilla activity within South Vietnam began to slow down markedly, and the question must be asked as to whether this attempt by the government to win the allegiance of the villages could have succeeded. The answer may well be that it could – but the shield of US might needed to protect the South from the experienced Army of North Vietnam was about to be removed, and this would change the situation once again.

it more difficult for the insurgents to oppose the Vietnamization and pacification programmes. The Phoenix Program too probably hit the VC leadership (as well as resulting in many innocent deaths). With the Paris peace talks under way, many communists must have felt (as did many Americans) that they did not want to die in a war that was coming to an end. The number of VC defectors who took advantage of the South Vietnamese government's policy of offering an amnesty to deserters from the communist side increased greatly during 1969-70, and although only a relatively small number of these were 'genuine' defectors, according to the then head of the US pacification programme, William Colby, even this number marked a significant advance.

Uncertain future

So during 1970, Marvin the ARVN was doing better. He was not quite on top of the situation, but he was seeing a way of getting there. He still needed, however, US aid in massive quantities. 'We live with the military assistance of the US. Without that aid our army would die.' So said one prominent commander. Yet the US was now committed to pulling out its ground troops, and was talking with the North Vietnamese in Paris. The future was still very dark.

During 1969 American strategy in Vietnam underwent a major change. Gone were the days of actively seeking main force battles with the NVA; instead, the priorities were Vietnamization and a gradual withdrawal of US units. On 1 February General Abrams introduced his 'One War' plan, combining the main-force and village wars and preparing the ARVN to conduct both simultaneously.

This new approach took a variety of forms. In the northern provinces of ICTZ, where the 3d Marine, 5th Infantry, and the 101st Airborne Divisions were still stationed, the previous emphasis on physically blocking NVA infiltration routes was dropped in favour of more mobile operations, designed to disrupt NVA/VC supply bases. Operations such as Dewey Canyon (22 January-18 March) and Apache Snow (10 May-7 June) saw US and ARVN units move together into the Da Krong and A Shau valleys with just such an aim in mind. On the coast the 1st Marine and Americal Divisions, with ARVN units attached, protected Hue and Da Nang, even to the extent of mounting amphibious landings to clear offshore islands such as Go Noi (26 May) and Barrier (7 September).

Further south, in the Central Highlands, the US 4th Infantry Division continued to cover the Cambodian border, but the main mobile operations occurred around Saigon. The capital was shielded by the 1st Cavalry, and 1st and 25th Infantry Divisions, with Australian, Thai and ARVN formations in attendance. They conducted sweeps towards the border and set up patrol bases, protected by sensors and airpower. These bases inevitably attracted NVA attacks. In April, Patrol Base Frontier City was hit, followed by Fire Support Base Crook in early June. But lengthy battles were avoided.

By early 1970, with Vietnamization continuing apace, the emphasis of the war had been shifted to the border north of Saigon, the intention being to provide a clear-cut victory to boost ARVN morale and destroy NVA sanctuaries in Cambodia. Spearheaded by US units, restricted to incursions of no more than 30 kilometres, a series of ARVN attacks took place in May and June (Operations Toan Thang 43, Toan Thang 44 and Binh Tay). Success was mixed, but the reality of Vietnamization could not be ignored. Even in ICTZ, where US forces constructed and manned firebases to support the ARVN, the levels of combat were curtailed: when Fire Support Base Ripcord was hit in April, for example, the allies chose to withdraw rather than fight a major battle. It was a sign of the times.

423

HOT TUBES

Mortars could be a real help to a grunt in need. They were portable, easy to use and flung out a lot of explosive. But Charlie had them too – and that wasn't such good news

'Incoming!.....Mortars!' It's the rule. The first man to hear the distinctive *whoosh* of a mortar shell yells the warning, then hits the dirt. Everyone around him flops as fast. If he's made a mistake his buddies might curse and swear at him. But if he's right, lives are saved.

After the first or second time, you don't make mistakes about incoming rounds. If you do, you're dead. You learn quickly to tell mortars from rockets and artillery. By the third or fourth time under fire, you can figure whether they will hit on you, nearby, or far enough away not to bother. But you always, repeat *always*, hit the dirt. Better dirty than dead.

What is even better is throwing mortar rounds right back at the enemy, giving him a taste of the hot tubes. Best of all, of course, is to hit him first, to cream him right out of the blue. For that warm and fuzzy feeling in enemy countryside, there's nothing like a whole load of fire support on call. To the infantry rifle company, that means having your own three 81mm mortars ready to drop HE or

Above: While this US mortar team cover their ears, Charlie best be covering his eyes – there's a present coming his way. The Americans usually deployed the battalion mortars in Fire Support Bases like this one. Mobile support was available from medium mortars mounted on APCs.

Willie Petes onto the enemy when you need to.

Grunts see two big advantages in mortars. First, they are both offensive and defensive weapons, and real cute for lobbing shells over obstacles and on top of the enemy, reaching him where rifles and machine guns can't. Second, they belong to the company or battalion and are on call in seconds. Mortars are easy to use, relatively lightweight, and can lay heavy firepower on an enemy in a hurry.

US rifle companies in Vietnam were authorized three 81mm mortars, model M1, which had a range of 3000 metres. Each mortar was served by a squad of six men. When companies took to the field in search or patrol operations, most commanders set up the mortars at a patrol base.

To speed the rain of steel on the enemy when needed, planned 'concentrations' were arranged. These used easily identified landmarks in a unit's area of operations. The men in the mortar platoon's Fire Direction Center (FDC) used these landmarks to calculate the firing data for each mortar.

To prepare for action, the mortar squad leader designated a spot for the weapon and a general direction of fire. Then the crew would move slickly into its well-oiled routine. First, assistant gunners swiftly hacked out a shallow square pit to the baseplate's dimensions. Then the baseplate was dropped into the pit and stamped firmly into place. With barely a pause, the tube was locked onto the baseplate and the bipod assembly slipped over the tube. At the same time, red and white striped aiming stakes were hammered into the ground several metres in front of each tube. Finally, an optical sight was clamped onto the bipod mount. This helped the team to make precise adjustments in elevation and deflection.

Break out the ammo

While the gunner was aligning the mortar precisely with the aiming stakes, other members of the crew methodically laid out ammunition. A few rounds of each type were broken out of the shipping boxes: a dozen high explosive rounds weighing 3.3kg each; six WP rounds at 5kg apiece; and six illuminating rounds at 4.6kg each.

Sitting on the ground, the gunner aligned his sight on the pre-set landmark. Then he made fine adjustments from exact information provided by the man at the Fire Direction Center, a few metres behind the tubes. Usually, a couple of rounds were fired from the tube into a safe area to settle the baseplate more solidly into the ground.

At the FDC position, the 'computer' – a man who had to be good at maths – used an M-10 plotting board to calculate firing data. His job was to solve, by trigonometry, the exact direction and distance from each mortar to the target. Working out deflections for each tube, the human computer passed his handiwork to the gunners.

Gun-target distance was measured directly from the board. Knowing the type of ammunition to be used and the distance to the target, the man

at the M-10 plotting board consulted prepared firing tables. Through a combination of adjustment in tube elevation and depression, and varying the propellant charges attached to the mortar round, it wouldn't take him long to work out the precise range needed. Range error was a few metres, but most of the rounds loosed off at that setting would explode where the pinned-down grunts wanted them to.

Left: One third of a mortar squad stand behind their weapon – teamwork was crucial if a mortar was to be used to optimum effect. Below: Paratroopers of the 2d Battalion, 101st Airborne transport 4.2 inch mortar rounds to a gun position during Operation Wheeler. If a battalion was operating on foot and needed to give support to its forward troops as they advanced, the usual method was to split the mortar section into pairs of 'tubes'. These pairs moved alternately with two mortars always ready to fire.

1970

CHAPTER 82

1970

Infantry platoon leaders arranged fire support plans with the mortar crews. Those plans were integrated into the company's fire plan. This also included supporting fire from the battalion 4.2in mortars and artillery 105mm howitzers. This added up to a pile of fire support. But the M1s were always the first to be called on.

The moment this happened, the platoon leader screamed a curt command to his Radio Telephone Operator (RTO) or Forward Observer (FO): 'Fire concentration, location...' The order sped down the line, from the RTO to the FDC to the mortar crews, who immediately adjusted their tubes.

Meanwhile, the projectiles were being readied. Safety clips were pulled off the fuzes. The first round was handed carefully to the assistant gunner. From the squad leader came the command: 'Hang it in the tube!'

The assistant gunner hung the round inside the tube, ready to drop it on command. At the order 'Fire!' he released the round. Everyone held their ears and crouched down. The round dropped down the tube, hit the fixed firing pin, the propellant charge exploded, and the round shot out of the tube and arced through the sky towards its target. 'On the way!' was radioed to the FO.

Fire for effect

Up ahead, the FO counted off the seconds from the round being fired, watching and waiting for it to hit. Then, if corrections were necessary, he made them. His method was simple, but the effect was deadly. First, bring the rounds in on top of the general target area. Second, bracket the target with one round over and one round short, setting up the pigeon. Finally, split the bracket neatly down the middle and smear the target. Command for that is 'Fire for effect'.

Mortarmen love to hear 'Fire for effect'. Time for

Below: Catering for the choppers. Leathernecks of 2d Battalion, 9th Marines prepare to fire an 81mm mortar to suppress enemy mortar fire, while a CH-46 Sea Knight touches down in the LZ. In Vietnam, with the high availability of helicopters, it was easier to fly the 'mortar baseplate' than have it leapfrogging forward on foot. Right: Hang it in the tube! A shell about to be dropped into the mortar at a permanent fire position. Most shells used point-detonating fuzes but some could be fitted with a proximity fuze to give an airburst.

their skill, training and teamwork to pay off in steel being dumped right on top of the enemy. A good 81mm mortar crew can fire at a rate of 30 rounds per minute. That means the first two rounds are just reaching the target when the last one is dropped down the tube. With three tubes firing as fast as possible, that firepower can break an enemy attack or slow it while heavier firepower is coming up. Even more useful were recent US developments in field radar. When the radar locked onto incoming rounds, it quickly calculated and displayed the firing point, bringing 90 rounds of bad news onto surprised enemy gunners!

Light my fire

In night defensive positions, the mortar concentrations were calculated on likely avenues of approach and enemy assembly areas. Illumination is the 'round of choice' for night defence. An outpost hearing enemy movement to the front, reports it. The platoon leader or company commander calls for 'Illum' at a certain concentration. It arcs high into the sky, peaking over the target. A bright illuminating flare hung from a small parachute ejects, and flutters slowly earthward. Its harsh white light illuminates the area. The enemy are caught in the glare, transfixed like rabbits, and it's like open season.

After a sustained fire mission – say 30-60 fast rounds – the mortar tubes heated up. Burning residue from the propellants lurked in them. Then it was time to give the tubes a quick swab and let them cool for a minute or so before resuming. An astute mortar platoon leader never let all three tubes heat up at once. He spaced their fire missions so high explosive was always on the way. The maximum rate of fire was used only in emergencies – usually the *sustained* rate (5-6 rounds per minute) was used. Accuracy was better than numbers.

No gaps from hot tubes was the watchword.

VIET CONG MORTAR POWER

When attacking US bases and airfields, the mortar was the communists' standard weapon

If the mortar hadn't existed at the start of the Vietnam war, the Viet Cong and NVA would've had to invent it. Easily portable and simple to operate, it was. ideally suited to the terrain of South Vietnam. The communist forces, wary of awesome US firepower, could set up a mortar team out of enemy sight, loose off two or three rounds at maximum range and, due to the mortar rounds' long flight time, be moving away before the first had reached the target.

When attacking a US base, the VC most commonly used either mortars or single-shot rockets. The advantage the mortar had over the rocket was its greater accuracy, which allowed it to be used against point targets. The rocket was employed purely as an area weapon.

The VC and NVA deployed a wide variety of mortars, ranging in size from the 50mm M41 to the breech-loaded 160mm M43. One of the most common types, particularly with the VC, was the light mortar Type 63. This 60mm weapon has a convoluted history.

Originating in pre-World War II France, it was adopted by the US. The American version

Below: The elusive Viet Cong sprint across a paddyfield while a mortar team gives support.

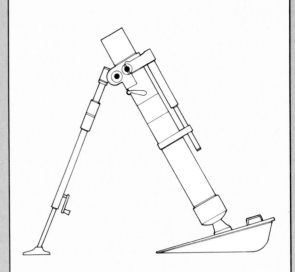

TYPE 63 MORTAR

Calibre: 60mm
Weight: 12.3kg
Barrel length: 610mm
Maximum range: 1530 metres
Maximum rate of fire: 20 rounds per minute

was then copied by the Chinese Nationalist forces as the Type 31. This in turn provided the basis for a Chinese communist variant – the Chincom Type 63. This updated variation on the Type 31 was designed with the emphasis on irregular and guerrilla warfare and was used extensively during the Vietnam war. It was simple, reliable and at 12.3kg it could easily be carried by one man. The NVA added their own modification, attaching a carrying handle to the barrel.

The barrel, baseplate and bipod were arranged so the unit could be carried without dismantling the mortar. Once at the firing site, the mortar could be emplaced, sighted and ready to fire within a matter of seconds.

The mortar bomb has a teardrop-shaped steel body, a nose fuze and tail fin assembly and is packed with an explosive such as TNT or with white phosphorus or an illumi-

nant. An ignition cartridge with primer (like a shotgun shell) sits in the tail and variable numbers of propellant increment charges are clipped onto the tail fins.

Medium mortars were popular with both sides in Vietnam, the communist forces using a variety of Soviet and Chinese 82mm designs and a copy of the American 81mm M1 mortar. There was little difference in this proliferation of communist designs, although some Chinese and older Soviet models had wheels at the end of their bipods, a feature which allowed them to be towed by the muzzle.

Although the communist weapons were 82mm, they could fire NATO 81mm rounds. US mortars could not fire communist rounds. NVA mortars fired high explosive, fragmentation and smoke rounds. The M1 copy was popular with the NVA as it could be broken down into three one-man loads.

VETS AGAINST THE WAR

Being a pot-smoking hippie and being against the war was one thing. Being there, being decorated, being crippled and being against the war was quite another. And the vets who changed their mind about US involvement often had to suffer hostility from their former buddies to make their point. Once, soldiers had donned olive drabs in the service of their country and Lady Liberty, believing passionately in the cause that their leaders were espousing. Now, six years later, they weren't so sure. Barricaded inside the Statue of Liberty, they spoke out against the war

An Open Letter to

As a result of our action at the Statue of Liberty, and because of widespread feedback from Vietnam veterans all across the land, we have now gained a consensus of opinion which allows us to make this statement.

Each Vietnam Veteran who has barricaded himself within this international symbol of liberty has for many years rationalized his attitude to war. When we were in Vietnam we excused our actions because we thought that we had no choice. After coming home we excused bitterness because we thought that it would entitled to it. Last spring we threw our medals into the dirt because we thought it would excuse our guilt, and because we thought that it would help end the war.

Now, as we sit inside the Statue of Liberty, having captured the hopes and imaginations of a war-weary nation, we have run out of all excuses. We can no longer tolerate the war in Southeast Asia regardless of the color or its dead or the method or its implementation.

Mr. Nixon: You set the date...we'll evecuate

Vietnam Veterans Against the War

Far left: On 28 December 1971, 16 Vietnam veterans occupy America's symbol of freedom, the Statue of Liberty in New York harbour. To draw attention to their protest they send an open letter (left) to President Nixon and hang the Stars and Stripes upside down out of the observation platform in the statue's crown. Many Americans were aghast at what they saw as such abuse of their nation's flag.

Top: The weather's right. But this is not Saigon. The vets are awaiting capture at the 1972 Democratic convention in Miami.

Above: Crippled vets defy the Supreme Court in a demo in DC.

Right: Draped in the flag – for warmth not patriotism.

A year in the Nam was a long time, and things in the World could change during that period. For some grunts, returning to the US was a painful experience

'**H**owzit going, baby killer?' That's what the man said to me when I walked down the corridor of Oakland air terminal. That bit of shit was slung in my face by a stoned-out, long-haired freak. It stung.

It was my third day back in the States. I was in uniform, still suffering the 18-hour flight from Nam and disorientated.

Oakland terminal was a far cry from the war I'd been fighting about 10 days earlier. Most people simply ignored me. I was an embarrassment to them. I represented the United States in Vietnam. I was the war made flesh, not some item on the evening news. By 1971, a lot of Americans were brainwashed by the media and protest movement

GOING HOME

Left: September may be along way away, but you still marked off the days left before you could return to the safety of home. Below left: Waiting for a plane out of Da Nang USAF base. Below: Relaxing before catching the big bird home. The map of 'the world' is festooned with messages.

into believing Vietnam was wrong: that we, and not the North Vietnamese, Chinese and Soviets, were the evil aggressors in a country fighting for survival. We warriors were blamed for the war but, whether the war was right or wrong, most of us simply went where Uncle Sam told us to go.

There were four of them, unwashed, unshaven, wearing tie-dyed T-shirts and headbands and Army field jackets, giggling their disjointed way up the terminal corridor. I hadn't seen anything like them for a year. They saw me coming the other way, and stopped. When I was close enough to see their dilated, blood-shot eyes and smell them, one stepped out, partially blocking my way.

'Howzit going, baby killer?' His comrades started giggling again.

I thought about it. I really did. Should I smash this asshole in the face? Would it accomplish anything? The corridor was crowded, full of tunnel-visioned transients ignoring the confrontation between the soldier and hippies.

All I wanted was a drink

What the hell. I was in United States Army uniform, and NCOs didn't punch civilians in airports no matter how obnoxious they were. I just paused for a moment and stared, and wondered if the reason I had fought in Vietnam was standing in front of me, stoned on drugs and smelling like shit. God, I hoped not.

They finally stumbled off and I heard something like 'Army motherfucker' drift over from the retreating little mob, and more bent laughter. I was suddenly bone-tired and emotionally exhausted. All I wanted was a drink and to go home.

Uncle Sam had given me 30 days leave after Vietnam before I had to report to my next duty assignment. Los Angeles was as big and busy as when I'd left, even more so. It took some getting used to the fact that danger now came from freeway traffic and smog rather than booby-traps and VC bullets.

We fought to stay alive

I slept something like 15 hours my first day back. My dad was good enough to leave me alone for the next few days. My brother had spent a year as a combat pilot in Vietnam, so my dad had been through it before. He figured, rightly, that I needed some time to get my bearings.

A couple of days later we went out to dinner and talked about Vietnam. I didn't have much to say at first. What did come out was the funny stuff, crazy grunts and officers I'd known, bush rats in the bunkers – useless drivel. Then I asked him what everyone back home thought about Vietnam.

'Riots, protests where they burn the American flag. Everyone seems to want us out of there,' he said, taking another sip of his drink.

'What do you think?' he asked. He was a man who had survived the depression, World War II and Korea. 'Can we win? Should we be there?'

My gut reaction was to say yes. Yes, we should be there. Yes, we can win. But I wasn't so sure

1970

CHAPTER 83

VETERANS SPURNED

Vietnam veterans had severe psychological problems for many years after returning Stateside. But to what extent did public reaction to the war exacerbate the problem?

Many returning veterans have had problems of adjustment into civilian society. It has not been unusual for men to feel that their sacrifices have not been sufficiently appreciated, nor to experience psychological problems long after the end of their service.

After World War I, the number of disability awards to former British servicemen increased significantly between 1921 and 1929 because many psychological scars did not become apparent for some years. Nevertheless, there was something different about Vietnam.

Of the 3,402,100 US servicemen who served in Southeast Asia between 1964 and 1973, some 2,594,000 served within the borders of South Vietnam. About 80 per cent made a successful transition to civilian life, but there was still an unusually high proportion of veterans who were not so easily assimilated. Possibly as many as 700,000 veterans developed some symptoms of what was officially accepted in 1980 as Post Traumatic Stress Disorder (PTSD), a condition similar to that described as shell shock in World War I and as battle fatigue in World War II. About 10 per cent were diagnozed as suffering from the disorder itself.

However, while the nature of the war contributed to the development of such psychological problems, many difficulties also stemmed from the widespread feeling on the part of all veterans that they were being forced to shoulder the nation's collective guilt, or shame, or humiliation. There was no official homecoming beyond the welcome from family or friends and, even then, there might be little real understanding or sympathy.

One veteran, who later became Lieutenant-Governor of Massachusetts, recalled waking up yelling while on a domestic flight soon after returning home: 'The other passengers moved away from me – a reaction I noticed more and more in the months ahead. The country didn't give a shit about the guys coming back, or what they'd gone through. The feeling toward them was, "Stay away – don't contaminate us with whatever you've brought back from Vietnam."'

Although many veterans were aware of the hostility towards the war amongst the US public, few were prepared for the level of hostility directed towards themselves. Some joined the anti-war movement, possibly seeking a kind of emotional catharsis for their guilt feelings as well as approval and acceptance. Many waited years for the understanding they craved, a process that has been assisted in no small way by the unveiling of the Vietnam Veterans' Memorial (paid for by public subscription and not government funds) in Washington in November 1982 and the new readiness of Americans to come to terms with their past.

about that. The Paris peace talks had sapped the will to win, if we'd ever had it in the first place. I knew that in my own platoon, we fought only for the platoon, not any great ideals about liberty or freedom or stemming the communist tide. We fought to stay alive.

I was getting drunk. Maybe it was the only way I could talk. 'Yeah, we should be there, for all the right reasons. Should we pull out now? Christ, I don't know. Too many damned good people are fucked up or dead fighting that war, and I can't – won't – even think that it was for no reason at all.

'Shit, we could have won. The grunts and everyone else did their job, kicked Charlie's ass...the goddamn politicians didn't give us a chance to win.'

Paternal wisdom

I got a little loud, and some of the other diners shot dirty looks my way. I stared back, thinking that right now a bunch of grunts were getting their asses shot off, or eating tinned ham and lima beans, huddled in a crumbling and muddy bunker, waiting for some VC sapper to crawl up and end dinner with a grenade. But these assholes didn't care a bit. I was furious at them.

My dad understood. 'It's not their fault. They only know what they read in the paper and see on TV.'

'Well, what do you think?' I asked him.

'If we're not going to win it, then I don't want any more boys dying,' he said. God, was it that simple?

I went through a couple of days of hard, steady drinking, trying to sort it out in my mind. There was no escaping what my dad had said. He didn't say the war was wrong, just that if we weren't going to try and win it, we should cut our losses and get out. It was hard to swallow because the

Above: Army Spec. 4 Jimmy Jones, 21, gets an ecstatic welcome home from his family in Missouri. Left: Members of 'Vietnam Veterans Against the War' are arrested on the steps of the Supreme Court in Washington after an 'End-The-War' demonstration.

Vietnam war would then be such a damned waste. I wasn't hyped on war for its own sake: it was simply the end result when the political process had failed. Now, even the process of war had failed and this was something the United States had never had to face before. We were confronted with 'peace with honor' – which, in my book, meant surrender. It made me mad.

I didn't have the answers

None of my close childhood friends had had to go into the service. Only one had wanted to enlist, but he was rejected on medical grounds. When I went to talk to them I think they provided me with a fairly accurate reflection of middle-class American thinking. Of my group of five old friends, one supported our involvement. The rest thought I was kind of stupid for going to Vietnam, and one even called the Viet Cong the 'real heroes' in Southeast Asia. I haven't seen him since.

Mostly, they couldn't understand what we were trying to accomplish in Vietnam. I was their first real live contact to the war, and they thought I should have all the answers. I didn't.

Only Chuck, my life-long friend who was pro-Vietnam, didn't press me for scholarly geopolitical answers. The rest seemed to think that I was walking proof of the futility of America's Vietnam policy. If I couldn't tell them exactly what Vietnam was all about, then who could?

I saw Chuck more than the rest of my friends during my leave. When we all got together, conversation was strained and empty. Vietnam wasn't discussed, and I was too far away from their daily lives to make any meaningful comment.

Conservation and therapy

Over whiskey, coffee and cigarettes, Chuck let me use him as a sounding board. I hit him with my impressions and feelings about the United States I had walked back into, and he'd gently set me straight when I missed the mark. No, not all Americans thought GIs were baby killers. In fact, there had been a number of demonstrations *against* the so-called 'peace' protests. Yes, it's true that most Americans were tired of the war, but many still believed in what we were doing. He showed me some articles and books explaining the full implications of a communist-dominated Southeast Asia and what America stood to lose if we just walked away, and I read them.

In turn he dredged out of me details of the war, what it was like to survive ambushes and fire-fights, the endless days and nights of patrols, the terror that can freeze the body and soul, like waking up alive buried in a coffin.

It was great therapy. I was able to unwind a coiled spring inside me that I didn't even know was there. I found I missed my old platoon, and I even found myself missing the war. Combat, as anyone who's experienced it can tell you, is as potent as any narcotic ever developed by man.

I reported in to my next assignment feeling like I was ready, and able, to go back to work. I was made an instructor, teaching young recruits the finer points of M16 marksmanship.

I recalled the line with which my own instructors three years earlier had uniformly prefaced their lessons: 'When you get to Vietnam....' I started using it too. Some of these kids would go to Vietnam whether their country supported them or not. They might survive the war, then come home to face pretty much what I'd experienced. I hoped it would be easier for them.

Below: Troops who have attained 'DEROS' status ponder on the likely reception they will get in the US. Will they be heroes or criminals?

GUNSLINGERS

Compared with the Cobra, earlier helicopter gunships were slow and unwieldy. In the Cobra, you had speed and firepower, and the communists soon realised that these birds spelt danger

O n his first tour in Vietnam, John B. Morgan III went down with his bird (see chapter 7). He survived the crash of his chopper, and his tour. But later he was to return to Nam, to the red dust of Pleiku. This time he wasn't flying a slick. He was flying a gunship – the ultimate gunship, the AH-1G Cobra, designed as a result of lessons learned in Vietnam.

Huey Cobras weren't the improvised gun platforms found in the early years of the war. They weren't troop-carrying UH-1A slicks, laden down with 30-calibre machine guns. Nor were they UH-1Bs converted with factory-made kits. Nor were they the souped-up UH-1C with Emerson Quad 'flex' guns, 38 2.75in rockets and two M60 door guns.

Hot choppers

They weren't even the CH-47A Chinook 'Go-Go' birds that so impressed the grunts when three came in on trial. The pilots weren't much impressed when two of them went down though, one of them in an accident where the 20mm cannon's mounting pin broke during a firing run, letting the gun flip skyward and take out the forward rotor blades. All on board were killed.

No, John B. was flying the AH-1G Huey Cobra, the meanest mother ever to take to the skies:

'I went to the 4th Aviation Battalion, the very same one I had come in-country with in January

Above: Banking steeply, a US Navy Huey unleashes a 2.75in rocket. This chopper was working in conjunction with two River Patrol Boats on the delta. Above left: As plumes of smoke rise from the jungle, a Huey inspects its handiwork. Left: Its Quad mount bristling with weaponry, a Huey sends a rocket into the jungle.

1970

1970

1967. This time it was Company B, the gunship company. They were in the process of turning in their Charlie model gunships for Cobras. It involved a round trip to Vung Tau to drop off the UH-1C and pick up a brand new AH-1G.

Tactics were pretty simple

'Flying guns isn't as rewarding as slicks. Unless there was a combat assault to cover, we spent a lot of time on standby, either down at the operations shack on the airfield, or at the 2d Brigade's forward HQ at a place called the Oasis.

'We worked in pairs – always. Two ships made up a gun team. We had four Cobra teams and four Loaches [Hughes OH-6As] which were used for scouting. The company never did get rid of all the "C" models while I was there. I believe we had two teams of "C" models up until the time I went home.

'Tactics were pretty simple. While one Cobra fired at the bad guys the other ship was going outbound on a racetrack pattern to position him-self at the point where he could cover his partner's break and begin firing himself. There were some unwritten rules: you never overflew friendlies while making a gun run. The falling brass would confirm their worst fears that we were trying to do them in as well. And never overfly the target.

We never killed any friendlies

'The front-seat man fired the turret and the back-seat man, usually the aircraft commander, fired the fixed wing stores and flew the aircraft. Our ships were adorned with a black ace of spades symbol on either side of the cockpit, advertising our radio call sign "Gambler". For the most part we maintained a pretty good reputation among the folks we worked for. We never killed any friendlies while I was there and we usually got the job done even in marginal weather and at night.

'The Cobra had a Huey heart in that its drive train and rotor systems were interchangeable with the UH-1. But the fuselage was different –

EYE-WITNESS

John B Morgan III was shot down flying a Huey in Nam. Completing that tour, he came back for more, returning to fly Cobras.

435

only 36in wide, to reduce frontal area and provide tandem seating for only two. It was red-lined at 190 knots and that's fast for a helicopter. It would do it in a dive, but not straight and level. Loaded with fuel and ammo 120-130 knots was good.

Gatling guns and grenades

'The rotor head and blades were from the UH-1C and differed from a UH-1A in that they were about 26in wide, which gave it some strange handling qualities.

'We were armed with several different kinds of weapons. The turret had one six-barreled electric Gatling gun, which fired 7.62mm ball ammo. As I remember, there was a selector switch on the turret sight in the front seat which would change the rate of fire from 2000 to 4000 rounds per minute. To the left of the gun, in the turret, was a 40mm grenade launcher which fired belt-fed gre-

Above right: The ground crew open up a Cobra and prepare her for another mission. Right: A pilot's eye view from a Huey cockpit.

Bell UH-1C

Max speed: 204km/h
Range: 511km
Weight: 2116kg
Armament: 4 x 7.62 mm
machine gun
38 2.75in roc

GUNSHIP ADVANCES

The US Army was quick to realize that the Huey UH-1 armed helicopter was, at best, a temporary expedient, thrown together to satisfy a need for escort and gunship capabilities in Vietnam in the early 1960s. A purpose-built design, incorporating machine guns and rockets without affecting performance, was essential. Although this was technically feasible, the project soon got bogged down. In 1965, a compromise had to be accepted – an interim rather than an ultimate design – out of which the Bell 209/AH-1G Cobra emerged.

Important as the first helicopter designed specifically for an attack role, the Cobra took the powerplant, rotor and transmission of the UH-1 and added a new streamlined fuselage, within which the pilot and gunner sat in tandem. The initial armament was a single 7.62mm rapid-fire minigun, mounted in a turret beneath the nose, but this was soon replaced by a twin turret

system. Stub wings were added, onto which were fitted pod-mounted 2.75in rockets, 7.62mm machine guns or 20mm cannon. With a top speed of 352 km/h and an effective range of 574 kilometres, the Cobra had a lot to offer.

Once deployed to Vietnam in late 1967, the Cobra played an integral part in the airmobility concept, providing 'Pink Teams' responsible for seeking out and destroying the enemy on the ground. Working in co-operation with an OH-6 Loach scout helicopter, a typical team flew into battle at about 610m (2000ft), ready to engage targets with a devastating display of agility and accurate firepower. The sudden appearance of Cobras over hot LZs often marked the difference between success and failure for ground forces. Their firepower enhanced the troops' ability to hit back at NVA or VC ambushers even when the latter 'hugged' their enemy in an effort to avoid air attack.

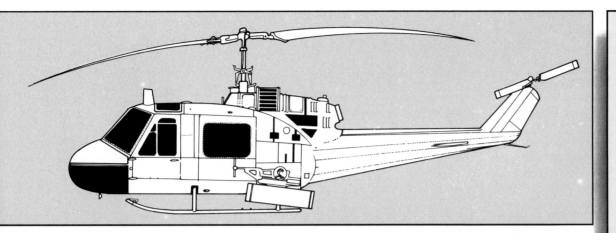

THE GUNSHIP CONCEPT

From the start of the Vietnam war it was recognized that transport helicopters were vulnerable to ground fire and that some form of escort and ground-attack capability was needed to protect them. To a certain extent, fixed-wing aircraft could provide such capability, but they lacked the close-in accuracy so essential during a landing operation and were, of course, under Air Force rather than Army control. Some pilots began to fit machine guns to their CH-21 Workhorses but something more precise was clearly needed.

It began to be provided in mid-1962, when UH-1 Hueys arrived in Vietnam. Equipped with .30in machine guns and 2.75in rockets, the Hueys quickly carved out a role as escort helicopters, capable of laying down accurate suppressive fire as the transports went in.

The Hueys soon replaced the CH-21s in the transport role as well, allowing fully integrated airmobile companies to emerge. By late 1964, special Eagle Flights had been formed, comprising a command-and-control helicopter, seven unarmed transports, five armed escorts and a medevac machine each. These became the models for more sophisticated airmobile tactics in both the 1st Cavalry and the 101st Airborne Divisions as the war progressed.

But the UH-1 had its limitations, particularly in terms of weight, for the addition of weapons and gunners to a basic transport design inevitably affected performance. What was needed was a purpose-built gunship and this was provided in September 1967 with the deployment of the AH-1G Cobra. With its combination of speed, agility and firepower, it ensured that the gunship took its place as an integral part of the airmobility concept.

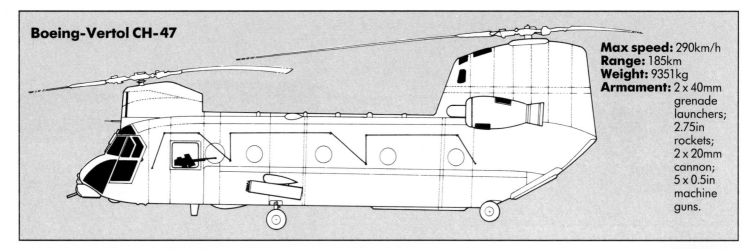

Boeing-Vertol CH-47

Max speed: 290km/h
Range: 185km
Weight: 9351kg
Armament: 2 x 40mm grenade launchers; 2.75in rockets; 2 x 20mm cannon; 5 x 0.5in machine guns.

1970

ARVN AND AIRMOBILITY

The US military machine threw up some of the most sophisticated technology ever seen on the battlefield. But with the advent of 'Vietnamization', would the ARVN be left out in the cold?

Airmobility, using transport helicopters and gunships to project forces deep into enemy-controlled territory, was an all-American concept. As such, it had its roots firmly in the American approach to war, substituting technology for manpower wherever possible, and it was heavily dependent upon American money and know-how. Only the Americans could have made it work in the 1960s and the success it enjoyed in Vietnam was bought for a high price in terms of financial and technological commitment.

This left the South Vietnamese a bit out in the cold. Although ARVN troops took part in airmobile operations – indeed, before the deployment of US main-force units to Vietnam in 1965, their participation was guaranteed – they tended to be passive contributors to the concept, using the mobility provided but being excluded from the more active roles. Few South Vietnamese helicopter pilots were trained for gunship duties in the 1960s and the record of co-operation between ground and air units in the ARVN was not impressive. As with so many aspects of the fighting, the South Vietnamese had grown used to gunship support being provided by the Americans – with all their advantages of specialized training and sophisticated equipment.

Thus, when the Americans began to withdraw in 1969-70, there were limits to how much of their tactical approach they could transfer. Helicopters were provided and extra pilots trained, but the close co-ordination of effort so central to airmobility could not be created overnight. Furthermore, it could be argued that airmobility had less relevance to the war once the emphasis had shifted from main-force battle to border surveillance and pacification.

nades at a rate of about 400 per minute. You could shoot either the launcher or the gun but not both.

'The launcher was good for working brush or areas where targets were indistinct. The projectiles were quite slow and as a result required a higher trajectory and longer time to impact than the minigun.

A red tornado of death
'The turret would traverse about 110 degrees to each side, so it could be used to cover part of a break outbound. At night the minigun was awesome. There was one tracer in five and, at the rate they were going out, it looked like a red tornado funnel

weaving death to and fro.

'Fixed on the stub wings were several kinds of pod. My ship had two self-contained minigun pods, one on each inboard hardpoint. They contained 1500 rounds each and fired together. By working tail rotor pedals and cyclic the ship could be made to pitch and yaw, directing this fire about 30 degrees, left and right, up and down. On the outboard hardpoints I had two 19-round rocket launching pods, one left and one right. They fired a 2.75in folding fin air-to-ground rocket.

'These rockets could be quite accurate in the hands of an artist, but they still took skill to fire. Upon leaving the tube they would weather-cock

Above inset: Loading a chopper's steely pit. Above: With its narrow cross section and deadly array of armaments, the HueyCobra was 10,000lb of instant, skyborn death.

into the relative wind. So to get them to go straight you had to be in perfect trim and not pitching up or down from an established dive angle. Working these in near friendly positions was a job left to experienced hands. One guy I knew could fire rockets while making his break, and by kicking the ship out of trim at the moment of launch, could direct them into what seemed to be a 90-degree turn back to the target.

'Rockets were fired by depressing a thumb button on the cyclic stick. Depress it once and one rocket would launch from each pod. A selector on the armament panel could change that to two or three or all the way to 19 pairs. Usually they were fired in pairs in order to get on target, wasting a minimum of ammunition. We had several war-

Above: Making final adjustments to a 2.75in rocket pod. The rockets came in 10 or 17lb warhead versions, in HE and in WP. Variations on one theme: skyborn destruction.

1970

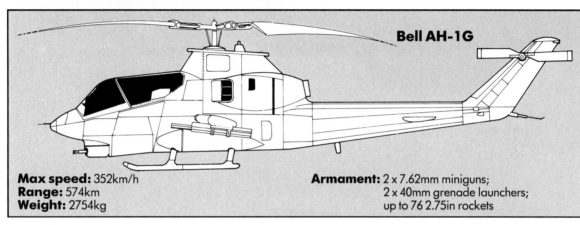

Bell AH-1G

Max speed: 352km/h
Range: 574km
Weight: 2754kg

Armament: 2 x 7.62mm miniguns;
2 x 40mm grenade launchers;
up to 76 2.75in rockets

Right: A group of Hueys and Cobras wait for another operation. During 1970 and 1971, the Cobras came into their own, smashing NVA armour even in poor weather.

heads these rockets would launch. A 9lb high explosive, an 18lb high explosive, a white phosphorus and anti-personnel flechette rounds called "Nails".

'We heard that the NVA called the flechette round "The Silent Death", due to the lack of any explosive charge. They were accelerated to a supersonic speed by the rocket motor. At burn out, the decelerating forces caused the plastic casing to break open, emitting a red dye marker and 5000 nails. They were fired from a low angle in order to obtain a long, wide impact zone. In Vietnam's climate even small wounds from these devices were said to be almost fatal.

'Most of the time when the guns showed up the bad guys would head for the hills. It made for more relaxed flying – a lot less stressful than flying slicks. We lost only one ship while I was there. Our home airfield was rocketed just before sundown and even though a huge thunderstorm was about to descend on us, some desk jockey ordered the standby guns out to find where they were launched. The Cobra didn't make it back. It crashed into Dragon Mountain while it was trying to get back to base camp. Two Loaches from some neighbouring units went down in the same storm. No-one survived.'

Left: Carrying the ammo for a gunship's grenade launcher. Above: Patrolling the delta.

FNGs

If you're new, you've got a problem. The VC don't make allowances and you can bet your life the rest of your platoon won't either

At some time in our lives, we're all new guys. Whether it's at a new job, school or military unit, we've all got to learn to settle in, learn the ropes and get to know – and get along with – the people already there. Usually (unless you're a complete ass) those folks will try to help you fit in, to find your niche. But not in Vietnam. Not by a long shot.

I've never really been able to put my finger on it; why a soldier new to a combat unit in Vietnam was treated as a non-person, a pariah to be shunned and scorned, almost vilified, until he passed that magic, unseen line to respectability. I can't think of too many other wars or conflicts where that happened.

They even got homesick

There were a few obvious reasons, of course. New meat, or 'Fucking New Guys' (FNGs) if you prefer, were at once a liability to a close-knit, seasoned bunch of jungle fighters. They talked too loud and made too much noise while moving around, didn't know what kit to take into the bush or even how to wear it properly, couldn't respond to basic combat commands, fired too much ammo, and tended to flake out on even the easiest 10-klick moves. An' Christ, they even got homesick. Useless as tits on a boar hog, or so the old guys figured.

But there were other reasons for that kind of thinking. They weren't obvious, and I doubt even consciously considered, but they made most combat infantrymen in Vietnam anti-FNG.

FNGs, after all, were an unknown factor. Old-timers, on the other hand, could be read like a basic primer. Everyone knew what everyone else was capable – or incapable – of doing on patrol or in combat. Liabilities were considered and accounted for. Assets were used to best advantage. A raised eyebrow or flick of the finger could tell volumes about enemy locations or danger areas. A half grin or shake of the head could easily summarize a man's feelings about an upcoming operation or the last 24 hours.

The platoon was a family in the closest sense of the word. They were tighter than blood relatives, fought like crazed wildcats with each other when the time was right, and would stand off the entire outside world when one of their own was threatened. A poor FNG just didn't stand a chance in hell of bonding with this bunch...well, until he became part of it.

And there were other reasons why the FNG was destined to become the platoon's version of Typhoid Mary upon arrival. He represented too many things that combat troops – immersed in a vicious, small-unit war half-way around the world – didn't want to think about. An FNG was straight out of the Land of the Big PX. Just last week he was lazin' and gazin', eating ice cream and hugging those big, beautiful round-eyed American women, driving around the block with jams blasting out of the music machine. Old-timers resented the hell out of that because it was the FNG, and not them, who had the closest link to The World.

Living up to a legend

The old army marching song went: *Ain't no use in lookin' back, Jody's got your Cadillac; Ain't no use in going home, Jody's got your girl and gone.* Well, to those grunts who'd been humping the bushes for six, or eight, or 10 months, FNGs were always the proverbial Jody.

If that wasn't enough, the FNG – although he didn't know it – stood for two other things in the eyes of the platoon: the platoon's legendary grunt, and themselves, when they were FNGs.

For whatever reason, small combat units in Vietnam always seemed to create a legend around someone who had served in the past. 'Christ, remember ol' Skate? That mother was the baddest gook killer/point man/machine gunner/chow hand/card player/tunnel rat/scout/beer drinker (and on and on) we ever seen.' No matter if Skate had left last week or last year, poor FNG had to fill his shoes – at least in the eyes of the platoon. Only he didn't know anything about it. If ol' Skate had been a wicked M60 gunner, then by God FNG had better be good too if he wanted acceptance – and FNG surely wanted that more than anything else in those first few days. Until he made a name for himself in some other way, he was tagged with fulfilling the legend (true or not) of some ghost from the past.

And then there was the 'I went through it, so you have to go through it too' syndrome. Every member of that platoon had been an FNG once himself, and he remembered, usually painfully, what it was like. It's an aberration of the military combat psyche that when we experience pain or unpleasantness, we want others to go through the same trauma. Sadistic? You bet. And in Vietnam, sadism of some sort – physical, mental or emotional – was the rule rather than the exception. Like a school first-termer in a room of school-leavers, that poor sucker was in for harassment and abuse until he, in turn, was senior enough to administer the same to his juniors. Yeah it was childish,

For the fresh-faced FNG (previous page) Vietnam was especially hard. Apart from the fears and ever-present dangers, he also had to contend with the oppressive heat and humidity (above) and diseases such as foot rot (left). While he had the occasional solace of a letter from home (right), he was aware that his new 'buddies' wouldn't mourn too much if he got killed or wounded. Most of them probably didn't know his name.

especially for stone-killers in a combat zone. But it was there, and it was a fact of life.

One time, my battalion had been airlifted up to Kontum in the Central Highlands to help run some pretty intense ground ops against a number of slick VC units bent on taking the AO for their own. ARVN wasn't having much luck; it seems the Corps bosses, political appointees from Saigon, couldn't (or didn't want to) get a grip on the situation.

He was nervous and scared

I was a sergeant squad leader/acting platoon sergeant by then, and we ran into a lot of small-unit stuff trying to locate Charlie and force him to stand and fight – so we could blow the shit out of him with artillery and airpower. It never really developed that way, but we did ace a few gooks – and lost some of our people in the process.

My company got in four or five replacements to fill the gaps. A couple were old in-country bush rats, and a couple were FNGs fresh from the States. I got one of the latter for my platoon. I remember that he was immediately tagged with the nickname 'Pot', because he was a small guy and his steel pot seemed twice as big as it would have on someone larger.

They'd come in on the log bird late one afternoon, and I picked up Pot at the company command post. On the way back to our part of the perimeter, I briefed him on what was happening

for the night, told him I'd square him away the next morning, and then turned him over to the Speedy Four running my own squad. I had more important matters to take care of.

Later that night I made quiet rounds of the perimeter, checking guards. As the FNG, Pot had been tagged with the 0230-0330 shift. This was the worst of the lot, because there would be little time for any sleep before stand-to. 'Everything OK?' I whispered. He was nervous and scared, understandably so. 'I don't know what to do sarge,' he answered, a kid lost in a strange country with an even stranger war. 'Keep your eyes open, don't shoot anything, and wake someone up if you get really worried,' I told him. I was more interested in his staying awake and keeping the AO secure than settling his fears.

Bitten by a snake

Our company moved out on a sweep just after first light, and I didn't get a chance to talk with Pot. About 1000, I got the word a man was down. 'Snakebite, sarge. Hit him in the neck. Better get a medevac in here or he's gone.' It was Pot, and I felt strangely relieved. It wasn't someone I knew. Or really knew, anyway.

We got him out on a bird, with medics pumping him full of drugs. I don't think I ever knew the kid's real name; he never came back, and I never found out what happened to him. He was, after all, just another FNG.

US CASUALTIES

The controversy over American casualties at Hamburger Hill in May 1969 – a week in which 242 servicemen had died overall – underlined the need for Nixon's Administration to reduce losses and the harrowing sight of coffins arriving by air back in the US from Vietnam (above). On 15 July, therefore, Secretary of State Melvin Laird told the Senate Foreign Relations Committee that, although no change had yet been made in the orders given to MACV to maintain pressure on the communists, policy was under review. Laird also revealed that Nixon had made the avoidance of US casualties a primary MACV objective – something Nixon himself was to emphasize when meeting Creighton Abrams on 30 July.

Although the steady Vietnamization of the war was likely further to reduce American deaths, it was clear that Nixon's willingness to escalate the conflict if deemed necessary might run counter to his avowed aim of reducing casualties. This aspect of Nixon's policy – as with the incursion into Cambodia in 1970 – was also likely to provoke domestic outrage.

In 1969, 9249 Americans died in Vietnam – many as a result of the mini-offensive with which Hanoi had greeted Nixon's inauguration. But, thereafter, the casualty rate did drop significantly. In January 1968, there had been 1202 deaths from hostile actions, a rate of 2.4 per 1000 men in Vietnam. By 1972, this figure had been reduced to 0.1 per 1000.

The monthly casualty rate was also halved in 1970. Thus, while 222,351 Americans became casualties during Johnson's four years of office between 1965 and 1968, the figure was reduced to 122,708 during Nixon's first term from 1969 to 1972.

On 20 April 1972, a North Vietnamese SAM exploded in mid-air a few feet away from Major Ed Elias's RF-4C Phantom. The violent blast wrenched metal, severed hydraulics and disabled the Phantom's electrical system. There was no way home. 'Eject, eject' Elias intoned, talking to his weapons systems officer, Captain Ernest (Woody) Clark.

Falling apart and leaving behind a fatal trail of red-orange fuel-fire, the Phantom tumbled into a hillside and exploded. Two parachutes unfurled over the North Vietnamese paddy fields as Elias and Clark floated down to earth in a heavily populated sector of Ho Chi Minh's homeland. NVA troops fanned out below the two men. Elias landed in the middle of several dozen of them and was immediately taken prisoner.

Clark was luckier. He came crashing down in heavy brush some distance from the enemy troops. His bleeper – a tiny hand-held survival radio – was working and he was able to talk to friendly aircraft overhead.

Once again, as happened so often during the air war, a man was down. It was a basic rule that when one of your guys was trapped in enemy territory, you made every effort to get him out – no matter

Whenever a US pilot was shot down, an operation swung into action to rescue him. The key parts of this operation were daring helicopter crewmen and A-1 Skyraiders giving close support

what the cost. The elaborate mechanism for a combat rescue swung into motion.

The attempt to rescue an airman downed in North Vietnam could mean assembling hundreds of men and aircraft. For a successful rescue, it could be necessary to have F-105 Wild Weasel aircraft to suppress SAMs, Phantoms to fly cover, KC-135 tankers to provide the gas to get everybody into the rescue area, OV-10 Pave Nail Broncos to direct rescue efforts at night, A-1 Skyraiders to provide direct support to the downed airman and HH-3E Jolly Green Giant or HH-53C Super Jolly helicopters to make the actual rescue: a complicated business.

To illustrate the importance placed on rescue missions, in one rescue attempt three helicopters were downed by ground fire, an OV-10 Bronco destroyed by a direct hit from a SAM, seven crewmen killed, one captured and one was himself rescued after 10 days on the ground – all the result of an attempt to save just one man. But no one considered this to be false economics. Every airman who flew against heavily defended North Vietnam was re-assured by knowing that if he happened to be unlucky, a rescue attempt would be on the way.

Perhaps the most important men in the whole elaborate operation were the enlisted para-rescue specialists – also called Para-Jumpers or PJs – aboard the helicopters. These men were trained in parachuting, helicopter rescue work, medicine and survival under the the most extreme conditions. There was even a distinctive uniform with a maroon beret and bloused trousers over combat boots for the elite PJs. In Vietnam, some PJs became legendary.

Sergeant Chuck Morrow spent two tours in Southeast Asia and was awarded three Silver Stars, five Distinguished Flying Crosses and numerous Air Medals. All for combat rescue missions flown deep into North Vietnam.

Crashing down on top of the H-34

Airman First Class Duane D Hackney, a PJ with the 37th Aerospace Rescue and Recovery Squadron, appeared in numerous after-action reports and established a magnificent combat 'save' record. During one mission, Hackney searched for a downed pilot in the underbrush of a North Vietnamese jungle. He found the injured pilot, strapped him to a Stokes litter and both of them were winched up towards the helicopter. However, they were spotted by North Vietnamese troops, who immediately opened fire. As the pilot pulled the HH-3E up, an enemy gunner found his mark and the Jolly Green began to burn. Hackney quickly put a parachute on the injured man and pulled one on himself. Suddenly, the helicopter exploded and Hackney was thrown out, his chute opening just above the trees. The second HH-3E – the 'high bird' – rushed in and its PJ went down to search for survivors. He found only Hackney, dazed, but not seriously injured.

A month later, on 13 March 1967, Hackney was

Left: Alone in the jungle, a pilot would pop a smoke flare so the Jolly Green could find him. The D/F fix was not enough to pinpoint a downed airman under the jungle canopy, but the smoke invited the unwelcome attention of the NVA too. Below: A pilot is down! The rescue team rush to their Jolly Greens.

1970

RESCUE MISSION

COMBAT RESCUE

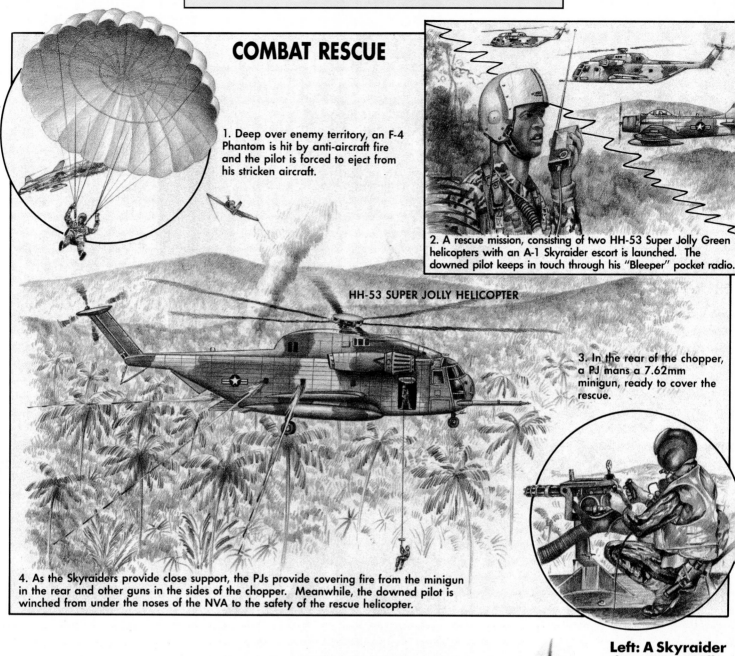

1. Deep over enemy territory, an F-4 Phantom is hit by anti-aircraft fire and the pilot is forced to eject from his stricken aircraft.

2. A rescue mission, consisting of two HH-53 Super Jolly Green helicopters with an A-1 Skyraider escort is launched. The downed pilot keeps in touch through his "Bleeper" pocket radio.

HH-53 SUPER JOLLY HELICOPTER

3. In the rear of the chopper, a PJ mans a 7.62mm minigun, ready to cover the rescue.

4. As the Skyraiders provide close support, the PJs provide covering fire from the minigun in the rear and other guns in the sides of the chopper. Meanwhile, the downed pilot is winched from under the noses of the NVA to the safety of the rescue helicopter.

1970

Left: A Skyraider drops two 500lb napalm pods to defend a downed pilot and protect the rescue helicopters that are on their way.

one of two PJs aboard an HH-3E Jolly Green flying just south of the DMZ, over enemy-controlled territory. A Marine H-34 Huey was down and its survivors reported NVA closing in for the kill. A second Marine chopper crew heard the transmissions and turned their larger H-46 towards their beleaguered comrades. Hackney's Jolly Green arrived in time to see the H-46 get hit and go crashing down on top of the first helicopter that had gone down.

On the ground, the Marines gathered their injured and set their defences against an enemy that was closing in from all sides. Above them, in the door of the HH-3E, Duane Hackney watched as A-1 Skyraiders darted in to blast the NVA. When the Skyraiders had laid down a smoke screen, the pilot cautiously moved the Jolly Green over the embattled Marines. As soon as the chopper came to a hover, Hackney was on the Stokes litter and on his way to the ground. He loaded as many injured men as he could onto the litter and rode up with them.

Just as Hackney and the last wounded Marine got in the door, the pilot's warning light came flashing on. With bullets smashing into the fuselage, the pilot pulled the chopper up and headed to Da Nang. Meanwhile, Hackney tended to the wounded in the back. Suddenly, he slumped to the floor. An enemy bullet had grazed his helmet and knocked him out. He soon regained consciousness, however, and continued to set fractures, tend head wounds and apply tourniquets. Hackney received the Air Force Cross for that day's work, another award to add to his growing collection. Described by a fellow PJ as 'modest, shy and baby-faced', Hackney was detained by Air Force police when he returned Stateside, until a telephone call verified that he was, indeed, authorized the huge array of medals he was wearing.

A clanking machine

If PJs like Morrow and Hackney were crucial to the success of combat rescue, so too were the others aboard the rescue chopper. An HH-53C Super Jolly Green carried a pilot, who was always in command and responsible for the helicopter's role in a mission, and a co-pilot, who provided a second pair of eyes and ears, as well as an extra hand on the throttle. Of the three PJs on board, one operated the helicopter's 7.62mm six-barrel GAU-2A/B miniguns.

But a helicopter, even with a highly trained crew on board wasn't going to be much use if it couldn't reach the survivor on the ground. To open up a landing zone and keep the enemy troops at bay, the Air Force began using A-1 Skyraiders – better known by their radio callsign 'Sandy'.

The Sandy dated back to 1945. It was an ancient clanking machine that belched smoke and oil. One pilot complained that if the enemy didn't kill him, then he'd probably die after skidding on one of the many oil slicks that adorned the runway at Da Nang. They might have been old, but A-1s were sturdy, tough and could stay overhead for

long periods when a rescue required it.

Above all else, the Sandy could carry a mind-boggling selection of ordnance. On a typical mission, an A-1 would carry a centreline fuel tank, a 7.62mm minigun on one 'stub' (inboard wing pylon) and an additional fuel tank on the other. Pods containing 2.75in folding fin aircraft rockets (FFARs) and six 100lb Willy Pete (white phosphorus) bombs, to make smoke to shield the path of an incoming rescue helicopter, were also carried.

The Sandy was the key to success when a man was down. In the RF-4C Phantom shootdown, survivor Woody Clark was in contact with Sandies but was told that a rescue would not be immediately possible. Darkness was closing in, and rescue forces would have to wait until the next day before attempting to snatch Clark from the clutches of the North Vietnamese. The lone survi-

Below: Once the PJ has located his man, both of them have to be winched back aboard the hovering helicopter – no easy task if the airman is injured and they are under fire.

1970

Above: Rescuing an airman in enemy-held territory was no milk run. Rescue helicopters got hit and downed too. Many had miniguns mounted on their back ramp to lay down suppressive fire. Left: A Jolly Green refuels in the air from a KC-135 tanker.

vor passed the night bedded down in a gully.

The next morning, Sandies and F-4 Phantoms prowled the area but could not immediately re-establish contact with Clark. One of his wing men at the 14th Tactical Reconnaissance Squadron at Udorn, Captain Donald S Pickard, buzzed the hills and valleys, trying without success to get a D/F (direction finding) fix on his bleeper. It was not until the end of the second day that rescue forces got a fix and were able to confirm that Clark

was still alive and free. Pickard then devised a plan to drop medicine, food and other vital supplies to Clark inside a Phantom centreline fuel tank. Once again, however, darkness prevented any rescue attempt.

On the third day, Woody Clark had plenty to think about. North Vietnamese forces around him were considered too thickly concentrated for a pair of HH-53C choppers to attempt a rescue.

'The bad guys are awfully close'

When, on the fourth day, an HH-53C chopper finally slipped through low, clinging fog and got close to Clark, the PJs aboard the chopper were determined. One laid down fire with a 7.62 mm minigun while another helped the pilot home in on Clark's bleeper. 'The bad guys are awfully close to him,' the pilot noted. 'That's what makes it interesting,' one of the PJs commented.

Clark had probably despaired of ever getting out of North Vietnam, so the appearance of a camouflaged HH-53C high over his head must have been a beautiful sight. A PJ came floating down with a rescue hoist, grabbed Clark, and lifted him up into the chopper. Although famished, Clark was in good shape – and astonished, for while being lifted into the helicopter he could see NVA troops within a few hundred yards of where he'd been hiding. He was out.

EXTENDING THE WAR

Above: After artillery and airstrike prepping the US Army's armour leads the way into Cambodia. The grunts were determined to seek out their enemy.

US troops moved into Cambodia in search of the elusive communist HQ. Arms and ammunition caches were uncovered, but the guy in the COSVN T-shirt got clean away

The guys had had it up to here. They'd all lost buddies in combat up near the Cambodian border while the gooks would scuttle back to their sanctuaries laughing at them. So when a plane load of generals turned up at Quan Loi they weren't at all unhappy. Sooner or later they'd be going in. Guys were taking bets on it. You didn't usually get a whole bunch of brass up in that area. Soon the place was full up with helicopters, hundreds of them. Something was definitely in the wind.

For the grunts, the incursion into Cambodia was an act of revenge, though some of them had to be bullied into it. 'My orders were for Vietnam, not Cambodia,' complained one. 'But it was either Cambodia or the LBJ [Long Binh Jail].' The brass saw it as a good way of hurting the enemy. But Nixon believed that this, at last, was the crucial test of America's – and his own – moral fibre. 'I would rather be a one-term president,' he said on TV, 'than see America accept the first defeat in its 190-year history.'

Of course, he knew there'd be trouble. For the folks back home the war seemed to be winding down. Last week they'd heard that another 150,000 of their boys would be coming home. Suddenly it would seem like Nixon was escalating it again. It would be his war. The demonstrators would be out on the streets again. The media would be bleating. The Congress would get cold feet and some would even say it was illegal.

The ARVN wanted revenge

But Richard Milhous Nixon was not the kind of a guy who backed down when the going got tough. When, as Eisenhower's vice-presidential running mate, he was accused of corruption, he appeared on TV with his household accounts and even introduced his dog Checkers to the nation. No, Nixon could handle a little thing such as adverse public opinion over the invasion of a neutral country.

Besides, his ally, the new premier of Cambodia, Lon Nol, 'invited' him in and Nixon promised to 'scrupulously observe the neutrality of the Cambodian people'. Unfortunately, the ARVN, who had gone into the Parrot's Beak, didn't feel the same way. After the massacre of the Vietnamese living in Cambodia when Lon Nol took over in 1970, which had sent bodies floating down the Mekong, the ARVN also wanted revenge – but not just against the NVA.

Tanks and APCs move in

On 1 May, the US Army bulldozed into the Fish Hook. First there was an artillery bombardment and an airstrike to soften up the salient, then two columns of tanks and APCs of the 11th Armored Cavalry, followed by Sheridan reconnaissance vehicles and M48 Patton tanks moved forward. The helicopters of the 1st Air Cav swooped in, expecting to come under fire from radar-controlled machine guns at any minute.

The Americans were certainly ready for heavy resistance. Two NVA regiments were supposed to be in the area that straddled the border. But the grunts found there wasn't anyone there. In the first two days, only eight Americans were killed and 32 wounded. And they claimed only 476 enemy KIA, 160 of them victims of air attacks.

The NVA staged small delaying actions, usually crushed by machine guns, cannon fire and airstrikes. Only at the small Cambodian town of Snuol did the NVA show any inclination to stand and fight. As American tanks approached through a nearby plantation they came under heavy fire from troops dug in on the edge of the town. US helicopters were peppered with anti-aircraft fire.

Backing off, the US tanks started to pound the town with their 120mm cannon. Once the NVA gun emplacements were taken, the Americans sent in a column of nearly a hundred Sheridan reconnaissance vehicles. They met a hail of mortar rounds and smallarms fire. They had to back out to regroup and then return to take out building

after building. This small Cambodian town suffered a two-day bombardment of shells, rockets and napalm, introducing a new word Namspeak – 'To snuol': to utterly obliterate. Over 90 per cent of the town was reduced to rubble.

When American ground troops eventually went in they captured one NVA anti-aircraft gunner, who had been ordered to stay behind and fight the American tanks. The bodies of four dead civilians lay in the street, one of them a young girl.

'We didn't want to blow this town away,' said Lieutenant-Colonel Grail Brookshire. 'But it was a hub of North Vietnamese activity and we had no choice but to take it.' His men grabbed what loot they could from what was left of the shops.

Right: A trooper warily probes the entrance to a concealed supply dump. As the advance into the Fish Hook proceeded, the dumps got larger and the finds more spectacular.

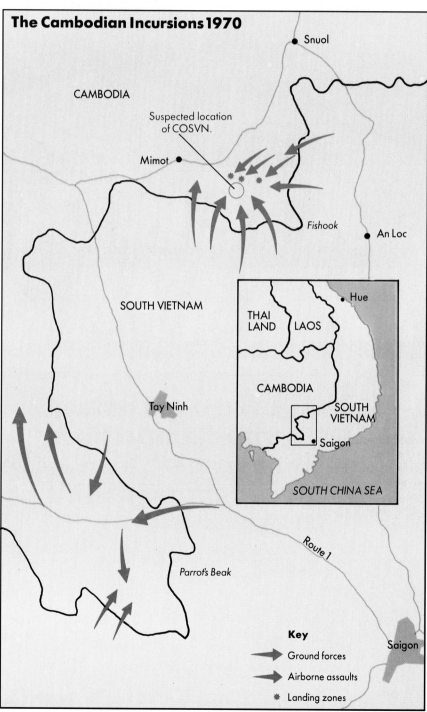

The Cambodian Incursions 1970

CAMBODIA

Snuol

Suspected location of COSVN.

Mimot

Fishook

An Loc

SOUTH VIETNAM

Tay Ninh

Parrot's Beak

Route 1

Saigon

THAILAND

LAOS

Hue

CAMBODIA

SOUTH VIETNAM

Saigon

SOUTH CHINA SEA

Key

Ground forces

Airborne assaults

Landing zones

Grunts went out to question villagers and were told of a massive NVA compound in the jungle. Jets went in and stripped away the trees while Loach helicopters searched the area. Eventually a pilot spotted a well-camouflaged hootch and a company was sent in. They found the place well guarded. That night they picked off the guards with a series of ambushes.

For Nixon it was like Christmas

Next day, beneath layers of jungle foliage, they found concealed log huts, bunker systems, bamboo walkways, bicycle paths, street signs, garages for trucks, chickens, a pig farm, mess halls, a firing range, even a swimming pool. The grunts called the two-square-mile complex 'The City'. There were 400 thatched huts in all, with sheds and bunkers stuffed with clothes, medical supplies and food. Over the next week 182 separate caches of weapons and ammunition were found – one contained 480 rifles, another 120,000 rounds of ammunition.

A couple of days later a helicopter spotted four trucks on a jungle trail. Ground troops went in and, after fierce fighting, the NVA scattered, leaving behind the biggest cache taken in the war – more than 6.5 million rounds of anti-aircraft ammunition, half a million rifle rounds, thousands of rockets, several General Motors trucks and even telephone switchboards. The grunts called it Rock Island East after the Rock Island Arsenal in Illinois.

But Nixon had promised something else: 'The headquarters for the entire Communist military operation in South Vietnam' – the fabled COSVN. MACV had a precise map reference for it. It wasn't there. It was claimed that The City was it, but none of the documents, bunkers or equipment there proved it. The search continued, unsuccess-

CAMBODIAN INCURSIONS

The operations which were to have such far-reaching political repercussions began with a limited ARVN foray into Cambodia on 14 April 1970. On 29 April, Lieutenant-General Do Cao Tri threw 12,000 ARVN troops into the 'Parrot's Beak'. Two days later, US and ARVN units commanded by Brigadier-General Robert Shoemaker plunged into the other Cambodian salient jutting into South Vietnam, the 'Fish Hook', in Operation Toan Thang ('Total Victory') 43, aimed at locating COSVN, the communist headquarters supposedly directing the war in the South. While the 3d Brigade, 1st Air Cavalry took up screening positions to the north and west, armour from the 11th Armored Cavalry, the 2d Battalion, 34th Armor and the ARVN 1st Armored Cavalry drove in from the south and east. US infantry and ARVN airborne troops were also deployed to close the net.

However, earlier ARVN probes and preparatory bombing robbed the enterprise of tactical surprise. When the operation terminated on 30 June, there had been only limited contact with communist units believed to include the NVA 7th and VC 5th and 9th Divisions. The subsequent Operation Toan Thang 44 by the US 1st Brigade, 25th Infantry, along the Rach Beng Go river (6-14 May), the push by the 1st Air Cavalry northeast of Bu Dop (6 May - 20 June) and Operation Binh Tay ('Tame the West') by the US 4th Infantry Division and 40th ARVN Regiment (6-16 May), also lacked hard contact. What was achieved, however, was the location of major communist logistic bases.

'The City', discovered on 7 May, yielded 1282 individual and 202 crew-served weapons, 1.5 million rounds of smallarms ammunition, 30 tons of rice and 16,000lbs of corn. The following day, discovery of 'Rock Island' yielded 329 tons of munitions. The Cambodian operations disrupted communist plans, but at the price of incurring prohibitive restrictions on the future employment of US troops outside South Vietnam.

CAMBODIA'S BALANCING ACT

Cambodia was little touched by the war until the late 1960s, its fragile neutrality being maintained by the delicate balancing act performed by Prince Norodom Sihanouk. Elected king by the Royal Council in 1941, Sihanouk had abdicated after the country became independent in 1954. Winning the 1955 elections, he then served as prime minister until 1960, when he became head of state.

Initially, he had sought United States' protection but had then turned to China in 1963 and broken off diplomatic relations with Washington two years later. Sihanouk then acquiesced in Hanoi's use of Cambodian territory to infiltrate into South Vietnam, a 'Sihanouk Trail' taking supplies from the port of Sihanoukville (later named Kompong Som) to communist sanctuaries in eastern Cambodia.

Sihanouk became alarmed by the threat posed by the communist presence and began edging back towards the United States in 1967. He made it known that he was not opposed to the Americans engaging in 'hot pursuit' across the Cambodian frontier, and he re-opened diplomatic relations in July 1969.

Four months earlier, Nixon had authorized B-52 strikes over Cambodian territory, the resulting refugees placing considerable pressure on the economy and causing discontent in the towns.

Discontent also affected the army and, when Sihanouk went to France in January 1970 for his annual obesity cure, his prime minister, Lon Nol, orchestrated anti-Vietnamese riots. Sihanouk chose to go to Moscow to seek a Soviet restraining hand on Hanoi but, on 18 March, Lon Nol deposed him. Sihanouk went to Peking and formed a coalition National United Front Party for Kampuchea, including the hitherto unsuccessful Khmer Rouge communists. Still popular in the countryside, Sihanouk's appeal to the peasantry to rise against Lon Nol gave the Khmer Rouge new legitimacy and forced Lon Nol to appeal for US assistance. Henceforth, Cambodia could not escape becoming part of the wider Southeast Asian war.

1971

The NVA delayed the advance, before melting away. As always there were the wounded to attend to (above). Above right: At 'The City', men of the 79th Engineer Group are stunned at the tons of supplies they have uncovered. Below: Heavy artillery support comes from firebases established as the troops press on.

fully. As one US intelligence agent said: 'We're still looking for the guy in the COSVN T-shirt.'

For Nixon it was like Christmas. In just two weeks the operation had culled 4793 smallarms, 730 mortars, over three million rounds of rifle ammunition, 7285 rockets, 124 trucks and some two million pounds of rice. He ordered another 31,000 US troops into Cambodia to take out all the sanctuaries along the border.

But in the US, the reaction was stronger than Nixon had imagined. At Kent State campus four students were shot dead protesting against the invasion. Congress was hostile and Nixon was forced to give a firm undertaking to withdraw US troops in three to seven weeks and that they would penetrate no deeper than 21 miles into Cambodian territory.

The ARVN had performed well

The problem for the generals was that the 21-mile limit left the NVA with plenty of room to organize a counter-offensive. And they did not have enough men to shift the weapons and supplies they were

finding. Bulldozers cleared more than 2000 acres of jungle, making road and helicopter landing zones, and the grunts struggled day and night to shift the caches they'd found. The 1st Air Cav alone flew more than 6436 sorties in order to carry some 25,000 tons of captured materiel out of Cambodia.

What couldn't be shifted had to be destroyed. Engineers bulldozed reinforced bunkers and blew up tons of supplies. On 30 June, all US ground troops were back in Vietnam and Nixon pronounced the operation a success.

During the Cambodian incursions, 354 Americans were killed and 1689 wounded. During the same period the ARVN reported 866 killed and 3274 wounded. Nixon noted that more than a year's worth of supplies and weapons had been captured and, he reckoned, 11,349 enemy troops killed – though even the CIA called this body count 'highly suspect'.

The ARVN had performed well. Not limited by the 21-mile limit or the 30 June withdrawal, they found a new fighting spirit in Cambodia.

M48A3 PATTON MEDIUM TANK

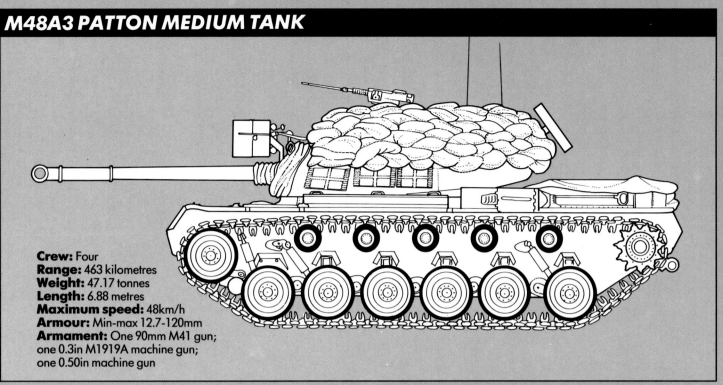

Crew: Four
Range: 463 kilometres
Weight: 47.17 tonnes
Length: 6.88 metres
Maximum speed: 48km/h
Armour: Min-max 12.7-120mm
Armament: One 90mm M41 gun;
one 0.3in M1919A machine gun;
one 0.50in machine gun

THE PATTON GOES TO VIETNAM

The Vietnam war saw tanks employed in a variety of roles. Whether facing NVA infantry or tanks, the M48A3 performed well

Because of the rivers and canals of the Mekong Delta and the highlands north of Saigon, the traditional role of the tank was curtailed in Vietnam. Nevertheless, armour was deployed throughout the war and occasionally given a major part to play, such as in the 1971 invasion of Laos. The chief American tank used during the conflict was the M48A3 Patton.

Entering service in 1963, the M48A3 was a development of the early 1950s' M48, a tank that stemmed from the World War II M26 Pershing.

The M48's high rate of fuel consumption had given it a range of only 120km. This critical deficiency was overcome in the M48A3 by installing a more efficient Teledyne Continental diesel engine and a larger fuel tank.

With an increased number of track return rollers (five instead of the three found on the M48A2) and vegetation cutting bars fitted to the front of the tank, the M48A3 was a popular, 'jungle-crushing' fighting vehicle that performed reliably, except for some engine overheating and mud clogging the tracks.

The M48A3's main armament was the 90mm M41 gun, a weapon that proved a match for the 100mm guns of the NVA T-54/55s – the M48A3 out-

fought these Soviet designs in tank-to-tank combat. The main gun also proved effective in combined infantry/armour operations, where canister and beehive rounds were used. A 'flamethrower' round, introduced in 1968, made every tank into a potential flamethrower – instead of the usual jet of flame, the new round burst into flame on hitting the target. M48A3s were widely used for destroying Viet Cong

bunkers using high explosive rounds. The weight of the tank frequently caused VC tunnels to cave in.

With experience gained from Vietnam, several modifications were made. These included new brakes, improved driver control, a new inflatable turret seal and the addition of protection for the turret stowage rack. Some vehicles were fitted with a turret riser which enlarged the commander's cupola.

With infantrymen clinging on to the turret, an M48 of the 9th Armored Division moves through Saigon during 'mini-Tet'.

1971

EYE-WITNESS

Rod Macon served three tours with Military Assistance Command, Vietnam Special Operations Group, and was wounded three times. He now lives in Florida with his wife and four children.

Heavy-duty recon and high-level assassinations, both part of the menu for the SOG. They went into Indian country loaded for bear, knowing that capture by the VC was a fate worse than death

SPECIAL

Getting to Nam was no express trip for this soldier. Before I got the order for my trans-Pacific excursion, I'd worked my way through over two-and-a-half years in training. From Basic and Advanced Infantry Training at Fort Jackson, South Carolina, through the NCO Academy, jump school and Ranger School at Fort Benning, I'd sweated up to the JFK Special Warfare School, Fort Bragg. At Bragg I qualified in guerrilla warfare, small-arms and counter-intelligence operations.

I finally made it to Vietnam, in November 1971.

From there I was sent to Da Nang, where I was attached to G Company Rangers for my preliminary in-country training on reconnaissance ops. Then it was a step up to MACV Special Operations Group CCN (Command and Control North), which ran all clandestine ops in I Corps, northern Laos and North Vietnam.

Most of our external missions were quick in-and-out recons to locate enemy concentrations and set up standard airstrikes or B-52 Arc Light raids. We were also tasked with assassinating high-level Viet Cong or NVA officials or officers. We inherited this after the demise of the CIA's Phoenix Program. The Agency still had excellent on-the-ground assets in the North Vietnamese local governments, as well as in Laos and South Vietnamese villages. If the Agency guys got word, for example, that a couple of NVA colonels were coming down near the border for an inspection or planning session, we'd go in and try to get them.

We went in loaded for bear

Although I was on two ops into the Parrot's Beak area in Cambodia, as well as a few into North Vietnam, most of my external operations were into Laos. My deepest penetration was about 20 klicks into Laos for an assassination mission, which turned into a complete screw-up. We'd hit a heavy contact and were trying to get away when I stopped to give covering fire and was overrun by the NVA. This NVA actually took me out with the butt of his AK-47. He laid me out cold but must have decided I was dead, because he left me there. If it hadn't been for one of our Nungs who came back for me, I probably wouldn't be here today.

We used the Nungs a lot. They were definitely some bad dudes you didn't want to mess with. Real pros. They were also unbelievably loyal and trustworthy – there were a number of occasions when they went back into serious Indian country to rescue wounded Americans.

Not long before the Vietnamese Tet holiday in 1971, we received intelligence that NVA and local Viet Cong forces were building up strength at a place less than 10 klicks inside Laos. My team –

went in loaded for bear. My personal weapons included a Swedish K sub-machine gun, a sawn-off 12-gauge pump shot-gun shoved down the top of my rucksack with 24 rounds of OO buckshot and 10 'flechette' rounds, a Browning High Power and my Gerber fighting knife. I also carried two Claymores, two pounds of C4 plastic explosive, six frag and two concussion grenades, two white phos grenades and two smoke grenades, plus a bundle of canteens.

The insertion went smooth as honey

We each had our personal first aid kits and seven packs of freeze-dried LURP rations – one pack per day – and underneath the rucks we wore STABO extraction harnesses. This all came to about 120 pounds. At the time, I only weighed 148 pounds soaking wet!

Each team was basically divided into two. If our mission was compromised by a contact or had been spotted, one half would take off for the extraction point while the other half would try to disappear and continue the mission. It was a tactic that worked pretty well on occasion.

We boarded our slicks and departed around

OPERATIONS GROUP

Above: His M60 and ammunition at the ready, a SOG operative takes five. Right: Checking that the PRC-25 is in A1 condition. The radio was the only link between the SOG team and air support in enemy territory.

Recon Team 'Python' – was tasked with going in to check things out. The afternoon before, we received a briefing from one of the Agency people assigned to us. He told us that there was an obvious build-up of forces, but no-one knew why. Our job was to determine whether the NVA were there to supply the Viet Cong, or to assist them on ops. As with most missions of this kind, it was emphasized that it was strictly a recon; we were not – repeat not – to make contact.

After the briefing, we pulled our equipment and went over the operation in detail. Even though we would make every effort to avoid a contact, we still

0330 the next morning and flew to our Forward Operations Base (FOB) near the Cua Viet River, northwest of Khe Sanh. There were four slicks and two gunships riding shot-gun. Another slick-and-gunship-team broke off before we reached the border and flew to another location a few klicks the other side of where the Viet Cong-NVA force was reported to be. Without being too obvious about it, they tried to get themselves spotted. The idea was that they'd be our decoys and direct any unwanted attention away from us.

The insertion went smooth as honey. We were on the ground and already setting up a perimeter

Top left: Taking a last look at the chopper that has set it down, a SOG team moves off into the jungle. Below left: An MACV-SOG base camp in the Central Highlands. SOG teams in Laos worked alongside local Nung tribesmen, usually in teams of four to six Americans with 10 to 12 Nungs. Below: They are still only in their early teens, but the ravages of war have given these two fighters a maturity way beyond their years.

before the pilots were pulling collective to get out of there. It was still at least 30 minutes before sunrise and as soon as the slicks were gone and we decided there was no-one waiting for us, we checked to see that everyone was okay, checked our equipment and maps and moved out.

For the next four or five hours, everything was still going smooth. I was working trail behind my half of the team when we hit an old French logging road. The forward half of the team moved in ones and twos across the road. As soon as they got across, the whole world opened up on us.

Tortured by the Viet Cong

We hit the ground and returned fire with everything we had. From the volume of fire coming at us, we knew we'd hit something big and that there was no percentage in hanging around.

When they sprang the ambush, all our training and experience went into the automatic mode. My half of the team laid down maximum covering fire so the first half could get back across the road. As soon as they were across, they went through our position and set up covering fire behind us. We'd then withdraw back through their position and lay down covering fire for them. This way, we could keep the enemy under constant fire while we put some distance between us and them.

The team leader was already on the radio to our FOB radio relay team, to advise that we needed immediate air support and extraction. By this time, we had two Nungs KIA plus two Nungs and two Americans wounded. We were withdrawing as fast as possible, having already dumped our rucks and any other non-essential equipment.

The trail half of the team would set Claymores, running the tripwires across our tracks. As soon as the enemy tripped one, we'd lay into them hard and start running again.

I suppose the one thing in the back of our minds was getting captured. Capture by the NVA wouldn't be pleasant, but if the Viet Cong got us...they had very special treatment for any SOG team member. We once found two of our people they'd captured. They'd been strung up by their ankles, gutted and their genitals had been cut off and stuck in their mouths. We had no intention of letting them get their hands on us.

The slicks came in hot

Soon our radio relay team called back to say that not only were the extraction slicks en route, but that it was 'no sweat' on the air support – we had two F4s in-bound at that time. We called them, using our callsign 'Dirty Trick'. The flight leader's voice coming back at us was pure heaven.

We were still moving as fast as we could, and the bad guys were right on our butts. We hit an open area and as soon as we were across it, stopped and laid everything we had into the other side. About that time we saw the two F4s.

The first F4 came in fast and low, releasing his entire load of Delta twos – 500 pounders – a little west of where we wanted. About 10 seconds later, the second F4 put half his load right on target. Before the smoke had cleared, we were running again, beating feet through the woods as fast as we could go. By now, we had been running and fighting for over two hours. We went straight past our primary extraction point, hoping to give the people behind us a false indication, and humped hard for the second.

At the second extraction point, the slicks came in hot and our people were diving on board before the skids even touched the ground. Heavy fire was already coming from the treeline to our left and one of the slicks was hit hard and went in, the pilot and crew chief both dead. Some of us got to the Huey – which was already starting to burn – and got the co-pilot and door gunner out while the four gunships riding shot-gun for the extraction opened up on the treeline.

TANGLED LAOTIAN POLITICS

As part of the Geneva Agreements of July 1954, Laos was established as an independent state, governed by Prince Souvana Phouma. From the start, he faced entrenched opposition, chiefly from the forces of the communist Pathet Lao, which were led by his half-brother Prince Souphanouvong. As the Pathet Lao controlled the two northernmost provinces of Phong Saly and Sam Neua, close to the Chinese border, the new country was virtually guaranteed to experience civil war, a fact which led to the creation of a strong neutralist faction, which was determined to prevent outside powers from further fuelling the political divide.

In 1957 Prince Souphanouvong agreed to a coalition with his half-brother, but the experiment was short-lived, leading to a period of anti-communism in Laos, supported by the Americans. This deepened the political rift, particularly when, in 1960, General Phoumi Nosavan seized power in a right-wing coup. Neutralists under Captain Kong Le (supported by Souvana Phouma) staged a counter-coup, triggering an all-out civil war. The Americans, fearing some sort of deal between the neutralists and communists, rebuilt a right-wing front under General Nosavan and Prince Boun Oum, but Kong Le managed to survive. By

July 1962 the demands for neutrality were strong enough to receive international backing at Geneva.

But this could not be expected to last. Both the North Vietnamese and the Americans had used the cover of the civil war to increase their influence in Laos, and throughout the 1960s the country became a secondary theatre of the Vietnam war. The North Vietnamese violated Laotian neutrality by developing the Ho Chi Minh Trail along the border with South Vietnam and, in response, the Americans showed scant regard for the Geneva Agreements, mounting increasingly violent air attacks on the Trail in Laotian territory.

At the same time, the CIA funded both the Royal Laotian Army and the Meo tribesmen as anti-communist forces.

The process culminated in the joint US/ARVN incursion into Laos in February 1971 (Operation Lam Son 719). NVA counter-attacks, forcing the ARVN to pull back, marked a turning-point in the war. Thereafter, the communists gradually gained the initiative inside Laos. Although a ceasefire was imposed in 1973, the existing government – by now denied US backing – was too weak to withstand the Pathet Lao/NVA offensive in 1975. Since then, Laos has been little more than a dependency of Vietnam.

Above: Rigging up a Claymore anti-personnel mine. Below: Waiting for the enemy to show himself. Note the head-band, the preferred SOG wear. Other SOG equipment was invariably 'sterile' – nothing could be identified as being US-made. All manufacturers' labels were removed and no ID or papers were carried, other than a medic alert bracelet in cases of penicillin allergy.

I was the last man on the last slick and I was hollering 'GO! GO! GO!' as I dived through the door. As the pilot was getting us out of there, we could feel and hear rounds going through the fuselage and tail. He kept the nose down, dragging the skids through the tree tops and going balls to the wall until we were out of range. Only then could we take stock of our losses. Incredibly, we had no more wounded.

Intelligence later learned that instead of being inserted the planned eight to 10 klicks from the suspected Viet Cong-NVA concentration, we'd actually landed about one-and-a-half klicks from two reinforced NVA battalions. The only things that saved us were experience, a lot of hard fighting and lady luck.

LAM SON 719

L am Son 719. I only remember that last great US/South Vietnamese gasp in fragments, like dog-eared photographs hastily thrown into a scrapbook without much rhyme or reason. I was pretty much a new guy in late January 1971 when we got the word: 'There's a big op coming down. ARVN's jumping the border into Laos to kick some ass and take names.' 'Bout friggin' time, most of the old hands said. They were tired of fighting the ARVN's war.

We pulled out of Quang Tri on a late-January morning, cold and damp from the mist that hung low to the ground. We were ready for a fight, but no one knew what we might run up against. The rumour mill had run amok: we'd be facing 10 reinforced NVA divisions; we were invading North Vietnam, Laos or Cambodia; advance units from the 101st Airborne had been annihilated at Khe Sanh. And on and on they went. We just didn't know.

Bombs out of the blue

I was riding in the back of an M113A1 with the APC's two M60 gunners and a couple of my guys. Our armoured column was just a small part of the overall push up to Khe Sanh, which was to be the primary forward US operating base.

We rumbled over the Quang Tri river up Route 1, then pushed west along Route 9 when we hit Dong Ha. Our initial excitement was wearing off by now, as it always does when nothing happens. We chomped on cold C-rations, smoked cigarettes and waved at little Vietnamese kids standing by the road, shouting out for candy and 'numba one smoke-smoke, GI?'

For the life of me I don't remember now where we were when the first incoming mortar rounds hit. It was in a stark, tropical green valley, probably somewhere between The Rockpile and Khe

EYE-WITNESS

The author, John Morris, served seven years in the US Army and reached the rank of infantry squad leader during the Vietnam war. He was awarded the Bronze Star, Purple Heart and the Vietnamese Cross of Gallantry.

Americans watched as the ARVN rumbled into Laos, kitted out with white scarves and huge grins. The smiles wouldn't last

CHAPTER 89

Operation Lam Son 719

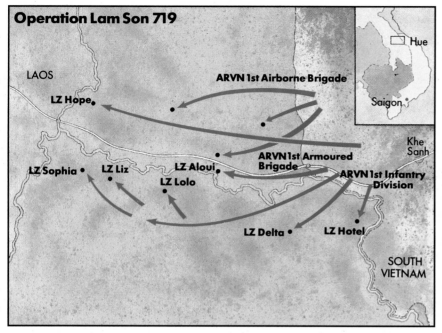

Far left: The long road home. Battered in Laos, the ARVN limp back into Vietnam. Below left: Does a wealth of weaponry supply confidence? Maybe not. Below: Firepower from above. A Sky Crane lifts a 105mm piece into Laos. Right: Colonel Ho Trang Hau, deputy commander of the ARVN Airborne, scratches his head and ponders the way ahead.

LAM SON 719

Authorized on 18 January 1971, Lam Son 719 took its name from the site of a Vietnamese victory over the Chinese in 1427. Its objective was to drive a 15-mile wide corridor to Tchepone, 22 miles inside Laos along Route 9 and a strategic junction on the Ho Chi Minh Trail.

Phase One (Dewey Canyon II) began on 30 January, securing Route 9 inside South Vietnam and re-establishing Khe Sanh as a logistic base. On 8 February, Phase Two saw 12,000 ARVN troops, commanded by Lieutenant-General Hoang Xuan Lam, strike into Laos. The ARVN 1st Armored Brigade moved along Route 9, while airborne troops and Rangers secured firebases on the hills to the north. The advance went well until heavy NVA counter-attacks developed from the north on 12 February. Ranger firebases became untenable by 22 February and the Airborne Division was also forced out of its positions by PT-76 and T-54 tanks.

Xuan Lam changed his original plans and the 1st Infantry Division was lifted in a series of bounds along the escarpment. Two battalions were flown direct from Khe Sanh to seize Tchepone on 6 March: it was the longest-range heliborne assault of the war.

Phase Three had been intended as a lengthy clearing operation but, suffering heavily, Lam ordered withdrawal (Phase Four) on 10 March. It turned into a rout, with only US airpower saving the ARVN from extinction.

It was all over by 24 March, with ARVN casualties estimated at nearly 10,000 — nearly 50 per cent of the total committed to Laos. The Americans, who had been confined to a supporting role, had lost 107 helicopters and 176 aircrew.

Sanh. Route 9 had been chopped out of the mountains along the northern slopes, with a river running along the valley floor on our left, then more green, foliage-tangled mountains rising up on the south. It was beautiful in the sense that a coiled, rearing and weaving Cobra is beautiful – but still deadly enough if you take your eyes off it.

CRUMP, CRUMP, CRUMP...bright flashes and smoke partially hidden by tightly packed trees, bush and shrub. Charlie's first salvo impacting high on the hills above us. CRUMP, CRUMP, CRUMP...a couple of mortar rounds drop off in the valley, but one smacks close to the road near a tank about 100 metres ahead. Twilight's creeping in and the flashes of high-explosive 82mm rounds take on a firework effect of light and colour; white,

blue, orange and red balls and streaks of gasses and fragments and earth shoot across our little stretch of exposed road, bouncing off armoured skins with hisses, thuds and deadened metallic clangs.

A hail of rounds drop in and around our column, and there's nowhere for us to go. Just straight-up mountain on the right, and straight-down valley on the left. Not ideal armour country, so drivers slam their feet to the floor and rev down the road, hoping no-one up front throws a track, or gets hit and blocks the road.

Counter-battery fire from 105s starts pounding the other side of the valley and the reverse slope, trying to suppress the mortars. We hear rounds flying parallel to us, ripping up the air then

Left: A pallid corpse clashes with sporty neckerchieves as the hammer comes down on the ARVN in Laos. Above: As the NVA bear down on them, aerial fire support is limited and the South Vietnamese try to lever themselves out of trouble with the arty. Above right: US troops supporting the ARVN take a break in Khe Sanh. Far right: Hand ups! The NVA capture a couple of APCs. In fact, the picture looks suspiciously posed – the armour looks as if it has taken root.

dropping down to become bright sparks against a fading green backdrop. WHUMP, WHUMP, WHUMP...'Get some!' 'Fry those fuckers!' I hear those shouts over the roar of engines and incoming 82mm rounds and my own pounding heart. I'm probably shouting too.

Something shatters the air, waves of heat, noise and metal fragments blast against our APC. The driver yanks back on the steering levers and I'm thrown forward against the left-side sixty gunner. The other gunner is spraying 7.62mm rounds in frenzied bursts up the mountainside, red tracers sucked into the bush and vanishing, but some ricocheting off rocks straight up into the darkening sky.

Rocket attack

'RPG!' somebody yells out, and my ear picks it up over the howling, insane drum beat of M60s, M16s, .50 cals, M79s, screaming engines and incoming rounds.

Our track commander, a sergeant I don't know, grabs my shoulder. 'Come on...gotta get those fuckers...let's go!' He jumps out of the hatch and over the side, .45 in his hand. I jump out after him. He waves like mad at the two tracks behind us, the only ones who could direct fire at our part of the mountain. They wave back, and lift their fire higher up.

It seems like an alcoholic's dream now, following that guy from tree to rock, stumbling along up that goddamn hill in the near dark. Rounds crack

WHY WAS THE WAR EXTENDED?

The expansion of the Vietnam war into both Cambodia and Laos contradicted the 'Nixon Doctrine' of 1969 that was designed to prevent US troops from fighting on foreign soil. But were there valid causes for widening the conflict?

From the beginning of the US involvement in Vietnam, there had been military pressure to extend operations into Cambodia and, especially, into Laos. Since the earliest days there had been limited incursions, of dubious legality, into Cambodia by covert teams of US volunteers and local mercenaries. In March 1969, airstrikes by B-52s were extended into Cambodia. Large-scale incursions by land forces began in March 1970.

The primary reason that the Nixon administration gave for escalating the war into Cambodia had always been the need to disrupt the communist logistic and support systems in that country. However, while Hanoi had 40,000 troops in Cambodian bases, largely supplied through the port of Sihanoukville, State Department and CIA analysts doubted the logistical significance of Cambodia itself, and saw the Ho Chi Minh Trail as the more potent supply route.

Another stated objective was that, with the start of the process of Vietnamization, the ARVN needed time in order to survive, and that could only be won by disrupting the communists across the frontier. Nixon's military advisers had warned him that further large withdrawals of US troops from Vietnam could only be achieved if enemy bases in Cambodia were destroyed.

The incursion into Cambodia, from April to June 1970, had offered the further possibility of setting back NVA offensive preparations until at least the following dry season as well as easing pressure on Prime Minister Lon Nol, who had seized power from Prince Sihanouk in March 1970. The Laotian incursion, from February to March 1971, was also timed to effect maximum disruption of the communist build-up and delay any major offensive until the following year. Therefore, it can be seen that Lon Nol's public appeal for assistance on 14 April 1970 had only legitimized a decision already taken. Lon Nol himself was not told of the scale of the operation that had been planned.

Nixon was concerned to safeguard US withdrawal, but he also intended to exert pressure on Hanoi in the peace negotiations. To facilitate this, Nixon put great trust in his 'madman' ploy, the hope that a heavy blow against Cambodia would help to convince Hanoi that the US president was capable of anything, even perhaps adopting a nuclear option.

But in reality, a major factor in escalating the war did reside in Nixon's contradictory and unstable psyche in 1970. He was enraged by Congress thwarting him on domestic policies, and furious about press revelations of US bombing raids on Laos. He was contemptuous of the US peace movement, and indeed often displayed this in callous public statements.

In the event, the Cambodian incursion aroused considerable domestic opposition, Congress repealing the Gulf of Tonkin Resolution on 24 June 1970 and prohibiting employment of US troops inside Cambodia beyond 30 June. The Cooper-Church Amendment in December 1970 imposed a further prohibition on using US troops outside South Vietnam, hence the need to use the ARVN alone in Laos in 1971. That second incursion persuaded Daniel Ellsberg to go to the *New York Times*, which began serializing 'The Pentagon Papers' on 13 June 1971.

over our heads and splatter around us on the ground, ours or Charlie's or both. Then we both hear the WHOOSH and see the flash of an RPG firing just off to our left and below.

·45 rounds per menace

Someone down on the road sees it too and starts spraying the area with machine-gun fire. We drop down, but not quick enough. I take a round in my M16; I think I do anyway, because it's yanked out of my hands and propelled into the bush. The sergeant is hit and I can see blood on his leg and back. Then there's movement in front of me. Shadows moving fast, not running, but ducked low and skimming over the ground, coming right toward us. I pick up the .45, point it and start firing. I even count the rounds. I stop at seven, fumble another magazine out of the sergeant's webbing, fire again, release the empty magazine, slam another in, release the slide and fire again. A Vietnamese with the RPG launcher pops up in front of me, out of nowhere. I don't even think, but nail him in the head with the barrel of the .45. Then I hit him again, and again, until he goes down.

No more moving shadows. My ears are still ringing, but it's now pretty quiet. Only an occasional burst of machine-gun and M16 fire. 'Hey!' I yell towards the road. 'I need some help up here.'

Days spent at Khe Sanh, where the only organized activity seems to be the monotonous, late afternoon incoming rocket barrage. Choppers

them, and they finally grin back. 'This shit sucks,' one of them says. We share cigarettes and agree with that.

I'm at the end of Khe Sanh's airstrip, helping unload supplies flown in by the big, twin-rotor Chinooks. I'm standing on the edge of the chopper pad when one flies in, and its prop wash literally blows me off the pad. I tumble down the side, and I can see the flight engineer hanging out of the bird, laughing from under his flight helmet. Yeah, very fucking funny.

Big grins and berets

We're moved to the old Special Forces camp at Lang Vei, up along the Laotian border, to run local security patrols. Route 9 runs right by the camp, and we watch scores of ARVN tankers ride by into Laos, red berets, white scarves and big grins, rumbling off to war. Up above, swarms of American choppers and jets cloud the sky from first light to last. We patrol and patrol, listen to arty fire and watch aircraft swoop into attack runs as they drop behind distant mountains. Once in a while we spot a bird trailing smoke limp back into Vietnamese airspace. One of our jobs is to secure downed aircraft if they crash in our AO, but none come our way. We hear things aren't going well across the border, and then we see it. ARVN tankers stumble into Lang Vei, no pretty berets or clean, white scarves this time around – and no tanks either. A chaplain gives them food and water. Air Cav and 101st Airborne slicks, nearly bursting with ARVN troops, bounce into Lang Vei, disgorge their shit-scared cargo, then lift off to go back for more. Bullet holes and jagged rips in the Hueys' thin skins, and blood splattered everywhere, tell us about conditions in Laos.

Shoot for a Star

Our brigade commander flies in, white-handled pistols on his hips. He says there's an enemy armour threat, and he'll award a Silver Star to the first tank crew at Lang Vei that knocks out an NVA PT-76. Muffled and uneasy conversation among our tankers. Most of the main guns haven't been bore-sighted. The brigade CO flies out again, and there's some talk about bailing out if NVA tanks are sighted. No-one knows what's going on.

We're among some of the last troops to fly back to Khe Sanh. Someone's scratched out a sign that reads: 'Will the last GI leaving Lang Vei please turn out the lights.' I'd see similar signs in Quang Tri and Cam Ranh Bay before my tour was over.

I'm at Fort Ord, California. I'm called into the adjutant's office. 'You're going to receive the Bronze Star for Valor' he says. 'Why?'

He reads the citation. Credited with killing that RPG team back in the valley, thus saving countless American lives, etcetera, etcetera.

It comes back to me in a rush, but only in fragmented and disjointed pieces, just like the rest of those miserable months of Lam Son 719. A scrapbook of black and white memories, frayed at the edges, and probably best forgotten.

– hundreds of them – coming in and taking off. We're sitting in a bunker, listening to the screech of Charlie's welcome wagon fly overhead and impact around the airstrip. Three young warrant-officer helicopter pilots tumble into our bunker in a tangle of arms and legs. They stare at us, wide-eyed and panting from fright and the run from their birds to the nearest safe hole. We grin at

Above: The scramble to get out. ARVN troops hurry for one of the limited-edition trips home.

DID THE ARVN CRACK?

There is no doubt that the attempt to raid the Laotian panhandle was a disaster. But does the blame for this rest with the South Vietnamese alone?

The last 12 days of Lam Son 719 saw the unedifying spectacle of American helicopters coming out of Laos with panic-stricken ARVN troops clinging to the skids. Undoubtedly, the operation was a major disaster that offset the relative success of the ARVN during the Cambodian incursions a year earlier. But, in many respects, the failure was not surprising.

US troops and, crucially, US advisors were not able to accompany the ARVN into Laos due to the political restrictions imposed by Congress. Although the Americans were able to provide logistic and tactical air support, with over 2000 aircraft and 600 helicopters made available, the ARVN was accustomed to having American advisors co-ordinate fire support – few of its Forward Air Controllers could speak English well enough to do so. The persistent low cloud and mist, the heavy anti-aircraft fire, and the NVA tactics of 'hugging' ARVN positions also contributed to the difficulties in providing the South Vietnamese with adequate fire support. Indeed, President Thieu claimed the Americans reduced flights when they began to take heavy aircrew losses.

Another factor was that ARVN operational strength was hopelessly inadequate for a task the Americans had once calculated would require 60,000 men. As it was, the NVA hurled at least 36,000 men at the ARVN's narrow corridor. Neither ARVN Rangers nor the Airborne Division were equipped to deal with armoured assault, and the deployment of the 1st Infantry Division to the southern escarpment was a major miscalculation. Supposedly elite troops performed dismally, but it should not be forgotten that retirement under sustained pressure is one of the most difficult of all military operations. Abrams felt Thieu lost his nerve in authorizing retreat, but the decision was understandable given the losses incurred among the ARVN's best formations and the knowledge that major NVA offensives were yet to come. While the failure of Lam Son 719 had a telling effect on South Vietnamese morale, one year later these same units would stem the tide of the NVA's Easter invasion.

DRUGS

In the Nam, drugs were both illegal and dangerous. But that didn't stop grass and opium from flourishing in the boonies and back at base. But heroin was the final nail in the coffin for most addicts

1971

I had never even seen a joint during the early and mid 1960s when I was a student at a large East-coast university. Our campus had only a handful of hippies and they tended to keep to themselves. Like the overwhelming majority of students, my choice of consciousness-altering refreshment was beer.

I'd read about GI drug use in Vietnam and was curious about it. During my first month or so in-country, however, I was afraid to bring up the subject. After all, drug use was highly illegal. If you got caught possessing marijuana or opium or any other illegal drug, you could expect a court martial. This typically resulted in a big fine, a reduction in rank and time in Long Binh Jail. Then, after you got out of LBJ, you still had to serve your remaining time in Vietnam.

Dishonourable discharge

Even worse, a drug-possession conviction could mean getting booted out of the service with a dishonourable discharge. A dishonourable discharge meant you were ineligible for any GI Bill or Veterans' Administration benefits. In addition, most prospective employers shy away from hiring people with 'bad paper' discharges. In 1969 and 1970 alone, some 16,000 GIs were dishonourably discharged for drug possession.

In the early years of the war, from 1965 to 1967, drug use among GI's was not widespread, and it certainly was not a big problem. For those who did

Above and left: The lonely hell of drug addiction. For these GIs, on an Army drugs rehabilitation course, the posters' warnings came too late.

use drugs while they were in Vietnam, the overwhelming favourite was marijuana, although opium, barbiturates and amphetamines were all widely available.

Government officials were involved

During the late 1960s and early 1970s, however, drug use in some units in Vietnam reached near epidemic proportions. And the choice was not the soft drug marijuana, but the powerfully addictive heroin. A report issued by the Pentagon in 1973 estimated that 35 per cent of all Army enlisted men who'd served in Vietnam had tried heroin and that 20 per cent were addicted to it at one point during their tour.

Why was drug use so extensive in some units in Vietnam? For one thing, the young soldiers were no different to their civilian counterparts back home – in the late 1960s and early 1970s, marijuana use especially was widespread among high-school and college-age Americans. Second, Southeast Asia was (and remains) one of the world's biggest illegal drug centres. Locally-grown marijuana and opium cultivated in the Golden Triangle (where Laos, Thailand and Burma meet) was easily obtainable throughout Vietnam and at very low prices. There were even rumours that the South Vietnamese Air Force and Navy, working with high ranking officials in the governments of Ky and Thieu, ran the opium-smuggling operations. Finally, the frustration of fighting a protracted, dirty little war, while life at home went on seemingly unaffected, raised in many American troops a desire to escape the reality of Vietnam with drugs.

Fear of undercover agents

In my case, I was simply curious about the stuff. About a month after I arrived at my rear-echelon unit in II Corps, early in 1968, I smoked dope for the first time. It turned out that the guys I worked with were all nightly dope smokers. But they had kept the news from me because new guys were universally distrusted. The military was famous

Below: The trappings of the alternative lifestyle. In Vietnam, as in San Francisco, New York and London, the explosion in drugs use gave rise to a wide range of related paraphenalia, such as growers' guides. But, as in the West, dabbling in soft drugs soon gave way to a more deadly fixation – the steady increase in the use of heroin.

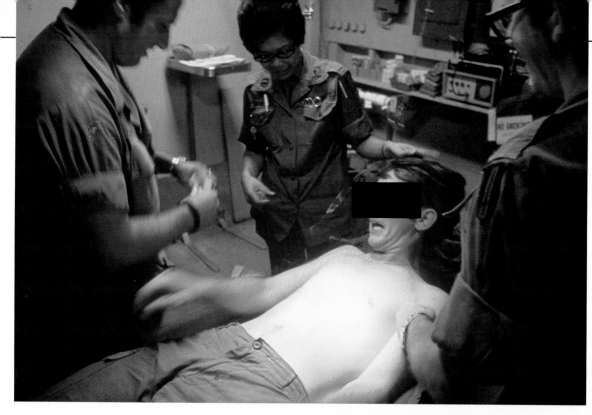

Left: Undergoing a methadone cure for heroin addiction. The patient and the Army medical staff may be having a laugh, but drug addiction in the US armed forces in Vietnam was no joke. Apart from the obvious dangers, a grunt who was stoned out of his head in a combat situation was a threat, not only to himself, but also to his buddies.

for planting undercover agents in units like mine, to spy on drug users. My buddies waited a month before they invited me to go into the neighbouring town and buy some dope.

That night I joined them and tasted the sweet-smelling marijuana for the first time. Wanting to fit in, I pretended that I'd smoked regularly back home. The truth was, I'd never even smoked tobacco cigarettes and hadn't the slightest idea how to inhale. I wound up smoking an entire joint of the immensely powerful Vietnamese marijuana that night. But I just sort of swirled it around in my throat, and never inhaled it into my lungs. I didn't get high.

I became a regular pot smoker

But that didn't stop me from coming back the next night to try again. This time I managed to swallow the fragrant smoke and hold it in my lungs for a while before exhaling. I got stoned, very stoned. It was a delicious feeling – all my senses were heightened. The night colours seemed especially sharply focused. Jokes seemed hysterically funny. The music someone was playing on a guitar sounded sharper and more rhythmic than anything I'd ever heard. I got enormously thirsty and someone handed me a cold can of soda. I felt as if I was being tickled by an icy sweet waterfall as I let the soda trickle down my throat.

For the rest of my tour I was a regular among the nightly pot smokers. We changed our meeting places from time to time. Eventually, we wound up in bamboo-curtained sections of the barracks, where we smoked, relaxed, joked around, listened to rock music on our PX-bought Japanese stereos and munched candy and other snack foods sent from home. Sometimes we'd amble over to the Enlisted Men's club and have a cold beer and listen to music on the juke box or from a live Filipino band. Sometimes we'd sit under the stars and ponder the Vietnamese night. Once in a while

we'd stare in awe as a Puff the Magic Dragon gunship spewed a steady stream of red tracers onto distant hilltops.

They looked like real cigarettes

We bought our dope in the town or from young Vietnamese boys who worked on our compound. The going price was about a dollar for 10 thick, hand-rolled cigarettes. For 10 dollars you could get a coffee can full of loose marijuana, enough to last our crowd for weeks. Marijuana was also sold packaged in what looked like real tobacco cigarettes, inside packs and cartons of authentic-looking American brands such as Winston. But the price of the phony cigarettes was too expensive (I don't remember what they went for, but it was at least 10 or 15 dollars a carton). So we stuck with the loose stuff, which we smoked in corncob pipes or as pre-rolled joints. Sometimes, when we went

Above: Instant oblivion, under the ministrations of a mama san. But opium could only make you forget for a brief period, it did not make the war go away. As the war became increasingly senseless, more and more US servicemen turned to drugs, making a small problem into a major one.

465

into town, we'd pay a few bucks extra and have mama-san at the dope-seller's house paint some opium on the joints.

At first, I made a point of never getting high during work hours or when I had guard duty. But some of my buddies seemed to smoke all day and night. I remember walking to the mess hall before sunrise and in the pre-dawn darkness seeing orange glows bobbing down the hill. Some of the hard-core smokers were having their first joints of the day, on the way to breakfast.

Eventually my pattern was: finish my paper-work job at seven, take a shower, eat chow, get high. Later on in my tour, as I was getting shorter and shorter, I started smoking earlier and earlier in the day. And I even smoked some nights on guard duty. But I quit that. It was too scary sitting out there on the perimeter all by yourself, stoned. I'd start hearing things, seeing things. One night I remember seeing what I absolutely knew was a VC sapper about 50 metres straight in front of me. I stared and stared at him as I locked and loaded my M14. After a minute, I saw that the VC sapper was actually a tree, swaying in the wind.

He took LSD before shipping out

Our group of dope smokers, probably about 20-25 guys out of our 200-man company, was a close-knit lot. We distrusted strangers, especially new guys who wanted to join the group. One time a new guy, with the longest hair any of us had ever seen in the Army, was assigned to our company. He soon figured out who the smokers were and asked to join the group. We treated him as though he had the plague. We figured anyone with hair hanging over his ears had to be an undercover cop trying to look like a hippie GI. It turned out the guy actually was a hippie GI. He told us later, after we'd accepted him into the group, that he'd decided to take LSD the night before he was due to ship out for Vietnam, and didn't come down from the drug until he was in the airplane, winging over the Pacific.

In our unit, drugs turned out to be a unifying force between blacks and whites. The races tended not to mingle. The black guys had their own tables in the mess hall and the EM club, and their own bars and whorehouses downtown. But when it came to smoking, the racial barriers seemed to lift. Nearly every night there'd be groups of blacks and whites getting together to get high. Somehow, doing this illegal act bound us together.

The Lieutenant wanted to join in

Only one career sergeant and only one officer smoked with us. Sergeant M, who'd been in for a decade, made a regular habit of visiting our nightly pot and music parties. We felt no fear smoking with him. He even tipped us off in advance of the occasional shakedown – the un-announced, middle-of-the-night searches for dope and other illegal items – conducted by his sergeant cronies. Of course, we rarely hid our dope in our lockers; we usually had it in special hiding places

Above: A warning before returning to The World. The problem of drugs in Vietnam was not confined to Southeast Asia. There was also the added fear that GIs returning Stateside would import drugs into the US. Left: A typical haul from a drugs raid.

outside the barracks. But occasionally someone kept a small supply by his bunk and we appreciated Sergeant M's tip offs.

The officer, Second-Lieutenant B, came up to us one night and asked if he could join the party. We were stunned at first, thinking the worst: that he was going to bust us. But this young rookie lieutenant just wanted to blend in with the guys. I guess the non-fraternization-with-enlisted-men lesson of officer training school never took with him. But he quickly learned it from us. We were more than a little uneasy smoking with him and let him know it. The green LT never came back.

I left Vietnam before heroin became a big problem in some units. During my time there I knew of no one who used the stuff. My group

smoked marijuana. One or two guys would sometimes go into a dope den in town and smoke opium. A few bought barbiturates over the counter at a Vietnamese pharmacy. I tried those downers once and all I did was promptly fall asleep.

So my experiences with drugs in Vietnam were basically positive. When I returned to the States early in 1969, I became a regular user of marijuana. As did virtually all of my friends. I smoked almost daily for the next six years.

But I quit smoking in the mid 1970s and nearly all of my friends stopped using drugs, as well. These days drugs are a memory. But, looking back, I have to say that drugs helped me through the rough spots. Drugs weren't the reason I survived a year in Nam. But they helped.

Below: The wounds of a secret war. A ravaged GI displays the scars of his heroin addiction. For him there is the prospect not of a Purple Heart, but of a long, hard road back to health after succumbing to the temptations of hard drugs.

Above: An Army medic hands out pills to GIs kicking their drug habits.

Above: Re-educating ex-drug users into a healthier life-style.

Above: Ex-addicts recovering at a US Army drugs re-habilitation camp.

One of the greatest ironies of the Vietnam war took place at the conference tables of the peace talks. Nixon's envoy, Henry Kissinger, a man who had once supported the widening of the war, would later be awarded the Nobel peace prize for his part in the Paris Accords, signed by himself and his North Vietnamese counterpart, Le Duc Tho, on 24 January 1973. The peace process required both formal and informal discussions...

THE PARIS

PEACE TALKS

Above, far left: Away from the conference table, National Security Adviser Henry Kissinger (right) and North Vietnam's principal negotiator, Le Duc Tho, reach some sort of private accord. Above: The Americans wanted an oblong table, the North Vietnamese a square. The compromise was round. Above, far right: Kissinger and Le Duc Tho in graver mood with Le Minh. Right: Away from the conference table, delegates would meet informally at Kissinger's rented villa at Saint-Nom la Bretêche. Left: Le Duc Tho and his deputy, Xuan Thuy, arrive at Le Bourget after a trip back to Hanoi. Far left: Kissinger, his deputy Alexander Haig, and the US delegation share a joke with the North Vietnamese negotiators. But it was no joke for South Vietnam.

Operations Menu and Freedom Deal took US firepower into Laos and Cambodia. The bombings were secret, illegal and pretty hairy

1971

THE SECRET BOMBINGS

Left: An A-1 Skyraider – affectionately known as the 'Spad' – is loaded up with napalm bombs, before flying out on a secret bombing mission over Cambodia. Above: The night sky lights up with an eerie glow as napalm bombs explode over the target.

EYE-WITNESS

Richard S. Drury, awarded the Silver Star, flew missions over the Ho Chi Minh Trail in Laos.

Flying the 'Spad' – Douglas A-1 Skyraider – over Laos was a hairy job at the best of times. The communist anti-aircraft gunners were not short of practice, and a pilot shot down over the jungle could be lost forever. Many were. Meanwhile, the US government denied they even existed.

One of the pilots flying the A-1 with the 1st Special Operations Squadron was Richard S. Drury. He describes one night mission that he flew three days before Christmas:

'We launched into the night on our expedition to northern Laos. My wingman pushed in his power seconds after I started rolling and was off somewhere around the 4000ft mark, utilizing the A-1 pilot's usual fancy footwork and ability. It was as black as dreamless sleep. Once away from the base we were over jungle, and either we made the transition to instruments or hoped that the powers that be lifted us to cruising altitude. Sometimes they didn't.

We could see the muzzle flashes

'"Climb check," I muttered into my mask. The A-1s had been running terribly, their engines being a conglomeration of re-manufactured parts, and night flying was a true test of one's fortitude. That which was ordinarily an almost imperceptible vibration during day flights was easily construed to be a major structural crisis at night. The air was dingy with the smoke of burning rice crops, a little oriental trick to make the flyer's world a little less than magnificent below eight or nine thousand feet. Los Angeles smog was about half as bad. Actually, the legitimate farmers were just doing

Above: A USAF bombardier prepares some CS gas canisters, destined for targets in Laos or Cambodia during America's highly controversial 'secret war' in Southeast Asia.

471

their antique jobs and old Charlie was picking up the idea just to make the visibility worse. In the rice-burning season, Laos itself is almost invisible. Unless, that is, a pilot decides to run into it in a dive or something like that. And at night we could see the muzzle flashes of the bigger guns. One could tell there was ground down there somewhere. Other than that, we were on instruments, sometimes even during the day. The smoky film did make for some extravagantly red, burning sunsets, also like Los Angeles in the late afternoon of a smog alert. Our night wasn't in the middle of the season though; it was the beginning really, and we were quickly on top and in the moonlight. "I'm level. Back to cruise power," I said to my wingman, now just a voice on the radio and lost to sight.

Radio contact is made

'We had been assigned to work with an FAG (Forward Air Guide) known as "Kingpin". He was situated in some lofty mountains nearly two hours away. At least that was where he was reported to be. We had a set of co-ordinates and were out doing our night time-and-distance flying once again.

Right: The view from the cockpit of an A-1 Skyraider as a flight of 'Spads' sets off on another mission over Cambodia. Below: A USAF bombardier checks the fuze settings on a load of napalm bombs before yet another secret bombing raid. The disclosure of the raids resulted in violent demonstrations, both in the US and around the world.

Top: A Forward Air Controller (FAC) checks on the damage after a US bombing raid. Above: B-52s rain death and destruction on Vietnam's neighbours. Below: KC-135 tankers refuelling F-4 Phantoms in mid-air.

SECRET BOMBINGS

The US had been bombing Cambodia for four years before President Nixon admitted it publicly. But what considerations prompted this drastic escalation of the conflict in Southeast Asia?

On 9 February 1969, General Abrams formally requested B-52 strikes against communist 'Base Area 353' in the Fish Hook region of Cambodia, close to the border with South Vietnam, northwest of Saigon. Convinced that this was the site of COSVN HQ (the communists' elusive Central Office for South Vietnam), he advocated a single, concentrated blow to disrupt NVA bases in the border area. Renewed NVA/VC attacks on Saigon on 23 February seemed to confirm Abrams's suspicions and to justify his suggested course of action.

Abrams's request was granted by President Nixon on 17 March. Early the following morning, 48 B-52s carried out the first in a series of strikes, codenamed Operation Menu, which was to continue, in conditions of utmost secrecy, until 26 May 1970. They were then widened out to cover vast tracts of Cambodian territory in Operation Freedom Deal. The bombing did not cease until August 1973.

Nixon was aware that these airstrikes constituted a direct violation of Cambodian neutrality, but felt that they were justified for a number of reasons. The purely military considerations were obvious: not only would a perceived NVA build-up in the border regions be disrupted, 'buying time' for Vietnamization and US troop withdrawals, but the communist supply route through the port of Sihanoukville (Konpong Som) would, for the first time, be interdicted. At the same time, the attacks would offer support to the rulers of Cambodia in their efforts to rid their country of growing communist influence, while indicating to Hanoi that the Nixon Administration was, despite its policy of troop withdrawals, both willing and able to use force in Southeast Asia. Finally, as The *New York Times* put it in 1973, after the existence of the raids had been 'leaked', the airstrikes were also a way of testing 'the general process of gradually substituting helicopters and attack planes for foot soldiers' in the Administration's efforts to maintain the security of Vietnam. To Nixon, these were tempting arguments.

HOW THE NEWS LEAKED OUT

The bombing of Cambodia, initiated on 18 March 1969, was meant to be strictly secret. Each B-52 strike under the Menu/Freedom Deal codenames was briefed for targets on the South Vietnamese side of the border, with only the pilots and navigators being told that, once over the target area, their Combat Skyspot radar controller would give new co-ordinates which would take the bombers into Cambodia. Once the raid was over, ground controllers were to destroy all evidence of the diversion, shredding documents and reporting that the attacks had taken place, as planned, inside South Vietnam.

But secrecy was difficult to maintain. As early as 26 March 1969, The New York Times carried a report, written by its Pentagon correspondent William Beecher, which stated that 'B-52 bombers have raided several Viet Cong and North Vietnamese supply dumps and base camps in Cambodia'. The public did not react, although President Nixon, angry at the leak, authorised the FBI to investigate Beecher, tapping his phone and monitoring his movements in the first of a series of illegal acts which were to culminate in the Watergate scandal of 1973-74.

By then, further evidence had emerged about the bombing, chiefly from officers deeply concerned about their role in the deceit. Major Hal Knight, a radar supervisor for the area between Saigon and the Cambodian border in 1969, wrote to his Congressman in December 1972. At much the same time, Captain Gerald Green, an FAC pilot at An Loc in 1969, reported that he had flown over devastated areas of Cambodia in the aftermath of B-52 strikes. The Senate Armed Forces Committee responded by calling for USAF records of bombing at that time and, when these failed to detail the Cambodian attacks, an investigation began. In mid-1973, it was obvious that responsibility for the cover-up lay in the White House itself.

Time about up, I attempted radio contact in the idiot English we had developed. I twirled the knobs of the VHF radio and gave it a go. "Hello Kingpin. This is Hobo. You hear me?" Silence. A 37mm airburst miles away. The sound of my engine. "Kingpin. Hobo. How you hear?" Checking the map with my flashlight, I decided that we were somewhere over where he ought to be. Heading and time was all we had. "Kingpin, damn it. You hear Hobo?"

There was a crackling of the radio static. Then a very distant voice. "Hobo. Kingpin. You come help Kingpin?" That, I thought, was brilliant and intelligent. No Kingpin, we just happen to be about 400 miles from home and were wondering what you were doing tonight! But we had to be nice. After all, the poor fellow was down there in the night and someone was trying to kill him with a mortar, or something. "Yes Kingpin, Hobo come help you. You have bad guys?"

Misled by the enemy

"Rager, rager, Hobo. Have many, many bad guys. They all around. They shoot big gun at me." Maybe it was so. No muzzle flashes could be seen though and perhaps the fight in question was strictly a smallarms affair. But the "big gun" wording made me think it might be a mortar. If there was smallarms return fire then it made things easier. It could even be interesting. It sounded like rain on tin and put those little holes in the airplane. Usually, that was about all it did. The big guns were different. "OK, Kingpin. You give us co-ordinates where you are. We come help you." I flipped the flashlight on and got ready to copy his numbers. "Hobo, Kingpin. I have co-ordinates..." I copied them and checked the map. Then I called my wingman. "Hey. You copy that? Either the guy

doesn't know where he is or he's a hundred miles from here." Sometimes the "find me puzzle in the sky" was normal with an FAG, like hide-and-seek. Then again, we sometimes got voices that gave a position to hit and, on checking, found the location to be on designated areas of friendly troops. One of the enemy had a radio and was trying to get us to bomb the friendlies. Then we would hurl obscenities at each other.

'Bad guy in valley'

'We went back to basics. "Kingpin, this is Hobo. You hear my airplane?" It usually worked. "You standby, Hobo. I go listen."

'Silence. The little man was climbing out of his hole and peering into the night sky. He was soon back. I was still in a left-hand orbit. "Hobo, Kingpin. I hear your airplane. You come nort maybe two mile." Swell. I drove on 'nort' for a minute or so. Nort was Laotian for north and rager was Roger. "Hey Kingpin. You hear my airplane now?" By that time I was looking over the fuel supply. With some unusual forethought, someone had ordered a full centreline tank, so we still had enough 115/145 grade fuel for another hour of playtime, as it was called. "Rager, rager, Hobo. You over my position now."

'We had finally narrowed our position down to within a few miles of dark surround. The mountains were high and a cruising altitude of 10,500ft didn't put us all that far over them. There was an immensely deep valley below. "Kingpin. Hobo see big valley. Where are you?" "Rager, Hobo. Bad guy in valley. You put bomb in middle of valley." With such a pin-point target there was obviously no hesitation. A few 500lb bombs spread around in the night would be harmless. "Look here, Kingpin, I want to know where YOU are." It wasn't in the rules to bomb Kingpin himself. "Hobo, Kingpin on top of mountain. You bomb bad guy." That was better. "OK, Hobo drop bomb in valley."

'The depths of that valley were as black as could

be. The moon lit the tops and spread dim light a ways down into the valley, but that was about all. Setting the wing station selector to the left stub which held a 500lb napalm, I peered into the murk and hit the mike button. "I'm in hot from the west." I left a single fuselage light on so that my wingman would be able to see where I was going. If I was lucky, I might even be in the right valley. I wasn't too worried about anti-aircraft fire from that location – not hitting the ground was foremost on my mind.

The sky was like a bowl of milk

'Rolling over partly on instruments, partly in the moonlight, I stabilized near a 40-degree dive and looked through the gunsight to the valley below. I was closing rapidly as I descended below the tops of the mountains. My "unhesitating bravery" was running thinner as the altimeter unwound and I immediately thought, now, look here old boy, if he's up there and I'm down here, then what the heck? I won't be dropping anything on him so why press this attack? I hit the release button, felt the loss of five-hundred pounds, and grunted under a three-G pull-up. The nape splashed like one giant flash bulb in my rearview mirrors and made the sky look like a bowl of milk. Back to instruments. Kingpin let us know that he was enjoying the show from his position above.

"'HOBO! You have number one bomb! *Ver-ry* good. You do same again.""OK, Kingpin, we'll put it right there." I did, and after swapping altitudes, my wingman did too. The valley wasn't dark any longer. It was a mass of little fires and splotches of sparkling 20mm hits. Kingpin thought the whole thing was delightful and, if nothing else, we kept him company for a while on an otherwise lonely night. As we climbed back to altitude I think it was entirely without precedence that Kingpin said: "And to you, Hobo, a good night." Ah, the Christmas spirit.'

Far left: A grinning US serviceman manhandles a huge drum of the highly controversial napalm. Left: A suspected Viet Cong base in Laos is hit by one of the secret US raids, this time using conventional high-explosive bombs.

THE A-1 SKYRAIDER

The peculiar circumstances of the war in Southeast Asia required more than just fast-jets. Indeed, in certain situations, where the target took time to locate or the support had to be delivered close-in, the jet could be a positive liability. What was needed was a slower, piston-engined aircraft, capable of carrying a hefty weapons load. The Douglas A-1 Skyraider fitted the bill exactly.

First sketched out in 1944 in answer to a US Navy demand for a new carrier-borne torpedo/dive-bomber, the prototype XBT2D-1 did not fly until March 1945 and therefore entered service too late to see any action in World War II. With its powerful Wright R-3350 radial engine, the production AD-1 (the designation was altered to A-1 in September 1961) could carry 3630kg of munitions on 15 strongpoints beneath the fuselage and wings. But, with the introduction of jet-engined aircraft, the Skyraider's value as a military aircraft seemed to be severely limited.

This could not have been further from the truth. During the Korean War (1950-53), Navy and Marine Corps Skyraiders performed so well that the design was described as 'the best and most effective close support airplane in the world'. Although production ceased in 1957, enough A-1s still existed to ensure them a place in the Vietnam conflict. Loaded with bombs, rockets, napalm, mines, torpedoes or depth-charges and armed with 20mm cannon, the aircraft played a crucial role in close ground (and naval) support.

Most A-1s served with the Navy, Marines or South Vietnamese Air Force, but a number were also employed by the USAF for special operations. These included sowing sensors along the Ho Chi Minh Trail, escorting HH-3 'Jolly Green Giant' helicopters on rescue missions and supporting covert forces in Laos. Altogether, about 1000 Skyraiders saw service in Southeast Asia.

Above: An A-1H Skyraider on a mission over Northern Laos. It is armed with rockets and Cluster Bomb Units (CBUs). Top: Skyraiders delivering napalm on a target in Cambodia. One of the work-horses of the US air effort, the Spad fulfilled a number of roles in the Vietnam war.

MERCENARIES ON THE TRAIL

The CIA case officers who organized the elite of the Royal Lao Army into hard-hitting guerrilla units were a far cry from the James Bond-type spies usually associated with 'Spook' intelligence gathering and interdiction

It's damp and cold under the low canopy of untended coffee bushes, interlaced with jungle vines and forest foliage. Suddenly, the silence is shattered by the tearing sound of an M16. Another burst of fire and then silence again. There's no return fire since everyone is hugging the earth. After a muttered conversation in Lao, Captain Boon-su waves his men forward. An NVA knapsack, complete with three B40 rocket rounds, is lying at the entrance to an earthen bunker. The two Laotian troops on point had surprised an NVA soldier, fired, but missed as he disappeared with his B40 launcher, leaving his pack behind.

The troops soon find a dozen more bunkers. They are over one metre deep and well camouflaged by jungle shoots and flowers planted in a shallow layer of earth on top of log roofs. As bunkers go they are airy, with two or three entrances each. Some even have duckboard walk-

Left: Blacked up and anything but green, this trooper heads up river.

ways. The bunker complex extends about 100m from the dirt track on which the patrol has been advancing.

The track the team are working is Route 16, part of Hanoi's Ho Chi Minh Trail network in southern Laos. The 30-man patrol is part of a CIA Special Guerrilla Unit (SGU), Group Mobile (GM) 33, commanded by Lieutenant-Colonel 'Black Bear' Bounthavi and directed by a CIA case officer, call-sign 'Leon'.

On the case

'Leon' is one of a handful of Americans in Laos. They are called 'case officers' and are known by their radio call-signs: 'Kayak', 'Bamboo', 'Hog', 'Greek', 'Mule', 'Montana' etc. They aren't James Bond-type spies but highly professional soldiers who have already completed tours of duty in South Vietnam with elite outfits, such as SOG and SEALs. They are based at three main locations: Nam Yu, in northern Laos, Long Chen near the southern edge of the Plain of Jars, and Pakse, a town on the Mekong river. In Laos, these case officers are working under contract to the CIA Plans and Operations Section at Langley, Virginia: the section responsible for world-wide paramilitary operations.

A case officer in Laos has to be a jack of all military trades. He's responsible for combat tactics, directing combat, intelligence gathering, command and control during US Air Force and Navy airstrikes, artillery adjustment, calling in medevac helicopters and co-ordinating food and munitions drops, often under communist shellfire. (A major hazard for supply planes was landing on a strip which had just been overrun by communist troops. In one instance the NVA laid out the call sign 'N-November' to lure an approaching Helio Courier in. But they had laid out the orange marker panels so neatly, in contrast to the irregulars who just tossed the panels down haphazardly, that the US pilot guessed the true situation and opened out his engine again just short of the strip and escaped!) Case officers are responsible for regiment-sized units' logistics and finances, with authority over millions of dollars worth of US government equipment and a cash fund that runs into hundreds of thousands.

Capture Front 'Y' headquarters

The men are tired and tense. The 950 man GM has been here in the Ban Phone valley for almost three weeks now and virtually every day has clashed with enemy troops. Route 16, which runs along the Ban Phone Valley, links Thateng at the western end of the valley with Ban Phone at the eastern end, a distance of about 30 kilometres. It forms an important crosslink between two south-running parallel roads, 23 and 96, down which much of the North Vietnamese traffic travels. It is a kind of switchpoint and tran-shipment centre,

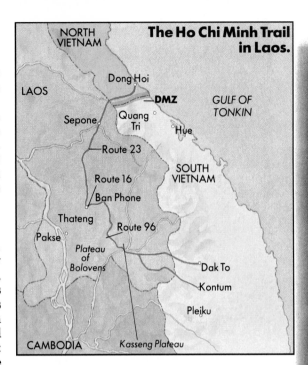

The Ho Chi Minh Trail in Laos.

NORTH VIETNAM
LAOS
Dong Hoi
DMZ
GULF OF TONKIN
Sepone
Quang Tri
Hue
Route 23
SOUTH VIETNAM
Route 16
Ban Phone
Thateng
Route 96
Pakse
Plateau of Bolovens
Dak To
Kontum
Pleiku
CAMBODIA
Kasseng Plateau

with materiel and NVA troops heading east for the fighting in South Vietnam and Cambodia, or west to confront Laotian Army forces on what the NVA call Front 'Y'.

GM 33's mission here has two objectives: capture Front 'Y' headquarters and destroy North Vietnamese trucks, supply caches and logistics personnel in the Ban Phone Valley.

Into the gap

It's been planned as a spoiling operation. The SGUs will concentrate on ambushes, harassment and the destruction of enemy headquarters and communications. Their attacks have been timed so as to take advantage of a gap that the CIA has found in the NVA rear. Hanoi's Front 'Y' force, which is supposed to be responsible for Route 16's defence, is otherwise occupied. It is busy attacking other targets in southern Laos. According to intelligence reports, only two North Vietnamese infantry companies plus logistic personnel are at present on Route 16.

The operations are launched in mid-November 1971 from CIA airstrips on the eastern Bolovens Plateau. One GM makes a fast two day march into Thateng, and GM 33 helicopters into an LZ about five klicks from Ban Phone, achieving complete surprise. Two six-man NVA patrols, unaware of the Laotian's arrival, wander into ambushes and are wiped out. Alarmed by the shooting, some 20 NVA pop out from among the sunflowers on the outskirts of Ban Phone. Seven of them are killed in the brief firefight which develops as the Vietnamese scatter for safety into the undergrowth. Documents found in an underground 'office' reveal that the bunker complex, with US parachute material spread across the ceilings, is the 49th North Vietnamese Army field hospital. It's pretty well equipped. There are medicines, bandages, surgical instruments and even some microscopes

THE PATHET LAO

One of the many confusing aspects of the Laotian conflict was that a government led by one royal half-brother, Prince Souvanna Phouma, was opposed by another royal half-brother, Prince Souvannouvong (above), heading a communist movement.

When the French gave Laos limited autonomy in 1949, Souvanna accepted. Souvannouvong, however, rejected the settlement and helped found the Neo Lao Issara ('Lao Freedom Front') in 1950. At the same time, a Lao People's Liberation Army, which actually predated the Front, became established in the north east.

The Neo Lao Issara – renamed the Neo Lao Hak Sat ('Lao Patriotic Front') in 1956 – was directed by a People's Party of Laos formed in March 1955. This secretive party, which numbered perhaps 14,000 members in 1968, controlled the Front and army through a Central Committee on which Souvannouvong was an influential but not necessarily dominant figure. Souvannouvong participated in coalition governments with Souvanna between 1957 and 1958 and again in July 1962. The communists, who became popularly known as the Pathet Lao ('Land of the Laos'), finally withdrew from the coalition in 1963.

The war took on an almost familiar pattern of the Pathet Lao advancing westwards each dry season (November to April), only to be driven back by the Royal Laotian Army and Vang Pao's army of Meo tribesmen. However, the annual stalemate changed in 1971 when Hanoi's greater commitment enabled the 35,000-strong Pathet Lao to take Long Cheng and all but capture the administrative capital of Vientiane.

CIA UNDERCOVER OPERATIONS IN LAOS

At its height, the CIA operation in Laos tied down the bulk of two NVA divisions, which would otherwise have been available for deployment in South Vietnam. But did such successes justify the nature of the CIA presence in Laos?

The Central Intelligence Agency (CIA) was created in 1947 to gather and assess information on America's 'enemies' world-wide. In the prevailing atmosphere of 'Cold War', these enemies were invariably seen as the forces of communism and, as Southeast Asia was an area susceptible to communist expansion, the CIA soon became deeply involved in Vietnam, Laos and Cambodia.

This involvement took a variety of forms beyond the compilation of routine intelligence assessments. As early as 1954, Colonel Edward G. Lansdale organized 'stay-behind' squads of anti-communists in Hanoi as the French pulled out, and it was one of his groups, led by Major Lucien Conein, that poured acid into the city's petrol supplies in an effort to halt all public transport. At the same time, the CIA's own airline, Air America, began to deliver supplies to the Laotian government to sustain its fight against the Pathet Lao. Indeed, as CIA operations in Laos grew, Air America, along with Continental Airways, came to provide a fleet of about 60 unarmed workhouse aircraft, from single-engined planes to large C-123 transports, and a wide range of helicopters.

Another approach was to ensure the survival of existing non-communist regimes, and here the success was more concrete, although hardly less controversial. In the early 1960s, Lansdale ensured the survival of President Diem in South Vietnam, partly by using CIA funds to bribe his opponents to rally to the government. However, this did not prevent the CIA from giving covert support to the dissident generals who overthrew Diem in 1963. Despite vigorous denials, a similar policy may have helped Lon Nol to seize power from Prince Sihanouk in Cambodia seven years later. It was in Laos, however, that the Agency carried out its most extensive operations in Southeast Asia.

It maintained a network of over 200 grass and dirt airstrips scattered across the Laotian mountains. Some of these strips were of high strategic value, such as the one at Pathi Mountain in northeast Laos, close to the border with North Vietnam. This housed CIA officials, a USAF detachment, a navigation beacon and electronic aids to guide US aircraft based in Thailand onto bombing targets in the North Vietnamese Red River Delta. On 11 October 1968 the garrison at the Pathi Mountain base was wiped out, with just one CIA official surviving. The USAF was blind without Pathi's beacons.

The CIA managed to establish a pattern of activity which was to continue until the US withdrawal in 1973 and the communist victory two years later. The idea of 'stay-behind' squads, for example, was developed into one of infiltration, with CIA-trained South Vietnamese commandos being sent into the North by sampan or by parachute, to gather information and spread unrest. Few of the groups survived, raising serious questions about the effectiveness of CIA policies.

In Laos, a combination of North Vietnamese gains and the ineffectiveness of the Royal Lao Army sparked the CIA's quasi-guerrilla strategy. The CIA recruited the best Royal Lao Army officers and built the South Laos provincial Auxiliary Defense Companies (ADCs), which they had already been using for armed reconnaissance on the Ho Chi Minh Trail's west rim, into Special Guerrilla Units (SGUs), which case officers paid and controlled directly.

The CIA also used its funds and training facilities to establish anti-communist groups among various tribes in Southeast Asia. The process began in Laos, where the Meo people were trained and supported in their fight against the Pathet Lao. By the early 1960s, this process had been extended to the Montagnard people of the Central Highlands of South Vietnam, out of which emerged the effective Civilian Irregular Defense Groups (CIDGs), run by US Special Forces. The CIDGs were used not just to defend tribal areas, but also to mount covert cross-border raids into Laos and Cambodia. Unfortunately, when this was extended elsewhere, under the auspices of the Civil Operations and Revolutionary Development Support (CORDS) Program, it came up against a strong Viet Cong infrastructure. Attempts to eliminate this – the Phoenix Program – brought the Agency into disrepute. And when the US pulled out of the region the various tribes were simply left to their fate. The Meo held out as long as they could in northern Laos but were gradually all but wiped out. Caught between the communist forces and the Thais they were just so much cannon-fodder in another of the CIA's dirty wars.

manufactured in East Germany. But no patients.

At Thateng the Lao commander, Major Van Thong, reports that his men have caught the North Vietnamese loading up before fleeing, and have killed 10 of them. This time the NVA react quickly and pull west, realizing that their first priority is to protect the Front 'Y' command group. The Laotians lose 25 killed and 60 wounded as enemy infantry lay down heavy fire, giving the HQ staff time to slip away.

Deadly games

In the next three weeks a deadly game of hide and seek ensues between the SGUs and the North Vietnamese defenders. The Vietnamese split into small teams. While the surviving North Vietnamese logistics people try to empty as many of their supply caches as they can before the Laotians find them, the Vietnamese infantry, operating in two, three or four-man groups and armed with B40 rocket launchers, try to hold the Laotians back by ambushing them in the maze of small paths twisting through the luxuriant undergrowth.

However, the Laotians are also operating in six-man reconnaissance teams and 30-man combat groups. They aren't defending fixed positions and are stopping to rest only a few hours at a time. They enjoy numerical superiority, and they know the terrain well because many are local men and are getting information from the local Lao valley people. The haul of North Vietnamese material mounts: nine Russian trucks with spares, a gasoline dump, over 40 individual weapons and 41 tons of rice. GM 33's losses so far are five killed and 17 wounded. Captain Boonsu's 30-man patrol is part of a final attempt by GM 33 to add to this haul before terminating the operation.

Truck trashers

The patrol's objective is a Vietnamese truck park, reported by local Lao villagers to be seven klicks further east along Route 16. The patrol has been ordered to look for additional North Vietnamese garage and storage areas en route and to destroy any bunkers, supply caches or trucks it finds.

The patrol has spent a sleepless night. At about 0200 hours a communist team bumps the patrol 'sonnette', a two-man listening post located just outside the patrol's bivouac in a clump of trees. Bursts of AK-47 fire bring twigs down on the men's heads, and they reply with M79 grenade launchers and Claymore mines, firing into the moonlit elephant grass. The shooting lasts only two minutes before the communists break contact. Next morning there's blood on the grass and a gory piece of green shirting. Seems an enemy soldier's day has been spoilt.

The bunker complex is empty and Boonsu wants to find the truck park before the NVA soldier who escaped reports our location. To speed things up, and to swing the odds in the patrol's favour, Boonsu radios for an NVA truck that had been captured earlier in the operation. A 'Raven',

Below left: A chopper lands at a rough strip in Laos and is loaded with supplies flown in by the CIA's Air America. Right: the author and three Nung troops in Laos. Below: Speeding along the Ho Chi Minh Trail, camouflaged trucks transport troops of the NVA's 10th Engineering Corp. Bottom: Pathet Lao forces attack an enemy position with B40 rocket launchers.

1971

479

an American Forward Air Controller (FAC) flying an O-1 spotter plane, moves in overhead to call down air support if necessary. The truck which arrives is a dark green three-tonner, a Russian 'Autobha', camouflaged with a framework of ash staves, bamboo wickerwork and sacking.

Six Laotians change into North Vietnamese uniforms and, AK-47s slung, climb into the cab and cluster over its roof while everybody else lies down among the old rice sacks on the truck floor, weapons at the ready. The patrol is now moving faster than the NVA would have estimated and so has the element of surprise if it meets them further on.

Raven goes blind

But there's no enemy around. The patrol bounces four klicks along Route 16, then another kilometre into the truck park reported by the villagers. There are five Russian two-tonners and an American jeep, parked about 200m apart. The Raven upstairs has lost the patrol because of the thick forest cover and heavy camouflage over the truck park. The Lao pop a smoke grenade and lay it on a truck bonnet, but the red smoke dissipates along the bottom of the forest canopy. The Raven radios that he still has no visual contact.

The Lao thrust thermite grenades under bonnets and into all the vehicle engines, including

their own. Then a fast trot south away from the noise, smoke and flares to throw any pursuers off the scent, before turning west to rejoin the GM for the airlift out.

Fish paste and rice surprise

The Lao, without steel helmets, wearing canvas boots, living off sticky rice balls, fish paste, peppers and greens and with only weapons and ammo to carry, can really shift. Moving swiftly over open ground that's too wide to go around, the patrol stumbles across a North Vietnamese rice cache piled under nine houses on stilts, only two of which show signs of being inhabited.

The NVA certainly know how to hide things. US pilots had just assumed this was an ordinary village. The Lao burn everything by shooting flares into the rice piles. This has displeased someone. As the patrol pulls out there is a sharp snapping sound and everybody drops flat. A Soui Kha tribesman, many of whom have followed their leader, Sithone Kommadam, and joined the Pathet Lao, has fired at the patrol with a wooden crossbow. The nine-inch wooden bolt, pencil slim and with a fire-hardened tip, takes all a trooper's strength to pull from the tree where it's embedded.

By evening the patrol reaches a helicopter LZ guarded by another group from GM 33. Yet another mission has been successfully accomplished.

Below: A suspected NVA storage position is discovered and destroyed by a CIA guerrilla unit. The NVA were past masters at disguising such caches — from the air they would look like innocent villages or houses. Here, a CIA unit happens upon just such a rice store and destroys it with flares.

Nixon called the protesters 'bums' and others talked about unleashing the dogs of war. But then the Ohio National Guard shocked America

KENT STATE

Above: The National Guard is not national at all. It is an Army and Air Force reserve organized at state level, but can be called into service by the president as well as the state governor. During the Vietnam war, many joined it to avoid the draft. They received minimum training and were expected to turn out for any emergency. Some of the air wing served in Vietnam. The rest saw service at home, quelling riots and anti-war demonstrations. They were called in from policing a teamsters' dispute to Kent State.

On 1 May 1972, a bomb exploded in a bathroom inside the Pentagon. It had been detonated by the underground anti-war protest organization, the Weathermen, and was the last whimper of the campaign of protest that had reached its climax one weekend two years before.

That weekend had ended in bloodshed. Around 1225 on Monday, 4 May 1970, members of the Ohio National Guard shot students at Kent State University. Four students – Allison Krause, Jeffrey Miller (a registered Republican), William Schroeder (an ROTC member) and Sandra Lee Sheuer (who was passing on her way to class) – lay dead and 10 others were wounded. These weren't blacks rioting in the ghetto, or yellow people in a far away country. They were white, middle-class kids on a relatively quiet campus in middle America. The body count had finally come home.

Not that this was entirely unexpected. The anti-war protesters had already won a notable victory in hounding Johnson from office and engineering the defeat of his successor as Democratic nominee, Hubert Humphrey, in the 1968 presidential election. But what they got in his place in the White House was Republican Richard Nixon, who was no friend of theirs.

He promised to pull American troops out of Vietnam, though, and he seemed to be doing it.

481

1972

But on 30 April 1970, he announced that US forces were again escalating the war by invading neutral Cambodia. Demonstrations exploded on college campuses across America. Nixon responded by calling the demonstrators 'bums'. The previous year be had ostentatiously watched a college football game on TV while 250,000 fellow Americans had demonstrated against the war in Washington. And the Governor of California, Ronald Reagan, justified the shooting and killing of a white demonstrator during the People's Park protest in Berkeley by saying that 'once the dogs of war are unleashed, you must expect these things will happen'.

On Friday, 1 May, Kent State history graduate students calling themselves World Historians Opposed to Racists and Exploitation – WHORE – organized a rally opposing the war at noon at the Victory Bell on the Commons, an area of grass in the middle of the campus. Around 500 people attended and witnessed the burial of a copy of the Constitution to symbolize its murder by President Nixon. Jim Geary, a student who had won the Silver Star in Vietnam with the 101st Airborne, burned his discharge papers. The organizers called for another rally to be held on the same spot at noon on Monday, 4 May, to protest against the war in Vietnam, the invasion of Cambodia and to push for the closure of the university's Reserve Officers Training Corps (ROTC).

The president of the university monitored the protest. Reassured by its peaceful nature, he left that afternoon for a weekend in Iowa.

Drinking on the Strip

That Friday night began as most Friday nights did at Kent State. Students went drinking in the Ron-de-Vou, Big Daddy's and The Cove along the Strip. But the topics of discussion that night soon changed from the New York Knicks-Los Angeles Lakers basketball game to Cambodia and Vietnam.

On the street, beer glasses were thrown at police cars. A crowd began shouting '1-2-3-4, We don't want your fucking war'. Soon a human chain was blocking traffic on Water Street and drivers were being asked about their views on the escalation of the war. A trash bonfire was lit in the middle of the street and a group of protesters moved down the street doing some $10,000-worth of damage.

Mayor Leroy Statrum returned to the city after midnight and declared a state of emergency and established a 2300 hours curfew for the city, 0100 for the campus. He also closed the bars, which swelled the crowds on the streets. Deputies dispersed them with tear gas, forcing them out of the city centre towards the campus. But by 0230 the town and campus were quiet.

On Saturday, 2 May, the Ohio National Guard told city officials that if they were called in they would assume total control of the university. This was not challenged by either city officials or university officers. The Mayor announced a 2200-

0600 curfew for the city and an 0100 curfew for the campus. But later, largely on the basis of false rumours that the Weathermen had been behind the previous night's disturbances, he decided to call in the National Guard.

That evening, around 1500 students milled around the campus shouting political slogans, letting off firecrackers and throwing the odd rock. The old wooden barracks which housed the Kent State ROTC became a target and people began shouting 'Get it' and 'Burn it'. Rocks and a garbage can were thrown through ground-floor windows and the building was soon on fire. When the fire department attempted to put it out, their hoses were cut. The fire appeared to go out, only to blaze up again after live ammunition stored in the building went off. Around 2200, the National Guard went in with drawn bayonets and tear gas and cleared the campus.

On the Sunday morning, the Governor of Ohio,

Right: The war had three faces. Behind the mask of Vietnam lurks the face of Johnson. Behind those of Laos and Cambodia is Nixon. Below: Daniel Ellsberg – he provided the evidence, in The Pentagon Papers, that succeeding administrations had not been telling the truth about the conduct of the war.

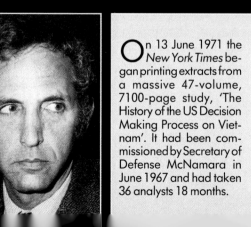

On 13 June 1971 the *New York Times* began printing extracts from a massive 47-volume, 7100-page study, 'The History of the US Decision Making Process on Vietnam'. It had been commissioned by Secretary of Defense McNamara in June 1967 and had taken 36 analysts 18 months.

THE PENTAGON PAPERS

Only 15 copies were printed and it is still unclear why McNamara should have wanted to produce a document that detailed the growth of US commitment in Southeast Asia between 1954 and 1968, especially as the text revealed 14 years of government deception, cynicism and incompetence and detailed a calculated escalation of America's role in the war.

One of the analysts, Daniel Ellsberg, had been a keen supporter of McNamara and US involvement. However, he became disillusioned by what he learned and was influenced by the protests of the National Moratorium on 15 October 1969. Accordingly, he began secretly to photocopy the study and pass pages to Senator William Fulbright. In the wake of the ARVN incursion into Laos, however, Ellsberg decided to send further copies to the press.

Nixon slapped an injunction on the *New York Times*, only for the *Washington Post* to begin printing more extracts. When the *Post* was silenced by injunction, papers in Chicago, Los Angeles, St Louis and Boston took up the challenge until, on 30 June, the Supreme Court refused to uphold Nixon's attempt to gag the press.

Meanwhile, Ellsberg and another colleague, Anthony J. Russo, were indicted for theft. The charges were finally dropped in May 1973 after the discovery that Nixon had authorized the burglary of Ellsberg's psychiatrist. It had been carried out by a group of White House staff.

Jim Rhodes, came to Kent and described the events of the previous two nights as 'probably the most vicious form of campus-oriented violence yet perpetrated by dissident groups and their allies in the State of Ohio.' He pledged to use 'every form of law' to control them. The 'troublemakers' were 'worse than the brown shirts and the communist elements, and also the night riders and the vigilantes. They are the worst type of people that we harbor in America.' It was the last weekend of his election primary campaign for the Republican Senate nomination.

Students gathered at the Victory Bell again at 2245 only to be told that the curfew had been moved from 0100 to 2100. And at 2100 the Ohio Riot Act was read to them and they were given five minutes to disperse. The crowd broke into two groups, one heading towards the president of the university's house and the other into the town where they sat and sang 'Give Peace a Chance', while a helicopter with a searchlight trained on them circled overhead. The students wanted to talk with President White or Mayor Statrum in order to present their demands – the withdrawal of the National Guard, the lifting of the curfew and an amnesty for those students who had been arrested. At 2300 the Riot Act was read again.

On Monday, 4 May, between 1500 and 3000 students were gathering at the Victory Bell for the

A LOSS OF INNOCENCE?

The foreign policy of the USA had always been portrayed as morally just. But Vietnam made the American public wonder if their crusaders really were on the side of the angels.

United States' foreign policy has always been cloaked in the rhetoric of crusading. Many Americans believed that their 'intervention' in other countries' affairs was somehow different from the 'interference' of other powers and was in the interests of a higher morality. This feeling had characterized Woodrow Wilson's '14 Points', Franklin D. Roosevelt's 'Four Freedoms' and John F. Kennedy's 'Commitment to the defense of the West'.

However, it all went sour in Vietnam as a result of a combination of factors – the bombing of North Vietnamese cities, the burning of South Vietnamese villages, the disintegration of the American army and the corrupt nature of the Saigon regime that was being supported. All of this was faithfully captured by the media and transmitted into living rooms across America.

Gradually the perception that the war at all levels might be going rotten began to sink in. There was the uncovering of the My Lai massacre and the revelation that Cambodia was being secretly bombed: in both cases there were attempts at a cover up.

Then the Pentagon Papers revealed that such cases were just the tip of the iceberg. For a generation the question was inevitable: if the US was fighting a just war, why did it need to lie and cheat its own people? If you supported the war, you condoned the cheating, or you opposed the war and condemned your government.

rally, called on Friday. The Governor had unlawfully banned all – including peaceful – demonstrations and was determined to clear the area. At 1150 a military jeep carrying guardsmen and a campus policeman with a bullhorn appeared with the latter shouting: 'This crowd must disperse immediately. This is an order.'

The students responded with shouts of 'Seig Heil' and 'Pigs Off Campus'. And they rang the Victory Bell usually sounded after football games. The National Guard commander, General Canterbury, ordered his men to load their weapons with live ammunition and to put on their gas masks. He then ordered the 100 troopers on the top of a grassy knoll, known to trysters as 'Blanket Hill', to fire tear-gas canisters into the crowd. But the students threw the gas canisters back, shouted obscenities and threw rocks and concrete.

'They're firing blanks'

When the guardsmen ran out of tear gas canisters, around 40 of them moved down the hill to confront the crowd. Several times they assumed firing positions to scare the demonstrators. But eventually they were forced back. A single shot was heard, then there was a salvo from the troopers on the knoll lasting for about three seconds. In all, 61 shots were fired. No warning was given. The students did not even know the guardsmen's rifles were loaded.

'They're firing blanks,' said one student, 'otherwise they would be aiming in the air or at the ground.' Some of them may have. But others, unbelievably, fired directly into the crowd. Shrieks and moans filled the air. Four were dead, 10 wounded. One student was paralyzed from the waist down with a bullet lodged in his spine. Ignoring his cries for help, the guardsmen marched away. The days when hippie protesters put flowers in the barrels of soldiers' guns were gone.

President Nixon's first response was that 'when dissent turns to violence it invites tragedy'. Over

150 colleges were closed or on strike in the days after the killings and 100,000 protesters marched on Washington, DC. But 'hard hats' broke up a student demonstration on Wall Street – while police looked on.

The Weathermen set up a National War Council. They bombed the home of a judge trying black radicals, planned an attack on an army dance at Fort Dix, shook the New York City police department with an explosion, blew up a ladies' room in the US Senate, hit a bathroom in the Pentagon and killed one and wounded three in a bomb attack on the Army's Mathematics Research Center in Wisconsin. Over 5000 bombs went off in all. But the anti-war protest had been taken out of the hands of the students by trades unionists, veterans and the media, who were just as determined to get Nixon as to end the war.

The attempt to justify the shootings as self-defence received a blow when the results of an FBI investigation were leaked. This concluded that: 'The shootings were not necessary and not in order,' and 'We have some reason to believe that the claim by the National Guard that their lives were endangered by the students was fabricated subsequent to the event'. Even so, the guardsmen were found not guilty when they were brought to trial.

But eight and a half years later, the defendants signed a statement expressing regret and admitting responsibility for the shootings. And on 4 January 1979, in an out-of-court settlement, the parents and students received $675,000 from the State of Ohio.

Facing page: The Kent State campus – the Commons viewed from Blanket Hill, shortly before the shooting. Below: After the demonstration was brought to its bloody end the National Guard marched away – leaving the students to tend their wounded and mourn the dead.

PROTEST IN THE USA

Following the demonstrations outside The Pentagon in October 1967 and the violence at the Democratic Convention in August 1968, the peace movement became more fragmented. The militancy and violence frightened many away, while others were pacified by Nixon's promises to end the war. Other issues, such as black power, also served to divert attention from the anti-war movement – even on the campuses, where support had been strongest.

However, in September 1969, a former McCarthy activist, Sam Brown, created the Vietnam Moratorium Committee with the intention of showing that protest was not confined to students. 15 October 1969 was designated Moratorium Day and a wide cross-section of American society peacefully demonstrated its disaffection with the war.

The Moratorium brought 250,000 people onto the streets of Washington and between 13-15 November another 500,000 took to the streets again in response to the committee's call. But it was Nixon's Cambodian incursion in 1970 that led to an explosion of protest. There was ferment on the campuses and, amid widespread violence, four died at Kent State. These protests demonstrated a change in the anti-war movement. Everyone knew that American troops were being withdrawn; it was the speed of the withdrawal and Nixon's personal handling of the war that was now faulted.

1971 saw renewed protest at the invasion of Laos, with large demonstrations in Washington and San Francisco on 24 April. May witnessed clashes between Washington police and the May Day Tribe, with 12,000 arrests. Nixon's expansion of the war into Cambodia and Laos had given the anti-war movement a renewed vigour and in November 1971 there were large anti-war rallies in 16 cities. Because the protest was now directed at Nixon's handling of the war it was able to keep its focus, and 1972 saw more demonstrations against Nixon's decision to renew the bombing campaign.

By the beginning of 1972 there were only about 156,800 US troops left in Vietnam. Throughout the period of the incursions into Laos and Cambodian (1970-71), the US armed forces were shrinking in size, as the government of Richard Nixon did its best to bring the boys back home, and end direct US involvement in the war.

There was still fighting, though. Early in 1971 the 101st Airborne carried through a series of operations against suspected NVA areas in the Central Highlands. This involved the by-now

The era when American servicemen humped the boonies in search of the enemy was drawing to a close. For most grunts it was simply a matter of staying alive for a few months more. By 1972, the war had gone sour

THE US WITHDRAWAL

usual routine of sweeping through wide stretches of inhospitable countryside, but with a difference. The NVA no longer had any interest in inflicting large-scale casualties on US forces – they knew that the Americans would be on their way home sooner rather than later, and so they tended to avoid contact. Maybe a few rockets or mortar shells would let the grunts know that there were still some hostiles out there in the dense vegeta-

tion of the hills – but when they came across a bunker complex, the Americans usually found it abandoned. There was none of the bitter fighting that had characterised earlier contact in the region.

Towards the end of the year, the 101st took part in Operation Jefferson Glenn, in Thua Thien Province, establishing firebases and conducting sweeps through wide sectors. The operation ended

US PRESENCE IN 1972

When the US withdrawal began in June 1969 there were 544,000 American servicemen in South Vietnam. By December 1971, 156,800 remained and Nixon had announced his intention to reduce this figure to 139,000 by 1 February 1972.

Moreover, the majority of those remaining were support elements and not combat troops. The 101st Airborne Division had begun pulling out on 31 January, leaving the 3d Brigade, 1st Air Cav, and the 1st Aviation Brigade in the vicinity of Saigon, and the 196th Infantry Brigade on perimeter defence at Da Nang. In the whole of I and II Corps Tactical Zones there was less than the equivalent of a division of US personnel left.

Headquarters had been severely pruned and several bases were either closed down entirely or handed over to the ARVN. Most US advisers had also departed. Those remaining were only at ARVN corps, division and province level. Allied formations had gone as well, although the Koreans had agreed to retain two divisions – albeit at reduced strength – until the end of 1972. The 3d Brigade, 1st Air Cav, saw minor action at the beginning of the NVA Easter Offensive, but it was soon relieved by the ARVN 18th Division and pulled back to the Bien Hoa-Long Binh-Saigon complex.

The Easter Offensive did nothing to arrest the speed of US disengagement. Both the Air Cav and the 196th were withdrawn in late June to leave just 31,900 American servicemen. The last two remaining combat units – the 1st Battalion 7th Cavalry (part of Task Force Gary Owen) and the 3d Battalion 21st Infantry – left in August to bring the total down to around 25,000 by the end of the month. However, it is significant that the withdrawals did not include 13,000 seamen stationed off the coast with the US 7th Fleet, and 47,000 US airmen in South Vietnam and Thailand. Their presence guaranteed South Vietnamese survival in late 1972: in their absence, the beleaguered state would collapse three years later.

PARIS PEACE TALKS

Between 1965 and 1968, constant contacts between intermediaries from Hanoi and Washington, and the rumours of peace that they generated, helped to halt the bombing of the North several times.

In September 1967 Johnson offered a complete suspension of bombing in return for 'meaningful negotiations', and on 31 March 1968 bombing was restricted to south of the 20th parallel.

On 3 April Hanoi signalled its agreement to talk, and Johnson pulled the bombers south of the 19th parallel. Preliminary negotiations opened in Paris on 10 May, and Johnson offered to suspend bombing altogether, providing Hanoi did not violate the DMZ, shell South Viet-

namese cities, or attack unarmed reconnaissance flights.

On 31 October, Johnson finally suspended all air and naval activity against North Vietnam and announced that talks would begin in Paris the following week. In fact, it was not until 25 January 1969 that plenary talks were opened between the United States, the North and South Vietnamese, and the VC. In August, Nixon's National Security Adviser, Henry Kissinger, opened parallel secret negotiations in Paris with the head of the North Vietnamese delegation, Le Duc Tho.

However, all talks foundered on two contentious points: American insistence that there be a mutual withdrawal as a precondition of a ceasefire, and Hanoi's

insistence that the withdrawal be preceded by Thieu's removal and replacement with an interim coalition administration which included communists.

While Nixon and Kissinger could not afford to delay, Hanoi treated the negotiations as part and parcel of the protracted struggle. Nixon and Kissinger attempted to outflank Hanoi by reaching new agreements with Moscow and Peking and by escalating the war as required. However, in October 1970, the Americans were compelled to accept the principle of a standstill ceasefire in place, and by April 1972 had also dropped their insistence on a mutual withdrawal. Hanoi had to accept the continuation of Thieu's rule – at least for a while.

Far left: The rituals of retreat. An MP carefully folds the Stars and Stripes, an act that was repeated all over South Vietnam as US troops packed their bags and moved Stateside. Above: A Lockheed C-141 Starlifter at Da Nang Air Base prepares to ferry a batch of US troops back to The World. The high ideals and hopes of 1965 had long since vanished, and all the Americans wanted now was out.

in October 1971: it was the last large-scale US deployment of ground troops in the combat role.

Although large-scale operations were running down, the day-to-day patrolling and security movements continued. 'Dynamic defense' was the new description. Specially designated zones within rocket-firing range of large towns, cities or major installations – the so-called 'rocket belt' – were made the target of repeated sweeps.

Morale, already at a low ebb during 1970, declined still further during 1971 and the first months of 1972. All attention was focused on the peace talks in Paris: more than ever, all grunts could see their ticket home on the horizon, and they didn't want to die in the last phase of what now seemed a futile war.

Military police were busy as 1971 drew to a close. In September they had to besiege 14 soldiers of the 35th Engineer Group who had barricaded themselves into a bunker and refused to come out; in October, in a camp near Da Lat, a Military Police task force had to be flown in by air to protect the commanding officer. Fragging had reached such proportions that an attempt had been made

1972

GOING HOME

When John Morris caught a plane Stateside, he shared part of his journey with an Air Force Chief Master Sergeant. This is the Chief's story.

The World Airways' military-chartered stretch DC-9 stood waiting for us on the tarmac at Cam Ranh Bay. It looked good. But then a Gypsy Moth, if it could have flown us out of Vietnam and back to The World, would have looked good too.

A couple of hundred of us, outfitted in Army summer-dress khaki and Air Force pale blue, crowded aboard. We held our collective breaths as the plane took off, then clapped and cheered when the wheels came up. We were on our way home.

I was sitting in a port side aisle seat, and an Air Force Chief Master Sergeant was sitting across from me. I was still having some problems with my left knee, so I asked him if we could change seats so that I could stretch my leg out into the aisle. No problem. We started chatting.

The grizzled old Chief told me that, after 38 years in this man's Air Force, he was heading home to retire. His last three tours in Vietnam and Thailand had helped him to see the light.

We put down in Yakoda Air Force Base in Japan to refuel, drop off some supplies and pick up a few more. We wandered around the terminal, picking up trinkets and souvenirs, then reboarded about an hour later.

I noticed the Chief had a couple of bags he hadn't deplaned with, bags that clanked and tinkled suspiciously.

It's worth noting here that military-chartered civilian aircraft flew under the same rules as military aircraft. In other words, no booze was allowed on the aircraft.

Chief, as a senior Air Force NCO, knew those rules as well as anyone. But when he pulled out a bottle of Bacardi 151-proof rum and two cans of Coke, it was obvious he didn't give a damn.

It took the stewardesses a little while to catch on. I guess it happened when Chief leaned over with the bottle to fill up my can, nearly impaling a bubbly little blond in her World Airways' uniform.

'Sir, you cannot drink on this aircraft.'

'Missy, don't worry. I won't spill on anyone,' the Chief replied.

'Sir, I will have to have that bottle. Open containers are not allowed.'

'Missy, you can have it when it's empty.'

'Sir, if you don't cooperate, I'll have to contact the flight deck.' She tried to fix the Chief, who was used to staring down generals, with a stern glare. It didn't work. Chief just smiled and topped off his can of Coke with more rum.

Moments later, the first officer came down the aisle. He was a kid, maybe his first time around as an FO (First Officer). Hell, anyone under 50 was probably a kid to Chief.

I don't know what the FO was expecting, but it sure wasn't a sleeve full of stripes and a chest overflowing with medals. He started the same routine as the stewardess, but Chief just ignored him. His rum-and-Coke took precedence.

Finally, the FO brought out his last, and biggest, guns. 'Buddy, if you don't hand over that bottle, we're going back to Yakoda, and I'll have the security police escort you off this aircraft.'

No-one in his right mind calls a Chief Master Sergeant in the Air Force 'buddy' – Chief, sergeant, or even 'hey you', but not 'buddy'.

The Chief put his can on the fold-down tray in the next seat and stood up. His 5ft 11ins, eight rows of ribbons, an armful of stripes on a crisply pressed uniform, and tanned and creased face, was an imposing sight. The First Officer backed up a step or two.

'Sir, first, I am not your "buddy",' the Chief began, his command voice rumbling from his chest.

'Second, I am heading home to retire after spending the last 40 months in Southeast Asia. Third, you can fly to Yakoda or Foggy Nuts, North Dakota, for all I care. I personally know every airbase commander and his staff no matter where you land, and I can guarantee it'll be you who gets escorted off, not me.'

Chief paused to let that sink in. Then he said: 'Any questions, mister?'

Some GI a few rows up shouted out: 'Tell him, Chief!' But the Chief cut him down with a look that would freeze fire. He wasn't out to humiliate the FO or start a mutiny. He just wanted to be left alone to enjoy his last flight home.

The FO left without a word and went back to the flight deck. The Chief and I tucked into our next round of rum-and-Cokes. Then the pilot came rolling down the aisle, eyes flashing. He was no rookie. World Airways was probably his last stint before retirement.

He stopped at our row, gave me a quick glance then settled his attention on the Chief, who by now was standing again. In a second the captain's experienced eye sized the Chief up for what he was – a professional career Air Force NCO who was not out to cause undue trouble if he was left alone.

The captain leaned over to Chief's ear and spoke softly, but with the authority due to him as aircraft commander.

'Chief, drink yourself into oblivion. You deserve it. But if you give my aircrew so much as half of a hard time, or fuck up my airplane in any way, I will personally throw you overboard at 36,000 feet. Copy that?'

Two iron wills locked horns for a brief moment, then Chief smiled. 'Roger that, sir. It's a real pleasure to fly under your command.' They understood each other.

I bailed out of the Bacardi a little while later, and drifted off into a fitful doze. The Chief was still knocking them back, last I remember.

I woke up sometime later, and the aircraft was quiet. Lights were dimmed, slumbering bodies stretched out all over. I looked over at the Chief. He was sitting ramrod straight, eyes closed, not a hair out of place, with his hand curled around a glass. One of the stewards had brought it to him, filled with ice.

'You OK, Chief?' I asked softly.

He didn't move for a moment, then his hand uncurled from the glass. He closed his fist, then popped his thumb straight up. Yeah, I guess everything was OK with the Chief: he knew he was going home.

on the man's life two nights running. Not until the MPs had been in residence for a week could discipline be restored. Perhaps the worst single incident to befall US forces in 1971 was the disaster at Fire Support Base Mary Ann. Situated in Quang Tin Province, the base was garrisoned by men of the 196th Infantry Brigade. They had got into bad habits, barely mounting a worthwhile guard at night, and in March the NVA took full advantage. It is estimated that about 50 NVA soldiers broke in one night. They caused widespread damage, and over 100 US troops were knifed or shot while sleeping.

Civilian antagonism

If the war was going sour for the US soldiers desperate to get home, by early 1972 Vietnam itself had gone sour on the Americans. While US money had funded businesses – from prostitution to antique shops – many Vietnamese had been prepared to accept the less palatable aspects of the American presence. But when the troop numbers began to decline, anti-American feeling became more overt. What would happen to the tens of thousands of Vietnamese who had obtained jobs in and around the enormous base areas of Da Nang and Cam Ranh Bay? They could hardly expect to feel grateful when the GIs began to depart.

In the big towns, gangs of youths made life very unpleasant for Vietnamese girls seen with Americans. US sources estimated that up to 1000 'confrontations' per month were occurring between US troops and Vietnamese civilians. There were reports of young Vietnamese trying to beat up and even castrate Americans found on their own, and US personnel were advised not to wander alone in Saigon – a far cry from the balmy days of 1965, when US soldiers had been greeted with garlands.

They refused to go on patrol

In 1970, student protests against the Americans had started – in Qui Nonh (after a US soldier had accidentally killed a Buddhist student) and then spread to Saigon. All Vietnamese descriptions of these riots made one thing clear – the students were not supporters of the communists. They were just manifesting a widespread anti-American feeling. Vice-President Ky encouraged such feelings; he called the US government 'bad and unwelcome masters' and denounced 'unreasonable meddling'.

Marines had been the first ground combat troops into Vietnam; the final Marine combat units left Vietnam in June 1971. The 173d Airborne, which had been involved in some of the earliest fighting near Saigon in 1965, left in August.

The 101st Airborne was one of the last formations to see real combat, during January 1972, but by this date the US ground troop combat role had almost disappeared. When the Northern invasion took place in March 1972, there was no plan to increase US involvement on the ground (in the air

was another matter). And what attempts were made to use US troops to bolster the ARVN were unsuccessful: in April, members of the 196th Infantry Brigade refused to go out on patrol when ordered to do so in support of ARVN operations.

The 1/7th Cavalry remained in Vietnam until August 1972 – not doing very much but serving as a reminder of the early days. The Air Cavalry had blunted the first big NVA offensive in autumn 1965. Now, almost seven years later, the last grunts were going home.

By civilian airliner (far left) and by Naval transports (top), US troops departed South Vietnam in droves throughout 1972. For the few who remained (above), the rule was to stay alive.

THE EASTER

Camp Carroll never knew what hit it. At around two in the morning of 30 March 1972 the silence was brutally shattered by the roar of incoming shells. Explosions and screams split the night and pandemonium broke loose. Within a couple of hours, over 2000 shells had visited death and destruction on the beleaguered outpost. The long-awaited NVA offensive had arrived.

Camp Carroll managed to hold out against this ferocious assault but, for its battered ARVN garrison, their worst fears had been confirmed. Accelerated US troop withdrawals had left only 7000 of their ground combat troops in South Vietnam, and it had been decided to let the ARVN fight the ground war on its own, while the US would restrict itself to supplying air cover. So now the North had picked up the gauntlet.

Camp Carroll's experience that night was not

an isolated one. All along the line south of the DMZ, ARVN-manned firebases came under instant and sustained bombardment from Soviet-supplied rockets, 130mm field-guns – which outranged any US combat field piece – and 152mm howitzers. Around 12,000 rounds were expended in this softening-up exercise, and then the ground troops attacked. In the biggest communist assault since the siege of Khe Sanh in January 1968, four complete NVA divisions, including the veteran 304th and 308th, comprising in total 40,000 men, and supported by 200 Soviet T-54, T-55, T-34 and PT-76 tanks, poured southward across the DMZ.

The areas closest to the DMZ had been left lightly defended by just the greenhorn ARVN 3rd Division. Not surprisingly, it had little hope of withstanding the unbridled fury of the NVA assault. As its raw and inexperienced troops were forced to retreat, the firebases fell, one by one. Fuller, Mailoc, Halcomb, Pioneer, Charlie 2, as

INVASION

The firebases fell one by one as General Giap hurled his army against South Vietnam during the 1972 invasion. Whole provinces succumbed to the Northern warriors. Was this the day of reckoning?

THE AIMS OF NGUYEN HUE

Hanoi's aims in Nguyen Hue (the offensive named after the 18th century king who united all Vietnam) were varied. There was the hope that, if the ARVN could be smashed on the battlefield, the war would be over. But even if this could not be achieved, there were other advantages.

The offensive was designed to damage the Vietnamization and pacification programmes which had put the Viet Cong on the defensive. As well as wanting to prove Vietnamization a failure, the North Vietnamese wished to damage the ARVN, both materially and psychologically, and to undermine the stability of President Thieu. Hanoi also hoped to gain as much territory as it could before any truce and thereby accelerate negotiations on its own terms. Finally, Hanoi may well have hoped that a major offensive would help damage Nixon's chances of winning the presidential election and result in a 'dove' being elected.

Giap therefore decided that the time was ripe to use a conventional invasion in strength. Virtually the whole of the NVA was committed to an invasion of the South and, in the early hours of 30 March, the Easter Offensive began.

In typical fashion, Giap launched the offensive on several fronts. The first prong swept directly south across the DMZ into I Corps Tactical Zone, westwards from Laos and north from Cambodia through the A Shau valley. The second prong, in II Corps, began with a drive through Loc Ninh and on to An Loc, which guarded Route 13 to Saigon. The third prong erupted in III Corps, with the NVA advancing on Kontum and striking into Binh Dinh Province, with the aim of cutting South Vietnam in two.

The offensive also aimed to gain control of as much as possible of the rich and populous Mekong Delta. By June, the Viet Cong had overrun or occupied more than 100 abandoned government posts in the region, while pacification programmes had crumbled in several key provinces such as Chuong Thien and Dinh Tuong.

well as two smaller observation posts, all wilted under the furious enemy pressure. Within five days virtually all of the northern half of Quang Tri Province was in the hands of the NVA 304th Division, and only the provincial capital of Quang Tri itself was still in ARVN hands. Its fall seemed only a matter of time.

The second thrust

Then, on 5 April, the second thrust of the offensive was opened. It came from a totally unexpected direction, over 600km to the south, where a further 15,000 troops, also heavily supported by artillery and tanks, erupted out of their Cambodian bases and punched into Binh Long Province, just over 100km north of Saigon.

The first wave of the southern thrust fell upon ARVN troops near Tay Ninh but, as reinforcements were rushed to the area, it was realized too late that this attack was only a feint, as the main

assault was launched by three full NVA divisions to the northeast. They overran Loc Ninh and severed Route 13 between Saigon and An Loc. In the north, Camp Carroll finally fell, as did The Rockpile, while Firebase Bastogne came under siege. Inside a week of the offensive being launched, a 25km strip between the DMZ and the Cua Viet river was in North Vietnamese hands.

It was fast becoming apparent that a primary NVA aim of the offensive, to demoralize and discredit the ARVN – and to demolish President Nixon's policies of Vietnamization and pacification into the bargain – was about to be realized. To make matters worse, bad weather and low, scud-

Left: The ARVN took massive casualties, but held on. Above left: There were still US troops in country but this was the ARVN's fight. Above: The ARVN in action in Quang Tri Province.

1972

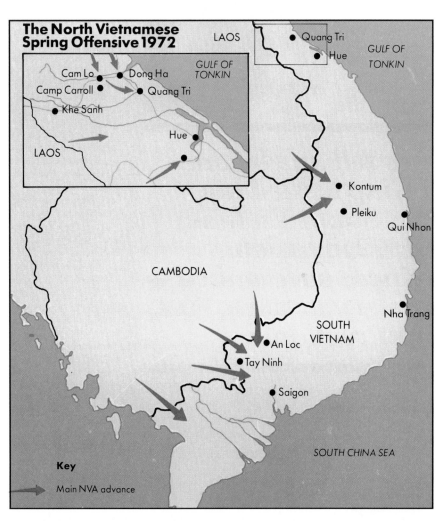

The North Vietnamese Spring Offensive 1972

LAOS
GULF OF TONKIN
Quang Tri
Hue

Cam Lo
Dong Ha
Camp Carroll
Quang Tri
Khe Sanh
LAOS
Hue

CAMBODIA

Kontum
Pleiku
Qui Nhon

SOUTH VIETNAM

Nha Trang

An Loc
Tay Ninh

Saigon

SOUTH CHINA SEA

Key

→ Main NVA advance

ding clouds – the monsoon season was due shortly – kept most of the formidable US arsenal of strike aircraft languishing idle on the ground. This meant that the ARVN, trained to the US pattern of working directly with heavy air support, was severely weakened in its capability.

Never bombed like this time

However, President Nixon, undeterred, dispatched an armada of extra planes to Southeast Asia, including 20 additional B-52s. He also ordered the US carriers *Midway* and *Saratoga* to the South China Sea, bringing the full US complement there up to six (already on station were the *Coral Sea*, *Hancock*, *Kitty Hawk* and *Constellation*). So when, on 6 April, the weather finally improved, Nixon ordered massive strikes against NVA positions on and around the DMZ. 'The bastards have never been bombed like they're going to be bombed this time,' he declared. The naval contribution came not only from the aircraft carriers but also from shelling by almost 20 destroyers and cruisers lying offshore. In the air, flying over 200 missions in three days, the US planes pulverized their targets.

But the pilots soon discovered that the NVA had added a new weapon to their arsenal – SAM missiles, which claimed several US planes. And, for the first time, the Seventh Fleet was attacked – MiG attacks wounded four sailors on the destroyer *Higbee* while shore batteries hit the *Buchanan*, killing one and injuring seven.

The US air bombardment of the North and the NVA in the South may have helped shore up the

morale of the South, but the ground-war situation was looking bleak. An Loc was under siege and then, on 23 April, the third thrust of the Nguyen Hue offensive opened, again in a wholly new area. It was aimed at Kontum in the Central Highlands, and was designed to cut South Vietnam in two. As with the previous thrusts, it was heralded by massive NVA artillery fire brought to bear on surrounding firebases, and soon the strategic town of Tan Canh, which blocked the northern route to Kontum, was in NVA hands, as its ARVN garrison panicked and fled. Meanwhile, the ARVN 22nd Division, having borne the brunt of the NVA 320th and 2nd Division assaults, began to dissolve as it withdrew to Kontum. So the South Vietnamese command decided to withdraw it and reform it in the rear. It was replaced by the ARVN 23rd Division, shoehorned into Kontum just one day before the NVA arrived in force. For the moment, Kontum was relatively safe, but it was a rare respite for the South Vietnamese. The very next day, 24 April, Dak To fell.

For the ARVN, the last days of April were ones spent in hell. On the 27th the NVA, having committed five whole divisions to their northern front, renewed their offensive there. Firebase Bastogne managed to survive a tear-gas attack but elsewhere the hapless rookies of the ARVN 3rd Division, having withstood a month of being pounded and mauled, finally broke. It was a miracle that they had lasted so long. The Cua Viet river line was now breached and the communists poured through, swiftly overrunning Dong Ha. Their progress was helped by the weather, which

once again was too bad to permit air support for the ARVN. The road to the South now lay wide open, and the communists advanced through Quang Tri Province, moving ominously towards Quang Tri City itself.

The NVA advance on the other two fronts was likewise steady. In the Central Highlands the ARVN surrendered control of the district town of Hoai An and the An Loa valley. The equivalent of three NVA divisions harassed the South Vietnamese forces and laid siege to seven firebases west of the provincial capital of Kontum, while other communist troops cut the main supply route, Highway 19, between Pleiku and the coastal town of Qui Nhon, and inflicted heavy casualties on a South Korean division that tried to

Above: Casualties mounted and all looked lost for the ARVN as the NVA moved forward to take advantage of US troop withdrawals. But the South still managed to hold out. Left: The roads were packed with refugees fleeing towards Saigon by any means possible. Centre left: Panic seized northern cities as people desperately tried to escape the fighting. Far left: Some were evacuated by plane and helicopter, others just took to the roads. They were heading for the relative safety of the south and Saigon. Three years later, however, there would be no place left to run.

1972

reopen the road. But here at least air support was possible, and B-52 strikes inflicted enormous casualties on the NVA 28th Regiment.

In the south, the NVA had reached to within 60km of Saigon itself. About 100km southwest of An Loc they surrounded the Cambodian town of Svay Rieng, astride Route 1, which links Phnom Penh to Saigon. In the Mekong Delta, Viet Cong guerrillas mounted rocket attacks on the provincial capitals of My Tho and Can Tho and took over areas vacated by those ARVN troops that had moved north to defend An Loc, which was now under siege.

The fall of Quang Tri City, on 1 May, was perhaps the nadir for the ARVN in the offensive so far, and highlighted one of its fundamental weaknesses: its antiquated and perniciously inefficient officer system. Despite the fact that, under the Vietnamization programme, the Pentagon had sent some 12,000 ARVN officers to the US for advanced training, for an army at war the ARVN relied to a frightening degree on an officer corps drawn from the upper reaches of society, political

Left: An American adviser and an ARVN officer with captured enemy tank. Despite the NVA onslaught the ARVN managed to mount a counter-offensive – and win through.

THE BLUNTING OF NGUYEN HUE

In the Easter Offensive of 1972 North Vietnam committed virtually its entire army in an invasion of the South. US airpower notwithstanding, why did the NVA fail?

By the end of September 1972, with the fighting in South Vietnam back to pre-offensive levels, the NVA attempt to overrun South Vietnam was seen to have failed. During the six months of the Easter Offensive Hanoi had committed 14 divisions and 26 independent regiments – virtually all that they had – but they had failed to topple President Thieu's regime.

True, pacification had been set back owing to the ARVN being tied up in the fighting, and the percentage of South Vietnam's population under communist control had risen from 3.7 before the offensive to 9.7 at its close. Crucially, though, the ARVN was still very active, and could only have gained in confidence from its recent successes.

A fundamental element in the strategy employed by Vo Nguyen Giap, North Vietnam's Minister of Defence and the commander-in-chief of its army, was his insistence on attacking on several different fronts at the same time, rather than concentrating his forces at one point. For example, if one or more of the NVA divisions used to attack An Loc and Kontum had been employed instead in the northern sector of the offensive, the momentum of the communist attack there might well have continued until at least Hue was captured. If this had happened, the survival of the South would have been seriously in doubt. Indeed, the NVA compounded their error by pausing for three weeks after reaching the Cua Viet river, allowing the ARVN time in which to move up reinforcements.

A further problem was that Giap's commanders lacked proper experience of co-ordinating attacks which combined infantry, tanks and artillery. (For example, NVA tanks at An Loc and Kontum found themselves bogged down in the rubble ensuing from NVA artillery bombardments and were thus highly vulnerable to the defenders.) Also, tanks were frequently sent into attack without any infantry support, and were often wasted in quasi-static battles instead of utilizing their mobility, by-passing towns like An Loc and pressing on towards Saigon.

Another failing was that NVA commanders tended to waste the numerical superiority they had achieved by massing their troops at chosen points, and by initiating repeated shock assaults which produced very heavy NVA casualties and eventually left them outnumbered.

In addition, Giap, normally a master logistician, seems to have underestimated the effects of aerial interdiction of their supply routes. Heavy bombing by the US of communist supply dumps and communications lines destroyed a great deal of supplies being moved south. There were several reports of NVA tanks running out of fuel.

But the question must still be asked whether, in the eyes of Giap and indeed Hanoi generally, the offensive had in fact failed. The North Vietnamese did not regard the war as needing to be of limited duration – 'We shall fight for 1000 years' was their cry. Furthermore, they did end 1972 in control of more of the South than they had at the start of the year. As always, Giap had hedged his bets. He may have missed a golden opportunity, but he had still strengthened his position.

appointees, and men influenced by corruption.

In Quang Tri, the NVA tanks smashed through the town's northern defences, aided by the fact that the 3rd Division's flank had been exposed by a failure of co-ordination among its senior officers. But worse was to come, for when the divisional commander, Brigadier-General Giai, ordered a withdrawal, the sight of him and his staff cravenly leaving the city on a US helicopter sparked panic among the troops. As thousands of dispirited South Vietnamese troops swelled the human river of desperately fleeing civilians on Route 1

leading to Hue, NVA artillery shelled the road, inflicting 20,000 casualties.

Deserters would be executed

But now came a turning point in the fortunes of the ARVN. Pressured by his US advisers, and realizing that the South was all but lost, President Thieu finally put military considerations before political ones and acted decisively. He relieved Giai of his command (he was later court-martialled for abandoning his position in the face of the enemy) and the regional commander of the northern sector, the flamboyant Lieutenant-General Ngo Dzu, suddenly suffered a 'heart flutter' and was also relieved.

Giai was replaced by General Ngo Quang Truong, in many people's opinion South Vietnam's best officer, who was also put in charge of all ARVN forces on the northern front. He immediately issued orders that all deserters and looters would be executed. He reinforced the northern sector with the elite ARVN Marine and Airborne Divisions and quickly established a new defensive line 40km north of Hue, along the My Chanh river. So, although the NVA brought in their 312th Division from Laos, they were unable to break through to Hue.

South Vietnamese morale received another boost on 8 May when the US Navy mined North Vietnamese ports, including Haiphong. Just over a week later the ARVN 23rd Division in Kontum, supported by B-52s and US Army choppers with TOW anti-tank missiles, managed to withstand attacks by the NVA 2nd and 320th Divisions.

The tide turns

The tide was now definitely turning. By the end of May the NVA were on the retreat from Kontum, fleeing back to their bases in Laos. The ARVN counter-attack, spearheaded by the 1st Infantry, Marine and Airborne Divisions, and massively supported by B-52s and US fighter-bombers, continued its momentum. On 18 June the long and bloody siege of An Loc was finally lifted and at the end of the month the ARVN counter-offensive north of Hue began. 19 July saw operations starting in Binh Dinh Province to regain three northern districts, whose capitals were recaptured two weeks later. Finally, on 19 September, the ARVN Marines hoisted their flag over the rubble of Quang Tri Ctiy.

Although the northern part of Quang Tri Province was to remain in NVA hands, the South had survived.

Above: Supported by the mining of Haiphong harbour, B-52 airstrikes and US fighter-bombers, the ARVN found the will to strike back. After six months they had managed to claw back some of the territory they had lost.

DEATH CHARGE

Machine guns that can cut a man down from a terrifying distance, mortar rounds that crump in with deadly precision, sniper fire from the tree-line. Moving forward to engage the enemy in a firefight, the infantryman can expect death to engulf him from any direction. But when two of your men are down and screaming for help, fear takes a back seat. Photographer Terry Fincher, on patrol with an ARVN militia unit, took this remarkable series of pictures after contact was made with the NVA.

DEATH CHARGE

Bottom: Hitting hard contact on the edge of a clearing, the ARVN militia pour fire into an unseen enemy, trying to take the heat off forward elements that have been cut off when the NVA opened up.

EYE-WITNESS

Photographer Terry Fincher (above) spent many months in Vietnam, covering the war for *Express* newspapers.

Far left: Hearing the agonized screams of their stricken comrades, the militia decide not to wait for armoured support and sprint forward into a gauntlet of fire. Under covering fire, the wounded are dragged out of the killing zone. (right). Meanwhile, American M113s, brought up from the rear, move in to engage (centre right). It is at this moment that the NVA decides to carry out a tactical withdrawal, vanishing into the dense forest. **Bottom right:** Fallen colleagues are carried by members of the ARVN militia.

497

When NVA armour seemed poised to crush the defenders of An Loc, true grit and American airpower saved the day

AN LOC UNDER SIEGE

This Easter the ARVN were to have their own cross to bear. With only a skeleton US presence in the country, the South Vietnamese armed forces were now standing on their own size six, combat-booted feet – on the ground if not in the air. Trouble had been expected south of the DMZ, where US Intelligence had picked up a heavy NVA build-up. But the area to the north of Saigon had been presumed safe – no large-scale communist preparation had been detected here. This illusion of safety was soon shattered.

Assisted by artillery and tanks – ageing T-34s and more modern T-54/55s – the NVA fell on the unprepared ARVN units near Tay Ninh, running up rapid successes after the first round of fighting on 2 April. ARVN forces were sucked into the defence of Tay Ninh, but this was merely a feint. The real attack came on 5 April, three days later, overrunning the town of Loc Ninh to the north-east. On the same day the NVA 7th Division moved behind An Loc and cut Route 13 – the road to Saigon now lay open to the invaders.

A fight to the last man
Undeterred by the grave situation up near Hue and the danger of other enemy offensives else-where, President Nguyen Van Thieu decided to stand and fight for An Loc. Although he had little

Left: Apprehensive yet defiant in their bunker, ARVN troops armed with M16s await the next communist assault on An Loc. Many observers thought that the ARVN would not be able to withstand the offensive, but at the end of the day the warriors of the South had proved them wrong. Above: Soviet-built tanks burn amid the rubble of devastated An Loc. The rubble caused by continual NVA artillery barrages had rendered the streets of the city largely inpenatrable to the NVA armour.

option – this provincial capital was only 90 kilometres from Saigon – by declaring that An Loc should be held, Thieu gave it a symbolic importance beyond its strategic value.

The town's population of 17,000 had been swollen by 6000 men of the battered South Vietnamese 5th Division and 2000 refugees from Loc Ninh. The defenders faced two problems: little artillery and no overland supply line.

As Loc Ninh collapsed, two ARVN Ranger battalions were rushed to An Loc to support the units already in the city. These were followed by another couple of Ranger units. Finally, on 13 April Thieu committed his own guard, the 1st Airborne Brigade. They were ordered to fight to the last man.

The Airborne began a slow and costly march up Route 13. Their troubles were often compounded by the half-hearted attitude of the ARVN 21st Division, dragged up from the Delta to secure Route 13. One journalist recalls meeting this motley crew. 'I drove past one regiment of the 21st lounging on the side of the road – after I had been assured the route ahead was clear. But less than three miles farther on, communist mortar shells rained down on us and we hurriedly sped back, again passing the 21st Division troops – who were still resting.'

Confident that they could crush An Loc with their sheer weight of numbers and firepower

superiority, the NVA started the squeeze. Kicking off with a 7000-round-a-day shell overture, what was to be a minor epic of a siege began on 7 April. From tree-covered cliffs and rubber plantations overlooking the town, round after round of artillery, mortar, rocket and tank fire poured in. Several shells landed on the overcrowded hospital, located near the South Vietnamese Army headquarters. 'The wounded were everywhere,' said ARVN captain Le Van Tam. 'Children, pregnant women bleeding, the old. They were dying and no-one was able to help them.'

The smell just got too bad

Around 1000 refugees squashed into the Catholic church, where they had little food and water and were under constant bombardment. The defenders buried 350 soldiers in a mass grave. 'During the first week we just stacked up the bodies, 60 or 70 a pile,' said a US advisor who helicoptered in and out of town. 'But eventually the smell just got too bad.'

Yet this awesome bombardment was to prove a mistake. It reduced large areas of the town to rubble and in the process made the town easier to defend. The communist forces had an opportunity to realize this the following day when they attempted to take the town.

They were met with a pulverising show of strength from the extremes of the US air inven-

tory – dragonfly HueyCobras unleashing a breath of fire from tree-top level and gargantuan B-52s releasing hell's own ordnance from the roof of the sky. As if this wasn't enough, AC-119 Stinger and AC-130 Spectre gunships joined the fray. The 105mm howitzer that equipped the AC-130E could smash any tank open like a celestial nut-cracker, as could the TOW (Tube-launched, Optically-tracked, Wire-guided) missiles on the Cobras of the 1st Cavalry Division. Six T-54/T-55s found this out to their cost when they drove down An Loc's main north-south street in a determined attack on the ARVN Command Post. The lead tank was taken out with an M72 LAW, an anti-armour weapon that came into its own during the Easter invasion. The ARVN commander then cleared three Cobras to attack the remaining tanks. Four were put out of action.

'Go away from Vietnam'

Not that US air power was always so effective – one pilot, Lieutenant-Colonel Stephen Opitz, had to watch helplessly as machine-gun fire from his AC-130 splashed impotently off the side of a T-54 as it overran an ARVN position. As a multitude of

WHY DID THE ARVN STAND FIRM?

The South Vietnamese army held fast at Easter. Did it do so on its own merits?

When the NVA opened its offensive on 30 March 1972, the ARVN seemed incapable of withstanding the pressure. As the 3rd Division fell back from the DMZ, it revealed all the inherent weaknesses of the Southern forces: officers fled, soldiers threw down their weapons, desertion rates rocketed and territory was abandoned without a fight. Further disasters around Quang Tri City in April – by which time NVA attacks to the north of Saigon and in the Central Highlands had led to yet more loss of ground – merely reinforced an inevitable conclusion: man for man, the ARVN was not a match for the NVA.

Yet the fact remains that by late May all three NVA assaults had been blunted. In the northern provinces, Hue had been saved, while

further south Kontum and An Loc had held out, like rocks in the path of the communist advance. It was a remarkable reversal of fortune.

The reasons are many and varied. Clearly, ARVN resolve had been strengthened once the soldiers realized that they were fighting for their country's survival, and the disasters of April did force President Thieu to abandon his previous policy of promoting political allies within the armed services, turning instead to more able, if uninfluential, officers. But there was more to it than that, for regardless of the fighting qualities displayed by some ARVN units – notably the 1st and Marine Divisions around Hue – there can be little doubt that they depended heavily upon American firepower to survive. Air and naval strikes saved Hue, while at An Loc it was the destruction of seven NVA regiments by B-52s that marked the turning-point in the battle. In Kontum, the bombers even hit targets inside the city. If this awesome power had not been available the ARVN would probably have collapsed – a fact which boded ill for the future, when US aircraft and warships would not be on call.

Above: An NVA tank lies abandoned in a landscape stripped bare by repeated airstrikes. It was US airpower, provided by B-52 bombers supported by F-4 Phantom jets (left) that played a crucial part in helping the defenders of An Loc to weather the NVA siege.

aircraft buzzed over the town, things got hectic. As one A-37 pilot recalls:

'I had just completed a pass over An Loc when an NVA soldier comes on my radio as clear as could be. "Go away from Vietnam, American GI," the voice said. "The people do not want you." I wish he would have talked a little bit longer so I could have got a fix on him. It would have given me a great deal of pleasure to drop a 500-pounder on his head.'

'That place is like the Alamo'

In the face of this airborne defence, the attackers could neither consolidate nor extend their gains. They settled down for a siege, strengthening their anti-aircraft defences as they attempted to sever An Loc's aerial link with the outside world.

On the first day of battle, the South Vietnamese had been forced to end efforts to keep An Loc fed

Right: A lone ARVN trooper looses off with his M16 just outside An Loc. Below right: For this young South Vietnamese soldier, the war is over. He is being transferred to hospital, where his leg will be amputated. It was the stoicism and newly-discovered fighting spirit of the ARVN that enabled them to hold out for the three months that the siege lasted.

and watered using Chinooks. 'That place is like the Alamo,' said one US pilot. Another flier added, 'The NVA let one or two birds come in, then open up with heavy machine guns and blow the daylights out of the third.'

Supplies had to be sneaked in

With the airfield closed, the Vietnamese and the Americans were forced to try to supply the besieged town with low-altitude, low-speed drops by transports, mainly C-130s. The first five US Hercules swooping in were riddled with anti-aircraft fire, one being shot down. This method was then replaced with high-altitude radar-controlled parachute drops. Most of these drops landed in enemy territory and, by 23 April, the relieving forces had resorted to sneaking in and dropping supplies at night.

As the town struggled through its second week of siege, the relief force was getting near An Loc. The approach of this Asiatic variation on the 7th Cavalry prompted the NVA into launching their biggest artillery attack to date, on 27 April. Despite the proximity of the relief force, the communists still straddled Route 13 and the air remained the town's only supply route, a situation that better parachutes and guidance techniques improved every day.

The infantry swarmed down

Worried by the approach of the potential reinforcements, the NVA threw caution to the wind and began a renewed attempt to overrun An Loc through sheer weight of numbers. American gunships found that increased enemy flak forced them up to altitudes where they simply couldn't provide their formerly withering fire, and on 11 May the North Vietnamese forces launched a

Left: Exhaust fumes billowing, a B-52 launches into the sky on its way to An Loc. Despite the pin-point accuracy achieved by the B-52 pilots during the sustained bombing, the NVA attackers dug in on the front line managed to withstand the aerial barrage far longer than was thought possible. With napalm raining down upon their heads, they were still careful not to give away their position by returning fire.

major assault. Infantry, backed by a battalion of tanks and yet another artillery barrage, swarmed down.

In response, the Americans directed every B-52 in Southeast Asia against the attackers. Zeroing in with pre-planned bombing patterns, the awesome concentration of bombs shattered this attack and then beat off further attacks on 12 and 14 May. Shocked by this display of airborne firepower, the NVA moved away from An Loc in an attempt to block the progress of further relief columns. But their offensive was now broken – the ARVN had survived and An Loc had not been surrendered. The city was relieved for a second time on 9 June and communist forces were cleared from the surrounding countryside by 12 June. The siege of An Loc, the most protracted single episode of the NVA Easter 1972 offensive, during which perhaps half of the town's inhabitants and some 10,000 communist troops were killed, was declared over on 18 June.

Warning for the ARVN

Despite the fact that An Loc was held, Route 13 remained closed and by August all ARVN bases between An Loc and Chon Thanh, 30 kilometres to the South, had to be abandoned. The communist sanctuaries over the border remained intact and, although An Loc had been a great victory, it also revealed how much the ARVN remained dependent on US air support. The full consequences on this dependency were to emerge three years later, in April 1975.

The NVA Attack on An Loc

Snuol

CAMBODIA

Loc Ninh

Quan Loi

An Loc

Dong Xoai

Chon Tanh

Tay Ninh City

Lai Khe

Svay Rieng

Ben Cat

Route 1

Bien Hoa

LAOS

CAMBODIA

SOUTH VIETNAM

Saigon

SOUTH VIETNAM

Key
The North Vietnamese advance

US AIR SUPPORT

When NVA divisions invaded South Vietnam on 30 March 1972, they advanced beneath a protective umbrella of surface-to-air missiles (SAMs) and anti-aircraft guns. Combined with their decision to attack at a time of monsoon cloud, this was symbolic of their major fear: despite troop withdrawals and Vietnamization, the Americans still retained a formidable air capability in Southeast Asia.

It was a well-grounded fear, for President Nixon's immediate response to news of the invasion was to reinforce the squadrons already available, despatching extra USAF and Marine Corps units from Japan and South Korea to bases in Thailand and South Vietnam. By late May, more

than 700 American aircraft had been tasked to support the ARVN in its life-or-death struggle against the NVA.

These included 170 B-52s, each capable of dropping 24,500kg of bombs in a single mission. Flying from bases in Thailand and Guam in three-aircraft 'cells', the Stratofortresses were guided onto their target 'boxes' (each measuring one kilometre by three kilometres) by ground-based radar. The results were impressive. On 11/12 May, for example, during the battle for An Loc, B-52 cells arrived over the disputed area every 55 minutes for more than 30 consecutive hours, destroying NVA regiments as they massed for attacks on the beleaguered town.

Nor was this all, for despite the appalling flying conditions, more precise close-support aircraft – F-4s, F-105s, AC-119 and AC-130 gunships, and attack helicopters – also made an appearance, called in by O-1 Bird Dog or OV-10 Bronco FACs (Forward Air Controllers). Preceded by F-4 or F-105 'Wild Weasels' seeking out and destroying SAM sites, the attackers launched laser-guided, cluster and conventional bombs to devastating effect. In the northernmost provinces alone, between 1 April and 15 August, an estimated 285 NVA tanks were destroyed from the air. Against such a weight of airpower, the NVA stood little chance of decisive victory.

DISPOSABLE TANK DESTROYER

Light enough for the infantry to carry as an instant armour-piercing punch, the M72 LAW emerged as a valuable weapon in stopping NVA armour

Effectively a replacement for the 3.5in M20 'Super Bazooka', the M72 HEAT (High Explosive Anti-Tank) LAW ('Light Anti-armour Weapon') was a light-weight, one-shot, disposable rocket launcher, a miniature anti-tank weapon capable of penetrating 300mm of armour-plated steel.

Since it weighed in at just under two-and-a-half kilograms, a pair of M72s could easily be carried by an infantryman, and the weapon's theoretical ability to penetrate the thickest armour with its shaped charge made it useful baggage.

The LAW consisted of two concentric tubes. The outer, fibreglass tube carried the pressel-switch trigger mechanism and the pop-up sights. The inner, aluminium one contained the missile. To arm the weapon, the two covers were first removed from the open ends of the launcher. The two tubes were then pulled apart until they clicked into a single, elongated tube.

After the weapon had been sighted and the back-blast area of about 10 metres checked clear, the safety handle was pushed forward to the 'arm' position and the rocket released by pressing the trigger.

Fired from the shoulder, the rocket was fin stabilised in flight and detonated when impact with the target caused a piezo-electric crystal in the nose to send a charge to the fuze at the base of the warhead.

The M72 suffered from two drawbacks. Its small warhead, short range and clumsy sighting arrangement meant that the rocket had to be used with a marksmanship that only came through repeated firings. But because the LAW was employed as an 'extra' infantry weapon, troops generally received insufficient instruction on how to knock out tanks and destroy bunkers with it. A case in point was the weapon's combat debut against tanks — Soviet PT-76s — at Lang Vei in 1968. One tank was hit nine times, yet still came on.

The second problem was that when M72s had been stored in bunkers for any length of time, they had a tendency to fail due to corroded electrics. Though US troops usually received insufficient training with the LAW, the ARVN did tend to get the necessary instruction, and as a result of their better training were able to use the LAW to great effect against NVA armour during the 1972 Easter invasion.

Above: A grunt adorned with three M72 LAWs.

M72 66mm HEAT ROCKET LIGHT ANTI-ARMOUR WEAPON

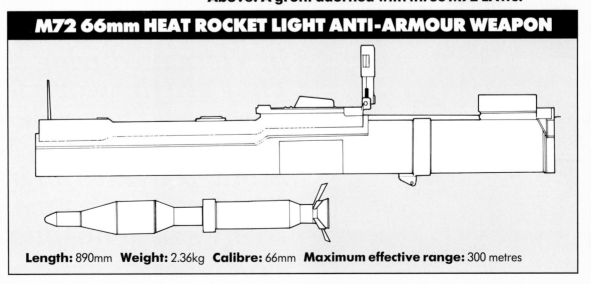

Length: 890mm **Weight:** 2.36kg **Calibre:** 66mm **Maximum effective range:** 300 metres

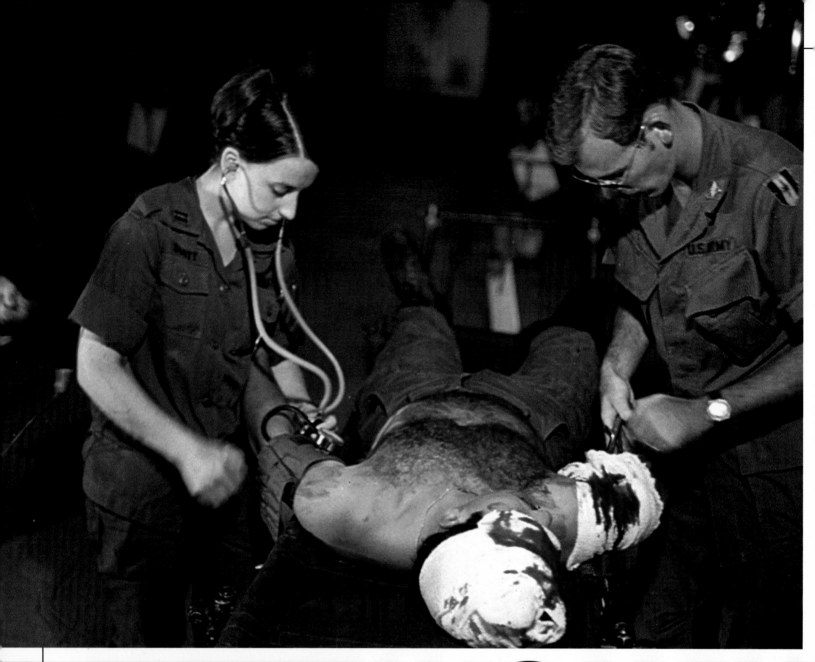

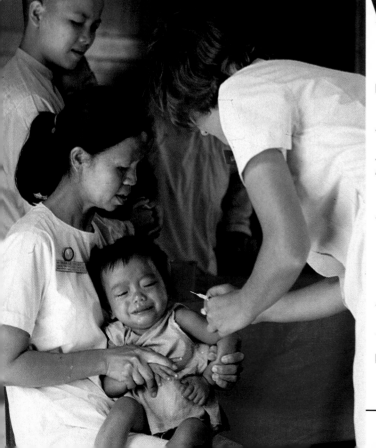

WOMEN

Almost 10,000 women served in Vietnam during the war. They are the war's forgotten heroines. The president of the Vietnam Veterans, Mary Stout, provides an insight into life –and death – in one of the Army's field hospitals

Left: The wounds of war. Covered in blood, and with bandages swathing his head and the remains of his right arm, this GI is in good hands. However, medical aid was not confined to the military, nor was the nursing staff exclusively American. Below left: A British nurse inoculates a Vietnamese child in Saigon. Below: Working against time in the cramped conditions of a field hospital.

1972

Vietnam was the place where my friends had gone, my friends from Fort Ord. The nurses I lived and served with, the young officers I had met at social gatherings at the Officers' Club and night spots in Monterey and Carmel. Vietnam was the place my father asked me, his only daughter and youngest child, not to volunteer to go to. Vietnam was the place that needed my skills to care for wounded young Americans. The call to Vietnam was irresistible, and so I went.

The 2d Surgical Hospital of the 1st Air Cavalry Division, in the mountains at Camp Radcliff, An Khe, was a conglomeration of prefab 'Quonset' huts and wooden buildings that housed the wards, emergency room, operating rooms, pharmacy, laboratory, X-ray, mess hall and headquarters. It was surrounded by tents of various sizes that housed the staff. There were seven other women in my tent. Each of us had a six by 10ft cubical, separated by bamboo mats hung like walls from the inner wooden frame of the tent. A metal cot with mosquito netting, a narrow wall locker and anything else we could scrounge, build or have our parents send us, made up the furnishings of each little room. 'Keep the mosquito net tucked in all the time' the nurses told me. 'It keeps the bugs from crawling in during the day and the rats out at night.' There were some specimens of the bugs kept in jars in the lab; centipedes eight inches long and kadydids with wings as large as my splayed hand.

We worked eight-hour shifts for the most part, and I was assigned to various units: intensive care, post-op and medical wards. Our wards were full, but the pace seemed slow and we had time to learn new skills in the caring for battle casualties.

The doctors were doing cleft lip and palate repairs on Vietnamese children, and skin grafts on Vietnamese burn victims. I spent my free days going to neighbouring villages on the Medical Civilian Aid Program (MEDCAP), visiting other hospitals and friends in Pleiku and Quin Nuon, doing laundry and writing letters home.

The wards were full

Six months after I arrived we moved the hospital to Chu Lai, on the coast in I Corps. We were housed in wooden buildings with screens on the outside – no need for mosquito nets – but An Khe was a vacation compared to Chu Lai. For me, the move changed the whole face of the war. We had gone as part of the Americal Division. It was around 105 degrees when we were setting up the hospital and, within a couple of days, the wards were full and we were on 12-hour shifts. After a few weeks I asked to be assigned permanently to the intensive care/recovery room. In my memory, the ward will always look enormous. In reality, however, it never contained more than 12 intensive care and six recovery beds.

Many soldiers needed amputations

Sometimes we opened another small ward next to intensive care. This turned a room normally used for post-op into another intensive care unit when we could no longer hold the numbers in our regular unit. Our job was to get the patients stabilized enough to move them to a post-operative ward or medical ward, or else prepare them for evacuation to another hospital. That usually took about three to five days.

Many of the soldiers needed amputations. Others had large gaping wounds that had to be cleaned four to six times a day. The wounds were

IN THE NAM

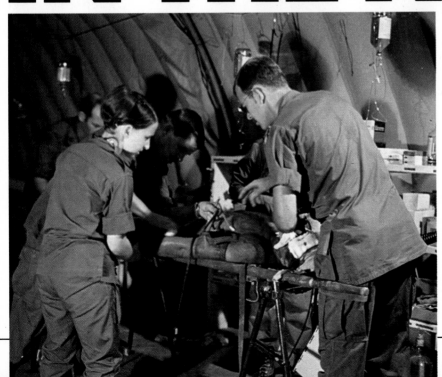

left open to prevent infections, and we had to give massive doses of antibiotics and morphine to ease the pain. Everyone had intravenous fluids. There were lots of chest tubes, catheters, blood infusions and nasal oxygen tubes to be watched. Patients went into shock and had blood reactions on a regular basis. Somehow we knew how to take care of all that. When patients 'got shocky' the team went into action – blocks under the foot of the bed, blood ordered, doctor notified, constant attention given. If there was a cardiac arrest we started resuscitation in a heartbeat. We were all able to save many lives.

The soldiers always told me that, in the field, the guys said that if you got to the hospital you had it made. Maybe that's why it was always such a shock to lose someone. I knew what the wounded had been through to make it to our ward. I knew what the medics in the field did to save their lives. I was aware of the kind of chances Medevac helicopter crews took to get them out of the field. I spent three weeks in the emergency room and I knew first-hand the quick reactions and heroic work of the triage teams. I witnessed the dedication and expertise of the surgical teams. At least 15 people had done all that was humanly possible to keep each soldier we got alive, and so any death touched all of them. But none of us had enough time to grieve when a man didn't make it through – there were many others who needed our care.

I hoped their families knew that we had cared and that we had done our best to save their sons. We tried to make sure that no-one died alone.

There were just too many patients
The wounded soldiers were men to be proud of. Their spirit was incredible and they seemed to care more about their buddies than they did about themselves. They worried about the guys they had left in the field and asked about the patient in the next bed. The ones with no feet worried about the ones with no legs. And even when THEY were in pain, they asked ME how I was doing.

I remember the generator going day and night and bathing the wards in constant electric light. We tried to bring a soothing darkness to the wards when we could, but most nights there were just too many patients who needed constant attention, and never enough individual lamps to provide the lighting. Many men remember the moaning above all else. I, however, do not. Perhaps, just like a mother can distinguish the cry of pain in her child from other cries, I became attuned to the sounds of distress.

The artery was pumping blood out
One evening as I was filling out some paperwork at the nurses' desk I heard a moan, the special kind. Right across from the desk was a young soldier, Steve, who had a very bad leg wound. The guys who brought him out from surgery told us that in the emergency room he had begged the doctors not to take his leg off. They had put in an arterial graft, but were very worried that it might not hold because there was so much damage. Steve was positioned right across from the nurses' desk so we could keep a close eye on him. Several days after the initial surgery, he was taken back and a new graft put in because the first one was leaking. Again, he had begged them not to take his leg.

It was a full week later when I heard that special moan. I was worried. Steve was so pale. 'What's wrong Steve?' I asked. 'I don't know Lieutenant, I

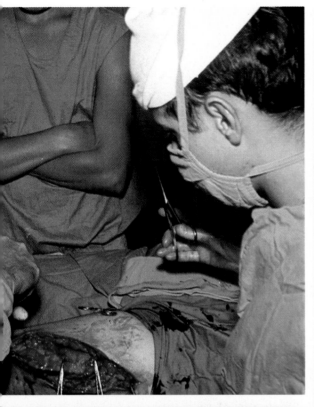

Left: A nurse attempts to bring succour and relief to the inhabitants of war-torn Saigon. Above left: Surgeons work patiently and confidently on a dangerous chest wound. Above: Wounded US personnel await airlift in a USAF medical evacuation plane at Cam Ranh Bay Air Base. According to recent statistics, over 150,000 US troops were hospitalized for wounds during the war. It is to the credit of the medical staff that the majority survived.

don't feel good.' His skin was white, cold and clammy and his pulse was weak. I threw back the blanket only to see a huge pool of blood under Steve's leg. As I tore off the dressing, my suspicions were confirmed – the new graft had blown and the artery in Steve's thigh was pumping blood out with each of his weakening heartbeats. I put my bare hand in his leg and pinched off the artery as I called for shock blocks, blood, his doctor and a corpsman to put on gloves and take my place.

'I don't want to die!'

Even with all the activity, the ward seemed strangely calm. I kept talking to Steve, telling him it was going to be okay. Silently I was saying to myself 'Don't die, don't die!' As the surgical team rolled Steve's bed through the doors to the operating room for the third time, I heard him say, 'Take it off, Doc, I don't want to die.' A few days later Steve was wondering what it was going to be like living without his leg. I hope he made it.

There are so many young men to remember and wonder about. Johnny Darling, however, is the only patient whose full name I remember. He was in my fiance's company out in the field when he tripped a mine and lost both his feet. I tried to get him to eat carrots, telling him my dad had always told me they would make my hair red. Johnny didn't seem to think red hair looked too great on black men. A couple of years back I talked to another nurse who was there with me. She's like me – still wondering what happened to all those guys who passed through our wards.

A CARRIER AT

1972

You may not be the guy who sits in the cockpit, but you see that airplane as your baby. And you can't loosen up until she's home

At 0200 hours I'm kicked out of my bunk by a buddy. Deep inside the ship I ignore the cold and thrash into my utilities while others sleep. The USS *America* (CVA-66) churns through the Gulf of Tonkin on Yankee Station, turning into the wind for a night launch. Even in the bowels of the ship, where my world consists of an 8x4 bunk, wall locker and toilet kit, you can feel the mighty ship pressing its continual contest with the cruel sea. You can hear the indefinable sounds of a carrier underway at night – a faint, distant creaking, the barely audible purr of turbines, a clacking from a faulty air conditioner.

A dozen other sailors are in motion around me, using the head, shaving, performing that wake-up ritual of dousing your face with cold water and shaking it off. It's incredible how these men perform this routine in a ghostly near-silence, out of deference to those who sleep at this hour.

I'm an E-4, an assistant plane captain on an A-7C Corsair attack aircraft of squadron VA-86, the 'Sidewinders', one of six squadrons in the *America*'s embarked air wing.

We're on a Westpac (West Pacific) cruise which will keep us away from our home base at Norfolk, Virginia, for five months. It is September 1972 and the *America* is involved in the Linebacker bombing campaign against North Vietnam.

Working round the clock

My job is straightforward. I'm to assist Petty Officer Engels, crew chief for A-7C Corsair number 156799, in getting the plane ready for launch and in recovering it after the mission. If time permits, I'll perform maintenance/check-up work on other Corsairs belonging to the squadron.

The pilot of our plane tonight is Lieutenant J.G. Murphy. He'll be number two in a two-plane division hurtling aloft after dark to search for Wiblicks. That's a WBLC or Water-Borne Logistics Craft. Much of the war is being fought by daylight against targets deep in the enemy's homeland, but the *America*'s is a round-the-clock

WAR

operation and it's important to harry the boats infiltrating supplies into South Vietnam.

I leave my billet (which I share with 88 other sailors – our bunks are stacked three deep), climb up two levels, and reach the flight deck via the passageway between the ready rooms. Known as 'Broadway', it leads to the outside iron staircase on the starboard side of the ship. Tonight we won't have to bring any aircraft up from the workshop below decks. Our Corsairs are already in a 'six pack' on the flight deck near the carrier's island. Working with flashlights (attached around our necks by cord, lest they become a hazard on the crowded deck), Engels and I perform a walk-around check of airplane 156799, looking for a sign that anything might be wrong.

By God, that plane is mine

You have to understand the fierce pride of personal ownership that I get when I'm working on old 799. Sure, it has the pilot's name stencilled on one canopy rail and my boss Engels' name, as crew-chief, on the other. But by God, that airplane is *mine*. Like every man who works on a naval aircraft, I feel a keen sense of personal responsibility, knowing that the pilot's life may depend on how well I keep the Corsair flying.

We check everything – control surfaces, cockpit, instruments, air intake...you name it. It's as if 799 is being scrutinised under a microscope.

This plane's 'gripe sheet' indicates a persistent problem with the electrical system, so I get an electrician who checks it over and pronounces it okay. We review the bomb-load of six 600lb Mark 81 bombs hung under the Corsair's wings. At 0300, while we're completing a readiness check on the A-7C, the pilot, Lieutenant Murphy, is getting a weather briefing and being told that if he can't

The busy routine on USS *America*. Below: The hectic flight deck. Below far left: Arming up. Below centre: An A-7 Corsair blasts into the sky.

find a Wiblick he ought to keep his eyes open for a Luctar. That's Navy slang for a lucrative target.

The A-7C eats people

In these pre-dawn hours, a time of wind and cold and discomfort, our job is gruelling physical work. Once it becomes time to start the engines we have to be extremely careful. The droop-mouthed Corsair – with its low air intake and no grille between inlet and engine – eats people. More than any other naval aircraft, our A-7C can ingest anything from a monkey wrench to a human being. It can be, and has been, fatal to the careless deck hand.

Soon pilot Murphy is in the airplane, starting up, taxiing forward to position himself on the catapult for launch. My work on 'our' airplane is done for the moment but other hard-working deckhands attach the launch bridle, check the weight of the aircraft, and finally use *America*'s massive steam catapults to send Murphy and his flight leader slamming into the sky. As I watch the two Corsairs climb towards the North Vietnamese coast I reflect upon all the men around me who help to get them there...

The men behind the scenes

To keep a carrier air wing in combat you need more than mechanics, electronics technicians, fuel handlers and armament specialists. You also need to keep alive this floating city from which aviators come and go. This takes food, drink, a laundry, a dry cleaners, air conditioning, communications. The Hollywood stars of an attack carrier like the *America* are the brightly-clad deck crewmen who risk their lives daily to attach a catapult bridle to a revved-up Intruder, or who manoeuvre Phantoms and Corsairs around the crowded deck in a blurred cacophony of noise and motion. But don't ever tell me that we could run

the war without a 14-hour day from that crewcut Texan kid who works the ovens in the bakery, or the sweat and toil of that skinny black guy from Chicago who types up the ship's drill bulletin, the Plan of the Day. The cook, the tailor and the typist may not get into the credits like a missile guidance technician or a catapult launch chief do, but it takes an intense commitment by every last man-jack aboard the 1047-foot, 60,300-ton *America* to keep the carrier and its air wing in the war.

And how about the medics? Too often, we've had to pull a pilot out of a bullet-riddled aircraft. Some guy suffering from a gut wound, a spraying by hot metal fragments, or grievous burns. The medical technicians and doctors who labour on our wounded deserve all the credit they can get. They were particularly important on those occasions during the Vietnam war when a carrier at sea was decimated by a lethal fire. It happened to the *Oriskany* and later to the *Enterprise*.

There's no time to worry

Worth thinking about. Anything is worth thinking about to escape from my worries. I'm racked by the gut-wrenching knowledge that *my* airplane and *my* pilot are now up there in the black night, closing with the enemy. Did I check that instrument panel warning light carefully enough yesterday? Did we miss anything in our walk-around check this dark morning? Should we have worried more about the electrical system? We want Lieutenant Murphy to go into battle with the best damn airplane on the carrier...

But there's no time to waste thinking, not on a carrier. With Engels and some others, I join a work party to get the hangar at the 0-4 level ship-shape. By 0600 we are working in a yellow glare, stowing gear, moving aircraft around, cleaning up, tackling an unexpected maintenance problem with

Above: Clouds of black smoke rise from the burning flight deck of the nuclear powered aircraft carrier, USS *Enterprise*. The risk of accidental fire was a constant and lethal threat to carrier crews, and one that claimed many lives. Above right: Aviation ordnancemen roll 500lb bombs across the flight deck to waiting attack aircraft prior to another bombing mission over North Vietnam. Right centre: Relaxing amidst the instruments of death. Crew members calmly eat their dinners in a mess hall that is also being used as a bomb store.

another plane. There's no more time to worry about Murphy.

Aboard *America* are a ship's complement of 2800 men (150 officers and 2650 enlisted) plus 2150 in the carrier air wing: a total of 4950 souls.

A chief looks after his men

The officers? Well, the skipper is in charge. No doubt about that. The skipper of a carrier is always a naval aviator and senior captain who has previously commanded a smaller vessel. The XO (Executive Officer) may be a captain or senior commander, and he's the 'hard ass' who whips things together and makes them work. Perhaps third in importance is the Air Operations Officer, called the Air Boss. He looks down at *America*'s six-acre deck from 'Pri-Fly', atop the steel island, and makes decisions about the movement, launch and recovery of aircraft to keep the choreography of the flight deck functioning smoothly. When an Alpha Strike of 28 to 36 aircraft is returning to the carrier, several perhaps with battle damage, at the same time that a combat air patrol must be launched, the Air Boss sorts out the priorities and

Below: An assistant catapult officer on the USS *Oriskany* gives the ready signal to an F-8 Crusader.

decides who moves first.

Then there are department heads. But for us in the wing, the two most important officers are our CAG (carrier air wing commander) and our squadron CO. Every one of these men, all the way down the line, is a seasoned professional.

The *real* glue that holds the ship together is the chief. A chief petty officer may be a grizzled old salt or a modern-day technocrat. Either way, he swings his weight. You screw up, he'll hang you. You do it right, he'll make sure you get some recognition. A chief watches out for his men. One hard-working Corsair wrench monkey desperately needed leave to go home and straighten out a bad marital problem. Our chief arranged the trip by applying a rather liberal interpretation of the regulations. In return, he retained a good worker.

It would be nice to have the luxury of going down to 'Combat' (the *America*'s Combat Information Center, also called CIC) to listen to radio traffic and find out how Murphy is doing in my 'personal' A-7C Corsair. No such luxury is permitted. We're busy working on other airplanes until the word comes that Murphy is on final approach

Above: Careful where you lay your head. Below: The strain shows after a mission.

and has 'called the ball'. This means that he has lined up with the light on the cambered deck (the 'ball') which tells him that he's on a glide path for a perfect 'trap', or carrier landing. We scramble up to deck to watch him land.

Checking for bullet-holes

Murphy makes a nice approach in the dim light that precedes dawn, tailhook hanging down. He catches the number three wire and comes slamming to the deck. All of his bombs are gone. We learn later that he and his division leader located some North Vietnamese sampans along the coast, dropped flares, and bombed 'em. There was only light gunfire from the boats which apparently missed, but we still have the job of checking over every inch of the Corsair for bullet holes. We don't even get a chance to talk with the grinning Murphy as he heads for his debrief. As a gesture of thanks to his plane captain, he swats Engels on the behind, then trundles off with his flight gear.

Murphy's mission was, for me, only the start of the day. At about 0700 we'll prepare the Corsair for another mission. Murphy may fly her again – two combat missions a day is not unusual – or another pilot may take her. This time, it may be another two-ship mission or it may be an Alpha Strike to Hanoi...

We'll be at it about another six hours. Finally, at about 1400, I'll be free for a meal and then some sleep before waking up to start over again.

The all-important mail

During the line periods our life on this ship is one of almost completely uninterrupted work. The North Vietnamese have not actually challenged our fleet, not yet at least, so we are not always at full General Quarters, but we're constantly aware of the war and there are few breaks. The big event is the twice-weekly arrival of the carrier onboard delivery C-1A cargo plane which brings the all-important mail from home. Perhaps today I'll be able to grab a few minutes to finish a tape I'm sending home and get it on the next outgoing. But there'll be little time for other pleasures. The war continues...

A B-52 may pack the firepower, but it can't shake off an incoming SAM. With four engines out, it's your job to nurse the aircraft back to base

EYE-WITNESS

John D. Mize, now a retired major living in Rapid City, South Dakota, believes that he survived his mission over Hanoi because of providence. His stongest wish is for the public to recognize the men who fought with him during the 'Eleven Day War'.

LINEBACKER

1973/4

During the 'Eleven Day War' of 18-29 December 1972, more than one-third of Strategic Air Command's B-52 force was pitted against North Vietnam in a costly round-the-clock campaign which ultimately pressured Hanoi into negotiating a conclusion to America's longest war. Captain John D. Mize and the crew of B-52D Stratofortress 56-0599, assigned to the 307th Strategic Wing at U-Tapao, Thailand, were among the participants in this campaign, codenamed Linebacker II.

Mize's B-52 bored towards Hanoi on the night of 27 December. The pilot and members of his crew could see six or seven SAMs whooshing past in the dark sky like roman candles.

From his lonely berth in the rear of the B-52, Tech Sergeant Peter E. Whalen, the bomber's fire control operator (FCO), or gunner, peered out. He described it later: 'When the SAMs come up through the clouds, you can see a bright glow as the rocket fire reflects on the cloud. The clouds magnify the light and make the SAM look bigger than it really is.'

By this time, North Vietnam's defences were confused and ineffective. No MiG dared to venture into the night. In kneejerk fashion, the SAMs were being fired in salvoes but were wildly inaccurate because of what the bombing had done to

Top centre: A fighter pilot gives the all clear. Right: Hi tech killing power descends towards rural Vietnam, courtesy of Strategic Air Command.

their radars. As his B-52 approached its target – one of the SAM sites ringing Hanoi – Captain Mize saw no fewer than 15 SAMs darting around wildly in the sky.

Like other Stratofortressses in the 'cell' (a formation of three ships), Mize's B-52 sent its load of 84 500lb bombs falling towards the target. A few seconds later, a lucky-SAM hit defied all logic and sent shrapnel hurtling around the bomber's cockpit area. Flying shards of steel tore into Captain Mize's body at several points, bringing sudden pain and bleeding in the left thigh, lower left leg and right hand.

More shrapnel pummelled the tail of the great bomber, wounding gunner Whalen. The sudden

damage knocked out the electrical system, plunging radar navigator Captain Bill North and navigator Lieutenant Bill Robinson into darkness. Both were in the bowels of the aircraft unable to see out. North, too, was cut up by flying metal.

The impact of the SAM 'near miss' threw pilot Mize forward in his narrow steel seat and sent the bomber lurching to the side. On the instrument panel, engine fire-warning lights spelled trouble. The Stratofortress dipped and began plunging towards the earth, falling several thousand feet in a few seconds. Captain Mize struggled with his controls and found that three of the eight engines were out.

It took a near-superhuman effort for the badly

Top left: An RB-66 Destroyer sits at the apex of the 'V' and guides in the Phantoms. Bursting with electronics, the RB-66 made for accurate bombing. Above left: Tooling up an A-6 with full metal destruction.

1973/4

Above: Ready to play its part in Operation Linebacker, a Crusader strains at the carrier's catapult. This Christmas the US was intent on giving the North Vietnamese everything it had.

injured Mize to bring the giant Stratofortress back into level flight. Most of the power boost on the controls was gone, and it was the bulky Mize's sheer will against the 185,000lb bomber.

The pilot ran a hurried check of his crew to determine their injuries, grateful that the intercom was still functioning. After a quick check of battle damage, Mize decided that he could keep the crippled aircraft in the sky long enough to find a safer location for the crew to eject. He was talking with Robinson about their position and about alerting rescue forces when a fourth engine began to die on the port side of the B-52.

Mize later acknowledged that he was not the first man to fly an eight-engined B-52 on four

engines, but his modesty overlooked the fact that all four lost engines were on one side of the bomber, all four good engines on the other.

Furthermore, almost none of the bomber's equipment was working properly. With half of his automatic navigation equipment blown away, Robinson had to use airspeed and distance-travelled calculations to aid Mize in nursing the B-52 toward Thailand.

The pre-deployed rescue forces were fully alerted and a C-130 flying command post met Captain Mize's bomber near the border of North Vietnam and Laos. By now, the condition of the aircraft had worsened. Flames were spreading along the fuselage and the crew were making a

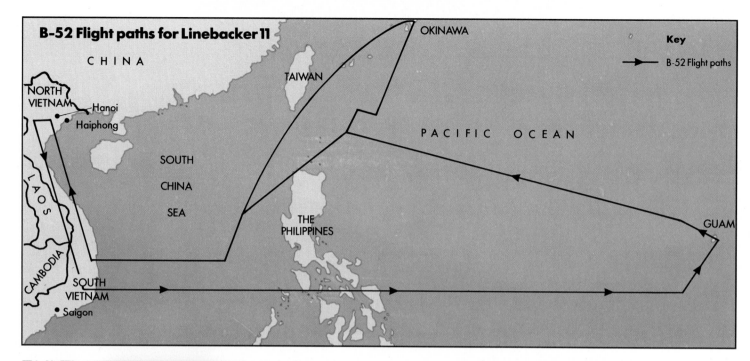

B-52 Flight paths for Linebacker II

CHINA

NORTH VIETNAM
Hanoi
Haiphong

LAOS

CAMBODIA

SOUTH VIETNAM
Saigon

SOUTH CHINA SEA

TAIWAN

OKINAWA

THE PHILIPPINES

PACIFIC OCEAN

GUAM

Key
→ B-52 Flight paths

1973/4

final check of their ejection procedure. It looked like time to get out. But Robinson cautioned Mize that they were over jagged mountain ridges. If they could continue another 30 miles they would have flat paddy fields to come down in.

With four engines and electrical power only for the cabin lights and radio, Captain Mize continued to struggle for altitude and sought to reach the safer location recommended by Robinson.

Altitude was of critical importance. Mize flew the airplane by sheer brute force, descending about 1500ft to pick up airspeed, then climbing 1000ft. More than an hour after dropping his bombs near Hanoi, Mize finally reached hospitable terrain over Thailand.

A battered bomber

The situation then deteriorated rapidly. The bomb-bay door fell open, one landing gear started cycling maddeningly up and down. Mize felt a kind of death throe run through the giant airplane. He ordered the crew to eject.

Four men threw themselves out into the night, including co-pilot Captain Terrance Gauthers. Bill Robinson, however, did not eject – he pulled the handle but nothing happened.

'Climb out!' shouted Mize. He wanted Robinson to jump through the hole which had been opened up by Bill North's ejection seat. Robinson got up to do this, and no longer could the two men communicate by radio. Captain Mize continued to wait, postponing his own ejection until he could find out if the navigator had gotten out safely.

There was now a deadly serious waiting game in which, no longer able to talk to Robinson, Mize could only attempt to retain control of the B-52 long enough for the navigator to jump. By now, the only lighting in the B-52 was in the forward cabin. Flames were spreading from the wing. Captain Mize continued to struggle with the controls but

Right: 'A Big Ugly Fat Fucker' gets unleashed in the east. When a B-52 was overhead, you wouldn't know about it until you heard the whistle of the bombs.

the bomber was falling relentlessly.

Robinson had, unknown to the pilot, leaned into space and opened his parachute manually. Rescue forces had set up a string of aircraft and helicopters which followed the path of the crippled B-52, setting up a mass pick-up for the men ejecting from the bomber.

As the electrical system in the cabin finally went out, Mize knew he had no choice. Certain now that Robinson had gone, he ejected.

In the night and cold of the Thai jungle, helicopters homed in on the URC-64 bleeper radios that were carried by each crewman: all six men from the bomber being rescued within 15 minutes of Captain Mize's ejection. The captain's struggle during the final moments in the life of the B-52, and especially his effort to save crewmate Robinson, were reflected in Mize's eventual award of the Air Force Cross, the second highest American decoration for valour. As the only SAC recipient of this award in the Vietnam conflict, Captain Mize was given the honour by General John C. Meyer, Commander-in-Chief, SAC.

THE LINEBACKER RAIDS

On 8 May 1972, in response to continued NVA attacks on the South, President Nixon suspended peace negotiations in Paris and ordered the release of American airpower over North Vietnam. Under the codename Linebacker, Northern ports were mined and there was sustained bombing of military targets throughout North Vietnam, with the exception of a 40-48km 'buffer zone' along the Chinese border and, initially, a 16km 'restricted zone' around Hanoi and Haiphong.

The Americans made full use of electronic devices to disrupt air-defence systems and were able to achieve impressive pin-point destruction using television- and laser-guided 'smart' bombs. When the bombing was suspended on 23 October, over 41,000 aircraft sorties had been flown and 155,548 tons of bombs dropped. The movement of supplies through Northern ports had virtually ceased, the rail link with China had been severed, marshalling yards, oil-storage facilities, SAM sites and airfields had all been hit. As the North Vietnamese were willing to resume negotiations, Linebacker seemed to have worked.

But a peace settlement proved elusive and, on 18 December, Nixon ordered a new air campaign to break the deadlock. For the next 12 days (except for Christmas Day), US aircraft pounded targets in and around Hanoi/Haiphong in an operation known (unofficially) as Linebacker II. For the first time, B-52s were used. Losses were not light – 26 aircraft were shot down, including 15 B-52s – but the results were devastating. When Nixon recalled the bombers on 30 December (by which time they had dropped a further 20,370 tons of bombs), the North had lost over 1000 dead, its internal communications and electrical power grid had been disrupted and its air force had ceased to exist. On 8 January 1973, negotiations were resumed.

Far left: During Linebacker II, the groundcrews broke their backs, often putting in 24-hour stints to keep their planes in bombs. The North replied with 1000 SAM launches and as many MiGs as they could get up. Above: The legacy of Linebacker. B-52 crews would rarely see what happened after they opened their bomb doors. From several miles up in the sky the battered North must have seemed a remote land.

CHAPTER 100

SMART

BOMBS

Ordinary bombs just weren't good enough, so Uncle Sam set the lab boys to work on a new generation of high-tech explosives such as the Walleye

The spirit of Dr Frankenstein was at work in Vietnam. By the time the Americans called a halt to the bombing of North Vietnam, in January 1973, he had breathed life into several bombs that could see and think and manoeuvre clumsily, and were powerful enough to strike terror in the hearts of the population of a small country somewhere in Southeast Asia.

The problem was that most bombs were dumb. After you dropped them out of the plane they fell straight down and, in operations like Rolling Thunder, they too often did little more than churn the bomb craters made the last time the B-52s came over. After 873 US sorties with dumb bombs – in which 95 American planes were lost – the Thanh Hoa Bridge in North Vietnam remained stubbornly intact. So Dr Frankenstein's laboratory came up with the smart bomb. And in 1972, a single eight-plane squadron armed with laser-guided 'intelligent' bombs attacked and the heavily defended bridge came tumbling down.

To make a smart bomb, you take the body of a dumb bomb and give it a brain. The first intelligent bombs were made in World War II, but with the advance in miniaturized electronics they came into their own in Vietnam.

Laser-guided destruction

The US Navy's Walleye glide-bomb was the first. It was a standard 850lb high-explosive bomb with a TV camera in its nose. The camera could be used to lock the bomb onto the target before it was dropped, then, using its tail fins, steer the bomb down its glidepath as it fell.

Commander Homer Smith was the first man to use one in combat. In an attack on the NVA barracks at Sam Son, Smith watched on his cockpit TV screen as the bomb homed in on its target and plunged in through a window.

Above left: One intelligent bomb could do the work of countless 'dumb' bombs – it only takes one hit in the right place to bring down a bridge. Left: A Phantom drops a Paveway laser-guided bomb (LGB). The centre-line fuel tank obscures a second LGB. Above: The top plane is carrying a Paveway laser-guided bomb under its right wing and the Pave Knife laser designation-pod under its left.

The problem was that locking the Walleye onto its target took about 15 seconds of straight and level flight before the pilot could drop the bomb and turn away. This was a gift for the anti-aircraft gunners and Walleye-equipped aircraft suffered an average of four times as many hits from anti-aircraft fire as conventional 'dumb' bombers. In addition, early Walleyes were found to be too small to be really effective against hardened targets.

The US Air Force preferred laser-guided bombs (LGBs) to the Navy's electro-optical guidance systems, and they dropped some 25,000 Paveway LGBs during the war. First introduced in 1968, the Paveway made use of standard dumb bombs, to which a laser seeker unit and a steering wing assembly were added. The seeker unit detected light reflected off the target when it was illuminated by a laser designator. The bomb then steered itself onto the target with the rear-mounted fins. The laser target designator could be either ground-based or airborne. If it was airborne it could be mounted on the attack plane or another aircraft.

Paveway was usually carried by an F-4 Phantom fitted with the Pave Knife designation-pod as well as the Paveway bomb itself. Pave Knife was fitted with a low-light TV camera system which would work in daylight or at night. The operator used this to identify the target on a 5in Sony display in the rear cockpit and fix the laser designator on it before the bomb was dropped. This system gave LGBs a circular area of probability of 30ft. That meant that 50 per cent of the time the bomb would land within 30ft of the target. Conventional dumb bombs had a 420ft circular area probability. It was later claimed that in attacks on night-time truck traffic on the Ho Chi Minh Trail by specially equipped B-57s, 80 per cent of the laser-guided bombs dropped landed within 15ft of their aiming point – even in total darkness!

Fire and forget

But Frankenstein really began turning uncomfortably in his grave when the Pentagon scientists put a computer brain into their smart bombs. They mounted a Walleye camera on a 2000lb bomb and used it as the eyes of a mini computer. Once the pilot aimed the camera at the target, the computer mapped the pattern of light and dark around it in its memory. Then it used this map to

519

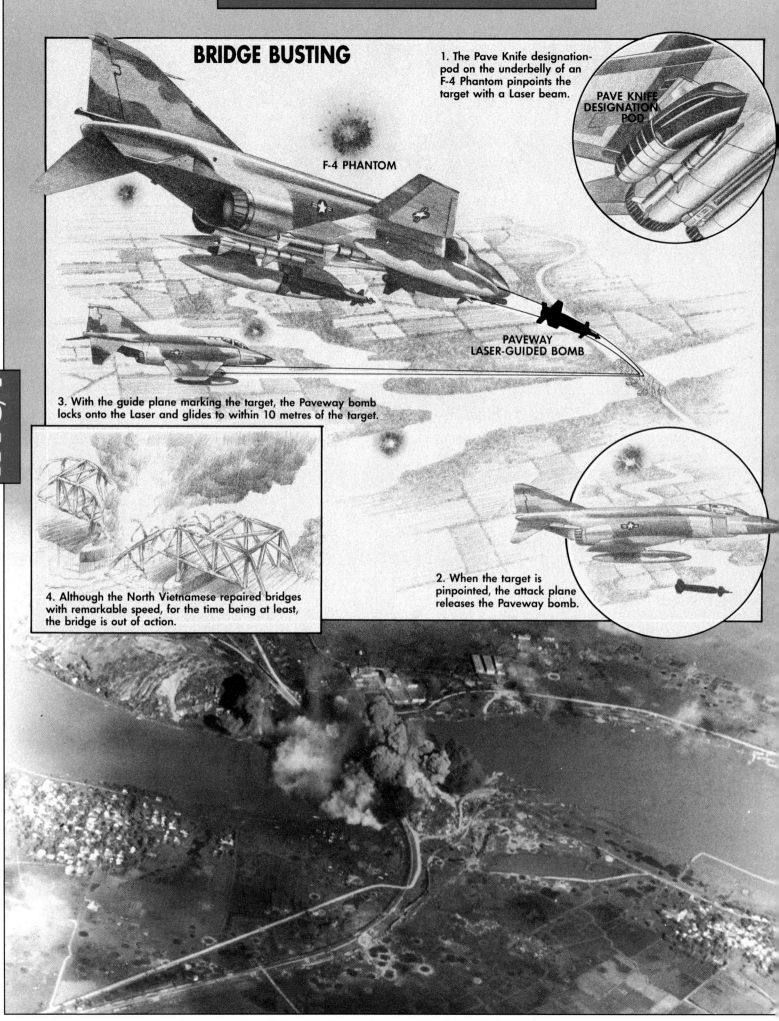

BRIDGE BUSTING

1. The Pave Knife designation-pod on the underbelly of an F-4 Phantom pinpoints the target with a Laser beam.

PAVE KNIFE DESIGNATION POD

F-4 PHANTOM

PAVEWAY LASER-GUIDED BOMB

3. With the guide plane marking the target, the Paveway bomb locks onto the Laser and glides to within 10 metres of the target.

2. When the target is pinpointed, the attack plane releases the Paveway bomb.

4. Although the North Vietnamese repaired bridges with remarkable speed, for the time being at least, the bridge is out of action.

1973/4

guide the bomb onto the target, while the pilot headed for home. It was, in effect, a 'fire-and forget' bomb. By 1972, Walleyes could glide to their targets from as far away as 32 miles and could be fitted to virtually any American combat plane.

Nixon's designation for the renewed bombing in May 1972, 'Linebacker', was apt. Frankenstein's monster sure had the build for that position. But like any American footballer, even Boris Karloff in bolts and big boots would need the rest of the team around him. Not even remotely-targeted bombs were enough to keep US pilots and planes safe over the defences of North Vietnam. Planes certainly could not venture out alone. During the

THANH HOA BRIDGE

Completed in 1964, the Thanh Hoa road and railway bridge, spanning the Song Ma river to the south of Hanoi, was a key target in American efforts to destroy the internal communications system of North Vietnam. As early as 3 April 1965, as part of Operation Rolling Thunder, 46 USAF F-105 Thunderchiefs, armed with Bullpup air-to-ground missiles and 750lb general-purpose bombs, flew against the bridge, but without success. Despite scoring hits on the superstructure, the American pilots could only scorch the paintwork.

With a massive central pillar of reinforced concrete and heavy steel trusses set into hills on either bank, the bridge – known to the Vietnamese as the Ham Rung (Dragon's Jaw) – proved too tough a target to be destroyed using existing 'dumb' weapons.

Between 1965 and 1968 more than a hundred attacks were carried out, initially by the USAF and then, from June 1965, by US Navy aircraft when Thanh Hoa became part of the Navy's Route Package IV. The raids were expensive – Thanh Hoa rapidly became one of the most heavily defended locations in North Vietnam – but the best that could be achieved was a temporary closure while repairs took place. When Rolling Thunder ended, the Dra-

gon's Jaw was still open.

What was needed was a guarantee of pin-point bombing accuracy; this did not emerge until 1972, when Thanh Hoa reappeared on the target lists as part of Operation Linebacker. By then, the Americans had developed TV- and laser-guided 'smart' bombs and these were used to devastating effect.

On 27 April F-4 Phantoms of the 8th Tactical Fighter Wing scored a number of hits. On 13 May they returned to finish the job. As the western span of the bridge collapsed under the impact of 15 laser-guided bombs, the toughest target in Vietnam finally went down.

Linebacker missions, what the North Vietnamese dubbed the American 'air pirates' set sail in giant convoys, a strike package which gave the bombers air-to-air refuelling, airborne rescue facilities, fighter escorts, an airborne command and control capability, and electronic warfare defences. The Linebacker package mustered for an attack on the Paul Doumer bridge and the Yen Vien railway yard on 10 May 1972 contained no less than 85 support aircraft. These included 24 involved directly in providing electronic warfare cover. All this to sustain just 32 F-4 strike aircraft.

Chaff, echo and jam

The first aim of this operation was to knock out the Spoonrest and Fansong radars used to control the North Vietnamese anti-aircraft and SAM missile defences. The bombers and their 30-strong fighter cover each carried one or more radar jammers mounted in pods either in the Phantoms' forward Sparrow bays or slung under the inboard wing pylons. There were eight F-4 chaff bombers which dropped strips of aluminium foil or metalized fibreglass to further confuse the radar with false echoes, 12 F-105 Wild Weasel defence suppression aircraft to detect and attack the radar installations, and four EB-66 stand-off jamming platforms.

These platforms arrived in the target area ahead of the main formation and set up race-track flight patterns outside the enemy's defensive zone, blasting the airwaves with nearly a hundred radar jamming transmitters mounted in their bellies.

The Weasels then moved in. Operating in pairs, they used anti-radar missiles (missiles that home in on radar transmissions) and cluster bombs to destroy the threatening transmitters. Then the eight chaff bombers laid a corridor of reflective chaff ahead of the main strike force to mask it from the enemy's other radars while it ran up to take out the main targets.

Such technical sophistication was undreamt of by Dr Frankenstein. But though his monster terrorized people, at least Dr Frankenstein was concerned with creating life. The Frankensteins whose inventions terrorized the skies of Vietnam were only concerned with destruction.

Above: A Phantom drops its bombs. Far left: Their effect would be much like this dumb-bomb attack on the Ninh Binh railway bridge 30 miles north of Thanh Hoa – spectacular, but when the smoke cleared the bridge was still standing. Left: the bridge after being hit by LGBs dropped by a carrier pilot.

HANOI UNDER SIEGE

For 11 days, the people of Hanoi listened for the sounds of approaching aircraft and rushed for cover as bombs descended from the air. Meanwhile, SAMs and aircraft joined battle

522

EYE-WITNESS

The author is a member of the Vietnamese community and does not wish to be identified.

Above left: A SAM in waiting. Left: 'precision bombing' results in distress and agony for the civilians. Far left: Has this child just been bombed back to the conference table?

For those of us in Hanoi during the Christmas of 1972, there seemed no safe place from the bombs. Not since World War II had such a heavy rain of death fallen on an innocent civilian population. The Americans maintained that precision bombing techniques were being employed. It did not appear like that to us.

For 12 days over Christmas, that traditional time of peace and goodwill, over 400 US Navy and Air Force fighter-bombers and 100 B-52s of the Strategic Air Command flew from their bases in Thailand and Guam, from aircraft carriers offshore and from Tan Son Nhut, to unload their deadly cargoes on our capital, Hanoi, and the harbour city of Haiphong.

The people of those cities lived quiet, difficult lives made poor by the bombing in the countryside and the war in the South. We were non-combatants in a divided, war-weary country, who had never fired a shot in anger and who, until now, lived in relative safety. Now we were being bombed with an intensity which beggared the imagination and for reasons which had little to do with military necessity and everything to do with

political strategy.

Since the Operation Rolling Thunder bombing raids began in 1965, the whole of the North, except Hanoi and Haiphong, had suffered air strikes of every kind: napalm, white phosphorus, anti-personnel mines, high-explosives and defoliants. Every bridge, road junction, rail depot and factory had been hit, rebuilt, camouflaged, hit again, moved and rebuilt. The Americans were bombing a poor farming country, not a modern industrial economy. They were running out of targets and, by October 1972, they were running out of time.

On 18 December, on Kissinger's advice, President Nixon launched the first air raids on Hanoi and Haiphong, in order to 'bomb them back to the conference table'.

I was at work in the office when the air raid siren

Above left: For those North Vietnamese children not evacuated, the bombing tended to interrupt school work. Above: Bomb shelters in the streets saved a lot of lives and allowed life to go on in Hanoi and Haiphong with some semblance of normality.

523

1973/4

first howled its urgent call across the rooftops. It would sound at all times for the next 12 days (excluding 25 December), haunting our days and nights, disturbing our sleep, breaking our meals, disrupting our work. Despite the constant threat of the bombs, we tried to continue normal life. People adapted very quickly: shops stayed open, people whose work kept them in town stayed at their posts and remnants of family life continued. The children and the elderly were evacuated to the countryside and nobody knew when they would see each other again.

Everywhere on the streets, there were individual and communal bomb shelters where you were supposed to take cover when the siren called. They were a nuisance because you had to step round them all the time, but they helped save many lives. As a tactic, the Americans would sometimes send over a single plane or a pilotless drone to set off the alarm and disrupt the pattern of our lives. Other times, waves of invisible B-52s, high up in apparent invincibility and escorted by fighters, would send down strings of bombs to

Left: Hanoi's air defences fire a SAM at an American strike aircraft. Right: If the pilot does not spot the SAM early enough, he has no chance. Far right, top: Hanoi's air defences claim another victim. Far right, below: SAMs were the main, but not the only reason for the high attrition rate of US planes. This pilot is ejecting over the Gulf of Tonkin because he has run out of fuel.

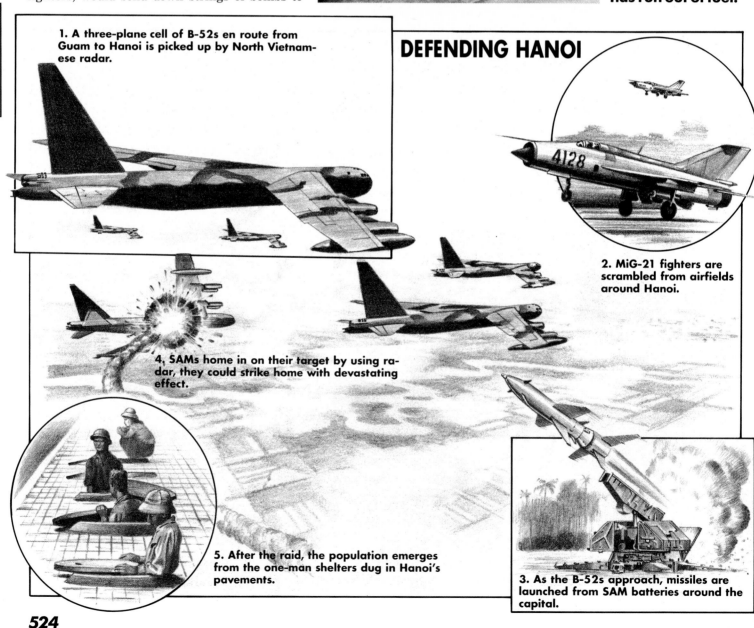

1. A three-plane cell of B-52s en route from Guam to Hanoi is picked up by North Vietnamese radar.

DEFENDING HANOI

2. MiG-21 fighters are scrambled from airfields around Hanoi.

4. SAMs home in on their target by using radar, they could strike home with devastating effect.

5. After the raid, the population emerges from the one-man shelters dug in Hanoi's pavements.

3. As the B-52s approach, missiles are launched from SAM batteries around the capital.

1973/4

erupt in destructive chaos.

The Americans used the raids to terrorize us, to fray our nerves by the mere threat of bombing at any and all times. The siren would sometimes sound up to 20 times a day. The raids continued at night, forcing us out of our beds into the winter cold and down cramped, dark shelters. Some people, like myself, just refused to go down into the shelters and stayed to watch the Soviet-built missiles streak up on a bolt of light to hit back at the enemy planes.

Our air defence forced their planes high up, where it was hoped it would be almost impossible

BOMBED TO THE TABLE?

Linebacker II inflicted massive damage on the North Vietnamese war economy. But did the operation make any real difference to Hanoi's bargaining position?

In the immediate aftermath of Operation Linebacker II, when the US administration claimed that the North Vietnamese were willing to enter 'more meaningful' negotiations in Paris, it was widely thought that the bombing of Hanoi had had a decisive impact on the outcome of the war. At first glance, this analysis of Linebacker's effect on the negotiations in Paris would not seem unreasonable. But there is one fatal flaw in this analysis – the final terms of the Paris Peace Accords were, in fact, very similar to those agreed by Le Duc Tho and Henry Kissinger back in October 1972.

As early as May 1982, Kissinger had appeared to move away from his negotiating stance on a mutual withdrawal of US and NVA troops from South Vietnam, and Le Doc Tho had seen this compromise as an indication that the Americans were anxious to reach an agreement before the presidential election. Accordingly, in October 1972, he put forward a set of proposals that would allow an immediate ceasefire. Kissinger saw this as a breakthrough.

Thieu, however, was unimpressed. He refused to allow North Vietnamese troops to remain in the South and publicly denounced the terms of the draft agreement as a sign of American betrayal. Nixon backtracked – much to the consternation of Kissinger – and ordered his envoy to present Thieu's 69 amendments to the communists. The talks fell apart, and Nixon gave the order to commence Linebacker II.

The bombings stopped on 30 December. Yet four days earlier, it had been the Americans who had indicated their willingness to re-enter negotiations. Kissinger and Le Duc Tho resumed their meetings in Paris on 8 January, and Thieu was sent an ultimatum by Nixon: 'You must decide now whether you desire to continue our alliance or whether you want me to seek a settlement with the enemy which serves US interests alone.' Thieu relented, and the Paris Accords were signed on 27 January 1973.

It is clear that Linebacker was not primarily intended to pressurize Hanoi into modifying its negotiating position, as the terms of both the October 1972 draft treaty and the Paris Peace Accords were virtually identical. Instead, Nixon had wanted to convince President Thieu that American airpower would be on hand to crush any attempt by the North to break the armistice.

Linebacker had not been intended as an instrument of diplomacy, and the Christmas Bombings did not, despite Nixon's statements to the American public, bring the North back to the conference table.

for them to aim with any accuracy. Even before the Christmas bombing, we had proved just how effective our anti-aircraft systems were. On 17 October, we brought down the 4000th American plane since 1964. The victim was nothing less than an F-111, the supersonic swing-wing fighter-bomber which was then the latest in aviation technology.

Hanoi was ringed by radar, linked to surface-to-air missiles and fighter planes. The MiG 17s and 21s were scrambled on first warning of enemy intrusion and attempted to intercept away from the Hanoi area. Those that got through were targeted by the SAMs, anti-aircraft cannon and heavy machine guns.

Americans say they bombed military or economic targets and claimed we placed them next to

Below: A missile team scramble. US 'air pirates' are on their way. Bottom: American claims of precision bombing were often hard to reconcile with phtographs showing the destruction of some civilian areas.

our schools and hospitals. These are just excuses for the terrible civilian casualties they caused. The schools and hospitals were built in the time of the French, before the hostilities, and we were not so stupid as to draw fire on our own children and sick by placing potential targets next to them. Their claims to 'precision bombing' cannot stand up to the sight of whole neighbourhoods flattened, like the densely populated Kham Thien area, or the 1000-bed hospital of Bac Mai, which were both hit by bombs.

Hydrogen bombs and bamboo cages

So when the planes were hit, our spirits soared. In 12 days, Hanoi claimed 81 aircraft downed, of which 34 were the hated B-52s. Imagine our delight when we gathered round the twisted metal hulk of an American plane and saw just how vulnerable they were. These were the most advanced planes in the world, flown by the best-trained, best-equipped air force; the B-52s, designed to fly thousands of miles and drop hydrogen bombs. And here they were, lying at our feet and their crews captive in bamboo cages.

Apart from the two cities, the bombs fell on the huge networks of dykes in the countryside. There were terrible floods, destroying homes, farms and ruining the harvests.

On 30 December, Nixon called off the bombing and nine days later talks resumed in Paris. Le Duc Tho, our chief negotiator, did not budge from the position he held before the bombing. The American changes were not accepted. Nixon caved in and the Peace Accords were signed by North Vietnam and the US on 27 January, much as they had stood the previous October. Our people's iron resolve and belief in fate had borne fruit. We had survived the might of the US.

CHAPTER 102

As Cambodia's saxophone-playing and flamboyant leader amused himself at court, the Khmer Rouge placed the country on a collision course with tragedy

Early in the 1960s, the playboy Prince Norodom Sihanouk, ruler of Cambodia, invited one of his political opponents, the dedicated communist teacher and journalist Ieng Sary, to spend an evening at the royal palace in Phnom Penh. As a little joke, the prince had arranged an after-dinner treat – imported pornographic movies. The serious-minded Sary sat stony-faced as the French erotic acrobatics flickered on the screen, to roars of appreciation from the royal entourage. When the communist made his excuses and left, Sihanouk commented gleefully: 'Ieng Sary will have to go through terrible self-criticism tomorrow!'

Below: A Cambodian government soldier lets rip with his M-60 in a desperate attempt to stem the tide of the Khmer Rouge advance.

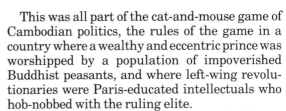

CAMBODIA TORN APART

1973/4

This was all part of the cat-and-mouse game of Cambodian politics, the rules of the game in a country where a wealthy and eccentric prince was worshipped by a population of impoverished Buddhist peasants, and where left-wing revolutionaries were Paris-educated intellectuals who hob-nobbed with the ruling elite.

Some observers thought that Cambodia during the early 1960s was near to paradise, with its fertile ricefields, classical culture, awe-inspiring monuments, beautiful women and perpetually smiling people. The 'Khmer smile', however, was a mask. Behind it lay a very unpleasant set of conflicting interests, and a capacity for ruthless, gratuitous cruelty that was to reach its terrifying climax after the communist victory in 1975.

The rise of the Khmer Rouge

Sihanouk understood all too well the nature of his country, and that of his countrymen. Though he was a less than admirable figure and dominated by self-interest, in the 1960s he was walking a tightrope. By delicate political manoeuvres he was managing to balance a pro-American right-wing faction, associated with the army and Marshal Lon Nol, against the communists, whom Sihanouk himself would later dub the 'Khmer Rouge' or 'Red Khmers'. And this balancing act was carried out against the background of the first of the great conflicts of Cambodian life – fear and hatred of neighbouring Vietnam.

When the Vietnamese communists began establishing bases in Cambodia during 1964 and 1965, there was little Sihanouk could do. He had

downgraded his right-wing army; he could not risk conflict with this well-armed, experienced foe. So he came, in effect, to a deal with the Vietnamese communists. They could maintain their cross-border sanctuaries, and even bring in supplies through the port of Sihanoukville. But they would not interfere in Cambodian internal affairs.

Cambodia's own communists did not, at this stage, seem a serious threat to Sihanouk, since they were basically concerned with petty ideological class arguments conducted in the living rooms of Phnom Penh, and in the mid-1960s there were only a few scattered communist guerrillas, based in remote rural areas. Furthermore, the peasants revered their prince as a Buddhist king with religious and political significance.

What the communist leaders could play on, however, was a deep hostility between rural and urban areas, a hostility enshrined in tradition and folk tales, as well as having practical causes. The Cambodian peasants owned barely enough land for subsistence. Merchants from the towns bought peasant rice cheaply and sold seed at high prices. Moneylenders and tax-gatherers exacted their depredations too.

In 1967, the Khmer Rouge was able to profit from an outbreak of peasant discontent. The Vietnamese communist forces were buying rice at good prices from the peasantry. But in 1966, a right-wing government was elected after a campaign of intimidation and corruption, and it decided to use the rice harvest of 1967 for export. It moved into the villages to force the peasants to hand over the surplus, but offered prices well

Left: Cambodian government forces crouch low in the brush, waiting to spring an ambush on communist rebels. Below: The Khmer Rouge on patrol, armed with an assortment of weapons including Chinese-made B40 rocket launchers. A large number of Khmer Rouge recruits came from village youths in remote rural areas. Their food was requisitioned from refugees, who themselves were being supplied by international relief agencies; food for peace financing war.

By December 1973 Phnom Penh was within range of Khmer Rouge artillery (right), but the communists chose to apply a slow strangulation to the city rather than assault it directly. Below right: Prince Sihanouk.

below what the NVA was prepared to pay.

In the ensuing peasant violence, government officers were hacked to death. The communists associated themselves with these revolts, and Sihanouk rounded on the left, forcing any remaining communists out of the capital and taking fierce reprisals. Whole villages were razed, and suspected ring-leaders hung from trees with their stomachs slit open, to die in slow agony.

When the army crackdown started, the Khmer Rouge leadership retreated to the remote mountains of northeastern Cambodia, an area inhabited by hill tribesmen who defended their territory against incursions with swords, spears and crossbows. They had little reason to like the central government, and they provided willing recruits to a growing guerrilla army.

By 1968 the communists were well established in the northeast, and a small but intense war was under way. It reflected yet another of the contradictions within Cambodian society: gratuitous violence that lurked behind a gentle facade. Two examples will suffice: two children, accused of acting as couriers for the Khmer Rouge, had their heads sawn off with the razor-sharp leaves of palm fronds; 40 schoolteachers thought to have left-wing leanings were bound hand and foot and thrown over a cliff.

The US had backed a loser

By 1970, the Khmer Rouge had not yet made effective inroads into the allegiance that the mass of the peasantry still felt for their prince. But they were building a firm base, and Sihanouk himself was wobbling on his tightrope. For the US bombing of NVA sanctuaries in Cambodia was destabilising large areas. The Vietnam war was about to spill over into the land of the Khmer smile.

Perhaps Cambodia was doomed anyway, but it was still unwise of Sihanouk to take a holiday in France in March 1970. In his absence, Lon Nol took power in a bloodless coup, and immediately called for American help to drive out the North Vietnamese. Even if the CIA did not plan the coup, they had long encouraged and financed Sihanouk's enemies. Naturally, the United States now backed the anti-communist Lon Nol.

Yet in reality the coup was a disaster for the US – and for Cambodia. As soon as Lon Nol's troops

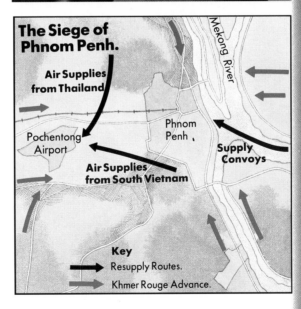

The Siege of Phnom Penh.

Air Supplies from Thailand

Pochentong Airport

Air Supplies from South Vietnam

Mekong River

Phnom Penh

Supply Convoys

Key
Resupply Routes.
Khmer Rouge Advance.

moved against the communist bases along the South Vietnamese border, the NVA counter-attacked, driving deep into Cambodia. Pressure from US and South Vietnamese forces at their backs only encouraged them to press further towards Phnom Penh. By the late summer of 1970, they controlled over half of the country.

KHMER ROUGE LEADERSHIP

When the Cambodian Communist Party achieved victory in 1975, brutally implementing its plans for an agrarian utopia, the systematic mass murder and idealistic return to the land was to become identifiable with one name: Pol Pot.

Pol Pot was in fact the meaningless political pseudonym adopted by Saloth Sar, the Paris-educated son of a minor Cambodian official.

Saloth Sar returned from Paris in 1953 and within a decade had joined with other communists to create a party in Phnom Penh. At the First Party Congress in September 1960, Tou Samoth, the only attending communist leader from the First Indochina War, was chosen as head and named party secretary. Saloth Sar was elected to the third position, with his friend Ieng Sary capturing the fifth.

Early in 1963, Samoth disappeared on the way back from a secret trip to Hanoi. He was presumed murdered and, after a special congress, Saloth Sar was chosen as his replacement, Ieng Sary following him up the ladder to third place in the party structure. Sar, remembered by his brother as a plodding, dedicated student, had matured into a handsome, determined politician with a gift for remaining cool in the confused world of Cambodian politics.

Sar's party left Phnom Penh in early 1963, initially heading for the safety of the Cambodia-Vietnam border. From there they moved to the northeastern highlands. Here, isolated, Sar emphasised the purity of self-sufficiency, a concept that became his overriding concern.

The communists launched their first offensive in January 1968 and fought increasingly effectively against the Cambodian Army until 1975 After the communist victory, Pol Pot put his ideology into practice. The Khmer atrocities, in the words of author Stanley Karnow; made 'the Nazi holocaust seen tame by comparison'.

Lon Nol's army was a rabble of ill-trained recruits, many of them schoolchildren, led by officers with no grasp of military tactics but with a well-developed talent for lining their own pockets. Their 'phantom' soldiers became a legend: fictitious troops were invented so that the officers could embezzle their pay, and arms and ammunition were sold to the enemy as an everyday business operation. Lon Nol himself, a deeply superstitious man of limited intelligence, recommended sacred talismans and magic rituals to ensure safety in battle, and even consulted astrologers to determine strategy. Once again, the Americans had backed a loser.

But Lon Nol was certainly sincere in his hatred of the Vietnamese, communist or not. Immediately after the coup he started a campaign of terror against the half-million Vietnamese living in Cambodia – mostly tradesmen or clerks. Soon, hundreds of bloated Vietnamese corpses were drifting down the rivers into which they had been dumped by Lon Nol's soldiers. In 1971 the Khmer Rouge carried out their own purge of Vietnamese in the villages they controlled, and of pro-Vietnamese elements in their own ranks.

There were plenty of recruits

At the time of Lon Nol's coup, the Cambodian communists were still very limited in influence and military strength. But Prince Sihanouk changed all that. Resurfacing in Peking, he set up a government of national unity that included the Khmer Rouge. He called on all loyal subjects to rise up against Lon Nol, a call that greatly influenced the Cambodian peasantry. Both China and, crucially, North Vietnam, agreed to support Sihanouk's government-in-exile, which in practice meant giving military support to the Khmer Rouge. Pol Pot and the other hard-line Khmer Rouge leaders despised Sihanouk and distrusted

Below: Selective bombardment left parts of Phnom Penh devastated, as the Khmer Rouge bid to wrest control of Cambodia from the corrupt and wavering government. The tightrope that Sihanouk was walking so precariously was about to snap, plunging Cambodia into the dark of Year Zero.

the North Vietnamese, but they bided their time, exploiting Sihanouk's popularity to achieve influence over the peasants, and North Vietnamese military strength to drive back Lon Nol.

Between 1970 and 1973 the Khmer Rouge, rather than fighting, devoted their efforts to establishing a firm base among the peasants inside the now extensive North Vietnamese-controlled area of Cambodia. Their readiness to work hard in the fields, their lack of corruption and their concern for the peasants' welfare impressed those whose initial suspicions had been allayed by the magic name of Sihanouk. There were plenty of willing recruits for the guerrilla force, all of which were painstakingly trained and indoctrinated. By 1973 the Khmer Rouge had a disciplined army of about 40,000 at their disposal.

A brutal transformation

The peace agreement between the United States and North Vietnam in January 1973 had an immediate and dramatic effect on Cambodia. As the NVA withdrew once more to the border areas, leaving the Khmer Rouge to do their own fighting for the first time, US airpower, banned from Vietnam and Laos, was turned on Cambodia in a concentrated campaign of devastation. It took a heavy toll of the Khmer Rouge guerrilla army as it fought its way towards Phnom Penh; it also completed the destruction of the Cambodian economy and ruined the country's traditional peasant society. Peasants were now divided into two groups: refugees who fled to Phnom Penh, swelling its population to four times the pre-war number, and those who stayed behind in the Khmer Rouge areas, to be regimented into the guerrilla war-economy. It was at this time that the communists began their brutal transformation of rural Cambodia, forcing all the peasants into co-operatives where every hour of the day was regulated and controlled, imposing an iron discipline by terror. People who disagreed just disappeared. Money was abolished in the 'liberated' areas, so that 'Angka', the Organization, could control all rice supplies and other trade. Buddhist monks were set to work in the fields and traditional ceremonies disappeared. It was brutal, but it worked. The Khmer Rouge could feed their army; Lon Nol could not feed his.

Completing the stranglehold

By the start of 1974, with the American bombing halted, the guerrillas were dug in within shelling range of Phnom Penh. Captured US 105mm howitzers provided the firepower for a bombardment that caused hundreds of casualties before government troops temporarily forced the Khmer Rouge back from the city's defensive perimeter. But all roads into Phnom Penh were cut off. The only lifeline for the besieged population and Lon Nol's army was the Mekong river, bringing supplies up from South Vietnam. The Khmer Rouge decided against a direct assault on the city and set out instead to complete the stranglehold.

Above: Government troops engage the Khmer Rouge. Right: A river boat skipper keeps his head down. With all roads into Phnom Penh cut, the city had to be supplied via the Mekong river. Between January 1973 and January 1974, 92 per cent of the city's rice, fuel and ammo came in this way. Thereafter, the US undertook supply by civilian aircraft. But, despite a daily quota of 1088 tons, flown in by up to 42 flights a day, it was not possible to supply sufficient food, and artillery fire made resupply increasingly dangerous.

Lon Nol's troops actually outnumbered their guerrilla enemies. However, despite being backed by the US, it was all they could do to hold a defensive line around Phnom Penh, about 25 kilometres out from the city. Moreover, even in these desperate straits, the traditional corruption continued to absorb most of the leaders' time and energy – and most of the Americans' money. Food distribution was manipulated for profit and soldiers went unpaid – on several occasions they refused combat until money turned up. For the better-off citizens of Phnom Penh, an easy routine continued as if in a hypnotic trance. No-one worked in the afternoons, and students were not conscripted because it would interrupt their education. The contrast with the Khmer Rouge, geared up for war, could not have been more stark.

They are the ones who mourn, the ones left behind to sit alone and weep. They are the refugees on the road out of Hue. They are the dead, heaped in the ditches of My Lai. Their eyes have lost all innocence, from gazing too long on horrors yet untold. Their voices are mute, save for a keening protest that is drowned in the babble of war. They are the civilians. They are the victims.

MEN, WOMEN

From Phnom Penh to Xuan Loc, from Laos to the Mekong Delta, the civilian populations of the war-torn countries of Southeast Asia bore the brunt of the suffering engendered by 30 years of conflict. Left: Crying for help, a bleeding Chinese woman is comforted following a rocket attack on Phnom Penh.

AND CHILDREN

Far left: As the ARVN crumble, the panic-stricken civilian population attempts to secure the few seats available on a US aircraft. Above: Two who escaped. Their innocent faces belying the horrors they have witnessed, two small children sleep aboard a helicopter amidst a few pitiful belongings. Left: ARVN Rangers near the Cambodian border gaze down upon a scene they have witnessed too many times on too many roads. Holding the lifeless body of his young son, a father looks up in helpless sorrow, his eyes framing the eternal question: Why?

533

With the signing of the Paris Peace Accords and the exchange of POWs, Americans wanted to write off the war as a bad dream

THE SOUTH ABANDONED

In April 1973, Graham Martin, a frail but determined US politician, flew in to Tan Son Nhut airfield at Saigon to take up his post as the new US ambassador to South Vietnam. He was confident about the future, and a firm supporter of the Thieu regime. For although the US was pulling its armed forces out of Southeast Asia, the future did not look too bleak. The balance of power in the region was not irretrievably swinging towards the communists, and there were many factors in favour of the government of the South.

In any comparison between the ARVN and the communist forces, the communists could in no sense be said to be waiting to gobble up a defence-less morsel. A prominent communist commander, General Tran Van Tra, has since published a record of the NVA discussions during this period. His account was rapidly suppressed when it came out in 1982; it does seem to give an accurate indication of the problems facing the NVA.

First of all, the NVA had suffered heavy losses in the 1972 offensive, and its sources of manpower were not inexhaustible. Morale was also a problem. The ceasefire may have removed the Americans from the equation, but the use of their airpower had not necessarily been ruled out. And airpower on its own was a considerable disincentive to any future communist offensive. The present phase of the struggle for South Vietnam had been going on since 1965 – and after eight years of non-stop, steadily escalating conflict, the communists were in some ways back where they had started. They controlled only about 25 per cent of South Vietnam's territory, and 15 per cent of its population. In 1965 they had seemed on the verge of victory – now they still had a long way to go.

Marvin expands

In addition, the South had been steadily expanding its armed forces since 1970, and by 1973 had over one million men under arms. These men were well equipped with US weapons – the ARVN had about four times as many artillery pieces as the NVA, for example.

By the summer of 1973, President Thieu felt strong enough actually to take the offensive against certain communist enclaves, in the Delta and near the Cambodian border. He was confident that if a crisis occurred he could rely on US airpower to help his forces out.

Unfortunately for Thieu, however, the airpower that he counted on would never be forthcoming. Even before Ambassador Martin arrived in Saigon, an event of crucial importance for US attitudes had occurred. The release of the last American prisoners of war by Hanoi, in March 1973, marked a key point in US involvement in

Above left: An ARVN soldier kicks up some dust. Left: Ford, Nixon and Kissinger wrap up an unpopular war. Right: As ground changed hands, refugees poured in streams.

Southeast Asia. As far as the American public was concerned, and as far as most US politicians were concerned, they now wanted just to forget the whole episode. As the haggard faces of the POWs grinned with relief at getting home, so the nation decided that the war was over.

President Nixon had, indeed, promised Thieu late in 1972 that US aid would continue to be available in large quantities, and US airpower would be deployed in support of the ARVN. In fact, one of the aims of the Linebacker II raids on North Vietnam in December 1972 seems to have been to reassure Thieu. 'You have my absolute assurance that if Hanoi fails to abide by the terms of this agreement it is my intention to take swift and severe retaliatory action,' Nixon had written to Thieu in November.

Nixon wavers

In public, however, Nixon was rather less forthcoming, restricting himself to a public address that declared: 'We shall continue to aid South Vietnam within the terms of the agreement...We shall do everything the agreement requires of us, and we shall expect the other parties to do everything it requires of them.'

In March, Nixon responded strongly to reports that the North was building up its forces. He made a public statement that implied he was consider-ing bombing the North again; and Secretary of Defense Elliot Richardson also hinted at a resumption of bombing. But these statements were made before the final POWs had come home. After that, the whole landscape began to change.

The unmentionable war

President Thieu visited the US in 1973. Few prominent politicians were willing to meet him; Vietnam had become a dirty word, a subject that few wanted to be associated with. On 30 June, Congress passed an important bill, cutting off the funding of US activity in Southeast Asia, a measure that was to become effective as of 15 August. Nixon and Kissinger were still intent on continuing the bombing of communist concentrations in Cambodia, but found that this too was no longer possible.

On 7 November 1973, Congress brought into force the War Powers Act. This gave Congress control over the president's use of American troops abroad – a very significant weakening of the president's powers in terms of Vietnam. This was a far cry from the Gulf of Tonkin Resolution that, in 1964, had given Johnson a free hand.

The differences between 1964 and 1973 were vast. Not only was the US war weary, it no longer trusted its president. The slow but steady uncovering of the Watergate scandal was destroying

Below: A reluctant ARVN was encouraged to go out and fight for space. As the ceasefire approached, both sides went out to take control of as much land as they could – when the ceasefire came into operation, the Saigon regime and the communists would hold the areas they had. The North termed their territorial patchwork the 'leopard spots'.

Above: An exchange of prisoners. When US POWs had been brought home, interest in the war rapidly declined. Below right: For the children, hi-tech military hardware was part of growing up.

confidence in the government. As each new level of criminal activity was revealed, so a presidency that had conducted a bold, successful foreign policy took on the mantle of a shabby bunch of crooks, run by a foul-mouthed fixer. By late 1973, Nixon was fighting for his political life; by August 1974 he had resigned rather than face impeachment proceedings.

One of Nixon's last acts as president was to sign a bill that put a ceiling of 1 billion dollars on aid to South Vietnam. Within a few days of his resignation, this figure was reduced to 700 million dollars by the House of Representatives. Nixon's succes-

sor, Gerald Ford, was not a political heavyweight. In the 1960s, Lyndon Johnson had described him as a man who 'could not chew gum and walk straight'. Ford's response to the Congressional cut in aid was to assure Thieu that 'our support will be adequate.' Hardly the most inspiring offer of help.

By the middle of 1974, US commitment to South Vietnam had degenerated to a level that ruled out military action. The strong shield of air cover that had destroyed the communist formations in 1972 was no longer available. No more Americans would be expected to die on behalf of a small country in Southeast Asia.

PARIS PEACE ACCORDS

When negotiations were reopened in Paris on 8 January 1973, agreement was quickly reached on essentially the same terms as those put forward by Hanoi in October 1972, namely a ceasefire in place in return for US withdrawal and an exchange of prisoners. The ceasefire was signed by representatives of the US, North Vietnam, South Vietnam and the Provisional Revolutionary Government of the Republic of South Vietnam — the Viet Cong — on 23 January, to come into effect at 2359 GMT four days later. There was then a 60-day period in which the exchange of prisoners, US and Free World troop withdrawals

and the establishment of the status of those missing was to be accomplished by a Four Party Joint Military Commission (FPJMC) based in Saigon.

The FPJMC's work ended on 29 March with a total of 587 American POWs repatriated and 23,516 US and 30,449 Free World servicemen withdrawn from South Vietnam. A Four Party Joint Military Team (FPJMT) then continued to attempt to trace the missing until the US delegation was withdrawn in April 1975. The agreement was overseen by an International Commission of Control and Supervision (ICCS) from Canada, Poland, Indonesia and Hungary.

1973/4

The ink had hardly dried on the paper before North and South tried to gain the upper hand. As for the Control Commission, according to the US 'it couldn't control shit'

THE FRAGILE CEASE FIRE

I t was an awesome sight. We were standing in front of a huge arch that towered above the devastated plain like the entrance to the gates of hell. From the writing and signs over the brickwork, we gathered that this was the beginning of Viet Cong territory. Up until then we had had a fairly uneventful trip. I had decided to drive north from Saigon to try to find out exactly where the ceasefire line – or more accurately, the new front line – cut across Route 13, the scene of heavy fighting the previous year.

Just over 40 kilometres outside Saigon, we saw a group of Vietnamese civilians on heavily-laden Honda scooters waiting at a road block while government troops checked their papers. The soldiers waved us through without stopping us because, we were told later, they thought we were members of the International Control Commission. Minutes later, we were alone. On both sides of the badly damaged tarmac road the detritus of war built up: rusting tanks, wrecked lorries,

EYE-WITNESS

Peter Scholl-Latour is a West German television reporter who has covered French involvement in Indochina, American involvement in Vietnam and the devastation of Cambodia. In his writings he reveals a wide knowledge of the peoples of Southeast Asia and compassion for their sufferings.

bombed-out dug-outs and gun emplacements. There was something oppressive about this hostile, deserted landscape.

I was standing with my film crew and Jean-Louis Arnaud, a French journalist. As we were setting up the tripod for the film camera under the arch, we heard a rustling noise in the tall clumps of grass around us. A ring of 20 soldiers in green uniforms began closing in on us, automatic rifles at the ready. There was no mistaking who they were – the round, green jungle hats, the AK-47s, the baggy trousers, the Ho Chi Minh sandals: they were either Viet Cong guerrillas or North Vietnamese regulars, and we were their prisoners.

'Don't try to escape'
We were driven to a wooden barracks that was a kind of official checkpoint. Communication was difficult, and we had no idea which of them was supposed to be the officer on duty: the communists had no insignia to indicate rank. They told our interpreter, Thanh, that they thought our status

Despite the January 1973 ceasefire, the war continued as Hanoi infiltrated its forces into the South (right). Below: From left to right, Indonesian, Canadian, Hungarian and Polish members of the International Commission of Control and Supervision (ICCS). Ceasefire violations by both sides were much in evidence (left and opposite page). Indeed, the ICCS was obstructed to such an extent that Canada left the four-party commission in disgust in July 1973 and was replaced by Iran. The proposed elections in South Vietnam never materialized and all attempts at a political settlement had ended by the close of 1973.

as journalists was extremely suspect and that they had no way of guaranteeing we weren't CIA agents.

Towards evening a rather gruff young political officer turned up, accompanied by six armed men. We were escorted to a jungle hide-out through a landscape devastated by B-52 airstrikes. After a short time we came on a few bamboo huts and a dug-out. Thanh translated a warning given us by a man who was obviously some sort of captain. 'Don't try to escape,' he told us. 'We've laid mines right round the camp and you will almost certainly tread on one.' The soldiers (by now we knew they were a regular unit from the North) watched us like hawks but were always well behaved.

Prisoners of the communists

We were brought some rice and hot water, plus a few stalks of some unidentifiable green vegetable. The soldiers were given the same meagre helping of food as we were. The captain then showed us to a big plank bed.

A major aspect of the ceasefire was the exchange of POWs. Behind the formal signing ceremonies (above left), there was joy and hope. Whether you were an NVA conscript longing for your village in the North (below left), or a USAF officer whiling away the time talking with an opposite number (right), the end was the same. When you got off the bus at Gia Lam airport (below), there was nothing more to worry about but getting on that plane and winging it back to The World. Below right: Operation Homecoming. The faces of these men say it all: they're going home.

We were woken the next morning by the noise of hens clucking and the sentries shouting. The captain told us we would be kept prisoner for at least a few more days. As we had neither soap, shaving gear nor towels, he would allow Thanh to leave the camp and return with all the basic essentials required. I handed Thanh a piece of paper. But instead of putting down what we needed, I wrote on the back in English: 'We are prisoners of the Viet Cong near Route 13. Please notify German embassy in Saigon for release. Help!' I warned Thanh to be careful of the South Vietnamese police and said that under no circumstances should he come back to the camp. I felt quite pleased at having beaten the professional conspirators of the North Vietnamese underground at their own game.

The radio gave us hope

Towards midday we were transferred to a new hide-out – a large camp in the middle of the jungle that seemed to be a staging post for one of the North Vietnamese battalions. The actual front itself was no more than five kilometres away, and at night we could hear artillery fire in the distance. We were taken to our roofed-over trenches and hung up our green hammocks and mosquito nets. The captain said that the food in the revolutionary army was fairly basic, but assured us that the water we were given had been boiled and was completely germ-free. I told him we could make do with very little food. We liked rice, and so long as we could mix some nuoc mam (a pungent fish sauce) with it we would be perfectly satisfied. The captain looked rather embarrassed when I said this. 'Nuoc mam is a luxury for us,' he said. 'We just

use salt water to season our rice.'

The guard detailed to watch us never took his eye off us for a second. Fortunately, they gave us a radio to help pass the time. That evening, the BBC World Service newsreader announced that a German television crew and a French correspondent had been taken prisoner by the communists. So Saigon did, in fact, know about our disappearance. We offered up a silent prayer of thanks to Thanh.

Invited to make a film

In the afternoons we could hear people shouting and a ball being thrown around – the North Vietnamese enjoyed volleyball in their off-duty hours. At night the troops would sit together and sing revolutionary songs. Most of the time our captors seemed to take hardly any notice of us and, while we kept insisting that we were innocent journalists, our pleas were met with stony-faced silence. By our third day in captivity the outlook didn't look too good.

On the afternoon of the third day, a mud-caked Honda drew up outside our hut. A green-clad soldier came straight over to us, shook our hands and welcomed us to the 'liberated zones' on behalf of the National Liberation Front of Vietnam: 'I have good news for you,' said Commissar Huyn Ba Trang. 'Our liaison officers in Saigon have clearly established that you are journalists. That means you are no longer our prisoners, so from now on you should consider yourselves our guests. If you should like to film the liberated zone and make a report on us, then please feel free to do so.' The guards who had glared at us suspiciously only that morning now became smiling and friendly. We were even served tea in an empty grenade case.

SOUTH VIETNAM, 1973-1975

Even before the ink had dried on the Paris agreements, Hanoi and Saigon were struggling to make territorial gains before the ceasefire took effect.

Since the communists had suffered heavy losses during the 1972 Easter Offensive, the ARVN more than held its own during 1973. Indeed, it had won back about 15 per cent of the country by the end of the year.

The North had suffered badly through reductions in the aid that it had been receiving from both China and Russia. The protracted Sino-Soviet split, which at times had resulted in border clashes, forced Mao Zedong to contemplate a reconciliation with the US in order to offset the Soviet menace. This resulted in President Nixon's historic visit to Beijing in February 1972. Having tied the withdrawal of US troops from Taiwan, an island much coveted by China, to an early solution to the Vietnam conflict, Nixon turned his attention to the Soviet Union. His visit to Moscow in May 1972 was returned by Premier Leonid Brezhnev the following year.

Hanoi, however, was determined to rebuild in the South and by the end of 1974 had not only increased its total forces – both combat and support elements – from 150,000 to 300,000, but had also constructed an all-weather road network from Quang Tri Province to the Mekong, a major airfield at Khe Sanh and an oil pipeline as far south as Loc Ninh.

Throughout 1974 Hanoi had begun to exert additional pressure in areas such as Quang Nam and Quang Ngai. Ben Cat was the scene of heavy fighting in May 1974 and two ARVN airborne brigades had to be rushed to restore the situation at Thuong Duc in August, following heavy communist pressure around Da Nang. The military situation was grim in both Military Regions 1 and 2. ARVN forces in the former were severely stretched, and in Military Region 2 a tenuous hold was maintained only over the major cities of the Central Highlands and the main lines of communications to the coast.

541

COULD THE SOUTH HAVE SURVIVED?

The Paris Accords were supposed to give the South the opportunity to consolidate in order to fight their own war. But did those high hopes have any chance of success?

The crucial difference between the Geneva Agreements of 1954 and the Paris Accords of 1973 was that the former had removed communist regular forces from South Vietnam while the latter had not. Thus, from the very beginning, Saigon faced a difficult military situation even though Hanoi's forces were still relatively weak after the disasters of the Easter Offensive of 1972. Moreover, US aid was being curtailed by the Paris Accords and by increasing Congressional restrictions placed on the Nixon and Ford Administrations – aid was fixed at a ceiling of $1 billion for 1974 and cut in October of that year to $700 million for 1975. However, North Vietnam was also experiencing cuts in the aid it was receiving from Moscow and Beijing.

An additional problem for Saigon was that its purchasing power also decreased as a result of the economic crisis consequent on the oil price rises imposed by Arab states following Israel's victory in the Yom Kippur War of October 1973. The scarcity of oil not only deprived the armed forces of fuel but also increased inflation generally. Between January 1971 and September 1974 the price of food alone shot up by a staggering 313.8 per cent, with ARVN personnel in particular having to resort to 'moonlighting' in order to earn enough to support their families. Although US aid had been cut back, however, Thieu's government possessed enormous stockpiles of weapons and ammunition that had been flown in during Operation Enhance Plus in late 1972. Over two billion dollars' worth of equipment had been supplied by the US, but Thieu seemed unable to ensure proper distribution. It did not help that the South lacked any wider cohesiveness. Regionalism, ethnic and religious diversity and political factionalism all undermined national consensus, while the widespread corruption at the highest levels of government and society robbed Thieu's administration of any legitimacy. What reform there had been – such as the Land to the Tiller Program – had come too late, and even Thieu's sacking or re-assignment of over 2500 officers, officials and police in 1974, in response to a campaign by the Catholic-backed People's Front Against Corruption, drew only cynical reaction.

Despite protestations of an administrative revolution, Thieu also further weakened local autonomy in 1973 and 1974 by abolishing the election of hamlet chiefs, placing regional and popular forces under military rather than local control and re-instituting the central appointment of local officials. Hanoi faced difficulties, but these appeared slight compared to those of Saigon.

After that we were allowed to wander around the camp with our cameras and tape recorders exactly as we pleased. The soldiers, burly peasant lads between 18 and 28, were open and friendly. The only portraits they had on the walls were of Ho Chi Minh.

When it got dark in the evenings we would go and sit with the soldiers, stumbling blindly through the vegetable patches they had planted, hoping to find some relief from the mosquitoes in the smoke of the camp-fire. We asked them how much longer they thought they would have to wear the green uniform of the revolutionary soldier. The verdict was unanimous: 'Until Vietnam is one country again and we have carried out the task handed down to us by Ho Chi Minh.' The words were empty rhetoric, learned parrot-fashion. And yet, coming from these young men, they had real sincerity and spontaneity.

We decided that we would take up the North Vietnamese offer to make a film of the area. We drove about 30 kilometres in the direction of An Loc, heading for the village of Minh Hoa. Our guides were anxious that we should show the civilian as well as the military side of the revolution. At the time of our arrest, the communists already controlled substantial areas of South Vietnam. But only five per cent of the population – roughly one million people – lived in these remote and inhospitable 'liberated zones'. Since the ceasefire agreement, which had effectively ratified the presence of 150,000 North Vietnamese regulars south of the 17th parallel, Hanoi had lost no time in extending its military infrastructure in the region.

An official welcome

Our arrival in Minh Hoa caused something of a sensation – ours were the first white faces the villagers had seen since the revolutionary army had marched into the area. Before the fighting had started they had worked on the rubber plantation, but now they looked like they had fallen on hard times. There were plenty of signs that the Northern troops were in command here, and loudspeakers kept on booming out battle-songs and rousing speeches through the deserted main street of the village. We were officially welcomed by the local party and army officials in a bamboo hut specially erected for the occasion.

Next morning we watched a political gathering. We were told that every family in the village had sent along at least one representative. The leader of the revolutionary committee called for an increase in farm production and 'self-reliance', and announced preparations for the forthcoming national holiday on 2 September. At the close everybody gave the customary three cheers, but their faces remained blank. We saw no signs of revolutionary fervour among the listeners.

We returned to our original camp along Route 13 and got ready to go back across the frontier. It was still dark when we set out to walk the seven

Opposite page: NVA officers on board a US helicopter oversee Operation End Sweep, the clearing of North Vietnamese ports of mines sown by the US Navy in mid-1972. The operation, carried out by US Task Force 78, was completed in July 1973. Above: An electronic mine detector, designed to trail in the water, hangs from a chopper.

kilometres to Route 13. We were accompanied by an escort of heavily-armed guards, but this time they were there to protect us. Eventually we arrived back at the Viet Cong arch. There, hidden in the bushes, were our two cars.

One kilometre over the border we were stopped by a group of South Vietnamese soldiers. Three of them squeezed into the car beside us. We continued driving until we came to a South Vietnamese regimental camp. A pencil-slim paratroop major with a pale blue silk scarf around his neck greeted us: 'You're very welcome here...You're probably fed up eating rats – I imagine that's the best the communists could do for you in the way of food.' He handed each of us an ice-cold bottle of Coca-Cola. All that week as we had sat sipping our tepid water in the camp we had dreamed of the moment when we would taste our first Coke. At last the moment had arrived. We threw back our heads and gulped it down, but somehow the drink tasted flat and stale.

US MK2

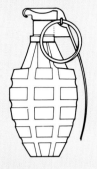

Weight: 595g
Blast radius: 10 metres
Fuze delay: 4-5 seconds
**Average throwing
distance:** 30 metres

US M26

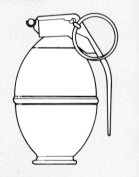

Weight: 425g
Blast radius: 10 metres
Fuze delay: 4-5 seconds
**Average throwing
distance:** 40 metres

USSR RGD5

Weight: 310g
Blast radius: 20 metres
Fuze delay: 3-4 seconds
**Average throwing
distance:** 45 metres

GRENADES IN VIETNAM

Differing widely in size, sophistication and effectiveness, a host of grenade designs were flung throughout Vietnam

Dangling from the webbing of the NVA, ARVN and US soldier and tucked into the VC's black pyjamas, a variety of grenades found their way into the Vietnam war.

The communist forces employed grenades ranging from the World War II vintage Soviet F1 and RG42 hand-grenades, to the state-of-the-art RGD5 hand-grenade.

The F1 and RG42, respectively shaped like a 'pineapple' and a tin can, were typical hand-thrown grenades with similar fragmentation radii of 20 to 25 metres and a throwing distance of around 40 metres. The RGD5 was the Soviet successor to the F1 and was able to pack a similar blast despite having only half the F1's weight.

Towards the end of the war, the NVA began using the RKG3 anti-tank hand-grenade. A supplement to the RPG7 grenade launcher, this stick grenade had a cloth drogue in the handle which was pulled out when the grenade was thrown. This armed the weapon, stabilized its flight and allowed the grenade to drop on armoured vehicles from above – their weakest point. The RKG3 could penetrate almost 120mm of armour.

On top of the supplies of grenades they received from the North and the grenades they captured or stole from the Americans, the VC proved to be experts at manufacturing grenades in the field.

After completing the risky operation of extracting explosive from undetonated American bombs and shells, fragmentation material was gathered from a variety of sources. Casings were fashioned from US tins, scavenged from the rubbish US forces left behind.

The US Army and ARVN used two main types of high-explosive grenade in Vietnam, the Mk2 hand-/rifle-grenade and the M26 hand-grenade. The M26 was a smooth-bodied grenade which would send 1000 fragments out to 10 metres, with a 50 per cent hit probability against men standing in the open.

The Mk2 was broadly similar to the Soviet F1 but suffered a problem with its base plug, which was apt to fly up to 200 metres on detonation, endangering the thrower.

Aside from these high-explosive grenades, the allies also had at their disposal a variety of gas and smoke-grenades. The gas-grenades had been developed for riot control and usually contained CS gas. These were used extensively against VC tunnel complexes. The one smoke grenade that troops thought produced a workable smoke-screen was the white phosphorus-filled M34. But because even a strong man could only just throw it far enough not to be hit by its spray of burning phosphorus, and because of its vulnerability to stray bullets and fragments, many thought it was too dangerous to carry in combat.

USSR RKG3

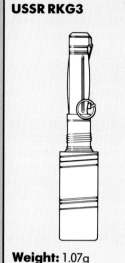

Weight: 1.07g
**Armour
penetration:** 125mm
Fuze: impact detonation

US M34

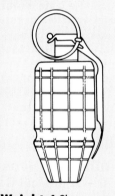

Weight: 1.9kg
Blast radius: 25 metres

USSR F1

Weight: 600g
Blast radius: 20 metres
Fuze delay: 3-4 seconds
**Average throwing
distance:** 35 metres

Above: In the field, equipped with M26 and Mk2 grenades.

THE ROAD TO VICTORY

The plan had been to prepare the ground for a full-scale invasion in 1976, but that soon changed when the ARVN crumbled into disarray. After 10 years of struggle, the NVA smelled victory

During the months of July, August, September and October of 1974, all the agencies of the General Staff were bustling and tense. The revolution in the South had soared since the March 1974 Resolution. The situation on the battlefield was developing to our advantage. When we discussed the strategic combat plan for 1975, the question was raised what should be the principal battlefield.

In II Corps, which included the Tay Nguyen, the enemy had only two main-force divisions, and these had to be spread out both to hold all of the provinces of the Tay Nguyen and to protect the coastal provinces. The conferees unanimously approved the General Staff's judgement and chose the Tay Nguyen as the main field of battle for large-scale offensives in 1975.

Prospect of victory

By March a whole Saigon main-force army was fleeing at full tilt, abandoning the whole Tay Nguyen. It was indeed a knockout blow. The enemy was reeling and in disorder.

On 15 March, 1975, I received a cabled reply from the Political Bureau, signed by Le Duc Tho, and one from the central Military Committee, signed by Vo Nguyen Giap. At a meeting in Hanoi,

Previous page: A captured M48 tank in the vanguard of the NVA advance. Below: Against a backdrop of billowing smoke, NVA troops overrun Tan Son Nhut Air Base.

members of both bodies had carefully read the telegram I sent from the front on 14 March, agreed with our assessment and accepted our proposals.

In 1968 and 1972 we had mounted big attacks in the Tay Nguyen, but there had been no tremendous lightning victories like those of this year. Now there was a clear prospect of us liberating the Tay Nguyen. If we acted quickly and well, we might finish before the 1975 rainy season.

Da Nang in chaos

After we won our big victory in the Tay Nguyen, Zone 5's party committee and its front command, in a sharp response to the new opportunity, abandoned their plans to advance to the south and changed the thrust of their attacks to the north in order to establish the conditions for the liberation of Da Nang.

By 25 March, the Central Military Committee and the General Command, concluding that after losing Hue, Tam Ky, Quang Ngai and Chu Lai, the enemy could not hold Da Nang even if they tried, decided to open the offensive for Da Nang under these guiding principles: 'In the best time, most rapidly, more daringly, most unexpectedly and certain to win.'

After 25 March, the city of Da Nang was in chaos. The enemy had to abandon their plans to

regroup and began to use Boeing 727s to evacuate the American advisers and a portion of the Saigon forces.

The Political Bureau met again, and that historic meeting decided: 'Our general strategic offensive began with the Tay Nguyen campaign. A new strategic opportunity has come, and conditions allow an early completion of our resolution to liberate the South. We resolve to rapidly concentrate our forces, weapons and material to liberate Saigon before the rainy season.'

Our troops roared forward

In their hour of agony, the enemy were completely mistaken in their assessment of us. Naturally it was no longer any surprise to them that we were mounting sustained attacks throughout South Vietnam, but clearly they did not yet know the direction or timing of our actions, the forces we would use, our manner of fighting, our strategic intentions, or the extraordinary efforts we would make to seize this new opportune moment. If the enemy were completely surprised in the Tay Nguyen, they would be even more surprised in Saigon.

The slogan, 'All for the front, all for victory!' had become a reality in this high point of the final phase of the resistance against the United States.

Right: The morning after the fall of Hue. As panic and confusion grips the South, ARVN troops mix with civilian refugees in a Vietnamese Navy boat at Da Nang. Below: Displaying the order and discipline that enabled the North to prevail after years of struggle, victorious NVA troops parade outside the Presidential Palace in Saigon, which is adorned with a banner showing the face of Ho Chi Minh.

Below: As the NVA advance, an ARVN soldier evacuates his family. Left: An NVA tank in Saigon. Opposite page: After the victory, an NVA trooper returns north with presents for his family.

The great rear, the socialist North, rapidly marshalled all its human and material strength for the battlefield, for the great front lines of the South. Night and day our troops roared forward, advancing at lightning speed, in high spirits and confident of victory.

Spring was returning to the grassy hills and sun-drenched mountains. The rubber forests that stretched as far as the eye could see were putting out new leaves. Setting up positions southwest of Saigon was a real exploit for the army, because the geography here made it difficult to deploy a large force, especially their heavy weapons. There were few roads for motorized artillery; in fact, it could be said that the sole route was across exposed marshlands.

'H' hour approaches

After our offensive against Saigon during Tet Mau Than in 1968, the enemy had ridiculed and blustered, 'The Vietcong will never again have the strength to attack Saigon.' Today as we looked at the field positions we had set up, with the close co-ordination between our troops inside and outside Saigon, and saw the firm operational areas we had captured, as we determined the objectives we would strike right from the outset, calculated the time, and completed our final tasks before 'H' hour – the final 'H' hour in the history of our people, and also the biggest 'H' hour in the history of our people for more than a hundred years – we were pleased, happy and proud.

In all of Saigon-Gia Dinh, the largest city in Vietnam, with hundreds of thousands of enemy troops deployed in inner and outer rings of defensive positions, we chose only five of the largest objectives for certain capture. Those were the quisling General Staff headquarters, 'Independence Palace', the Special Capital Zone headquarters, the Directorate-General of Police and Tan Son Nhut airfield. These targets were the most important nerve centres of the Saigon army and the quisling administration.

The guns open fire

On 22 April, the campaign headquarters rechecked the official plan for the Ho Chi Minh campaign one final time, and spread out the campaign resolution, a map with fresh red markings indicating the directions of all our units' attacks on Saigon-Gia Dinh.

At 1700 hours on 26 April, the first guns of the Ho Chi Minh campaign opened fire. The plan specified that on the morning of 27 April there would be a barrage of attacks from all directions on the outskirts of Saigon. On 29 April the barrage of attacks on the centre of the city would begin.

On the afternoon of 28 April, a flight of five captured A-37s had taken off to strike Tan Son Nhut.

When our planes had reached Tan Son Nhut, the enemy control tower stared and asked, 'A-37s, what squadron are you from?' Our fighters answered, 'American made planes here!' The ex-

THE INVASION PLAN

During 1974 the forces of North Vietnam made steady gains in the South. Inflation was hitting the ARVN hard; the Thieu regime was unable to control corruption, and was incurring severe internal criticism which it met by cracking down on dissent; and, most important, US support was being reduced. There was a big question mark over whether US airpower, the saviour of the South in 1972, would be available.

Encouraged by Southern weakness, the Northern forces were building up their strength. Road systems made the Ho Chi Minh Trail into an efficient all-weather highway, and a pipeline now followed the Trail. By late spring 1974, the communists had retaken all the territory the ARVN had taken in the Delta in 1973. The balance of forces had decisively shifted in the North's favour.

In October 1974, General Tran Van Tra, a leading communist commander in the South, advocated an offensive into Phuoc Long Province, about 100km north of Saigon. The Northern politburo, mindful of the losses incurred in the 1972 offensive, were cautious; but the general's plan was given an initial go-ahead. The result was a spectacular success, with the province capital falling to NVA troops on 6 January 1975.

US response to this reverse was muted – no promise of more direct or indirect aid. The lack of US funding meant the South had to ground over 200 planes, cutting airlift capacity by 50 per cent. But the Soviet Union now began to step up help to Hanoi, and General Van Thien Dung was sent South to take control of a major offensive.

Dung's strategy was to hit through the Central Highlands to Ban Me Thuot, cutting the South in two; smaller attacks would tie the ARVN down in the northern provinces. The main intention was to gain territory to form the basis of a decisive offensive in the following year, 1976.

In fact, victory for the North came one year earlier, in 1975.

plosions struck Saigon and pillars of smoke rose high into the air. Our daring bombing raid destroyed a number of enemy airplanes, including American planes on evacuation missions. The enemy no longer had any place which was secure, no place where they could go to escape our punishing blows.

As 'H' hour approached a deep-strike unit including one tank brigade and one infantry regiment assembled secretly in a rubber forest south of Dau Giay to await the order to advance into Saigon. Our fighters were sitting ready in trucks, wearing neat new uniforms, and all red armbands so they could recognize each other easily when they entered the city.

'Defend to the death'

With leafy branches camouflaging people and vehicles, the whole unit roared off at 1500 hours on orders from the Second Army Corps command, truck after truck, bravely advancing toward the centre of Saigon. That imposing and historic sight as they moved out for the concluding attack of the war was truly unprecedented.

As we listened to the overall report of the situation, we all felt it had worked out well. General Cao Van Vien, chief of Saigon's General Staff, had fled before the ink on his signature was dry on the orders to 'defend to the death, to the very end, the portion of land that remains.'

Ho Chi Minh campaign headquarters was bustling with activity the night of 29 April. Flashlights, hurricane lamps and headlamps burned bright in every hut and along every road. Behind the combat operations room a battery of combat telephones worked incessantly. By 2400 hours on 29 April, 1975, the body of forces for the attack on Saigon was poised like a divine hammer held aloft, and the enemy about to be dealt a punishing blow shook and trembled in fright watching the hammer descend.

'Total victory is ours'

As it unfolds our history occasionally repeats itself. As with our forefathers in those nights before their final strategic general offensives against other invaders, our fighters on the Saigon front on the night of 29 April and early the next morning were restless, determined to win lightning victory. In those sacred hours, in this the final day of the period determined by the Political Bureau for the liberation of Saigon, the fighters wrote on their helmets, on their sleeves, on their gun slings the immortal proclamation of President Ho Chi Minh:

'Forward! Total victory is ours!'

THE 1975 INVASION

The NVA offensive in the Central Highlands, the key move in Dung's strategy, opened on 1 March 1975. After a feint towards Pleiku, the NVA cut ground links with Ban Me Thuot and their tanks roared into the town, with the ARVN fleeing before them. It was in communist hands by 13 March.

President Thieu now made two critical decisions. He ordered ARVN units in the Central Highlands to pull out of Pleiku and Kontum, to counter-attack Ban Me Thuot; while in the North, ARVN units were to abandon Quang Tri.

In both the North and the Central Highlands, these orders led to panic and disaster. A retreat under enemy pressure is possibly the hardest military manoeuvre, and the ARVN was simply not up to it.

Millions of civilians added to the confusion. In the northern provinces, Hue fell on 25 March, and Da Nang, where the great US base had been, on 30 March, amid scenes of confusion as thousands tried to get out of the cities.

In the Central Highlands, too, a stream of deserting soldiers (above) and civilians was the only hindrance the NVA now faced. By 1 April, the Central Highlands were effectively in communist hands.

The speed of this collapse surprised the NVA commanders. The question now was whether Thieu could hold the rich southern provinces before the rains came and slowed NVA operations – the race for Saigon was on.

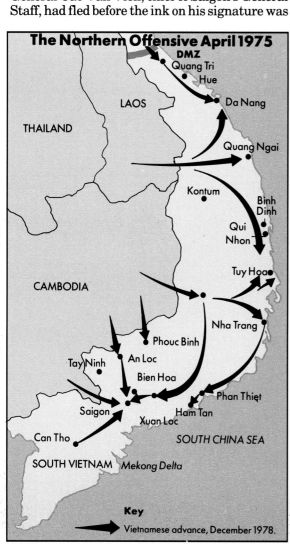

The Northern Offensive April 1975

DMZ
Quang Tri
Hue
LAOS
Da Nang
THAILAND
Quang Ngai
Kontum
Binh Dinh
Qui Nhon
Tuy Hoa
CAMBODIA
Nha Trang
Phouc Binh
An Loc
Tay Ninh
Bien Hoa
Phan Thiet
Saigon
Ham Tan
Xuan Loc
Can Tho
SOUTH CHINA SEA
SOUTH VIETNAM Mekong Delta

Key
→ Vietnamese advance, December 1978.

NVA TRACKS HEAD SOUTH

By 1975 the NVA were driving south with large numbers of tanks. The T-54/55 was the best they had.

The NVA first employed tanks south of the DMZ in 1968 but it was not until the 1972 Easter Offensive that they used them in large numbers. They then began using armour to spearhead infantry attacks, and at the apex of these formations came T-54/55 main battle tanks (MBT's).

The T-54's development can be traced to the classic T-34 design, the Soviet use of armour in World War II giving rise to their first post-war design in the T-44. This tank had problems with its turret design, cramping of the crew and with the installation of the 100mm D-10T main armament. By 1947 these shortfalls were largely overcome in a new prototype design, the T-54, a tank that was to give rise to the T-55 and T-62. The T-54 and its variants were to be built in greater numbers than any other Soviet tank after World War II.

The T-54's four-man crew was placed in a welded hull divided into three compartments. Power was provided by a 12-cylinder, water-cooled diesel engine which, because of its high alloy content, increased the risk of fire, to which the tank was particularly prone.

The cramped crew quarters, lack of hydraulic driving assistance, bouncy torsion bar suspension and a tendency for the tank to shed dead track made the T-54 an irritating vehicle to drive.

Compared with US Army and ARVN tank crews, NVA tankers were badly trained and their commanders poor at co-ordinating their armour with infantry attacks and artillery. This meant that the T-54/55 was less effective than it might have been. Though it had a 100mm main gun, the T-54/55 was lightly armoured compared to the opposing M48A3s. When the two met, the T-54/55 usually lost.

The 100mm main armament had been developed from a naval gun of the same calibre and, with the HVAPDS-T (High-Velocity Armour-Piercing Discarding Sabot-Tracer) shell, could penetrate well over 200mm of armour at 1000 metres. Only 34 rounds of 100mm ammunition were carried and because of the rounds' weight, and the fact that the gun had to be ele-vated after each firing for the ejection of the case, rate of fire was limited to a maximum of four rounds per minute. Another major drawback was that the main armament could only be depressed to -4 degrees, which made firing from a hill or reverse slope almost impossible.

The T-54's fire-control system involved co-ordination between the commander's binocular sight and rangefinder and the gunner's telescopic sight, and was slow and inaccurate compared with Western MBTs' fire control systems.

The T-55 had an almost identical external appearance to the T-54 but, in addition to incorporating the infra-red sights and snorkelling equipment of the T-54A, it featured a more powerful engine and more space for main-gun ammunition.

Although usually recorded as T-54/55s, many of the MBTs in NVA service were in fact Chinese T-59s, copies of the T-54A which differed only in minor details.

T-54 MAIN BATTLE TANK

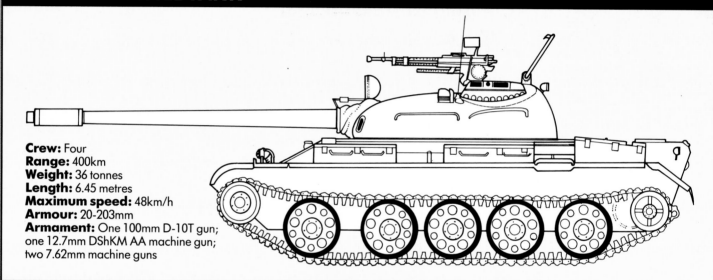

Crew: Four
Range: 400km
Weight: 36 tonnes
Length: 6.45 metres
Maximum speed: 48km/h
Armour: 20-203mm
Armament: One 100mm D-10T gun; one 12.7mm DShKM AA machine gun; two 7.62mm machine guns

---

Below: Flying a red flag, a T-54 enters Saigon.

There was an unrealistic atmosphere in Saigon as South Vietnam went through it's final death throes. Da Nang had fallen and now the NVA had surrounded the last ditch town of Xuan Loc which sits across Route 1. In the fishing port of Vung Tau, a boat drifted into the dockside loaded with a cargo of human sardines, all jammed together and only three days ahead of the communist steamroller. The exhausted refugees were ordered to keep moving south again.

The same tragic story was being repeated on Route 1, where there was another enemy waiting – the baking sun, which was keeping the temperature hovering at around 95 degrees, day after hopeless day.

Gone was the American air support; the South was on its own. With Saigon only one hour away, the ARVN dug in at Xuan Loc and fought a desperate battle to halt the advance of the NVA

LAST STAND AT XUAN LOC

Sheltering from the scorching heat under umbrellas or sheets of scrap iron, the refugees took their rest; small children carried their even smaller brethren on their backs, and everywhere the meek and mild had to fend for themselves.

That's why life seemed so unrealistic in Saigon, only 40 kilometres away, where a normal existence still seemed possible. Many people simply refused to believe that Saigon would fall. The coffee shops and restaurants were all open and the city dwellers carried on with their business as if everything was normal.

EYE-WITNESS

The author, Terry Fincher, was a reporter and photographer for the *Express* group newspapers during the Vietnam war. He covered the fall of Xuan Loc.

Journalists and photographers who were covering the final days of the war found it a very different business from when the Americans were there. Gone were the facilities of the US forces: no flak jackets, no tin helmets and no air transport to get you to and from the front. Instead, you hailed a taxi outside your hotel. If the driver was agreeable you'd ask him to take you to Xuan Loc, which was now besieged and under attack and heavy shelling by communist forces.

On the drive north, I saw that Route 1 was crowded with refugees heading south and fleeing

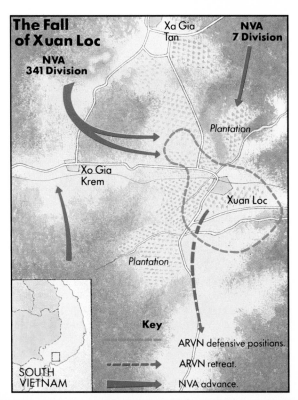

The Fall of Xuan Loc

Xa Gia Tan

NVA 341 Division

NVA 7 Division

Plantation

Xo Gia Krem

Xuan Loc

Plantation

Key

SOUTH VIETNAM

→ ARVN defensive positions.
--→ ARVN retreat.
→ NVA advance.

the communist advance. They were travelling by foot or, if lucky, by battered cars, motor bikes, and three-wheeled taxis. Rich and poor alike had loaded all the worldly possessions that they could carry onto any available form of transport. Perched on the top were the children and the aged. Some of the refugees had nothing, lacking even shoes to keep out the blistering heat of Route 1.

There were several check-points along the road to Xuan Loc, where identification papers were checked and re-checked. It seemed like just another useless bureaucratic order amongst all the chaos and hardship.

In a great open space outside the last small village before Xuan Loc, large Sikorsky helicopters that had been left over from the days of US involvement were landing more wounded: more refugees to join the exodus south after having been flown out from the fighting.

In by chopper
South Vietnamese troops were also waiting there to be choppered into the besieged town. They looked remarkably young, with clean uniforms and equipment not yet stained by the red dust which covered everything else.

Previous page: Bloodied and confused, the wounded at Xuan Loc. Below: NVA soldiers, captured during the height of the battle. The fighting raged for two weeks, with the ARVN troops and the South Vietnamese Air Force's cluster bombs inflicting heavy losses on the NVA. Even General Van Thien Dung admitted that the ARVN at Xuan Loc were a 'desperate, diehard enemy'.

It was here also that a dead North Vietnamese officer lay on a stretcher. His arm, stiff with rigor mortis, stuck straight out as the dust from the helicopter's wash blew around him. Soldiers and children stopped and stared listlessly at this now harmless enemy.

As we pushed on relentlessly as far as we could go, something warned us it was dangerous to proceed any further. Heavy, incoming shell fire could be heard just ahead and the road was deserted except for the odd refugee hurrying past. With me were two newspaper colleagues from the London *Sunday Times*, Philip Jacobson and the late Steve Brodie, a photographer. We got out of our car and watched a company of South Vietnamese soldiers hurrying across the road. They also seemed very young and, like the others, clean, as if they had only just arrived at the front. It was then that some incoming mortar rounds exploded nearby. We were the first to hit the ground; the reaction of the troops was a lot slower than ours.

Soon they were sheltering in a rubber plantation, spread out and less exposed. We ran back to our taxi, but had to dive into a ditch alongside our driver as some further mortar rounds came crashing in. It was pointless to try to go any further since it was obvious that the road ahead was in communist hands and that they were zeroed in on our position.

Getting back into our battered old taxi, a big, automatic Chevrolet, proved yet another bad experience. The driver had flooded the engine in his haste to get our of there, and we could only retreat in fits and starts, stalling frequently. We passed the body of a refugee who lay alongside the road, entangled with his bike. He had not been there before.

For several days running we made this same journey, returning each evening to Saigon. But at least we could get a respite from the extreme heat and refresh ourselves, unlike the refugees.

One morning I was having breakfast with Sandy Gall, the English television reporter, on the rooftop restaurant of the Caravelle Hotel. White table-cloths, polished cutlery and delicate flowers decorated the tables. The ritual of tea and toast made the war seem like a scene from a surrealist movie. Saigon was its usual self: a hot haze filtered the early sun through the open windows, the noise from the early morning traffic could be heard buzzing below us.

North by taxi

Suddenly, an A-37 screamed over the city, not much higher than our rooftop haven. As it disappeared into the distance over the Presidential Palace, we wondered what it was all about. Somebody remarked that it 'must be for morale purposes'. Once again the A-37 came in flying low, only this time it was firing its guns. We barely had time to be shocked before we saw it unleash a high explosive bomb, aimed straight at the palace. Everybody in the vicinity who had a weapon started shooting in a vain effort to down the aircraft along with its pilot – obviously a deserter – who would soon be landing in communist-held Da Nang.

Within half an hour I was once again making my way north by taxi, up Route 1 towards Xuan Loc. However, this time the front was just that little bit nearer Saigon, and it was impossible to get into Xuan Loc.

Eventually the pressure exerted by journalists forced the South Vietnamese military to lay on a

Above: As 40,000 North Vietnamese troops got a stranglehold on Xuan Loc, refugees fled in their thousands. When Xuan Loc fell and Saigon stood next in line, President Thieu resigned and the South prayed for a ceasefire. None came, and Vietnamese civilians and soldiers alike continued to suffer. Grabbing any transportation from wheelbarrows to bicycles, the refugees loaded up and fled. Where to wasn't clear anymore.

helicopter. It was decided that only 25 – including myself – would be taken in and that an ARVN officer would accompany us. He pointed out the dangers since we would be flying in low over enemy-held territory. Also, the town itself was being heavily shelled. Thousands of rounds had landed near the cathedral, flattening much of the town centre.

We flew low and fast at tree-top height, and landed on a dusty road on the outskirts of the town. Great clouds of dust filled the hot air as helicopters brought in supplies and evacuated the wounded and the refugees.

Tour by truck

We were taken by truck on a conducted tour of the area around the cathedral, past ruined buildings which were smouldering after the recent ferocious shelling. In the market place a wounded North Vietnamese prisoner was being treated by a South Vietnamese soldier, and in a rubber plantation on the edge of town blindfolded prisoners sat on the red earth.

After being briefed at the front line by an officer whose haggard face clearly showed the strain, it was time to leave Xuan Loc and to rendezvous with our helicopter pick-up. There was desperate

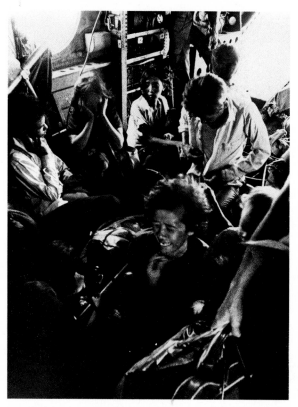

Left: This Vietnamese mother made it aboard the helicopter but any sense of relief is hopelessly tainted – her daughter was left behind. Nonetheless, these Vietnamese were the envy of many – they'd succeeded where hundreds had failed. Anxious and confused, the refugees have no idea where the chopper is taking them, and even less idea of what to expect when they get there.

ABANDONED BY THE US?

Much of the blame for the final collapse of South Vietnam has been laid at the door of the US and its failure to come to the aid of the South in its hour of need. But is this too simplistic an explanation?

'Today, Americans can regain the sense of pride that existed before Vietnam. But it cannot be achieved by refighting a war that is finished...These events, tragic as they are, portend neither the end of the world nor of America's leadership in the world.'

With these words President Ford, speaking on 23 April 1975, a week before the fall of Saigon, seemed to be relegating Vietnam to the history books.

From the beginning of the crisis which was to culminate in the fall of Saigon, the South Vietnamese leadership had clung to the hope that the Americans, somehow, would save the day. In 1972, communist attacks had been blunted by American airpower; three years later, a repeat performance was expected, in line with promises made by President Nixon at the time of the Paris Accords in early 1973.

But American politics had changed since then. Nixon, disgraced by the Watergate scandal, had resigned in August 1974 and his successor, Gerald Ford, was in no position to offer direct military support to the South, even if he had wanted to. American public opinion, relieved by the apparent end of the war in 1973, was hardly likely to back a recommitment of forces to Southeast Asia, and this was reflected in the existence of a Congress hostile to any such moves. Critics of the US stance over this crisis in South Vietnam's history point to the War Powers Act of November 1973 and the cuts imposed by Congress on economic assistance for the South, which reduced a request by Ford's Administration for $1.45 billion for the fiscal year 1974-75 to $700 million, as proof that it was primarily

Congressional antagonism that ultimately condemned the South.

Yet this is too simplistic. To begin with, Congress was merely reflecting US opinion, which was by this time strongly against any continuation of US involvement in Southeast Asia. Indeed, this reflection of public opinion can be seen in all branches of the US government machine, from the Pentagon to the Executive itself.

In March 1975, President Thieu travelled to Washington to plead his case in person. Although he received a favourable response from Ford and support from the Army Chief of Staff, General Weyand (who, after a fact-finding visit to Saigon, urged an additional cash input of $722 million), Thieu's mission ended in failure. It is indicative, though, that the support suggested by the powers that be in the US was purely financial. There had not even been any suggestion of deploying US airpower, which had been so effective in thwarting the Easter Invasion of 1972.

The truth of the matter is that South Vietnam largely had only itself to blame for the position it now found itself in. In 1973 the ARVN had been in a relatively strong position. But a combination of inefficiency, complacency, and the corruption that was endemic at all levels of both the military and the government had eroded whatever strength the ARVN may have had. While Thieu was pleading for extra aid, there were huge stockpiles of US equipment lying idle in South Vietnam, steadily deteriorating due to a combination of poor maintenance standards and corruption. (In fairness it should be pointed out that there were similar stockpiles in the US itself, condemned to remain there by a combination of lack of interest and bureaucratic red tape.)

The inescapable conclusion is that the US, internally riven and demoralized by 10 fruitless years of war, and the political scandals which largely sprang from the war, was in no mood to throw good money after bad, let alone more of its young men. By 1975 South Vietnam was doomed and, however reluctantly, the US recognized this fact.

pushing and shoving as refugees and wounded soldiers tried to get onto the helicopters. Our conducting officer was already on board and he was shouting over the noise of the engine, telling us to get on ourselves.

I clambered up and was pulling young children and babies onto the helicopter when it suddenly took off. People were still trying desperately to get on. Some fell off, including a little girl who had been hanging grimly onto the superstructure. Her grief-stricken mother had to be restrained by other refugees from jumping off the helicopter as it was gaining height. I felt so guilty – should I have stayed on the ground, pushing more children on board? I took out my camera and began taking pictures of the woman. I had to do something to hide my feelings.

Back in Saigon the final days of the war were now very close. The airline offices were full with the rich who were rushing to get out. On the day that Xuan Loc fell I left Saigon for home via Bangkok. Bangkok, a city full of tourists enjoying the life of luxury hotels and all the fun that a Far East holiday tour has to offer. I myself was full of tragic memories of the plight of the refugees, of the hardships and the loss of loved ones, a tragedy that is still happening today.

Top right: An ARVN soldier helps an injured civilian as his comrades file aboard a Chinook. Right: Dust flies and trees bend as another Chinook touches down. Helicopters buzzed the skies, but there simply weren't enough of them. Below: More of the endless stream of wounded are evacuated from Xuan Loc. Without US air support, the town was doomed.

The optimism that had carried Saigon through the war had vanished, swept aside by news of the enemy advance. NVA tanks were at the gates and the party was over

n April 1975 in Saigon, we ran. We ran for news, shelter, rumour, escape plans, hope. Everywhere it was the same story – confusion, panic, anxiety. Time was running out. The city was encircled, shells and rockets were pounding the outskirts. Soon it would be the airport, but the river was still open. The word was that people were getting out by boat. What should we do? Should we wait? Should we take our chances now; which route should we take? Plans were made, changed, dropped. Confidences exchanged. Money was counted – but still no-one knew what to do. The war was coming to an end and Saigon was our last refuge.

THE FALL OF

The armies of the North had swept through the country and now their tanks were just outside the city itself. We inside the city had been following the rolling advance of the past few weeks with flags on a map. Every day more flags turned red until we found ourselves as the next government flag. The enemy was at the gates.

There was a day which marked the inevitability of collapse. When it came, people saw the truth of disaster. It was Monday, 21 April, the day President Thieu resigned. The situation was so hopeless, there was no longer any point clinging to power. If Thieu was giving up, there was no hope left for any of us. But more than that, everyone felt a deep sense of betrayal.

Below: On the morning of 30 April, the first NVA tank follows standard-bearing troops into the grounds of the Presidential Palace. Below left: Victory belongs to the men of the North.

SAIGON

In his two-hour resignation speech, Thieu said the Americans had paid for the war in money, while we the Vietnamese had paid in blood. Why shouldn't the Americans share the sacrifice? People took this to mean we had fought the war because we had been paid for it. It angered everyone. But it also scared everyone, since the one man who really knew what was going on was abandoning his post. Earlier that same day, the besieged town of Xuan Loc had finally fallen to the North.

But even before Thieu's resignation, people knew the situation was rapidly worsening. Ever since the Northern offensive broke on 10 March, when three crack NVA divisions overran the town of Ban Me Thuot, the news had all been bad. Our own army simply unravelled before the advance. Provincial towns fell or were simply given up – Hue, Da Nang, Pleiku, Kontum. On our map, we watched the government areas left over from the 1972 ceasefire – the 'leopard spots' – dissolve. Each day, we speculated about the territorial and political concessions the government would make, to save what was left of the South. But, implacably, the advance rolled on.

Bad news and worse news

All through the month of April, we knew the US Congress was holding out against an emergency $722 million military aid package, but when we saw the last shipment of artillery arrive, without shells, the army lost hope utterly. We were hungry for news, listening to the Voice of America, the BBC, the Australian news services. Each wave of refugees brought fresh news from the provinces and the level of fear rose still higher. Saigon was run on rumours. And as things got worse, the rumours grew more fantastic.

Everyone talked of a bloodbath. The communists would kill all civil servants and journalists. In their view, or so we thought, journalists would be among the first to go because they were seen as an extension of the psychological war being waged.

The communists would confiscate everyone's money, leaving only a little, to make everyone equal. They would force all the single women to marry communist soldiers, especially wounded soldiers. And the painted fingernails of our women would be torn off to show they no longer lived in a frivolous capitalist society.

Although we feared the enemy, the evils were actually being done by our own soldiers, the very ones who were supposed to protect us. Refugees told of being run off the road by soldiers in hijacked vehicles as they fled from the front. Tales were told of murder, rape and robbery of civilians as marines shot their way onto ships bound for the south. At Puh Quoc Island, a staging post for refugees outside Saigon – they were kept there for fear of communist infiltrators – the colonel in charge stopped a marine coming ashore, searched him and found his arms covered in wristwatches. He ordered him shot as an example.

Another ominous sign of the war coming to Saigon was the bombing of the presidential palace

itself. Early one morning, an A-37 jet, piloted by a defecting South Vietnamese air force officer, made three passes and hit the palace on the last run. Not much damage was done, Thieu was untouched, but morale fell. Prices rose alarmingly in Saigon as the news got worse. When we heard of the US aid cut, people started hoarding – some to speculate against future shortages, others simply to use up money which would be of no use or confiscated under the communist regime. All this time, shops and restaurants stayed open and were full of people. Customers sat and stared, stirring their coffee endlessly, waiting.

People committed suicide out of despair, among them those who had left the North 20 years before. They feared that they would be marked down for revenge.

In such a climate, it was difficult to know who to trust, who to share an escape plan with. You might be tricked and robbed, or might find it was someone who would denounce you to the communists after the fall. But you needed contacts, people who knew other trusted people, who could get you

passage on a boat or a plane. There were exit visas and passports to organize. So every day, you ran around town, running to work – people still went to work but no work got done, of course – running to see family, to see friends, to meet contacts, to see, to hear, to be reassured. When there was a 24-hour curfew, it was unenforceable.

When the shells and 122mm rockets started falling, you could feel the earth shake and people threw themselves to the ground. The rockets slammed in and around Tan Son Nhut airport and

Left: Sporting shorts and automatic rifles, Viet Cong supporters follow the NVA into Saigon. Below: Gatecrashing at the palace. As NVA armour crashes towards the Presidential Palace, a symbolic final breakthrough is added to military victory. The palace would soon be renamed Doc Lap, 'The Palace of Liberation'.

THE CURTAIN FALLS

Saigon was strangely quiet as the last US helicopters departed early on the morning of 30 April. The panic of the last few days had subsided and, with the exception of the looters, the streets were deserted. Everyone was waiting for the communists to arrive.

President Duong Van Minh ('Big Minh'), who had been appointed less than 48 hours earlier, was hoping that a battle could be avoided. On 29 April he had sent representatives to meet the communists at Tan Son Nhut, in the hope that negotiations were possible now that two of the North's main conditions – the withdrawal of all US troops and the resignation of Thieu – had been met. He was to be disappointed: instead of negotiating, the communists introduced a new condition: 'the dissolution of the puppet military and police.' Minh had little choice but to comply.

At 1020 hours on 30 April, Radio Saigon called on the people to stand by for a presidential announcement. A few

moments later, Minh made his speech: 'I believe firmly in reconciliation among all Vietnamese. To avoid needless bloodshed, I ask the soldiers of the Republic to put an end to all hostilities. Be calm and remain where you are. To save the lives of the people do not open fire...'

As the words echoed through the streets of the city, relayed by loudspeakers, the looters began to drift away, clearing the roads for an unopposed NVA advance. At 1215 hours, T-54 tanks appeared in front of the Presidential Palace. An NVA sapper team raced ahead to plant their flag on the presidential balcony, before bursting into the conference room where Minh and his aides were waiting. Political officers joined them in time to hear Minh announce: 'We have been waiting for you so that we can turn over the government.' The reply was curt: 'You have nothing left to turn over. You can surrender unconditionally.' The communists had won.

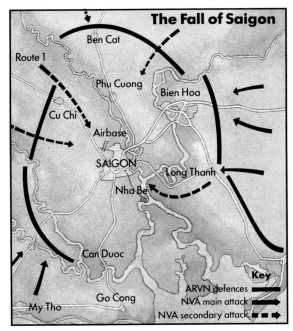

The Fall of Saigon

Ben Cat

Route 1

Phu Cuong

Bien Hoa

Cu Chi

Airbase

SAIGON

Long Thanh

Nha Be

Can Duoc

Go Cong

My Tho

Key
ARVN defences
NVA main attack
NVA secondary attack

we were afraid no planes could get out. People flocked along the road to get to the airport before it was closed and were killed by the artillery rounds: their bodies lying in the dust for days. No-one seemed to care anymore.

Night and day, we could hear government planes bombing the NVA just outside the city. There were no more B-52 raids, but the air force used 500lb bombs and one truly terrible weapon, the CBU-55. This bomb detonated with a gigantic explosion which incinerated and blasted everyone for a huge distance, suffocating victims further out by burning up all the oxygen in the area. It was gruesome but it did not halt the offensive.

When American radio started playing strange notes, we knew it was the signal for their long-awaited evacuation. People sped off to the gathering places – the university, behind the cathedral, the US embassy.

On the road to the airport, there were cars left abandoned, their keys still in the dashboard. We saw the helicopters and C-130 Hercules transports leave, loaded with their human cargoes. With the Americans finally departing, it was all over. I saw a soldier of one of the elite units, on guard outside the presidential palace, with tears streaming down his face. He just stood and cried in public.

On 30 April, General Minh declared the surrender over the radio. The war was lost. Soldiers stripped off their uniforms. There was wholesale looting. There were many poor people in Saigon and they broke into the houses of the rich who had left. Fear uncovers hidden strength and I saw quite small people carry off huge objects – beds were a particular favourite.

Cycling communists

Petrol was siphoned out of cars to be sold immediately on the pavements. Those who had money left went out and bought a bicycle in the belief that it was a badge of simple living and would be well looked on by the communists – even though bicycles were really expensive. Others bought anything they caught sight of, tinned milk, biscuits, chocolates, little luxuries that would soon vanish.

Some just gave their money away. It was no longer of any value. Their world had ended. The city which had been the centre of their lives was to be conquered territory, occupied by invaders. They felt twice betrayed, by their allies and then by their own leaders who had deserted them. And now it was over, we were still scared but we had stopped caring. A sense of fatalism descended.

There was a strange feeling of relief, after the weeks of climbing anxiety. When we saw the first communist troops – the creatures we had feared as if they were wild animals – we were struck by how ridiculously young they were. They seemed no more than children. Some of us instinctively offered them food, as if they were our kith and kin, which they were. Our conquerors marched in like long-lost sons.

THE FALL OF THE CITY

By 28 April 1975 Saigon was surrounded. As a total of 16 communist divisions (140,000 men) closed in, the defenders – about 60,000 ARVN soldiers, drawn from the remnants of a variety of broken units – fell into a state of near panic. Few areas of the city were adequately defended and military cohesion had virtually disappeared. The US evacuation efforts, centred on Tan Son Nhut airfield, did little to relieve the atmosphere of defeat, while the appointment of General Duong Van Minh as president merely smacked of desperation.

Minh's inaugural speech, relayed by TV and radio to the city's frightened populace that morning, held out a slender hope of negotiation, but few believed in it, particularly when North Vietnamese pilots, flying captured A-37 fighter-bombers, raided Tan Son Nhut a few minutes later. That evening, General Van Thien Dung, NVA commander in the South, ordered a final push to secure the city.

The attack began at 0400 hours on 29 April, with NVA artillery and rocket strikes on Tan Son Nhut. US C-130s were hit, effectively halting fixed-wing evacuation. Although elements of the South Vietnamese Air Force took off under the command of ex Vice-President Ky, they could find few targets and soon ran out of both ammunition and fuel. Minh formally requested the Americans to pull out of Saigon, hoping that this would persuade the communists to compromise, but when his offer of talks was rejected that night, it was obvious that the time for negotiation was over.

The evacuation of the US embassy (Operation Frequent Wind) gathered pace and, as the last CH-46 lifted off soon after dawn on 30 April, the NVA penetrated the city. Spearheaded by T-54 tanks, they entered the Presidential Palace at 1100 hours, seizing the reins of government a few minutes later. The occupation of Saigon, in stark contrast to the rest of the war, had been a relatively bloodless affair.

OPERATION

When Bing Crosby starts crooning White Christmas, even though it's 105 degrees and rising, activity at the American embassy climbs to fever pitch. Option IV has begun

Above: Mid-afternoon, 29 April, and the gathering crowds are desperate to cross the barbed wire and get into the embassy complex. US boots, fists and rifle butts will be needed to keep the Vietnamese out.

Saigon in late April 1975 was a city of rumours. Rumours that the Americans had won a last-minute peace agreement from the North, that there had been a coup in Hanoi and the NVA would be pulled back and, of course, that the B-52s would arrive overhead and save Saigon as they had done in 1972. However, it was not to be. Deep down inside, the people probably knew it. All those who could get out certainly did. Commercial flights from the airport were full – packed with the wealthy and whatever they could carry. American companies had begun to withdraw their employees in March and special flights were laid on for American bankers and their families.

The US authorities had prepared an emergency plan in case of a Northern invasion – Operation

Frequent Wind. There was also a vague plan to evacuate the 200,000 or so South Vietnamese who would be at risk should the North take over. However, the planners had not counted on the speed with which the NVA swept down through the South and they had never expected the final ARVN retreat to turn into the rout that it so quickly became. Furthermore, Graham Martin, the US ambassador to South Vietnam, had decided – for good or ill – to delay any evacuation until the last possible moment, in the hope of avoiding a panic. When, in the third week of April, Washington finally ordered the evacuation of all non-essential personnel, it soon became clear that, although it had been estimated that there were about 7000 Americans in need of evacuation, the true figure was nearer 35,000. With the ARVN crumbling, time was running out.

Chaos from the start

Ken Moorefield was special assistant to the US Ambassador in Saigon and was working at Saigon's Tan Son Nhut Air Force Base when the evacuation was stepped up on 20 April. He describes the chaotic scenes around the base: 'We had a mandate to take only Americans and their dependants. Initially, I even tried to get people married or to adopt children...The first day there were only 300-400 refugees, but we were quickly up to thousands...I was still in a sense fighting. Battling for whatever manoeuvring room was left to save peoples' lives.'

The NVA were getting closer all the time. Moorefield continues: 'The people who were at the evacuation centre were panicked already. Terribly panicked. They'd already escaped from some other part of the country in most cases. They had already suffered the traumatic and dramatic collapse of the country.'

Things were starting to get out of hand. At Tan

THE AFTERMATH

The main thing Western journalists remaining behind in Saigon noticed was the silence. 'Big Minh' broadcast the surrender over the radio at 1020 on 30 April and soon the streets were full of discarded uniforms as soldiers and police melted back into civilian life. Northern flags began to appear as the tanks and then the infantry of the NVA 324th Division entered Saigon. A single tank crashed through the gates of the Presidential Palace at 1215, then obligingly recreated the scene, as Western cameramen had missed it first time around. It was to be a media war to the very end.

Communist cadres began to emerge – four of them took over the building to prevent incriminating files on South Vietnamese officials being destroyed.

Memories of the Hue massacres in 1968 had led to fears of a bloodbath in Saigon, but it did not take place. Instead, the crowds mingled with the young Northern troops who were taking in new sights and sounds. The black-market traders continued to do good business and the troops camped out in the streets and open spaces.

The broadcast announcing that Saigon was now Ho Chi Minh City brought about an abrupt change, however. On 1 May the bars, brothels and all places 'for American-type activities' were closed.

A communist newspaper, the *Giai Phong*, appeared on 5 May, a census of inhabitants was begun and registration for the supporters of the old regime was announced on 6 May. Despite all the hopes, it was not, after all, going to be like old times.

FREQUENT WIND

Son Nhut there were desperate South Vietnamese troops who would obviously be at risk when the North won. Ugly scenes developed as soldiers and civilians fought and pushed each other off the evacuation planes. Many Vietnamese pilots took matters into their own hands and flew themselves out. Swarms of helicopters landed on US carriers in the South China Sea. When the decks were full the helicopters were pushed overboard. Other pilots, seeing that there was no more landing space available, hovered near the ships and then made a desperate leap into the ocean, hoping to be picked up.

At 0400 hours on the morning of 29 April 1975 the NVA began shelling Saigon itself. The explosions woke Moorefield and he made his way back to the airfield: 'The air base was being rocketed when I arrived there. Helicopters and airplanes

Above: Americans hurriedly embark on the trip of a lifetime – the limited edition flight to safety. Right: From inside the embassy, US troops act as ambassadors for exclusivity – a lucky few get out, while a less fortunate many are left to contemplate their bleak future.

1975

LEFT TO THEIR FATE?

On 29 and 30 April the Americans evacuated approximately 8000 people from Saigon roof-tops, yet many South Vietnamese who had helped the Americans and could have been targets for execution were left behind. Why?

The US ambassador in Saigon, Graham Martin, later claimed that 22,294 South Vietnamese employees of American agencies were safely evacuated from the country in April 1975. However, this was less than a quarter of an estimated 90,000 such employees excluding dependants. For example, of 1900 Vietnamese CIA employees, only 557 escaped, and only 218 from 1122 employees of Special Assistant to the Ambassador for Field Operations (SAFFO), the successor to CORDS, got out. Even worse, in the haste to escape, tons of sensitive documents naming US employees were left intact.

Many 'high risk' South Vietnamese were left behind, including members of the Special Police Branch, the Central Intelligence Organisation (CIO), defectors and counter-terrorist agents from the Phoenix Program. Indeed, in the last frantic moments of the evacuation, prominent South Vietnamese politicians and a South Korean general were left behind in the embassy compound, while those arguably less at risk, such as bar girls, were evacuated.

The fact that so many employees did escape was due to the efforts of individuals such as US Defense Attache, Major-General Homer Smith, to circumvent official policy by organizing illegal 'black flights'. The difficulty arose because both Secretary of State Kissinger and Ambassador Martin frustrated evacuation plans until it was far too late. Kissinger was still seeking a compromise in diplomatic negotiations with Hanoi, while Martin was determined to maintain the illusion of support for South Vietnam for fear of triggering an even faster collapse. The US Immigration and Naturalization Service was also wary of relaxing its rules to allow in large numbers of refugees at a time when the US economy was in recession. The matter was further complicated because, until 25 April, Congress was opposed to any suggestion that a US military presence might be required to allow orderly evacuation. Only State Department and Commander-in-Chief, Pacific Command (CINPAC) pressure made Martin act, while President Ford authorized military cover for evacuation as US commander-in-chief without Congressional approval.

Left: Vice-President Ky with his family en route to Tan Son Nhut airfield. Below left: A motley flotilla of Vietnamese craft make their way towards the American fleet. Right: A chopper is dumped from the US carrier *Blue Ridge* to make space for others to land during the closing stages of Frequent Wind.

were trying to get off the ground to escape...The city was in flames, the communists had the city surrounded with missiles. We realised we were down to hours, if not minutes.'

News of the rocket attacks on the airport prompted a series of top-level emergency meetings in Washington. Within hours the order came through from President Ford: Martin was to evacuate all Americans remaining in Saigon. He visited Tan Son Nhut and saw the chaos. It was enough. As Major-General Homer Smith pointed out to him: 'Either we go with Option Four or we're going to look pretty stupid or pretty dead'.

Chopper cavalry

As soon as Martin gave the go-ahead for the final evacuation, a flight of 81 helicopters flew from the US fleet – which had been carefully assembled off the coast – to Tan Son Nhut airport, which by now was under sporadic North Vietnamese sniper fire. The shelling had made it impossible for aircraft to land and the arrival of the helicopters prompted an outburst of real joy. A force of 865 Marines was dropped off to keep the area secure. Then, despite worries that the NVA might at any moment bring SAMs into action against the helicopters, the evacuation continued, with the helicopters flying southwest over barracks reserved for ARVN dependants and in the process receiving over 100 rounds from M-16s and M-79 grenade fire. The flight had clearly begun. It did not do so, however, without touches of bureaucratic red tape. For instance, Martin would not permit local employees of the IBM subsidiary to evacuate since they had to process the payroll for the Saigon government!

By 1930 hours the helicopters, which had flown continually to and from the carriers, had succeeded in getting almost all of the people out. Forty minutes after leaving Vietnamese soil, the evacuees were on board a US Navy carrier.

All that could be done now was to complete the evacuation by clearing everyone out of the US embassy. Moorefield had been looking for stragglers and found himself outside the embassy in the late afternoon, in the midst of the thousands of Vietnamese who were trying desperately to find a way inside. He recalls: 'I finally pushed my way through the crowd and got to the front gate. I caught the attention of one of the Marine guards, who opened the gate for me. I slipped inside. The rest of the late afternoon and early evening, I looked to see what needed to be done and helped pull some people over the back wall. Evacuation by helicopter was ongoing.'

Room at the top

The helicopters had to land on a pad on the top of the embassy roof and this in itself caused further problems: 'We were dealing with a 90mph prop blast and there was no guard-rail. For people who were tired, fatigued or disoriented, it was somewhat dangerous. One of our Marines had fallen off the helicopter pad onto the roof below and cracked his skull.

'I spent the rest of the night up there. During the wee hours of the morning I had plenty of time to think. It was a rather calm and reflective opportunity – there was an opportunity to reflect on the full extent of our damage and our loss.'

Associated Press photographer Neal Ulevich also found himself in the midst of the throng outside the embassy as the airlift was beginning: 'We knew the Marines would take us in. We had to get in close. Thousands of Vietnamese were at the wall, hoping to climb over and into a helicopter. The Marines were pushing them back to keep the embassy from being overrun, allowing only westerners and a few Saigon officials inside.

'Vietnamese began to crawl over the barbed wire on top of the wall, like commandos. One man caught his leg and fell. He dangled upside down, hanging by a lacerated leg.

'The Marines spotted us. Our group pushed nearer the wall. The crowd pressed closer. A youngster, perhaps 18, and half American, clung desperately to my neck. "I will die if I stay" she cried out.

Inside the embassy

'Mothers held their children above the mass of people for Marines to take them inside. One of my cameras disappeared. Then my watch was gone. The Marines, still kicking Vietnamese, started grabbing westerners by their collars and hauling them up.

'Once inside the embassy, it was easy. The embassy compound was in chaos, but a quiet man with a .45 calibre pistol in his belt led us to the inner court where Marines in combat gear guarded the walls.

'He led us into a building to make our way to the roof. Waiting in the corridors, we saw men calmly destroying code machines with hammers. The place was littered. Offices were now deserted.

'Telephones were ringing and no-one was answering them. We were nearing the end.

'We heard the roar of the helicopter settling down on the embassy roof and we climbed the staircase. The Marine CH-46 was waiting when we emerged, its twin rotors turning great arcs in the drizzly greyness. Suddenly we were airborne and the lights of Saigon seemed like gems growing dimmer and smaller.'

Americans only

At about 0400 hours on the morning of 30 April, 1975 direct orders were received from Washington that only American staff were to be evacuated from that moment on. When the next chopper arrived, Moorefield escorted Ambassador Martin onboard. There were still 300-400 Vietnamese outside the embassy. Moorefield recalled the last frantic minutes before leaving the compound: 'The next helicopter came in. I put the last remaining American citizens onto the helicopter. There was no-one left. I decided at that point that my job was done. There was nothing left to do. I got on the helicopter and went.'

In just over 40 minutes Moorefield was safe onboard a US carrier. He was among the lucky ones who were able to get away; who could say goodbye to a war they had been unable to win and a people they had never fully understood. The same day, those who didn't get out began a lifetime under communist rule.

FREQUENT WIND

It was not until 9 April 1975 that the Americans began detailed planning for an evacuation. The US Army Attaché, Colonel Wahle, outlined four possible options: Options I and II were step-by-step airlifts; Option III was a combined air and sea lift; while Option IV was a heliborne lift from Saigon itself (above). In addition to the embassy, 13 buildings were selected as potential LZs.

Americans were told to listen to US Armed Forces Radio for a coded message – 'Mother wants you to call home' – and a weather report: 'It is 105 degrees and rising', followed by Bing Crosby's recording of 'White Christmas' – repeated every 15 minutes.

Off the coast, US Navy Task Force 76, with the carriers Hancock, Okinawa and Midway waited with 81 helicopters. Aircraft from Task Force 77 were to fly air cover. Operation Frequent Wind – Option IV – began at 1108 hours on 29 April. The evacuation from city roof-tops ended at about 1830 on 29 April but that at the US embassy continued until 0430 the following day. During those 18 hours a total of 1373 Americans, 5595 South Vietnamese and 85 'third country nationals' were evacuated – 2100 from the embassy itself. The last of the 865 Marines used to secure the embassy – 11 men carrying the flag – left at 0753.

In addition to the official evacuation, 41 South Vietnamese Air Force aircraft loaded with air crews and their families made for the task force.

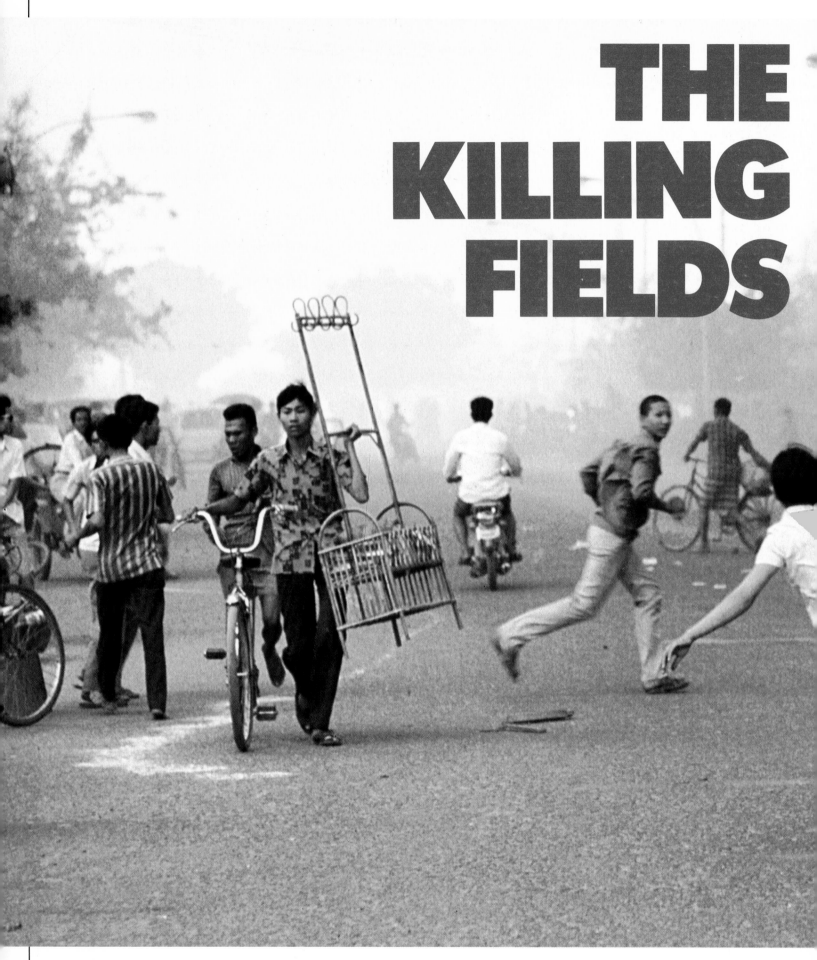

THE KILLING FIELDS

Tightening their stranglehold over Phnom Penh, the Khmer Rouge moved in for the kill. For many, it would be a slow death

Above: Khmer Rouge guerrillas on the outskirts of Phnom Penh await the final push on the Cambodian capital. Left: As communist shells bombard the city, panic-stricken civilians flee in terror. However, there was to be no hiding place. Some of the fiercest fighting in defence of Phnom Penh was that conducted by US deserters, drug peddlars and black-marketeers who had come to Cambodia from Saigon when South Vietnam's capital had fallen two years earlier.

Just one hour into 1975 a barrage of artillery and rocket fire from around the city of Phnom Penh announced the beginning of the final Khmer Rouge offensive. It was not swift to succeed, but it was sure. Some 5000 guerrillas were positioned along the banks of the Mekong between the city and the South Vietnamese border, preventing supply convoys from getting through to the capital. There were virtually no reserves of rice and shortages were felt almost immediately. For Cambodia, the 20th century was drawing to a premature end.

On 6 March, the Khmer Rouge howitzers advanced to within range of the airport. Year Zero was coming ever closer. All efforts by government forces to drive back the encircling guerrillas failed. The Khmers crept nearer and nearer to the heart of the city. Meanwhile, the US Congress had washed its hands of Cambodia. There would be no more money and no return of the B-52s. The Cambodians were on their own.

Conditions in Phnom Penh were appalling. Rocket and artillery fire battered the city streets. The peasant refugees were starving, the hospitals were out of medical supplies. Government soldiers carried on a meaningless fight until 16 April; then it was all over.

At dawn on the 17th, the austere army of teenage peasant guerrillas marched into Phnom

565

Penh along the once-smart boulevards. The expressionless self-control of the Khmer Rouge struck the first note of terror in the city's inhabitants. The guerrilla fighters were impervious to argument, bribery or sentiment. They had known nothing in their lives but the brutality of war – mutilated corpses as much a part of daily existence as a bowl of rice. And they had learnt to obey without question the orders of their political leaders. Phnom Penh could read its fate in their hard, worn and implacable faces.

Death or slavery

The evacuation of the city began that same afternoon – 17 April. The whole population was ordered to leave on foot for the countryside. No exceptions were allowed: even the hospitals were emptied. For many, already weakened by malnutrition or disease, it was a death march. As the great exodus stumbled out of the city into the unknown, under the eyes of the impassive Khmer Rouge, the dead fell by the roadside and were left where they lay.

Watchful soldiers looked out for signs of easy-living, education, wealth or power. Anyone with good clothes, soft hands, or a well-fed look was pulled out of the human stream and interrogated. If they naively admitted to being one of that elite of Phnom Penh – a bureaucrat, businessman, doctor, teacher or engineer – they were immediately taken away and shot. 'Class vengeance' was a favourite slogan of the Khmer Rouge. Other massacres took place in the city itself. The Khmer Rouge broadcast an order for all leading officers and officials of the previous government to present themselves at the Ministry of Information. Most, fearing worse treatment if they refused, turned up as ordered. All were killed.

Once, the tree-lined streets of the Cambodian capital had reeked of colonial charm like a cheap imported Parisian perfume. Behind the French facade of pavement cafés and chic *haute cuisine* restaurants, the pleasures of the East had proliferated in the opium dens and the brothel houseboats of the Tonle Sap. But the opulence of the capital was but a fading memory for the thousands of city dwellers now marching towards a life of slavery in the countryside.

Marching towards Year Zero

The decision to empty Phnom Penh after victory had been taken by the Khmer Rouge leadership back in February 1975, because it seemed to provide the answer to three problems. First, there was the question of political control – the Khmer Rouge felt that they were not yet ready to run the country in the conventional sense. The staunch communist cadres who would be responsible for organizing the new society numbered only 14,000. Even their young peasant army was not numerous enough to control the millions of inhabitants of Phnom Penh. But if the city dwellers were dispersed to the countryside, it was argued, they would be too disorganized and disorientated to

OPERATION EAGLE PULL

Just as Ambassador Martin's diplomatic manoeuvring was later to delay the evacuation of Saigon, Henry Kissinger's determination to maintain a 'stabilizing' American presence in Cambodia caused considerable anxiety to the US ambassador in Phnom Penh, John Gunther Dean. Dean asked for his staff to be evacuated as early as 3 April 1975, as the Khmer Rouge closed rapidly on the doomed city. But Kissinger declined, since he was negotiating to bring Prince Sihanouk back to the capital for a compromise peace. With the city airport closed by

Khmer Rouge bombardment on 11 April, Kissinger finally relented and Operation Eagle Pull commenced.

The US Seventh Fleet's amphibious task force – Task Force 76 – already had elements to carry out a heliborne evacuation using the USS *Okinawa* in the Gulf of Siam. At 0600 hours on 12 April, Dean sent out messages to members of the Cambodian government and other prominent politicians offering places on the choppers in two-and-a-half hours time.

However, the only Cambodian politician to accept Dean's offer was the acting president,

Saukham Khoy. The prime minister, Long Boret, and others on the Khmer Rouge death list of 'Seven Traitors', declined the offer, refusing to leave their homeland. At 0900 hours the first of 36 CH-53 helicopters set down close to the embassy, to disgorge 360 Marines as a security force to secure the perimeter and protect the evacuees. Just after 1000 hours, 82 Americans, 35 other non-Cambodians and 159 Cambodians (mostly embassy employees and their families) had been safely evacuated. Watched by a small crowd, the last Marines lifted off at 1113 hours.

offer any real resistance. Evacuation would thus manufacture the conditions for total power.

Second, there was the problem of the Cambodian economy. The guerrilla war and the American bombing had laid waste much of the land. Rice stocks were almost exhausted but the Khmer Rouge refused, as their most fundamental principle, any help from abroad. The economy would have to be rebuilt by the Cambodians themselves, by turning the whole country into a work-camp.

A diet of lizards and toads

Finally, the evacuation of Phnom Penh was seen as a great leap forward towards the ideal communist society of which the Khmer Rouge leaders dreamed. At a stroke, the city dwellers lost all their property and became peasants. Those who would not or could not accept this change would be killed. With urban corruption eradicated, a totally new society would be built on fresh foundations – work, revolutionary purity, national independence. It was Year Zero: the country was to be built again from nothing.

The beginnings of the new society already

Below: Running for cover from the communist bombardment, US Marines land near the US embassy in order to evacuate American personnel and selected Cambodians. Left: Stone-faced and implacable, the Khmer Rouge enter Phnom Penh. Not for them, however, the indulgence of victory celebrations. Within hours they were overseeing the enforced evacuation of the entire civilian population.

existed in the 'liberated' areas that had been under Khmer Rouge control during the war. Here, money and private property had been abolished and all the population grouped in co-operative farms, where the peasants worked from dawn to dusk in return for a meagre portion of food doled out by the Khmer Rouge authorities. These 'old people', the peasants already in the co-operatives, now had to take in the 'new people', the deportees from the city. When the city dwellers who survived the long gruelling march from Phnom Penh arrived at the co-operative that was to be their new home, they did not receive a warm welcome.

Their incompetence at work in the fields earned them the contempt of the 'old people', and could get them executed for 'economic sabotage'. Many soon succumbed to hardships that the peasants had learned to endure: back-breaking work, starvation and lack of medical care. The 'new people' died like flies. The attitude of the authorities was summed up in a slogan: 'If you keep this man there is no profit. If he goes there is no loss.'

Minorities exterminated

The identity of the leaders who were imposing this fate on Cambodia remained for a long time a mystery. Pol Pot, Ieng Sary, Ieng Thirith and Khieu Samphan – the small clique of Paris-educated intellectuals in control of the Khmer Rouge – set up their power centre in the ghost city of Phnom Penh and from there imposed an iron grip on Cambodia. The country was divided into zones, and each zonal party secretary was answerable to the central authority in Phnom Penh, while each co-operative ruling committee was answerable to the head of the zone. But the population had never heard of Pol Pot and his

THE NEWS GETS OUT

After the Americans had evacuated their embassy on 12 April 1975, at least 700 Europeans remained in Phnom Penh. Among them were a handful of journalists, including Jon Swain of the London *Sunday Times* and Sydney Schanberg of the *New York Times*. When the Khmer Rouge finally entered the city on 17 April most foreigners, including Swain and Schanberg, ended up at the French embassy.

They were not evacuated from the embassy for three weeks, and were able to glimpse something of the forced evacuation of the city's inhabitants.

Schanberg was able to file his first report on 8 May. That same month, refugees began to arrive in Thailand with stories of Khmer Rouge atrocities. Most of what happened in Kampuchea has been reconstructed from their harrowing accounts.

Observers such as Francois Ponchaud and the *Reader's Digest* staffers, John Barron and Anthony Paul, were also able to glean additional information from careful scrutiny of the broadcasts of Radio Phnom Penh, 'The Voice of Democratic Kampuchea'.

However, the full extent of the massacres only became apparent after the Vietnamese invaded Kampuchea in December 1978; Hanoi publicised the excesses of Pol Pot (below) and the Khmer Rouge to justify its invasion.

1975

colleagues – orders were issued simply in the name of Angka, the Organization. Only Prince Sihanouk, officially still leader of the movement that had overthrown Lon Nol, was widely known. The country's new rulers had no time for Sihanouk, however, now that he had served their purposes in achieving victory. The prince returned to Phnom Penh, only to be put under house arrest. In January 1976 the monarchy was officially abolished and the following March Sihanouk announced to his people his retirement from politics 'to have more time for private life'. Cambodia was renamed the Democratic Republic of Kampuchea.

Throughout 1976, Pol Pot and his colleagues pressed forward towards their ideal society. Private eating was abolished – all food had to be consumed in communal canteens from stocks controlled by the Khmer Rouge. Any attempt to improve one's diet, even by picking wild fruit or vegetables, could lead to execution. Some turned

to a diet of lizards, toads and earthworms. Family relations were discouraged. Children in the co-operatives slept in dormitories away from their parents. Youngsters were encouraged to spy on their parents and denounce them if their behaviour was judged impure by the standards of Angka. With the teachers and intellectuals exterminated, there was no education of the young, simply a brutal process of indoctrination. Different members of a family were sometimes drafted into work brigades and sent to opposite ends of the country. There was no postal system or telephone, so once contact was lost, they were unlikely to meet again. All private pleasures were forbidden. Sex outside marriage was punishable by death.

Executions, carried out either on the orders of the secret police or of the co-operative ruling committee, were as discreet and mysterious as Angka itself. People disappeared in the night; it was not safe to ask where they had gone. Some were killed on a pure whim – to possess thick-

Above: So-called 'Mobile Brigades' at work on dykes in Kampuchea. The construction of dams and irrigation works was a national obsession under Pol Pot. However, the reign of terror in Year Zero was to produce more sinister landmarks – the killing fields, stacked high with human skulls.

lensed glasses, for example, made you a target for Pol Pot's butchers. The favourite method of execution was a blow to the back of the head or neck with the base of an axe-head. Bullets were in short supply. Disembowelling and burying alive were also favourites, with the victims usually required to dig their own graves. Whole truck loads of people vanished without trace. Keeping a firm grip on the reign of terror in the villages was simple for the Khmers. A few rotting human remains, scattered along the trail into the village, would suffice. Rumours of victims suffering grotesque torture – throats sawn by razor-sharp reeds or serrated palm fronds – had the same chilling effect. At first, it was chiefly the 'class enemy' which was targeted – anyone who was not born a peasant or worker, or who had education. Then there were national minorities – the Chinese, the Vietnamese, the Cham Muslims. Pol Pot believed in the purity of the Khmer race as firmly as Hitler had believed in the superiority of the Aryans. Minorities were systematically exterminated.

A web of paranoid fantasy

From the start of 1977, however, the executioners increasingly turned against the Khmer Rouge themselves, especially those in the party from a 'bourgeois' family background. They were blamed for the continued failure of the economy. There were still food shortages. Irrigation projects and dams, built by hand without expert engineers to supervise the work, fell apart as soon as it rained. There could only be one reason for these setbacks – sabotage and conspiracy. Torture centres like Tuol Sleng in Phnom Penh were used to 'uncover' conspiracies that implicated ever more people in a nightmare web of paranoid fantasy.

The killings had become so random and widespread by mid-1977 that Pol Pot himself tried to call a halt. In September 1977 he went public for the first time, making clear his own dominant role and that of the Communist Party in Kampuchea. In an address to the people, he claimed to have liberated them from 2000 years of 'despair and hopelessness'. But most of his speech was devoted to the need to defend Kampuchea against foreign aggression.

Death to all party members

The Khmer Rouge had always distrusted Vietnam, and there had been border clashes immediately after the fall of Phnom Penh, back in 1975. In the second half of 1977 this border conflict flared up again. A new instruction went out: death to all party members connected with Hanoi. Then it was the turn of the Eastern Zone leadership, accused of not fighting hard enough against the Vietnamese. In the early months of 1978, most of the Eastern Khmer Rouge cadres were purged. Some, however, took refuge in Vietnam, including the man who would later replace Pol Pot, Heng Samrin. The scene was set for the Vietnamese invasion that would put an end to the Khmer Rouge tyranny on 21 December 1978. Kampuchea was to be 'liberated' once more.

No-one knows how many people died on the killing-fields of Pol Pot's Kampuchea, nor what proportion of deaths were due to malnutrition or disease, as against deliberate execution. One estimate is two million dead, but this is probably far too high, even if all the victims of the civil war and the American bombing are included. In the end, the numbers do not matter. A whole society was destroyed and nothing but terror erected in its place. The war, and the Cambodian communist experiment that followed it, was a human catastrophe.

1975

Right: The telegraph operator is named Ton. He is 13 years old. The mechanic on the same 50-ton Chinese-built ship is 17. Their 38-year-old captain was neither a fisherman nor a seaman before he was assigned this job. But he was a loyal cadre. Some of those recruited for naval duties had never even seen the ocean before.

1975

Right: When the Khmer Rouge took control of Phnom Penh, a population of two million was herded into the countryside. The city became a ghost town, haunted by the souls of those executed on the spot when they refused to leave. Hundreds more were butchered for being 'tainted' by education. As many as 20,000 people would die while marching to the new agrarian society of the Khmers.

YEAR ZERO

Time stood still when the Khmer Rouge marched into the Cambodian capital, Phnom Penh. Then, slowly but surely, the hands on the clock-face started moving backwards. Convinced that they were the prophets of a new era, Pol Pot and his followers were attempting to transform an entire country into an agrarian utopia. This was Year Zero, an experiment that placed Cambodia/Kampuchea on a collision course with tragedy

Left: The US had poured aid into Camdodia at a staggering rate of one million dollars per day. But now, with the arrival of Year Zero, money lost all value. Strewn around the streets of Phnom Penh like confetti, it was ignored by passers-by. To be found with a wallet of cash could provoke 'class vengeance' and lead to instant execution.

Right: Out with the old and in with the new. Sophisticated foreign machinery lies cannibalized in one of Phnom Penh's scrap-yards. Together with all signs of 'bourgeois aspirations', foreign influences were ruthlessly exterminated by the Khmer Rouge. Purity had replaced opulence in the new order.

Left: As human ants till the fields, Pol Pot realizes his dream of a peasant state. Despite a healthy level of production in some areas, however, rations were steadily reduced.

A typical Khmer slogan was 'with rice we can have everything.' But for many Cambodians the only arable land was the killing fields, where the harvest was death (below).

1975

The story of Southeast Asia after 1975 has been one of perpetual struggle between warring countries and guerrilla groups. The Americans have long since left, but still the conflict continues

While the fall of Saigon led to the reunification of Vietnam, it failed to put an end to the suffering in Southeast Asia. Indeed, the prime minister of Singapore, Lee Kuan Yew, remarked in January 1979 that the thousands of refugees from Indochina's continuing wars were 'victims of peace'.

THE CONTINUING

To many Vietnamese, final decision and a united nation came as something of a relief after 15 years of more or less non-stop war. But as time passed, the new regime alienated various social and racial groups.

Not unexpectedly, defeat brought retribution to the supporters of the South Vietnamese government, though by no means on a scale that approached the revenge meted out by the Khmer Rouge in Kampuchea. There were undoubtedly some summary executions, however, while prominent government supporters were committed to 're-education' camps. It was estimated that, as late as 1986, as many as 50,000 people were still being detained as political prisoners, with many more lesser officials and soldiers being submitted to 're-education'.

Another aspect of communist rule was 'socialist transformation', which forced 700,000 people out of Ho Chi Minh City (formerly Saigon) and into

'New Economic Zones'. An estimated 1.3 million people were relocated from urban areas to the countryside. For those more at home with life in the towns and cities of South Vietnam, adjusting to the deprivations of rural life was an enormous task. They were further alienated by campaigns against vestiges of Western culture, and meanwhile, peasants found it difficult to adjust to state ownership of land – not to speak of communist drives to weaken the hold of traditional religion. And southerners resented being ordered around by men from the North.

Currency devaluation saw the life savings of the middle classes plummet, and a ruthless assault on 'bourgeois trade' from 1978 onwards affected large numbers of ethnic Chinese, whose business acumen and tireless labours had previously dominated the South's business community.

Traditional Vietnamese-Chinese hostility was

Above: In Vietnam the 10,000-day war was over, but Southeast Asia would be racked with conflict for years to come. For these boat people, the struggle was far from ended. Above right: After the communists reunited Vietnam, those who had been 'led astray' were re-educated in camps like this.

572

1975

WAR

magnified by deepening conflict with the Chinese-backed Khmer Rouge in Kampuchea, and the maltreatment of ethnic Vietnamese there. The result was that pressure was put on the Chinese to leave Vietnam – either by boat or directly across the border into China. Many Vietnamese left also, creating a refugee problem of enormous proportions.

By August 1979, an estimated 865,000 people had fled from Vietnam either by land into China or by taking to the sea in whatever vessels they could muster. The latter, known as the 'boat people' where given little welcome in the countries to which they fled, none of which, for understandable reasons, proved welcoming.

The flight of the ethnic Chinese from Vietnam, as well as that of ethnic Vietnamese from the excesses in Kampuchea, was also indicative of a resurgence of traditional national antipathies once the common external enemy – the United

WAS THE DOMINO THEORY RIGHT OR WRONG?

Eisenhower spoke of 'a row of dominoes' in Southeast Asia, waiting to be knocked over by communist insurgency. The domino theory became the basis for US involvement: but was it a profound misreading of the situation?

The 'domino theory' was first recognized by President Eisenhower's administration of the 1950s, although its seeds were sown in the late 1940s. There was a fear of a spreading monolithic communism directed from Moscow.

America had witnessed communist-inspired insurgency in Greece, Malaya, French Indochina and the Philippines in the late 1940s. In 1949 Mao's communists gained power in China and in June 1950 communist North Korea invaded South Korea. It began to look as if Southeast Asia was in danger of falling completely under communist influence. Eisenhower's Secretary of State, John Foster Dulles, spoke in March 1954 of the dangers of communist aggression being extended. A month later, on 7 April 1954, Eisenhower expressed fears about the possible fate of Southeast Asia: 'You have a row of dominoes set up, you knock over the first one, and what will happen to the last one is the certainty that it will go over very quickly.' With insurgency still continuing in Malaya and the Philippines, it appeared to Eisenhower that Southeast Asia and possibly Australasia could be at risk.

In the early 1960s the Kennedy administration held the same beliefs; Vice-President Johnson remarked in May 1961 that the loss of South Vietnam would mean fighting on the 'beaches of Waikiki'. Kennedy sent US troops to Thailand in May 1962 and extended covert assistance to Laos. However, even by this early date, flaws in the argument were appearing. Insurgency was defeated in both Malaya and the Philippines and, even as US troops were arriving in South Vietnam in 1965, communists were being massacred in Indonesia.

South Vietnam, Laos and Cambodia succumbed to communism in 1975, but by then attitudes had changed. The Sino-Soviet split and Nixon's visits to Moscow and Beijing had shown that the idea of monolithic communism was a myth in world terms. Since then, even within Southeast Asia, the perspective has changed considerably. Vietnam invaded Kampuchea, and Vietnamese forces are still there, and China attacked Vietnam in 1979.

The other Southeast-Asian dominoes have so far survived and the relative prosperity of the area is in stark contrast to the situation within communist Vietnam. What the domino theory did not take into account was the intense national rivalry – between Khmers, Vietnamese and Chinese – that was only masked, not obliterated, by a commitment to Marxism.

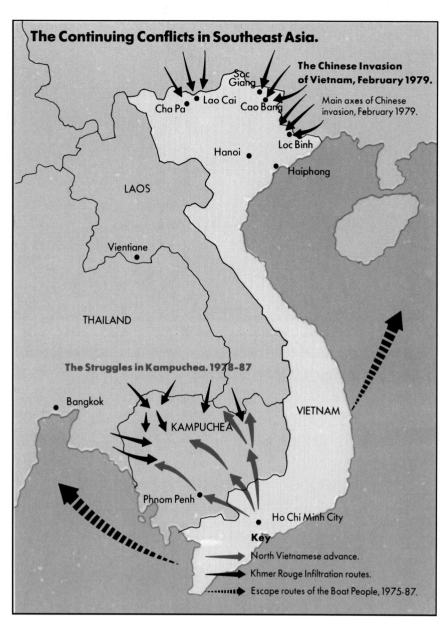

The Continuing Conflicts in Southeast Asia.

The Chinese Invasion of Vietnam, February 1979.

Main axes of Chinese invasion, February 1979.

Sac Giang

Cha Pa • Lao Cai • Cao Bang

Loc Binh

Hanoi •

• Haiphong

LAOS

Vientiane •

THAILAND

The Struggles in Kampuchea. 1978-87

Bangkok •

KAMPUCHEA

VIETNAM

Phnom Penh •

Ho Chi Minh City •

Key

North Vietnamese advance.

Khmer Rouge Infiltration routes.

Escape routes of the Boat People, 1975-87.

1975

States – had gone. Little love was lost between the Khmers of Kampuchea and the Vietnamese, the former considering that they had been deserted when Hanoi had accepted peace terms in 1973. Indeed, even as the ink was drying on the ceasefire agreement between Vietnam and the Americans, US bombers were still flying regularly over Cambodia. There was also considerable resentment on the Khmer side – primarily over the use to which the North had put Kampuchean territory during its war against the US and Saigon. In addition, both Kampuchea and Vietnam had conflicting territorial gains, notably over islands in the Gulf of Thailand. Similarly, the Vietnamese laid claim to large tracts of Chinese territory.

Clashing with the Khmers

The Khmer Rouge made a limited incursion into Vietnamese territory in April 1977 and again in September. The Vietnamese retaliated by throwing six divisions into Kampuchea in December 1977 as a clear warning to Pol Pot, who nevertheless chose to ignore the signs and promptly broke off diplomatic relations with Hanoi. The Vietnamese offered a demilitarized zone, but Pol Pot rejected all further overtures and clashes continued. Accordingly, on 3 December 1978 a former Khmer Rouge commissar named Heng Samrin was appointed head of a Vietnamese-sponsored Kampuchean National United Front for National Salvation. On 25 December, 100,000 Vietnamese and 20,000 United Front troops invaded Kampuchea. Out-gunned, the Khmer Rouge abandoned Phnom Penh and took to the jungles. Samrin's People's Republic of Kampuchea was instituted on 7 January 1979, supplanting Pol Pot's Democratic Kampuchea.

Meanwhile, Sino-Vietnamese relations had worsened considerably. Vietnamese rapprochement with the Soviet Union, Hanoi's invasion of Kampuchea, accompanied by the persecution of

Above right: China 'teaches Vietnam a lesson', as Chinese artillery shells a Vietnamese hamlet. However, Chinese forces performed poorly during their 1979 incursions. Far right, top: Vietnamese anti-communist guerrillas, operating in the Mekong delta. Below right: Vietnamese artillery attempts to repel the Chinese invaders.

574

FRIENDS OR ENEMIES?

From the very beginning of the US involvement in Vietnam, one of the strangest features was that, although the Americans were ostensibly defending the South Vietnamese government, in fact there were always severe strains in the relationship.

As early as 1956, President Eisenhower's adviser in Saigon, General Collins, had recommended that Diem be abandoned, and although the US eventually decided to back

him, he was ditched in the end, in 1963. Of the group of generals that succeeded Diem, the most popular was General 'Big Minh', but the Americans did not find him to their taste either, and engineered his removal from power.

During the period of main-force US involvement, the Americans shored up President Thieu – but a thorn in their side was the attitude of Air Marshal Ky, the flamboyant vice-president, who was constantly and

publicly urging the Americans to take the war directly to the North. As US forces began to run down in the early 1970s, Ky became more aggressive in his attacks on American policy, claiming that: 'The Americans are here to defend their interests, which do not always correspond with those of Vietnam.' He argued that it was necessary to 'greatly reduce the influence of the Americans – the sooner the better.'

By the autumn of 1972,

Thieu also was in direct conflict with the Nixon administration. Kissinger had negotiated a deal that would bring US troops home, and give peace with honour; but Thieu realized that the settlement would put his regime in grave danger. It was his intransigence that prevented a treaty being signed before January 1973 – in one meeting with Kissinger, Thieu, weeping, accused the Americans of colluding with the Soviet Union and China to destroy South

AMERICA AND SOUTHEAST ASIA SINCE 1975

In negotiating the Paris Accords, President Nixon pledged reconstruction aid for the two Vietnams. Following its victory two years later, Hanoi indicated its willingness to open normal diplomatic relations with the United States in return for payment of $3.25 billion. Negotiations were opened in December 1975 and Henry Kissinger initiated an exchange of diplomatic notes in March 1976. However, the negotiations foundered on the issue of the MIAs – the Americans still classed as missing in action. Hanoi released the names of 12 missing pilots as a gesture of goodwill in August 1976 but this was not regarded as sufficient by Washington, which vetoed Hanoi's application to join the United Nations in November of that year.

Subsequently, President Carter sent a presidential commission to explore avenues of conciliation. The American veto on Hanoi's application to the UN was dropped in September 1977 and Carter also relaxed a trade embargo. However, normal diplomatic relations were not resumed.

Since taking office in January 1981 President Reagan's administration has moved to bolster those countries seemingly threatened by Vietnamese ambition, notably Thailand, and, as recently as 1986, Congress voted 'non-lethal aid' for the non-communist partners in Sihanouk's Coalition Government of Democratic Kampuchea – the organization fighting the Vietnamese forces occupying Cambodia.

the ethnic Chinese in Vietnam, eventually proved too much for the regime in Beijing. China speeded up its normalization of diplomatic relations with the United States and, once the Vietnamese had invaded Kampuchea, began to make clear its intention to meet aggression with aggression.

On 17 January 1979 some 85,000 Chinese troops of the Forty-First and Forty-Second Armies – later reinforced to 200,000 men – invaded Vietnam at three widely dispersed points. China was, or so it thought, going to teach Vietnam a 'lesson'. The main thrusts were directed at the important centres of Lao Cai, Cao Bang and Lang Son. Even though the best Vietnamese troops were in Kampuchea, the 60,000-strong defensive force – mostly border troops and regional soldiers – was still able to hold off the People's Liberation Army, which had seen no active service since the Korean War (1950-53). The Chinese later admitted to 20,000 casualties and, once they had taken Lang Son on 5 March, began to withdraw after announcing that Hanoi had been suitably 'punished'.

The events of 1978 and 1979 have cast long shadows over the whole of Southeast Asia. Serious clashes have continued on the frontier between China and Vietnam, the most serious in 1981 and 1984. Similarly, the Vietnamese maintain an army of occupation in Kampuchea in support of Heng Samrin, whose government is still not recognized by the United Nations.

The Khmer Rouge, who are still officially recognized as the legitimate government, continue to fight a guerrilla campaign from across the Thai frontier. The situation is further complicated by the presence, alongside the Khmer Rouge, of non-communist guerrillas. A former Cambodian

Vietnam.

After the signing of the peace accords, Thieu's relations with the American political establishment became eroded still further. The corruption at all levels of South Vietnamese society was heavily criticized, and in spite of a vigorous defence by Ambassador Martin, few members of the Senate or the House of Representatives wished to associate themselves with the South Vietnamese leader.

When Thieu fled South Vietnam in April 1975, just before Saigon fell, he expressed bitter feelings about the US, claiming that their failure to defend him had been 'an inhumane act by an inhumane ally'. But in truth, the Americans had not so much been an inhumane ally as unable to trust fully any South Vietnamese government. One of the great paradoxes of the Vietnam war was that the US did not really like or admire the government it was ostensibly supporting.

1975

Above: A Khmer Rouge guerrilla, fighting to topple Heng Samrin and the People's Republic of Kampuchea. The Khmers operate from across the Thai border and are still recognized as the country's legitimate government.

some reported joint military operations by the Khmer Rouge and the KPNLF in 1986 but, for the most part, operations appear to be separate.

Tussling with the Thais

The Vietnamese have reacted to this continuing guerrilla war with annual dry-season (October to April) offensives as in 1980/81 and 1981/2, with that in 1984/5 apparently driving the ANS out of its headquarters at Tatum and the KPNLF from its base at Ampil. Almost inevitably, the fact that the guerrillas routinely seek refuge in Thailand has led to clashes between Thai and Vietnamese forces, the most serious of which occurred in 1980. Consequently, Thailand has faced increased fears for its own security and has received United States military assistance. Thailand is also a member of the Association of South East Asian Nations (ASEAN), an organization originally conceived in 1967 as a means of furthering social and economic development among its members, the other founders being the Philippines, Malaysia, Singapore and Indonesia. ASEAN has sponsored numerous anti-Vietnamese resolutions at the UN, that of November 1985 being the seventh. However, the military threat posed by Vietnam and by increased Soviet naval activity in the South China Sea has compelled ASEAN to consider a more military orientation. Vietnam has attempted to exploit the differences that do exist between the member states, who were joined by Brunei in 1984, but without notable success. The Vietnamese announced partial troop withdrawals from Kampuchea in July 1982, April 1983 and June 1984, but showed no signs of leaving the country. Indeed, they rejected the proposals by Sihanouk in March 1986 for a political settlement based on a four-party coalition in Kampuchea, withdrawal of Vietnamese forces under United Nations supervision, and an interim government pending free elections.

The key to the future of the region remains the extent of Hanoi's ambition and how far this might be tempered by, on the one hand, a desire to improve diplomatic relations with the United States and, on the other, by any thaw in the relationship between Vietnam's backer – the Soviet Union – and her principal rival – China. Vietnam is now heavily dependent upon the Soviets who, by 1979, were giving the Vietnamese economic aid to the tune of two million US dollars a day, in return for which some 80,000 Vietnamese were working in the Soviet Union, and the Soviet Navy was taking advantage of facilities at Cam Ranh Bay and Kompong Son. The Soviets still have an interest in diverting Chinese attention southwards, while China continues to be concerned by the prospect of encirclement by the Soviet Union and its clients. Consequently, Beijing attempts to back both the Khmer Rouge in Kampuchea and the Meos inside Laos.

With the network of diplomatic, military and economic alignments as they exist today, the prospects for peace in Southeast Asia are grave.

prime minister, Son Sann, leads the Khmer People's National Liberation Front (KPNLF), which had an estimated 14,000 adherents in 1986, while the ubiquitous Prince Norodom Sihanouk leads the Moulinka movement whose National Army (ANS) numbers perhaps 10,000. The Khmer Rouge, whose nominal leadership has been held since 1979 by Khieu Samphan in an attempt to make the organization more respectable in international eyes, has some 35,000 men.

In June 1983, a somewhat fragile Coalition Government of Democratic Kampuchea was established, with Sihanouk at its head, to coordinate all three anti-Vietnamese factions. However, Sihanouk in particular has dismissed Pol Pot's reported retirement from the Khmer Rouge's Supreme Military Commission as a 'farce', and it is clear that major differences remain between the coalition partners. There were

MISSING IN ACTION

Operation Homecoming brought the POWs back. But are there Americans still captive in Southeast Asia?

HANOI: RELEASE OUR POW–MIA

National League of POW/MIA Families, 1608 K St., NW, Wash., DC 20006

Previous page, top: The dead are flown home. But did the remains always match up with the name on the coffin? Bottom: a bumper sticker produced by the National League of POW/MIA Families.

Today, 15 years after the signing of the Paris Peace Agreement, members of the National League of American Prisoners and Missing in Southeast Asia believe that POWs are still being held in Vietnam, Kampuchea and Laos. Although the story is one of conflicting reports and a wealth of unsubstantiated evidence, many Americans believe that their government has so far failed to come clean on this burning issue.

By the end of March 1973, Operation Homecoming was over and 591 American prisoners of war

had returned home from Vietnam. A mere nine came home from Laos, men who had been captured by the NVA in Laos and then passed on to Hanoi. As the servicemen stepped onto United States' soil, satellite television relayed the joyous reunions to screens across the land. Now, surely, the war was finally over.

President Nixon claimed that all POWs had been brought home, and little thought was given to the 2500 men still listed as missing in action. Only the friends and families of those who had not come home seemed to care. As the Nixon Administration began to sink into the mire of Watergate, the MIAs were written off. The intelligence community – the CIA, the Defense Intelligence Agency (DIA) and the National Security Agency (NSA) – kept quiet. Yet NSA, responsible for monitoring enemy radio traffic throughout the war, was perfectly aware that almost 300 men on their list of 'captured alive' pilots had not been repatriated. General Eugene Tighe, the head of the DIS, put the figure of those expected to return, but did not, at around 400-500.

Today, 2413 men – or their remains – have yet to return from Southeast Asia. The majority belong to the Air Force (899), followed by the Army (702), Navy (480), Marines (289), civilians (42), and Coast Guard (1). Over half of these are believed to have been killed in action, remains never recovered. The rest are listed as Prisoners of War/Missing in Action (POW/MIA). The total includes 549 men missing in Laos and a further 82 in Kampuchea. People believe that many of these men are still alive, still held captive after an interval of 15 years.

Tracking the POWs

As the Vietnam war grew in scale, increasing numbers of US servicemen had become separated from their units in jungle firefights, or else ejected from their stricken aircraft over enemy territory. It was down to the intelligence community to collect information on the whereabouts of these POW/MIAs, aided by captured documents, enemy POWs and refugee interrogation reports. Together with reports from their own agents, electronic radio traffic eavesdropping and photographs taken by spy planes and satellites, the majority of enemy POW camps were located. A list of men believed to be held captive was then compiled.

A CIA report in November 1970, using 'confirmed information', listed prisons in Laos where POWs were being held. These included Ban Na, Kay Neua, Khamkouane and Hang Long. Aerial photographs were produced as evidence. But in 1973 when Hanoi was asked for the return of the prisoners in Laos, the reply was 'Go talk to the Pathet Lao.' Back then, the US did not recognize the Pathet Lao and to date, not one POW, aside from the nine captured by the North Vietnamese and moved straight to Hanoi, has been repatriated by Laos.

The evidence *seems* to suggest that American

Below left: Two captured US airmen being escorted to a North Vietnamese press conference. The world's media would focus on this disorientated pair. The capture of many others would remain undetected, their fate uncertain. Right: Identified as Lieutenant Robert Shumaker, this American pilot bailed out of his stricken aircraft over Hanoi.

servicemen – either alive or dead – are still in Laos. Yet some doubts remain. At the time of the 1970 report, the CIA was practically running the war in Laos, and may well have exaggerated the reports of POW camps in an effort to justify American presence in an area outside the borders of South Vietnam. The truth of the matter is shrouded in mystery.

The majority of the pilots were shot down over

Below right: Remains officially identified as those of Master Sergeant James Fuller. Authorities outside the Army claim this is scientifically impossible.

North Vietnam. Assuming they survived the crash of the aircraft and were not killed by the militia, they would have been passed to the communist authorities. Most surfaced in the prison system and were returned to the US in 1973 – less those killed through torture or inadequate medical care. A number, however, were known to have been captured alive but never showed up in the prison system.

There has been speculation that some of the missing were 'Moscow bound': passed on to the Soviets who would have jumped at the opportunity to 'debrief' them on their specialized knowledge. This theory is by no means implausible. Among the pilots and aircrew who floated down to enemy soil were electronic warfare experts,

POW SIGHTINGS

Although there is a lack of hard evidence concerning live POWs, there is no shortage of refugee reports. The following are only two examples of sightings among the large number received by the National League of Families:

'I was an ARVN officer and company commander, Marines, and was captured by the Viet Cong at the Thach Han river in June 1974. I want to provide you with information on a number of American prisoners which I knew of while I was in captivity in the Khe Sanh area near the Lao border. I escaped from the Viet Cong in 1978 and made it to America just five months ago...I can give you the

names of two American prisoners still alive in the Viet/Lao area...'

Another report received by the National League of Families came from a CIA-trained Special Forces paratrooper who had spent 15 years in communist prisons in North Vietnam: 'During the time I was imprisoned in Hanoi I heard a number of American POWs. I have heard their voices and have heard the cadremen say that they were downed pilots undergoing re-education. They were held nearby, separated from me by a high wall.'

The source goes on to say that at the end of 1978, he and 130 American POWs were transferred

to Thanh Hoa. While in Thanh Hoa, the former paratrooper said that he saw about 30 Americans being held in three separate camps about seven kilometres from each other. He added that the POWs were divided into separate camps so that the communists could keep a closer guard. In conclusion, the source states: 'The POWs I saw were very thin, they were covered with scabies; there was just skin and bone left on them. They could hardly walk, yet they were forced to carry wood from the forests. They often fell down. Sometimes they were beaten by the guards. These are things I saw with my own eyes.'

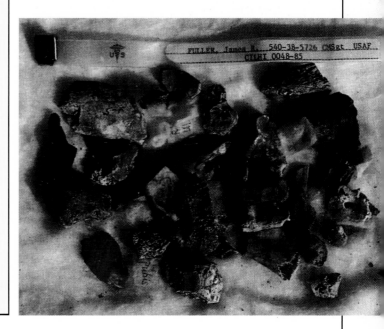

INESCAPABLE DESTINY OF U.S. PIRATES THAT COME TO SOW CRIMES.
The body of one of the two pirates flying U.S. aircraft downed
by the armed forces of HANOI (2102N/10551E) at H Village in the
suburbs of HANOI around 1500 hours 31 October 1967.
[Bao Doi Nhan Dan (V), HANOI, 1 Nov 67]

Above: A photo released by the North Vietnamese of a dead US airman. He was Stephen J. Nott, navigator to Major Hugh Fanning, who reports suggested was captured alive. In 1984, the Vietnamese returned what they claimed were Fanning's remains. His wife Kathryn (above far right) was told that her husband's dental records matched those of the remains and that he had been wounded in the head. Ten months later, when she was allowed access to her husband's forensic file, Kathryn Fanning learned that there had been no skull and no teeth.

weapon systems officers and operators of the latest technology, such as that used in the AC-130 Spectre gunships or the SAM suppressor Wild Weasel F-105s. Anyone with knowledge of the new 'smart bombs' would have made a fine catch, as would the crews of the new F-111 swing-wing fighter-bomber. There is every chance that the Soviets would have seized the opportunity to interrogate these men.

Vietnamese insurance

Some of the pilots possessed other specialized knowledge that would have been of interest to the Soviets. Lieutenant-Colonel Iceal Hambleton was a 53-year-old navigator in an electronic counter-measures EB-66 that was shot down just south of the DMZ in the midst of the Easter Invasion of 1972. Hambleton had been the assistant Deputy Chief of operations of a Strategic Air Command missile wing before he went back to the cockpit, and had a head full of top-secret war plans. He was so important to the US High Command that the 11-day operation to rescue him, before he fell into enemy hands, was the largest Search and Rescue operation mounted during the war.

Another factor that must be considered during any analysis of the POW/MIA problem is that of money. President Nixon had informed the North Vietnamese that they would be given aid and reparations to the tune of three billion dollars. But Congress cut the purse strings, Nixon resigned over the Watergate scandal and the money was never paid. There are those who see this as a possible explanation for the Socialist Republic of Vietnam retaining some prisoners as an insur-

ance policy against an uncertain future. The POW/MIA League cite the experience of the French following their withdrawal from Indochina as an example – for the last 30 years, the French government has been paying millions of dollars each year for the return of remains and live POWs.

Forgotten Soldiers?

In the eight years immediately after Operation Homecoming, the Nixon, Ford and Carter Administrations paid little attention to reports of live Americans still being held in Southeast Asia. Sixty-seven such sightings were made between 1973 and 1979. Doubts as to the authenticity of live sightings remain, however. The involvement of the French and Americans in Southeast Asia has left hundreds of Caucasian-looking men and women in Laos, Kampuchea and Vietnam, and there may be a correlation between sightings of live POWs and these descendants of mixed parentage.

Nevertheless, the National League of POW/MIA Families continued to lobby succeeding Administrations to obtain the fullest possible accounting of the Americans still listed as missing. A small number of remains were handed over to the US prior to 1980, and these were sent to the Army Central Identification Laboratory in Hawaii (CIL-HI) for identification, prior to release to their families for burial. After 1980, as the Reagan Administration accelerated negotiations with a view to obtaining a full accounting, Hanoi responding by despatching a growing number of remains to the US. No live POWs have surfaced, however, with the exception of a Marine who returned home in 1979. Although court-martialled and accused of collaborating with the enemy, he claims to have seen groups of American POWs in North Vietnam between 1973 and 1979.

Since the fall of South Vietnam, Laos and Kampuchea, a wealth of intelligence information has appeared in the form of refugee reports. Vietnamese boat people and those trekking overland into Thailand have provided almost 1000 first-hand sightings of live Americans. The DIA has dismissed 211 of these as untrue, and claims to have resolved a further 641. A total of 137 sightings are still under investigation.

US commitment

Both President Reagan and Vice-President Bush have shown their commitment to resolving this issue: 'If we can get hard evidence that Americans are still being held in Vietnamese prisons, we're pledged to do whatever is necessary to get them out.' Such evidence has, however, so far eluded the POW/MIA League.

Although the POW/MIA League has dismissed the possibility that a high-level conspiracy exists within the US, there are some who accuse the government of holding back, and even falsifying, information on live POWs. Indeed, there is one part of the POW/MIA jigsaw that lends a certain amount of credence to this theory.

During the last two years, with an increase in the number of remains returned, a story of gross incompetence – or intrigue – is emerging. At first, the bereaved families had accepted the remains of their loved ones in good faith and laid them to rest with full military honours. Some, however, still had their doubts. When some remains were exhumed for a second opinion, the relatives found that, far from containing full skeletal remains, the contents of the coffins often contained little more than a handful of small pieces of bone.

Forensic evidence

One of the eminent anthropologists called in by some of the families was Professor Michael Charney, the Director of the Forensic Science Laboratory of Colorado State University. In 1986, Charney told a House Armed Services Subcommittee that, of the 20 sets of remains that he had examined, only two could be positively identified. On one occasion, CIL-HI had informed a relative that her husband had been identified by his dental records and an X-ray of his skull. When the remains were later exhumed, the skull and teeth were missing. The entire identification procedure had been fabricated.

Either the CIL-HI had been overzealous, or it had received pressure from above to falsify documentation. Further investigations followed. Captain Thomas Hart had been the pilot of an AC-130 gunship shot down over Laos on 21 December 1972. In February 1985, a joint Laotian/US excavation team examined the burnt-out wreck of the aircraft and found the remains of the 13 crew. At least, that's what the relatives, including Anne Hart, were told by the CIL-HI.

There had, in fact, been 14 men in the gunship when it crashed. Charney maintained that only one set of bones could be positively identified, and

Anne Hart was now convinced that someone up above was telling lies. Her evidence was convincing. In July 1973, seven months after Thomas Hart's aircraft had been shot down, and five months after the signing of the peace accords, a US spyplane photographed the message 'TH 1973' freshly cut in elephant grass 250 miles from the crash site. Anne Hart had only found out about this in 1983, when a reporter handed her a copy of the photograph. Two further sources have subsequently confirmed that similar symbols were found near the crash site, together with five parachutes. It is difficult to reconcile this information with the findings of CIL-HI.

The question still remains – do the governments of the Socialist Republic of Vietnam, Laos and Kampuchea know far more about the fate of the men still unaccounted for than they are willing to admit?

No solution

It is hard to imagine that successive US administrations have collaborated in a conspiracy designed to stifle information relating to US servicemen missing in action and POWs still alive in Southeast Asia. The Vietnamese have always maintained that if there are any POWs still living in Southeast Asia, they are being held outside the areas of their jurisdiction. The US points to top-level meetings with Hanoi's representatives and contends that everything possible is being done to repatriate the remains of US servicemen – official government policy denies the possibilty of living POWs.

Neither the US nor the Vietnamese have anything to gain by covering up. Precisely the opposite, in fact. But there are so many inconsistencies still unresolved. Perhaps the full story will never be known.

Above: Major Hugh M. Fanning's wife Kathryn. The military claimed to have identified her husband from his remains. It was later concluded that the remains could not be identified as those of Hugh Fanning...or anyone else.

Right: American officials meet with the Vietnamese authorities to organize the return of the remains of American servicemen. When the Americans asked about the fate of prisoners held in Laos, they were told 'Go talk to the Pathet Lao'. Only nine POWs ever came out of Laos.

COST OF THE WAR

Add up the amount spent by the US on the Vietnam war and it runs into billions. But what about the disabled vets, the blow to national pride and the scarred landscape of Vietnam?

CHAPTER 112

As a simple mathematical equation, it seems so easy. If the number of enemy you kill is larger than they can afford, you have to win in the end. So ran the US military's theory of body-count, the yardstick by which it gauged its success in the Vietnam war. But for the US public and, increasingly, the politicians, such an accounting system was, at best, spurious and, at worst, self-deluding and courting disaster.

As Sir Robert Thompson, chief of the British advisory mission to Vietnam in the early days of the war, has said, 'If one side has costs which are indefinitely acceptable to it' – and by this he meant the North – 'and imposes on you costs which are not indefinitely acceptable to you, it does not matter what happens in the battles.'

When one looks at these costs it is not hard to see why so many Americans turned against the war. By June 1974, the US Department of Defense estimated that the total cost of the war – that is the cost over and above what would have been spent on defence in peacetime – currently stood at a staggering $145,000 million at 1974 prices. But the drain on America's resources did not stop there. The inevitable wartime economic inflation, lost production, the continuing loan repayments and the benefits paid to veterans of the war had still to be accounted for. It has been estimated that the final figure will be something in the region of $300,000 million; about $1100 for every American citizen – man, woman and child.

The Vietnam conflict was a war in which vast quantities of bombs and shells were expended and the cumulative cost soon became astronomical. During the bombing campaigns against North Vietnam, Laos and Cambodia, and the close air support missions flown in support of operations in South Vietnam, American aircraft dropped some eight million tons of bombs, four times the quantity dropped during the whole of World War II. On each mission flown by a B-52 heavy bomber, $80,000 went out through the bomb-bay doors. Looking at the figures for one year alone gives some indication of the cost involved in fighting the air war. In 1966 148,000 missions were flown by fighter bombers and heavy bombers over North Vietnam during the Rolling Thunder campaign. In all, this amounted to $1247 million, and that figure does not take into account the 818 aircraft lost on operations. The total tonnage of bombs dropped was a staggering 128,000.

But was this massive expenditure justified by the amount of damage it wreaked on the North? Figures for North Vietnamese losses during the war can only be estimated, but it is reckoned that in 1966, actions by US aircraft cost the North Vietnamese economy and military effort some $130 million. When the costs involved are compared with the damage done, one comes up with a figure that shows the American air war to be less than cost effective: for every dollar's worth of damage inflicted on the North, the United States had to spend $9.6.

The air war was also very expensive in terms of the number of aircraft lost. Helicopters were the most vulnerable. During the conflict the US lost 4865 choppers – at a quarter of a million dollars apiece – and a further 3720 other aircraft of various types.

The cost in lives

Although the air war was by far the most expensive single area of operations, the war on the ground was by no means cheap. Again, high-technology weaponry and huge expenditures of ammunition were to blame. On an average day at the height of the fighting American artillery was loosing off some 10,000 rounds of high explosive shells. With each shell costing something in the region of $100, the fire support for infantry operations alone was setting the American taxpayer back one million dollars per day.

The American system of one-year tours of duty was also very costly. Of the 27 million draft-aged Americans of the Vietnam generation, some 10 per cent served in the Nam. Hundreds of thousands of men were drafted – the bureaucracy involved in this one area alone was massive – and then armed and trained, and that was all before they got anywhere near the battlefields of Vietnam. Operating a US division cost 20 times as much as a South Vietnamese division.

The bare statistics for the cost of the war to the North pale when compared with the money pumped into the Vietnam war by the USA. Verifiable figures for military expenditure are still extremely sketchy, but it is reckoned that the North's defence budget ran into $3560 million for the years 1965 to 1971. Without the financial support of the Soviet Union and China, however, the North would have been hard pressed to sur-

The cost in men, the cost in land. Top left: The Vietnam Veterans' Memorial in Washington, D.C. Dedicated on 13 November 1982, it helps to address the guilt suffered by vets and their families since the war ended. As one parent said: 'My son was killed, and I can't bring it up during a party.' Left: A Vietnam vets' counselling service tries to repair some of the damage to those who 'survived'.

vive. Estimates put the Soviet contribution to the war at $1660 million and the Chinese at $670 million over the same period, thus boosting the total budget available to the North to $5890 million. However, when the final figures are totted up, the amount available to South Vietnam's war effort was still 17 times greater than that available to the North.

But the cost of the war stretches far beyond the bottom line on a financial balance sheet. In human terms, America got off very lightly. In a war that lasted nearly 15 years, 46,370 US servicemen died in battle, more than 10,000 died from non-combat-related causes and a further 300,000 were wounded. When one thinks that there were 57,470 British casualties – nearly 20,000 of which were fatal – on the first *day* of the battle of the Somme in July 1916, the American losses seem small by comparison. In fact, with an average loss rate among American forces running at 1.8 per cent per annum, the grunt on the ground had only a one in 55 chance of being killed.

His South Vietnamese counterpart in the ARVN, however, was not so lucky. The ARVN lost some 2.5 per cent of its men every year, amounting to 184,000 soldiers killed between 1961 and the January 1973 ceasefire.

Accurate statistics for North Vietnamese and

A LESSON LEARNED

It took almost a decade for the US Army to recover from the trauma of Vietnam. When the last American soldiers were withdrawn in 1973 and, more particularly, when the NVA marched into Saigon two years later, it seemed as if all the sacrifices of the war had been in vain. Something had gone wrong; the army had clearly failed in its appointed task.

Analysis of this 'failure' began immediately. A number of reasons were put forward: that the army had, in fact, fought well, but had been denied the victory it deserved by unnecessary political control; that preoccupation with the main-force war against the NVA had diverted attention from the insurgency in the villages of the South; that the army's emphasis on technology and firepower had prevented the sort of face-to-face combat so essential for victory; that

the army had been 'tail heavy', deploying a huge logistic back-up which cut down the number of combat troops available; that the individual soldier (especially the draftee) had lacked the motivation and training needed to face the problems of Vietnam.... And so the list went on.

Some solutions were easy to put into effect. As early as 1973, the draft was ended and an all-volunteer force reintroduced, enabling more sustained training, especially in basic military skills such as leadership, initiative and weapons handling. There was even talk of adopting an American version of the much admired British regimental system, within which the ordinary soldier would feel loyalty towards a unit rather than his immediate buddies.

But the process went much deeper, manifesting itself in growing de-

mand that, in any future war, the army should not be expected to fight with its hands tied behind its back. Instead, it should be given a general objective by the politicians and allowed to achieve that by 'fighting to win'. In August 1982, this was put forward as a central feature of AirLand Battle, a new doctrine within which the army and air force, by making full use of surveillance and target acquisition techniques (some of which had their origins in the Vietnam war), would be able to take on and defeat a numerically superior enemy force. The emphasis continued to be on technology and firepower, and nowhere was there any mention of counter-insurgency, but by clarifying the army's role in future war, the doctrine did much to restore the pride and professionalism so cruelly shattered in Vietnam.

Viet Cong losses are far more difficult to calculate due to the difficulty in identifying real military as opposed to civilian deaths among the guerrilla forces, but estimates have put the figure as high as 900,000 killed between 1961 and 1974. That is nearly four times the number lost by the American and South Vietnamese forces put together.

The ongoing legacy

But the real victims of the war in Indochina were the civilian populations. Despite the intentions of the US, most of rural South Vietnam came to be regarded by the US forces as a virtual 'free-fire zone' where they could shell, bomb and napalm at will. Hamlets and villages were often torched or, like Ben Suc during Operation Cedar Falls in 1967, completely wiped off the face of the earth. Fearful of being caught up in the deadly crossfire on their doorsteps, the South Vietnamese peasants and farmers, with their families in tow, fled their villages in search of safety. Many of the rounds fired and bombs dropped failed to detonate and an estimated 27,000 tons of unexploded munitions were left behind in the earth. Today, these souvenirs of a war fought over a decade ago still pose a grave threat to farmers tilling their fields.

A further expensive legacy inherited by the Vietnamese – primarily those of the South – was a country severely ravaged by US defoliants such as napalm and the more insidious Agent Orange. It has been estimated that two-thirds of the South Vietnamese population of 18 million was displaced during the war as the land suffered the impact of some 10 million tons of bombs and shells and 55,000 tons of defoliating agents. Munitions

significant effect on the world's balance of power. Further, and perhaps even more crucial, is the effect the war has had on the US political system. The fall-out arising from the various political scandals which had their roots in the war – Watergate, the Pentagon Papers – has resulted in a deep-seated and enduring antagonism between the executive and legislative branches of the US government. Never again, or at least not for a very long time, will Congress be prepared to trust the President unequivocally. This can be seen not only in measures such as the War Powers Act of 1973, but also in the furious argument currently raging over funding for the Contras.

Today, Vietnam remains a country shattered by war. While gigantic bomb craters disfigure the countryside, its people continue to live in the terrible poverty created by the economic strain of keeping the war going. For America, the price of victory in South Vietnam finally became too high in lives and dollars and it was left to the Vietnamese to pay it.

and defoliants severely damaged 32 per cent of the total land area of the South while three per cent was totally devastated. About one fifth of all timberland was destroyed; croplands, water and food supplies were all contaminated, and there has been a serious rise in babies born either handicapped or severely malformed. It is an ongoing legacy of death.

The political price

While the war displaced whole villages and chewed up the surrounding countryside, it also exacted a terrible toll of civilian casualties. Incidents like the massacre at My Lai have become notorious, and there has been fierce controversy over the real figure for civilian deaths in the Vietnam conflict. Edward Kennedy's Senate committee on refugees estimated 430,000 South Vietnamese civilian deaths between 1965 and 1974, and over a million wounded or injured. Later estimates put the figure lower, at 250,000 dead and 900,000 wounded. Even the lowest estimates provide a rate of around five civilian deaths for every American serviceman killed. No accurate figure can be found for the number of civilians killed in the whole of Indochina during the war but it is considered to be in excess of a million deaths.

Another long-lasting and far-reaching cost of the war incurred by the US was a political one. Commentators have pointed to the so-called 'opportunity costs' of the war, claiming that while the US poured billions of dollars into the Vietnam theatre, the Soviet Union was able to continue to invest in strategic systems which have had a

Above: A meeting of the Vietnam Veterans Association of America. One of their major battles has been to gain official recognition of Post Traumatic Stress Disorder (PTSD). It is estimated that as many as 40 per cent of Vietnam vets suffer the debilitating effects of PTSD: guilt at being a survivor, alienation, and an alarmingly high suicide rate. Top right: Some vets have been so unable to adapt themselves to civilian life after their experiences in Nam that they can only live in the wild. Bottom right: Defoliated land remains in Vietnam.

VIETNAM ON FILM

EYE-WITNESS

Marc Leepson is the books editor of, and a regular contributor to, *VETERAN*, the monthly magazine issued by the Vietnam Veterans of America.

From Graham Greene to Oliver Stone, writers and directors have tried to capture the Vietnam experience on film. Usually, however, Hollywood turns fact into fiction

Vietnam vets were in two minds about *Platoon*. Here for the first time was a movie about Vietnam written and directed by a Vietnam vet. All the action was set in Vietnam and the film tried to portray the horrors of this most horrendous of wars, so different from the pro-war propaganda of *The Green Berets*, the introspection of *The Deer Hunter*, the multi-million-dollar spectacle of *Apocalypse Now*, the sentimentality of *Coming Home* and the empty exploitation of Rambo. On the other hand, *Platoon* came 15 years after the event.

Oliver Stone's *Platoon* burst upon the scene in December 1986. Its story of the war, told from an infantryman-in-the-trenches perspective, struck a chord with the American public. Made for a mere $7 million in 11 weeks in the Philippines, the movie nonetheless evoked the feel of the horror of Vietnam more realistically than anything previously put on celluloid. The critics raved, the public responded in kind, and *Platoon* became a mega-hit.

Platoon also ushered in what some called The Year of the Vietnam Film. In 1987, Hollywood

released four other major Vietnam films: Stanley Kubrick's five-years-in-the-making *Full Metal Jacket*, Coppola's *Gardens of Stone*, a story about the war set in and around Arlington National Cemetery in Virginia, *Hanoi Hilton*, a prison drama revolving around shot-down US pilots, and *Hamburger Hill*, the story of one of the war's bloodiest battles. *Full Metal Jacket* and *Hamburger Hill* received mixed reviews. Both were hits at the box office. *Gardens of Stone* and *Hanoi Hilton*, though, were critical and popular duds.

Television joins in

American television also caught the mood. In 1987 the first Vietnam combat TV series, CBS's *Tour of Duty*, hit the small screen, along with *Vietnam War Story*, a 90-minute trilogy of fictionalized Nam stories that appeared on Home Box Office, the largest pay cable channel.

The fact that four movies and two TV shows on Vietnam appeared directly after *Platoon* was mainly coincidental. All were in the works long before Oliver Stone's movie hit the theatres. Nevertheless, *Platoon*'s financial success made Vietnam hot and TV companies were not slow in scheduling Barry Levinson's *Good Morning, Vietnam*, starring Robin Williams as a whacky GI disc jockey in Vietnam, *Bat-21*, a true war story with Gene Hackman and Danny Glover, *Saigon*, a murder mystery with Gregory Hines and Willem Dafoe (Sergeant Elias in *Platoon*), *Born on the Fourth of July*, the real-life story of ex-Marine and anti-war activist Ron Kovic, and *Flight of the Intruder*, which takes a *Top Gun*-like look at the air war in Nam. All this is a far cry from the distinct lack of interest the entertainment industry showed towards Vietnam in earlier years.

The early years

One of the first films that dealt with Vietnam was *The Quiet American* (1957), based on the Graham Greene novel. The movie, which starred World War II hero-turned-actor Audie Murphy, turned Greene's story upside down. In Greene's book, the title character, Pyle, is an idealistic, simplistic American CIA operative who comes to a fictional Vietnam and self-confidently goes about helping the people avoid the evils of communism. In the movie Pyle – based, perhaps, on CIA man Edward

Hollywood's view of Vietnam has shifted from *The Quiet American* (top left), in which Graham Greene's anti-Americanism became anti-communism, via the gung-ho *The Green Berets* (below), to the stark realism of *Platoon* (opposite, right and above).

G. Lansdale – is a hard-working hero, cruelly slain by the treacherous communists. Five years later, in *The Ugly American*, Hollywood again turned the plot of a popular book about Vietnam upside down. This time, the book's crooked, self-serving American ambassador, played in the film by Marlon Brando, in a Vietnam-like country becomes a devoted, heroic freedom fighter. In those days, Americans could do no wrong.

Following *The Ugly American*, no movies of note dealt with Vietnam until John Wayne released *The Green Berets* in 1968. In this, the overweight, ageing, toupeed Wayne posed unconvincingly as a Special Forces colonel leading a team of heroic men against a fanatical, cruel enemy. The film, which contains a classic cinematic error – a shot of the sun sinking in the East – was as unrealistic as it was politically hawkish. It was the good guys versus bad guys, cowboys versus Indians. When it was shown to the troops in Vietnam, they howled in derision.

The crazed veteran

While *The Green Berets* was essentially pro-war propaganda, the anti-war case was put by the documentary *In the Year of the Pig*, which showed the war from the North's point of view and won its director, Emile de Antonio, an Oscar in 1969. But America was so widely divided on the war that studios dared not risk their money. Any movie about the war was bound to alienate, not just large sections of the audience, but large sections of the film industry too. Instead, directors made their comments indirectly through war films like *Catch 22* and *M*A*S*H* – set in World War II and Korea respectively but with distinctly Vietnam attitudes – and westerns like *The Wild Bunch* and *Ulzana's Raid*.

Meanwhile, the Vietnam vet became a shorthand for madman. Going through the Vietnam war was such a powerful experience it could turn you into the vengeful psychopath of *Taxi Driver*

Right: Martin Scorsese's *Taxi Driver*, in which Robert De Niro plays the Vietnam vet who progresses from urban avenger to would-be political assassin. The film showed that Hollywood was more prepared to examine the severe psychological problems of Vietnam veterans than was the general public. Below: Christopher Walken, terminally hooked on the random violence of war, plays Russian roulette in a Saigon gambling den in *The Deer Hunter*. Below right: A photo-call on the set of *The Deer Hunter*. The film used the Vietnam war as but one episode in the maturing of a group of friends. Below left: The British success *The Killing Fields*.

or, later, the benign visionary of *Birdy*.

In 1976, in *Tracks*, Hollywood began to take a sideways look at the Vietnam war again, through the eyes of a veteran travelling across the US by train with the remains of his dead buddy in a coffin.

During that same period, TV was also taking an oblique squint at the Vietnam war. Vietnam vet as walking timebomb became a stock character in nightly cop operas like *Kojak*. But the press was not all bad. The hero of Hawaii-based detective series *Magnum* is a Vietnam vet and relatively sane. *Magnum* also marked the return of the 'soul' to American TV – that is, the lead actor's voice-over reveals his innermost thoughts, thoughts which in Magnum's case often revolve around Vietnam. And then there is *The A-Team*.

A Special Forces A-Team who fought in Vietnam, they have been wrongly accused of some heinous crime by the high command and are on the run to prove their innocence. They make a

RAMBO

John Rambo is to the average soldier in Vietnam what Superman is to the average cop. He is pure cartoon fantasy. But Rambo, as portrayed by the muscular, inarticulate Sylvester Stallone (above) in *First Blood* (1982) and *Rambo: First Blood, Part II* (1985), is perhaps the best known cinematic Vietnam veteran.

In both movies former Green Beret John Rambo takes his revenge on both America and the NVA in orgiastic outpourings of violence. In *First Blood* he wreaks havoc in a small town after the sheriff does him wrong. In *Part II* Rambo single-handedly takes on the US military and political establishment – not to mention what appears to be the entire Vietnamese army – to rescue some POWs and take his bloody revenge for the war. This time, he asks, do we get to win?

Both movies were roundly denounced by the critics but they did very well at the box office. So why have the preposterous Rambo films won such wide audiences? Many people presumably go to see them simply to be entertained by their non-stop action. Others evidently buy the easy answers that Stallone provides. So we didn't win the first time – send in Rambo. Never mind the fact that Stallone sat out the war with a series of draft deferments.

Sylvester Stallone has voiced admiration for the Vietnam vets, but many believe his films demean every American who fought in Vietnam. He does so by diminishing their opponents. In *Rambo*, where an American battalion would have failed, one soldier-as-cowboy can do it all. Still, for those who still believe that it is impossible for America to lose a war, the Rambo fantasy gives some comfort.

living by helping out people in trouble. These are definitely the good guys of prime-time TV – they did their duty in that crazy Asian war and were let down by incompetent generals, self-serving politicians and everyone on the make back home.

In all these TV programmes, Vietnam became part of America's romantic history. The heroes had been there and, presumably, been heroes there too. But Vietnam was essentially off-stage, always.

It was not until 1977 that Hollywood touched upon the war directly again. This time, in *The Boys in Company C*, director Sidney Furie came up with a low-budget amalgam of World War II-type action and cynical Vietnam war pessim-

Apocalypse Now was Francis Ford Coppola's allegorical study of the Vietnam war and the nature of evil. Above: An Air Cav squadron in a dawn attack on a coastal village. Top: Martin Sheen, a Special Forces operative who was tasked to 'terminate' Marlon Brando 'with extreme prejudice'. Right: Brando's renegade army, spawned by brutality.

ism. Next came the big-budget, solidly anti-war *Coming Home*, in which Jon Voight gave a convincing, sympathetic portrait of a severely disabled Vietnam vet. Hal Ashby's film won Voight and Jane Fonda, who played the wife of a career Marine who falls in love with the iconoclastic Voight, Best Actor and Best Actress Oscars. The movie called attention to the problems of wounded vets, but it over-simplified the big questions about the war. *Go Tell the Spartans*, also released in 1978, presented another negative view of the war. This time, though, it came from an ageing army major, played by Burt Lancaster, who finds out from personal experience that the US effort is doomed. The same year, the film *Dog Soldiers* showed the corruption of America's involvement seeping back into the US via heroin shipments.

Michael Cimino's *The Deer Hunter*, which also came out in 1978, won three Academy Awards, including Best Picture. The movie showed what happened to three buddies from a steel-mill town in western Pennsylvania after volunteering to

fight in Vietnam. One is killed, one badly wounded and the other returns home mentally disturbed. Critics complained that it unfairly depicted the Viet Cong as blood-thirsty killers and the Americans as innocents in a corrupt land. Essentially, however, although the film took its kudos and its box office from Vietnam, it was about blue-collar second-generation immigrants in the US and used the Vietnam war only as part of the backdrop.

Hollywood bites the bullet

Apocalypse Now, Coppola's $31 million film, came out the next year and won awards, large audiences and its share of controversy. It took Joseph Conrad's story *Heart of Darkness* into the belly of the Vietnam beast. Some considered the movie a bombastic, surreal masterpiece of irony, the quintessential anti-war movie. Others called it glorified violence. Either way the Vietnam war was only the background, the stage on which Coppola could parade his real concerns.

After 1979, Hollywood took another Vietnam vacation. But in 1984, the British production *The Killing Fields*, became the first movie to address the subject of what had happened in Southeast Asia – though it looked at Cambodia in Year Zero. Then, at the end of 1986, Hollywood bit the bullet with *Platoon*.

Platoon's political message is never spoken aloud. But it is palpable. The first Vietnam vet to write and direct a Nam movie, Oliver Stone's message is that war is hell and that Vietnam had its own special form of hellishness. He brings the village-burning, the gang-raping and the fragging before the cameras to make the point. For the first time, the American movie-goer looked Vietnam squarely in the eye.

Differing viewpoints

In *Platoon*'s wake came Stanley Kubrick's *Full Metal Jacket*, which the London-based American produced, directed and co-wrote from a book, *The Short Timers*, by Gustav Hasford. This quite realistic movie – though it was shot in England – tells the story of a group of Marines from their days in boot camp to their passage through the Battle of Hue in 1968. Unlike Kubrick's first war movie, *Paths of Glory, Full Metal Jacket* is not an out-and-out anti-war film. The closest Kubrick comes to getting out the soap box is a scene in which the Marines get interviewed before TV cameras during a break in the action. But what comes through is a disillusioned frustration with the war, not passionate anti- or pro-war sentiment.

The fourth big Vietnam movie of 1987, *Hamburger Hill*, contained action scenes that stand up to the best in *Platoon*. But its political point of view has more in common with John Wayne's than Oliver Stone's. It takes shots at the anti-war movement and the media, and the message seems to be that if the protesters had co-operated and the TV had told a fair story, things might have turned out differently in Vietnam.

Tim Page came of age as a photojournalist in Vietnam. Now, more than ten years after the 'liberation' of the South, he travels back to a land ravaged by war

TEN YEARS AFTER

Flying into Hanoi's Gia Lam airport, you get an immediate idea of how difficult it is to fill in a bomb crater in a landscape predominantly composed of paddy fields. It is a bleak drive downtown into the former enemy's capital, where the evidence of the war's length and brutality is everywhere. Bombed out factories, partially rebuilt; wrecked bridges, still standing alongside their replacements; a marshalling yard full of shot-up railroad cars and carriages; a patchwork of B-52 bomb craters. Slowly, the Vietnamese are rebuilding. They're accomplishing this with the same tenacity and dogged dull perseverance with which they fought and won the 10,000-day conflict.

The light in Tonkin is grey and dismal and a depression hangs over a group of people toiling in the mud beside the two-lane, French-built, dyke-top highway. You cross the Red River now on an enormous concrete span that has been constructed with Russian aid. Hanoi's colour is a dirty stucco, overlaid with peeling green and pastel shaded shutters. The city does not emit real joy – even the street lights go off at ten. Authority has clamped down on its very soul. The women wear drab, quasi-military pyjamas. Most of the men

Main picture: The wreckage of war and the plodding feet of time immemorial.

project a steady stream of imported Russian, Bulgarian, Romanian and other Eastern-bloc epics. The nascent film industry is now housed in the notorious POW camp, the Hanoi Hilton, its cell doors and barred windows still intact. It is also chilly in Hanoi: the seeping *crachin* mist affects the mood of the town.

Fly into Saigon, renamed Ho Chi Minh City after its 'liberation' on 30 April 1975, and you taxi past empty blast-proof aircraft hangars before encountering a graveyard of rotting planes and choppers, abandoned a decade ago. Forlorn Hueys, their innards and engines gone, droop their rotor blades as bamboo and jungle push up through the shattered plexiglass. Lines of C-46s, C-47s and C-130s slump, undercarriages awry and props adrift, ghostly shells of their former selves. The drive downtown is in the familiar, reckless traffic of snarling Hondas and scooters. There are more bicycles, fewer cars. The air still hangs hot and heavy, redolent with the smoking fumes of Russian gasoline, fuel so impure that it reduces the engines of the many abandoned US-built cars to metal that is suitable only for recycling at the mills opposite the old US base at Long Binh.

Unnatural resources

Recycling is big business in today's Vietnam. Conservative estimates suggest that they have enough scrap to keep their foundries turning out reinforcing rod, plate and girders for reconstruction for the next 15 years. The Japanese are prime customers for the high quality ingots of melted down, US-forged gun barrels and armoured vehicle steel. A Hitachi-built factory nearby turns out simple electrical appliances, such as hot rings and fans, the raw material coming from the thousands of wrecked airframes and abandoned communications gear. Local home guard units have been re-issued with captured carbines and M16s. Clapped-out jeeps and three-quarter tonners double as staff cars and buses. The world's fifth largest standing army is in dire need of transportation. (There are rumoured to be a few operational Hueys still working up along the Cambodian border.) During the Tet holiday the street stalls along Le Joi had children's toys all carefully crafted out of scrap a decade old. There were planes and choppers heat-stamped out of plastic GI water bottles and school satchels made from old ammo pouches.

Since the war a whole new generation of children has gone through the education system, attuned to a dogma that is gradually relaxing as 'glasnost' creeps east through the satellites. Mother War is still the principal core of the teaching curriculum. Liberation, unification, the struggle; these dominate the philosophy of the 24 million Vietnamese that have been born since 1975. It is one of the world's most horrendous growth curves, especially as the inefficient state agricultural system cannot produce enough rice, much less market produce, for home production.

dress in something ex-army; the traditional pith helmet is still standard headgear.

Traffic is sparse, bar the never ending flow of bicycles, all of which are without bells or lights. Trams that left France in the 1920s still clank through the paved, narrow streets. The centre of the city is unscathed, marred only by the dank air-raid shelters that still remain.

There is little to do or see as a tourist in Hanoi, apart from Ho's mausoleum, the Central Market at the end of Silk Street and the big and small lakes. There are three private restaurants and only two hotels where a foreigner can stay. Rats are as numerous as bicycles. *La Revue de Samedi* claims a strip act and rock and roll; in reality it's as tame as a church hall theatrical. The cinemas

Above Left: Artefacts from the 10,000- day struggle litter post-war Vietnam. Here, an air raid bell fashioned from a shell case hangs silent outside Ho Chi Minh's home town in Lang Sen district. Ho and the bombers are gone, but this battered chunk of metal lingers on. Right: The Americans lashed Vietnam with every calibre of artillery imaginable. The legacy is a cratered landscape and seemingly endless deposits of shell cases. These are used for building, and also recycled to help the battered Vietnamese economy. For shell collectors like this, the going rate is eight dong for a hundred. Below left: Landscaping courtesy of the US Air Force. After years of attention from the world's most powerful airborne earth-moving corporation, Vietnam now has a countryside dotted with lakes and unexploded bombs.

Right: After the war the oriental ornamentation of the South was replaced with the clean lines and determined expressions of socialist art. This statue is a memorial to the atrocities of My Lai. Below: Remembering the war and its dead — lighting incense beside the graves of liberation fighters.

Should a surplus be produced in the south, the transportation is too poor to allow its movement and distribution to the people in a less fertile area. Virtually every bridge, culvert and ferry north of the 17th parallel was destroyed. It took three years to get the first train running between Hanoi and Ho'ville, and even now locomotives must be changed five times, as the patched-up bridgework will not support heavy loads. They plan to install newly-donated Belgian engines and cars, making the trip 'foreigner-compatible', as it was in the days when Noel Coward wrote *Mad Dogs And Englishmen* whilst riding its length in the 1930s.

The state has also been re-educating hundreds of thousands of employees and troops of the old, or 'puppet', regime. Most Americans and many South Vietnamese believed that there would be

instant and indiscriminate mass liquidations after the South's 'liberation'. Doubtless quite a few scores were settled. But the majority of those connected with the US reign had to report for basic re-training. Even so, thousands perished in camps which had been established in the most inhospitable tracts of the country, and even in areas that had once been the sites of furious battles. In the Ca Mau peninsula and in the notorious V Minh forest – both old Viet Cong havens and therefore free fire zones – the new inmates had to establish pineapple and banana plantations. In an atmosphere heavy with bugs and malaria-carrying mosquitoes, the first step was to clear the mass of unexploded ordnance. The cheapest method was human mine detectors. Clearing the unsuccessful McNamara Line, south of the DMZ, 1700 men –

Above: After the war, when Vietnam was desperately short of transport, traditional modes like these primitive Tonkinese wheelbarrows came into their own.

mostly ex-ARVN – were killed or maimed removing, it is claimed, 17 million pieces of live ordnance.

Nearby, at the old US Marine combat base of Con Thien, there is the largest *Liet Si*, or martyr's cemetery, in this unified country. It contains over 23,000 markers for the troops lost in action, in campaigns from Cua Viet to Khe Sanh, and it includes those who died keeping the strategic Ho Chi Minh Trail open. The graveyard and adjacent sculpture garden, situated in a poisoned, bomb-pocked landscape, is a sad place, with no birds to exorcise the ghosts of the war. A tall, concrete obelisk, officially called the Unification Memorial, stands in the centre of the kilometre-square park.

Inland, along Route 9, lies the old Marine base of Khe Sanh. Today it is a gulag for recalcitrant Bru tribespeople: the Montagnards who were Special Forces mercenaries. Now they till a few vegetables and make handicrafts for export. They are prisoners in a town constructed out of recycled airfield plating, beaten out oildrums and bunker sections. The veranda of the coffee shop on the main street – which was once the perimeter track – is made out of 105mm shell cases, pounded in upside down, and the porch is supported on barbed-wire stanchions. The old A-Team camp, three klicks away, is now a rock quarry, the foreman being an ex-NVA platoon commander wounded whilst over-running the command bunker in 1968.

Everyone over the age of 15 has a war story, which is told in a matter-of-fact fashion, and with that bland, unemotional way that the Vietnamese have learnt to adopt. There is little room for feelings in a state where survival remains the principal motive. Among the southerners there is still a yearning for the old times, for the Yankee presence and the fast life with its material wealth. This is probably felt strongest in the old I Corps HQ of Da Nang. Over half-a-million ex-ARVN are still stranded here and the mood is one of resentment: it is unwise for a round-eye to wander the streets alone at night. Knifings of Russian seamen are not unknown, though not officially admitted. The enormous bases at Marble Mountain and China Beach are no more, though out at the main airbase the last departing US unit's insignia, a viking figure, still adorns the hangars. As you catch your turbo-prop Antonov you watch MiGs taxi out of the emblazoned doors. The planes are a reminder of the constant threat posed to Vietnam by China.

It is impossible to escape the past. The war remains everywhere: in the landscape, in the blind creeping through the streets, the pension-less amputees begging at the bus stations, the public transportation made up out of old military buses and trucks, many of their engines converted to charcoal burning. Vietnam is a wreck trying to draw itself into the mainstream of the 20th century with minimal help or aid, a pariah in the psyche of the industrial West.

I drove 16,000 miles in today's Vietnam, searching for its soul, researching my own. The names were only yesterday – Chu Lai, Qui Nhon, Pleiku, An Khe, Nha Trang, Ban Me Thuot, Can Tho – but it was 20 years ago that I had lived them. It was weird to realize that I could drive with no problem virtually anywhere, in places where once all that could be expected was an ambush or a mine.

It is still Vietnam, still stunningly beautiful, scarred by what we did to it, haunted by an Agent Orange sunset, a nightmare on our collective TV screens. An apocalypse that the Vietnamese have to deal with daily but one that we can sideline.

Vietnam, the body and conscience of our time, the dragon apparent still defensively breathing fire on two frontiers.

Below: The Hanoi to Ho Chi Minh City express approaches Ham Rong Bridge at Thanh Hoa. It was not until three years after the end of the war that a train connected the two cities.

BIBLIOGRAPHY

1. Background: The Indochina War

Blum, Robert. *Drawing the Line: The Origin of Containment Policy in Southeast Asia.* New York: W.W. Norton, 1982.

Bodard, Lucien. *The Quicksand War: Prelude to Vietnam.* Boston: Atlantic Brown, 1967.

Ennis, Thomas. *French Policy and Developments in Indochina.* Chicago: University of Chicago Press, 1956.

Fall, Bernard. *Hell in a Very Small Place: The Siege of Dien Bien Phu.* Philadelphia: J.B. Lippincott, 1966. *Street Without Joy: Insurgency in Indochina 1946-63.* Harrisburg, PA: Stackpole Books, 1963.

Hall, Daniel. *A History of Southeast Asia.* St Martin's Press, 1955.

Hammer, Ellen. *The Struggle for Indochina.* California: Stanford University Press, 1954.

Kalb, Marvin and Abel. *Roots of Involvement.* New York: W.W. Norton, 1971.

Kolko, Gabriel. *Vietnam: Anatomy Of The War 1940-1975* London: Allen and Unwin, 1986.

Long, Ngo Vinh. *Before the Revolution: the Vietnamese Peasants under the French.* Cambridge, Massachusetts: MIT Press, 1973.

Santoli, Al. *To Bear Any Burden* London: Sphere, 1986.

Shaplen, Robert. *The Lost Revolution.* Harper and Row, 1966.

Warner, Denis. *The Last Confucian.* New York: Macmillan, 1963.

2. US Involvement 1965-75: General

Ambrose, Stephen. *Rise to Globalism.* New York: Viking Penguin Ltd, 1971.

Austin, Anthony. *The President's War.* Philadelphia: J.B. Libbincot, 1971.

Berman, Larry. *Planning a Tragedy: The Americanization of the War in Vietnam.* Norton, 1982.

Bonds, Ray. *The Vietnam War.* New York: Crown Publishers, 1979. *The Vietnam War: The Illustrated History of the Conflict in Southeast Asia.* New York: Crown Publishers, 1983.

Bowman, John. *The World Almanac of the Vietnam War.* New York: Bison Books, 1985.

Braestrup, Peter. *Big Story.* Colorado: Westview Press, 1977.

Burchett, Wilfred. *Vietnam: Inside Story of the Guerrilla War.* New York: International Publishers, 1965.

Caputo, Philip. *A Rumor of War.* London: Macmillan, 1977.

Cincinnatus. *Self Destruction: The Disintegration and Decay of the United States Army during the Vietnam era.* New York: W.W. Norton, 1978.

Cooper, Chester. *The Lost Crusade.* New York: Dodd, Mead, 1970.

Destler, I.M. and Lake, Anthony. *Our own Worst Enemy.* New York: Simon and Shuster, 1984.

Emerson, Gloria. *Winners and Losers.* New York: Random House, 1976.

Fitzgerald, Frances. *Fire in the Lake: The Vietnamese and the Americans in Vietnam.* Boston: Atlantic-Little Brown, 1972.

Frost, Frank. *Australia's War in Vietnam.* Sydney: Allen and Unwin, 1987.

Gershen, Martin. *Destroy or Die: The True Story of My Lai.* New Rochelle: Arlington House, 1971.

Harrison, James. *The Endless War: 50 years of struggle in Vietnam.* New York: Free Press, 1982.

Herring, George. *America's Longest War: The United States and Vietnam 1950-1970.* New York: Wiley, 1979.

Kahin, George and Lewis, John. *The United States in Vietnam.* New York: Dial, 1967.

Karnow, Stanley. *Vietnam: A History.* New York: Viking, 1983.

Kinnard, Douglas. *The War Managers.* Hannover, New Hampshire: University Press of New England, 1977.

Lewinski, Jorge. *The Camera at War.* New York: Simon and Shuster, 1978.

Lewy, Guenter. *America in Vietnam.* New York: Oxford University Press, 1978.

Maclear, Michael. *The 10,000 Day War.* New York: St Martin's, 1981.

Oberdorfer, Don. *Tet: the Turning point of the Vietnam War.* New York: Da Capo, 1983.

Palmer, Bruce. *The 25 Year War: America's Military Role in Vietnam.* Lexington: University of Kentucky Press, 1984.

Palmer, Dave. *Summons of the Trumpet: US-Vietnam in Perspective.* San Raphael CA: Presido Press, 1979.

Peers, William. *The My Lai Inquiry.* New York: Norton, 1979.

Rosser-Owen, David. *Vietnam Weapons Handbook.* Wellingborough: Patrick Stephens, 1986.

Sharp, U.S. *Strategy for Defeat: Vietnam in Retrospect.* Novato, California: Presidio Press, 1978.

Stanton, S.L. *Vietnam Order of Battle.* US News Books, 1981.

Stanton, Shelby. *The Rise and Fall of an American Army: US Ground Forces in Vietnam 1965-1973.* Novato, Calif: Presidio Press, 1985.

Thompson, Scott and Frizzell, Donald. *Lessons of Vietnam.* New York: Crane, Russak, 1977.
The Vietnam Experience Time-Life books. *Setting the Stage. Passing the Torch. Raising the Stakes. America Takes Over. A Contagion of War. Nineteen Sixty Eight. Combat Photographer.*
Fighting for Time. South Vietnam on Trial. Rain of Fire. Fall of the South. A Nation Divided. A Collision of Cultures. A False Peace. Tools of War. Thunder From Above. The Aftermath. A War Remembered. Boston: The Boston Publishing Company.

Turley, William. *The Second Indochina War.* New York: Westview Press, 1986.

Walt, Lewis. *Strange War, Strange Strategy.* New York: Funk and Wagnall, 1976.

Wilcox, Fred. *Waiting for an Army to Die: The Tragedy of Agent Orange.* New York: Random House, 1983.

Willenz, June. *Women Veterans: America's Forgotten Heroines.* New York: Continuum, 1984.

3. The Air War

Ballard, Jack. *The United States Air Force in Southeast Asia: Fixed Wing Gunships.* Washington DC: US Government Printing Office, 1982.

Berger, Carl. *The United States Air Force in Southeast Asia.* Washington DC: US Government Printing Office, 1977.

Buckingham, William. *Operation Ranch Hand: The United States Air Force and Herbicides in Southeast Asia, 1961-1972.* Washington DC: US Government Printing Office, 1982.

Burbage, Paul. *The Battle for the Skies over North Vietnam, 1964-1972.* Washington DC: Government Printing Office, 1976.

Chinnery, Phillip. *Air War Vietnam.* London: Bison Books, 1987.

Drendel, Lou. *Air War over South East Asia: A Pictorial Record, Vols 1,2 and 3.* Carrolton, Texas: Squadron/Signal Publications, 1982-84.

Huey. Carrollon, Tex: Squadron/Signal Publications, 1983.

Francillon, Rene. *Vietnam Air Wars.* London: Hamlyn, 1987.

Lavelle, A.J. *Airpower and the 1972 Spring Invasion.* Washington DC: US Government Printing Office, 1976.

BIBLIOGRAPHY

The Battle for the Skies over North Vietnam. Washington DC: US Government Printing Office, 1976.

The Tale of Two Bridges. Washington DC: US Government Printing Office, 1976.

Thompson, James. *Rolling Thunder*. Chapel Hill: University of North Carolina Press, 1980.

Tilford, Earl. *Search and Rescue in Southeast Asia 1961-1975*. Washington DC: US Government Printing Office, 1980.

4. Naval Operations

Croizat, Victor. *Vietnam River Warfare 1945-75*. Blandford Press, 1986.

Fulton, William. *Riverine Operations 1966-1969*. Washington DC: US Government Printing Office, 1973.

Tulich, Eugene. *The United States Coast Guard in Southeast Asia During the Vietnam Conflict*. Washington DC: United States Coast Guard Historical Monograph Program, 1975.

Uhlig, Frank. *Vietnam: The Naval Story*. Annapolis, Maryland: Naval Institute Press, 1986.

5. Ground Force Operations

Carhart, Tom. *Battles and Campaigns in Vietnam*. Greenwich, Connecticut: Bison Books, 1984.

Del Vecchio, John M. *The 13th Valley*. New York: Bantam Books, 1982.

Dunstan, Simon. *Vietnam Tracks: Armor In Battle 1945-1975*. Novato, California: Presidio Press, 1982.

Garland, Albert. *Infantry in Vietnam: Small Unit Actions in the Early Days 1965-66*. Nashville: Battery Press, 1967.

Nolan, Keith. *Battle for Hue: Tet 1968*. Novato, California: Presidio

Press, 1983.

Pisor, Robert. *The End of the Line: the Siege of Khe Sanh*. New York: Norton, 1982.

Schell, Jonathan. *The Village of Ben Suc*. New York: Knopf, 1967.

Schlemmer, Benjamin. *The Raid*. New York: Harper and Row, 1976.

West, Francis. *Small Unit Action in Vietnam: Summer 1966*. New York: Arno Press, 1967.

6a. Ground Force Units

Fenn, Charles. *The First Air Cavalry Division in Vietnam*. New York: W.M. Lads Publishing Co, 1967.

Kelly, Francis. *US Army Special Forces 1961-1971*. Washington DC: US Government Printing Office, 1973.

Mertel, Kenneth. *The Year of the Horse: Vietnam First Air Cavalry in the Highlands*. New York: Exposition Press, 1968.

Padden, Ian. *The Fighting Elite: US Air Commando*. New York: Bantam Books, 1985.

The Fighting Elite: US Army Special Forces. New York: Bantam Books, 1985.

The Fighting Elite: US Rangers. New York: Bantam Books, 1985.

Simpson, Charles. *Inside the Green Berets*. London: Arms and Armour Press, 1983.

Stanton, Shelby. *The Green Berets at War: US Army Special Forces in Asia 1956-75*. Novato, California: Presidio Press, 1986.

Starry, Donn. *Mounted Combat in Vietnam*. Washington DC: US News Books, 1981.

6b. US Army Vietnam Studies

Airmobility 1961-81. Base Development. Cedar Falls-Junction City. Command and Control. Communications-Electronics 1962-1970. Field Artillery 1954-73. Logistic Support. Mounted Combat in Vietnam. Reorganisation for Pacification Support. Riverine Operations-1966-1969. Role of Military Intelligence 1965-1967. Sharpening the Combat Edge. Tactical and Material Innovations. US Army Engineers 1965-1970. US Army Special Forces 1961-1971. War in the Northern Provinces 1966-1968. Allied Participation. Development and Training of the South Vietnamese Army 1950-1972. Washington DC: Department of the Army.

6c. US Marine Corps Vietnam Operational Histories

US Marines in Vietnam 1954-64: the Advisory and Combat Assistance Era, 1977. US Marines in Vietnam 1965, The Landing and the Build-up. US Marines in Vietnam 1967. US Marines in Vietnam, January-June 1968. US Marines in Vietnam, July-December 1969. US Marines in Vietnam, 1969. US Marines in Vietnam, 1970-1971.

US Marines in Vietnam, 1971-1973. US Marines in Vietnam, 1973-1975. Washington DC: History and Museums Headquarters, US Marine Corps, 1977-1985

7. Politics and Dissent.

Baskir, Lawrence and Strauss, William. *Chance and Circumstance: The Draft, the War and the Vietnam Generation*. New York: Knopf, 1978.

Elliott-Bateman, M.R. *Defeat In the East*. Oxford: OUP, 1967

Ellsberg, Daniel. *Papers on the War*. New York: Pocket Books, 1981.

Ezell, Edward. *The Great Rifle Controversy*. Harrisburg: Stackpole, 1984.

Left: A mud-splattered tanker watches intently for the NVA while a wounded grunt (above) is carried out of the Nam.

Gabriel, Richard and Savage, Paul. *Crisis in Command*. New York: Farrar, Straus and Giroux, 1978.

Fall, Bernard. *The Two Vietnams: A Political and Military Analysis*. New York: Praeger, 1963.

Halberstam, David. *The Making of a Quagmire*. New York: Random House, 1964. *The Best and the Brightest*. New York: Random House, 1972.

Johnson, Lyndon. *The Vantage Point: Perspective of the Presidency 1963-1969*. New York: Popular Library, 1971.

Just, Ward. *To what end: Report from Vietnam*. Boston: Houghton Mifflin, 1978.

Kearns, Doris. *Lyndon Johnson and the American Dream*. New York: Harper and Row, 1976.

Pentagon Papers. 2 editions:-Gravel ed. Boston: Beacon Press 1971. New York Times ed. Toronto: Bantam Books, 1970.

Powers, Thomas. *The War at Home: Vietnam and the American People*. New York: Grossman, 1973.

Schandler, Herbert. *The Unmaking of a President: Lyndon Johnson and Vietnam*. Princeton: Princeton University Press, 1977.

Thompson, Robert. *Defeating Communist Insurgency*. New York: Praeger, 1966. *No Exit From Vietnam*. New York: McKay, 1970. *Peace is not at Hand*. New York: McKay, 1974.

Wheeler, John. *Touched with Fire: the Future of the Vietnam Generation*. New York: Franklin Watts, 1984.

Zaroulis, Nancy, and Sullivan, Gerald. *Who spoke up? American Protest against the War in Vietnam 1963-1975*. New York: Doubleday, 1984.

8. Eye-witness Accounts and Memoirs.

Albright, John. *Seven Firefights in Vietnam*. Washington DC: US Government Printing Office, 1970.

Anderson, Charles. *The Grunts*. Novato, California: Presido Press, 1976.

Anderson, William. *Bat-21*. New York: Bantam Books, 1983.

Baker, Mark. *Nam: The Vietnam War in the Words of the Men and Women who Fought There*. New York: William Morrow, 1981.

Blakey, Scott. *Prisoner of War: The Survival of Commander Richard A. Stratton*. New York: Anchor Press/Doubleday, 1978.

Broughton, Jack. *THUD Ridge*. New York: Lippencott, 1969.

Butler, David. *The Fall of Saigon*. New York: Simon and Schuster, 1985.

Clark, Johnnie. *Guns up!* New York: Ballantine Books, 1984.

Donovan, David. *Once a Warrior King*. London: Weidenfield and Nicholson, 1986.

Downs, Frederick. *The Killing Zone: My Life in the Vietnam War*. New York: W. W. Norton, 1978.

Drury, Richard. *My Secret War*. New York: Martin's Press, 1979.

Ehrhart, William. *Vietnam Perkasie*. New York: Kensington Publishing, 1983.

Giap, Vo Nguyen. *Unforgettable Days*. Hanoi: Foreign Language Publishing House, 1978.

Goldman, Peter, and Fuller, Tony. *Charlie Company: What Vietnam did to US*. New York: Morrow, 1983.

Grant, Zalin. *Survivors*. New York: W. W. Norton, 1975.

Herr, Michael. *Dispatches*. New York: Knopf, 1978.

Herrington, Stuart. *Silence was a Weapon: the Vietnam War in the Villages*. Novato, Calif: Presidio Press, 1982.

Kissinger, Henry. *The White House Years*. Boston: Little Brown, 1974.

Lunn, Hugh. *Vietnam: A Reporter's War*. Queensland: University of Queensland Press, 1985.

McCauley, Lex. *The Battle Of Long Tan*. London: Arrow Books Ltd, 1987.

Marshall, Samuel. *Vietnam: Three Battles*. New York: Da Capo Press, 1971. *Ambush: The Battle of Dau Tieng, War Zone C, Operation Attleboro, and other Deadfalls in South Vietnam*. New York: Cowles, 1969. *Battles in the Monsoon: Campaigning in the Central Highland, South Vietnam, Summer 1966*. New York: Morrow, 1968. *Bird: the Christmastide Battle*. New York: Cowles, 1968. *The Fields of Bamboo: Dong Tre, Trung Luong and Hoa Hoa: Three Battles just Beyond the China Sea*. New York: Dial, 1971. *West to Cambodia*. New York: Cowles, 1968.

Mason, Robert. *Chickenhawk*. New York: The Viking Press, 1983.

McDonough, James. *Platoon Leader*. New York: Presidio Press, 1985.

McKay, Gary. *In Good Company*. Sydney: Allen and Unwin, 1987.

Nixon, Richard. *The Memoirs of Richard Nixon*. New York: Grosset and Dunlap, 1978.

O'Brien, Tim. *If I Die in a Combat Zone*. London: Calder and Boyars, 1973.

Parish, John. *A Doctor's Year in Vietnam*. New York: Bantam Books, 1986.

Risner, Robinson. *The Passing of the Night: My Seven Years as a Prisoner of the North Vietnamese*. New York: Random House, 1974.

Rutledge, Howard and Phylis. *In the Presence of Mine Enemies*. New Jersey: Fleming H. Revel and Co, 1973.

Sack, John. *Lieutenant Calley: His own Story*. New York: Viking, 1971.

Santoli, Al. *Everything We Had: An Oral History of the Vietnam War*. New York: Random House, 1981.

To Bear any Burden. New York: Ballantine Books, 1985.

Scholl-Latour, Peter. *Eyewitness Vietnam*. London: Orbis, 1981.

Snepp, Frank. *Decent Interval*. New York: Random House, 1977.

Stockdale, Jim and Sybil. *In Love and War: the Story of a Family's Ordeal and Sacrifice During the Vietnam Years*. New York: Harper and Row, 1984.

Terry, Wallace. *Bloods: An Oral History of the Vietnam War by Black Veterans*. New York: Ballantine Books, 1985.

Trotti, John. *Phantom Over Vietnam*. New York: Presidio Press, 1985.

Webb, James. *Fields of Fire*. Englewood Cliffs, New Jersey: Prentice-Hall, 1978.

Westmoreland, William. *A Soldier Reports*. Garden City, NY: Doubleday, 1976.

9. South Vietnamese Forces.

Dawson, Alan. *55 Days: The Fall of South Vietnam*. Englewood Cliffs, New Jersey: Prentice Hall, 1977.

Hosmer, Stephen. *The Fall of South Vietnam: Statements by Vietnamese Military and Civilian Leaders*. Santa Monica: Rand, 1978.

Ky, Nguyen Cao. *Twenty years and Twenty Days*. New York: Stein and Day, 1976.

Long, Nguyen. *After Saigon Fell*. Berkeley: University of California Press, 1981.

Pilger, John. *The Last Day*. New York: Vintage, 1976.

Smith, Harvey. *Area Handbook for South Vietnam*. Washington DC: US Government Printing Office, 1967.

Trung, Ngo Quang. *The Easter Offensive of 1972*. Washington DC: US Government Printing Office, 1980.

Territorial Forces. Washington DC: Center for Military History, 1981.

Turley, G. H. *The Easter Offensive: Vietnam 1972*. Novato, California: Presidio Press, 1985.

Vien, Cao Van. *The Final Collapse*. Washington DC: Government Printing Office, 1980.

Vien, Coa Van, and Khuyen, Dong Van. *Reflections of the Vietnam War*. Washington DC: US Government Printing Office, 1980.

10. Communist Forces.

Burchett, Wilfred. *Grasshoppers and Elephants: Why Vietnam Fell*. New York: Urizen Books, 1977.

Don, Tran Van. *Our Endless War: Inside Vietnam*. Novato, California: Presidio Press, 1978.

Dung, Van Tien. *Our Great Spring Victory*. Foreign Broadcast Service Supplement, 1972.

Fenn, Charles. *Ho Chi Minh: A Biographical Introduction*. New York: Charles Scribner's Sons, 1973.

Giap, Vo Nguyen. *Dien Bien Phu*. Hanoi: Foreign Language Publishing House, 1962. *Big Victory, Great Task*. New York: Praeger, 1967. *Banner of the People's War: The Party's Military Line*. Novato, Calif: Praeger, 1970.

Johnson, Chalmers. *Autopsy on People's War*. Berkeley: University of California Press, 1973.

Loconture, Jean. *Ho Chi Minh: A Political Biography*. New York: Random House, 1968.

Ngan, Nguyen Ngoc. *The Will of Heaven*. New York: Dutton, 1981.

Nguyen, Hung. *Communist Offensive Strategy and the Defense of South Vietnam*. Journal of the US Army War College, Winter 1984.

O'Neill, Robert. *General Giap: Politician and Strategist*. New York: Praeger, 1969.

Pike, Douglas. *History of the Vietnamese Communist Party*. Palo Alto: Hoover Institution, 1978.

Viet Cong: The Organisation and Techniques of the National Liberation Front of South Vietnam. Cambridge, Massachusetts: MIT Press, 1966.

The Viet Cong Strategy of Terror. Saigon: US Information Agency, 1970.

Smith, Harvey. *Area Handbook for North Vietnam*. Washington DC: US Government Printing Office, 1967.

Tang, Troung Nhu. *A Viet Cong Memoir*. Washington DC: Harcourt Brace Jovanovich, 1985.

Taylor, Maxwell. *Swords and Plowshares*. New York: Harpers, 1959.

Taoi, Doan. *The Vietnam Gulag*. New York: Simon and Schuster, 1986.

Tra, Tran Van. *Ending the 30 years War*. Ho Chi Minh City: Literature Publishing House, 1982.

Webb, Kate. *On the Other Side: 23 Days with the Viet Cong*. New York: Quadrangle, 1972.

An uncertain face scans a landing zone.

11. Cambodia and Laos

Burrs, Richard and Leitenburg, Milton. *The Wars in Vietnam, Cambodia and Laos, 1945-1982: A Bibliographic Guide*. Santa Barbara: ABC-Cleo Information Services, 1984.

Becker, Elizabeth. *When the War was Over*. New York: Simon and Schuster, 1986.

Hinh, Nguyen Duy. *Lam Son 719*. Washington DC: US Government Printing Office, 1981.

Issacs, Arnold. *Without Honor: Defeat in Vietnam and Cambodia*. Baltimore: Johns Hopkins Press, 1983.

Kiernan, Ben. *How Pol Pot Came to Power*. New York: Schocken Books, 1985.

Paschall, Rod. *White Star in Laos: A Study in Miscalculation*. Carlisle Barracks, Pennsylvania: US Army Military History Institute, 1985.

Ponchard, Francois. *Cambodia: Year Zero*. New York: Holt Rinehart and Winston, 1978.

Shawcross, William. *Kissinger, Nixon, and the Destruction of Cambodia*. New York: Simon and Schuster, 1979.

Stevenson, Charles. *The End of Nowhere: American Policy Towards Laos Since 1954*. Boston: Boston Press, 1973.

Sutsakhan, Sak. *The Khmer Republic at War and the Final Collapse*. Washington DC: Indochina Monograph, US Army Center of Military History, 1980.

Tro, Tran Dinh. *The Cambodian Incursion*. Washington DC: Indochina Monograph, US Army Center of Military History, 1979.

Vongsavanah, Solitchay. *RLA Operations in the Laotian Panhandle*. Washington DC: US Government Printing Office, 1981.

INDEX

Right: The Vietnam perspective – the thousand-yard stare.

WAR '65

Like all wars, Vietnam began with a series of threats. On 2 March 1965 those threats took a new turn when 100 US jet bombers took off from Da Nang to strike targets inside North Vietnam. It was the first air raid that could not be justified as a retaliation and began America's graduated bombing campaign - Operation Rolling Thunder.

The object of Rolling Thunder was to slow down the supply of arms and men from North Vietnam and to threaten the communists into a negotiated peace. It succeeded in doing neither, but having committed America to a plan of action, it raised the price of failure. Six days later, on 8 March, 3500 US Marines landed at Da Nang to defend the airbase. War was escalating with a logic of its own.

Rather than being forced into a negotiated peace by this growing display of US military muscle, the Viet Cong grew ever more resolute to win. By the end of May, it looked as if they might succeed. As the monsoon rains opened up, the Viet Cong and North Vietnamese Army staged a series of lightning attacks on government forces. With entire regiments of the South Vietnamese Army decimated, General Westmoreland asked on 2 June for US troop strength to be increased to over 200,000. The need for a major US offensive was growing every day.

When the assault came it was sudden, dramatic and victorious. Operation Starlite began on 18 August, a combined land, air and sea attack that caught the Viet Cong wholly by surprise. It taught many lessons, but the most valuable were those learnt by the Viet Cong. If they were to win this war, their advantage lay not in open combat, but in covert, guerrilla attacks. At the same time, President Johnson was making draft evasion a prisonable offence; the pattern of the Vietnam War was being set.

MARCH

2 100 US jet bombers strike military targets in North Vietnam as America begins its graduated bombing campaign - Operation Rolling Thunder.
8 Two Marine battalions, totalling 3500 men, land at Da Nang to guard the airfield. US forces in Vietnam now total 27,000.
9 President Johnson authorises use of napalm by US planes bombing targets in North Vietnam.
14 Stepping up the pressure in North Vietnam, America bombs military and naval targets on Conco Island, off the North Vietnamese coast.
23 Britain pledges support for President Johnson's Vietnam policy.
31 Although ready to authorise US troops to go on the offensive, President Johnson denies that he knows of a 'far-reaching strategy' for developing the war in Vietnam.

APRIL

3-5 Operation Rolling Thunder is extended to cover non-military targets in North Vietnam.
4 With US support, the ARVN destroys a communist enclave in the U Minh forest, killing 258 Viet Cong. Australian Prime Minister Robert Menzies praises America for accepting the challenge to 'human freedom'.
7 President Johnson says America is ready to begin 'unconditional discussions' to end the war. He offers a $1 billion aid programme for Southeast Asia.
11 North Vietnam rejects Johnson's peace plan.
15 In the biggest air strike of the war, 230 South Vietnamese and American fighter-bombers drop 1000 tons of bombs on a Viet Cong forest stronghold.
17 As the US affirms commitment to the bombing campaign in the face of international pressure, 15,000 students stage a protest march in Washington.
20 Restrictions limiting US Marines to an eight-mile radius of the Da Nang airbase are lifted.
21 A Buddhist monk publicly burns

himself to death in Saigon as a protest against the war. Pictures of the ritual suicide are relayed around the world.
24 President Johnson officially declares Vietnam a 'combat zone', meaning that all soldiers will receive combat pay and tax advantages.
26 US Secretary of Defense Robert McNamara reveals that the war is now costing America $1.5 billion a year.
26 Johnson defends US bombing raids, saying, 'our restraint was viewed as weakness. We could no longer stand by as attacks mounted.'
29 US air strikes claim 70 Viet Cong deaths, while South Vietnamese troops kill 84 more, taking 31 prisoners.

Rolling Thunder: An F-4 Phantom sets out on another mission.

MAY

3-12 3500 men of the 173d Airborne Brigade arrive in Vietnam, the first US Army combat unit to join the conflict.
7 Congress approves President Johnson's request for a further $700 million for the war.
10 ARVN troops flee from a battle with the Viet Cong near Saigon when they become frightened by the sound of their own planes flying overhead.
13 America halts bombing of North Vietnam to see if Hanoi will compromise on peace conditions. With guerrilla attacks increasing daily, the Viet Cong stage a daylight attack on a textile mill just five miles north of Saigon.
16 A university 'teach-in' is held in Washington in protest against the war as opposition within the American academic community intensifies.
19 America resumes bombing of North Vietnam.

1965

22 The mother of a US college student who has been showing Viet Cong propaganda films asks for his scholarship to be revoked.
24 Cyrus Eaton, an industrialist working for world peace, reports from a recent trip to the USSR that the Soviet President has warned that the world is threatened by nuclear war within four weeks if US aggression continues. The ARVN launch a major offensive on Viet Cong enclaves in Kontum. The Viet Cong keep in hiding to prepare their own attack.
29 Viet Cong emerge from secret camps to mount a devastating attack on the South Vietnamese 51st Regiment - effectively destroying it as a fighting force.

JUNE

1 President Johnson requests $89 million for economic aid to Southeast Asia.
7 General Westmoreland reports from Vietnam that 'battle losses have been inordinately high'. Fearing for the success of the US involvement, he asks for American troop strength to be increased from 50,000 to over 200,000.
10-13 Viet Cong attack a Special Forces camp and district headquarters of the ARVN at Dong Xoai, initiating the fiercest fighting of the war so far and causing the ARVN some 900 casualties. Heavy US strikes eventually drive off the Viet Cong who lose 350 men in ground combat and nearly twice that number in bombing raids.

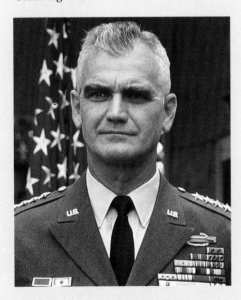

Escalation: On 2 June General Westmoreland demands 150,000 troops.

12 Roman Catholic opposition forces President Quat to resign as leader of South Vietnam.
16 Secretary of Defense McNamara announces 21,000 troops to be sent to Vietnam, bringing the total to 74,500.
18 The Vietnamese Air Force commander, General Nguyen Cao Ky, becomes the new premier of South Vietnam.
22 US planes bomb targets only 80 miles from the Chinese border, the

Rising Casualties: the US suffered 5687 wounded and 1241 killed in 1965.

deepest raids into North Vietnam so far.
28-30 US forces launch their first major offensive on a Viet Cong enclave 20 miles northeast of Saigon, but fail to make contact with the enemy.

JULY

1 The Viet Cong infiltrate the Da Nang airbase, destroying three planes and damaging three others.
8 At a court-martial in Okinawa, an American Captain pleads not guilty to feigning mental illness while serving in Vietnam.
8-13 Britain sends an MP to Hanoi to persuade the North Vietnamese to reconsider peace negotiations. He is rebuffed.
11 America reveals that it is prepared to bomb any part of North Vietnam.
12 Lieutenant Frank Reasoner becomes the first Marine to earn the Congressional Medal of Honor while serving in Vietnam.
15 Premier Ky is quoted in an English newspaper as saying that Adolf Hitler is one of his 'heroes'.
24 The Pentagon reports that since 1961 US wounded in Vietnam outnumber those killed by 5 to 1.

28 In a major turning point of the war, President Johnson announces that US troops in Vietnam will be increased to 125,000 and monthly draft calls raised from 17,000 to 35,000.

AUGUST

3 CBS TV shows pictures of men of the 1st Battalion, 9th Marines, burning down most of the village of Cam Ne, six miles west of Da Nang,

against a report that the Viet Cong had long since left the village. The report sparks off international indignation.
5 Viet Cong attack the Esso storage terminal near Da Nang and destroy 2 million gallons of fuel - almost 40% of the US supply.
7 The Chinese government warns that it may send forces in to fight for the communists.
8 US planes launch a major air strike on Viet Cong positions in South Vietnam.
12 President Johnson claims that the US would not continue to fight in Vietnam 'if its help were not wanted and requested'.
13 ARVN troops kill over 250 Viet Cong in the Mekong Delta.
18-23 US Marines launch Operation Starlite - their first major ground action of the war. With aerial and naval support, Marines destroy a Viet Cong stronghold near Van Tuong. The Viet Cong are caught by total surprise and lose most of their 1st Regiment.
31 President Johnson signs into law a bill making it a crime to destroy or mutilate a draft card, with penalties of up to five years in prison and a $1000 fine.

WAR '65

In its bloodiness and intensity, the war in Vietnam entered a new phase in the closing months of 1965. It was a phase that was ushered in on 11 September by the arrival of the first full division to be sent to Vietnam – the 1st Air Cavalry Division (Airmobile).

With its helicopter mobility, the 1st Air Cav was to spearhead a new and aggressive stage in America's 'search and destroy' offensives. When US planes initiated a major bombing campaign to cut off the supply of arms and men through the Ho Chi Minh Trail, ground forces were ready to stifle the growing presence of the NVA.

Their chance came after the 1st Air Cav had helped repel a Viet Cong attack on the Plei Me camp on 19 October. Seizing the iniative, Westmoreland sent his forces into the jungles of the Ia Drang Valley, beginning a month-long campaign that was to see some of the bitterest fighting of the war to date. By 20 November, half of a full NVA division had been destroyed.

While the campaign may have been a success, victory was achieved at a high price. US losses increased rapidly, and the nature of the war was soon to change even further. Instead of pressing for immediate victory, Hanoi recognised that the NVA advantage lay in a war of attrition and a weakening of US morale.

At home, that morale was under increasing attack from the anti-war movement, now growing in numbers as the scale of America's involvement became more apparent. But the protesters were to have little impact on the Pentagon. By December, over 200,000 more troops were prepared for combat in Vietnam and the Arc Light bombing campaign was extended to cover Laos. A cease-fire at the Christmas of 1965 seemed to offer the last, slim chance of an honourable peace.

SEPTEMBER

2 United States announces that over 100 US servicemen are volunteering every day for service in Vietnam.

3 US and ARVN planes fly a record of 532 missions in one day.

5 Senator Richard Nixon affirms his support of US policy on a visit to Saigon, saying: 'There is only one basis for negotiations...a communist withdrawal.'

7-10 US and ARVN troops begin Operation Piranha – an attempt to destroy the remainder of the Viet Cong 1st Regiment after Operation Starlite. Storming a Viet Cong stronghold, the US claims 200 enemy dead – although most are the wounded survivors of the earlier operation.

11 The US 1st Cavalry Division (Airmobile) begins to land at Qui Nhon, bringing US troop strength in Vietnam to about 125,000.

18-21 US troops strike at An Khe in one of the biggest engagements of the war so far. The US claims 226 Viet Cong killed.

20 America loses seven planes in raids over North and South Vietnam.

23-29 The South Vietnamese government executes three communist agents at Da Nang by night to prevent foreign photographers recording it. Hanoi announces the execution of two US prisoners, held since 1963, as 'war criminals.'

30 America reveals that troops are using non-toxic smoke, spread with crop dusters, on suspected Viet Cong hideouts. Two USAF jets are shot down while bombing the Minh Binh bridge, near Hanoi.

OCTOBER

During this month, the remainder of the US 1st Infantry Division arrives in Vietnam to join its 2d Brigade for combat operations in III Corps. South Korea deploys ROK (Republic of Korea) Capital Division to join 101st Airborne Division for combat operations in II Corps.

5 US government authorizes use of tear gas by troops in Vietnam.

6 US B52s bomb suspected Viet Cong bases near the Cambodian border.

10-14 US 1st Air Cav joins with ARVN marines to strike at 2000 NVA troops in the Central Highlands.

15 At a pacifist rally, David Millar, a relief programme volunteer, becomes the first US war protester to burn his draft card in contravention of the law. He is later arrested by agents from the Federal Bureau of Investigation.

16 Protests against US policy in Vietnam are held in 40 American cities, as well as in London, Rome, Brussels, Copenhagen and Stockholm.

19 NVA troops launch a major assault on an ARVN/US Special Forces Camp at Plei Me. With the help of the 1st Air Cav, ARVN reinforcements repulse the attack. With the camp secured, General Westmoreland decides to seize the advantage and send in the 1st Air Cav to 'find, fix and defeat the enemy forces that threatened Plei Me.'

22 Pacific commander Admiral Grant Sharp claims that allied forces have 'stopped losing' the war.

23 The Americans for Democratic Freedom denounce a probe into suspected communist influence on the war protest as a blatant attempt to 'stifle criticism' of government policy.

27 Viet Cong commandos damage and destroy a number of allied aircraft in two separate raids on US air bases.

US scepticism: Robert McNamara voices grave doubts over the war.

1965

Ia Drang: A hot LZ and the most savage fighting to date.

30 Led by five recipients of the Congressional Medal of Honor, 25,000 people march in support of America's action in Vietnam. US planes accidentally bomb a friendly Vietnamese village, killing 48 civilians and wounding 55 others. Ten miles from Da Nang, US Marines repel a Viet Cong assault, killing 56 guerrillas. A search of the dead uncovers a sketch of Marine positions on the body of a 13-year old boy who had been selling drinks to Marines the previous day.

NOVEMBER

1-20 Members of the 1st Air Cav begin an assault on NVA forces in the Ia Drang Valley. It turns into the bloodiest battle of the war to date, decimating the NVA 33rd Regiment and ending with the virtual elimination of the Air Cav's Company C in a single ambush.

2 As a war protest, a 32-year old Quaker from Baltimore sets fire to himself in front of the Pentagon.

5 Senator Robert Kennedy defends 'the right to criticize and the right to dissent' from US policy in Vietnam and claims that donating blood to North Vietnam is 'in the oldest tradition of this country.'

19 Using string bows, Viet Cong guerrillas fire arrows dipped in rancid animal fat at US troops guarding the air base at Qui Nhon.

22 The Chairman of the House Armed Services Committee, L. Mendel Rivers, calls for the bombing of Haiphong and Hanoi, saying that it is 'a folly to let the port of Haiphong and military targets of Hanoi remain untouched while war supplies being used against our troops are pouring into port.' Two US Navy nuclear-powered ships, an aircraft carrier and a guided missile frigate, join the 7th Fleet and take up positions off Saigon.

27 The Pentagon demands that US troop strength be increased from 120,000 to 400,000 men. Nearly 35,000 war protesters circle the White House for two hours before moving on to the Washington Monument where they are addressed by Dr Benjamin Spock and the wife of Martin Luther King.

27-28 Viet Cong guerrillas attack a South Vietnamese regimental headquarters at the Michelin rubber plantation inflicting heavy casualties.

30 Secretary of Defense McNamara warns that there is no guarantee of US military success, saying that now: 'US killed in action can be expected to reach 1000 a month and the odds are even that we will be faced in early 1967 with a 'no-decision' at an even higher level.' British Foreign Secretary Michael Stewart visits Moscow in an effort to persuade Soviet leaders to help restart the Geneva conference on Indochina. Andrei Gromyko, the Soviet Foreign Minister, rebuffs him, saying that peace talks cannot begin until America withdraws all troops and ceases its bombing of North Vietnam.

DECEMBER

US Third Brigade, 25th Infantry Division, deployed to Vietnam for operations in II Corps. US Navy establishes River Task force for naval operations in II Corps.

4 Viet Cong guerrillas blow up a Saigon hotel housing US soldiers, killing eight servicemen and civilians and wounding 137.

7 McNamara warns President Johnson that the NVA and Viet Cong 'continue to believe that the war will be a long one, that time is their ally and that their staying power is superior to ours.'

8-9 US aircraft launch Operation Tiger Hound, a major attack on transport routes between North and South Vietnam to reduce enemy infiltration.

8-19 A joint US and ARVN assault routs Viet Cong forces in the Que Son Valley, but with the loss of two ARVN battalions.

9 An article in *The New York Times* reports on the failure of US bombing raids to effectively slow down the passage of NVA forces and supplies into South Vietnam.

14 A US opinion poll shows that only 20 per cent of Americans believe that America should have withdrawn from Vietnam before troops became involved in the conflict.

15 In the first air raid on a major industrial North Vietnamese target, US planes destroy a thermal power plant at Uongbi.

16 General Westmoreland sends a memorandum to Defence Secretary McNamara requesting 443,000 troops by the end of 1966.

24-25 The Christmas period is marked by a truce, originally proposed by the Viet Cong. Hoping to persuade the communists into peace talks, America accepts the truce and refrains from bombing until 31 December.

26 US and ARVN forces abandon efforts to extend the Christmas truce in ground warfare after extensive Viet Cong attacks.

From defence to offence: The 1st Infantry Division arrives in force.

WAR '66

A glimmer of hope that the war in Vietnam might end through a negotiated peace had flashed briefly on the horizon at the end of 1965. By the end of January 1966 such hopes were to be firmly doused by American jet bombers. To the North Vietnamese, the 37-day halt in air attacks was nothing more than a deceptive trick; to presidential advisor Maxwell Taylor, Hanoi had failed to respond to 'the sincerity of our peaceful purposes'. A deadlock ushered the war into another bitter phase.

When the air raids restarted, they drew ever closer to Hanoi and Haiphong – targets which the US had earlier avoided. By the beginning of April, B-52 strategic bombers were joining the assault on NVA supply routes for the first time, as the North Vietnamese stepped up their resistance with the help of Soviet-made MiG jet fighters.

On the ground, Korean, Australian and New Zealander troops joined US forces in the bloodiest search-and-destroy missions to date, centering on Operation Masher/White Wing. Beginning on 24 January, allied troops joined up across corps boundaries and for more than forty days swept across the Binh Dinh province, taking an estimated 2,389 enemy casualties – another elusive victory in this war without frontiers.

But by the time the 1st and 25th Infantry and 173rd Airborne were taking the search and destroy initiative into overdrive, the US was to face a set back from its own allies. As the swelling numbers of US servicemen gave Saigon the dimensions of a US base, the endemic corruption of Premier Ky's government led to a Buddhist armed uprising. With the virtual seizure of Da Nang and Hue by rebel forces, America was caught in the crossfire of civil unrest which was to prove a continuing problem.

JANUARY

1 US Senator Strom Thurmond calls for the use of nuclear weapons in Vietnam if there is no other way of bringing about victory. A Chinese newspaper dismisses the roving ambassadors sent out before Christmas to explain US policy to world governments as 'monsters and freaks'.
6 A Special Forces camp at Khe Sanh is attacked by Viet Cong forces with 120mm mortars – the first time this weapon has been used.
8 Senate Majority leader Mike Mansfield delivers a pessimistic analysis of the war, warning that the whole of South East Asia 'cannot be ruled out as a potential battlefield'. A US Senate report estimates that the communists can deploy 230,000 men, including 59,000 'full time' guerrillas.
8-14 Operation Crimp is launched, a large scale US-Australian drive against the 'Iron Triangle'. An extensive network of tunnels is destroyed, but in terms of the body count the operation is disappointing.
15 Amid growing concern about the plight of US prisoners of war, an anti-war organisation announces that the Viet Cong have agreed for POW's mail to be sent via Algeria.

17 Douglas Ramsey, a US diplomat, is abducted from his car by Viet Cong guerrillas.
19 101st Airborne, South Korean and ARVN troops begin Operation Van Buren in the rice fields of the Phu Yen province.
24 Secretary of Defense McNamara recommends to President Johnson that yet more US troops should be committed to Vietnam, raising the number to 400,000 by the end of 1966. He warns, however, that increased troop levels will not ensure success.
24 1st Air Cavalry join with allied troops to launch Operation Masher/ White Wing – the greatest search and destroy mission yet seen in Vietnam.
28 General Westmoreland asks for 16,000 more troops in addition to the 443,000 already requested.
31 US resumes bombing of the North after a 37-day pause. Five days earlier, General Maxwell D. Taylor, former ambassador to Saigon, had said the bombing halt had 'shown ...the sincerity of our peaceful purposes.'

FEBRUARY

6-9 President Johnson and South Vietnamese Premier Ky meet in Hawaii. The US President offers to extend his 'Great Society' (plan for social reform) to Vietnam, saying, 'We are determined to win not only military victory but victory over hunger, disease and despair'.
7 The political and military

Search and destroy: Troops set out on Operation Masher.

Right: A North Vietnamese soldier on the Ho Chi Minh Trail.

problems of the Saigon regime are starkly illustrated by the revelation that its village pacification programme was so inefficient that it would take up to six years to gain control of a rural province. US planes strike a military training centre at Dien Bien Phu.

11 Johnson announces a gradual increase in the numbers of US troops in Vietnam (currently totalling 205,000). A former US sergeant alleges that US Special Forces are trained to torture prisoners.

16 Evidence that the war is spreading to neighbouring countries comes with the news that communist troops had clashed with Laotian government forces inside Laos.

17 General Taylor claims that the purpose of Rolling Thunder is to 'change the will of the enemy leadership', and that in Vietnam America will prove that 'wars of liberation' are 'costly, dangerous and doomed to failure'.

23 The Allied mission in Saigon discloses that 90,000 South Vietnamese soldiers deserted in 1965.

25 Elements of the 1st Infantry destroy three Viet Cong camps and an arms factory during Operation Mastiff in the Boi Loi woods.

MARCH

4-6 7000 Marines and ARVN troops launch Operation Utah, destroying half of a 2000-strong NVA regiment in the Quang Ngai province.

7 USAF and USN planes fly 200 sorties over North Vietnam in the heaviest raid of the war so far.

8-11 A Special Forces camp at A Shau, 60 miles from Da Nang, is evacuated after an overwhelming NVA attack. The US commander claims that many of the Vietnamese under his command were secret Viet Cong sympathisers.

9 US authorities admit to destroying 20,000 acres of crops to deny food to the Viet Cong, causing outraged protests from the American academic community.

10 A violent Buddhist campaign to oust Premier Ky follows the decision of South Vietnam's ruling junta to dismiss Lieutenant General Thi, a leading Buddhist.

16 Reporting on his recent visit to Vietnam, US Representative Clement Zablocki claims that for every Viet Cong guerrilla killed in

Premier Nguyen Ky.

recent search and destroy missions, six civilians have died.

23 Rejecting a Soviet invitation to a communist party congress, China charges Russia with collaborating in a US 'plot' to impose peace talks on North Vietnam.

25 Radio stations in Hue and Da Nang are taken over by Buddhists and their supporters, demanding the resignation of Premier Ky's military government.

26 In one of many demonstrations, 25,000 protesters march against the war in New York City.

31 The US Marine Corps announces that 1382 Viet Cong have been killed in a series of six operations around Chu Lai and Phu Bai during March.

APRIL

US 25th Infantry Division deploys to Vietnam from Hawaii for operations in III Corps. US Navy begins Operation Game Warden to interdict weapons and supplies coming to Vietnam via the waterways of the Mekong Delta. On the ground, in Operation Abilene, the 1st Infantry Division sweeps through Phouc Tuy province.

1 The mayor of Da Nang openly joins with anti-government forces. Rebel troops in South Vietnam begin establishing independent control of the city. Viet Cong commandos blow up a Saigon hotel housing US troops.

3 Premier Ky stuns reporters by saying that Da Nang is 'held by communists and the government will undertake operations to clear them out'.

4 US F-4C Phantom bombers

attack the main supply link between North Vietnam and Nanning, China, destroying road and railway bridges.

5 Premier Ky leads government forces into Da Nang. Finding the roads blocked, he begins talks with the mayor as the US, keen to avoid interference, begins to withdraw some personnel from Hue, Da Nang and other trouble spots.

11 The US government reveals that political turmoil in South Vietnam is severely disrupting military operations. The strains of combat flying are revealed when the USAF announces that no aircrew could fly more than 100 missions over North Vietnam.

12 B-52 strategic bombers are used for the first time against the North. The determination of the US to prevail in the air war is indicated by the dropping of one million tons of bombs on the Mugia Pass in an attempt to slow the passage of guerrillas along the Ho Chi Minh Trail.

13 The Viet Cong launch one of their most successful guerrilla attacks yet on Tan Son Nhut airport, Saigon. Using mortars and smallarms, a 30-man unit destroys 12 helicopters and nine aircraft, causing 140 US and Vietnamese casualties.

17 Elements of the 1st Infantry Division begin a two-month search and destroy operation in the Rung Sat Special Zone. The US bombing campaign in the North escalates when Navy and USAF planes begin the closest raids to Hanoi and Haiphong of the war so far.

23 For the first time, North Vietnamese planes make a major effort to oppose a US air raid. 16 MiGs clash with US planes.

24 In Operation Birmingham, the 1st Infantry Division heads north of Tay Ninh, but only makes squad- and platoon-sized encounters.

Air war: B-52 bombers are used for the first time.

WAR '66

In the summer months of 1966, the war in Vietnam was growing increasingly into a major conflict that was threatening to engulf the world. Frustrated by the failure of Rolling Thunder to quell the resistance of North Vietnam, America once again raised the stakes – directing bombers ever deeper into the Hanoi and Haiphong area and, on 30 July, intentionally attacking the Demilitarized Zone (DMZ) for the first time.

Vietnam's neutral neighbours, Laos and Cambodia, found themselves in the firing line; more dangerously, China's own border territory was under threat. Both the Soviet Union and China were thrown into a closer kinship with Ho Chi Minh, while even Britain, a supporter of President Johnson's policy under Harold Wilson's premiership, nervously disassociated itself from this latest escalation of the war.

On land, as in the air, US military command made attacking infiltration points from North Vietnam a priority. Operations Hastings and Paul Revere, in the border regions of the North and Central Fronts, were both aimed at NVA entry routes as the search and destroy strategy progressed with a new fury and intensity. NVA forces were being successfully engaged, but it was proving impossible even to restrict communist infiltration to a constant level.

Elsewhere in the South, Premier Ky released his full military might on Buddhist rebel forces, reclaiming Da Nang and, on 22 June, taking control of Quang Tri – the last anti-government stronghold. Intensified guerrilla activities were promised to coincide with the coming election, but the immediate fears of a Buddhist uprising had been allayed.

MAY

2 US Defense Secretary McNamara reports that North Vietnamese infiltration into the South is running at 4500 men a month – three times the 1965 level.
10 ARVN units, along with troops of the 3d Brigade, 25th Infantry Division, launch Operation Paul Revere to counter possible NVA offensive activities against Special

War in the Highlands: The 101st Airborne in Operation Hawthorne.

Forces border camps at Duc Co and Plei Me.
15 Premier Ky's decision to despatch 1500 ARVN troops to Da Nang sparks off another wave of violent protests by Buddhist dissenters.

JUNE

2 US 1st Division and ARVN 5th Regiment begin Operation El Paso II in Binh Long province. In Kontum province in the Central Highlands, troops of the 101st Airborne and ARVN forces commence Operation Hawthorne/Da Nang 61 in an attempt to withdraw the Tou Morong Regional Force back to Dak To.
4 A three-page advertisement against the war appears in the *New York Times*, signed by 6400 academics.
11 Private Adam R. Weber, a black soldier in the 25th Infantry Division,

is sentenced to one year's hard labour for refusing to carry a rifle because of his pacifist convictions.
20-26 Operation Nathan Hale is fought in the vicinity of US Special Forces camp at Dong Tri by elements of the 101st Airborne and Ist Cavalry Divisions.
21 Rejecting a new American proposal for peace talks, Hanoi reiterates its demand that an unconditional bombing halt precede negotiations.
25 After smashing anti-government resistance in Saigon, Hue and other major cities, Premier Ky appeals for conciliation and forgiveness for the 'misunderstandings of the past'.
29 In a major escalation of the war, America bombs targets close to Hanoi and Haiphong, destroying an estimated 50 per cent of the North's fuel supply.
30 Peking claims that US planes killed three people during an attack on Chinese fishing boats in international waters.

JULY

1 US Air Force and Navy jets begin a major campaign to wipe out fuel installations in the Hanoi-Haiphong area. China reacts by calling the bombing 'barbarous and wanton acts that have further freed us from any bounds of restrictions in helping North Vietnam'. All but essential war workers are evacuated from Hanoi.
5 As Britain and France, among others, condemn the air raids, Johnson declares: 'I cannot

617

understand the thinking of any country...that says we should sit by while these men...[are] killing our Marines.'

6 Pentagon reports that 80-90 per cent of North Vietnam's fuel supplies have come under attack and 55 per cent destroyed as US air raids intensify.

6-9 Hanoi Radio reports that several captured US pilots have been paraded through Hanoi in front of angry crowds.

7 A House of Commons motion is passed upholding Harold Wison's support of American policy, but dissociating Britain from the raids on the Hanoi-Haiphong area.

8 Premier Ky embarrasses the US government by calling for an all-out invasion of the North.

11 The US bombing campaign against Laos intensifies; over 100 raids a day are now being flown against the Ho Chi Minh Trail, compared with under 50 a day at the beginning of the year.

15 Operation Hastings/Deckhouse II is launched by US Marine Corps and ARVN troops against the 10,000-strong NVA 324B Division in Quang Tri province. It is the largest

New pressures: Johnson takes advice.

combined operation of the war up to this time. The NVA suffers 882 casualties.

20 Johnson warns North Vietnam that holding war crimes trials for Americans will produce serious repercussions.

29 Terry Sullivan, one of many pacifists in America who protested against the war by destroying their draft card, is given a year's prison sentence.

30 For the first time in the war, US aircraft bomb the Demilitarized Zone after a reported sighting of NVA troops crossing through it into South Vietnam.

Air assault: An A-1 Skyraider loads up for a close-air support mission.

AUGUST

3 In the follow-up to Operation Hastings, Marines begin Operation Prairie – a sweep just south of the DMZ against three battalions of the NVA 324B division. It is to result in 1397 known enemy casualties by 19 September.

9 USAF jets mistakenly attack two South Vietnamese villages 80 miles south of Saigon, killing 63 and wounding over 100 civilians.

10 Troops of the 1st Battalion, 5th Marines fight a bitter battle against NVA forces in Quang Tin province.

13 Prince Sihanouk, ruler of neutral Cambodia, bitterly attacks America for bombing Thlock Track, a village near the South Vietnamese border.

23-29 The US freighter *Baton Rouge Victory* hits a Viet Cong mine in the Long Tao river, 22 miles south of Saigon. Seven crewman are killed and the half-sunken ship blocks the link between Saigon and the sea.

28 Soviet newspapers report that North Vietnamese fighter pilots are being trained at a secret air base.

29 Peking charges that US planes sank a Chinese merchant ship and damaged another in the Gulf of Tonkin.

30 Hanoi announces that China has signed an agreement to provide non-refundable economic and technical aid to North Vietnam.

SEPTEMBER

1 President de Gaulle of France condemns US policy and calls for an

American withdrawl from Vietnam, while on a visit to Cambodia.

6-9 Three army privates are court-martialled in New Jersey for refusing to go to Vietnam. The court rejects the defense argument that the war is illegal and immoral.

9 Reports emerge that America is planning a massive increase in its aerial crop-destruction campaign against Viet Cong territory.

11 South Vietnam holds an election for its constitutional assembly. It is boycotted by many Buddhists and two and a half million people in Viet Cong controlled areas are prevented from voting.

12 500 US planes bomb coastal targets, transportation lines and supply areas in the heaviest raid of the war so far.

14 Operation Attleboro begins near the Cambodian border, 50 miles north of Saigon, although the first major contact does not take place until 19 October. At its peak, 20,000 US and ARVN troops are involved.

16 Reports emerge that US troops burned down Lien Hoa, a South Vietnamese village, by lighting the straw roofs with matches.

16-19 China claims that US planes have twice attacked Chinese territory on recent raids. The US concedes the possibility of some incursion into Chinese territory.

19-23 B-52 bombers carry out heavy raids against North Vietnamese targets in the DMZ.

23 America reports that US planes are defoliating jungle areas just south of the DMZ.

WAR '66

By October 1966, America's graduated bombing campaign – Operation Rolling Thunder – had been raging for 18 months in an attempt to halt the passage of arms and supplies down the Ho Chi Minh Trail and to force the communists into a negotiated peace. But Rolling Thunder had failed on both counts. To step up the pressure and achieve some tangible results, it was now decided to push the operation into its most violent phase to date.

Flying over 25,000 bombing sorties a month, American planes drew ever closer to Hanoi itself. By 2 December they were striking targets a mere five miles outside the city; by 13 December bombs were falling on the very edges of Hanoi – and, according to some reports, destroying outlying villages and hamlets. On 26 December, as a new wave of international criticism surfaced, US officials admitted that 'it is sometimes impossible to avoid all damage to civilian areas.'

In the South, America's search and destroy campaign pressed ahead with some success. Near the Cambodian border, Operation Attleboro was concluded with over 1100 reported enemy casualties, while at the very end of the year South Vietnamese troops mounted a massive drive against one of the Viet Cong's best-fortified strongholds – the U Minh Forest in the Mekong Delta. With both the US Air Force and Navy bombarding the area, 6000 ARVN troops staged a lightning four-day attack.

The New Year would see no abatement of the pressure, and the human cost continued to spiral upwards. Over 5000 US servicemen had been killed and 37,738 wounded in 1966. More worrying, however, was the enormous number of civilian deaths in this war without frontiers.

OCTOBER

1 US planes attack the city of Phuly, 35 miles south of Hanoi. It is later reported that all the homes and buildings have been destroyed.
2-24 Troops of the 1st Air Cav mount Operation Irving, a major search and destroy mission aimed at clearing the NVA 610th Division out of the Phu Cat mountain area. 680 enemy casualties are reported.
3 The Soviet Union claims that an undisclosed amount of military and economic assistance will be given to North Vietnam.
4 B-52 bombers attack supply and staging areas in the DMZ.
13 US aircraft fly a record 173 multi-plane missions over North Vietnam.
15 US troops move into Tay Ninh province near the Cambodian border and sweep the area in search of Viet Cong as part of Operation Attleboro.
17 Units of the 196th Infantry Division arrive in Vietnam to join Operation Attleboro in III Corps.
18 Newly arrived 4th Infantry Division, elements of the 25th Infantry Division and 1st Air Cav launch Operation Paul Revere IV near the Cambodian border of Pleiku province.
24-25 Johnson meets with allied leaders in Manila. They sign an agreement pledging to withdraw troops from Vietnam within six months if 'North Vietnam withdraws its forces to the North and ceases infiltration of South Vietnam'.
25 Units of the 1st Air Cav launch Operation Thayer II in Binh Dinh province. US anti-shipping operations off the North Vietnamese coast intensify in the Dong Hoi area. After a gunnery duel between US destroyers and shore batteries, America begins a four-week series of attacks that results in the sinking of more than 230 communist vessels.
27 China attacks the proposals of the Manila conference, calling the troop withdrawal 'out and out blackmail and shameless humbug'.
31 US Navy boats intercept and sink 35 junks and sampans crossing the Mekong Delta.

NOVEMBER

1 The Viet Cong stage two separate guerrilla attacks in Saigon to coincide with celebrations for South Vietnam's National Day.
2 Former vice-president Richard Nixon criticizes the Manila Conference for not taking a hard enough line. In particular, he takes issue with the pledge to withdraw US forces from South Vietnam if North Vietnam withdraws its own troops.

US forces move in to continue Operation Paul Revere.

1966

3 The US Department of Defense plans intensified bombing of the North as reports emerge that attacks on oil facilities have done little to slow down the passage of arms and supplies into the South.

4 Reacting to Nixon's criticism, President Johnson claims that Nixon confuses rather than clarifies issues.

5 Three days before the US Congressional elections, Secretary of Defense McNamara says that 'no sharp increases' are planned in the number of air strikes over Vietnam. He also reveals that America will increase its troop presence in 1967, although the number of men drafted will be less than current levels.

5-6 After suffering heavy losses, the 196th Infantry Division are withdrawn from action in III Corps.

7 McNamara faces a storm of student protest when he visits Harvard University.

12 A report in the *New York Times* claims that because of corruption and black marketeering in Saigon, 40 per cent of US aid to Vietnam fails to reach its destination.

13 138 prominent Americans sign a document urging 'men of stature in the intellectual, religious and public service communities' to withdraw their support for critics of America's policy in Vietnam.

14 McNamara issues a report claiming that increasing the number of US troops in Vietnam has failed to bring about a significant rise in enemy casualties.

Saigon bombing: A wounded Vietnamese crawls to safety.

18 The American National Conference of Catholic Bishops confirms its support for US actions in Vietnam. Two US destroyers shell a North Vietnamese radar site two miles north of the Demilitarised Zone.

23 US destroyers bombard a flotilla of communist supply barges off the south coast of North Vietnam.

30 China claims that US bombers attacked a fleet of Chinese fishing boats in international waters off the Gulf of Tonkin, killing 14 sailors and sinking five boats

DECEMBER

US 9th Infantry Division is deployed to Vietnam from Fort Lewis, Washington, for operations in III Corps. US Air Force Tactical Fighter Wing deployed for combat operations in II Corps.

The USS *Pickering* attacks communist shore targets.

1 US 25th Infantry Division launches Operation Ala Moana in an effort to keep the Viet Cong away from the rice-producing areas adjacent to the Ho Bo and Boi Loi Woods.

2 US Navy jets strike five miles outside Hanoi in the closest raid to the city since 29 June. Further north, two major North Vietnamese fuel depots are bombed. A record eight US planes are lost in one day.

4 A Viet Cong guerrilla unit penetrates the 13-mile defence perimeter around the Tan Son Nhut airport. They succeed in damaging one aircraft before being driven off.

5 The US destroyer *Ingersoll* is damaged during a battle with a North Vietnamese coastal battery.

7 Tran Van Van, a leading member of the South Vietnamese Constituent Assembly, is killed by Viet Cong terrorists in Saigon.

8-9 North Vietnam rejects a proposal by President Johnson for a joint discussion of fair treatment and possible exchange of prisoners of war.

10 Governor-elect Ronald Reagan declares that he favours 'an all-out total effort' in Vietnam.

13-14 Drawing ever closer to Hanoi, US bombers attack a truck depot two miles south of the city. One French journalist reports that the village of Caudat, outside Hanoi, has been 'completely destroyed by bombs and fire'. The raid brings international condemnation.

14-16 General Westmoreland denies that US bombers have attacked non-military targets in Hanoi.

18-20 US B-52s, operating from Guam, bomb North Vietnamese supply bases just south of the DMZ, where Intelligence believes the NVA 324B division is preparing for a fresh offensive.

20 China alleges that the Soviet Union, 'in collusion with the United States', is 'resorting to the dirty tricks with the aim of compelling the Vietnamese people to lay down their arms and give up the struggle!'

25 The *New York Times* releases a major report describing the damage done to several North Vietnamese cities by intensified US bombing.

26 The US Defense Department concedes that North Vietnamese civilians may have been bombed accidentally by missions against military targets.

27-31 US planes drop hundreds of tons of bombs and napalm in the Mekong Delta. It is followed by an attack by 6000 South Vietnamese troops on a major Viet Cong stronghold in the U Minh forest. The operation ends with 104 Viet Cong reported killed and 18 captured.

WAR '67

Following the New Year's truce at 0700 on 2 January 1967, America was ready to shoulder an ever-greater burden of the Vietnam war. The arrival of the 9th Infantry Division on 1 January brought US troop strength to a massive 380,000 men. More significantly, the Combined Campaign Plan drawn up by US and South Vietnamese commanders meant that from now on US forces would take on the principal role in *all* offensive campaigns against the communists, leaving ARVN troops free to lead the bulk of the pacification programme.

This development – merely a confirmation of the way things had been going – had come about because US commanders were determined to seize the initiative and take the ground war into a new phase. For too long US commanders had suffered from the threat of secure communist strongholds in the heart of South Vietnam, centring on the infamous Iron Triangle. While authorisation was given for artillery fire and defoliation missions in the DMZ in the northern provinces, Operations Cedar Falls and Junction City were large scale, multi-divisional offensives designed to challenge the enemy in its lair near Saigon. Destroying entire villages and forests in their wake, these operations revealed that America was now impatient to bring the war to a swift conclusion.

In many ways, however, these massive search and destroy missions were playing directly to Viet Cong strengths. Fighting a war of attrition, the communists could withdraw in the face of a full-scale attack, only to regain the area once American forces had left. And inspite of impressive body counts, the VC tactic of wearing out America's will to fight on seemed already to be paying dividends as opposition to the war grew in the USA.

JANUARY

1 5000 men of the 9th Infantry Division arrive in Vung Tau, bringing the total of US troops in Vietnam to 380,000. Operation Sam Houston – a renewal of frontier observation operations by the 4th and 25th Infantry Divisions – begins in II Corps (Pleiku and Kontum provinces).
2 Seven MiG-21s are destroyed by US F-4 Phantom jets in the largest air battle of the war.

US forces launch the biggest search and destroy campaigns so far.

3 Remarks made by North Vietnamese Premier Dong lead to international speculation that the North might be softening their position on negotiating an end to the war. However, seven days later, Ho Chi Minh says that Hanoi's previously announced four-point plan for peace 'can be reduced to one: The United States should quit Vietnam'.
4-5 A British plan for an international peace conference is rejected by the communists.
5 1st and 25th Divisional troops are moved into position on the flanks of the Iron Triangle under the cover of search and destroy missions Fitchburg and Niagara Falls.
6 Operation Deckhouse V begins. Special Landing Force (SLF) Marines and ARVN troops operate in the Mekong Delta against an enemy stronghold, the Thanphu Secret Zone until 16 January but with little success.
8 Units of the 1st Aviation Battalion along with the 1st and 25th Infantry Divisions begin Operation Cedar Falls in the Iron Triangle.
9 The 11th Armored Cavalry begins a sweep through the Iron Triangle as the main initiative of Cedar Falls gets underway.
10 To the anger of the US, UN Secretary-General U Thant publicly scorns the idea that South Vietnam is vital to Western security. In his State of the Union address, Johnson announces that although America faces 'more cost, more loss and more agony' in Southeast Asia, 'We will stand firm in Vietnam'.

13 After a controversy over civilian deaths from American air raids, the US temporarily halts the bombing of the Yenvien marshalling yards, Hanoi.
18 On a 'goodwill' tour of New Zealand, South Vietnamese Premier Ky is called 'a murderer' and 'a miserable little butcher' by the Labour leader of the opposition, Arthur Calwell.
23 Senator William Fulbright attacks US policy in Vietnam in an influential book entitled 'The Arrogance of Power' in which he advocates face to face talks between Saigon and the Viet Cong.
25 Cedar Falls ends with an estimated 750 enemy casualties. Large numbers of invaluable documents are captured.

1967

Air war: US bombers attack targets close to Hanoi.

27 America reiterates its 14-point plan for peace. Operation Desoto is launched by Marines of I Corps in Duc Pho. By the time it ends in April, some 43 square kilometres of the area will be firmly under military control.

FEBRUARY

1 Operation Prairie II begins, a search and destroy mission carried out by 3d Marine Division south of the DMZ. It is to end on 18 March with 694 reported NVA losses.
2 Johnson dismisses recent peace 'feelers' from Hanoi with the comment, 'As of this moment, I cannot report that there are any serious indications that the other side is ready to stop the war'. Operation Gadsden begins in War Zone C to cover the build up for Operation Junction City.

Johnson faces the press.

A member of the 25th Infantry Division at ease.

5 Student leaders meet in Washington and call for an end to conscription. ARVN forces begin the use of defoliant agents in the DMZ.
8-10 In the US a national 'Fast for Peace' is held by religious groups to atone for the war.
8-12 A truce is observed over Tet, the lunar New Year.
9 US Secretary of State Dean Rusk states that Hanoi must reciprocate by scaling down its military activities should the US bombing campaign be halted. The demand is rejected by the North.
11 lst Air Cavalry Division begins Operation Pershing in Binh Dinh province.
14 Another diversionary offensive, Operation Tuscon, allows the 1st Division to move into position for Operation Junction City.
22 The US escalates the war by permitting the use of artillery against North Vietnamese territory and (on the 26th) dropping mines into Northern rivers. Four ARVN battalions and 22 US battalions begin Operation Junction City in Tay Ninh and bordering provinces. At the University of Wisconsin hundreds of demonstrators protest against the presence of recruiters from the Dow Chemical Company, which makes napalm for use in Vietnam, on campus.
25 Elements of the US 1st Infantry Division uncover and destroy three Viet Cong camps and an arms factory in the Boiloi forest. Units of the 3rd US Marine Division clash with NVA troops at the Khe Sanh base.
28 First contact with a major Viet Cong unit of Operation Junction City is made when a company of the 16th Infantry wins a firefight near Route 4.

MARCH

8 US Congress passes a bill supporting the use of armed force in Vietnam and authorising the expenditure of $4.5 billion.
10-12 US bombers raid a steelworks 40 miles from Hanoi in a further expansion of the air war.
18 South Vietnam's constituent assembly agrees on a new democratic constitution that will lead to a civilian government. Elections are planned for the autumn. Thailand agrees to provide base facilities for B-52 bombers. In Saigon US officials agree to give South Vietnam a further $150 million in aid, taking the total aid granted in 1967 to $700 million.
20-21 At a conference with Johnson in Guam, Ky is critical of US restraint, asking 'How long can Hanoi enjoy the advantage of restricted bombing of military targets?'

Cutting the supply routes

21 640 Viet Cong are reported dead in a battle in Operation Junction City. lt is revealed that Johnson exchanged diplomatic notes with Ho Chi Minh in February, but the North Vietnamese leader rejected an offer of direct negotiations with the US.
27 US Air Force Captain Dale E. Noyd sues in court to be reclassified as a conscientous objector to the Vietnam conflict. His petition is to be turned down in June.
28 A group of US Quakers sail a yacht into Haiphong harbour loaded with $10,000 dollars of medical aid for the North.

WAR '67

The greatest single offensive of the war so far, Operation Junction City, ended on 14 May 1967. It had been a heavy blow against the communist forces. The US claimed over 2700 VC killed; 5000 bunkers and military installations destroyed; 500,000 pages of documents seized, and US troops penetrating previously unassailable areas. However, alarming flaws in the US strategy were becoming apparent. The allies were too weak to hold the cleared areas, and communist troops soon returned to War Zone C. Worse, the communists, not the Americans, held the initiative – despite being inferior in firepower by a ratio of about five to one. All too often, US forces merely reacted to communist moves.

Back in the US, the anti-war debate became increasingly bitter. Television was bringing the horrors of the war directly into the living rooms of American citizens, leading many to question US policy. Yet many still gave their whole-hearted support to the war: 70,000 marched in a pro-war demonstration in New York in May. President Johnson was now under siege from two sides: those demanding less military involvement, and those demanding more.

Hanoi, however, also had problems. The heavy losses in the South were forcing the dispatch of 10,000 men a month just to keep the numbers up. The communists were being drawn into debilitating fighting in previously safe sanctuaries such as the Iron Triangle, and the continuing US air raids were striking at important centres: central Hanoi, Haiphong, and MiG bases. So although the North Vietnamese will to fight was unimpaired, the politburo was suffering in the war of attrition. While the Americans were still there fighting, communist victory was not in sight.

APRIL

1 United Nations Secretary-General U Thant suggests that the US should begin a 'standstill truce' in Vietnam, only firing back if fired upon. The last major battle of the second phase of Operation Junction City is fought, between 1st Battalion, 26th Infantry, US 1st Division, and Viet Cong troops at Ap Gu, 70 miles from Saigon. The US force is supported by nearly 180 fighter-bombers. The US claim that 591 Viet Cong are killed, for only 10 Americans killed and 64 wounded.
2 Viet Cong sources claim that 864 US troops became casualties in the Ap Gu battle on 1 April, in addition

Thieu says invade the North.

to 22 aircraft. Local village elections are held in South Vietnam under the new constitution. The election is marred by Viet Cong terrorist attacks.
6 2500 North Vietnamese and Viet Cong troops attack the northern city of Quang Tri. The defending ARVN Division loses over 200 men. 250 Viet Cong POWs are freed from the provincial jail, and centres of administration and an ARVN base are attacked. For the first time, an NVA force attacks across the Benhai River bridge, which spans the border between the two Vietnams. As a result, Nguyen Van Thieu, the South's head of state, threatens to bomb Hanoi or even invade the North as 'a natural act of self-defence'.
7 Operation Desoto ends.
10 First B-52s arrive in Thailand. Previously they had operated from Guam.
11 US forces reveal that Moscow and

Peking have reached an agreement on sending supplies to North Vietnam. However, on 30 April the Chinese Communist Party newspaper, describes the Soviet leaders as 'a pack of rank traitors', 'shameless scabs' and 'No. 1 accomplices to the US gangsters'.
12 28 US servicemen become casualties in a mortar attack on Chu Lai airbase.
13 Viet Cong troops sabotage two bridges between Quang Tri and Da Nang, disrupting US supply routes to the DMZ.
14-17 US units, including 3000 men of 2d Brigade, 1st Air Cavalry Division, are dispatched to the north of South Vietnam to reinforce units under pressure from the NVA. These forces later form part of Task Force Oregon.
14 Former Vice-President Nixon, on a visit to Saigon, says that 'this apparent division at home' is 'prolonging the war'.

Protest grows at home.
15 Saigon announces the construction of a fortified barrier six miles long, two miles to the south of the DMZ. It is intended to combat infiltration from the North. Huge anti-war marches are held in New York and San Francisco. By a conservative estimate, 195,000 people take part. Phase II of Operation Junction City is halted.
18-20 At the annual meeting of SEATO ministers, Hanoi is attacked 'for its aggression by means of armed attack'.
19 US suggests widening the DMZ by 20 miles with all forces being withdrawn behind it. Two days later Hanoi rejects this idea. Operation

1967

Prairie III in the Khe Sanh area ends. US sources claim 252 communist dead and 128 weapons captured. The operation has cost the Marines 56 dead and 530 wounded. Operation Prairie IV is commenced the following day.

20 Haiphong, North Vietnam's principal port, is bombed for the first time.

21 Operation Union I begins, launched by US Marines against the 2d NVA Division in the Que Son Basin in the north of South Vietnam. US Secretary of State Dean Rusk expresses 'regret' that civilian casualties might occur as a result of raids on 'essential military targets'. Operation Oh Jac Kyo I, which began on 7 March comes to an end. This is the largest operation the South Koreans have yet mounted. The area of operations is the central coast of II Corps and there are 831 known enemy casualties.

22 Task Force Oregon, a 15,000 strong US army formation, is established in the northernmost provinces (I Corps) under the command of General William B. Rosson, to free Marines for offensive actions.

24 General William Westmoreland causes a storm of criticism by suggesting that anti-war activity in the US 'gives him (the enemy) hope that he can win politically that which he cannot accomplish militarily'. Westmoreland goes on to state that his troops in Vietnam 'are dismayed, and so am I by recent unpatriotic acts at home'.

24-5 During Operation Prairie IV a major battle erupts for control of three hills overlooking the US base at Khe Sanh, south of the DMZ. Half of the combat strength of two battalions of 3d Marines become casualties, and the defeated NVA lose 764 dead.

25 US planes mistakenly attack a British freighter, the *Dartford*, in Haiphong.

28 Westmoreland addresses Congress and declares that 'Backed at home by resolve, confidence, patience, determination and continued support, we will prevail in Vietnam over the communist aggressor'. Hill 861 at Khe Sanh is taken by the 3d Marine Regiment.

29 Former President Dwight D. Eisenhower states 'America doesn't have to apologize for her part in the war. She can be proud of it'.

MAY

1 US Secretary of State Dean Rusk alleges that North Vietnam has turned down at least 28 proposals for peace talks. Henry Cabot Lodge is replaced as US ambassador to Saigon by Ellsworth Bunker.

2 A mock war crimes tribunal in Stockholm, organized by the 94-year-old British philosopher, Bertrand Russell, condemns the USA for atrocities committed in Vietnam.

4 In response to a suggestion by a member of the House Foreign Affairs Committee that the US threaten Hanoi with nuclear weapons, Rusk states that the US is 'not contemplating any nuclear ultimatum' to force North Vietnam into negotiations. NVA troops attack a US Special Forces base at Lang Vei, near Khe Sanh, and cause over 100 casualties for only 5 NVA dead. The Soviet Union reveals details of an agreement that will provide

COSVN eludes Junction City.

'hundreds of millions of roubles' of food, weapons and economic aid in 1968.

8 The Marine base at Con Thien, an important observation point south of the DMZ, is attacked by the NVA. As a result Washington authorizes US troops to fight in the southern portion of the DMZ.

10 More than 80 colleges across the US participate in a 'teach-in' organized by anti-war groups.

11 In a pessimistic address in New York, U Thant suggests that 'direct confrontation' between the US and China is likely, and that 'we are

witnessing today the initial phase of World War III'. Operation Crockett (aggressive patrolling around Khe Sanh) begins.

13 70,000 people march in New York in support of US policy in Southeast Asia, in a demonstration organized by a captain in the city's fire department.

14 Operation Junction City is concluded; communist casualties are claimed as 2728 dead and 34 prisoners.

17 Operation Union I in Quong Tin Province ends with the communists suffering 865 casualties.

18 US and ARVN troops move into the DMZ for the first time, in a series of operations that last until 26 May. US sources claim 789 enemy killed and NVA command structures disrupted. But allied losses are also heavy: 164 killed and over 1000 wounded.

19 Central Hanoi is bombed for the first time by US naval aircraft. The target is the largest electrical power plant in North Vietnam.

22 President Johnson publicly urges Hanoi to join him in leading 'our people out of this bloody impasse' by accepting a compromise peace.

26 Operation Union II begins.

31 Operation Prarie IV in the DMZ ends. The 3d Marine Division has suffered 1400 casualties and killed 505 enemy.

The House Un-American Activities Committee claims that the massive anti-war demonstrations of 15 April were communist inspired. This report is denounced by Reverend Bevel, a prominent clergyman and anti-war activist.

JUNE

1 Marines begin Operation Cimarron near the DMZ. The operation lasts until 12 July but with little concrete result.

2 Marine Operation Union II is halted, 701 communists and 110 Americans were killed.

23 Johnson meets with Alexsei Kosygin, the Soviet Premier, in New Jersey.

30 It is decided by the South Vietnamese Armed Forces council that Nguyen Van Thieu will run for the Presidency in September with Nguyen Cao Ky as his running mate. In May, Ky had announced that he was running for President.

WAR '67

July to September 1967 were among the most important months of the war. Vietnam was devouring lives, money and equipment at an awe-inspiring rate, but to the American military it appeared that the war was being won. In the Mekong Delta the 9th Infantry Division riverine patrols were opening up an area previously dominated by the Viet Cong. The Air Cavalry were exerting US influence in their sector, while around the DMZ the Marines seemed to be achieving success in a conventional struggle with the NVA. And in August President Johnson lifted many of the restrictions placed on the bombing of North Vietnam.

In September, a significant decision was made which epitomised the US response to the problems of the war: the use of high technology. The 'McNamara Line' was to be built along the DMZ. Linked to this were a series of Fire Support Bases. But the system possessed major flaws which even US technology could not cure.

Measured in terms of bombs dropped and villages destroyed in actions such as Operation Malheur, the US pacification effort – its attempt to control the countryside – looked impressive. However, such measures failed to come to terms with the need to satisfy the peasantry, particularly over land ownership. Therefore, in spite of the August election, the South Vietnamese regime remained unpopular.

In the summer, Giap published a book entitled 'Big Victory, Great Task' in which he analysed the lessons learned in the fighting against the Americans. Convinced that he had found a winning strategy, he succeeded in persuading his colleagues to order a major offensive in early 1968. With hindsight, it is possible to recognise this decision of July 1967 as the turning point of the war.

JULY

2 3d Marine Division begins Operation Buffalo in DMZ to combat NVA efforts to seize the key position of Con Thien. The operation ends on 14 July with 701 NVA dead.

7-11 Secretary of Defence McNamara visits South Vietnam amid demands by Westmoreland for 200,000 reinforcements. President Johnson agrees to send another 45,000 troops. Ellsworth Bunker, US ambassador to Saigon, expresses confidence in the long-term success of the 'Pacification' programme.

10 141st NVA Regiment attacks the ARVN base at An Loc (60 miles from Saigon) but is repelled. 173d Airborne Brigade takes heavy casualties in action at Dak To.

12 China alleges that US jets fired missiles at a Chinese border post.

16 3d Marine Division launch Operation Kingfisher, which continues into October.

19 The South Vietnamese election campaign begins amid opposition claims of harassment by government forces.

23 An NVA incursion force from Cambodia suffers heavy losses in a fire fight with 4th Division at Ducco.

29 134 men are killed by a fire on board the aircraft carrier USS *Forestall*.

AUGUST

2 Operation Malheur, conducted by Task Force Oregon, ends, having distributed 23 million leaflets since 11 May. 869 communists have been killed, 8,885 civilians evacuated and their villages burned in an attempt to deny the Viet Cong shelter.

8 President Johnson approves the extension of Operation Rolling Thunder to include previously forbidden targets in North Vietnam.

9 Operation Cochise begins in Que Son valley but the 1st Marine Division makes little headway.

Elements of 1st Air Cavalry (2nd Battalion 8th Cavalry) launch an air assault on a VC stronghold in the Songre Valley.

Meanwhile, other elements continue with Operation Byrd, a pacification mission in Binh Tzuan province. The bulk of the Air Cavalry is committed to Operation Pershing against the NVA 610th Division in Binh Dinh Province.

11 US planes bomb road and rail links in the Hanoi-Haiphong area. For the first time US aircraft are authorised to bomb within 25 miles of China, and strike within 10 miles of the border. One Democrat compares the raids with a hypothetical Chinese strike in Mexico 'within 10 miles of the Rio Grande' and asks how America would react to that.

13 B-52s hit NVA targets north of the DMZ.

16-23 Johnson's broad interpretation of the 'Gulf of Tonkin' resolution is attacked at meetings of the Senate Foreign Relations Committee by the

Riverine forces open up the Mekong Delta

Right: A US Special Forces advisor in the Central Highlands.

1967

chairman William Fulbright, who feels that Johnson has no mandate to conduct the war on the present scale.
18 A major contribution to the Vietnam debate is made by Governor Ronald Reagan of California. He demands a US withdrawal from Vietnam, saying 'my idea of honourable disengagement is that you win the war. I can't technically say how you'd do it, but some experts have said too many qualified targets have been put off limits to bombing.'
22 The Chief of Staff of the US Air Force, General John P. McConnell states before a Senate Committee that adopting a graduated bombing policy in 1965, rather than launching a massive blow to destroy 94 targets in 16 days, was mistaken. Three days later McNamara admits that the bombing of the North has not materially affected Hanoi's 'war-making capability'.
27 Reports circulate that North Vietnamese jets are operating from China. At least 355 people are killed in a Viet Cong offensive throughout South Vietnam.
28 US officials admit to 'a serious increase in frequency of ineffectiveness' of the M-16 rifle.
29 Writing in a Communist newspaper, General Giap says Johnson is engaging 'backwards logic' in thinking that bombing the North would ease the pressure on the South. This follows claims by Admiral Grant Sharp that the US bombing was causing Hanoi 'mounting logistic, management and morale problems'.
31 A Senate Sub-committee calls for massive bombing of Haiphong port.

SEPTEMBER

1 North Vietnam Premier Phan Van Dong declares that 'US imperialism is aggressive and warlike by nature.

Premier Phan denounces the US

628

Senator Fulbright criticizes Johnson

All it wants is war'. He promises Hanoi will 'continue to fight'.
2 The military candidate for the South Vietnamese Presidency, Nguyen Van Thieu boasts about the freedom enjoyed by the press and the free speech granted to the opposition candidates during the campaign. The same day, the closure of two opposition newspapers is announced.

The NVA interrupt Operation Kingfisher with an offensive at Con Thien. Dong Ha base is also attacked,forcing the Marines to move a logistics centre back to Quang Tri. Con Thien is heavily shelled but the NVA assault is beaten off with heavy casualties.
4 Amid accusations of ballot rigging, the Thieu/Ky Presidential ticket is declared elected with 35 per cent of the vote. 1st Marine Division commence Operation Swift in Quang Nam and Quang Tin provinces. The offensive ends 12 days later claiming with 517 enemy troops killed.
5 The elite 2nd South Korean Marine Brigade begins Operation Dragon Fire in Quang Ngai Province.
7 Eleven Democratic senators propose that the war be discussed by United Nations. US ambassador to the UN Goldberg admits that he has discussed a new peace plan which involved some concessions by the US.

The US Defence Secretary, Robert McNamara, reveals plans for a barrier equipped with 'state of the art' electronic listening devices, to stop communist infiltration through the eastern end of the DMZ.
8 The 'McNamara Line', as it is called, is criticized by senior US military personnel including Westmoreland, who dislike the idea of static defence.
10 Cam Pha, a North Vietnamese port, is attacked by US planes: the first time the dock area of a Northern port has been subjected to air attack. Raids on the Hanoi and Haiphong

areas are carried out for the rest of the month.
13-16 One of the bloodiest of the Coronado riverine operations, Coronado V, is conducted by US 9th Infantry Division in the Mekong Delta. 213 Viet Cong are killed: US and ARVN casualties total 16 dead and 146 wounded.
14 Press reports indicate that Hanoi has expressed a willingness to engage in negotiations in three weeks' time if the US calls off its air raids on the North.
15 9th Infantry Riverine Force is ambushed during Coronado V. Following heavy airstrikes the Viet Cong are allowed to withdraw rather than risk a US defeat.
17 President Johnson is accused of 'effectively and brutally cancelling' a private peace initiative begun by a US journalist Harry Ashmore. *Centre* magazine alleges Johnson sent a negative letter to Ho Chi Minh after Ashmore had negotiated with Ho. Commenting on the story, Senator Fulbright says that it showed that US/North Vietnam negotiations could have begun had the US been more flexible.
19 173d Airborne Brigade and 1st Air Cavalry begin Operation Bolling, which lasts 501 days in Phu Yen province and yields 715 enemy dead.
21 3d Marine Division launch a major attack as part of Operation Kingfisher at Con Thien.
22 Andrei Gromyko, the Soviet Foreign Minister, denounces ambassador Goldberg's efforts to secure peace through the UN and claims that US 'aggression' in Southeast Asia threatens to escalate the war and endanger world peace.
27 Following the original Shenandoah operation, Shenandoah II is conducted for 54 days by 1st Infantry Division (Big Red One) in Binh Duong province, claiming 956 known enemy casualties. An advertisement headed 'A Call To Resist Illegitimate Authority', signed by over 300 influential people, appears in the press asking for funds to help a 'draft dodger' organisation.
29 In a speech loaded with veiled criticism of US opponents of the war, Johnson declares that 'protest will not produce surrender' because the US would 'provide all that our brave men require to do the job that must be done: and that job's going to be done'

WAR '67

With hindsight, it is possible to see that the last bloody months of 1967 were dominated by preparations for the Tet Offensive – the assault by the communist forces that was to shatter US complacency and bring about a turning point in the war. At the time, however, the view from Saigon and Washington was rather more rosy. Operation Rolling Thunder had forced – so it seemed – the North Vietnamese into a major concession, granted on 29 December: now they *would*, not just *might*, talk peace if the bombing of the North was halted. The US was cautiously optimistic, preparing the ground for talks by agreeing to the inclusion of the NLF in negotiations, to the evident disgust of Saigon.

The inauguration of Thieu and Ky as President and Vice President of the South Vietnamese Republic on 31 October offered hope that the Saigon regime had been legitimized.

In reality, the omens were clear enough for those who could read them. In an article in a Soviet paper on 21 October, General Giap had spoken of the imminent end of the guerrilla phase of the war and the beginning of operations 'employing large forces, forces that are growing daily'. Captured documents indicated the border battles were preliminaries to a major offensive.

On 8 December, William Fulbright denounced the conflict as an 'immoral and unnecessary war' and added that 'far from demonstrating America's willingness and ability to save beleaguered governments from communist insurgencies, all that we are demonstrating in Vietnam is America's willingness to use its B-52s, its napalm and all other ingenious weapons of "counterinsurgency" to turn a small country into a charnel house.'

OCTOBER

3 Operation Wallowa is begun by elements of 1st Air Cavalry Division in South Vietnam's northernmost provinces. The Cavalry task force is sent in to relieve pressure on the Marines, who are fighting a heavy series of engagements along the DMZ. US planes raiding North Vietnamese supply routes attack bridges only 10 miles from the Chinese frontier.

4 The communist shelling of Con Thien ends after heavy US airstrikes (part of Operation Neutralize – aerial bombing and artillery shelling of NVA gun positions near the DMZ) on NVA artillery positions.

5 Sources in Hanoi accuse the US of dropping anti-personnel bombs on a school in North Vietnam.

7 Speaking in Washington, Johnson declares that he is not going to gain cheap popularity 'by renouncing the struggle in Vietnam or escalating it to the red line of danger'.

10 US troops capture a Viet Cong document which sets out the attitude to coalition with the National Liberation Front (NLF – the political arm of the Viet Cong). The document envisages ultimate control being exercised by the NLF, despite the inclusion of non-communist members. The gist of the document is released on 15 December.

11 Operation Medina/Bastion Hill/ Lam Son 138 begins with 3d Marine Division in conjunction with ARVN troops and elements of the Marine Special Landing Force (SLF).

12 Operation Francis Marion, the 4th Infantry Division operation in Pleiku Province, Central Highlands, is combined with Operation Greeley to form Operation MacArthur, which continues until January 1969. Secretary of State Dean Rusk makes a controversial speech in which critics claim he invokes the 'yellow peril' of Chinese power.

14 A major NVA push begins against Con Thien, but is beaten off by 2d Battalion of 4th Marine Regiment.

21 686 people, including novelist Norman Mailer, are arrested in a massive anti-war demonstration as up to 150,000 march in Washington. In London, 3000 demonstrators attempt to storm the US embassy as anti-war and anti-US protests erupt across the world.

23-30 US aircraft launch heavy raids on the Haiphong-Hanoi region. Targets include some attacked for the first time, and range from bridges and airfields to the largest electrical plant in the North (bombed 26 August). US losses total 13 aircraft. Lewis B. Hershey, the director of the US conscription programme, is heavily criticized after he tells local boards to conscript anti-draft activists as early as possible.

29-4 November. Fierce fighting flares up around Loc Ninh, a rubber-plantation town north of Saigon and the site of a Special Forces camp. NVA and Viet Cong troops throw in mass assaults, but are repulsed by ARVN and 1st Infantry Division reinforcements. Allied losses are about 50; communist losses 'over 1000'.

31 The North Vietnamese government appeals to the international community to put pressure on Washington to halt the airstrikes on the North. President Thieu and Vice President Ky are sworn in in Saigon. A reception in the Independence Palace is marred by the explosion of three mortar shells on the lawn.

The Brown Water Navy steams into action.

1967

NOVEMBER

1 Operation Kentucky is begun by 3d Marine Division around Con Thien. This is a continuation of Kingfisher, halted on 31 October. Simultaneously, Operation Scotland begins around Khe Sanh (Quang Tri Province). This ends on 31 March 1968, with a bodycount of 1061.

2 A concession is made by the US in agreeing to allow NLF participation in debates on Vietnam at the UN in separate peace talks.

3-22 The heaviest fighting in the Central Highlands since the Ia Drang Valley battles of 1966 take place around Dak To. 1400 NVA are killed along with nearly 300 Americans.

6 A document is taken from the corpse of an NVA soldier at Dak To which reveals that the action there is a feint to lure US troops to the north of South Vietnam.

8 Westmoreland publicly declares that the aim of the NVA attack at Dak To is to steal the thunder of the recent inauguration of Thieu as South Vietnamese president.

11 President Johnson declares that 'our statesmen will press the search for peace to the corners of the earth', and suggests that peace negotiations should be held aboard a neutral ship at sea. Hanoi rejects these latest American overtures four days later. Operation Wheeler, conducted by the Americal Infantry Division (formerly Task Force Oregon), combines with Operation Wallowa. The Wheeler/Wallowa operations continue for exactly 12 months. By the end of December 1967, there are claims of 8188 enemy dead.

11 Viet Cong release three US POWs, including two blacks, as a response to the US anti-war demonstrations.

13 Operation Foster/Badger Hunt is conducted by 7th Marine Regiment and Marine Special Landing Force in Dai Loc and An Hoa areas. At its end on 30 November, 125 enemy have been killed and 11,500 refugees evacuated from communist-controlled regions.

13-16 President Johnson is briefed on the situation in Vietnam by Westmoreland, Ambassador Bunker, and the head of the CORDS programme, Robert W. Komer. The optimistic picture that they paint leads Johnson to state on television on 17 November that, while much

remains to be done, 'We are inflicting greater losses than we're taking...We are making progress.'

14 The highest ranking US officer yet to die in action is killed when his helicopter is shot down. Major-General Bruno Hochmuth was commander of the 3d Marine Division.

19-20 After reports appear in the US press that Cambodia is providing a haven for Vietnamese communist troops, relations deteriorate between Washington and Phnom Penh. On 24 November Prince Sihanouk, who strongly denies the claims, announces that US journalists are not welcome in Cambodia.

21 Westmoreland boldly declares to pressmen in the US that 'I am absolutely certain that whereas in 1965 the enemy was winning, today he is certainly losing.'

29 Robert McNamara announces his resignation as Secretary of Defence to become President of the World Bank.

30 A liberal Democratic senator, Eugene J. McCarthy, announces that he will run for president on a platform of the moral indefensibility of US actions in Vietnam.

US troops are lured to the north in preparation for Tet.

DECEMBER

1 A spate of reports begins to appear alleging contacts between NLF and US representatives. Nguyen Van Huan, an NLF official, is arrested apparently while on his way to meet the US Ambassador in Saigon.

4 Units of 9th Infantry Division and ARVN troops on river patrol in the Mekong Delta clash with 502d Viet Cong battalion and kill 235 VC. Saigon officials make clear their hostile attitude to NLF representation at UN talks.

7 Vice President Humphrey expresses the belief that not all of the NLF are communist and that the

Rolling Thunder – if bombing stopped, the North would talk.

non-communist elements might split off and negotiate with the Saigon government.

14 NLF's programme for reform is submitted to UN delegates. It includes a coalition government, free elections and land reform. It receives a hostile reception from US officials.

17 199th Infantry Brigade begins Operation Uniontown in Binh Hoa Province, and the South Korean Capital Division commences Maeng Ho 9 – a sweep through Binh Dinh Province which results in 749 known communist casualties.

19 Johnson praises Thieu's flexible and 'statesmanlike position' over the issue of negotiations with the NLF. The following day, Thieu makes it clear that he would be prepared to talk to individuals but not representatives of the NLF, which he does not recognize. Elements of Americal Division begin sweep in northern province of Quang Nagai (Operation Muscatine), which inflicts 1129 casualties in 175 days.

23 Johnson declares: 'From our course we shall not turn', and later that the communist enemy 'knows that he has met his master in the field'.

24 A Christmas truce begins which lasts until 30 December.

26 The Laotian government announces that a major push by the NVA has begun in southern Laos.

27 Cambodia announces that any US incursion would be resisted.

29 North Vietnamese Foreign Minister, Nguyen Du Trinh, publicly softens Hanoi's negotiating stance by declaring that talks with the US will begin after the bombing is ended.

WAR '68

As 1968 began it appeared that the US had the upper hand in Vietnam. But the Tet Offensive at the end of January was to shatter that illusion. The US public saw a supposedly beaten enemy waging war in the very heart of Saigon – even in the US embassy itself. The Viet Cong and NVA attacked in 36 of the 44 provincial capitals, 64 of the 242 district capitals and five of the six autonomous cities. TV pictures beamed into US homes told a story of US failure and communist success.

The overture to Tet was the siege of the firebase at Khe Sanh, near the DMZ. The defence of the base took on the proportions of the Alamo in the eyes of the US public. A major offensive – Operation Pegasus – was launched to relieve it. But it is arguable that by devoting so much attention to Khe Sanh the US played into the hands of the communists by diverting troops from areas earmarked by the enemy as the battlefields of Tet.

In military terms, though, Tet was a victory for the US/ARVN troops. The ARVN survived more or less intact, there was no popular, pro-Viet Cong uprising in the South, and the Viet Cong took such heavy casualties (perhaps 40,000) that it was almost wiped out as a fighting force.

Politically, however, Tet was a disaster for the US. Not only were the communists shown to be full of fight, but the destruction involved in crushing the offensive and the unsavoury methods of the Saigon regime shocked US audiences and called into question the morality of the war. The most prominent casualty of Tet was President Johnson. On 31 March he announced to the nation that he was not going to stand for re-election.

Coupled with the replacement of Westmoreland as MACV commander in June, it all seemed to confirm the total disarray of US policy in Vietnam.

JANUARY

30 December-2 January A New Year 'truce' is punctuated by frequent outbreaks of violence.
1 Ho Chi Minh announces that the coming year will bring military victories for the communist cause.
3-4 1st Air Cavalry are attacked by NVA units in the Que Son valley.
4 Secretary of State Dean Rusk reacts cautiously to hints of a softening of Hanoi's attitude towards peace talks.
5 US 11th Light Infantry Brigade arrives in Vietnam.
8 Viet Cong troops raid Khiem Cuong near Saigon.
12 US and Cambodia agree measures to exclude Cambodia from the war. Tension between the two states has been growing over alleged use of Cambodian territory as a refuge for communist troops.
13-15 US planes carry out heavy airstrikes against the Ho Chi Minh Trail.
15 In Saigon, Thieu makes a speech hostile to the idea of US-North Vietnamese negotiations.
21 US Marine base at Khe Sanh is attacked and besieged by NVA troops. Operation Lancaster II is commenced by 3d Marine Division.
30 Viet Cong launch a major offensive throughout South Vietnam on the first day of the Tet 'truce'. Hanoi announces that the offensive is to 'punish the US aggressors'.

A VC suicide squad attacks the US embassy in Saigon.

31 US embassy in Saigon is captured and held for six hours by 19 Viet Cong. All are killed when the embassy is retaken. Viet Cong troops also attack the Presidential Palace in Saigon. Eventually, 11,000 troops are committed to fight the 1000 Viet Cong in Saigon. The offensive is largely crushed by 10 February. The Citadel in Hue is seized by the Viet Cong and NVA, and 10 US Marines die reinforcing the ARVN.

FEBRUARY

1 A Viet Cong prisoner is summarily executed by Nguyen Ngoc Loan, Saigon's Chief of Police, in front of TV cameras. The resulting film footage badly damages Saigon's reputation in the eyes of the world. South Vietnam imposes martial law.
2 Johnson announces that the Tet Offensive is 'a complete failure'.
3 NVA troops gain control of Kon Tum in the Central Highlands. A senior US officer admits the US was taken by surprise by the offensive.
4 Washington decides to defend Khe Sanh rather than withdraw. The ARVN launch Tran Hung Dao, an operation in the Saigon area.
7 Lang Vei Special Forces camp is captured by the NVA.
8 Twenty-one Marines are killed in a day of heavy attacks at Khe Sanh. Heavy fighting occurs between the US 199th Light Brigade and Viet Cong at Saigon's Phu Tho racetrack.
10 A North Vietnamese newspaper describes Khe Sanh as America's 'Dien Bien Phu'.
11 11,000 additional ARVN troops are mobilised.
14 14 US planes launch a heavy raid on the Hanoi area.
16 After much public speculation, Johnson publicly denies that he is considering the use of nuclear weapons in Vietnam.
17 Units of 82d Airborne Division are sent to Vietnam.
18 In an apparent change of tactics, the Viet Cong shell South Vietnamese cities but launch few attacks.
21 US troops in Vietnam now total 495,000 men.
23 A heavy communist attack is launched at Khe Sanh to test the strength of the base's defences.
24 US sources admit that Tet has seriously damaged the Pacification

1968

programme in South Vietnam.

25 ARVN troops recapture the Imperial Palace in Hue. Three-quarters of the city had been destroyed. Westmoreland describes Tet as a 'military defeat' for the enemy.

MARCH

2 At Tan Son Nhut 48 men of US 25th Infantry Division are killed in ambush – one of the costliest ambushes of the war.

6 Fatalities for Tet are put at 50,000 communists, 11,000 ARVN, 2000 US and 7500 civilians.

11 Operation Quyet Thang begins in the Saigon region. 33 Allied battalions from seven formations are involved in the biggest operation yet. It continues for 28 days.

12 Peace candidate Senator Eugene McCarthy comes a close second to Johnson in the New Hampshire Democratic primary election.

13 The Saigon government announces plans to invade the North with a 'volunteer' force. Washington says no.

17 There are violent scenes outside the US embassy in London as 300 anti-war protesters are arrested and 50 people injured. Operation Duong Can Dan (People's Road) begins, conducted by 9th Infantry Division. On 21 May it is joined with an ARVN operation and inflicts over 1250 enemy casualties.

21 The *New York Times* publishes an optimistic report sent to Johnson by Westmoreland in January indicating that the President could have had little idea that an offensive

was imminent.

22 It is decided that Westmoreland will be replaced as US commander in Vietnam in June, and promoted to Army chief of staff.

25 Nearly 300 Viet Cong are killed during Operation Quyet Thang.

26 An NVA attack on a US firebase at Kon Tum in the Central Highlands is repulsed with heavy losses.

29 Three NVA POWs are freed by the US after talks between the two sides.

31 In a dramatic TV broadcast, Johnson announces he will not seek re-election. He also announces the limiting of air attacks on North Vietnam and challenges Hanoi to enter peace talks. Preliminary discussions begin immediately.

The second battle for Saigon is ended with bombs and napalm.

APRIL

1 Operation Pegasus is begun by 1st Air Cavalry to break the siege of Khe Sanh. US planes are forbidden to bomb north of the 20th Parallel, 225 miles north of the DMZ.

5 The siege of Khe Sanh is partially raised when 1st Air Cavalry reach the base. Operation Quyet Thang ends with 2600 communist casualties.

8 Operation Toan Thang (Complete Victory) – a major counter offensive – is launched around Saigon by Allies.

14 Khe Sanh is finally relieved.

27 US intelligence report reveals that 2000 extra supply vehicles have been identified on the Ho Chi Minh

Trail since the restriction of bombing. 200,000 students in New York City refuse to attend lectures as a protest against the war.

MAY

3 Paris is chosen as the site of peace talks between the US and North Vietnam.

5 A second battle for Saigon begins with a wave of Viet Cong ground attacks, accompanied by the shelling of 119 cities, towns and barracks. Fighting spreads to Saigon's Cholon district, Tan Son Nhut airbase and Phu Tho race track. Battle climaxes on 12 May with US jets dropping napalm and high explosives.

10 Paris peace talks open, but are almost immediately deadlocked.

17 Operations Nevada Eagle and Jeb Stuart III are launched by 101st Airborne and 1st Air Cavalry Divisions respectively, with a total of 5500 enemy casualties.

18 Operation Mameluke Thrust, conducted by 1st Marine Division in Quang Nam Province begins.

25 The third battle for Saigon begins, which lasts until 4 June. There is heavy fighting in Cholon suburb.

JUNE

11 Westmoreland returns to the US and is replaced in Vietnam by General Creighton W. Abrams.

28 A North Vietnamese official refers to the withdrawal of the US Marines from Khe Sanh as the 'gravest defeat' that the US had suffered so far.

General Creighton W. Abrams takes over from Westmoreland.

Right: Tunnels were a vital haven for the VC.

WAR '68

The second half of 1968 saw a shift of attention from the battlefield to political developments in Washington and the Paris talks.

It was an election year in America and Vietnam dominated the cut and thrust of the campaign trail. Johnson's withdrawal from the race led to Vice-President Hubert Humphrey receiving the Democratic nomination. But the Democrats were badly split and Humphrey was walking a tightrope – he could neither repudiate Johnson's policy nor easily defend it. The policy of his Republican rival, Richard Nixon, of promising on one hand an end to the war, whilst on the other refusing to reveal the exact nature of his plans for fear of upsetting any current diplomatic initiative, further dented the Democratic campaign.

After three US airmen were released by Hanoi, and the Americans released 14 North Vietnamese sailors later in the year, hopes were raised at the Paris talks that there would be more POW exchanges. The deadlocked talks were reinvigorated when the US agreed to stop bombing the North in return for Hanoi's agreement to respect the DMZ and stop shelling cities in the South. The talks were expanded to include Saigon and the NLF, a development which promised to give Humphrey's campaign a major boost. But only one day after the bombing ceased, Saigon refused to participate in the talks and thus wrecked the initiative. Nixon was duly elected.

The communists could look back on 1968 with satisfaction. They had taken heavy casualties, but in return they had unseated one US president, sown seeds of doubt in the minds of many Americans about the conduct of the war, helped cause deep divisions in US society and brought about a temporary end to the bombing of their cities.

634

JULY

1 Abrams replaces Westmoreland as MACV Commander.
1-16 A lull in the fighting, with the North initiating few attacks, appears to be connected with the Paris talks.
3 Hanoi releases three US airmen as a bargaining ploy at the peace talks, but Xuan Thuy, the chief North Vietnamese delegate at Paris, denounces US participation in the war.
5-7 US Marines kill 201 NVA at Gio Linh.
10 VC attack on Saigon is repulsed.
14-18 New US Defense Secretary, Clark Clifford, visits Saigon.
17 Operation Quyet Chien begun by three ARVN infantry divisions. It ends in March 1969, with communist losses estimated at 16,000.
19 Johnson consults with Thieu and calls rumours of a major US policy change 'absolute tommy-rot and fiction'.
20 South Vietnamese Vice-President Ky claims that: 'The only way to win over the Communists is by military strength. We cannot have any coalition with them.'
31 Admiral John McCain replaces Admiral U.S. Grant Sharp as CINCPAC.

AUGUST

2 ARVN begin Operation Lam Son 245 in Thua Thien Province. It lasts for 266 days and inflicts 630 communist casualties.
8 Richard Milhous Nixon and Spiro Agnew are chosen as the Republican presidential team. Nixon promises to 'bring an honourable end to the war in Vietnam'.
17 US reveals that over 2.5 million tons of bombs have been dropped on North Vietnam since 1965.
18 Fighting flares up in the South as communist forces resume a limited offensive.
19 Johnson challenges Hanoi to respond to his limitation of bombing. But he refuses to curtail other military activities in Southeast Asia.
21 25th Infantry Division clashes with Viet Cong near Saigon and reports 700 enemy casualties.
22 Saigon shelled for the first time since June.
23 The NVA besiege a US Special Forces camp at Duc Lap.
24 The 23d ARVN Division launches Tien Bo, a major operation in Quang Duc Province. It claims 1100 enemy losses in 17 days.
28 Democrats choose Vice-President Hubert Humphrey and Senator Edmund Muskie as their presidential team during a convention in riot-torn Chicago. Anti-war protesters fight with the National Guard and Police.
30 NLF proclaims that an offensive in succession to Tet has begun. Over

US Marines kill 200 Viet Cong at Gio Linh.

30 US troops of the 101st Airborne Division are killed by Viet Cong at Ap Trangdau.

SEPTEMBER

8 Troung Quang An becomes the first ARVN general killed in action when his aircraft is shot down. The commander of the 'Big Red One', General Keith L. Ware, suffers a similar fate on 13 September.
20 US defends the use of defoliants in Vietnam.
23 A heated row develops when UN Secretary General U Thant seems to encourage an anti-US resolution.
30 The 900th US aircraft is shot down over the North. Apparently trying to distance himself from Johnson's policies, Humphrey announces that, if elected, he would halt the bombing of the North.

1968

OCTOBER

1 Chinese Foreign Minister Chou En Lai offers China's support for 'heroic Vietnamese people'.
3 General Curtis E. LeMay, running mate of independent candidate George Wallace, causes a storm by seeming to advocate using nuclear weapons in Vietnam.
10 After rumours of an attempted coup, President Thieu asserts on national television that his government is under no threat. The previous day, however, ARVN troops in the capital had been put on a state of maximum readiness.
15 After a decrease in communist military activity it is revealed that NVA troops have withdrawn to border areas to regroup.
17 The *New York Times* reveals a US plan to halt bombing the North if Hanoi makes concessions.
21 US releases 14 North Vietnamese sailors.
24 The 5th Marine Regiment begins the 44- day operation Henderson Hill in Quang Nam Province.
26 US 1st Infantry Division troops are attacked in Tay Ninh Province.
27 In London, 50,000 protestors march in a demonstration against the war.
31 Five days before the Presidential election, Johnson announces on national television that, due to favourable developments in the Paris talks, he has ordered an end to Rolling Thunder.

B-52 crews take a break as Rolling Thunder ends.

NOVEMBER

2 Saigon announces they will boycott the Paris talks because of the presence of the NLF. It is later revealed that a prominent Nixon supporter influenced Thieu and Ky by offering them better terms if they refused to participate. Vice-President Ky is reported as saying: 'We can trust the Americans no longer – they are just a band of crooks.'
5 Eight years after being consigned to the political scrap-heap, Richard Nixon is elected President.

Nixon wins election.

8-9 B-52 airstrikes on communist bases near the Cambodia frontier.
11 Nixon is briefed at the White House. He promises that Johnson speaks for him on the war until he assumes office in January 1969.
15 US announces that the movement of military vehicles in southern North Vietnam has increased by 300 per cent since the bombing ended.

16 There are sharp diplomatic exchanges between Washington and Hanoi over alleged NVA activity in the DMZ.
26 After intense US pressure, Saigon announces that it will join in the Paris talks despite the presence of the NLF. US troops encounter NVA forces in the DMZ for the first time since the bombing of the North was ended.
29 Viet Cong High Command orders an all-out attempt to smash the Phoenix Program, an Allied bid to restore the pacification programme badly affected by Tet.

DECEMBER

1 9th Infantry Division begins Operation Speedy Express in the Mekong Delta. It results in a body count of nearly 11,000.
6 1st Marine Division begins Operation Taylor Common in Quang Nam.
8 South Vietnamese delegation, under the leadership of Ky, arrives in Paris. But the talks are held up by a wrangle over the shape of the tables. The US insist on oblong, and Hanoi on square.
14-16 B-52s used north of Saigon to forestall a possible enemy attack.
14 The total of US troops killed in Vietnam now exceeds 30,000.
24 Allied and communist forces begin a 24-hour Christmas truce.

WAR '69

The Nixon Administration came to power promising a different Vietnam policy to that of Johnson. While Nixon's rhetoric was remarkably similar to Johnson's, his policies were not. He introduced the concept of 'Vietnamization' to the war. This entailed re-equipping the ARVN so it would be able to stand alone against the communists, allowing a gradual US withdrawal.

Vietnamization did not satisfy the doves, but it was never intended to. It was aimed at the 'silent majority' of conservative Middle America which provided Nixon with much of his support. Nixon's stance came to be recognized as being concerned with reducing US casualties, and not against the war as such. By declaring (in the 'Nixon Doctrine') that there would be no more 'Vietnams', a major shift in US foreign policy was indicated.

The year began with Operation Rice Farmer, a joint US/ARVN effort, and the level of US involvement began to drop throughout 1969. At the end of November the 3d Marine Division was withdrawn, to be followed in a few weeks by the 3d Brigade, 82d Airborne Division and, less spectacularly, the Philippine Civic Action Group.

The fighting in 1969 did not reach the same level of intensity as it had done during the 1968 Tet offensive, but the VC spring offensive showed the continuing communist determination to carry the battle to the US troops, as did their autumn offensive, mounted despite the death of Ho Chi Minh in September. Also, the battle of Hamburger Hill in May was a brutal reminder that US soldiers were still dying. The revelation of the My Lai massacre underlined the plight of Vietnamese civilians. At home, the war continued to divide US society like no other. Vietnamization notwithstanding, America was not out of the woods yet.

JANUARY

1 A year-long operation by ARVN divisions in IV Corps, codenamed Quyet Thang, begins. Nearly 88,000 enemy dead are claimed by its end. President-elect Nixon nominates Henry Cabot Lodge, former US ambassador to Saigon, as senior negotiator at the Paris peace talks.
11 Two dozen South Vietnamese cities suffer a terrorist blitz from Viet Cong rockets and artillery.
22 Richard Milhous Nixon inaugurated as President of the US. Henry Kissinger made National Security Adviser.
22 Operation Dewey Canyon, the last major Marine operation of the war, begins in the Da Krong valley, north of the A Shau valley.
25 The first session of the Paris talks which include South Vietnam and NLF, as well as the US and North Vietnam, opens.

FEBRUARY

23 Viet Cong attack 110 targets in South Vietnam. Saigon is hit by rocket fire. Cities and bases are subjected to sporadic infantry attacks and shelling until April.
25 NVA break into a camp near the DMZ killing 36 Marines.
26 160 Viet Cong and 20 Americans killed in clashes in Saigon.

MARCH

4 Nixon threatens to resume bombing the North in retaliation for the Viet Cong offensive.
9 During a visit to South Vietnam, Defense Secretary Melvin R. Laird announces that he is going to ask Congress for more funds for the ARVN.
10 Hue hit by Viet Cong rockets.
15 Operation Maine Crag, a counterattack near the DMZ, begins. US troops go on the offensive in the DMZ for the first time since 1968.
18 US begin Operation Menu, the secret bombing of Cambodia. Operation Atlas Wedge is begun in Saigon area.

19 Defense Secretary Laird hints at Nixon's Vietnamization policy, saying he is working 'toward a situation in which US forces can be withdrawn in substantial numbers' from Vietnam.
27 Secretary of State William Rogers denies his thinking is accurately reflected by an aide's remark that the nation could be 'bought off' by the phased withdrawal of up to 60,000 troops per year from Vietnam.

APRIL

1 Laird announces details of 'Vietnamization'. Defence cuts of $613 million would be achieved by measures like a one-tenth reduction in B-52 raids.
3 US sources admit that US deaths in Vietnam, now at 33,641, have surpassed the numbers of US troops killed in the Korean War.
15 Operation Washington Green, a pacification effort in Binh Dinh Province by 173d Airborne Brigade, begins; it lasts until 1 January 1971 with over 1900 enemy deaths.
22 Operations Lam Son 277 and Putnam Tiger are begun by ARVN in Quang Tri and US 4th Division in Kontum and Pleiku Provinces respectively.
30 US troops in Vietnam peak at 543,400.

MAY

1 77-day Operation Virginia Ridge begun by US 9th Marines near DMZ.
8 NLF issues its peace plan. It gets a cautious welcome from the US.
10 Operation Apache Snow (9th Marines and 101st Airborne) commences in Thua Thien Province.
14 Nixon unveils plan for 'a peace we

Marines launch new offensives.

1969

can be proud of '.

14-18 Secretary of State Rogers visits South Vietnam and states that the US would uphold the right of the South Vietnamese to decide their own future.

16 Operation Lamar Plain begun by Americal and 101st Airborne Divisions in Quang Tin Province.

20 101st Airborne capture Hamburger Hill during Operation Apache Snow.

JUNE

8 Nixon meets Thieu and announces 25,000 US troops will be removed from Vietnam by the end of August.

18 Clark M. Clifford, former Defense Secretary, advocates a massive withdrawal of ground forces while keeping a strong air element to support the ARVN.

19 Nixon says he hopes to 'beat' Clifford's timetable of 250,000 men withdrawn by the end of 1970.

23-26 NVA besiege Ben Hat Special Forces camp.

JULY

8 814 men from 9th Infantry Division are flown back to the US – the first withdrawals under the new policy.

17 Secretary of State Rogers accuses

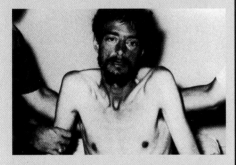

US POW rescued from the Delta.

Hanoi of 'lacking humanity' over US POWs, whose fate becomes a major issue in the course of the year.

21 Operation Idaho Canyon begun by 3d Marine Regiment in Quang Tri Province.

25 'Nixon Doctrine' is announced, ruling out future US involvement in a Vietnam-type war in Asia.

AUGUST

12 New offensive begun by VC, with attacks on 150 targets in South Vietnam.

SEPTEMBER

3 Death of Ho Chi Minh at the age of 79.

5 Lieutenant William Calley is charged with the massacre of 347 Vietnamese civilians at My Lai in March 1968.

13 After South Vietnamese President Thieu proposes elections to include the NLF, Vice-President Ky warns that any coalition with the NLF would provoke a coup within ten days.

16 Nixon orders the withdrawal of a further 35,000 US troops from Vietnam.

Ho Chi Minh dies in September.

OCTOBER

9 As the fighting slows and Vietnamization takes effect, US sources admit that only 64 Americans were killed in the week 28 September-4 October, the lowest weekly total since the end of 1966.

15 A 'Moratorium Day' against the

war attracts hundreds of thousands of demonstrators in major US cities.

19 Communist military activity intensifies, with battles in the Mekong Delta and northeast of Saigon.

NOVEMBER

3 Nixon makes a major televized speech on his Vietnam policy, appealing for national unity. He announces that US troops would be pulled out according to an 'orderly scheduled timetable.'

4 Congressional and public reaction to Nixon's speech is overwhelmingly

Nixon calls for national unity while Agnew attacks media bias.

favourable.

13 Vice-President Agnew attacks US media for bias in reporting on the war.

15 In Washington over a quarter of a million attend the largest ever anti-war demonstration.

DECEMBER

7 Operation Randolph Glen begun by 101st Airborne and 1st ARVN Divisions.

15 Nixon orders the withdrawal of 50,000 more troops from Vietnam, bringing the total reductions to 115,000.

20 Lodge quits as head US negotiator in Paris, due to complete deadlock in the peace talks.

31 US troops killed in Vietnam now 40,024.

WAR '70

This was the year when the Nixon administration drastically expanded the conflict in Southeast Asia. President Nixon and his influential National Security Adviser, Henry Kissinger, both believed that the war could not be won by purely military means. Firepower was to be used in combination with diplomacy to bring about a compromise peace which would allow America to exit from Vietnam with honour. Military successes would buy the US time for diplomacy to work, perhaps using China and the Soviet Union as levers on Hanoi, and allow time for Vietnamization to succeed.

The concrete expression of this policy came with the invasion of Cambodia in April. Intervening in the wake of a pro-American coup, ARVN and US troops attempted to sweep the Parrot's Beak and Fish Hook regions free of Vietnamese communists.

By the year's end, troop withdrawals had reduced the number of US soldiers in Vietnam to 334,600, with the monthly casualty rate halved. With both sides avoiding large-unit confrontation — the last major US ground operation took place in September — US casualties were mainly from booby traps, mortar attacks and sniper fire.

The process of Vietnamization was accelerating, with the majority of border defence now being undertaken by the ARVN. Together with this transfer of military operations, the attempt to win the 'hearts and minds' of the South Vietnamese population proceeded with the policy of pacification. A component of this, the controversial Phoenix Program and its supposed destruction of the VC infrastructure, was reaching its peak: by the end of 1970, the Saigon government claimed that 91 per cent of hamlets were secure, with local councils and chiefs freely elected.

JANUARY

2 Viet Cong's New Year truce ends.
8 At the Paris talks US suggests informal talks to end 'sterile debate', but Hanoi objects. The talks remain deadlocked.
17 Viet Cong order a massive guerrilla campaign to smash the Vietnamization programme.
30 Nixon warns that the rate of withdrawal of US troops from Vietnam depends on enemy actions, and that any escalation would meet with a firm response.
31 Over 100 bases are hit by communist missile fire in the worst attacks since mid-1969.

FEBRUARY

2 Heavy airstrikes are carried out on the Ho Chi Minh Trail by US B-52s in response to the upsurge of violence.
12 Amid US concern at communist successes in Laos, a major NVA offensive begins there. Reports circulate that for the first time US aircraft are bombing in support of the Laotian government.
20 Kissinger begins secret peace talks in Paris.
26 In response to domestic criticism of the US role in Laos, Defense Secretary Laird states that the President would ask Congress for approval, should ground forces be deployed in Laos.

MARCH

14 *The Columbia Eagle*, a US transport ship loaded with napalm, sails to Cambodia after two US seamen take control of the vessel as a

Sihanouk deposed in coup.

protest against the war.
16-22 'Anti-draft Week' in the US, sponsored by 'The New Mobe' (the New Mobilization Committee to End the War in Vietnam).
18 While on a visit to China and USSR, Prince Norodom Sihanouk, head of the Cambodian state, is deposed in a coup by General Lon Nol.
20 In a departure from the previous Cambodian position of neutrality, US and South Vietnamese planes and artillery aid Cambodian troops against Viet Cong on Cambodian territory.
27 ARVN troops carry out their first major ground operation on Cambodian soil.

APRIL

1 Communists launch new offensive in South Vietnam. Among other incidents, a Special Forces camp at Dak Seang is besieged by 2000 NVA troops.
4-5 For the first time in five months, there are serious clashes between

US uncover arms in Cambodia.

NVA and US troops near the DMZ.
20 Nixon announces the withdrawal of a further 150,000 troops by spring 1971.
29 US and ARVN forces move into Cambodia to destroy communist sanctuaries in the Parrots Beak and Fish Hook areas in the south of the country.

MAY

1 Nixon publicly refers to student anti-war activists as 'bums'. France leads world-wide condemnation of the invasion of Cambodia. China and USSR follow suit on 4 May.
1-2 Heavy US bombing raids launched against North Vietnamese targets.

Right: Time-out for a Marine in I Corps Tactical Zone.

Four students shot dead at Kent State.

1970

4 At Kent State University, Ohio, four students are shot dead by National Guardsmen during a protest against the invasion of Cambodia.
6 Viet Cong terrorist attacks in Saigon kill a record 450 civilians in one week.
7 10,000 ARVN troops are pulled out of Parrot's Beak at the conclusion of operations.
8 In contrast to the stated withdrawal date for US troops of 30 June, Saigon announces the ARVN will stay in Cambodia as long as they are needed. Nearly 1000 US troops are deployed in the Parrot's Beak.
9 US and South Vietnamese ships begin to blockade Cambodian coast.
12 Defence Secretary Laird promises to remove US troops from active service in Vietnam by mid-1971.
26 USAF begin Operation Freedom Deal in Cambodia.
31 South Vietnamese city of Da Lat is attacked by communist forces, who succeed in slipping into the city despite the presence of a large ARVN garrison.

JUNE

3 A new NVA/Viet Cong offensive begins in Cambodia. By 17 June Phnom Penh is almost cut off.
22 In Washington it is admitted that, contrary to earlier assurances, US planes have attacked targets deep inside Cambodia, beyond the sphere of operations of US ground forces. The controversial use of defoliants by US forces is brought to a halt.

29 The last of 18,000 US combat troops to serve in Cambodia, men of 1st Air Cavalry, withdraw.

JULY

13 The 101st Airborne Division inflicts heavy casualties on NVA 304th Division in operations near Khe Sanh.
23 Firebase Ripcord, close to the A Shau valley, is evacuated after intense fighting with NVA units since April.

The heaviest bombing for two years is carried out in November.

AUGUST

8 US military command confidentially instructs all commanders to say that US air raids in Cambodia are to protect the remaining troops in Vietnam and aid Vietnamization.
11 South Vietnamese forces take over from the US in defending along the Cambodian and Laotian borders.
24 Massive B-52 strikes along DMZ.

SEPTEMBER

5 The 101st Airborne Division (Airmobile), in co-ordination with the ARVN 1st Infantry Division, initiates operations in Thua Thien Province (Operation Jefferson Glenn). This is the last major military operation in which US

ground forces will take part.
7 A major attack by Cambodian loyalist forces commences, but makes little progress.

OCTOBER

7 Nixon proposes that a 'standstill' ceasefire begin, without prior troop withdrawals. His suggestions are well received at home but are rejected by the communists.
24-25 The ARVN begins two new drives into Cambodia.

NOVEMBER

21 A heliborne force lands at Son Tay, near Hanoi, in an attempt to rescue American POWs. The camp is found to be empty.
21-22 After an unarmed reconnaissance plane is destroyed, the heaviest raids on North Vietnam since the 1 November 1968 bombing halt are launched.

DECEMBER

10-11 Nixon and Laird warn Hanoi that more airstrikes might be launched if aggression continues.
22 US Congress prohibits use of US forces in Cambodia or Laos.
31 The US Navy hands over 125 vessels to the South Vietnamese.

WAR '71

The Vietnam war continued its devastation in 1971, as US operations expanded into both Laos and Cambodia. In 1970, the successes of communist Pathet Lao forces and the NVA, and the half-hearted response of the Laotian government, had led the Nixon administration to turn to the strategic bomber. B-52s devastated the countryside of Laos and made refugees out of 700,000 of the two million population.

But the bombing had little effect on the communists, so at the end of 1970 it was decided to embark on an invasion from South Vietnam by ARVN troops with US air support. However, Operation Lam Son 719 was an abject failure: communist traffic along the Trail actually increased during the operation, and ARVN deficiencies had been exposed. As Kissinger observed: 'the operation, conceived in doubt and assailed by scepticism, proceeded in confusion.'

Meanwhile US troop levels in Vietnam fell from 280,000 to 156,800. US casualties were also down: 1386 killed compared to 4204 in 1970. But these, set against ARVN losses of 21,500, and the fact that total US military deaths for the war topped 45,000, gave little comfort. Morale among US troops was low, drug addiction was approaching epidemic proportions, and refusals to obey orders and 'fraggings' of officers were increasing rapidly.

In the US, the war was putting the society under great internal stress as disaffection with the administration policy set in. The conviction of Lieutenant Calley for his part in the My Lai massacre created a storm of protest from supporters of the war, while the publication of 'The Pentagon Papers', which disclosed squabbles and duplicity within the Johnson administration, gave an opportunity for pro- and anti-war parties to re-fight old battles.

JANUARY

1 Congress bans use of US troops, but not airpower, in Laos and Cambodia.
3 Heavy B-52 airstrikes against the Ho Chi Minh Trail.
4 Nixon announces 'the end is in sight' for US combat role in Vietnam.
8 US planes launch strikes against North Vietnamese SAM sites.
17 ARVN troops attack POW camp in Cambodia but find it empty. When questioned, Nixon refuses to deny that an extension of the war into Cambodia is possible.
19 US planes launch heavy raids over Laos and Cambodia.
22 Communist forces shell Phnom Penh, the Cambodian capital.
30 Operation Dewey Canyon II, a preliminary to the allied invasion of Laos, is begun by the 1st Brigade, 5th Infantry Division (Mechanized) re-occupying Khe Sanh.

FEBRUARY

3 A new allied operation in the Fish Hook area of Cambodia is announced. Major fighting flares up in Laos as a communist offensive begins in the north of the country.
8 Operation Lam Son 719, an invasion of Laos by 12,000 ARVN troops supported by US aircraft, begins.
11 Washington denies claims that US troops are operating inside Laos.

Lam Son 719 brings the war to Laos.

17 Nixon refuses to limit US use of airpower. His popularity is at its lowest point since he took office.
20 President Thieu causes a political storm by implying that an invasion of the North is inevitable. Congressional opponents of the war try to curb the US president's powers to begin military action. At Phu Loc, Laos, an ARVN battalion is defeated by an NVA force and a firebase is captured.
22 The ARVN push into Laos grinds to a halt only 29km over the Vietnamese border. Bad weather and the necessity of removing captured arms caches are blamed.
27 An announcement that US troops are to be allowed to rescue airmen shot down in Laos is denounced by the North Vietnamese at the Paris talks.

MARCH

1 The Capitol building in Washington is damaged by a bomb planted as a protest against the invasion of Laos. The allied offensive resumes after a fortnight of stalemate with the capture of Tchepone, an important NVA logistic centre on the Ho Chi Minh Trail. The Phoenix Program is expanded in an attempt to destroy the Viet Cong political organization in South Vietnam.
10 China vows total support for North Vietnam's struggle against the US.
10 About one-third of the ARVN forces in Laos commence a withdrawal to Vietnam. US denies communist claims that this represents a defeat and calls it 'mobile manoeuvering'.
20 53 men of the 1st Air Cavalry refuse to obey an active service order, but no courts martial result.
22 Nixon defends Lam Son 719 while criticizing negative TV coverage of the campaign.
24 Operation Lam Son 719 is terminated four weeks early. The communists claim a significant victory. ARVN sources claim a bodycount of 13,700 and admit to allied casualties of 1146 dead.
25 US press sources claim that the ARVN has suffered 3800 dead in Laos.
31 Fire Base 6, near Dak To, is the scene of a long struggle between ARVN and NVA units. Losses are heavy on both sides. Lieutenant

1971

William L. Calley is sentenced to life imprisonment for his part in the My Lai massacre of 4 March 1968. His sentence provokes a storm of protest and is later cut to 20 years.

APRIL

7 Nixon defends his Vietnam record on national TV, pointing out the large numbers of troop withdrawals and restating his aim of bringing the war to an 'honorable' end.
14 Operation Lam Son 720 is begun in the A Shau valley as a sweep complementing the Laos operation.
19 Vietnam veterans in Washington

More US troops leave Vietnam.

begin a week of nationwide anti-war protests with a demonstration they dub 'Operation Dewey Canyon III'.
29 US losses in Vietnam top 45,000.

MAY

3-5 12,000 protestors are arrested in Washington during a further week of demonstrations.
26 NVA make an important gain with the capture of Snoul, in Cambodia.

JUNE

5-6 US helicopters and planes used in support of ARVN troops defending Fire Base Sarge near Khe Sanh come under heavy attack from NVA.
13 The *New York Times* serializes the secret 'Pentagon Papers', which reveal politically embarrassing decisions about the war made by previous administrations. Two days later, the government begins legal action to halt publication.
28 Daniel Ellsberg, who leaked the Pentagon Papers, gives himself up to

the police and is arrested.
30 The Supreme Court quashes attempts to suppress The Pentagon Papers.

JULY

1 6100 US personnel leave South Vietnam, the largest number ever to pull out on one day. At the deadlocked Paris Peace talks, the North proposes a new plan which would involve the release of all POWs and a US pullout from Vietnam by the end of the year.
9 Final US withdrawal from the DMZ. ARVN assumes allied role there.
15 Nixon raises hopes of an end to the war by revealing that he will be visiting Communist China in 1972, the first US president to do so.

AUGUST

2 US admits existence of 30,000 CIA-funded irregulars in Laos.
15 Cambodia demands withdrawal of South Vietnamese troops from that country due to alleged atrocities committed by them against civilians.
18 Australia and New Zealand announce accelerated withdrawal of their troops from Vietnam.

SEPTEMBER

6 13,500 ARVN troops with US air support begin Operation Lam Son 810, aimed at NVA bases near the DMZ by the Laotian border.

OCTOBER

3 Thieu is re-elected president in South Vietnam. All other candidates boycott the election, claiming that it is rigged.
9 A further case of 'combat refusal' occurs when men tasked to form a 1st Air Cavalry Division patrol 'express a desire not to go'.
29 US troop strength in Vietnam drops to 196,700, the lowest since January 1966.
31 The first of nearly 3000 Viet Cong POWs are released by Saigon.

NOVEMBER

12 A further reduction of 45,000 in US forces in Vietnam is announced, taking the total troop strength down to 156,800.
17 Moves to make further US involvement in the war impossible fail when the Senate rejects a bid to freeze military funds.
22 ARVN begins a new offensive into Cambodia, as the Khmer Rouge closes in on Phnom Penh.

DECEMBER

1 A major Khmer Rouge push around Phnom Penh causes a collapse in Cambodian morale, resulting in a rout of Cambodian Army forces trying to reopen Route 6.
26 The heaviest US airstrikes on the North since Operation Rolling Thunder was ended in 1968 begin and continue until the 30th.

With US air support the ARVN launch Lam Son 810.

WAR '72

On 30 March 1972 the North began a full-scale offensive against South Vietnam, escalating the level at which the war was to be fought. Since 1971, the USSR had been re-equipping the NVA with tanks, artillery, anti-aircraft missiles and all the paraphernalia of a modern, conventional army, in preparation for such a step.

General Giap, the architect of the offensive, decided on a strategy intended to stretch the ARVN to its limit. Three widely spaced thrusts were to be made: across the DMZ, into the Central Highlands from Cambodia, and from the south of Cambodia towards Saigon. It was hoped that the second thrust would cut South Vietnam in half and, faced with the occupation of major centres such as Hue and Quang Tri City, Thieu would have to capitulate.

In the event, although all US ground combat units had been withdrawn, the ARVN and US tactical airpower proved sufficient first to blunt and then to defeat the NVA offensive. Key cities such as Hue held out or were retaken, and the NVA's ability to fight on was placed under severe strain by the resumption of airstrikes on logistic targets in the North. In particular the mining of Haiphong harbour, where most Soviet aid entered North Vietnam, was a damaging blow.

Nixon proved ruthless in his use of strategic bombers as a military, diplomatic and propaganda weapon. The raids on Hanoi that he ordered late in the year gave the impression to the American public that he had 'bombed Hanoi back to the conference table.' But his real problem in the peace talks was the South Vietnamese government, struggling to avoid being abandoned. By the end of the year, however, the agreement Nixon wanted was just around the corner. The Americans were getting out and henceforth the South would have to fight on alone.

JANUARY

2 Nixon announces that up to 35,000 US troops will stay in Vietnam until the freeing of all US POWs has been secured.
3 In Laos, Long Thien base is abandoned to the Pathet Lao.
6 Washington announces the reduction of US troop levels in Vietnam to 69,000 by the end of April. This will entail the removal of 70,000 troops.
7 At Fiddler's Green firebase, 20 miles from Saigon, 18 Americans are wounded in a mortar attack.
21 Heavy B-52 airstrikes against the Ho Chi Minh Trail.
25 Nixon unveils a new eight-point peace plan, after secret talks between Kissinger and high-ranking North Vietnamese officials in Paris.

MARCH

10 US 101st Airborne Division withdrawn from Vietnam.
21 The Cambodian capital of Phnom Penh endures the most serious shelling of the war so far.
23 US boycott the Paris talks for an indefinite period. Nixon accuses Hanoi's delegation of failing to 'negotiate seriously.'
30 A massive NVA offensive, the largest since Tet in 1968, begins when four divisions cross the DMZ. The ARVN, taken by surprise, gives way under the onslaught.

APRIL

1 US air support for ARVN in the northern provinces is hindered by bad weather, including dense clouds.
2 Operation Freedom Train given go-ahead. US planes are to attack logistic targets up to 25 miles beyond the DMZ. NVA sweep through Quang Tri Province. Allied forces cut off in Quang Tri City and Dong Ha.

Le Duc Tho leads Hanoi's hard-bargaining team at Paris.

FEBRUARY

1 A new offensive is launched into the south of Cambodia by ARVN troops.
5 Hanoi rejects US peace plan.
10 Nixon reassures President Thieu that the US won't 'undercut' him.
16 NVA positions in and around the DMZ are hit in a series of 'limited duration' air attacks.
21-28 Nixon visits China.

5 NVA starts offensive into Binh Long Province. Communications within 40 miles of Saigon are cut off.
6 Better weather in Vietnam allows the full deployment of US aircraft, which hit targets in North Vietnam.
7 The town of Loc Ninh falls to the NVA, who also begin the siege of An Loc.
8 Fighting rages around An Loc as the 5th ARVN Division, ejected from Loc Ninh, struggles to hold on in the

1972

face of severe NVA attacks. B-52 strikes are made in the Kontum area.
10 A series of heavy airstrikes by B-52s, ranging 145 miles into North Vietnam, is begun by the US.
11 NVA besiege Fire Base Bastogne near Hue.
12 US hints that its troop withdrawal policy might be altered in view of the current offensive.
15 US bombs Hanoi and Haiphong.
15-20 A new wave of protests against the bombing results in hundreds of arrests across the US.
20 ARVN beat off an NVA assault on An Loc. In Cambodia, NVA move to within 40 miles of Saigon after the clearance of the South Vietnamese border east of the Mekong river.
27 Paris peace talks resume.
29 Kontum besieged by the NVA, who are now poised to drive to the coast, thus effectively cutting off the northern provinces from Saigon.

MAY

1 NVA capture Quang Tri City.
4 In contrast to the withdrawals of US troops, an additional 125 US aircraft are ordered to Vietnam. US and South Vietnam call indefinite halt to Paris peace talks.
8 In a major escalation of the war, Nixon orders that North Vietnamese ports, including Haiphong, are to be mined in an attempt to strike at Hanoi's supply lines. He offers an end to the action (codenamed Linebacker) and a complete withdrawal of troops in return for a ceasefire and the release of POWs.

Soviet merchant ships bring supplies to the North.

8-11 International outrage at Linebacker is paralleled in the US by anti-war demonstrations.
9 The mining of Haiphong harbour by US planes begins.

13-14 ARVN counteroffensive, backed by powerful US air support, begins in Quang Tri Province and around Hue.
15 US Army Vietnam Headquarters is decommissioned.
17 US reports indicate that Linebacker is damaging the North's war effort; US planes have destroyed roads, bridges, and oil installations, starving the NVA in the South.

JUNE

5 Hanoi reveals that Linebacker is causing severe economic problems.
18 Siege of An Loc ends as NVA withdraw in defeat.
30 General Abrams is replaced by General Frederick C. Weyand as Commander, MACV.

JULY

13 Paris peace talks resume.
14 Senator George McGovern, a long-term opponent of the war, is nominated as Democratic Candidate

War protest: Jane Fonda broadcasts for Hanoi.

for the 1972 presidential election.
18 Actress Jane Fonda broadcasts an anti-war message over Hanoi Radio, and is heavily criticized in the US.
19 ARVN troops begin a major offensive into Binh Dinh Province.
23 ARVN successes in Binh Dinh leave the NVA in control of only two towns: An Tuc and Hoaian.

AUGUST

19 McGovern attacks US pacification techniques of applying 'massive firepower and free-fire zones and [clearing] six million people out of their homes.'
23 Last US ground combat battalion in Vietnam, 3/21st Infantry, leaves.

SEPTEMBER

15 ARVN forces recapture Quang Tri City, with the claim that over 8000 NVA had been killed in the battle.
26-7 Against a background of rumours of major diplomatic developments, Henry Kissinger and Le Duc Tho, the chief North Vietnamese negotiator, hold the 19th of their private talks.
29 About one tenth of the entire North Vietnamese Air Force is destroyed in a series of devastating attacks by the USAF on airfields in the North.

OCTOBER

8 Le Duc Tho proposes a peace settlement which accepts in substance the US proposals, thus dropping demands for a political solution to accompany a military one.
18 Thieu rejects Hanoi's proposals, since he mistrusts US promises.
23 Nixon suspends the Linebacker raids. Interdiction raids on the south of North Vietnam continue.
26 Reporting on his talks with Le Duo Tho, Kissinger states that 'peace is at hand' in Southeast Asia.

NOVEMBER

7 Nixon re-elected US president.
11 Long Binh base turned over to ARVN, marking an end to direct US participation in the war.
20 US puts forward revized peace proposals, which are coldly received by Hanoi.

DECEMBER

4 Kissinger and Le Duc Tho hold private talks in Paris.
18 Following the breakdown of talks with Hanoi, Nixon orders the resumption of raids on cities, including Hanoi, in Operation Linebacker II. The bombing wrecks a large part of North Vietnam's infrastructure, and hence its war-making capacity.
30 Linebacker II is called off by Nixon, after US planes had delivered 20,000 tons of bombs. Linebacker II had been accompanied by a chorus of international condemnation.

Right: The Wall – the Vietnam War Memorial, Washington DC

WAR '73-'74

1973 was the year in which Richard Nixon finally disentangled America from Vietnam. But his claim to have achieved 'Peace with Honor' rang hollow in the ears of the South Vietnamese.

The Kissinger/Le Duc Tho accord allowed the US to withdraw its troops without losing too much face, but did little to secure the future of South Vietnam. Foreign troops were required to withdraw from Vietnam, which in practice meant US troops. Worse, a ceasefire 'in place' was arranged, which left the North Vietnamese in control of large areas of the South. Furthermore, the ARVN were virtually prohibited from trying to regain captured territory, since this would be a violation of the ceasefire. Only by being promised US air support in the event of a further communist offensive did Thieu acquiesce.

Throughout 1973 and 1974 communist forces built up their strength in the South, and a number of severe battles were fought. In Cambodia, the Khmer Rouge tightened their control over much of the countryside, and in Laos the communist Pathet Lao joined a short-lived coalition government.

A more insidious threat to the ARVN was the fact that the US had other major issues to deal with, such as the Watergate scandal, the SALT talks with the USSR, and the Middle East. South Vietnam became less of a priority: the 1974 military aid budget was slashed from $1.45 billion to $700 million. In December 1974 the North began to prepare plans for an offensive to win the war in 1975-6. Saigon, faced with a political and economic crisis, increasingly abandoned by the US, and with her armed forces badly hit by the world oil shortage, could not have relished the prospect of a major enemy offensive.

646

JANUARY

1 The US declares a 36-hour truce. In Congress, the Democrats table fierce anti-war resolutions.
2 NVA attack Route 1 north of Saigon. US resumes bombing of targets south of the 20th parallel.
7 North Vietnamese press claims thousands killed and Hanoi and Haiphong badly damaged by Linebacker II air raids.
8 Secretary of Defense Laird states that 'from a military viewpoint, the Vietnamization programme has been completed' and says he is sure that the South can now defend itself. Le Duc Tho and Kissinger resume secret talks in Paris. As the North renews offensive action, US bombers destroy 875,000 gallons of fuel at Da Nang in error.
13 Thieu demands an invasion of the North if the Kissinger/Le Duc Tho talks collapse, claiming 'Had we bombed North Vietnam continuously, had we landed in North Vietnam, the war would have been over by now'.
23 Nixon announces that Kissinger and Le Duc Tho have agreed 'to end the war and bring peace with honor'. The ceasefire will begin on 28 January.
27 As Laird announces the end of the draft in the US, Lieutenant-Colonel William B. Nolde becomes the last US serviceman to die in combat in Vietnam. Le Duc Tho calls the ceasefire a 'victory'.
28 The ceasefire begins, but there are many violations by both sides.

The ARVN: fighting alone.

FEBRUARY

5 Talks begin between the Saigon government and the Provisional Revolutionary Government of Vietnam (PRG), the political wing of the Viet Cong. They are swiftly deadlocked. International Commission of Control and Supervision (ICCS) and Joint Military Commission (JMC) members, who are to oversee the ceasefire, take up stations in South Vietnam.
7 With the end of the US role in the war, Canada recognizes North Vietnam. Other Western nations – but not the US – follow suit later in the year.
12 The exchange of POWs by all sides in the war begins.
14 First batch of released US POWs arrive in California as part of Operation Homecoming.
17 President Thieu forms Popular Front to fight for Peace and the Right to Self-Determination, a group of anti-Viet Cong parties.
20-27 As communists threaten Phnom Penh, US provides air support for Cambodian government forces.
21 Rebel Pathet Lao forces and the official government of Laos agree a truce and the establishment of a coalition government, thus ending two decades of civil war.
26 Saigon accuses Hanoi of installing anti-aircraft missiles at Khe Sanh (part of the NVA-controlled territory) in breach of the ceasefire.

MARCH

2 In Paris, 12 foreign ministers, including those of the US, South and North Vietnam, China, Britain and the USSR approve the January ceasefire agreement.
5 US and North Vietnam begin talks about possible aid for Hanoi.
17 US concerned that the communist military build-up in the South has continued, despite the ceasefire.
18 Major Floyd Thompson, the man held prisoner longer than any other US serviceman ever, is released. He was captured in March 1964.
29 Last US troops leave Vietnam. Nixon announces that, with the US military role in Vietnam officially at an end, 'the day we have all worked and prayed for has finally come'.

APRIL

4 After talks with Nixon, Thieu says he would 'never, never' ask US for direct military support.
9 Thieu denies that South Vietnam's gaols hold any political prisoners, only 'communist criminals'.
16 Hanoi accuses Washington and Saigon of breaches of the truce.

JUNE

4 US Senate approves bill blocking funds for US military activities in Southeast Asia, but Nixon lobbies to postpone the ban to enable the bombing of Cambodia to continue.

JULY

July – US Navy clear Northern ports of mines sown during Linebacker.
1 US Congress votes to end all bombing in Cambodia after 15 August.

AUGUST

15 US bombing of Cambodia is ended.
17 Washington reveals plans to withdraw US troops from Thailand.
22 It is announced that Henry Kissinger is to become US Secretary of State.
31 After heavy fighting around the city of Kompong Cham, forces loyal to Sihanouk launch a direct attack on it and make large gains.

SEPTEMBER

14 A provisional administration is formed in Laos which includes members of both the communist Pathet Lao and the former Laotian government.
22 Fighting rages at an ARVN base near Pleiku. Le Minh base is taken by an NVA force supported by armour, and an attempt to retake it on 25 October is bloodily repulsed.
29-30 Heavy fighting takes place at Kheim Hanh, when an ARVN sweep against Viet Cong forces backfires and an ARVN battalion is decimated.
30 Cambodian government forces complete the process of regaining Kompong Cham.

NOVEMBER

4-7 The fall of three ARVN bases in Quang Duc Province enables the communists to control the main communication route from Kontum and Pleiku to the south.

DECEMBER

3 Viet Cong raid oil-storage tanks 10 kilometres from Saigon and destroy 18 million gallons of oil.

1974
JANUARY

14 ARVN retake Le Minh base.
19 Changes in the South Vietnamese constitution extend the term of Thieu's presidency.
24-7 Phnom Penh, surrounded again by rebel troops, is heavily shelled after a month of rocket attacks.
27 Figures released by Saigon show that there have been 57,835 fatalities since the ceasefire.

MARCH

8 The return of POWs to their respective countries is completed.
16 There is confused fighting around Kontum. Both the ARVN and communists claim a victory.
18 The former Royal Cambodian capital of Oudong falls to Khmer Rouge troops.

APRIL

5 A new coalition government under Souvanna Phonma is formed in Laos with Pathet Lao participation.
16 Talks in Paris between the PRG and Thieu's government collapse.

MAY

2 ARVN forces fight their way through to the Ranger camp at Duc Heu, besieged by the NVA since late March.
17 As communist troops begin their largest offensive since the ceasefire, the battle around Ben Cat (55

kilometres north of Saigon) is begun, with a successful NVA attack on outlying posts.

JUNE

4 The ARVN 18th Division counter-attacks at Ben Cat and recaptures a village lost in May. The division is unable to make further headway and suffers losses of over 2500 over the next few days.

JULY

9-10 South Vietnam launches a series of airstrikes against communist targets in Tay Ninh Province. This initiates a period of severe conflict which peaks around 20 August, when ARVN and communist troops struggle for the control of Tay Ninh City.

AUGUST

9 Nixon becomes the first US president to resign. He is replaced by Gerald Ford.
15 NVA tanks break out from Ben Cat and get to within 25 kilometres of Saigon.

SEPTEMBER

16 President Ford offers amnesty to Vietnam-era draft evaders.
28 In the Northern provinces, NVA troops, after a series of successful pushes in July and August, close to within 25 kilometres of Hue. NVA pressure on the city is maintained throughout October.

OCTOBER

In the early part of the month, the North Vietnamese politburo tentatively decide on a major offensive in 1975.

DECEMBER

13 North Vietnamese offensive into Phuoc Long Province achieves major successes.
18 The politburo meets in Hanoi to plan an offensive for Spring 1975.

WAR '75

The Vietnam war, the longest conflict of the 20th century, finally came to an end in April 1975. Saigon, the South Vietnamese capital the US had fought for so long to defend, fell to the communists on the 30th. Phnom Penh, the Cambodian capital, had fallen 13 days earlier. In both cases the US had stood back, unwilling to intervene.

The North Vietnamese offensive which began in December 1974 was intended to gauge ARVN strength. However, the successes of the NVA in Phuoc Long Province led to a more ambitious offensive, the aim of which was to bring about the defeat of the South some time in 1976. Overrunning Ban Me Thuot, in Da Lac Province, the NVA quickly realized just how weak their opponents were.

Fearing that the NVA were poised to cut South Vietnam in two, Thieu ordered his crack Airborne Division to pull back to the south, and ARVN forces in the Central Highlands to abandon Pleiku and Kontum to regroup for a counter-offensive. Floods of refugees fled south, and the shaky morale and discipline of the ARVN began to crack.

Encouraged by these signs of the erosion of Saigon's will to resist, in March the politburo in Hanoi ordered an all-out drive to end the war in 1975. As a result, cities and provinces fell like ninepins to the victorious communist armies. Thieu resigned, but Saigon's belated attempts to negotiate with the communists were unsuccessful. With the fall of Saigon, the Vietnam war came to an end. In Washington, the US administration was forced to watch impotently from the sidelines as communism triumphed in Indochina. The longest and bloodiest American military adventure of the Cold War had ended in total and humiliating defeat.

JANUARY

1 Khmer Rouge attack the Cambodian capital, Phnom Penh.
3-4 Republican Cambodian troops counter-attack near Phnom Penh but are unable to break the siege.
6 With the fall of Phuoc Binh, the whole of Phuoc Long Province is in communist hands.
7 NVA seize and hold Ba Den mountain, 10km from Saigon.
11 US complains to the ICCS about NVA build-up in the South. The communists respond by denouncing US aid for Saigon.
12 US confirms making covert reconnaissance flights over Vietnam, after admitting giving technical aid to the ARVN. Both cases are violations of the 1973 peace settlement.
13 The town of Kien Tuong in the Mekong Delta is captured by NVA troops backed by tanks. Saigon claims major successes in airstrikes against NVA supply lines in the Central Highlands.
23 As the Khmer Rouge gain control of most of the Cambodian stretch of the Mekong, supply barges break the blockade of Phnom Penh for the first time in a month.
28 President Ford's request that Congress grant $522 million in extra military aid for Cambodia and South Vietnam is attacked by political opponents.
29 Saigon claims that ARVN forces have inflicted a significant defeat on the NVA 804th Division in the northern provinces.
30 Saigon moves against the anti-government Hoa-Hao Buddhist militia.

FEBRUARY

1 Father Thanh, a leading anti-communist South Vietnamese opponent of President Thieu, demands the latter's trial for treason.
3 Five anti-Thieu Saigon newspapers are shut down.
15 Two US companies join the Bird Air Company in flying supplies into besieged Phnom Penh. Little food

Phnom Penh: A last-ditch defence.

reaches the starving populace, however, most being reserved for the army.
26 In response to President Ford's appeal for military aid for Cambodia, George Mahon, a leading Democrat, comments: 'Ultimately Cambodia cannot survive, so why spend hundreds of millions of dollars more?'

MARCH

4 NVA 968th Division commences a diversionary offensive in the Central Highlands.
6 Henry Kissinger says that to deny money to South Vietnam would 'deliberately destroy an ally by withholding aid in its moment of extremis.' Ford rules out any US military intervention in Vietnam.
8 NVA capture Thuan Man in Quang Duc Province, weakening Saigon's hold over Route 14, a principal road in the Central Highlands.
11 Thieu decides to pull back from outlying regions and to concentrate troops in a strategic reserve.
13 NVA captures Ban Me Thuot, provincial capital of Da Lac Province in the Central Highlands, aided by a popular uprising. The ARVN 23rd Division is routed as its discipline collapses. South Vietnamese Air Force launches heavy airstrikes around Ban Me Thuot.
14 ARVN counter-attacks in Tay Ninh as communist threat to Saigon grows. Thieu orders that Pleiku and Kontum are to be abandoned to the communists. 400,000 refugees follow in the wake of the retreating ARVN.
17 A major NVA offensive around Saigon leads Thieu to order the ARVN Airborne Division, currently in Quang Tri, to deploy to defend the capital, thus dealing a fatal blow to ARVN resistance in the north.
18 The evacuation of Hue by the civilian population is ordered.

1975

19 Already suffering from a Montagnard revolt, a further blow is dealt to Saigon by the mutiny of four Montagnard units. The province in the extreme north of South Vietnam, Quang Tri, is abandoned by the ARVN. Thieu describes reports that the northern provinces have been abandoned by the ARVN as 'false and groundless rumours', declaring that: 'We are determined to defend our territory to the end.'

20 NVA take An Loc in Binh Long Province against minimal resistance.

22 NVA takes Gia Nghia, the ARVN's last toe-hold in Quang Duc.

24 Revolutionary forces seize control of Route 1.

Tuy Hoa: Refugees flee as the ARVN abandons coastal towns.

25 Hanoi aims for an end to the war in 1975, by attacking Saigon.

26 NVA moves into Hue as the garrison flees by sea to Da Nang.

27 Former Vice-President Ky demands that Thieu form a 'government of national salvation'. Two days earlier, Thieu had announced the beginnings of an attempt to form a broadly based war cabinet.

29 Da Nang, where the first US Marines landed in 1965, is taken by NVA forces. Reports suggest that the ARVN defenders of the town have become little more than an armed and disordered mob.

30 Hanoi attacks Ford's plans to evacuate civilians from Da Nang as contrary to the 1973 agreements.

APRIL

1 The Provisional Revolutionary Government (PRG) issues a charter for newly captured areas which includes the guarantee of democratic liberties and orders for civil servants employed by the Saigon regime to continue to work for the occupying forces. Qui Nhon is taken by the NVA. Little resistance is offered by ARVN forces. In Cambodia, the key town of Neak Long is captured by the Khmer Rouge. Cambodian President Lon Nol goes into exile, first in Indonesia and later in the US. He is replaced by General Sankhan Khoy.

2-5 ARVN abandons coastal towns, including Tuy Hoa and Cam Ranh, to the advancing revolutionary forces.

4 Thieu reconstructs his cabinet. He blames the loss of the northern provinces on desertions, cowardly commanders, the US and the fact that 'the armed forces did not have favourable conditions in which to fight'.

5 Successful Khmer Rouge attacks around Phnom Penh threaten the republican government's hold over the Cambodian capital.

6 Opposition leaders in Saigon denounce US plan to airlift 2000 war orphans from Vietnam for adoption in US as 'inhumane propaganda'.

7 Saigon shelled as communist forces close in on the capital.

9-10 At Xuan Loc, 60km northeast of Saigon, the 18th ARVN Division and elements of the Airborne Division succeed in repulsing NVA assaults. This is the first time in a month that the ARVN has seriously attempted to halt the communist offensive.

12 American personnel are evacuated from Phnom Penh.

14 Khmer Rouge begins final advance into Phnom Penh. The EEC refuses to condemn Hanoi as the aggressor in the war, despite US pressure.

16 The evacuation of US citizens and Vietnamese collaborators from Saigon speeds up as the communists close in on the city.

17 It is announced that the UN appeal for emergency relief for Vietnam has raised over $16 million, but $100 million is needed. Phnóm Penh is captured.

21 President Thieu resigns and is replaced by Tran Van Huong. The ARVN defenders of Xuan Loc, cut off by communist outflanking manoeuvres, are forced to retreat. The failure of the stand at Xuan Loc effectively spells the end for South Vietnam, as Saigon is now surrounded by 16 communist divisions.

23 It is reported in *The Times* that the conduct of the NVA in Da Nang had compared favourably with the unruly behaviour of the retreating ARVN, whose morale and discipline had broken down.

25 Thieu departs from Saigon to go into exile.

26 President Huong warns that Saigon could become a 'mountain of bones and a river of blood'. Ex Vice-President Ky denounces 'the [Vietnamese] cowards who are leaving with the Americans'. Two days later, Ky flies out to the US Seventh Fleet. After a pause of several days, the NVA recommence their offensive.

28 Huong resigns and is replaced as President by Duong Van Minh. President Minh appeals for a ceasefire with the communists, which is rejected out of hand.

30 At 10.15 am, President Minh says he is ready to transfer power to the PRG 'to avoid useless shedding of our people's blood.' Frantic crowds try to storm the US embassy in order to be airlifted out. At midday, communist forces enter Saigon.